THE
Phenomenology of Spirit
READER

SUNY Series in Hegelian Studies
William Desmond, editor

THE
Phenomenology of Spirit
READER

Critical and Interpretive Essays

EDITED BY
JON STEWART

STATE UNIVERSITY OF NEW YORK PRESS

Published by
State University of New York Press, Albany

© 1998 State University of New York

All rights reserved

Printed in the United States of America

No part of this book may be used or reproduced in any manner whatsoever without written permission. No part of this book may be stored in a retrieval system or transmitted in any form by any means including electronic, electrostatic, magnetic tape, mechanical, photocopying, recording, or otherwise without the prior permission in writing of the publisher.

For information, address the State University of New York Press, State University Plaza, Albany, NY 12246

Production design by David Ford
Marketing by Nancy Farrell

Library of Congress Cataloging-in-Publication Data

The Phenomenology of spirit reader : critical and interpretive essays / edited by Jon Stewart.
    p.   cm. — (SUNY series in Hegelian studies)
   Includes bibliographical references and index.
   ISBN 0-7914-3535-0 (alk. paper). — ISBN 0-7914-3536-9 (pbk. : alk. paper)
   1. Hegel, Georg Wilhelm Friedrich, 1770–1831. Phänomenologie des Geistes. I. Stewart, Jon (Jon Bartley) II. Series.
B2929.P384   1997
193—dc21   96-54245
                                                            CIP

10 9 8 7 6 5 4 3 2 1

Contents

Acknowledgments ix

Abbreviations of Primary Texts xiii

Introduction 1

Part I. Hegel's Preface and Introduction

1. John Sallis, Hegel's Concept of Presentation: Its Determination in the Preface to the *Phenomenology of Spirit* 25

2. Kenley R. Dove, Hegel's Phenomenological Method 52

3. Kenneth R. Westphal, Hegel's Solution to the Dilemma of the Criterion 76

Part II. Consciousness

4. Katharina Dulckeit, Can Hegel Refer to Particulars? 105

5. Merold Westphal, Hegel's Phenomenology of Perception 122

6. Joseph C. Flay, Hegel's "Inverted World" 138

Part III. Self-Consciousness

7. Howard Adelman, Of Human Bondage: Labor, Bondage, and Freedom in the *Phenomenology* 155

8. George Armstrong Kelly, Notes on Hegel's "Lordship and Bondage" 172

9. JOHN W. BURBIDGE, "Unhappy Consciousness" in
   Hegel: An Analysis of Medieval Catholicism? 192

PART IV. REASON

10. ALASDAIR MacINTYRE, Hegel on Faces and Skulls 213

11. GARY SHAPIRO, Notes on the Animal Kingdom
    of the Spirit 225

PART V. SPIRIT

12. PATRICIA JAGENTOWICZ MILLS, Hegel's *Antigone* 243

13. DAVID W. PRICE, Hegel's Intertextual Dialectic:
    Diderot's *Le Neveu de Rameau* in the
    Phenomenology of Spirit 272

14. KARLHEINZ NUSSER, The French Revolution
    and Hegel's *Phenomenology of Spirit* 282

15. MOLTKE S. GRAM, Moral and Literary Ideals
    in Hegel's Critique of "The Moral World-View" 307

16. DANIEL P. JAMROS, S.J., "The Appearing God"
    in Hegel's *Phenomenology of Spirit* 334

PART VI. RELIGION

17. JEAN-LOUIS VIEILLARD-BARON, Natural Religion:
    An Investigation of Hegel's *Phenomenology of Spirit* 351

18. HARALD SCHÖNDORF, S.J., The Othering (Becoming
    Other) and Reconciliation of God in Hegel's
    Phenomenology of Spirit 375

19. MARTIN J. DE NYS, Mediation and Negativity in
    Hegel's Phenomenology of Christian Consciousness 401

Part VII. Absolute Knowing and the Structure of the *Phenomenology*

20. Mitchell H. Miller Jr., The Attainment of the Absolute Standpoint in Hegel's *Phenomenology* — 427

21. Jon Stewart, The Architectonic of Hegel's *Phenomenology of Spirit* — 444

Bibliography: Works on the *Phenomenology* — 479

Index — 505

Acknowledgments

This collection would not have been possible if it were not for the generosity of the following journals and publishing houses in granting the reprint rights for the essays included here: Bouvier Verlag, *Clio, Graduate Faculty Philosophy Journal, Hegel-Studien, History of Philosophy Quarterly,* Humanities Press, *Journal of Religion, Mosaic, The Owl of Minerva, Philosophisches Jahrbuch der Görres-Gesellschaft, Philosophy and Phenomenological Research, Revue de Métaphysique et de Morale,* Suhrkamp Verlag, *Theologie und Philosophie,* and University of Notre Dame Press. A special thanks is due *The Review of Metaphysics* and Professor Jude P. Dougherty, whose unwavering support was crucial for the development of this project.

I would like to thank Professor Robert B. Pippin for his useful suggestions and encouragement. In addition, I am grateful to the contributors for their wiiling participation and positive feedback and suggestions on the various aspects of this collection.

Original Sources of the Essays

1. John Sallis, "Hegel's Concept of Presentation: Its Determination in the Preface to the *Phenomenology of Spirit.*" *Hegel-Studien* 12 (1977): 129–56. Also in his *Delimitations: Phenomenology and the End of Metaphysics.* Bloomington and Indianapolis: Indiana University Press, 1986, 40–62.

2. Kenley R. Dove, "Hegel's Phenomenological Method." *The Review of Metaphysics* 23 (1969–70): 641–61.

3. Kenneth R. Westphal, "Hegel's Solution to the Dilemma of the Criterion." *History of Philosophy Quarterly* 5 (1988): 173–88.

4. Katharina Dulckeit, "Can Hegel Refer to Particulars?" *The Owl of Minerva* 17 (1986): 181–94.

5. Merold Westphal, "Hegels Phänomenologie der Wahrnehmung." In *Materialien zu Hegels Phänomenologie des Geistes,* ed. Hans Friedrich Fulda and Dieter Henrich. Frankfurt a. M.: Suhrkamp, 1973, 83–105.

6. Joseph C. Flay, "Hegel's 'Inverted World'." *The Review of Metaphysics* 13 (1970): 662–78.

7. Howard Adelman, "Of Human Bondage. Labour, Bondage and Freedom in the *Phenomenology.*" In *Hegel's Social and Political Thought*, ed. Donald Phillip Verene. Atlantic Highlands, N.J.: Humanities Press, 1980, 119–35.

8. George Armstrong Kelly, "Notes on Hegel's 'Lordship and Bondage'." *Review of Metaphysics* 19 (1965): 780–802. Also in *Hegel: A Collection of Critical Essays*, ed. Alasdair MacIntyre. Notre Dame: University of Notre Dame Press, 1976.

9. John W. Burbidge, "Unhappy Consciousness in Hegel: An Analysis of Medieval Catholicism?" *Mosaic: A Journal for the Interdisciplinary Study of Literature* 11 (1978): 67–80. Also in his *Hegel on Logic and Religion: The Reasonableness of Christianity*. Albany: State University of New York Press, 1992, 105–18.

10. Alasdair MacIntyre, "Hegel on Faces and Skulls." In *Hegel: A Collection of Critical Essays*, ed. Alasdair MacIntyre. Notre Dame: University of Notre Dame Press, 1976, 219–36. © 1972 by Alasdair MacIntyre. Used by permission of Doubleday, a division of Bantam Doubleday Dell Publishing Group, Inc.

11. Gary Shapiro, "Notes on the Animal Kingdom of the Spirit." *Clio* 8 (1979): 323–38.

12. Patricia Jagentowicz Mills, "Hegel's *Antigone.*" *The Owl of Minerva* 17 (1986): 131–52.

13. David W. Price, "Hegel's Intertextual Dialectic: Diderot's *Le Neveu de Rameau* in the *Phenomenology of Spirit.*" *Clio* 20 (1991): 223–33.

14. Karlheinz Nusser, "Die französische Revolution in Hegels *Phänomenologie des Geistes.*" *Philosophisches Jahrbuch der Görres-Gesellschaft* 77 (1970): 276–96.

15. Moltke S. Gram, "Moral and Literary Ideals in Hegel's Critique of 'The Moral World-View'." *Clio* 7 (1978): 375–402.

16. Daniel P. Jamros, S.J., "'The Appearing God' in Hegel's *Phenomenology of Spirit.*" *Clio* 19 (1990): 353–65.

17. Jean-Louis Vieillard-Baron, "La 'religion de la nature'. Étude de quelques pagés de la *Phénoménolgie de l'esprit* de Hegel." *Revue de Métaphysique et de Morale* 76 (1971): 323–43.

18. Harald Schöndorf, "Anderswerden und Versöhnung Gottes in Hegels *Phänomenologie des Geistes*. Ein Kommentar zum zweiten Teil von VII. C. 'Die offenbare Religion'." *Theologie und Philosophie* 57 (1982): 550–67.

19. Martin J. De Nys, "Mediation and Negativity in Hegel's Phenomenology of Christian Consciousness." *The Journal of Religion* 66 (1986): 46–67.

20. Mitchell H. Miller Jr., "The Attainment of the Absolute Standpoint in Hegel's *Phenomenology*." *Graduate Faculty Philosophy Journal* 7 (1978): 195–219.

21. Jon Stewart, "The Architectonic of Hegel's *Phenomenology of Spirit*." *Philosophy and Phenomenological Research* 55.4 (1995): 747–76.

A NOTE ON THE TRANSLATIONS

Many of the essays featured in this volume appear here for the first time in English translation. The essays by Karlheinz Nusser, Harald Schöndorf, and Jean-Louis Vieillard-Baron were translated from their respective German and French texts by the editor of the present collection. These translations were executed in consultation with the original authors. Merold Westphal's "Hegel's Phenomenology of Perception" originally appeared in German as "Hegels Phänomenologie der Wahrnehmung," in *Materialien zu Hegels Phänomenologie des Geistes* (edited by Hans Friedrich Fulda and Dieter Henrich. Frankfurt: Suhrkamp, 1973). The English version of this text was furnished by the author himself and appears here for the first time. Where it was possible, an effort has been made in the translations to standardize the references to the *Phenomenology* to the established English translation of A.V. Miller (i.e., *Hegel's Phenomenology of Spirit*, Oxford: Clarendon Press, 1977).

Abbreviations of Primary Texts

Aesthetics I–II = *Hegel's Aesthetics. Lectures on Fine Art*, translated by T. M. Knox. Oxford: Clarendon Press, 1975.

Aesthetik I–III = *Vorlesungen über die Aesthetik*. SW vols. 12–14.

Briefe I–IV = *Briefe von und an Hegel*, edited by Johannes Hoffmeister. Hamburg: Meiner, 1961.

Difference = *Difference between the Systems of Fichte and Schelling*, translated by H. S. Harris and W. Cerf. Albany: State University of New York Press, 1977.

Differenz = *Differenz des Fichte'schen und Schelling'schen Systems der Philosophie*. GWe vol. 4, 1–92.

EL = *Hegel's Logic. Part One of the Encyclopaedia of the Philosophical Sciences*, translated by William Wallace. Oxford: Clarendon Press, 1975.

Enz = *Enzyklopädie der philosophischen Wissenschaften*. GWe vol. 19.

ETW = *Early Theological Writings*, translated by T. M. Knox. Fragments translated by Richard Kroner. Chicago: University of Chicago Press, 1948; reprint, Philadelphia: University of Pennsylvania Press, 1975.

First Philosophy of Spirit = *First Philosophy of Spirit*, in *G. W. F. Hegel, System of Ethical Life and First Philosophy of Spirit*, edited and translated by H. S. Harris and T. M. Knox. Albany: State University of New York Press, 1979.

GWe = *Gesammelte Werke*, edited by the Rheinisch-Westfälische Akademie der Wissenschaften. Hamburg: Felix Meiner, 1968ff.

History of Philosophy I–III = *Lectures on the History of Philosophy*, 3 volumes, translated by E. S. Haldane. London: K. Paul, Trench, Trübner, 1892–1896; reprint, Lincoln and London: University of Nebraska Press, 1995.

Jena System, 1804–5 = *G. W. F. Hegel: The Jena System, 1804–5. Logic and Metaphysics*, translation edited by John W. Burbidge and George di Giovanni. Kingston and Montreal: McGill-Queen's University Press, 1986.

JSE I–III = *Jenaer Systementwürfe*. GWe vols. 6–8.

Letters = *Hegel: The Letters*, translated by Clark Butler and Christian Seiler. Bloomington: Indiana University Press, 1984.

PG = *Phänomenologie des Geistes*. GWe vol. 9.

PH = *The Philosophy of History*, translated by J. Sibree. New York: Willey Book Co., 1944.

PhG = *Phänomenologie des Geistes*, edited by J. Hoffmeister. Hamburg: Meiner, 1964.

Philosophy of Mind = *Hegel's Philosophy of Mind*, translated by William Wallace and A. V. Miller. Oxford: Clarendon Press, 1971.

Philosophy of Nature = *Hegel's Philosophy of Nature*, translated by A. V. Miller. Oxford: Clarendon Press, 1970.

Philosophy of Religion I–III = *Lectures on the Philosophy of Religion*, translated by E. B. Speirs and J. Burdon Sanderson. London: Routledge and Kegan Paul; and New York: Humanities Press, 1962, 1968, 1972.

Philosophy of Spirit, 1805–6 = *The Jena Lectures on the Philosophy of Spirit (1805–6)*, in *Hegel and the Human Spirit*, translated by Leo Rauch. Detroit, Mich.: Wayne State University Press, 1983.

PM = *Phenomenology of Mind*, translated by J. B. Baillie. London: Allen and Unwin, 1931.

PS = *Phenomenology of Spirit*, translated by A. V. Miller. Oxford: Clarendon Press, 1977.

PR = *Hegel's Philosophy of Right*, translated by T. M. Knox. Oxford: Clarendon Press, 1952.

Propaedeutic = *The Philosophical Propaedeutic*, translated by A. V. Miller, edited by Michael George and Andrew Vincent. Oxford: Basil Blackwell, 1986.

RP = *Grundlinien der Philosophie des Rechts oder Naturrecht und Staatswissenschaft im Grundrisse*. SW vol. 7.

SL = *Hegel's Science of Logic*, translated by A. V. Miller. London: George Allen and Unwin, 1989.

SW = *Sämtliche Werke*. Jubiläumsausgabe in 20 Bden, edited by Hermann Glockner. Stuttgart: Friedrich Frommann Verlag, 1927–1940.

TJ = *Hegels theologische Jugendschriften*, edited by Herman Nohl. Tübingen: Verlag von J. C. B. Mohr, 1907.

VGP I–III = *Vorlesungen über die Geschichte der Philosophie*. SW vols. 17–19.

VPG = *Vorlesungen über die Philosophie der Geschichte*. SW vol. 11.

VPR I–II = *Vorlesungen über die Philosophie der Religion*. SW vols. 15–16.

Werke = *Georg Wilhelm Friedrich Hegel. Werke in zwanzig Bänden.* Frankfurt: Suhrkamp, 1970.

WL = *Wissenschaft der Logik.* GWe vol. 21.

WdL = *Wissenschaft der Logik,* edited by G. Lasson. Hamburg: Meiner, 1967.

Jon Stewart

INTRODUCTION

Hegel represents without question one of the most important figures in the European intellectual tradition. Most all of the major schools and movements of contemporary thought such as phenomenology, existentialism, Marxism, critical theory, structuralism, pragmatism, and poststructuralism have their origins in his work.[1] In addition, a number of disciplines such as intellectual history, sociology of knowledge, and hermeneutics find in Hegel an important forerunner. Reflecting on Hegel's influence, the French philosopher Merleau-Ponty writes that one can rightly claim "that interpreting Hegel means taking a stand on all the philosophical, political, and religious problems of our century."[2] However, Hegel's influence has been far from unproblematic, and his reputation has always been the source of a strikingly wide divergence of opinion, not the least of which is due to his profoundly obscure manner of expression. While many scholars are repelled by Hegel's language, regarding it as an obstruction to clear thinking and honest communication, others find in his neologisms and stilted prose a sign of the profundity of a thought that renders its darkest secrets only to the initiate. Due to these disputes, Hegel's influence and the true meaning of his philosophy have often been poorly understood. But, indeed, we must first come to terms with Hegel himself if our goal is to begin to develop an informed opinion about the major trends of contemporary thought which have their origins in his philosophy. Thus, as Merleau-Ponty says, "no task in the cultural order is more urgent than reestablishing the connection between . . . the . . . doctrines which try to forget their Hegelian origin and . . . that origin itself."[3] In short, if we are to be in a position to evaluate the current practice of philosophy in an informed manner, we must first return to Hegel.

The story of the influence of Hegel's philosophy is an extremely troubled one. In the Anglo-American philosophical tradition, his reputation has suffered for many years as a result of a number of misinterpretations, misconceptions, and outright caricatures of his thought. However, in the last few decades there has been an outpouring of literature on Hegel in the world of Anglo-American philosophy. What has been dubbed the

"Hegel renaissance"[4] has fortunately produced a body of literature that has gone a great distance toward correcting the numerous misconceptions surrounding Hegel's thought and toward reinstating the philosopher in his rightful place as one of the most important minds of the modern age.

The Importance of the *Phenomenology*

Hegel only actually wrote four full-length books in his lifetime: the *Phenomenology of Spirit*, the *Science of Logic*, the *Encyclopaedia of the Philosophical Sciences*, and the *Philosophy of Right*. Of all of Hegel's texts, it is his *Phenomenology of Spirit* which has been the most influential for the later development of European philosophy. This can be seen by a brief glance at the history of Hegel studies and the role played in it by the *Phenomenology*.

In France, Hegel had for many years been ignored, disregarded, and even derided until around 1930 when two events coincided to bring his philosophy into the mainstream in the French academic world[5]—a place which it since then has never fully relinquished. Perhaps the single most important event in French Hegel research was the influential lectures delivered by the Russian emigré Alexandre Kojève.[6] Between 1933 and 1939 Kojève lectured at the École des Hautes Études on the *Phenomenology* and handed down his provocative and highly idiosyncratic Marxist reading of Hegel to a whole generation of French intellectuals. Most all of the leading philosophers and social scientists in the French-speaking world of the day were in attendance, and in the years following Kojève's lectures, each of them reinterpreted and transformed Hegel's philosophy in a different and significant way. Thus, French phenomenology, existentialism, structuralism, and poststructuralism all in a sense had their start in Kojève's lecture hall. The second important event in French Hegel studies was the non-partisan work of Jean Hyppolite, which served to establish Hegel even more fully in the French academy. In two installments in 1939 and 1941, Hyppolite published the first French translation of the *Phenomenology*, and then in 1946, followed his masterful commentary on that text, which is still the most complete to date, namely his *Genèse et structure de la Phénoménologie de l'esprit de Hegel*.[7] Thus, Kojève and Hyppolite together served to introduce Hegel into the world of French letters. It is interesting to note that both men concentrated almost exclusively on the *Phenomenology*, making it by far the most important Hegelian text in the French-speaking world. The years that followed these events saw the French academy dominated by the new existentialist philosophy of Sartre, Camus, and Merleau-Ponty. In this atmosphere,

Hegel's *Phenomenology* was as alive as ever. Reflecting back on this period, Hyppolite writes, "After 1946, the *Phenomenology*—along with Sartre's *Being and Nothingness* and Merleau-Ponty's *Phenomenology of Perception*—became the fundamental book that was referred to in all French philosophical circles."[8] The chapter by the French Hegel scholar Vieillard-Baron, which is translated here for the first time, represents one of the most important contributions to our understanding of this text that issues from the French tradition of Hegel research.

Although the *Phenomenology* has never been *the* Hegelian text in German Hegel studies as it has been in the francophone world, it nevertheless still probably outdistances all other candidates as the most discussed and most disputed Hegel work in the German academy.[9] Ever since Haering's celebrated lecture in 1933,[10] which called into question the unitary structure of the *Phenomenology*, the overwhelming proliferation of literature that has appeared in response to this issue has given the *Phenomenology* the central position in German Hegel research that it still enjoys. Haering's thesis that Hegel changed his mind about the conception of the work during its composition set off a long debate which has still not been satisfactorily resolved.[11] Since then, we have seen the appearance of Scheier's detailed commentary on the *Phenomenology*,[12] which is the only one in any language to rival Hyppolite's in precision and detail. In addition to this, there have appeared a number of shorter studies[13] on individual sections which have continued to make the *Phenomenology* a theme of current debate in the classroom and in German journals. Essays from the well-known German Hegel scholars Nusser and Schöndorf have been allotted a place in the present collection as representatives of this important tradition of scholarship.

With respect to Hegel's influence on Anglo-American philosophy, it is useful to recall that there has been a long history of Hegelianism in both Great Britain and the United States.[14] In America two main schools of Hegel research arose in the middle of the nineteenth century in St. Louis and Cincinnati. Great Britain also saw important early expositors of Hegelian philosophy in men such as T. H. Green (1836–82), Edward Caird (1835–1908), and later F. H. Bradley (1846–1924), Bernard Bosanquet (1848–1923), and J. M. E. McTaggart (1866–1925). Although the *Phenomenology of Spirit* did not play a central role in these traditions, it has since come to the forefront of Anglo-American Hegel scholarship. Since the "Hegel renaissance," there have appeared a number of important works in English on the *Phenomenology*,[15] and it has established itself as one of the preferred Hegelian texts for classroom use.[16] In fact, in the Anglo-American world, the *Phenomenology* and the *Philosophy of Right* (complemented occasionally by the introduction to the

Lectures on the Philosophy of History) are virtually the only texts in the Hegelian *corpus* ever taught in American universities on a regular basis.

The Biographical Circumstances and the Composition of the *Phenomenology*

The *Phenomenology of Spirit*, which was originally published in 1807, was Hegel's first major philosophical work, and it represented the fruit of his six-year stay at the University of Jena, where he held his first real academic post. During his years as *Privatdozent* in Jena, he often made reference in his course announcements to a forthcoming work which would be a systematic statement of his philosophy.[17] Such a statement was particularly important to him at the time for two personal reasons. First, he had yet to achieve a philosophical reputation of his own. His friend and colleague Schelling had attained success very early, gaining recognition for his *System of Transcendental Idealism* (1800) and being awarded a professorship at Jena at the age of twenty-three. During Hegel's time at Jena, he was largely laboring in Schelling's shadow and for most philosophers at the time was seen as little more than someone in Schelling's school. Only when Schelling left Jena in 1803 was it possible for Hegel to establish his own academic identity. Thus, it was not by accident that Hegel at this time began work on the *Phenomenology*. A second reason for the importance of the *Phenomenology* for Hegel was a very practical one. Prior to Jena, he had worked long and bitter years as a house-tutor in Bern and Frankfurt. Only with the inheritance that he received upon the death of his father in 1799 was he able to try to embark upon a university career, which was a potentially hazardous undertaking financially since at the time the lectureships or positions as *Privatdozent* were unsalaried. As Hegel saw Schelling's star rising, he became increasingly aware of the need to produce his own philosophical system if he were to have any chance of one day securing a professorship. Like Schelling, who enjoyed success at a remarkably early age, Fichte, as a young man of twenty-nine, became a leading intellectual figure in Germany in one fell swoop with his *Attempt at a Critique of All Revelation* in 1792. In contrast to these two thinkers, Hegel was already in his mid-thirties and had yet to produce anything resembling a major work. Thus, the *Phenomenology* was for him to represent the first systematic statement of his thought and it would serve as an important stepping stone in his incipient academic career.

Manuscripts dating from the Jena years prior to the *Phenomenology* have been published and discussed at length in the literature.[18] These manuscripts, referred to as the *Realphilosophie* or the *Jena System*, represent a philosophical system which contains much of the structure and content of the later *Encyclopaedia*. This leads us to believe that while Hegel was working on his philosophical system, he was struck by the need to introduce or justify the system with another work. This might then have been the motivation behind his abandoning the system at that time and turning his attention to the *Phenomenology*.

The *Phenomenology* is thus intended as the introduction to his philosophical system and for this reason has become a useful text in courses on Hegel. In Germany there has been a long debate surrounding the question of the status of the *Phenomenology*. Many see the work not as an introduction to the system but rather as the actual first part of it. These controversies are based largely on philological evidence which seems to indicate that Hegel came to reconsider the conception of the book during its turbulent and hurried composition. According to this view, he originally conceived of the work merely as an introduction to a philosophical science; however, while he was writing, the text grew out of control in his hands, and it came to include material that belonged, properly speaking, to the philosophical system itself. Thus, it is argued, Hegel was obliged to change his original conception of the work from that of a mere preface or introduction to that of a substantive part of the system. This change in conception is allegedly reflected in the change in titles that the book went thorough.[19] First, the work was called *The Science of the Experience of Consciousness*, which was then later replaced with the title, *Science of the Phenomenology of Spirit*. The first title indicates that the work was merely supposed to explore the experience of consciousness, but with the change to the second title Hegel seems to acknowledge that the material treated moves beyond individual consciousness to a collective social-historical entity which he calls "spirit."

The ambiguity of the task of the *Phenomenology* comes out clearly in the introduction to the work itself where Hegel tells us, on the one hand, that at the end of the text's labyrinthine argument "consciousness will arrive at a point at which it gets rid of its semblance of being burdened with something alien, with what is only for it, and some sort of 'other,' at a point where appearance becomes identical with essence, so that its exposition will coincide at just this point with the authentic Science of Spirit."[20] This indicates that the goal of the *Phenomenology* is to dissolve the subject-object split and to reach the standpoint of Science, where such a split is no longer present. Thus, the experience of consciousness is prefatory to a Science which issues from it as a result. Yet, on the other hand, he writes, "the way to Science is itself already *Science*, and hence, in virtue of its content, is the Science of the *experience of consciousness*."[21] Here Hegel says explicitly that the *Phenomenology* is not merely an introduction but rather is itself already a science. These seemingly contradictory statements are representative of the central philological dispute surrounding the *Phenomenology*. Hegel explains the metamorphosis of the text at the beginning of the *Encyclopaedia*:

> In my *Phenomenology of Spirit*, which on that account was at its publication described as the first part of the System of Philosophy, the method adopted was to begin with the first and simplest phase of mind, immediate consciousness, and to show how that stage gradually of necessity worked onward to the philosophical point of view, the necessity of that view being proved by the process. But in these circumstances it was impossible to restrict the quest to the mere form of consciousness. For the stage of philosophical knowledge is the richest in material and organization, and therefore, as it came before us in the shape of a result, it presupposed the existence of the concrete forms of consciousness, such as individual and social morality, art and religion.[22]

Here Hegel indicates that the analysis had to proceed beyond consciousness to include more sophisticated forms of social and historical existence which were already implicit in it. Thus, on this account, the *Phenomenology* is much more than merely an introduction or an analysis of consciousness.

Although it is important to be aware of these arguments about the role and purpose of the *Phenomenology*, they are in the final analysis of concern primarily to the Hegel philologist. For this reason these discussions need not excessively exercise us here. The importance of the question of whether the *Phenomenology* is the first part of a science or an introduction to it are easily exaggerated and can stand in the way of attempts to examine the actual content of the work. Whatever the case may ultimately be, Hegel intended that the *Phenomenology*, of all his texts, should be read first, and this is one of the reasons why it plays such an important role in his *corpus*.

The *Phenomenology* in the Context of Hegel's Other Works

Napoleon's victory at Jena in 1806 caused the university to suspend its work, and Hegel found himself obliged to seek other employment. He worked for a time in Bamberg as the editor of a newspaper and later accepted a job as headmaster of a *Gymnasium* or secondary school in Nüremburg. There he completed his second major work, the *Science of*

Logic,²³ published in two installments in 1812 and 1816. This continuation of his career and biography also represents a continuation in the construction of his philosophical system.

The *Science of Logic* forms a natural sequel to the *Phenomenology*. As was indicated above, Hegel tells us that the goal of the latter is to justify the scientific standpoint. In the introduction of the *Phenomenology*, he explains that the task of that work is to examine critically the various natural points of view or prejudices of common sense. By means of the dialectical method, these views are scrutinized for consistency. Once a given view has proven to be inconsistent, it must be abandoned and a new one found to replace it. When these views have all been examined and the viewpoint of common sense overcome, then we reach the level of science. Each of the views of common sense is characterized by some form of dualism: subject-object, man-God, subject-subject, individual-community, citizen-state, and so on. By the time science is finally attained, these dualisms have all been shown to be no longer viable in the course of the various analyses of the *Phenomenology*. Thus, the central insight of science is the monism that absorbs and overcomes these various dualisms and thus attempts to come to terms with reality as a whole and not just with its component parts taken in isolation. The kind of philosophy that examines the whole is what Hegel calls "speculative philosophy." He characterizes this sort of philosophy by contrast to what he calls "dogmatism," which treats concepts individually and outside of their systematic context:

> Dogmatism consists in the tenacity which draws a hard and fast line between certain terms and others opposite to them. We may see this clearly in the strict "either—or": for instance, The world is either finite or infinite; but one of these two it must be. The contrary of this rigidity is the characteristic of all speculative truth. There no such inadequate formulae are allowed, nor can they possibly exhaust it. These formulae speculative truth holds in union as a totality, whereas dogmatism invests them in their isolation with a title to fixity and truth.²⁴

Dogmatism abstracts individual concepts from their organic unity. Speculative philosophy, on the other hand, rejects all absolute dichotomies and tries to see even apparently contradictory statements as parts of a unitary whole. The goal of the *Phenomenology* is thus to overcome the various dualisms of dogmatism and to reach the level of science at which the *Science of Logic* begins.

In his introduction to the *Science of Logic*, Hegel explains the role of the *Phenomenology* in terms of a deduction which is necessary as an introduction to science: "The notion of pure science and its deduction is therefore presupposed in the present work in so far as the *Phenomenology of Spirit* is nothing other than the deduction of it."[25] We can see the *Phenomenology* then as assuming the dualistic views of common sense and proceeding via a series of *reductio ad absurdum* arguments to prove them inconsistent. The task of the *Phenomenology* is thus to reach the monistic insight of science. The *Science of Logic*, then, assumes a monism and tries analytically to unravel what is bound up in this insight. It begins with the most basic category—pure being—and tries to unpack what is necessarily thought along with this category. In order to think pure being, Hegel argues, one must also be able to think nothing since the concept of nothingness is already analytically contained in the very concept of being. In order to think being and nothing, one must also be able to think becoming, and so on. In this way the universe of other categories is derived, the one from the other, and all of the concepts are shown to be interconnected in a complete system of thought.

In 1816, the same year that the second half of the *Science of Logic* appeared, Hegel returned to university life when he received a professorship at the University of Heidelberg. There he continued to develop his philosophical system, and in 1817 he published the *Encyclopaedia of the Philosophical Sciences*. In this work, the material from the *Science of Logic* that we know as the first philosophical science, is reworked and condensed in the form of the so-called *Encyclopaedia Logic* or the *Lesser Logic*[26] and is complemented by two new philosophical sciences—the philosophy of nature[27] and the philosophy of mind.[28] With the *Encyclopaedia*, Hegel completes his vision of the system of science. All of his later works are simply expansions on this basic outline.

Hegel left Heidelberg in 1818 to take up a distinguished professorship at the newly grounded University of Berlin, where he remained until his death in 1831. There in 1821 amid a tense political climate,[29] he published his last major work, the *Philosophy of Right*,[30] which constitutes the most complete statement of his political philosophy. As he tells us in his introduction, this work corresponds to the "Objective Spirit" section of the *Encyclopaedia* and is an elaboration of the material presented there. This is confirmed in the preface to the *Philosophy of Right*, where Hegel writes explicitly, "This compendium is an enlarged and especially a more systematic exposition of the same fundamental concepts which in relation to this part of philosophy are already contained in a book of mine designed previously for my lectures—the *Encyclopaedia of the Philosophical Sciences*."[31] Thus, the *Philosophy of Right* also forms a part of the philosophical sciences for which the *Phenomenology* prepared the way.

During his years in Berlin, Hegel gave extremely popular lectures on the philosophy of history,[32] aesthetics,[33] philosophy of religion,[34] and the history of philosophy.³⁵ At the peak of his career, he died suddenly during a cholera epidemic in Berlin on 14 November 1831. The years after his death saw the formation of the right and left Hegelians who battled for his heritage. The student notes from Hegel's lectures were collected and later published and today count as useful supplements to his published works. Through his writings and those of his influential students, Hegel has remained an influential figure in European philosophy up through our own day.

THE HETEROGENEOUS CONTENTS OF THE *PHENOMENOLOGY*

Much of the power and beauty of the *Phenomenology* is to be found in the extremely rich and diverse material which constitutes its subject matter. Here we find an account of Greek tragedy, medieval court culture, the pseudosciences of phrenology and physiognomy, forms of Romantic morality, Kantian ethics, traditional epistemological conundrums, sundry religious beliefs, and so on. The heterogeneous nature of the contents of the *Phenomenology* has posed great difficulties for commentators and has led to many mistaken approaches in the secondary literature.

In the face of the wide range of themes in the text, many commentators have simply concluded that the *Phenomenology* is an unsystematic and chaotic work. According to this interpretation, there is no single argument or guiding thread which runs through the entire text. Walter Kaufmann, an outspoken advocate of this view, writes, "One really has to put on blinders and immerse oneself in carefully selected microscopic details to avoid the discovery that the *Phenomenology* is in fact an utterly unscientific and unrigorous work."³⁶ Instead of a systematic text, the *Phenomenology* is seen simply as a patchwork of diverse discussions and analyses with no connection or relation. Thus, the view is that "The *Phenomenology* is a loose series of imaginative and suggestive reflections on the life of the spirit."³⁷ Kaufmann reduces the contexts of the book to the exigencies of the historical moment, claiming that, given the turbulent composition of the *Phenomenology*, we should not be surprised that the result was something chaotic and unsystematic: "The central point of our philological excursus is, of course, to show how Hegel himself handled his system: not as so much a necessary truth, deduced once and for all in its inexorable sequence, but rather as very neat and sensible way of arranging the parts of philosophy—not even the neatest and most sensible possible, but only the best he could do in time to meet the printer's deadline."³⁸ Kaufmann goes so far as to suggest that Hegel's preoccupation with the imminent birth of his illegitimate son was one reason for the confused and unsystematic structure of the *Phenomenology*. Although putting weight in these far-fetched biographical speculations is idiosyncratic of Kaufmann, the idea that the *Phenomenology* is an unsystematic text has many adherents in every tradition of Hegel research.

The natural result of the belief that the *Phenomenology* is an unsystematic text is that many essays and shorter works on the *Phenomenology* take certain themes or analyses out of their systematic context and use them as the focal point of discussion. Thus, Hegel's account of the Enlightenment, lordship and bondage, Stoicism, and so forth, are treated in an episodic manner with no attention paid to their role in the overall structure of the work. The strategy is to discover what insights Hegel has on the various topics he discusses without asking further to what use he intends to put them in his system. Kojève's interpretation is a good example of this tendency. By reading the entire text in terms of the lordship and bondage dialectic, Kojève overtly ignores Hegel's own claims about the necessity of the systematic structure of the *Phenomenology* and distorts the meaning of this individual section. This clearly represents a fundamental problem of interpretation since for Hegel these analyses are only meaningful in their systematic context.

Another obvious difficulty that arises from the heterogeneous content of the work is what can be referred to as the unevenness of many books on the *Phenomenology*. Many such works provide interesting and insightful accounts of some aspects of the book, while at the same time they seem to neglect others altogether. This is a natural enough tendency given that every commentator has his or her own strengths and weaknesses. It is, however, regrettable to the extent that each analysis and discussion in the *Phenomenology* is supposed to play a role in the overall structure of the work. As Kant says of his system, "For pure speculative reason has a structure wherein everything is an organ, the whole being for the sake of all others. . . . Any attempt to change even the smallest part at once gives rise to contradictions, not merely in the system, but in human reason in general."[39] Thus, we cannot ignore or treat lightly individual sections or parts of a systematic philosophy without doing damage to the whole. Ideally, Hegel's analyses would all be treated uniformly since they are all equally important in the systematic structure of the work. The problem with a number of approaches is that they badly distort Hegel's intention in the *Phenomenology* by ignoring the work's systematic structure. The goal of the present collection is to try to combat these problems by viewing the *Phenomenology* as a systematic text. There has, of course, been much debate about the nature of this structure, but no one can reasonably deny the fact that Hegel intended for there to be one, however complex, *ad hoc*, or disjointed it ended up being.

Hegel's Systematic Pretensions

One of the most celebrated slogans in the *Phenomenology* is "The True is the whole."[40] Understanding what Hegel means by this is crucial for an appreciation of the notion of system in his thought. In many places Hegel insists that philosophical knowledge must form a systematic structure. In the *Encyclopaedia Logic*, for instance, he says of the absolute Idea,

> The science of this Idea must form a system. . . . Truth, then, is only possible as a universe or totality of thought. . . . Unless it is a system, a philosophy is not a scientific production. . . . Apart from their interdependence and organic union, the truths of philosophy are valueless, and must then be treated as baseless hypotheses, or personal convictions.[41]

Also, in the preface of the *Phenomenology*, Hegel flatly claims, "The true shape in which truth exists can only be the scientific system of such truth."[42] This claim is echoed a little later in the preface, when he says, "knowledge is only actual, and can only be expounded, as Science or as *system*."[43] These unambiguous statements leave no doubt about the importance which Hegel ascribes to the systematic nature of the philosophical enterprise. In this general insistence on the systematicity of philosophical knowledge, Hegel in no way differs from the other major representatives of the German idealist tradition; Kant, Fichte, and Schelling no less ardently insist on systematic philosophy. The question that we must now address is how Hegel conceived of a systematic body of knowledge.

Perhaps the easiest way to understand his claims about speculative philosophy is to consider the example of a mosaic. A mosaic is, of course, an aggregate of tiles which, when seen at a sufficient distance, collectively form a picture or some kind of design. If one is too close, the general design becomes indiscernible, and, instead of seeing a picture, one can recognize the individual tiles. Hegel's conception of philosophy is something like this. Individual concepts and propositions are the analogue of the individual tiles in the mosaic. When these concepts are taken out of their larger context and treated alone as atomic entities, then they lose their true meaning, just as a tile abstracted from the mosaic of which it is a part, in a sense, loses its meaning. The concepts have the meaning that they do only in their particular relation to other concepts, just as a given tile has the meaning it does only by virtue of its particular place in the mosaic. The speculative philosopher is one who tries to see all of the concepts and propositions in their systematic connection.

Even concepts or propositions which seem at face value to be contradictory are rendered consistent once they are placed in their true systematic context. Hegel writes, "The Speculative stage, or stage of Positive Reason apprehends the unity of terms (propositions) in their opposition—the affirmative, which is involved in their disintegration and in their transition."[44] In a similar passage from the introduction to the *Science of Logic*, Hegel writes, "It is in this dialectic as it is here understood, that is, in the grasping of opposites in their unity or of the positive in the negative, that speculative thought consists."[45] Speculative philosophy thus overcomes contradictions by understanding the individual concepts in their proper relationships *vis-à-vis* one another.

The mechanism by which contradictions are overcome and dissolved is, of course, the dialectic. For Hegel, individual concepts are not simply negated by contradictions and then discarded only to be replaced by other notions; instead, the concepts are all linked together, and the one develops out of the contradictions implicit in the another. Hegel describes his conception of the dialectic with an organic metaphor:

> The bud disappears in the bursting-forth of the blossom, and one might say that the former is refuted by the latter; similarly, when the fruit appears, the blossom is shown up in its turn as a false manifestation of the plant, and the fruit now emerges as the truth of it instead. These forms are not just distinguished from one another, they also supplant one another as mutually incompatible. Yet at the same time their fluid nature makes them moments of an organic unity in which they do not conflict, but in which each is as necessary as the other, and this mutual necessity alone constitutes the life of the whole.[46]

As a plant grows and develops, specific forms and structures develop out of others; a bud, grows into a blossom and a seed into a stock. So also in philosophy individual forms or concepts develop out of one another. Seen from a certain limited perspective, the later forms appear to be the contradiction of the earlier ones, but when we examine the matter more closely, we find that they in fact belong to the same organic entity, just as the seed, the bud, and the blossom are all parts of a single plant. For Hegel, the goal of philosophy is to grasp this entire entity in its organic unity and to lay bare its principle of development. It is in this sense that the truth is the whole.

This account of the necessity of the system in Hegel's philosophy clearly demonstrates that the "patchwork" interpretations of the *Phenomenology* are fundamentally mistaken in their approach. If we neglect Hegel's insistence on speculative philosophy, then we risk missing the thrust of his philosophy entirely since for him systematicity is necessarily bound up with the project of philosophical enquiry as such and is not merely one approach among others. In this respect the content and the form of his philosophy cannot be separated without loss to the whole. Given Hegel's unambiguous account of the necessity of a systematic approach to philosophy, we as interpreters would do well to attempt to understand the parts of the *Phenomenology* in their systematic context.

THE *PHENOMENOLOGY OF SPIRIT* READER

The primary goal of the present collection is to make the *Phenomenology of Spirit* more accessible to students and general readers by making more readily available a number of influential interpretive essays. This task is necessitated by Hegel's dense language and the complexity of the text as a whole, which render the work rather daunting for the non-specialist. The essays, which have all been chosen for their clear prose and honest exegetical attempts to explain the individual sections at issue, should do much to eliminate the difficulty involved in a first reading of this difficult text. In order not to complicate matters for readers unfamiliar with traditional criticisms of Hegel's position or with critical debates in the literature, an effort has been made to select articles which are self-contained and primarily interpretive; for this reason, otherwise useful essays offering critical, philological, and historical accounts of the *Phenomenology* have been omitted. In addition, the present collection has tried to bring together the best things written on the *Phenomenology* by the most distinguished Hegel scholars in a way that would ensure something resembling systematic coverage.

The guiding idea behind this collection has been to try to present a picture of the *Phenomenology* as a systematic text, as Hegel himself intended. This idea is an attempt to improve upon the shortcomings in the literature on the *Phenomenology* outlined above: (1) the unevenness of many analyses, and (2) the patchwork or episodic readings. First, as was mentioned above, many commentaries on the *Phenomenology* fall short since the diversity of material often proves to be too great for the abilities of a single commentator. In this collection, the best material on individual sections by a number of different authors with different interests and specializations has been selected so as to obviate this problem. Second, the present collection attempts to avoid the patchwork readings of the *Phenomenology* both in its format and in its selection of essays. With respect to format, our volume closely follows the table of contents of the *Phenomenology* itself in order to avoid neglecting major sections. The essays together form a sort of dialogue with the *Phenomenology* itself. The goal here is to get as much coverage of the primary text as possible and to avoid lopsided readings that focus only on individual sections. The selection of essays was also informed by the desire to underscore the systematic nature of the text. Most of the authors featured here make some effort to situate the section at issue in the larger context of the work. Readings of this kind are intended as an alternative to the patchwork or episodic interpretive trend.

The long preface of the *Phenomenology* is one of the most widely read sections in the entire Hegelian corpus. There Hegel discusses his philosophical methodology at some length and tries to show how his conception of philosophy differs from that of his contemporaries. In his essay, John Sallis treats above all the first part of the preface, exploring some of Hegel's most famous methodological slogans. He takes seriously Hegel's claim that philosophy, since it is not esoteric and not immediately comprehensible to common sense, must offer an initial "presentation" of itself to allow the uninitiated to pass beyond the prejudices of common sense and to gain access to Science. Sallis sees the *Phenomenology* as the execution of this presentation and its preface as a presentation introductory to this presentation. The introduction to the *Phenomenology*, although considerably shorter than the famous preface, is by no means less important. There as well we find some of Hegel's most forthright statements about his conception of philosophy and about the methodology used in the work. It is in the introduction that he discusses his notion of dialectic, his doctrine of determinate negation, the phenomenological actor or the view of common sense which he calls "natural consciousness," as well as the role of the *Phenomenology* in relation to Science. This rich section of text is taken up by two chapters in the present collection. In his chapter, Kenley R. Dove examines the decisive issue of a criterion of truth internal to consciousness which Hegel discusses in his introduction. On the basis of his analysis, Dove argues that the methodology of the *Phenomenology* is in fact not dialectical; instead, he claims it is descriptive since it merely observes and describes the movement of consciousness. Kenneth R. Westphal offers an exegetical and critical discussion of the introduction, focusing on Hegel's attempt to come to terms with the paradoxes involved in positing any criterion for knowing.

It is with the "Consciousness" chapter that Hegel begins the actual march to scientific knowing. In the three sections of this chapter, he gives cutting criticisms of a handful of epistemological theories with deep roots in the tradition. Katharina Dulckeit's chapter treats the problem of reference in "Sense-Certainty," the first section of the "Consciousness" chapter. She argues, contrary to the accepted view, that Hegel in fact does not deny that reference to particulars is possible;

rather, in "Sense-Certainty" he attempts to give an account of the conditions which are necessary for such reference. "Perception," the second section of the "Consciousness" chapter, is treated by Merold Westphal's essay. Westphal locates the discussion of "Perception" in the context of the development of the "Consciousness" chapter as a whole, tracing the movement from knowledge based on sense to knowledge based on understanding. His employment of a number of parallel analyses in the history of philosophy such as those of Plato, Descartes, and Kant, elucidates many aspects of Hegel's dense discussion. The difficult and disputed "Force and Understanding" section is analyzed by Joseph C. Flay's article, which examines Hegel's celebrated yet deeply obscure account of the inverted world. Taking Hegel at his word, Flay tries to understand the figure of the inverted world as an absurd position and offers an account of how the dialectic is led from this absurdity to self-consciousness.

The "Self-Consciousness" chapter, with its famous discussions of the lordship and bondage dialectic and the unhappy consciousness, is for many commentators a preferred locus in the *Phenomenology*. In the present collection, two essays are devoted to the influential analysis of the struggle for recognition and the dialectical relation of the lord and the bondsman. In his chapter, George Armstrong Kelly outlines the distorting influence of Kojève's Marxist interpretation of this relation. Kelly argues that this famous dialectic is multilayered in its meaning and cannot be adequately understood in a one-dimensional way only via its social aspect as Kojève tries to do. He then offers a corrective reading of this analysis by sketching its heretofore neglected dimensions. Howard Adelman's essay includes a useful account of Hegel's extremely obscure analysis on life and desire before proceeding to analyze the dialectical movement of the lord and the bondsman. Adelman attempts to interpret and illustrate Hegel's account with reference to the story of primitive human relations in Genesis. The second famous discussion in the "Self-Consciousness" chapter is Hegel's account of the unhappy consciousness; the chapter by John W. Burbidge is dedicated to this. Burbidge, discussing the entire section "Freedom of Self-Consciousness," argues that the unhappy consciousness does not represent the particular historical moment of medieval Catholicism, as Baillie and others have assumed, but rather is a universal form of human consciousness.

The extended and difficult "Reason" chapter, despite its crucial role in the *Phenomenology*, has long been neglected, and the two essays offered here are meant to correct this trend. In Alasdair MacIntyre's seminal study "Hegel on Faces and Skulls," he examines Hegel's treatment of the pseudosciences of physiognomy and phrenology in the long and dense "Observing Reason" section. MacIntyre shows that surprisingly many of the key claims of these dubious intellectual enterprises are still alive and well today in a number of contemporary materialist doctrines. He thus demonstrates that Hegel's criticisms of these pseudosciences are not merely bygone chapters in the history of philosophy which we can comfortably forget, but rather are every bit as relevant for us as they were for Hegel and his contemporaries. Hegel's famous and ironical discussion of the "Spiritual Animal Kingdom" constitutes the first analysis in the third section of the "Reason" chapter and is discussed in Gary Shapiro's essay. Following Lukács' interpretation, Shapiro tries to make a case for the importance of this section in the overall movement of the work.

The "Spirit" chapter is one of the richest in the entire text. Here Hegel systematically examines the stages of world history beginning with the ancient Greek *polis* and working up to his own age. In her essay Patricia Jagentowicz Mills critically examines Hegel's famous discussion of Sophocles' tragedy *Antigone* with which the "Spirit" chapter begins. She carefully analyzes Hegel's account of the drama in both the *Phenomenology* and the *Philosophy of Right* and uses it as a measuring rod for understanding the role of women in Hegel's philosophy as a whole. In the second section of the "Spirit" chapter, which is entitled "Self-Alienated Spirit," Hegel analyzes Diderot's work *Rameau's Nephew* as an example of modern alienation. This section is treated by David Price's essay, which meticulously analyzes Hegel's quotations from Diderot's text in order to arrive at a general theory of how and why Hegel incorporates literary works and characters into his own philosophical system. Also to be found in the "Self-Alienated Spirit" section is Hegel's treatment of the Enlightenment, which is analyzed by Karlheinz Nusser's essay. In addition to his account of Hegel's view of the French Revolution, Nusser interprets the lordship and bondage dialectic as the first step toward a revolutionary theory and discusses in some detail the dialectical movement in "Spirit" that leads up to Hegel's account of the French Revolution. Nusser ultimately tries to resolve the apparent contradiction pointed out by Habermas that Hegel was an advocate of the French Revolution but at the same time a critic of individual revolutionaries. The final section of the "Spirit" chapter, "Spirit that is Certain of Itself," begins with "The Moral Worldview" and concludes with Hegel's famous account of the beautiful soul. Both of these important discussions are treated in this collection. Moltke S. Gram's essay examines this entire third section, beginning with the "Moral World-View" and moving up to the "Religion" chapter. By recreating the historical context, he tries to show that Hegel's targets in this section are the early German Romantics. In his conclusion, Gram, like Price, tries to give a general account of the meaning of literary works for the systematic structure of the *Phenomenology*. Daniel P.

Jamros in his essay treats the final discussion of this section "Evil and Its Pardon." He analyzes the role of conscience for Hegel and tries to show how it plays the crucial role in the transition from the "Spirit" chapter to "Religion."

"Religion," the penultimate chapter of the *Phenomenology* has been somewhat neglected in Anglo-American scholarship despite its crucially important role in the text. Here Hegel works through manifold forms of religious consciousness which culminate in Christianity. He dedicates the first major section of the "Religion" chapter to what he calls "natural religion." The essay by the French Hegel scholar Jean-Louis Vieillard-Baron has been included for its treatment of this material. The author situates Hegel's discussion in its historical context and gives a careful paragraph by paragraph analysis of the first form of natural religion, "God as Light." The third section in "Religion," entitled "Revealed Religion," contains Hegel's celebrated analysis of Christianity. This material is taken up by two essays in this collection. The German Hegel scholar Harald Schöndorf offers a detailed commentary on the actual experience of this form of consciousness, which constitutes roughly the second half of the "Revealed Religion" section. He demonstrates how the dialectical movement of the externalization and reconciliation of Christ plays the crucial role in Hegel's Christian theology. In his essay, Martin J. De Nys treats this same material in a more thematic fashion, specifically by examining the motifs of mediation and negativity in religious consciousness as they appear in these pages.

The final chapter of the *Phenomenology*, "Absolute Knowing" has been extremely controversial. Perhaps one of the reasons for this is that the conclusions that one reaches about this short chapter have far-reaching consequences for one's interpretation of Hegel's philosophy as a whole. In his essay, Mitchell H. Miller Jr., addresses the major issues posed by this final chapter. He reconstructs Hegel's account of the path to absolute knowing taken in the *Phenomenology* and offers an interpretation of the meaning of absolute knowing for Hegel's claims about the system. The final essay in this collection tries to give a view of the overall systematic structure of the *Phenomenology* in a manner consonant with Hegel's own systematic pretensions. Using key explanatory passages at the beginning of major sections of the work, the author sketches the interlinking architectonic structure of the work which is *ipso facto* offered as a refutation of the "patchwork" reproaches and interpretations of the *Phenomenology*.

The hope is that these essays together will be an aid above all to the student of Hegel and the non-specialist attempting to come to terms with this difficult thinker for the first time. In addition, for the professional philosopher and Hegel scholar, this collection conveniently brings together influential essays on the *Phenomenology* by some of the most distinguished contemporary Hegel scholars in the French, German, and Anglo-American traditions. Another goal of the present collection is to establish fruitful points of contact between these various traditions of Hegel scholarship by means of the essays translated here for the first time from French and German. The main objective of this collection is, however, to understand Hegel's philosophy as he intended it to be understood, namely, as a systematic enterprise. These essays will thus help us to correct the long-standing interpretive trend which views the analyses of the *Phenomenology* episodically. For these reasons, it is hoped that this collection will be beneficial to both students and scholars alike and will serve as an impetus for Hegel studies in the world of Anglo-American philosophy.

NOTES

1. Cf. Merleau-Ponty: "All the great philosophical ideas of the past century—the philosophies of Marx and Nietzsche, phenomenology, German existentialism, and psychoanalysis—had their beginnings in Hegel." "Hegel's Existentialism," in *Sense and Nonsense*, trans. Hubert L. Dreyfus and Patricia Allen Dreyfus (Evanston, Ill.: Northwestern University Press, 1964), 63.

2. Ibid., 63.

3. Ibid., 64.

4. See Henry Harris, "The Hegel Renaissance in the Anglo-Saxon World Since 1945," *The Owl of Minerva*, 15 (1983): 77–107; Frederick G. Weiss, "A Critical Survey of Hegel Scholarship in English: 1962–1969," in *The Legacy of Hegel: Proceedings of the Marquette Hegel Symposium 1970*, ed. J. J. O'Malley, K. W. Algozin, H. P. Kainz, and L. C. Rice (The Hague: Martinus Nijhoff, 1973), 24–48.

5. Cf. Jean Hyppolite, "La *Phénoménologie* de Hegel et la pensée française contemporaine," in his *Figures de la pensée philosophique: Écrits (1931–1968)*, tome I (Paris: Presses Universitaires de France, 1971), 231–41.

6. Alexandre Kojève, *Introduction à la lecture de Hegel* (Paris: Gallimard, 1947). Translated as *An Introduction to the Reading of Hegel*, ed. Alan Bloom, trans. J. H. Nichols (Ithaca, N.Y.: Cornell University Press, 1969).

7. Paris: Aubier, 1946. In English as *Genesis and Structure of Hegel's Phenomenology of Spirit*, trans. Samuel Cherniak and John Heckman. (Evanston, Ill.: Northwestern University Press, 1974).

8. Hyppolite, "La *Phénoménologie* de Hegel," 235.

9. Cf. Vojin Simeunivic, "Die Aktualität von Hegels *Phänomenologie des Geistes*," *Praxis* 7 (1971): 73–83; Bruno Puntel, "Hegel heute. Zur *Phänomenologie des Geistes*," *Philosophisches Jahrbuch* 80 (1973): 133–60.

10. Theodore Haering, "Entstehungsgeschichte der *Phänomenologie des Geistes*," in *Verhandlungen des III. Internationalen Hegel Kongresses 1933*, ed. B. Wigersma (Haarlem: N/VH.D. Tjeenk Willink & Zn. and Tübingen: J. C. B. Mohr, 1934), 118–36.

11. Cf. Hans Friedrich Fulda, "Zur Logik der *Phänomenologie* von 1807," in *Materialien zu Hegels Phänomenologie des Geistes*, ed. Hans Friedrich Fulda and Dieter Henrich (Frankfurt: Suhrkamp, 1973), 391–422; also in *Hegel-Tage Royaumont 1964: Beiträge zur Deutung der Phänomenologie des Geistes*, ed. Hans-Georg Gadamer, *Hegel-Studien*, Beiheft 3 (Bonn: Bouvier, 1966), 73–102; Otto Pöggeler, "Zur Deutung der *Phänomenologie des Geistes*," *Hegel-Studien* 1 (1961): 255–94; Otto Pöggeler, "Die Komposition der *Phänomenologie des Geistes*," in *Hegel-Tage Royaumont 1964. Beiträge zur Phänomenologie des Geistes*, ed. Hans-Georg Gadamer, *Hegel-Studien*, Beiheft 3. (Bonn: Bouvier, 1966), 27–74, also in *Materialien zu Hegels Phänomenologie des Geistes*, ed. Hans Friedrich Fulda and Dieter Henrich (Frankfurt: Suhrkamp, 1973), 329–90.

12. Claus-Artur Scheier, *Analytischer Kommentar zu Hegels Phänomenologie des Geistes: Die Architektonik des erscheinenden Wissens* (Freiburg and Munich: Verlag Karl Alber, 1980).

13. Klaus Kähler and Werner Marx, *Die Vernunft in Hegels Phänomenologie des Geistes* (Frankfurt: Klostermann, 1992); Matthias Kettner, *Hegels Sinnliche Gewißheit*. (Frankfurt and New York: Campus, 1990); Manfred Negele, *Grade der Freiheit. Versuch einer Interpretation von G. W. F. Hegels Phänomenologie des Geistes* (Würzburg: Königshausen und Neumann, 1991).

14. William H. Goetzmann (ed.), *The American Hegelians: An Intellectual Episode in the History of Western America* (New York: Knopf, 1973); David Watson, "Hegelianism in the United States," *Bulletin of the Hegel Society of Great Britain* 6 (1982): 18–28; David Watson, "The Neo-Hegelian Tradition in America," *Journal of American Studies* 14 (1980): 219–34.

15. Cf. bibliography.

16. Cf. Robert Solomon, "Teaching Hegel," *Teaching Philosophy* 2 (1977–78): 213–24.

17. Cf. Heinz Kimmerle, "Dokumente zu Hegels Jenaer Dozententätigkeit (1801–1807)," *Hegel-Studien* 4 (1967): 21–99.

18. These works are as follows in German: *Jenaer Systementwürfe I–III*, volumes 6–8 of *Gesammelte Werke*, ed. the Rheinisch-Westfälische Akademie der Wissenschaften (Hamburg: Felix Meiner, 1968). The English translations are as

follows: G. W. F. Hegel. *The Jena System, 1804–5. Logic and Metaphysics*, translation edited by J. W. Burbidge and G. di Giovanni (Kingston and Montreal: McGill-Queen's University Press, 1986); *The Jena Lectures on the Philosophy of Spirit (1805–6)* in *Hegel and the Human Spirit*, trans. Leo Rauch (Detroit: Wayne State University Press, 1983); *First Philosophy of Spirit* in *G. W. F. Hegel, System of Ethical Life and First Philosophy of Spirit*, ed. and trans. H. S. Harris and T. M. Knox (Albany: State University of New York Press, 1979).

19. For a complete account see Friedhelm Nicolin, "Zum Titelproblem der *Phänomenologie des Geistes*," *Hegel-Studien* 4 (1967): 113–23.

20. PhS §89; PhG 61–62. (PhS = *Phenomenology of Spirit*, trans. A.V. Miller [Oxford: Clarendon Press, 1977]; PG = *Phänomenologie des Geistes*, volume 9 of *Gesammelte Werke*, ed. Rheinisch-Westfälische Akademie der Wissenschaften [Hamburg: Felix Meiner, 1968–]).

21. PhS §88; PG 61.

22. EL §25; Enz. 50. (EL = *Hegel's Logic: Part One of the Encyclopaedia of the Philosophical Sciences*, trans. William Wallace [Oxford: Clarendon Press, 1975]; Enz. = *Enzyklopädie der philosophischen Wissenschaften*, volume 19 of *Gesammelte Werke*, ed. Rheinisch-Westfälische Akademie der Wissenschaften [Hamburg: Felix Meiner, 1968–]).

23. In English as *Hegel's Science of Logic*, trans. A.V. Miller (London: George Allen and Unwin, 1989).

24. Hegel, EL §32 Remark; *Werke*, 8: 98–99. (*Werke* = *Georg Wilhelm Friedrich Hegel.Werke in zwanzig Bänden* [Frankfurt: Suhrkamp, 1970]).

25. Hegel, SL 49; WL 33 (SL = *Hegel's Science of Logic*, trans. A.V. Miller [London: George Allen and Unwin, 1989]; WL = *Wissenschaft der Logik*, volume 21 of *Gesammelte Werke*, ed. Rheinisch-Westfälischen Akademie der Wissenschaften [Hamburg: Felix Meiner, 1968–]).

26. In English as *Hegel's Logic: Part One of the Encyclopaedia of the Philosophical Sciences*, trans. William Wallace (Oxford: Clarendon Press, 1975).

27. In English as *Hegel's Philosophy of Nature: Part Two of the Encyclopaedia of the Philosophical Sciences*, trans. A.V. Miller (Oxford: Clarendon Press, 1970).

28. In English as *Hegel's Philosophy of Mind: Part Three of the Encyclopaedia of the Philosophical Sciences*, trans. W. Wallace and A.V. Miller (Oxford: Clarendon Press, 1971).

29. Cf. Adriaan Peperzak, *Philosophy and Politics: A Commentary on the Preface to Hegel's Philosophy of Right* (Dordrecht, Netherlands: Martinus Nijhoff, 1987), 15–33.

30. In English as *Hegel's Philosophy of Right*, trans. T. M. Knox (Oxford: Clarendon Press, 1952).

31. Hegel, PR, preface, p. 1; RP 19. (PR = *Hegel's Philosophy of Right*, trans. T. M. Knox [Oxford: Clarendon Press, 1952]; RP = *Grundlinien der Philosophie des Rechts oder Naturrecht und Staatswissenschaft im Grundrisse*, volume 7 of *Sämtliche Werke*, Jubiläumsausgabe in 20 Bänden, ed. Hermann Glockner [Stuttgart: Friedrich Frommann Verlag, 1927–40]).

32. The standard English translation is *The Philosophy of History*, trans. J. Sibree (New York: Willey, 1944; New York: Dover, 1956; Buffalo, N.Y.: Prometheus Books, 1990).

33. The standard English translation is *Hegel's Aesthetics*, 2 vols., trans. T. M. Knox (Oxford: Clarendon, 1975). Cf. also the earlier translation: *The Philosophy of Fine Art*, 4 vols., trans. Franceis Plumptre Beresford Osmaston (London: G. Bell and Sons, 1920).

34. The standard English translation is *Lectures on the Philosophy of Religion*, 3 vols., trans. Ebenezer Brown Speirs and J. Burdon Sanderson (London: K. Paul, Trench, Trübner and Co., 1895; rpt. London: Routledge and Kegan Paul, 1967). New edition: *Lectures on the Philosophy of Religion*, 3 vols., ed. Peter C. Hodgson, trans. R. F. Brown, P. C. Hodgson, and J. M. Stewart (Berkeley, Los Angeles, and London: University of California Press, 1984).

35. The standard English translation is *Lectures on the History of Philosophy*, 3 vols., trans. E. S. Haldane and Frances H. Simson (London: Routledge and Kegan Paul, 1894–96); rpt. (Lincoln and London: University of Nebraska Press, 1995).

36. Walter Kaufmann, "Hegel's Conception of Phenomenology," in *Phenomenology and Philosophical Understanding*, ed. Edo Pivcevic (Cambridge: Cambridge University Press, 1975), 229.

37. Ibid., 220.

38. Walter Kaufmann, *Hegel: A Reinterpretation* (Notre Dame, Ind.: University of Notre Dame Press, 1978), 243.

39. Kant, *Critique of Pure Reason*, trans. N. Kemp Smith (New York: St. Martin's Press, 1929), B xxxvii–viii.

40. Hegel, PhS §20; PG 19. Cf. EL §16; Enz. 41–42.

41. Hegel, EL §14; Enz. 41.

42. Hegel, PhS §5; PG 11.

43. Hegel, PhS §24; PG 21.

44. Hegel, EL §82; Enz. 92.

45. Hegel, SL 56; WL 41.

46. Hegel, PhS §2; PG 10. Hegel uses the same metaphor in his lectures on the philosophy of history: "And as the germ bears in itself the whole nature of the

tree, and the taste and form of its fruits, so do the first traces of Spirit virtually contain the whole of that History." PH, p. 18; VPG, p. 45 (PH = *The Philosophy of History*, trans. J. Sibree [New York: Willey, 1944]; VPG = *Vorlesungen über die Philosophie der Geschichte*, volume 11 of *Sämtliche Werke*, Jubiläumsausgabe in 20 Bänden, ed. Hermann Glockner [Stuttgart: Friedrich Frommann Verlag, 1927–40]).

I

Hegel's Preface and Introduction

1

John Sallis

Hegel's Concept of Presentation

Its Determination in the Preface to the *Phenomenology of Spirit*

For the first issue of the *Critical Journal of Philosophy*, which appeared in January 1802, Hegel wrote a long introduction entitled *On the Nature of Philosophical Criticism in General and Its Relation to the Present Condition of Philosophy in Particular*. One of the issues taken up in this introduction is the peculiarly esoteric character of philosophy. Hegel writes that "Philosophy is by its nature something esoteric." He explains: "It is philosophy only by being opposed to the understanding and therefore still more to common sense [*gesunder Menschenverstand*]. . . . In relation to the latter the world of philosophy is in and for itself an inverted world."[1]

Philosophy is esoteric—and yet not in the sense that would entitle it to an indifferent aloofness. It is not such as can remain merely the esoteric possession of a few specially gifted individuals. Hegel is emphatic on this point in the preface to the *Phenomenology of Spirit*: the elaboration, the form, demanded of philosophy is precisely such as to render it universally intelligible, "capable of being learned and of thus becoming the property of all"—that is, such as to render it "exoteric."[2] Philosophy is esoteric in its way of comporting itself to its matter, its world an inverted world, but it is exoteric in that it offers to all who would undertake it the possibility of undergoing the inversion into philosophy. The formulation in the introduction of 1802 is succinct: "Philosophy must indeed recognize the possibility of the people elevating themselves to it, but it must not lower itself to the people."[3]

The peculiar esoteric character of philosophy prescribes the rigor demanded of the beginner who would elevate himself to philosophy: the displacement into philosophy requires a radical inversion. And this inversion has as an essential moment a disorientation so radical that only the name "scepticism" is appropriate to it. Yet being in another regard exoteric, philosophy is obliged to hold out to the beginner the possibility of entering into this disorienting inversion, of offering (in the strictest sense) an *introduction* to philosophy. The radically disorienting, inverting movement into philosophy must be *presented*. An initiatory presentation (*Darstellung*) is demanded. The *Phenomenology of Spirit* is intended to satisfy this demand.

Just as philosophy in the form of science cannot begin straightaway as though "shot from a pistol," just as it requires the prior presentation of the movement up to philosophy, so likewise, the initiatory presentation has its "prerequisite." The presentation requires a prior determination (appropriately preliminary) of the concept of presentation. Such determining—the introduction to the introduction to philosophy—proves actually to be an anticipatory leap, and as such its necessity for the presentation itself can, at best, be clarified only in and through the determination, not at the outset. Our task is to thematize this determination of the concept of initiatory presentation—or, more specifically, to exhibit it up to the point where its necessity for the presentation begins to show itself from out of the determination. We accordingly restrict our attention to the preface to the *Phenomenology of Spirit*—in fact, to its earlier sections. Rather than proceeding to that second phase, that more specific determination of the concept of presentation which Hegel carries out in the introduction, in which the considerations, becoming more "procedural," are narrowed down to that point at which the presentation itself can commence—rather than proceeding thus, we shall remain with the preface and attempt to think through to its end the connection between presentation and presented as this connection is manifest within that larger sphere opened up by the more dangerous anticipatory leap which Hegel dares in the preface.

THE FAILURE OF THE PREFACE

Of the nineteen sections into which the preface is divided,[4] the first is the most starkly reflexive. The theme with which the preface here begins is *itself*—that is, the idea of a preface as such. More specifically, it begins with a consideration of the questionableness that necessarily infests any preface to a philosophical work, a questionableness rooted in a basic conflict between the character of a preface as such and the demand under which philosophy stands.

Hegel begins: Such explanation as is customarily offered in a preface—an explanation of the aim of the work and of its relation to other treatments of the same subject—"seems in the case of a philosophical writing not only superfluous but in regard to the nature of the matter [*um der Natur der Sache willen*] even unsuitable and inappropriate" (PhG 9). The matter to which philosophical writing pertains is of such a nature as to render all such prefatory explanations inappropriate. More precisely, such explanations stand in opposition to the way in which philosophy must comport itself to its matter, to its way of having regard for the matter, its way of being for the sake of the matter, its letting the matter be: "For instead of occupying itself with the matter, such talk is always outside it; instead of abiding in the matter and forgetting itself in it, such knowing always reaches out for something else and really remains involved with itself rather than being involved with the matter and devoting itself to it" (PhG 11).[5] The way of comportment characteristic of prefatory explanations, hence, what is said in such explanations and the manner in which it is said—such "cannot hold as the way in which philosophical truth is to be presented" (PhG 9).[6] The preface determines preliminarily the nature of presentation, but such determining is not itself a presentation. The preface falls short of those very "standards" which it determines.

From the outset the preface is thus destined to fail; from its beginning it is already a failure. This character must be directive for the interpretation of the preface if such interpretation is to avoid duplicating in itself the violence which the preface does to the matter of philosophical thought. The interpretation is called upon to let the violence ultimately recoil upon and be absorbed by the preface, to let the matters themselves simply stand. There is required, on the side of the interpretation, a certain suspension of judgment regarding those matters, a certain "parenthesizing," which is also in a sense a complicity in the violence or, to the extent that it understands itself, more properly a restraint. This restraint is required most of all in those connections in which the preface is addressed to such matters as the true, knowing, the absolute, God. In *our* time the restraint is more difficult and the demand for it of an entirely different order to the extent that our time is determined by the "death of God"—that is, by the positive lack of a true that could stand correlative to knowing and converge with it in absolute self-consciousness—that is, by the negation of precisely those matters which Hegel's presentation would allow to show themselves as the matter of philosophy.

But the preface cannot allow them genuinely to show themselves. Measured by the demands of the matters themselves, it is a failure. This failure of the preface and its way of determining the further character of the preface are variously elaborated in the first section. Hegel draws a curious analogy between philosophy and anatomy: just as no one would suppose that he could learn anatomy merely by acquiring the general idea without mastering the particulars, so in philosophy mere consideration of aims and of other such generalities is inadequate to the matter itself. In fact, the inadequacy is much greater in the case of philosophy, it is even of an entirely different order; for, in the end, anatomy has no right at all to the name of science, and thus the very distinction between the actual elaboration and mere prefatory considerations breaks down, both being equally unscientific. The collapse of this distinction in the case of anatomy and the correlative breakdown of the analogy with philosophy serve, however, to render the distinction still more prominent in the case of philosophy. There is a fundamental opposition between a philosophical work and such general considerations as customarily go to make up a preface. This disparity generates, in turn, a disparity within the preface itself: "In the case of philosophy, on the other hand, there would arise the disparity that use would be made of such a way [i.e., an unscientific procedure, as in anatomy] and yet, by means of this way itself, it would be exhibited as incapable of grasping the truth" (PhG 10) Such a disparity characterizes the preface to the *Phenomenology of Spirit*: its procedure, its way of showing something, is such that the procedure itself gets shown up as inadequate. The preface is such as to revoke itself. Its exhibition of what is required in order to be equal to the task of grasping the truth recoils upon the preface itself, which manifestly does not meet the requirement thus exhibited. Nevertheless, in this self-revocation a certain content is preserved, namely, the determination of the nature of presentation; it is preserved inasmuch as it is carried over into *enactment*. The preface sublates itself; its fundamental movement is an *Aufheben*.[7]

Substance and Subject

The basis for the determination of the concept of initiatory presentation is prepared in sections 5–6 of the preface. Sections 7–8 explicitly carry through the determinations thus prepared. The subsequent sections of the preface are then devoted largely to elaborating the determination in various regards and to applying it to certain polemical contexts.

The preparatory sections will require our most careful attention and our most deliberate restraint. As guide for thematizing that basis which they prepare for the determination, we focus on three principal statements from these sections.

The first of these statements occurs at the beginning of section 5:

> According to my view, which must justify itself [only] through the presentation of the system itself, everything depends on comprehending and expressing the true not as substance but just as much as subject.[8]

Two general observations need to be made before we focus on the principal content of the statement. First, we note how the cast of the statement accords with the preliminary, prescientific character which both the determination and the provision of its basis have. The statement incorporates a self-characterization: Hegel is expressing his view (*Einsicht*) to which other views could be opposed, views whose claims to truth could not be effectively countered. Such expression does not belong to the presentation in the proper sense that is to be determined, and consequently what is expressed will eventually need to be genuinely established within the presentation. Second, we note Hegel's reference to "comprehending and expressing." This reference poses on the horizon two relevant dualities: the duality of presentation (the comprehending and expressing) and presented (that which is comprehended and expressed); and, within the presentation itself, the duality of comprehension and expression, of thought and language.

The true is to be comprehended and expressed "not as substance"—that is, not merely as substance, not as though it were substance and nothing more—"but just as much as subject." The true is to be taken as *both* substance and subject, yet in such fashion that the taking of it as subject involves a *negation* of the taking of it as mere substance.

In this context substance is to be understood primarily in the sense determined for it in Spinoza's *Ethics*: "By substance I understand that which is in itself and is conceived through itself."[9] Substance is that which is in itself in the sense of suffering no dependence on anything external to itself, which is absolved from all such dependence and in this sense absolute. Thus, Spinoza poses substance (i.e., the one substance, God) as encompassing both thought and extension as its attributes—hence, as encompassing both subject and object. But, in the end, substance as determined in Spinoza's work proves not to be so encompassing; as Fichte explicitly recognized,[10] substance as so determined remains bound on the side of things. Indeed, as Hegel notes in the present context, Spinoza's own age was outraged by his concept of God as the one substance because of "the instinctive recognition that self-consciousness was only drowned in it and not preserved." To take the true as mere substance is to remain on the side of the object, that is, to establish the identity of subject and object only on the side of the object. In the language of Hegel's *Differenz*-Schrift,[11] Spinoza's substance is, at best, merely an objective subject-object.

What is thus required is that the true be "just as much" subject, that it be not merely substance but also subject. In this connection, "subject" has, as the primary sense from which Hegel in reforming and further developing its sense will proceed, that sense determined for it in Fiche's *Wissenschaftslehre*: the subject "Has no being proper, no subsistence" [*kein eigentliches Seyn, kein Bestehen*] but rather is sheer "act" [*Handeln*] and nothing but act, specifically, the act of positing itself.[12] The subject is a movement of self-positing, hence, as both positing and posited, is "a necessary identity of subject and object: subject-object."[13] However, it is an identity of subject and object on the side of the subject, a subjective subject-object.[14] What is thus required is that it unite "with itself the being of the substance" (PhG 19), that is, that the true be both subject and substance. What is required is a synthesis which will yield the identity of subject and substance, that is, the identity of identity and non-identity.[15]

But everything depends on how this uniting of subject and substance is carried through, on whether it falls back into "inert simplicity" so as to end up presenting "actuality in a non-actual manner" (PhG 19f.)—that is, on whether this uniting results in an indifference with respect to subject and object in which the negation and opposition between them would be finally eliminated, so that the movement and struggle corresponding to such negation and opposition would be revoked ultimately, rather than being taken up into the end in the manner Hegel expresses by restoring to the word "actuality" the fundamental sense which the ancient philosophical tradition gave it. It is not sufficient that the true merely be *also* subject; rather, its way of being subject must be such as to sublate its way of being substance, its being-subject must constitute a sublation of its being-substance. This means that its being-subject must both negate and preserve its being-substance.[16]

Hegel's expression of the relevant negation consists mostly of a recapitulation of the general Fichtean determination of the nature of the subject. He begins: "The living substance is, further, that being which is in truth *subject* or, in other words, which is in truth actual only insofar as it is the movement of self-positing" (PhG 20). It is to be noted how Hegel refers here to *living* substance, which (to say the least) is meant to indicate substance in a sense which, in contrast to that determined in Spinoza's thought, does not remain merely on the side of things. Substance (as living) is in truth subject; that is, substance in respect of its being in the truth, in its character as constituting the truth, *is* subject. Substance, in that sense that would allow one to say "the true is substance," is such as to require that in the end one say instead "the true is subject." Furthermore, "end" is here to be understood as τέλος,[17] thus, in correlation with actuality in the sense of ἐνέργεια. Substance, as being gathered up into its τέλος, as actual, is movement—specifically, the movement of self-positing, the movement which, in the Fichtean determination, does not just belong to the subject but rather *is* the subject.

Hegel continues: "As subject, it is pure, *simple negativity* and thus the bifurcation [*Entzweiung*] of the simple." This means: As the positing of itself, the subject is both the subject (which posits) *and* the object (which is posited); the subject as posited is object, is what it is not, is pure, simple negativity. As subject, as positing of itself, it is a positing of bifurcation; it posits within itself the bifurcation into subject and object.

Hegel continues, describing the subject, which is the bifurcation of the simple: "or the doubling which opposes [*die entgegensetzende Verdopplung*], which again is the negation of this indifferent diversity and of its opposite." The bifurcation is an opposition *within* the subject; the opposition between subject and object is an opposition within the subject. Thus, it belongs to the movement of the subject (the movement which the subject *is*) to overcome the opposition, to negate the sheer diversity and reestablish its own unity. This overcoming, this reestablishing its own unity, is not merely something added on, as it were, to the subject's self-positing, to that movement of self-positing which the subject *is*. On the contrary, the movement of self-positing *is* such a reestablishing, of unity from out of diversity; it is a self-gathering—neither unity nor diversity but the gathering of diversity into unity. In Hegel's words "on this sameness which reconstitutes itself or the reflection into itself in being other—not an *original* unity as such or immediate unity as such—is the true."

The true is subject, that is, the movement of self-gathering into its end: "It is the becoming of itself, the circle which presupposes its end as its aim and has it for its beginning and which is actual only through its execution and end." The true is *not* substance: There can be "alongside" the subject no substance which, as object, would together with the subject constitute the true. There can be no such object, for the very distinction between subject and object is itself posited within the subject. The only being which, in the end, measures up to the Spinozistic criterion of substance is subject, not substance) only subject is "in itself" and "conceived through itself," whereas substance (as object) falls decisively within the sphere of the self-positing which is the subject.

Yet in the issue of subject and substance, there is not only the moment of negation but also that of preservation; the opposition between subject and substance is not simply abolished at the level of the true in its actuality but also preserved in a new form. This requirement, that a moment of opposition to the subject be preserved, suddenly bursts forth at the very center of the issue—bursts forth in a language of such sheer strength that it holds together as its content the utmost abstractness and the most stark concreteness. Hegel writes of how matters would stand if such a moment were lacking, if there were merely the moment of negation, if subject were just the negation of substance in the sense of excluding the latter from the true in its actuality: "Thus the life of God and divine knowing may indeed be spoken of as a playing of love with itself; this idea sinks to the level of edification and even insipidity when seriousness, pain, the patience and work of the negative are lacking in it." This playing of love with itself, this play of unification, of self-gathering into unity—what is that seriousness which, if lacking in the idea of such play, reduces what would be the idea of absolute knowing to the level of mere edification?

Hegel continues: "In itself that life is indeed untroubled sameness and unity with itself, which is not serious about otherness and estrangement, nor with the overcoming of this estrangement." Thus, that seriousness which is so crucial is a seriousness regarding otherness; and the insipid idea which fails to include this seriousness is an idea of the divine life merely as *in itself*. What is the character of this seriousness regarding otherness such that it shatters the untroubled unity with self of the divine life in itself? Seriousness about otherness can be thus effective only if it corresponds to an otherness which is in truth serious, a serious otherness. What, then, is other than life, knowing, subject? And how is it *seriously* other than these? The relevant otherness is simply that of object to subject. It is that otherness constituted by the subject-object bifurcation. What, then, is required in order that this otherness be a *serious* otherness? It is required that the bifurcation be no mere correlate of self-positing, that the otherness of object to subject not be such as to be immediately and totally dissolved into the subject's identity with itself. The bifurcation, the eruption of otherness, must be a rending, a tearing apart to which belongs the *pain* of dismemberment, a rending which no sheer self-assertion can heal but which requires "the patience and work of the negative." Serious otherness is no mere moment within the identity of the subject; and the overcoming of serious otherness is not to be accomplished by a mere positing of unity correlative to such identity, by a mere positing of a unity that would immediately abolish the diversity of dismemberment. What is required is rather the toilsome gathering of diversity into unity, a gathering which, in overcoming diversity, otherness, lets it nevertheless be preserved in a new form.

Referring still to the divine life regarded in itself, as lacking seriousness about otherness, Hegel continues: "But this in-itself is abstract generality in which is disregarded both the nature of this life *to be for itself* and thus the self-movement of the form." To surpass the level of mere edification, it is thus required that the divine life be regarded in its nature as being-for-itself. For it to be for itself means: to establish the unity of its self-identity (to posit itself) from out of an opposition of such seriousness as to require toil, an opposition of such seriousness that mere negation of it cannot stand, an opposition which, in being overcome, must also be preserved by being granted a new form, an opposition which must be *sublated*. The true is not merely the untroubled self-positing of the divine life, not merely "the pure self-contemplation of the divine"; it is such only *in itself*, not in its *actuality*. The true becomes actual only by troubling itself with the gathering of serious otherness into itself; the true in its actuality is the gathering which *forms* diversity into unity, the gathering movement of informing, "the self-movement of the form."[18]

Hegel concludes: "The true is the whole." He explains: "It should be said of the absolute that it is essentially *result*, that it is only in the end what it is in truth; and precisely in this consists its nature: to be actual, subject, or that which becomes itself." The absolute is the whole of that movement in which self-identity is reconstituted from out of a bifurcation involving serious otherness; it is the whole of the movement in which the otherness of what is seriously other is sublated and that other thus established in its proper identity with the subject; it is the whole of the movement of gathering diversity into unity. And yet, the absolute is *in truth* "only in the end," only as "result." In its way of being the true as such, the absolute is the whole of the movement of gathering *as itself gathered up* into its fulfillment in the end; for what gathers and what is gathered are established in their identity precisely through the gathering, and so the absolute is the self-gatheredness into the τέλος, that is, the absolute is ἐνέργεια.

The true cannot be merely substance in that Spinozistic sense that remains on the side of objects; the true must *also* be subject. Yet, the true cannot be merely both substance and subject; its being-subject must also sublate its being-substance. This means, first, that its being-subject negates its being-substance, that is, that there can be no mere substance (as object) alongside the subject, since the very distinction between subject and object is posited within the subject; and it means, second, that in its being-subject its being-substance is also preserved, namely, as serious otherness. Yet now it can be seen, further, that the being-substance which is sublated by being-subject falls as much on the side of the subject as on that of the object: the true in-itself, the divine life as lacking serious otherness, is substance—Hegel calls it "immediate substance"—which the subject, the true in its actuality, negates and preserves in that movement of self-gathering which it is.

Knowing as System

We are seeking to thematize the basis which Hegel lays in sections 5–6 as preparation for the determination of the concept of presentation. To this end, we have proposed to focus on three principal statements from these sections. The second of these statements occurs at the beginning of the next-to-last paragraph of section 6:

> Among several conclusions which follow from what has been said, one may be singled out: it is only as science or as *system* that knowing is actual and can be presented.[19]

We need to ask: From which of the previous considerations does this conclusion follow? And how?

It can be related, first of all, to the consideration of language, specifically, of the proposition, that occurs in the middle of section 6 (PhG 21–23). This consideration falls into two parts which are separated in the text by a paragraph in which Hegel develops his concept of actuality by bringing it into explicit connection with Aristotle's concept of purposiveness.

The first part of the consideration of language occurs as a response to those who would object to understanding the absolute as result, who would object to this on the ground that it introduces mediation into the absolute. Hegel answers this objection by showing how it is based simply on a misunderstanding of the nature of mediation and of the bond between mediation and determination. If the absolute is spoken of *immediately*, if one utters such words as "God," "absolute," "eternal," then the absolute *as* so expressed is merely something general, and such expression is hardly an adequate expression of the absolute. Such single words "do not express what they contain" (PhG 21)—just as the phrase "all animals" does not constitute a zoology. But if to such words anything else is added, if the transition is made to a proposition, then mediation is involved. If, for example, instead of saying merely "God," one says "God is the eternal," then there occurs within the expression the transition from God to something other, the eternal, and then the taking of this other back into God—that is, mediation, which Hegel defines as "nothing else but self-moving self-identity" (PhG 21). Without mediation there could be nothing beyond the mere uttering of names.

The second part of the consideration of language in section 6 is, in effect, an elaboration of Hegel's definition of mediation. In order to express the absolute more adequately than in the previously mentioned single words, one might employ the proposition "God is the eternal." Here one begins with the word "God," which, however, taken by itself, is "a senseless sound, a mere name"; only the predicate gives the name content (PhG 22). And so, one might well ask: why not just speak of "the eternal"? Why add the senseless sound in the first place? Hegel answers: "But this word signifies that what is posited is not a being or essence or mere generality but rather something reflected into itself, a subject" (PhG 23). The point is that the structure of the proposition anticipates the structure of the absolute as subject: it involves a transition into otherness (bifurcation) and the leading of this other back into the unity of the subject. Nevertheless, the structure of the proposition does *not* duplicate that of the absolute, does not mirror it perfectly; it *only* anticipates it: "The subject is accepted as a fixed point to which the predicates are affixed as to their support, by a movement which belongs to those who know about it and which is not supposed to belong to the fixed point; but only through this [that is, the recognition that the movement belongs to the subject itself] could the content be presented as subject." The limitation thus lies in the fact that the movement between subject and predicate is taken to belong to the one who knows or asserts the proposition, *not* to the subject itself, which is, rather, posited as a fixed point.

How is this consideration of language linked to that conclusion which Hegel draws: "It is only as science or as *system* that knowing is actual and can be presented"? It is linked, specifically, to that side of the conclusion which pertains to the presentation in general; this is indicated at the end of the consideration of language by Hegel's reference to what would be required in order for the structure of the proposition to be more than a mere anticipation of the structure of the absolute, in order that its content be, as Hegel says, "presented as subject." Such presentation would require that the subject (of the proposition) into which the predicate is taken back not be treated as fixed, as unaffected, unchanged, by the synthesis, that the movement not be regarded as belonging on the side of a detached knower who would have the proposition as object of his knowing. Rather, the subject must be treated as moved, as having become a different, more determinate subject by virtue of its taking of the predicate into itself. Yet this is precisely what a proposition is prevented from accomplishing by its static subject-predicate structure; a proposition can *only anticipate* that movement which the absolute is. The structure of the proposition is such that this movement of becoming determinate cannot be *presented* in a single proposition. This means that the conception of the nature of philosophy in terms of basic propositions [*Grundsätze*] or principles [*Prinzipien*], that conception which dominates almost all modern philosophy up to German idealism, is decisively transformed in Hegel's development of the issue of presentation. Any such proposition, 'if it is true, is also false insofar as it is merely a basic proposition or principle" (PhG 23). How, then, can the movement be presented? Its presentation will (at least) require a *system* of propositions, that is, a chair of propositions systematically connected in such a way that each proposition leads over to another which has as its subject that more determinate subject that results from the determination accomplished through the first proposition.[20] For the sake of presentation, the advance must be made not only from word to proposition but also from proposition to system of propositions. The absolute can be presented "only as science or as system."

Here it is appropriate to recall that peculiar disparity within the preface of which Hegel spoke at the outset, the disparity which gives to the preface its self-revoking character: it is to show that the way of showing characteristic of a preface does not measure up to what is required for a *presentation* of philosophical truth. Already this self-revocation is under way: the preface is not itself such a *system* of propositions as it has shown, to be required for the presentation of the truth.[21]

In the statement with which we are now concerned, there is a peculiar duality; Hegel referred not only to presentation but also to what is to be presented in the presentation. On the one hand, he says that knowing can be *presented* only as science or as system, the reference being primarily to the requirement that the presentation take the form of a system of propositions, in contrast, for example, to an attempt at presentation through an alleged basic principle. On the other hand, Hegel says also that knowing is itself actual only as science or system. Not only must knowing be presented as science or as system but also it *is* science or system; and only because it is such does its presentation stand under the requirement that it assume the form of science or system. Knowing, as actual, *is* system, and this is why it must be presented as system. A more fundamental sense of "system" thus begins to emerge: according to this sense, a system is not merely a system of propositions but rather a system of knowing, the system which knowing *is*. But what is this knowing which is actual only as system? It is the knowing *of* the absolute (in the double sense of the genitive). It is the self-knowing of the absolute, in which the absolute reconstitutes its self-identity from out of a serious otherness. Yet this movement of self-knowing is just the absolute itself; and so in its fundamental sense the system *is* the absolute.

In the first statement that we considered, Hegel calls the absolute "the true"; and, explicitly expressed "not as substance but just as much as subject," it is called "the true in its actuality," "the true as actual." In the second statement, on the other hand, he calls the absolute "knowing," or, more fully, "knowing as actual." The absolute in its actuality is called both "knowing" and "the true." But in so calling it, Hegel has let it become manifest why it may be called by both names: in its actuality, in that self-gatheredness into the τέλος, the absolute finds itself in the other so as to reestablish its own self-identity) such reestablishing, as sublation of the otherness of the object, and, hence, of the otherness of the known, *the true*—such reestablishing is thereby an establishing of the identity of knowing with the true. In its actuality the absolute is both knowing and the true, for in this actuality knowing and the true are identical; the absolute is, most properly, the movement of establishing this identity, the movement in which knowing and the true are gathered into their identity.

Spirit

According to the first principal statement, the absolute (the true as actual) is to be comprehended "not as substance but just as much as subject." If the terms are taken in the senses to which the development of this statement leads, that is, if substance is taken as the true in itself, as the "essence" (PhG 20), and subject as the true for itself, as the true in its actuality, then the result of this development may be expressed by saying: substance is essentially subject. The second statement—that "it is only as science or as *system* that knowing is actual and can be presented"—may be similarly abbreviated if the subordination of presentation to what is presented is taken as granted. It then says: knowing, that is, the absolute, that is, the true as actual, is system; that is, the true is actual only as system. The third of the statements, which stands at the beginning of the final, most crucial paragraph of section 6, brings the results of the other two statements together in the concept of spirit:

> That the true is actual only as system or that the substance is essentially subject is expressed in the representation which speaks of the absolute as *spirit*.[22]

In the paragraph which this statement introduces the basis is decisively laid for the determination of the nature of presentation.

The crucial connection is that of spirit to actuality: "The spiritual alone is the actual" (PhG 24). The determinations of spirit are thus to be worked out in terms of the concept of actuality, as the latter has been unfolded throughout sections 5–6. Hegel gives four determinations. First, spirit is "the essence or being-in-itself"—that is, it is immediate substance, the divine life as pure self-contemplation, as involving no serious otherness, as not having undergone the pain of that bifurcation which brings with it radical opposition. In this determination, spirit still lacks form and actuality, that is, it is not yet the concrete movement which forms diversity into the unity of the τέλος, into actuality; it is no more than the abstract, still indeterminate assertion of unity, the possibility of self-positing. Second, spirit is "that which relates itself and is determinate" (*das sich Verhaltende und Bestimmte*)—that is, spirit is that which can become determinate, which can concretely posit itself, *only* insofar as it relates itself to an other, only insofar as it undergoes that bifurcation by which radical opposition is brought forth. The third determination is stated together with the second, as though they were one: spirit is "that which is other and for itself" (*das Anderssein und Fürsichsein*)—that is, the other, which according to the second determination must be brought forth, is brought forth in a rending off spirit itself. It is an other which, however serious its otherness, is ultimately nothing other than spirit itself, an other in which spirit is object for itself. Fourth, spirit is that which "in this determination or being outside itself remains in itself—or it is in and for itself [*in dieser Bestimmtheit oder seinem Außersichsein in sich selbst Bleibende;—oder es ist an und für sich*]"—that is, spirit is the sublation of that bifurcation from which both otherness (being outside itself) and determinateness emerge; it is the gathering of otherness into itself, the positing of the identity of the other with what was subject in itself but is now, through this movement of determination, a reconstituted self-identity. In this fourth determination the others are gathered up: spirit is being-in-and-for-itself.

Hegel proceeds to develop a curious "doubling" of these determinations:

> This being-in-and-for-itself, however, it is first for us or *in itself*; it is the spiritual *substance*. It must also be this *for itself*, must be the knowing of the spiritual and the knowing of itself as the spirit. (PhG 24)

This doubling indicates a movement. It is a movement of spirit (as being-in-and-for-itself). But it is characterized in two somewhat different ways. This difference is decisive.

According to the first characterization, the initial term of the movement, namely, that *from* which there is movement, is being-in-and-for-itself (only) in-itself. This term Hegel describes as "spiritual substance." At the first level it has, in a sense, no lack: as spirit, as being-in-and-for-itself it has undergone the pain of bifurcation and the reconstitution of unity out of diversity. But, at the level of the "doubling" it is only substance, not yet subject; it lacks actuality. Yet the levels must be brought together, and that requires that his term be regarded as spirit in that condition in which that reunification, without which it would not be spirit, is indeed accomplished *but remains merely implicit*. It is the movement of gathering in that condition in which the moment of being itself gathered up, that is, the identity of what gathers with what is gathered, is still implicit. In this condition spirit is reunited with itself in the object; it knows itself in the object without, however, knowing that it is itself that it knows. The relevant movement is, then, from spirit in this condition *to* being-in-and-for-itself (also) for-itself—i.e., *to* spirit in that condition in which it knows itself explicitly in its other. Thus, the movement is a movement from spirit in-itself to spirit for-itself, to spirit which is actual in the highest sense. Yet spirit is itself movement; and so the movement being described is not something which spirit passively undergoes (in the sense, for instance, of a substratum that would remain unchanged through the movement), but rather the movement must belong to that very movement which spirit *is*.

But there is a second, quite distinct characterization given of this movement. According to this second characterization, the relevant movement is a movement from being-in-and-for-itself *for us* to being-in-and-for-itself *for itself*. Taken superficially, this characterization suggests that "we" know something about the absolute which it does not know about itself (namely, that it knows itself in its object). It suggests, in other words, that we know more about the absolute than it knows about itself, so that what would be required is that the absolute raise itself to that level of knowledge which *we* already have. The relevant movement would, then, be a movement by which spirit would come to know as much about its own self-knowing as we knew already before the movement. But clearly this suggested sense of the movement is a *comic sense*; and it collapses as soon as we ask seriously about such knowledge of the absolute as we would presume to have from outside the absolute. What must be the character of a knowing of the absolute in which we—or, more precisely, I—would be the subject of the knowing and the absolute its object? In order for it to be a genuine knowing, it must be true, that is, it must be a knowing of the true. But the development of the second of the three principal statements has shown that a knowing of the true in its actuality is precisely a movement in which is established the identity of knowing with the true. For genuine knowing there is thus required in the present case a movement through which the mutual externality of the I and the absolute would be retroactively revoked. In other words, the knowing must be such that what the subject knows in knowing the object is just itself and such that the subject comes to recognize this knowing *as* a knowing of itself. Thus, in knowing the absolute, the I would know itself *in* the absolute and would recognize its unity with the absolute.

Hence, in the course of knowing the absolute, the I would cease to be a subject situated outside the absolute; its knowing would be, as it were, appropriated to the self-knowing of the absolute.

What, then, is the character of the movement and of its terms? It is a movement *from* a knowing of the absolute which presumes to be outside the absolute and for which spirit would be merely in itself (i.e., its object) *to* a knowing of the absolute which knows itself as not being external but rather as belonging to the absolute's self-knowing. It is a movement of the knowing I *into* the absolute—that is, it is a movement by which the I's knowing is appropriated to the absolute's self-knowing. Considered with respect to its final term, it is a movement in which spirit becomes for-itself by appropriating the self-conscious I, the immediate *cogito*. Contrary to the comic sense at first suggested, the movement is not a movement of the absolute up to the I but of the I up to the absolute; yet even this conception grants too much externality and so requires qualification, for the I can move up to the absolute only because the absolute is already with it,[23] or, still more strictly, the movement is not something which the I accomplishes alone but is rather a movement of the absolute, that is, belongs to that movement which the absolute *is*. These qualifications point to a more fundamental perspective on the movement. If the absolute is absolute, then the I cannot have been initially outside it, so as then to undergo movement into the absolute. Rather, the I must already be in the absolute from the beginning, and the movement thus a movement within the absolute. It must be a movement by which the I, which takes itself to be outside the absolute, comes to the awareness that it is always already within the absolute.

Hegel's conclusion to section 6 poses the connection between spirit and science:

> The spirit which, so developed, knows itself as spirit is *science*. Science is the actuality of spirit and the realm that the spirit builds for itself in its own element.

Thus, science is not a theory about spirit, not an account of spirit—just as system is not merely a system of propositions. Rather, science *is* spirit in its actuality. Science *is* the absolute.

The posing of the identity between spirit and science brings to completion the preparation of the basis for the determination of presentation. With this completion two further issues are opened up which point ahead into the complexity of the problem of presentation.

The first concerns the title "System of Science," which Hegel places at the beginning of his work. The title now says: system of spirit in its actuality. Yet system in its fundamental sense is identical with spirit as actual, the gathering of diversity into the unity of the τέλος. Hence, the title, in this formulation as well as the first, just says the same thing twice—or, it says: system (science) which is spirit in its actuality. "System," "science," "spirit in its actuality"—in their fundamental senses all three say the same thing. And as long as one adheres solely to this fundamental sense, it makes no sense to speak of *Hegel's system*—or, at best, to speak in this way is only to allude to the problem of withholding from the primary sense of "system" (and "science") a secondary, yet in some measure distinct sense; it is to allude to the problem of presentation.

The second issue concerns the becoming of science—specifically, the way in which the sense of such becoming is determined by the posing of the identity of science with spirit in its actuality. Such becoming must belong (in a still to be determined way) to that movement of gathering which is spirit itself. The becoming of science must thus belong to science itself, just as the gathering movement of spirit is itself gathered up into the end. To the extent that the structure of presentation accords with that of what is presented, the presentation of the becoming of science, which Hegel is about to identify as the phenomenology of spirit, constitutes a part of science (as presentation). The presentation of the inverting movement into philosophy falls within philosophy and separates itself decisively from the (self-revoking) prefatory determination of the nature of presentation.

Presentation

In sections 5–6 Hegel has laid the basis for that determination of the concept of presentation that is to be carried out and elaborated in the subsequent sections of the preface. This basis consists primarily of the determinations of spirit and the peculiar "doubling" then built on these determinations, a "doubling" through which is distinguished, within that whole movement which is spirit as such, the particular movement from spirit in-itself (or for us) to spirit for itself (i.e., spirit in its full actuality). With this basis laid, Hegel proceeds in section 7 to introduce the issue of initiatory presentation and to relate it to that particular movement that has been distinguished.

Hegel introduces into the considerations the peculiar esoteric and exoteric characters of philosophy. These characters in their tension generate the problem of presentation, at least in its most immediate form as that of presenting the inverting movement into philosophy. The esoteric character is expressed first: "Science on its part demands of self-consciousness that it should have elevated itself into this ether to be able to live—and to live—with it and in it (PhG 25). Science—that is, in its fundamental sense, spirit as actual and, in its derivative sense, philosophy—brings a demand. It places this demand upon self-consciousness, that is, upon the individual I, the immediate *cogito*, which as such lays claim to knowing. The demand is that the I elevate itself "into this ether," that is, into the sphere of "pure self-recognition in absolute otherness" (PhG 24)—that is, up to the level of being-in-and-for-itself for itself, of spirit in its full actuality. That to which elevation is demanded is identical with that which places the demand. And what is demanded, the elevation of self-consciousness into the "ether," is precisely that movement which Hegel distinguished at the end of section 6: the movement of the I into the absolute.

Hegel proceeds to consider the exoteric character of philosophy: "Conversely, the individual has the right to demand that science should at least offer him the ladder to this standpoint and show him this standpoint within himself" (PhG 25). The ladder would lead from the I into the absolute—that is, it would make available to the I the way of that movement into the absolute—that is, it would *present* it. The ladder which the individual can rightly demand is simply the presentation of the movement into the absolute, of the movement up to philosophy. Yet how does the ladder, the presentation, lead the I to the standpoint of science? It does so, not in the manner of a mere connecting of two otherwise unrelated points, but rather, as Hegel says, by showing the individual "this standpoint within himself." The presentation is to let the standpoint of the I develop itself into what it already implicitly is, the standpoint of science.

However, the movement to be thus presented is not a mere uninterrupted, untroubled unfolding; it is not a movement lacking serious opposition, resistance, tension. In fact, the relevant tension has already come into view in previous considerations as the tension between the I's taking itself to be outside the absolute (such that the absolute would be its *object*) and the I's always already belonging to the absolute. Hegel now extends this into a fundamental tension between science and natural consciousness:

> If the standpoint of consciousness, to know of objective things in opposition to itself and to know of itself in opposition to them, is considered by science as the *other*—that in which it knows itself to be at home with itself, is considered rather as the loss of the spirit—so, on the other hand, the element of science is to it a distant beyond in which it no longer has possession of itself. Each of these two appears to the other to be the inversion of the truth. That the natural consciousness immediately entrusts itself to science is an attempt it makes, attracted by it knows not what, to walk for once also on its head. (PhG 25)

The opposition is fundamental. Science stands at the point of explicit unification of subject and object, of being-in-and-for-itself *for itself*, of "pure self-recognition in absolute otherness"; and at this point the I cannot remain outside as a subject having science (spirit) as its object; the I cannot have "possession of itself" in the sense on which natural consciousness insists. Natural consciousness stands at the point of *merely* implicit unification, and what it asserts is precisely the bifurcation into subject and object; at this point the movement of the I into the absolute is opposed and the I posited as subject over against object. Therefore, each "standpoint" appears to the other as a perversion, as inverted. The movement into philosophy is a radically disorienting, *inverting* movement.

At the end of section 7 the consideration of the movement into philosophy is explicitly connected with the previous characterizations of this movement (at the end of section 6). Hegel speaks of the demand that the I "which seems to itself to stand outside science" be appropriated to science, that the belongingness of the I to the absolute be made explicit, that science "show that and how" the I "belongs to it" (PhG 26). At the same time, this movement is precisely the becoming of science, that is, spirit's coming to be for itself:

> As lacking such actuality, it [science] is merely the content as the *in-itself*, the *purpose* which is still only something inward—not yet spirit, only spiritual substance. This *in-itself* has to express itself and to become *for itself*; this means: it has to posit self-consciousness as one with itself. (PhG 26)

It is now possible to formulate the issue of initiatory presentation, that is, to lay out the principal distinctions and questions. The most fundamental distinction is that between the presentation itself and that which is to be presented in the presentation. With respect to the presentation we can distinguish between two kinds of questions. First, there is the question of the *standpoint* of the presentation, that is, the question of its stand with respect to what it presents. Second, there is the question of the *form* of the presentation—a question for which Hegel has made preparations in his consideration of the way in which the demand for system is placed upon the presentation by the presented and in his consideration of the structure of the proposition, especially the way in which its structure anticipates the movement of the absolute itself.

On the other hand, that which is to be presented in the presentation is that particular movement which Hegel distinguished in his considerations at the end of section 6. It is a movement from being-in-and-for-itself in itself to being-in-and-for-itself for itself; and as such it is identical with the movement from being-in-and-for-itself for us to being-in-and-for-itself for itself. It is the movement of the I into the absolute—that is, the appropriation of immediate self-consciousness to the absolute.

What is especially important at this stage, as we approach the most fundamental development of the issue of presentation, is that we keep the principal items, presentation and presented, sufficiently distinct to allow their intertwining to unfold.

Presentation and Presented

In sections 5–6 of the preface the basis is prepared for the determination of the concept of initiatory presentation. This preparation consists in the distinguishing of the movement that is to be presented in the presentation. In section 7 the demand for initiatory presentation is then introduced and the movement previously distinguished is identified as that which such presentation is to present. With the presentation and the presented thus identified and distinguished, the task is to determine the precise manner in which they belong together.

Hegel expresses this determination in section 8. We shall attempt to work out the relevant determining methodically, in order then to be able to take up Hegel's expression at its proper level.

At the level of the mere distinction, there is the movement (from being-in-and-for-itself in itself to being-in-and-for-itself), and there is the presentation of this movement. The movement is a movement of spirit, of the absolute. The presentation of the movement would be accomplished by an I, an individual self-consciousness, outside the absolute. Clearly, however, this formulation cannot stand, and the items distinguished cannot remain so totally distinct. For, in this formulation, what is manifestly operative is the standpoint of natural consciousness: the formulation is, in effect, an affirmation of sheer bifurcation, of bifurcation between the moving absolute (as object of the presentation) and the presenting I (as subject of the presentation). Such an affirmation cannot stand because the very movement being presented (the becoming of spirit, of science) is an overcoming of such bifurcation, an inverting of natural consciousness. The character of that which is to be presented must be allowed to recoil upon the determination of its relation to the presentation; the recoil destroys the mere externality that natural consciousness would assert.

Even in the preparatory distinguishing of the movement to be presented Hegel already paints beyond such natural representation by giving a second characterization of the movement, a characterization by which the presenting I is drawn into the movement rather than being simply posed over against it. The movement is a movement from being-in-and-for-itself for us *to* being-in-and-for-itself for itself, and the movement so characterized amounts to a movement of the I into the absolute. Thus, there is the movement of the absolute and the movement of the presenting I into the absolute; that is, the movement of presentation is a movement into the very movement (i.e., the absolute) which it presents.

The connection between these two movements must be determined more precisely. So the question is: In what way can the presentation be a movement into the very movement presented? What must be the character of this *way* of movement into movement?

The general character of this way is already prescribed by the terms in which the way has become an issue. At a general level it may be said that there can be movement into movement only insofar as the first movement blends into the second. Thus, the presentation can be a movement into the movement presented only if it is of such a character that it comes to coincide with the movement of the presented. The problem is to determine the character of this "coming into coincidence," to exhibit it in terms of the specific character of the two movements involved.

The issue is no simple coincidence, no mere static coinciding, but rather a *coming* to coincidence. That which thus comes to coincidence brings something along to that with which it comes to coincidence, at least a doubling of self. Regarded from the end, the movement of presentation, moving into the movement presented, brings the latter to a completion) the presentation constitutes, in a still to be determined sense, the *completion* of the movement presented, it brings it into its final phase.[24]

Yet, on the other hand, the two movements are the same and not merely coincident in the end. Movement from spirit in itself to spirit for itself and movement of the I into the absolute—these were offered by Hegel as two characterizations of one and the same movement. But how can the presentation remain in any sense a presentation if it is simply the same as that which it presents? Clearly it cannot remain a presentation if it is *simply* the same as what it presents—that is, the relevant sense of sameness must be other than that of such simple sameness as would exclude all difference. There must be an element of difference which grants to the presentation its distance from the presented, even if the presentation should prove such as to abolish that distance in the end. Such distance is, of course, something utterly different from that distance of subject from object on which natural consciousness would insist.

How, then, can the presentation be the final phase of the movement, that which brings it to completion, and yet be in some determinate sense the same as the movement? Especially if we attend to the peculiar gathering character that belongs to the "ending" of the movement, which would constitute its "final phase," then it can be seen that there is only one way in which this is possible: the presentation must be a retracing of a movement which otherwise is already completed before the inception of the presentation. The presentation as a re-*tracing* is thus identical in content with the presented, but as a *re*-tracing it differs in form and has thus its proper distance. The presentation is to retrace the presented in such a way as to gather it into its τέλος. The presentation is a *gathering reenactment*.

In section 8 Hegel characterizes the presentation as such a gathering reenactment—that is, as recollection, which is further described as the movement proper to education. It is, more specifically, the recollecting of the past stages of spirit. It is a passage through the contents of the educational stages through which spirit has passed in coming to its present stage, a passage which reenacts, "relives" those stages, not in their original form, but "as shapes already cast off by the spirit": "The content is already actuality reduced to possibility, vanquished immediacy, and the shapes have been reduced to abbreviations, to simple determinations of thought" (PhG 27, 28). What are recollected are the past stages of spirit reduced to simple determinations of thought.

Hegel says that the content thus reduced is something possessed by spirit in its present stage; the reduced contents is its property. In other words, the past shapes of spirit are gathered up into spirit in its present condition. Rather than simply leaving its past stages behind in moving to new shapes, spirit reduces these stages in such a way that they can be gathered up into the new stage; with respect to its shape spirit is a movement of gathering into the τέλος. As so gathered the content of the past shapes of spirit are "property that has already been acquired by the general spirit which constitutes the substance of the individual" (PhG 27). They belong to spirit as substance, as still in itself to the extent of leaving the gathering of shapes implicit. The gathering has itself still to be gathered into the determination of spirit.

The recollection which the presentation is to accomplish is also a gathering. It is a passage which gathers up that through which it passes, which reenacts in such a way as to gather up that which it reenacts. That which it gathers up are just the stages through which spirit has passed; and it gathers these up in that form in which they now lie in spirit as its property, as thought determinations which are already gathered up. The gathering recollection is a regathering of what is already gathered; it is a regathering which reenacts the self-gathering of the shapes, which lets them show themselves as self-gathering, which thus lets the gathering be itself gathered into the determination of spirit. The presentation brings the gathering which spirit is to its completion by bringing to it the moment of its ending, the gathering of the gathering itself into the end; the presentation, leaving everything on the side of the presented, brings to it the doubling of explicit self-consciousness.

Hegel describes the movement of education, the enactment of initiatory presentation, from the point of view of the individual and from that of the general spirit. With respect to the former it consists fundamentally in his gaining what is already given over to him, in his appropriating his spiritual substance to himself as self-consciousness. From the point of view of the general spirit as substance "it is nothing else than that this acquire its self-consciousness [*sich ihr Selbstbewußtsein gibt*], bring forth its becoming and its reflection" (PhG 27). Initiatory presentation has its distance but only in order that it might properly "rejoin" the movement which is spirit itself and bring the latter to its completion, draw it into the end.[25]

The initiatory presentation, now explicitly identified by Hegel as a "*phenomenology* of spirit," presents the "becoming of science as such" (PhG 26). That is, it presents the movement from spirit in itself (i.e., spiritual substance) to spirit for itself—or, more specifically, the movement from "immediate spirit," which Hegel now identifies as "sensible consciousness," to genuine knowing, that is, spirit's knowing of itself. Yet what is distinctive about such presentation is the fact that it is no mere copy set over against an original already complete in itself. It is no mere copy, for it presents the relevant movement, the movement of spirit through its shapes, not in its "original" form, but rather as reduced to thought determinations, to property—that is, *as* already gathered up. Yet, even so regarded, that which is presented is not an "original" already complete in itself, of which the presentation would provide merely a pale reflection easily dispensed with. On the contrary, the presentation brings the reflection by which the presented first comes to its completion, by which spirit becomes for itself, by which the gathering (which spirit is) is itself gathered into the end.

Such is the "standpoint" of the initiatory presentation, that is, its *stand* with respect to what it presents. It is a stand which leaves everything on the side of the matter itself, which lets the matter be, not by turning away and ignoring it but by turning toward it and tending it. The presentation is to free the matter to itself, to let that self-gatheredness (which the matter is) come to fulfillment. The presentation is devoted to that midwifery which assists in the birth of the true; and to that extent it is Socratic.

But what is required in order that thought be able to tend the matter for thought, in order that it be able to free that matter to itself? Must not such thought already have presupposed something in order to occupy the standpoint demanded? Are its presuppositions not then foisted, in turn, upon the matter itself, in such a way that the presentation would end up binding the matter in alien forms rather than freeing it to itself?

Indeed, such thought must already presuppose something in order to attain the required stand with respect to its matter. However, what is of fundamental importance is that its presupposing is not such as to impose upon the matter something alien to that matter, as when, for example, an empirical concept is imposed upon a thing without regard for the nature shown by that thing. The thought which would present the matter has its proper directedness, and without such directedness it could never, for instance, present the transition from one shape of spirit to another, the transition which is unknown to the consciousness within those shapes. But the directedness, rather than imposing the transition onto the matter, only frees the transition that is already in the matter itself, only regathers what is already itself implicitly gathered, or, more precisely, lets it show itself as self-gathering. The presenting thought has undeniably a directness to unity; more precisely, it has a directedness to gatheredness as such, to unity in the sense of gathering unity. But it does not *impose* this unity upon the diversity that reigns among and within the shapes of spirit. Rather, it *holds out* this unity to the shapes, *lets* them develop into it, that is, lets them show themselves as already self-gathered into such unity.

Indeed, something is required of the thinking that would present the matter. Such thinking does not just observe—as Hegel himself finally grants when he comes to the end of the determination of the concept of initiatory presentation (PhG 74). Yet all that is required of such thinking is in service to that reticence capable of freeing the matter to itself.

It is to this stand of reticence that the determination of the concept of presentation would provoke one willing to undergo the inverting movement into philosophy. Indeed the preface does violence to the matter for thought—but precisely in order to contribute to drawing thought to that stand from which it can let the matter be.

Notes

Preparation of this study was made possible by a stipendium awarded by the Alexander von Humboldt-Stiftung.

1. *Jenaer Schiften 1801–1807. Werke* (Frankfurt: Suhrkamp, 1970), II:182.

2. *Phänomenologie des Geistes*, ed. J. Hoffmeister (Hamburg, 1964), 16f.; hereafter "PhG."

3. *Jenaer Schriften*, 182.

4. Following the division given by Hoffmeister, which is based on that given in the table of contents of the first edition of 1807.

5. Within the preface, see also the statements in sections 14–15, e.g., "scientific knowing, however, demands rather that one surrender to the life of the object" (PhG 45).

6. Thus near the end of the preface Hegel satirizes those who take that "royal road to science" which consists in relying on common sense (i.e., refusing to undergo the inversion into philosophy) and in reading reviews of and *prefaces* to philosophical writings—a "vulgar road [which] can be taken in one's dressing gown" (PhG 56–57), that is, which excuses itself from the "*Anstrengung des Begriffs.*"

7. For the purposes of this study it will suffice to let the usage of *aufheben* and its derivatives be governed by the sense determined in the early stages of the *Phenomenology* and expressed thus in the chapter "Wahrnehmung": "*Das Aufheben stellt seine wahrhafte gedoppelte Bedeutung dar, welche wir an dem Negativen gesehen haben: es ist ein Negieren und ein Aufbewahren zugleich*" (PhG 90). Hegel's more extended determination is given in *Wissenschaft der Logik*, ed. G. Lasson (Hamburg 1967), I:93–95. No English word suitably translates *aufheben*. However, because of the stylistic difficulty of retaining the German verb with its separable prefix, we shall resort to the frequently used translation *sublate*—which makes it necessary to insist all the more that the sense of the word be taken from Hegel's explicit determinations and not from extra-philosophical preconceptions.

8. "*Es kommt nach meiner Einsicht, welche sich [nur] durch die Darstellung des Systems selbst rechtfertigen muß, alles darauf an, das Wahre nicht als Substanz, sondern eben so sehr als Subjekt aufzufassen und auszüdrucken*" (PhG 19). "*Nur*" was added in the revisions for a second edition which Hegel began to prepare shortly before his death.

9. Part I, definition 3.

10. *Fichte: Grundlage der gesammten Wissenschaftslehre*. In *Werke* (rpt. Berlin, 1971), I:120–22.

11. *Differenz des Fichte'schen und Schelling'schen Systems der Philosophie* (Hamburg, 1962), 75ff.

12. *Erste Einleitung in die Wissenschaftslehre*, in *Werke*. I:440; *Zweite Einleitung in die Wissenschaftslehre*, in *Werke*, I.498.

13. Note added to the second edition of the *Grundlage* in 1802. In *Werke*, I:98.

14. Hegel, *Differenz*, 48, 75.

15. In the *Differenz*-Schrift (77) Hegel uses this formulation ("*Das Absolute*

selbst aber ist darum die Identität der Identität und der Nichtidentität") in showing how Schelling's thought goes beyond the limited standpoint (of subjective subject-object) to which Fichte remains attached. The formulation takes on added significance if contrasted with the corresponding formulation given in Schelling's *Darstellung meines Systems der Philosophie*, which was published the same year as Hegel's *Differenz*-Schrift; Schelling's formulation is: "*Die absolute Identität ist nur unter der Form einer Identität der Identität*" (*Sämmtliche Werke*, Abt. I/4.121). In the section of the *Phenomenology* under consideration, Hegel's mention of "intellectual intuition" is presumably to be understood as a reference to Schelling (cf. *Differenz*, 92f.).

16. Regarding the governing sense of "sublate," see note 7 above.

17. Cf. Werner Marx, *Hegels Phänomenologie des Geistes: Die Bestimmung ihrer Idee in, "Vorrede" und "Einleitung"* (Frankfurt: Klostermann, 1971), 98.

18. The connection at issue here between self-consciousness and serious otherness can be clarified by reference to Fichte. In Fichte's work there occurs a distinction which, granted certain fundamental differences, corresponds rather closely to Hegel's distinction between the true in itself and the true for itself. In the formulation given in Fichte's *Zweiter Einleitung* (1797), the relevant distinction is that between mere intellectual intuition, that is, self-reverting activity, which Fichte identifies as constituting the mere *possibility* of self-consciousness, *and* genuine (concrete) self-consciousness, that is, the positing of the I as determinate (*Werke*, I:459). In contrast to the sheer self-positing expressed in the first principle of the *Wissenschaftslehre*, which never occurs unmixed but is arrived at only by abstraction, concrete self-consciousness requires a genuine otherness, an otherness more radical than the always immediately surpassed otherness of abstract self-positing; it requires that a not-I be brought forth. As the matter is expressed in the theoretical part of the *Grundlage*: "An I that posits itself as self-positing, or a *subject*, is impossible without an object brought forth in the manner described (the determination of the I, its reflection upon itself as determinate, is possible only on the condition that it bound itself by an opposite)" (Werke, I:218). This means: The I's reflection on itself, that is, determinate self-consciousness, that is, a determinate I as such, is possible only if a not-I is opposed to the I. The matter is even clearer in the *Zweite Einleitung*: formulating the task of the *Wissenschaftslehre*, Fichte writes that it will be necessary to show "firstly, how the I is and may be for itself; then, that this being of itself for itself would be impossible, unless there also at once arose for it an existence outside itself"(*Werke*, I:458). In other words, opposition (negation) is required for determination, that is, the I can posit itself as determinate only in opposition to the not-I. Thus, for Fichte there is an intrinsic relation between genuine self-consciousness and serious otherness, and this relation has primarily to do with the possibility of determinateness in contrast to the total indeterminateness of the absolutely self-positing I of the first principle. This general connection which Fichte established between self-consciousness and serious otherness, the connecting of them through the concept of determination, remained decisive for Hegel.—On the other hand, the specific context of the connection was

transformed when Hegel, following the lead of Schelling, replaced the Fichtean not-I with an object capable of reflection into itself, capable of unfolding into an objective subjective-object. Regarding this development see Marx, *Hegels Phänomenologie des Geistes*, 61ff.

19. "*Unter mancherlei Folgerungen, die aus dem Gesagten fließen, kann diese herausgehoben werden, daß das Wissen nur als Wissenschaft oder als System wirklich ist und dargestellt werden kann*" (PhG 23).

20. Cf. PhG 53, together with Werner Marx, *Reason and World* (The Hague, 1971), 36.

21. It must be stressed that these considerations concern presentation *in general*, that is, they take no account of what is peculiar to an *initiatory* presentation or, therefore, of the specific way in which such a presentation would stand under the requirements here prescribed for presentation in general.

22. "*Daß das Wahre nur als System wirklich, oder daß die Substanz wesentlich Subjekt ist, ist in der Vorstellung ausgedrückt, welche das Absolute als Geist ausspricht*" (PhG 24).

23. Cf. Martin Heidegger, *Holzwege* (Frankfurt, 1957), 120.

24. Cf. Marx, *Hegels Phänomenologie des Geistes*, 103f.

25. It is in terms of this "distance" that the problem of the form and, more specifically, of the language required of an initiatory presentation would need to be developed. The basis for such a development is provided by Hegel's determination of the form of speculative presentation, which is carried out in section 17 of the preface and which is an extension of the considerations of language already given in section 6. The crucial point is that a speculative presentation is not the same as an initiatory presentation (cf. Marx, *Hegels Phänomenologie des Geistes*, 104); and thus the linguistic requirement under which the former stands cannot simply be carried over to the latter. In other words, it would be necessary to determine in precisely what measure an *initiatory* presentation stands under those requirements. The peculiar "distance" from the presented determines that measure, which may thus be posed (with respect to the single proposition as considered in section 6) as a general structural correspondence: to the extent that presentation is at a distance from the movement presented, so, to that extent the movement within the proposition will be referred to a knower outside the proposition rather than being actually the movement of the subject of the proposition.

2

Kenley R. Dove

Hegel's Phenomenological Method

There is probably no aspect of Hegelianism which was attracted more attention and occasioned more confusion than the so-called dialectical method. Every university student has doubtless heard at least one lecture on this "secret" of Hegelianism, whether in terms of the notorious triad: thesis-antithesis-synthesis, or in some more sophisticated terminology. This is particularly noteworthy, not only because it misrepresents Hegel, but because Hegel's *Phenomenology of Spirit* was probably the *first* philosophical treatise whose method was radically and consistently non-dialectical.[1]

What, then, is the method of Hegel's *Phenomenology* if it is not dialectical? Insofar as it can be characterized in a word, it is descriptive. The study of a science, in Hegel's sense, requires that the student, through a tremendous effort of restraint, give himself completely over to the structural development of that science itself. This, I take it, is what Hegel means by the famous phrase "*die Anstrengung des Begriffs*" (the effort of the Concept) (PhG 48). The true philosopher must strenuously avoid the temptation of interrupting the immanent development of the subject matter by the introjection of interpretive models; he must rather give up this instinctively felt prerogative or "freedom" and "instead of being the arbitrarily moving principle of the content," his task is "to submerge this freedom *in* the content and let the content be moved through its own nature, that is, through the self as the self of the content, and to observe this moment" (PhG 48).

But if the phenomenological method must not interfere with the movement of the subject matter, it must also abstain from a purely negative attitude *vis-à-vis* all content, for example, the stance of the disengaged analyst who removes all life from the content, going straight after its truth value by a more or less elaborate and systematic employment of the formal criterion of tautologyhood. This methodological device, which is of unquestionable value in the mathematical sciences, is totally inadequate in the field of philosophy. The abstract affirmations and negations evinced by a two-valued logic of tautological truths versus non-tautological falsehoods *eo ipso* exclude from consideration the characteristics of negation inherent *in* the subject matter itself. And it is precisely this internal negative movement which the Hegelian phenomenological method seeks to describe.

Since this method excludes the central criterion of formal or mathematical logic, it is natural to ask what sort of standard Hegel proposes to put in its place. His answer to this question, which constitutes the theme of the brief but all-important " Introduction"[2] to the *Phenomenology*, is also the clearest indication of his radical departure from the previous history of Western philosophy. He acknowledges (PhG 70; HCE 18) that if the *Phenomenology* were to be regarded as an exposition in which science is *related* to knowledge as it appears, or as an inquiry into the nature of human understanding or reason, then it would indeed, after the manner of a Locke or a Kant, require some sort of fundamental presupposition which could serve as a standard of measurement. But instead of adapting himself to this classical philosophical orientation, Hegel, to borrow a phrase from Kierkegaard, has found a way of "going beyond Socrates"—and Kant as well.[3] Unlike that of any previous philosophy, the method of Hegel's *Phenomenology* takes the "paradox of learning" of Plato's *Meno* (80d) in complete seriousness: "But here, where science makes its first appearance, neither science nor anything else has justified itself as the *essence* or as the in-itself" (PhG 70; HCE 18).

The argument of the "Introduction" divides itself at this point into three exceedingly compact and organically inseparable moments. The *first* concerns the abstract distinction between knowledge and truth on which all previous epistemological theories have turned. This distinction is based upon the observation that consciousness itself "distinguishes from itself something to which it at the same time *relates* itself" (PhG 70; HCE 19). The *determinate* aspect of this interrelationship, the something which is said to be *for* consciousness, the "being-for-another," is called knowledge. But, on further consideration, we also notice the side of that which is determined, namely the *determinable*. Or, to employ the expression of Brentano, consciousness is always consciousness *of*. This aspect of "being-in-itself," whether regarded as a material thing, an abstract entity, or a thing-in-itself, has tended to the associated in philosophical theory with *truth*, and philosophers have accordingly sought to establish criteria for determining the truth of knowledge.

It is particularly important to notice that Hegel does not join in this time-honored enterprise. From the viewpoint of the *Phenomenology*, the question of the truth *of* knowledge is not a matter of direct concern; it is, in the modern idiom, "bracketed." The only object with which the *Phenomenology* is concerned is knowledge as it appears, already organized in the form of a "science" involving some systematic distinction between knowledge and truth.[4] If, on the contrary, we were to concern ourselves with the truth *of* knowledge, that is, with what knowledge is in itself, then we should have to provide some standard whereby that truth could be determined. But it is clear that the truth thus attained, if indeed any such knowledge could be acquired, would not be the truth of knowledge, its being-in-itself; it could at most be *our* knowledge of it or its being-for-us. Moreover, as Hegel observes, the standard would be *our* standard and that for which our standard was to serve as a determinate "would not necessarily have to recognize it" (PhG 71; HCE 20).

The first moment of Hegel's methodical exposition therefore serves as a preliminary elucidation of what is implied by undertaking a phenomenological description of knowledge as it appears (PhG 66; HCE 13). Since the object of our inquiry is knowing, any distinction on our part between subject and object would be a playing with mere abstractions. *Our* object is at once and inseparably both the object-knowing subject and the object known-by-the-subject. Thus our object, consciousness or spirit, contains this subject-object distinction within itself and requires no further distinction by us.

The *second* moment of Hegel's argument is equally far-reaching and revolutionary though its philosophical significance can be no more than adumbrated here. It directly concerns the Concept (*Begriff*),[5] but it also involves a radically new insight into the perennial problem of time and eternity. Just as the object of knowledge is seen to fall *within* the object of *our* inquiry, Hegel also makes the unprecedented move of regarding the Concept as something completely within the temporal process of the consciousness or spirit under investigation.[6] Thus the Concept is not regarded as, in the Parmenidean tradition, identical with timeless eternity, or, after the manner of Plato or Whitehead, as an eternal object which "participates" or "ingresses" in the temporal realm of human experience or of "actual occasions." It is also to be distinguished from the Aristotelian and

Nietzschean interpretation of the Concept as something which, although falling, within time, for instance, as a "natural kind," nevertheless undergoes a cyclical process of eternal recurrence within time itself. For Hegel the Concept *is* time, and time is "the existentially embodied Concept itself" (PhG 558).[7]

Since the Concept is seen to fall within the knowledge we are investigating, it follows that "consciousness provides itself with its own standard, and the investigation will accordingly be a comparison of consciousness with its own self" (PhG 71; HCE 20). To understand how this comparison takes place, we must observe that, just as consciousness or spirit was seen to be at once both "subjective" and "objective," this same duality holds true for the Concept: consciousness itself distinguishes between (*a*) the Concept *qua* knowledge and (*b*) the Concept *qua* object. Hence there is within consciousness not only something which is taken to be *for it*; consciousness also assumes that that which is for it, is in-itself or has an independent status as well. Accordingly, we see that the Concept has two moments. If we take the Concept to be knowledge, then the standard for this Concept *qua* knowledge will be its object or what is said to exist in-itself. In this case the comparison will consist in seeing whether the Concept corresponds to the object, that is, what consciousness now regards as the standard of truth. But, on the other hand, if we take the Concept to be the object as it is essentially or in-itself, then the Concept itself will be the standard for the Concept *qua* known, that is, the Concept *qua* object of knowledge. Here the comparison consists in seeing whether the Concept *qua* known or *qua* object corresponds to the Concept itself.[8]

Although both aspects of the Concept must no doubt be taken into account in any adequate description of the knowing process—and an emphasis on one or the other has traditionally served as the touchstone for a realist or idealist epistemology[9]—Hegel's descriptive method seems, in this second moment of its explication, to be in danger of losing its purely descriptive character in virtue of the necessity of our determining which aspect of the Concept is to serve as the standard.

His answer to this problem is as simple as it is convincing, especially when the reader has followed the presentation through the section called "Consciousness." He observes, namely, that both of these processes are the same. The standard is selected by consciousness itself and, since both moments of the process fall within our object, that is, knowledge as it appears, any selection of standards on *our* part would be superfluous.[10] Needless to say, the adoption of such a purely descriptive stance does require a great deal of restraint; it is not the traditional way of "doing" philosophy.

The *third* moment in the development of Hegel's phenomenological method is guided by the observation that consciousness not only selects its own standard but is also the *comparison* of its knowledge with its own standard. This is based on the fact that consciousness is "on the one hand, consciousness of the object, on the other, consciousness of its self; it is consciousness of what to it is the true, and consciousness of its knowledge of this truth" (PhG 72; HCE 21). Consciousness is therefore both consciousness *of* something, and consciousness of its self.[11] In view of this characteristic feature of consciousness, it is at the same time conscious of its standard of truth and conscious of its knowledge of the truth in question. And since both the standard and the knowledge are for the same consciousness, their comparison is a fundamental feature in the movement of consciousness itself.

It is indeed true that consciousness' standard of truth is only a standard insofar as it is known by consciousness, that is, as it is *for* consciousness and not as it is in itself. And this observation has driven many less descriptive philosophers to some form of skepticism, for the presumptive standard does not really seem to be what it "ought" to be (namely, something independent of knowledge). Hence, it seems incapable of serving as a criterion of knowledge. But for Hegel, whose attention is steadfastly focused on the experience of knowledge as it appears, all such talk about "capacities" and "intentions" is beside the point.[12] The crucial point is that consciousness, in all the shapes of its appearance, *does* draw a distinction between its standard, or what the object is in itself, and its knowledge, or the being of the object *for* consciousness (PhG 72; HCE 22). And if, in the course of the comparison, consciousness should find that its standard and its knowledge do not correspond, it will, on the basis of its own assumptions, have to change its knowledge in order to make it correspond to its standard.

But it also follows from these same assumptions that a change in consciousness' knowledge *eo ipso* involves a change in its standard, for the standard was based upon the object and, indeed, upon the object *qua* known. Hence with a change in the knowledge for the sake of truth, the standard of truth is itself changed. Consciousness thus discovers that the process in which it placed its knowledge in *doubt*, all the while certain that it held a firm criterion for what the object of its knowledge was initself, turns out to be a movement in which it loses its own truth; the "path of doubt" (*Zweifel*) is transformed into "the way of despair" (*Verzweiflung*) (PhG 67; HCE 14). Moreover, this despair is not something arbitrarily imposed on consciousness from without; it is *immanent* in the very movement of consciousness itself. Thus, in Baillie's poignant translation, consciousness "suffers this violence at its own hands."[13]

The positive aspect of this third moment of Hegel's method is that the process of examining knowledge, which of necessity involves a standard, is actually (and equally necessarily) an examination of the standard as well. And with the emergence of a new standard, consciousness is confronted by an object which is for it new and now true. At this point in the exposition, one is nevertheless compelled to ask: "Whence this new object?" Or, more skeptically: "Isn't Hegel here attempting to justify that sleight-of-hand trick for which his dialectical method is so notorious?"

If this "new object" is in fact the product of Hegel's "dialectical method," the traditional charge against him is completely justified. But Hegel's method is radically *un*dialectical. It is the experience of consciousness itself which is dialectical and Hegel's *Phenomenology* is a viable philosophical enterprise precisely to the extent that it merely *describes* this dialectical process. The "new object" therefore must not be introduced by the philosopher; it must arise out of the course of the experience described—and not merely *qua* described, but through itself.

Experience itself is therefore described as dialectical to the extent that it generates new objects for itself. But the "new object" seems to be no more than a reflection on the part of consciousness, and a reflection which is not based on anything objective, but merely on its knowledge of its first object. The term "reflection," however, is misleading: it tends to suggest something which takes place immediately. But experience is a *process*, it is something which takes time; and the process of experience is precisely constituted by the alteration of its first object, and therewith its first standard. The alteration, in turn, must be seen as a negation of the *appearance* of the first object within consciousness' experience. Thus the negating process of alteration is not an immediate, empty, or abstract negation; the appearance which is negated has content and the alteration is a *determinate* negation (PhG 68; HCE 16) which, as the result of the negated appearance, also has a *content*.

Thus the "new object" is not simply the product of an immediate reflection; it is constituted by the process of negating the first object, "it is the experience constituted through that first object" (PhG 73; HCE 24). But Hegel's concept of determinate negation can only be grasped through a careful analysis of (I) the role of appearance in experience and (II) why "we" must describe the experience of consciousness as a phenomenon.

I

Hegel's concept of experience is both more restrictive and at the same time far more inclusive than what is usually understood by the word. And the intelligibility of the entire *Phenomenology* hinges upon a firm grasp of what phenomenal experience, knowing as it appears, consists in. In the first place, phenomenal experience is more restrictive than other philosophical interpretations of experience because experience, to be described as a phenomenon, must *appear*. Thus mere intentions, capacities, dispositions, meanings, and so forth, do not, as such, constitute experience. Insofar as such "mental entities" are recognized as the real content of experience, the attempt at phenomenological description is condemned to acknowledge the validity of Prufrock's claim: "That is not it at all, that is not what I meant, at all"; or the equally enigmatic "meaning" which is presumably expressed in the assertion: "The present king of France is bald."

For Hegel, on the contrary, genuine experience is a self-revealing process and philosophy is conceived as a description of this process, not as a systematic analysis of a presumed relationship between meanings and assertions. Experience is constituted by an *act*: something which is actually said or done. Experience is therefore revealed in language and work and what is so revealed can be *described*: it is an *act*, "and it can be *said* of it, what *it is*" (PhG 236). In the act, the "inexpressible meaning" is simply abolished, that is, it is expressed.

But if this restriction of experience to that which can be described appears to be a narrowing of what philosophers have usually understood by the term, the wealth of human experience[14] actually described in the *Phenomenology* is a most eloquent demonstration that Hegel's method is far more "empirical" than that of philosophers who call themselves "empiricists."[15]

The kinds of phenomenal experience described in the *Phenomenology* are basically two: (1) the acts of individual men considered in abstraction from their social and historical "world," and (2) the interaction of individuals within a community or a "world" in the course of its development (PhG 315). This emphasis on the forms of experience in the terms of the nature of the acting subject suggests[16] a systematic division of the *Phenomenology* into two parts. The first, covering the sections on "Consciousness," "Self-Consciousness," and "Reason," is a phenomenological description of man *qua* individual, or "natural consciousness," in the various shapes (*Gestalten*) of his theoretical (i.e., in language) and practical (i.e., through labor and work) struggle for truth. The second, spanning the sections from "Spirit" through "Religion" to "Absolute Knowledge," concerns the sequence of shapes assumed by man in his life with other men, that is, man *qua* spirit. Although Hegel himself is not entirely consistent in his account of the temporal relations between 'Spirit' and 'Religion' (compare PhG 476 with PhG 557), it is clear that the entire second half of the *Phenomenology* deals with the development of associated humanity. "All of the previous shapes of consciousness are abstractions from Spirit. . . . This abstractive isolating of such moments presupposes Spirit and requires Spirit for its subsistence" (PhG 314).

We have seen that the most critical precondition for a phenomenological description of experience is the actual *appearance* of experience itself. The term "appearance" has, however, two distinct usages in the *Phenomenology*, and Hegel's phenomenological method is bound to seem either exotic or capricious if these two usages are not distinguished. The first of these concerns the appearance *of* experience; the second concerns appearance *in* experience. A great deal of what is unique, and consequently "unfamiliar" about Hegel's method is based on his insight into and his consistent awareness of this twofold character of appearance throughout the *Phenomenology*. The appearance *of* experience is the condition necessary for the possibility of a phenomenological description; it is the basic (or direct) presupposition of the *Phenomenology* as a philosophical work. This presupposition must also be shared by the reader. We shall discuss this problem of the appearance *of* experience in section II. Here attention will be directed to the problem of appearance as it is revealed *within* experience.

The experiencing subject, either as an individual or a community, tacitly or explicitly presupposes a distinction between appearance and reality (*Wesen*), between knowledge and its standard. Appearance as such is taken to be something involving time; reality is felt to be something which is at least in principle timeless or somehow eternal (cf. PhG 558). But as long as this sense of the unchangeable remains a mere feeling, there is no experience in the proper sense of the word. Human experience must involve action, it must involve an expression of the inwardly felt reality—which as such is no reality. This is what Hegel means by an *act*: it is the revelation of "reality" through the process of letting it appear. Action, in turn, has two basic phenomenal forms: language and work.

Both forms of action entail an objectification of what is otherwise merely "meant," "intended," or "presumed" to be. Consequently the subject who actively expresses himself in the world of appearance puts himself at the same time under the risk that his sense of reality will be altered or perverted (PhG 237). The risk, however, is inevitable for the experiencing subject; the only seeming alternative is a solipsism of the present moment. But this is only theoretically conceivable as a "philosophical" stance which one tacitly "intends" or "means" to assume. As Hegel demonstrates in his opening chapter on "Sense-Certainty," it is impossible for this solipsism to say what it "means" because any saying involves *language* and language is a form of expression or objectification. But as objectified, such a "meaning" is patently contradicted: the solipsist's "here and now," once it has been written down, becomes a "there and then." In its actual appearance, in language, "meaning" must mix with time; and by this process its semblance of atemporal reality is simply negated.

But a negation of meaning-solipsism in no way entails a negation of that sense of eternal reality for which the language of sense-certainty is merely the most immediate expression. The entire course of human experience, both individual and collective, can be viewed as a series of progressively less immediate or more mediated expressions of this quest for certainty and truth in the form of something which will not, like Chronos, be devoured by Zeus.

Thus, with the negation of meaning-solipsism, the process of letting-appear begins once again; but this beginning of appearance within experience is not the same as its antecedent. The experiencing subject has changed; it has become a new subject through its objective activity. Perhaps it itself does not explicitly know this, but "we" do—and not because we have some special access to the inner recesses of its consciousness akin to that of the "omniscient narrator," which was once such a popular novelistic device.

The *Phenomenology* is not a work of that sort; in method of presentation as well as subject matter it is far more comparable to a dramatic work.[17] Like all literature, it is an expression in language; but unlike "ordinary language" and the language of pre-Hegelian philosophers, it is purely descriptive. The course of the dramatic development is only describable because it has appeared: because there have been actual appearances within experiences and because these appearances are susceptible of being discussed and have been discussed. Under these circumstances the development of human activity and the continual dialogue about human activity can be *comprehended* by those who have a descriptive guide and who are able to master the art of reading scientific descriptions. The guide in question is the *Phenomenology*; we shall now turn to the problem of its readers.

II

The reader's most obvious source of difficulty stems, of course, from the external literary form of the *Phenomenology*; it is at best a very peculiar kind of *Lesedrama*. But the dramatic development itself is systematically interrupted by what may be described—in the felicitous phrase of Brecht—as a *Verfremdungseffekt* (estrangement-effect).[18] Every reader of the *Phenomenology* has doubtless puzzled over the significance of the *wir* and the *für uns* which periodically come into view and break up the flow of experience described. In the preface, before the actual drama gets under way, it is of course clear that the "we" is to be taken in the sense familiar to readers of almost any philosophical work, namely, we philosophers who are following the argument in question.

The "Introduction" may be viewed as a transition from the ordinary philosophical usage of an editorial "we" to the problematical usage of the work itself. Here Hegel comes closest to giving an explicit account of how the term "we" is to be understood in the sequel. Yet even at this juncture the reader is forced to ask himself: "Who are 'we'?"

The problem seems to become critical at two points in particular. The first (at PhG 71; HCE 20) concerns the determination of what shall serve as a standard within experience: object or Concept. Hegel at first seems to suggest that "we" make the selection. But as the previous discussion has shown, he provides an answer which, in principle, preserves the purely descriptive character of his method. The second difficulty (at PhG 74; HCE 24) is, unfortunately, not so easily answered.

We have already seen the general relationship of consciousness to its object, the twofold character of the Concept, and how in the course of experience consciousness brings about both an examination of its standard and emergence of a new object. All of this is intelligible as a process which takes place within experience. We have also seen that experience itself involves, by its very nature, action and appearance. Hence the process of experience is not constituted by any hidden or "inner" meanings or intentions, that is, it is in principle describable. The problem which now emerges is that what is *for* consciousness a new object is *for us* a new attitude toward objectivity, a new shape or *Gestalt* of consciousness or spirit. In other words, whereas consciousness itself merely seems to be related to a new object appearing *within* experience, from *our* point of view, that is, the description of the appearance *of* experience, consciousness, the active protagonist, has itself changed.

"This way of observing the subject matter is *our* contribution; it does not exist for the consciousness which we observe. But when viewed in this way the sequence of experiences constituted by consciousness is raised to the level of a scientific progression" (PhG 74; HCE 24). On the one hand, therefore, "we" seem to be merely describing what the active experience of consciousness presents for phenomenological description; on the other hand, however, "our" observation is also seen to be an act (*"unsere Zutat"*) which plays a constitutive role in the drama as a whole. Moreover, as Hegel adds, without "our contribution," the drama of human experience could only have a skeptical conclusion, or rather, no conclusion at all.

In view of these considerations the descriptive character of the whole *Phenomenology* seems to become paradoxical, if not impossible. For if our observation is regarded as totally determined by the subject matter, the development of appearance within experience, then "we" may indeed observe the coming to be and passing away of various objects of experience, but the upshot would be no more than a chronicle tracing a formless flow of phenomenal content. Insofar as the description concerned historical phenomena, our viewpoint would be that of a skeptical relativism or historicism. This indeed has been a popular characterization of what Hegel's later philosophy of history-minus the absolute Idea—implies. And when we consider the radical temporalizing of the Concept in the *Phenomenology*, together with the conspicuous absence of talk about the absolute Idea, the method of this work seems to entail a distinctly relativistic orientation for the "we."

If, on the other hand, our description of the sequence of objects experienced is raised to the level of a scientific series simply in virtue of the fact that it is "we" who do the describing, that the description is "*unsere Zutat*," then "we" seem to be nothing short of the absolute itself. Either our description would be carried out *sub specie aeternitatis*, or "our" addition would have the significance of an arbitrary positing, or both.

Hegel's phenomenological method, for all its cogency in the treatment of appearance *in* experience, thus seems to entail an impossible dilemma with respect to the no less important and complementary question of the appearance *of* experience. Between the Scylla of relativism and the Charybdis of constructive metaphysics there seems to be no safe passage. In view of the absolutely critical nature of this problem, it will be well to consider at this point what Hegel scholars have had to say about the "we" in the *Phenomenology*.

As one might expect, Hegel's use of the term "we" in the *Phenomenology* has been recognized by most of his commentators as, in one way or another, in need of an explanation.[19] The explanations usually provided are, however, remarkably laconic. It will therefore be feasible to expedite our brief survey of these explanations by presenting and commenting on a selection of relevant quotations from the literature. In many cases, the passages cited will be coextensive with the total direct discussion of the problem in the work cited.

[HERBERT MARCUSE:] The reader who is to understand the various parts of the work must already dwell in the "element of philosophy." The "we" that appears so often denotes not everyday men but philosophers.[20]

[GYORGY LUKÁCS:] The characteristic mode of exposition consists in always clarifying for the reader that connection of the objective and subjective categories which remains hidden to the individual "shape of consciousness" then under consideration. . . . The dualism exists only for the "shapes of consciousness," not for the philosopher and consequently not for the reader. When Hegel . . . says that the decisive connections between objectivity and subjectivity are opaque for the "shapes of consciousness" but transparent *for us*, he means for the philosophical reader, who observes this process of evolution of the human genus from a higher plane.[21]

[NICOLAI HARTMANN:] With the term "we" Hegel means the accompanying philosophical comprehension. And therein lies the possibility for philosophy, in tracing the origination [of a new shape of consciousness], to grasp its necessity as well. For it is in virtue of this possibility that "this road to science is itself already a science," a science of the experience of consciousness.[22]

[JEAN HYPPOLITE:] That is why the necessity of the experience which consciousness undergoes presents itself under a double light, or rather that there are two necessities, that of the negation of the object, brought about by consciousness itself in its experience, in the examination of its knowledge, and that of the appearance of the new object which is formed through the earlier experience. (This necessity could be called *retrospective*.) This second necessity only belongs to the philosopher who rethinks the phenomenological development; there is in it a moment of the in-itself or "for us" which is not to be found in consciousness. . . . (The *Phenomenology* is *theory of knowledge* and at the same time *speculative philosophy*; but it is speculative philosophy only for us. . . . Which means that Hegel's *Phenomenology* is at the same time a *description* of phenomenal consciousness and a *comprehension* of this description by the philosopher.) . . . (The succession of the "experiences" of consciousness is thus contingent only for phenomenal consciousness. As for us who are gathering these experiences, we discover at the same time the necessity of the progression, which goes from the one to the other. The *Phenomenology* demonstrates the immanence of all experience in consciousness. Moreover, it must be recognized that this (synthetic) necessity is not always easy to grasp and the transition sometimes appears arbitrary to the modern reader. This transition also poses the problem of the connection between history and the *Phenomenology*.)[23]

[RICHARD KRONER:] In the *Phenomenology* there are thus two moving series running parallel to each other: that of the observed object, the wandering "soul" which passes from experience to experience, and that of the observer who surveys this progress from the end of the road and comprehends it as the self-actualization of the absolute. Each step which "natural" consciousness advances thus becomes a doubly necessary one; or *the necessity of each step appears under a double light.* On the one hand consciousness is urged forward on the basis of its own experience, . . . on the other hand, however, the necessity of the first self-movement is placed into the light of absolute knowledge and is comprehended as a necessity by the observer who has already reached that goal towards which consciousness directs itself and which in truth attracts the wandering ego to itself.[24]

[MARTIN HEIDEGGER:] Who are the "we?"
They are those who in the inversion of natural consciousness let it persist in its own meaning and opinion but at the same time and expressly look at the appearance of the appearing. This looking-at, which expressly watches the appearance, is the watching as which the skepsis fulfills itself, the skepsis which has looked ahead to the absoluteness of the absolute and has in advance provided itself with it. That which comes to light in thoroughgoing skepticism shows itself "for us," that is, for those who, thinking upon the beingness of being, are already provided with Being. . . .

The contribution accordingly wills the will of the absolute. The contribution itself is what is willed by the absoluteness of the absolute. . . . The contribution gives prominence to the fact that and the manner in which we, in watching, are akin to the absoluteness of the absolute.[25]

The passages here assembled provide an instructive spectrum of possibilities for envisaging the "philosophical we" but they also show how an interpretation of the "we" tends to govern—or be governed by—one's view of the *Phenomenology* as a whole. The following discussion will thus enable us not only to survey the field of Hegel scholarship through the prism of this vital issue; it will also afford an occasion for systematically developing the argument of this chapter.

The first point of critical importance that, consciously or unconsciously, divides these scholars is the degree of significance they attach to the inverted commas which they place around the "we" or "for us." Only Marcuse and Lukács draw explicit attention to the fact that the "we" refers to the *readers* of the *Phenomenology*. Thus the problem of the intelligibility of the dramatic activity to the "audience" is elevated to a position of prominence. When the "we" is understood to denote the readers such as you or I," then the *Verfremdungseffekt* serves to remind us (*a*) *that* we are the public, the audience, and (*b*) that *what* we as audience are seeing or have seen is an appearance in public space;[26] it prevents us from losing our descriptive orientation by, for example, becoming absorbed in the public action of the play as if it were the private experience of a protagonist.[27] It does not, on the other hand, estrange us from the standpoint of description, tacitly or explicitly suggesting that the "we" stands for some extraordinary intelligence which we readers see through a glass but darkly.

Marcuse's observation that the intelligibility of the *Phenomenology* is only open to those readers who "already dwell in the 'element of philosophy'" is clearly incontestable, but it is not clear from his remarks just what this "element" is. In a subsequent passage,[28] he suggests that this "element" is the philosophy of transcendental idealism; but this is also problematical since, as Hartmann points out,[29] transcendental idealism is not accepted in the *Phenomenology* as a thesis but is rather treated as a historical phenomenon, one of the stages of consciousness described. Although Hyppolite mentions the peculiar difficulties faced by "the modern reader" in following the transitions in the *Phenomenology*, as well as the problematical relationship of the *Phenomenology* and history, his extensive study has little to say about the specific preconditions for intelligible reading, whether in 1946 or 1807.[30]

The only writer who directly deals with this problem is Lukács. He suggests that the appearance of the various "shapes of consciousness" is intelligible for the philosophical reader because he (i.e., the "we") observes the developmental process of the human genus from a "higher plane." The higher plane is said to be that of "Objective Spirit" or the perspective of history.[31] This historical approach to the problem of the "we" is very suggestive, but in Lukács's discussion it has two distinct shortcomings as a general hypothesis: (*a*) the specific nature of the historical preconditions for the "we" is not developed (e.g., in connection with Hegel's references in the preface [PhG 15ff.] to "our age," ca. 1806, as a "new world") and (*b*) Lukács expressly limits this interpretation of the "we" to what he calls the "first part"[32] of the *Phenomenology*, that is, "Subjective Spirit." For the second and third parts of his triadically divided *Phenomenology* he offers no explanation for the "philosophical we"—which nevertheless continues to appear.

The citation from Hartmann adds to this discussion a recognition of the problem of "our" grasping the "necessity" in the sequence of consciousness' experiences, thus enabling "us" to raise this sequence to a scientific series, "a science of the experience of consciousness." But it is only Kroner and Hyppolite who develop the problem of the structure of "necessity" in the *Phenomenology*. In the terminology of this study, both scholars recognize that there is (*a*) a process of necessity *within* experience, the process in which consciousness judges its knowledge by its own standard and consequently tests its standard and alters its object, as well as (b) the necessity *of* experience as a noncontingent series observed by us. As the foregoing discussion has shown, it is this second kind of necessity which is most problematical and crucial for an understanding of the "Philosophical we."

It is noteworthy that, of the two, only Hyppolite speaks of this second necessity in terms of *appearance*. But it is appearance of a peculiarly "retrospective" nature. The "we" or the philosopher is said to be already (and not merely implicitly) at the level of "speculative philosophy" and, on Hyppolite's reading, the appearance *of* experience seems to provide the philosopher something like an *occasion* to rethink the phenomenological development, which he has presumably already, in some sense, experienced. In view of the historical preconditions for "our" phenomenological comprehension suggested by Hegel in the preface, this is at least a partially plausible assumption. One is, however, led to ask Hyppolite whether the standpoint of "speculative philosophy" is itself attainable without having *first* rethought the phenomenological development presented in the *Phenomenology*. This surely would seem to follow from Hegel's description of the *Phenomenology* as an *introduction*, and a necessary introduction, to speculative philosophy or, since for Hegel they are equivalent, logic (PhG 33).[33] Hegel observes that the "*System der Erfahrung des Geistes*" (system of the experience of Spirit) only embraces the *appearance* of this experience (PhG 33), and he clearly does not set down systematic philosophy as a precondition for grasping the systematic character of this experience. It is manifest that the reverse of this is proposed (cf. also, PhG 25ff. and WdL, I:30).

If, then, our critique of Hyppolite has hit its mark, Kroner's interpretation of the philosophical observer, or "we," is even less viable. Not mentioning the problem of the *appearance of* experience, he proceeds to assert that the "we" grasps the necessity in the sequence of natural consciousness' experiences from the standpoint of the goal toward which it is striving, from the *end* of its pathway, which the "*we*" recognizes as the "self-realization of the absolute." Kroner's version of the "we" has already arrived at the level of absolute knowledge. But if this interpretation were accepted, one could give no plausible answer to Hegel's "rhetorical" question: "one might simply dispense with the negative as something *false* and thus demand to be led to the truth without further ado; why bother oneself about that which is false?" (PhG 33).

The most detailed and provocative interpretation of the "we" problem in Hegel's *Phenomenology* is found in Heidegger's essay on "Hegel's Concept of Experience." He alone explicitly poses the question; "Who are the 'we'?" and his answer to the question constitutes the heart of his proposal for a reading of the entire book (*Holzwege*, 188; HCE 149).

Like the other commentators, Heidegger assumes that the "we" has some kind of privileged access to the absolute. But the superiority of the "we" over natural consciousness is not attributed to its "higher" historical standpoint (Lukács) or to its ultimately mystical and irrational intuition (Kroner). Heidegger's account is distinguished by the claim that the "we" is akin to the absolute through the fact that it lets consciousness be, that it keeps its own standards out of the self-investigation of consciousness. No one has seen more clearly than Heidegger that "our contribution" consists in the act of restraint in the face of the appearance *of* experience, that "our contribution" is the omission of all contributions (*Holzwege*, 174; HCE 128).

The peculiarity of Heidegger's interpretation is found in his tendency to identify the "we" of the *Phenomenology* with the fundamental ontologist of his own writings. Thus he refers to the consciousness described in the *Phenomenology*, natural consciousness, as "ontic consciousness" (*Holzwege*, 161; HCE 105), whereas the "we" is said to think "the beingness of being" and to be therefore "already provided with Being [*Sein*]." Heidegger accordingly reads the *Phenomenology* as "a dialogue between ontic and ontological consciousness" (*Holzwege*, 185; HCE 144) or between natural consciousness and absolute knowledge (*Holzwege*, 186; HCE 146). This dialogue is precisely what he regards as Hegel's concept of experience. The "we" is said to be receptive to that ontological dimension of consciousness' experience which remains invisible for natural or ontic consciousness because what appears *within* this experience excludes the appearance *of* experience for consciousness. But the "we," in its "thoroughgoing skepticism," does not interfere with the appearance *within* consciousness' experience and thus lets the "new object," and therewith the Being of experience itself, appear.

Heidegger's interpretation rests upon his contention that the term "Being" may be used to refer to what Hegel calls spirit (*Holzwege*, 142; HCE 69). But Hegel's sense of Being (i.e., spirit) is said to suffer from the forgetfulness characteristic of post-Socratic metaphysics in that Being is implicitly regarded as *will* (*Holzwege*, 187–88; HCE 148–49; and *Holzwege*, 120; HCE 30). The ontological knowledge of the "we" is therefore defective because (*a*) it has not yet made explicit and radicalized the traditional metaphysics of Being as will (an achievement Heidegger attributes to Nietzsche's writings on the will-to-power), and (*b*) it has not yet grasped the necessity of systematically destroying traditional metaphysics (the task which Heidegger himself claims to have undertaken). But Heidegger's interpretation of spirit in the *Phenomenology* as Being and Being as will rests upon his interpretation of the "we" as a mode of consciousness. For him, "Everything depends upon thinking the experience mentioned here [in the *Phenomenology*] as the Being of consciousness" (*Holzwege* 171; HCE 121).

The safest generalization about Heidegger's essay is that it uses the *Phenomenology*'s introduction as a touchstone for elucidating some important elements of his own fundamental ontology. As such it is a valuable document for the student who seeks to grasp the relationship between *Sein und Zeit* and the "late" Heidegger. And while it is in many respects a stimulating exercise for the Hegel student, it can be singularly misleading if taken literally as a commentary on the *Phenomenology*. For the *Phenomenology* is *not* an ontology (Hegel's *Logik* may be properly spoken of as his ontology[34]); it is a *phenomenology* and can only be understood if it is read as such.[35]

The most remarkable feature of Heidegger's interpretation of the philosophical "we" is that it focuses upon the dark passage in the next last page of the "Introduction" (PhG 74; HCE 24–25) dealing with *"unsere Zutat."* But perhaps this is not so remarkable after all, for when we look closely at the studies of Kroner, Hartmann, and Hyppolite, we find that their definitive utterances on the "we" also take the form of analyses of this passage (PhG 74). It seems to this writer a matter of no mean consequence that four of the six scholars cited tend so to limit their attention in defining a term on whose comprehension intelligibility in *reading* the *Phenomenology* hinges. And if, in addition, one recalls Hegel's frequent critical comments on prefaces and introductions to philosophical works, it is reasonable to assume that he too would be highly skeptical of a general definition which is based on a passage where, in the terminology of contemporary semantical theory, the term is, from the viewpoint of the work as a whole, metalinguistically "mentioned" rather than dramatically "used."

In point of fact, the term "we" and its variants are *used* repeatedly throughout the *Phenomenology*. Rather than adding any further speculations on the "real" meaning of *"unsere Zutat,"* perhaps it might be more fruitful to arrive at a comprehension of who "we" are through the process of "working the matter out." In the following paragraphs certain working hypotheses will be stated, but these can only be provisional; their only verification can be an enhanced comprehension on the part of a reader who works his way through the *Phenomenology* itself.

First, let us gather together the helpful suggestions which have emerged from our review of Hegel scholarship.

(1) Following Marcuse, our attention must be fixed on the problem of *intelligibility* in the *Phenomenology* and (2) with Lukács this intelligibility is to be sought, insofar as possible, in connection with the specific prerequisites for comprehension by "us" as intelligent (but also human)

readers. (3) As Hyppolite has pointed out, certain of these prerequisites are *historical*. (4) All the while, we must not forget that, as Hartmann observes, "we" must grasp the *necessity* in the development of the described consciousness' experiences. It will be of singular importance to comprehend just what this necessity consists in. (5) But our comprehension of this necessity will be clouded if we neglect to distinguish between the two parallel processes of necessity at work in the *Phenomenology*, as Kroner indicates.

The first and absolutely essential stage in the actualization of the reader's already implicitly philosophical (in Hegel's sense) comprehension (i.e., the first of the two processes of necessity) is found in working through the section called "Consciousness" (*Phenomenology* I–III). It is here that Hegel shows that the "we," *contra* Heidegger, cannot be understood as a mode of consciousness, for in his explication of the result of "Consciousness" (PhG 133–40) the "we" comes to see that the "I" of consciousness is first *constituted* through the intersubjectivity of the "we" and that the unity in question in the *Phenomenology* is not (as in Heidegger's interpretation) the unity of consciousness and Being but the "spiritual unity" in reciprocal recognition. It is this "spiritual unity" which constitutes the concept of spirit (*Phenomenology* 140–41). But the way out of consciousness' meaning-solipsism cannot be simply "pointed out"; it must be worked through. And in doing so the reader must note Hegel's peculiar use of the word "we" in this section. For it is only in "Consciousness" (and in subsequent references back to PhG I–III) that the "we" is seen to play the role (*zum Bei-spiel*) of the consciousness presented, to *speak* for it and *write* for it (PhG 81), immediately and passively *observe* for it (PhG 85), as well as *perceive* for it (PhG 95) and actively participate in its concept (PhG 103).[36] Moreover, "we" are able so to relate ourselves, not because it is some primordial experience and the "we" is "the absoluteness of the absolute" (with Heidegger), or because the "we" is a speculative Hegelian philosopher (with Hyppolite), or because the "we" enjoys the privileged access of absolute knowledge (with Kroner); both the consciousness in question and "we" ourselves are already in the element of *pre*-Hegelian philosophy.[37] Indeed, the section called "Consciousness" is the most clearly philosophical (when philosophy is understood as the theory of knowledge) of the entire work. And it is so because it must enable its readers to get beyond "philosophy," beyond the "love of knowledge," and thus to begin to know (PhG 12).

Hegel, contrary to many a legend, demonstrates in the *Phenomenology* a great respect for his readers. This, rather than his reputedly esoteric and didactic style, is a more probable source of "unintelligibility" to readers of the *Phenomenology*. He recognized that the individual reader has "the right to demand that science at least provide him with the ladder to this standpoint [the element of philosophy], and show him this standpoint within himself" (PhG 25). The ladder that Hegel extends in the opening three chapters of the *Phenomenology* is a "ladder language" quite unlike that of Wittgenstein's *Tractatus*: it *does* enable "our" theoretical orientation to rise above the level of solipsism, mystical or otherwise, because it destroys the "myth of meaning" underlying the "paradox of learning" which has plagued philosophical thought since Socrates.

In these chapters Hegel shows that meaning remains a myth and learning remains paradoxical as long as the ultimate subject is taken to have the egological structure of consciousness. Consciousness *is* dialectical because it presumes to give an account of its experience in terms of the ego and its other. But by playing the role of consciousness, *we* come to see at the end of *Phenomenology* III that consciousness' attempt at self-explication results, when pushed to the limit, in an inversion of consciousness and its world (PhG 121ff.). To see this inversion is "our contribution," an act of restraint through which we are finally able to relinquish the standpoint of consciousness.

We may agree with Heidegger that the *Phenomenology* presents us with a dialogue. But the protagonists are not the ontic and ontological modes of consciousness' experience. They are rather consciousness and spirit. The dialogue itself is consciousness' (not Hegel's) voyage to the discovery that it *is* spirit. For *us*, this dramatic dialogue begins when the concept of spirit reveals itself to us (PhG 140), when we no longer take ourselves to be substitution instances of the protagonist, consciousness. Heidegger's brilliant exposition of the "Introduction" founders on just this issue. He fails to see that the concept of spirit is inexplicable in terms of consciousness or its ontic and ontological modalities of experience. The "I" of consciousness must rather be grasped as constituted through the "we" of spirit. And when "we," the readers of the *Phenomenology* grasp this, the "we" becomes, for the first time, "we" in Hegel's distinctive sense of the word. As such, "we" are able to witness the dialogue between consciousness and spirit through which consciousness works out in concrete detail (PhG IV–VIII) what "we" have come to grasp merely *ex negativo* and in principle (PhG I–III).

In the concluding paragraph to the "Introduction," Hegel says "consciousness will reach a point (*Punkt*) at which it casts off the semblance of being burdened by something alien to it, something which is only *for it* and which exists as an other. In other words, at that point in the authentic science of spirit" (PhG 75; HCE 26). The suggestion which follows from the argument of this essay is that the "point" referred to is the transition to *Phenomenology* IV. "In self-consciousness, as the concept of spirit, consciousness has for the first time reached its turning point [*Wendungspunkt*]" (PhG 140).

These texts suggest that the *method* of Hegel's *Phenomenology* is developed in two stages. The first (PhG I–III) is a dialogue between consciousness and the "we" in which the 'we' participates. The result of this dialogue is that consciousness, through its inversion, comes to present itself to us as the appearance *of* experience, whose essence (spirit) "*we*" no longer distinguish from its appearance. Since "we" no longer interfere with consciousness (as at PhG 81, 85, 95, 103), "our contribution" becomes "the pure act of observation" (PhG 72; HCE 21). The second stage (PhG IV–VIII) is accordingly "the authentic science of Spirit," the *phenomenology* of *spirit* rather than consciousness. At this point "*we*" have grasped the essence of consciousness.

The "Introduction" ends with these words: "And, finally, when consciousness itself grasps this its essence, it will indicate the nature of absolute knowledge itself" (PhG 75; HCE 26).

Notes

All page references are to Johannes Hoffmeister's edition of *Die Phänomenologie des Geistes* (Hamburg: Felix Meiner Verlag, 1948).

1. Although scores of commentators, from Trendelenburg to Findlay, have denied that Hegel employed a consistently dialectical method (claiming on the contrary that his thought only attains its apparent dynamic through surreptitious appeals to experience), Ivan Iljin was, so far as I am aware, the first to develop the insight that "Hegel, in his philosophical method, was no dialectician" (Ivan Iljin, *Die Philosophie Hegels als kontemplative Gotteslehre* [Bern: A. Francke Verlag, 1946], 126). Iljin's argument, persuasive though it is, does not focus on the *Phenomenology*, but deals rather with Hegel's authorship as a whole.

2. A new translation of the "Introduction" to Hegel's *Phenomenology* has been published in Martin Heidegger, *Hegel's Concept of Experience*, with a section of Hegel's *Phenomenology of Spirit*, translated by Kenley Royce Dove (New York: Harper & Row, 1970), 7–26. This edition will be referred to as HCE.

3. Cf. Nicolai Hartmann, *Die Philosophie des deutschen Idealismus* (Berlin: Walter de Gruyter, 1960), II. Teil: *Hegel* (1929).

4. The term "science" is, of course, not to be taken merely in the restrictive sense of the natural sciences or any other formally organized discipline—although these too will come into view. What Hegel means by *Wissenschaft* here is a specific shape or *Gestalt* of consciousness or spirit which is *itself* constituted by a systematic mode of relating form and content, certainty and truth, subject and substance. Thus "*die Sittlichkeit*" is just as much a science as "psychology."

5. In view of the radical novelty of Hegel's use of the term *Begriff*, it is tempting to avoid translating it as "concept," the most obvious choice. Wallace and Baillie have presented cogent arguments for the term "notion." It has the advantage of suggesting a kinship with the Greek term νοῦς—and it has a systematic precedent in Berkeley's *Siris*. Unfortunately, the term carries with it irrepressible connotations of vagueness and imprecision.

6. For a discussion of the concept *qua* known by the philosophical "we," see below.

7. Cf. also PhG 38: "*Was die Zeit betrifft, . . . so ist sie der daseiende Begriff selbst.*" Both these passages are given an extensive and illuminating interpretation in A. Kojève, *Introduction à la lecture de Hegel: Leçons sur la Phénoménologie de l'Esprit*, ed. Raymond Queneau (Paris: Gallimard, 1947).

8. Hegel has in this analysis developed an important insight into the problematical relationship between the positive and negative senses of the Kantian thing-in-itself, that is, of the a thing-in-itself *qua* object (that which, according to the "Transcendental Aesthetic" of the first *Critique*, is said to be known) and the thing-in-itself *qua* noumenon. From the perspective of the *Critique of Pure Reason*, there is no unambiguous answer to Jacobi's well-known charge that Kant tried, against his own strictures, to have it both ways.

9. For Hegel's most explicit discussion of this question, see his Jena lectures of 1803–1804, first published in 1932 by Felix Meiner as *Jenenser Realphilosophie* I. See pp. 214ff.

10. In view of the endless polemics among Marxists and critics of Marx on the question of the "Hegelian method," it is interesting to note that this "method," is quite indifferent to the rival claims of idealism on the one hand and realism on the other.

11. But this aspect of human experience is not grasped by the reader of the *Phenomenology*, before he has followed the argument *through* the chapter on *Verstand*. N.B., PhG 128. As we shall see, an understanding of this characteristic feature of the PhG is essential for a demystification of the philosophical "we"; or, which is another way of expressing the same problem, it is essential to the intelligibility of the PhG as a philosophical work. This second aspect of consciousness must not be simply identified with that section of the *Phenomenology* explicitly called "Self-Consciousness." As a moment of human knowing, self-consciousness is a factor, however much explicitly emphasized, throughout the entire course of experience from "Sense-Certainty" to "Absolute Knowledge."

12. For a complementary formulation of this important methodological issue, see Hegel's Jena lectures of 1803–1804, *Jenenser Realphilosphie*, I:200.

13. Cf. *Hegel's Phenomenology of Mind*, trans. J. B. Baillie (London: Allen and Unwin, 1931), 138.

14. R. Kroner suggests that *Erleben* would be a more adequate term for what

Hegel describes as experience. Cf. Richard Kroner, *Von Kant bis Hegel*, vol. II: *Von der Naturphilosophie zur Philosophie des Geistes* (Tübingen: Verlag J. C. B. Mohr, 1924), 374.

15. This argument is forcefully developed by George Schrader in "Hegel's Contribution to Phenomenology," *The Monist* 48. 1:18ff, 1964.

16. The structure of the *Phenomenology* is so complex that nothing short of a detailed commentary could possibly do it justice. It is interesting to note that the only existing complete commentary on the *Phenomenology* divides the work into the two parts indicated above. Cf. Jean Hyppolite, *Genèse et structure de la Phénoménologie de l'Esprit de Hegel*, 2 vols. (Aubier and Paris: Editions Montaigne, 1946), 40 et passim. But Hyppolite's contention (p. 55) that "the *Phenomenology* was for Hegel, consciously or unconsciously, the means to deliver to the public, not a complete system, but the history of his own philosophical development," seems to commit that *intentional* fallacy which Hegel (PhG 227–301) subjected to such a devastating criticism. The most elaborate structural interpretation of the *Phenomenology* is given in the third appendix to Kojève's lectures, *Introduction à la lecture de Hegel*, 574–95.

17. Among existing works of drama, the one which immediately suggests itself for comparison is Goethe's *Faust*. An elaboration of this comparison between the *Phenomenology* and *Faust* may be found in Georg Lukács, *Goethe und seine Zeit* (Bern: A. Francke Verlag, 1947) and Ernst Bloch, "Des Faust-Motiv in der *Phänomenologie des Geistes*," *Hegel-Studien* 155–71.

18. Cf. Bertold Brecht, *Schriften zum Theater* (Frankfurt 1.1: Suhrkamp Verlag, 1957).

19. The problem of the "we" has, however, received scant attention in Marxist oriented studies dealing with the *Phenomenology*. It is, for example, not even mentioned by Bloch, *Subjekt-Objekt: Erläuterungen zu Hegel*, 2nd ed. (Frankfurt: Suhrkamp, 1962).

20. Cf. H. Marcuse, *Reason and Revolution* (Boston: Beacon Press, 1941), 94.

21. Cf. Lukács, *Der junge Hegel: Über die Bezichungen von Dialektik und Ökonomie* (Zurich and Vienna: Europa, 1948), 602–3.

22. N. Hartmann, *Philosophie des deutschen Idealismus*, 317.

23. Hyppolite, *Introduction à la lecture de Hegel*, 29–30. Cf. also pp. 81 and 104.

24. Kroner, *Von Kant bis Hegel*, II:369–70.

25. M. Heidegger, *Holzwege* (Frankfurt: V. Klostermann, 1957), 173, 175.

26. The most frequent contexts for the appearance of "we" in the main body of the *Phenomenology* are: *"jetzt sehen wir"* or *"wir sehen."*

27. Jacob Loewenberg's imaginative proposal that the "we" engages in an

alternating process of "histrionically impersonating" consciousness and experiencing its comic denouement systematically encourages this misunderstanding. The argument is formulated in Loewenberg's introduction to the Scribner edition of *Hegel Selections* (1929), in his two *Mind* articles (Oct. 1934 and Jan. 1935), and in *Hegel's Phenomenology: Dialogues in the Life of Mind* (LaSalle, Ill.: Open Court, 1965). Emil Fackenheim suggests that the reader of the *Phenomenology* is not the "we" but "must, as it were, hover *between* the viewing and the viewed standpoints" (*The Religious Dimension in Hegel's Thought* [Bloomington: Indiana University Press, 1967], 36). Unfortunately, the notion of "hovering" is never clearly formulated in Fackenheim's interesting book.

28. *Reason and Revolution*, 94.

29. *Philosophie des deutschen Idealismus*, 338.

30. Hyppolite does, however, offer a clue to answering this problem in a subsequent remark which does not directly deal with the problem of the philosophical "we": "but it is only the *universal individuality*, that which has been able to lift itself to absolute knowledge, which must find again in it and develop in itself the moments implied in its becoming. It is the same consciousness which, having reached philosophical knowledge, turns back upon itself and which, as empirical consciousness, goes upon the phenomenological itinerary. In order to indicate to others the road of absolute knowledge, it must find it back in itself. . . . That which for it is reminiscence and interiorization, must be for the others the road of their ascension. But this individuality itself, as far as it is individuality, carries necessarily elements of particularity; it is bound to time and for it the French Revolution or the period of enlightenment have more importance than other historical events. Isn't there an irreducible contingency in this?" Jean Hyppolite, *Introduction à la lecture de Hegel*, 50. Cf. p. 80.

31. Lukács divides the *Phenomenology* according to the triad of spirit in the *Encyclopedia*.

32. *Der junge Hegel*, 602.

33. Hyppolite takes up the question of the relationship of the *Phenomenology* to the *Logik* in the last chapter of his commentary. His discussion includes a, for this reader, novel argument showing how the *Logik* may be regarded as the standpoint *"für uns"* in the *Phenomenology* and the *Phenomenology*, reciprocally, as the standpoint *"für uns"* in the *Logik*. Cf. Hyppolite, *Introduction à la lecture de Hegel*, 560ff. But this discussion also leaves unanswered the problem of the philosophical "we" *qua reader* in the *Phenomenology*.

34. Cf. Heidegger's discussion of the *Logik* in his *Identität und Differenz* (Pfullingen: Neske Verlag, 1957).

35. Cf. T. W. Adorno's critique of Heidegger's Hegel interpretation in *Drei Studien zu Hegel* (Frankfurt: Suhrkamp Verlag, 1963), 69.

36. This is the only section of the *Phenomenology* which presents any *prima*

facie grounds for Loewenberg's interpretive notion of "histrionic impersonation." It is perhaps worth noting that Loewenberg's *Mind* articles mentioned above, written thirty years before his commentary on the *Phenomenology* as a whole, developed the "histrionic" thesis in connection with an analysis focusing on PhG I–III.

37. The term "pre-Hegelian" is to be understood in a systematic and not merely chronological sense.

3

Kenneth R. Westphal

Hegel's Solution to the Dilemma of the Criterion

Recently, problems about epistemic circularity, and more recently, Sextus Empiricus' "dilemma of the criterion" have been receiving thoughtful attention from contemporary epistemologists. Epistemic circularity is involved in using a source of belief in the process of assessing or justifying that source of belief; the dilemma of the criterion (quoted in the following section) concerns establishing basic criteria of justification in highly disputed domains. Because there are diverse and controversial views on this issue, how can basic criteria of justification be established without infinite regress, vicious circularity, or question-begging assumptions?[1] I think these problems deserve careful attention, but I don't believe contemporary epistemologists have fully realized how sophisticated a response Pyrrhonian skepticism requires.

Roderick Chisholm contends that there are three kinds of response to Sextus' dilemma:

1. Particularists believe they have various particular instances of knowledge on the basis of which they can construct a general account of the nature and criteria of knowledge.

2. Methodists believe they know the nature and criteria of knowledge, and on that basis can distinguish genuine from illegitimate particular instances of knowledge.

3. Skeptics believe that no particular cases of knowledge can be identified without knowing the nature or criteria of knowledge, and that the nature or criteria of knowledge cannot be known without identifying particular cases of genuine knowledge.[2]

Chisholm favors particularism, but thinks that any attempt to solve the problem must beg the question.[3]

Paul Moser has sought to avoid the dogmatism which arises from accepting either methodism or particularism by proposing to reach a "reflective equilibrium" between our considered judgments about epistemic principles and our clearest intuitions about particular cases of knowledge or justified belief.[4] There may be merit to this suggestion, but convincing reasons must be provided to suppose that we would equilibrate toward genuine principles of justification and genuine cases of knowledge or justified belief. Moser apparently discounts this problem because of his staunch justificatory internalism, which permits him to consider propositions as justified for particular persons, even if their principles of justification are not truth-conducive. As his recent work reveals, this is much more a capitulation to, rather than a solution of, serious skeptical challenges to knowledge and to our understanding of it.

Recently, Moser has argued for "conditional ontological agnosticism," the view that no agnostic-resistant, non-question-begging evidence for ontological claims (whether idealist or realist) can be found.[5] He contends that philosophy nevertheless can undertake important semantic, explanatory, and evaluative projects. His "explanatory project" addresses whatever constitutes the correctness of one's explanatory epistemic standards regarding the nature of justification; his "evaluative project" addresses whatever constitutes the correctness of the evaluative epistemic standards one uses to "discern" justified beliefs. These projects must avoid the dilemma of being either naive or viciously circular. Moser's "semantic project" purports to solve that dilemma through informative answers to questions about the point and significance of one's standards.[6] The explanations his three projects involve are avowedly "perspectival" because they are supported ultimately by the various semantic commitments, explanatory ends, and standards of success—in sum, by the conceptually relative "standpoints"—adopted by individual epistemologists.[7]

Moser contends that the dilemma he identifies for his explanatory and evaluative projects is more basic that Sextus' dilemma of the criterion.[8] In part this is because he accepts Chisholm's formulation of the dilemma in terms of justification,[9] instead of the criterial terms Sextus actually uses. This prevents him from recognizing how basic a problem

Sextus poses and how sophisticated Sextus is in parlaying that problem into objections to all sorts of philosophical endeavors. Moreover, Moser's case for ontological agnosticism is tantamount to the less sophisticated, more dogmatic cousin of Pyrrhonian skepticism, Academic skepticism.[10] Most important, however, is the fact that Moser doesn't recognize that direct permutations of Sextus' dilemma and its associated skeptical tropes arise for any attempt to assess the various explanations and evaluations offered by different epistemologists. Indeed, they arise for any attempt to assess the merits of various "semantic commitments" made by different epistemologists or of various "standpoints" they adopt. Acquiescing in "ontological agnosticism" and avowing "conceptual relativism" does not evade Sextus' challenging questions; quite the contrary.

Having once argued that epistemic circularity need not be vicious, William Alston soon had second thoughts:

> What I take myself to have shown in "Epistemic Circularity" is that epistemic circularity does not prevent one from showing, on the basis of empirical premises that are ultimately based on sense perception, that sense perception is reliable. But whether one actually does succeed in this depends on one's being justified in those perceptual premises, and that in turn, according to our assumptions about justification, depends on sense perception being a reliable source of belief. In other words, *if* (and only if) sense perception is reliable, can we show it to be reliable. And how can we cancel out that *if*?
>
> Here is another way of posing the problem. If we are entitled to use belief from a certain source in showing that source to be reliable, then any source can be shown to be reliable. For if all else fails, we can simply use each belief twice over, once as testee and once as tester. . . . Thus if we allow the use of mode of belief formation M to determine whether the beliefs formed by M are true, M is sure to get a clean bill of health. But a line of argument that will validate any mode of belief formation, no matter how irresponsible, is not what we are looking for. We want, and need, something much more discriminating. Hence the fact that the reliability of sense perception can be established by relying on sense perception does not solve our problem.[11]

Alston proposes several criteria for justifying doxastic practices. It counts in favor of a practice if it is more firmly established. This involves a practice being more widely accepted, more definitely structured, more important to guiding action, more difficult to abstain from, more innately based, or having principles that seem more obviously true. An acceptable doxastic practice cannot generate massive inconsistency, and persistent massive inconsistency between two practices indicates that at least one is faulty. Alston adopts a negative coherentism: an established doxastic practice is *prima facie* rationally acceptable in the absence of significant disqualifying reasons. More positively, a practice may generate "self-support" if it grounds our abilities to investigate how that practice is possible or grounds our abilities to engage in other effective practices. The more such self-support a doxastic practice generates, the more that counts in its favor. The failure to generate such "self-support" is a demerit. Analyzing doxastic practices in light of these criteria may help establish a rank ordering to which to appeal when massive conflicts arise among or within them. The aspirations of such "free-wheeling" philosophical analysis, within which every claim is open to criticism, are modest.[12] Even showing that there is no practical and rational alternative to believing that our general belief-forming practices are reliable faces epistemic circularity, and someone who does not accept the basic reliability of a source of belief cannot be justified in accepting it by an epistemically circular argument.[13]

Robert Fogelin has examined contemporary foundationalism, reliabilism, coherentism, and externalism, with Sextus' skepticism in view. He concludes:

> What I have tried to show, using a number of exemplary cases, is that Pyrrhonian skepticism, when taken seriously and made a party to the debate, is much more intractable than those who have produced theories of empirical justification have generally supposed. As far as I can see, the challenge of Pyrrhonian skepticism, once accepted, is unanswerable.[14]

I'm happy to add Fogelin's case studies—Bonjour, Goldman, Nozick, Dretske, Chisholm, Lehrer, and Davidson—to those I gave in my book—Descartes, Kant, Carnap, and Alston—to show that Sextus' skepticism is a serious problem deserving serious consideration. Unlike Fogelin I believe that our epistemological situation is good, not dire. The surprise is that the proper response to Sextus comes from a philosopher who is widely supposed to have had no theory of knowledge at all: Hegel. Hegel is an enormously sophisticated epistemologist whose views have gone unrecognized because his problems have gone unrecognized. Placing Sextus' dilemma of the criterion in the foreground solves this problem. In one way or another, the solutions posed in the literature require that we be self-critical in order, for example, to avoid dogmatism (Chisholm), to distinguish justifying from arbitrary reflective equilibria (Moser), to distinguish appropriate or adequate conceptualizations from inferior alternatives (Moser), or to distinguish genuine from sham self-support (Alston). Though not widely recognized, the real problem raised by Sextus' dilemma is to understand how self-criticism is possible. Hegel recognized this problem and developed a very sophisticated and powerful analysis of it.

Some of the importance and the difficulty involved in self-criticism can be seen by considering how Chisholm's three responses to the dilemma of the criterion highlight the fact that different philosophers make different assumptions about human knowledge and about how to analyze it. Such assumptions inform a philosopher's entire approach to epistemology, and they condition if not determine what, if anything, a philosopher will accept as credible. Because a philosopher's assumptions inform his or her theoretical formulations and his or her judgments about credibility, there is conceptual interdependence within the constellation of assumptions, principles, and paradigm examples comprised in any philosopher's basic approach to epistemology.[15] Philosophers take many different assumptions as points of departure; not all are equally credible. Can we distinguish more from less credible basic assumptions? If so, how?

A further difficulty is reflected in Alston's point about the limits of proof involved in epistemically circular arguments: there is a conceptual distinction between evidence one has and evidence one accepts. In particular cases of knowledge or belief, as well as in particular epistemic analyses, there may be a significant divergence between the evidence someone has and the evidence he or she accepts. This contrast reflects the fact that there is a conceptual distinction between apparent evidence and genuine evidence, and that in any particular case there may again be a significant divergence between them. These two distinctions are themselves distinct, and part of our challenge, both as cognizant agents and as epistemologists, is to align them, both in principle and in practice.

With these points in view, both the importance of and the difficulties involved in self-criticism can be suggested more clearly. In view of these four points—the interdependence among the basic assumptions, principles, and favored cases comprised in an epistemology; the distinction between having and accepting evidence; the distinction between apparent and genuine evidence; and the distinction between these two distinctions—can philosophers' basic epistemic assumptions be submitted to critical scrutiny? Can they be assessed without begging the question? If so, how?

Hegel's solution to the dilemma of the criterion provides a very sophisticated and powerful answer to these questions. Hegel's solution presents a series of "forms of consciousness" (explained below), each of which adopts a distinct set of assumptions about human knowledge and applies the principles implied or embedded in those assumptions to relevant examples of putative knowledge. The structure Hegel ascribes to forms of consciousness affords an internal critical assessment of the various assumptions and principles of knowledge those forms of consciousness illustrate. Even if we cannot justify a theory of knowledge to a skeptic who refuses to take *any* evidence or principle as credible, we still face a substantial problem providing a critical assessment of various epistemic assumptions and principles and achieving rational agreement among more credulous and credible epistemologists. Hegel solves this methodological problem, and in his substantive analysis of knowledge he shows how unwarranted the radical skeptic's refusal is to count anything as evidence or justification.[16] Hegel thus provides a theoretical solution to the dilemma which avoids vicious circularity, infinite regress, and self-certifying intuition. The assumptions he makes do not appear as premises in his proof, and ultimately they can be discharged through self-critical assessment of them.[17]

My discussion has four parts. I begin by discussing the dilemma of the criterion and its epistemological significance. As a first step in presenting Hegel's solution to this dilemma, I discuss his conception of "forms of consciousness." Hegel's main solution to the dilemma involves analyzing a conception of knowledge as a relation between knower and known. I conclude by briefly discussing a problem confronting Hegel's solution to this dilemma. Although I only discuss epistemology, the problem and reconstruction I offer extend quite directly to Hegel's concerns with ethics and action.

THE DILEMMA OF THE CRITERION AND ITS EPISTEMOLOGICAL SIGNIFICANCE

Hegel states that the aim of the *Phenomenology of Spirit* is to provide "insight into what knowing is."[18] Since there is severe and sustained disagreement on this topic, providing insight into the actual nature or structure of knowledge requires assessing competing views and defending one's own view. The methodological problem Hegel confronts in the introduction to the *Phenomenology* is how differing views of knowledge can be assessed, and indeed how this can be done without lapsing into dogmatism or begging the question against those who disagree. This problem was classically formulated as an argument purporting to show that no such assessment can be made because no criterion for such assessment can be established. This is the "dilemma of the criterion" propounded by Sextus Empiricus.

In his *Outlines of Pyrrhonism*, Sextus poses the following dilemma:

> In order to decide the dispute which has arisen about the criterion [of truth], we must possess an accepted criterion by which we shall be able to judge the dispute; and in order to possess an accepted criterion, the dispute about the criterion must first be decided. And when the argument thus reduces itself to a form of circular reasoning the discovery of the criterion becomes impracticable, since we do not allow [those who make knowledge claims] to adopt a criterion by assumption, while if they offer to judge the criterion by a criterion we force them to a regress *ad infinitum*. And furthermore, since demonstration requires a demonstrated criterion, while the criterion requires an approved demonstration, they are forced into circular reasoning.[19]

The problem posed is one of settling disputes—disputes about appropriate criteria for assessing knowledge claims. This kind of second-order dispute about what knowledge is could quickly develop from disputes about the way the world is. (I will call claims about the world "first-order" knowledge claims.) Insofar as establishing first-order knowledge claims involves demonstrating that those claims are warranted, second-order claims about what knowledge is and how to distinguish it from error would be invoked. Of course, these second-order claims, too, require warrants. Thus the problem of adjudicating among divergent claims to first-order knowledge recurs on a higher level as a problem of adjudicating among differing claims to second-order knowledge about what knowledge is. At this point, when what is called for are coordinated warrants for three types of claims (first-order claims, second-order claims about the principles warranting those first-order claims, and claims warranting these second-order claims), the problem may look insoluble. Sextus may well seem the wiser for having been compelled to suspend judgment by the multitude of divergent first principles propounded in various philosophies (OP I §§170, 178). Sextus uses this dilemma to try to undermine first-order knowledge claims. Hegel takes a methodological cue from Sextus' dilemma in recognizing that the dilemma arises and must be met at the second level of epistemological debate.

What can be done to solve this dilemma? What can be done to defend the claims made by a theory of knowledge? One ordinary strategy for defending claims to knowledge is unavailable here. In making claims about everyday things our beliefs are often justified by something that is not itself a belief or claim, such as being in a perceptual state. In the case before us, however, there is no such appeal to be made; we simply don't perceive what knowledge is in anything like the way we perceive tables and chairs.

Justifying a theory of knowledge involves appealing to further claims, which in turn require justification.

One negative condition for an adequate account of knowledge derived from Kant, and adopted by Hegel, is that any account of knowledge that cannot be known in accordance with its own principles is self-refuting: its very promulgation demonstrates abilities unaccounted for by that theory.[20] This is a powerful condition. However, this condition does not distinguish between theories of knowledge that are reflexively self-consistent in this way and a theory that is, in addition, true. Furthermore, Kant's condition doesn't address the problem of reaching agreement among dissenting epistemologists. Something more needs to be established in order to respond to Sextus.

What resources are there for addressing this problem? On the one hand, simply accepting various claims about what knowledge is leads to dogmatism, and Hegel called the trustworthiness of these claims into question. (One cannot simply accept all *prima facie* claims about knowledge because these claims contradict one another and so cannot all be true.[21]) On the other hand, simply rejecting such ideas altogether would leave us bereft of terms for even posing the problem, to say nothing of solving it. Thus some sort of *prima facie* cognitive abilities and terminology for analyzing these abilities must be granted in order to have a problem and a discussion of it at all. If there are reasons for questioning those *prima facie* abilities, then any solution to these difficulties will have to lie in the possibility of self-critically revising our *prima facie* understanding of knowledge. It must be *critical* revision because there are reasons to suppose that our understanding of knowledge is inadequate; it must be *self*-critical revision because there is need to avoid question-begging and dogmatism. Hegel's procedure for determining which *prima facie* claims are true is to examine a series of "forms of consciousness," each of which adopts a specific set of *prima facie* claims about knowledge. Hegel holds that the actual nature or structure of knowledge can be comprehended through examining the defects and proficiencies of a range of accounts of knowledge and its objects based on these *prima facie* ideas.

Forms of Consciousness

What is a "form" (*Gestalt*) of consciousness? A form of consciousness is an expository device consisting of a pair of basic principles. One of these principles specifies the kind of empirical knowledge of which a form of consciousness presumes itself capable. The other principle specifies the general structure of the kind of object which that form of consciousness presumes to find in the world. Taken together, these two principles constitute what Hegel calls a form of consciousness' "certainty" (*Gewißheit*). Idiomatically expressed, these principles specify what a form of consciousness is sure the world and its knowledge of it are like.[22] The principles at issue are categorial ones, for example, whether intuitive (a-conceptual) knowledge is humanly possible, or whether an ontology of sensa is adequate.

Considering these principles as a "form of consciousness" is neutral between a particular individual's consciousness and a group's collective outlook. Similarly, this device is neutral between historically identifiable, and summarily presented possible, views of knowledge and its objects. If Hegel is correct, historical epochs and extant philosophies are variations on, if not instances of, the forms of consciousness he recounts in the *Phenomenology*. This is because both forms of consciousness, as well as historically identifiable positions, all devolve from the real characteristics of consciousness. This is one point Hegel makes in claiming that his *Phenomenology* presents "the path of the soul which is making its way through the sequence of its own transformations as through way stations prescribed by its very nature" (PhG 55.36-39/H 67/PhS 49).

By grasping some aspect of its own nature as a cognizer, each form of consciousness adopts a particular principle concerning what knowledge is. Now any epistemic principle implies certain constraints on what the objects of knowledge could be. Therefore the adoption of an epistemic principle brings with it a concomitant ontological principle. To take examples from the first section of Hegel's book, the form of consciousness designated as "sense-certainty" holds that knowledge is unmediated by conceptions or inferences and that the world contains nothing but sheer particulars that can be grasped immediately. The form of consciousness called "perception" holds that cognition occurs by perceiving objects and using observation terms, and that the world contains multiply-propertied perceptible things. The form of consciousness called "understanding" holds that, in addition to perception, cognition requires inferences based on judgmental application of laws of nature, and that the world contains causally interacting substances structured by forces.

To take a pair of epistemic and ontological principles as a *form* of consciousness allows latitude for developing from less to more sophisticated accounts of knowledge and its objects based on each pair of principles. To take this pair of principles as a form of *consciousness* is to consider them only as they can be adopted and employed by consciousness in attempts to comprehend the world[23]—to make the kind of claims sanctioned by a conception of knowledge about the kinds of objects specified by a conception of objects. Indeed, a form of consciousness' epistemic principle is precisely a principle concerning how to apply its conception of objects to the world in order to comprehend the world. Hegel's neutrality on the question of who holds a given set of principles allows him to focus attention on the more important issue of the principles themselves in connection with their putative domains of application.

The conceptions Hegel proposes to examine in the *Phenomenology* include those of subject, object, knowledge, and world. However, these terms are too abstract to specify much of anything. So Hegel proposes to examine particular sets of specific versions of these conceptions through examining their ideal employment by each form of consciousness. "Each" does entail "every" here; Hegel thinks he can give an exhaustive list of the forms of consciousness. Hegel's defense of his own views about knowledge rests on their resulting from an internal, self-critical assessment of every form of consciousness and on that basis rejecting all alternative accounts of knowledge and its objects. (I comment on his problematic claim to completeness below.) Noting the proficiencies and deficiencies of each form of consciousness, and through that of each more specific interpretation of these abstract conceptions, will put us, Hegel's readers, in a position to understand the adequate specification of these abstract conceptions that Hegel purports to give at the end of the *Phenomenology*. Hegel's argument is thus a sort of argument by elimination, where he seeks to eliminate the errors but retain the insights of less adequate views through a self-critical process of revision.

Knowledge as a Relation

Hegel's defense of the possibility of self-criticism rests on two main points. First, being conscious is fundamentally a cognitive relation to the world, whether we realize it or not. (This may seem to beg the question in favor of realism, but it does not. Even subjective idealism has to account for the apparent dualism of subject and object.[24]) Second, this cognitive relation to the world has a certain structure that allows critical assessment and revision of conceptions of knowledge and of the world. If such self-criticism is possible, then Sextus is wrong to charge that vicious circularity and question-begging are ineluctable.

The Problem

Hegel begins his analysis of the structure of cognition by appealing to a common sense realism according to which the cognizant subject both relates itself to a known object and distinguishes itself from that object

(PG 58.23–35/PhG 70/PhS 52). Insisting that knowledge is a relation between subject and object does not seem to enable self-criticism. Indeed, it seems only to highlight the very problem that needs to be solved. If knowledge is a relation between subject and object, how can one tell if the object is as it seems to be? As Hegel notes,

> To be sure, the object seems to be for consciousness only as consciousness knows it; consciousness seems, as it were, unable to get behind the object in order to see it, *not* as it is *for consciousness*, but as it is *in itself*. Therefore consciousness also seems unable to examine its own knowledge by comparing it with the object. (PhG 59.35–37/H 72/PhS 54)

Because knowledge is a relation, any knowledge claim involves at least the conceptual distinction between the object itself and the object as it is taken to be. This conceptual distinction may well harbor a further distinction between the actual structure of the object and the content of the subject's cognitive state—ignorance, if not error. Hence on the face of it, any particular knowledge claim requires validation. However, any validation would involve further knowledge and claims. These further states and claims would involve the same conceptual distinction between object and cognitive state or claim and the same possibility of ignorance or error. So how could any cognitive state or claim be validated? One cannot simply compare one's putative knowledge with an unconceptualized "object itself," knowledge by direct acquaintance is not humanly possible,[25] so what could one do? Are we trapped within an opaque veil of representations? If not, how does insisting on knowledge as a relation between subject and object help to show that we're not? If there is a solution to this problem, it must be one of utilizing putative knowledge in a virtuously circular manner.

Surprisingly, Hegel seems to try to solve the problem of the circle of representations by simply reiterating the very problem itself:[26]

> But the difference between the in-itself and the for-itself is already present in the very fact that consciousness knows an object at all. Something is *to it* the *in-itself*, but knowledge or the being of the object *for* consciousness is *to it* still another moment. It is upon this differentiation, which exists and is present at hand, that the examination [of knowledge] is grounded. (PG 59.37–60.3/PhG 72/PhS 54)

Hegel claims here that the distinction between the object known (the "in-itself") and the knowledge of it (the "for-itself") is "available" (*vorhanden*) to consciousness, so that consciousness can examine its own knowledge of the object. Now in what sense, exactly, is this differentiation between the object and the knowledge of it available? As was just noted, this distinction is involved in the conception of knowledge as a relation, so that upon reflection one could recognize this conceptual distinction. Does simply recognizing the problem solve it? Hardly.

I contend that there is a crucial ambiguity in Hegel's text between two senses of "in-itself" and that there is an important set of distinctions that Hegel marks by using different grammatical cases. (Due to space considerations I will be brief about these arguments here.) Cataloging these distinctions generates a list of four aspects of knowledge as a relation between subject and object. Furthermore, because the "object" of any form of consciousness is twofold, both the world as an object of empirical knowledge and empirical knowledge as an object of self-knowledge, the initial list of four aspects of knowledge must be doubled into eight elements of consciousness as a cognitive relation.

The Eight Elements of Knowledge as a Relation

Hegel begins explaining how a form of consciousness can provide and revise its own criterion or standard of knowledge by refining a common sense notion of knowledge as a relation between subject and object:

> In consciousness, one moment is *for an* other; . . . At the same time, this other is to consciousness not only something *for it*; it is also [to consciousness] something outside this relationship or *in itself*: the moment of truth. Therefore, in what consciousness within its own self declares as the *in-itself* or the *true*, we have the standard by which consciousness itself proposes to measure its own knowledge. (PG 59.8–13/PhG 71/PhS 53)

This passage bears close scrutiny because the ambiguity of the phrase "in-itself" and an important grammatical case distinction are found here.

Two Senses of "In-Itself"

One sense of "in-itself" is that the object of knowledge is something unto itself, regardless of what may be known about it. The preposition "in" is not important; what is important is the object being what it is, with all of its properties known and unknown. In order to avoid question-begging, Hegel does not make claims about the structure of this object (at least not before the end of the *Phenomenology*). This sense of "in-itself" may be labeled as *The Object Itself* (*simpliciter*).

The second sense of "in-itself" is crucial to Hegel's project, for it is the standard that consciousness gives itself in order to assess ("measure") its own knowledge. Hegel describes this aspect of knowledge as "what consciousness within its own self declares as the *in itself* or the *true*" (ibid.). Hegel's inclusion of the word "declares" (*erklärt*) here is crucial, for it necessitates distinguishing this sense of "in-itself" from the previous one. If the object itself is something "outside" its relation to consciousness, then that object cannot be something simply "declared" by consciousness, for anything created by a declaration originates from, and so is what it is only within, some relation to consciousness. Furthermore, if the object itself were something created by consciousness' declaration, it would be misdescribed by calling it an "in-itself."[27]

What Hegel points out here is that by adopting naive realism, common sense adopts a conception of the world as being something unto itself. It is consciousness' having a *conception* of its object that Hegel signals by the phrase, "declares from within itself." Adopting a conception of the object known is precisely what happens in recognizing that the object known may not be as one takes it to be. What consciousness "posits" is the conception *that* the object it knows is what it is regardless of its being known.[28] This conception of the object is to be used as the standard for consciousness' cognitive self-examination. (How this conception could fulfill such a function is discussed shortly.) In order to emphasize that this aspect of knowledge concerns what consciousness takes its object to be, this aspect may be formulated as *The Object According to Consciousness* or, alternatively, *Consciousness' Conception of Objects*.

A Grammatical Case Distinction

In half a dozen passages in the "Introduction" Hegel distinguishes between those objects or aspects of knowledge that are *for* consciousness and those that are something *to* consciousness, a distinction between accusative and dative cases.[29] What is the significance of this distinction?[30] In the above passage, Hegel says that something's being *for* consciousness indicates that consciousness knows that thing, that consciousness is cognitively related to it. However, this is an *aspect* of knowledge rather than the whole relation. Hegel agrees with Kant that intuitions without conceptions are blind. Accordingly, there is no knowledge of an object without applying conceptions to it. The object's being something *for* consciousness results from the combination of the two aspects distinguished above (as two senses of "in-itself"): an object is something *for* consciousness when consciousness applies its conception of objects to an object itself. To put the same point slightly differently, an object is an object for consciousness insofar as consciousness takes that object to instantiate its conception of objects. This aspect of knowledge may be labeled *The Object for Consciousness*.

Hegel's distinction between dative and accusative (grammatical) objects of consciousness marks a distinction between levels of explicitness. What is *for* consciousness is something consciousness is explicitly aware of; what is *to* consciousness is something consciousness is aware of, but not explicitly so. Hegel's dative construction designates features of an object itself that are closely related to those features of that object explicitly captured by consciousness' conception of objects, but which are not themselves explicitly captured by that conception. These are parts or features of the object itself that consciousness has, so to speak, latched onto without yet understanding them. Consciousness' mistakings are takings nonetheless. The mistaken parts or aspects of the object itself fall into two cases. First, there are parts or aspects of the object itself of which consciousness is cognizant, but which do not figure centrally into its conception of objects. Second, there are parts or aspects of the object itself of which consciousness is not cognizant, but which are closely related to those parts or aspects of the object captured by consciousness' conception of objects. These "incidental" parts or aspects of an object are the first ones consciousness confronts in discovering the inadequacy of its conception of objects. This aspect of knowledge may be labeled *The Object to Consciousness*.

To summarize, the four aspects of knowledge as a relation distinguished so far are these:

The object according to consciousness

The object for consciousness

The object to consciousness

The object itself

For convenience, I have sometimes labeled the first of these "consciousness' conception of objects."[31]

Consciousness as Reflexive: The List Doubled

So far, knowledge has been treated generically as a relation between subject and object. But what objects does consciousness have knowledge of? In general, there are two: the world as an object of empirical knowledge, and empirical knowledge as an object of self-knowledge.[32] Self-knowledge is important to Hegel's project because the possibility of self-criticism requires that consciousness be able to reflect on itself and its activity. Indeed, consciousness takes on a particular form (and so is a particular form of consciousness) precisely by adopting, if only implicitly, a certain conception of what it, as a cognizer, is.[33] Consciousness' conception of knowledge both constrains what its conception of the world can be and it guides the application of that conception to the world. Because the "object" of any form of consciousness is this pair of objects—its own knowledge as well as the object known—the fourfold list of aspects of knowledge developed above forms two parallel lists of four elements, one list concerning the ontological side, the other concerning the noetic side, of knowledge. Each of these fourfold distinctions of elements of knowledge is generated in a manner parallel to that discussed above, by taking "the object" of knowledge to be first, the world, and then, empirical knowledge, as itself an object of self-knowledge. Hence there is no need to repeat that derivation again for these two special cases. The complete list of elements of knowledge as a relation is the following:

1. Consciousness' conception of the world:
   The World
   According to Consciousness.

2. The world taken as instantiating consciousness' conception of the world:
   The World
   For Consciousness.

3. Those elements of the world closely related to, but not included in, consciousness' conception of the world:
   The World
   To Consciousness.

4. The world as it actually is, with all of its properties known and unknown:
   The World
   Itself.

A. Consciousness' conception of knowledge:
   Knowledge
   According to Consciousness.

B. Knowledge taken as instantiating consciousness' conception of knowledge:
   Knowledge
   For Consciousness.

C. Those elements of knowledge closely related to, but not included in, consciousness' conception of knowledge:
   Knowledge
   To Consciousness.

D. Knowledge as it actually is, with all of its properties known and unknown:
   Knowledge
   Itself.

I grant that this double fourfold distinction of elements of consciousness as a cognitive relation to its objects is only tenuously indicated in Hegel's "Introduction." However, I maintain that these distinctions are to be found in the text and I would argue that it is only by making these distinctions that it is possible to construe the difficult remainder of the "Introduction."[34] This shows that these distinctions are operative in the "Introduction." If Hegel's analysis of knowledge as a relation is as rich as this list indicates, then he has a good deal to work with in defending the possibility of self-criticism.[35]

Hegel's Criterial Inference

The crucial question is this: How can consciousness determine whether its conception of the world corresponds to the world itself if consciousness has no access to the world itself except insofar as the world is for consciousness? Likewise, how can consciousness determine if its conception of knowledge corresponds to knowledge itself, if consciousness has no access to knowledge itself except insofar as knowledge is for consciousness? Hegel's answer to this double question can be seen by examining the eight elements of knowledge as a relation. Since the correspondence of conception and object is something that consciousness is supposed to be able to recognize that it has achieved, consciousness must be able to recognize this correspondence on the basis of its explicit awareness of certain of the elements of knowledge. The elements of which consciousness is (or at least comes to be) explicitly aware are its conceptions of the world and of knowledge and the world and knowledge for it (elements 1, A, 2, and B). Now it may seem that if these elements are all consciousness can work with, then its criterion of knowledge must be hopelessly subjective, in that the relevant standard would be "the object itself" and not just what consciousness takes it to be. This objection misses the main insight of Hegel's response to Sextus' challenge: Because the world for consciousness and knowledge for consciousness (elements 2 and B) result from consciousness' application of its conceptions of the world and of knowledge (elements 1 and A) to the world itself and to knowledge itself (elements 4 and D), the world itself and knowledge itself figure centrally into the world and knowledge for consciousness (elements 2 and B). Because the world itself and knowledge itself figure centrally into the world and knowledge *for* consciousness, *if* the world and knowledge *for* consciousness coincide with consciousness' conceptions of the world and of knowledge, then these conceptions also correspond to their objects, the world itself and knowledge itself. Conversely, if consciousness' conceptions of the world or of knowledge do not correspond to the world itself or to knowledge itself, then the theoretical and practical inferences consciousness bases on these conceptions will result in expectations that diverge from the actual behavior of the world or from actual cognitive practices. The experience of defeated expectations makes manifest a divergence between the world or knowledge for consciousness and consciousness' conceptions of the world or of knowledge, and so between these conceptions and their objects. What consciousness takes to instantiate its conception of knowledge or its conception of the world would be found *not* to instantiate those conceptions. This is why it is important to Hegel's method to consider principles in application to their putative domains, for so long as principles of knowledge or its objects are inadequate, any examples taken from those domains will be far richer in kind than is allowed by the principles under examination. By thorough and scrupulous application of epistemic and ontological principles, features of objects in their domains unaccounted for by those principles can be brought to light. Such discoveries may only require reconsidering the importance of previously recognized, though discounted, features of the objects or they may involve recognizing previously unknown features of knowledge or of the world. This is how categorial features of knowledge or of the world that are initially objects *to* consciousness become explicit *for* it. For example, the form of consciousness called "sense-certainty" finds that it is utterly unable to account for its ability to designate the particulars it knows without admitting the use of conceptions, and so must rescind its principle of aconceptual knowledge; the form of consciousness called "perception" finds that perception alone cannot determine that the perceived white, cubical, and sour properties all belong to the same grain of salt, and so it must grant that there is more to empirical conceptions than observation terms. By making previously unaccounted or unrecognized features of the world or of knowledge manifest in this way, defeated expectations supply information that can be used to revise conceptions of the world and of knowledge. The internal coherence of a form of consciousness is only possible if its conceptions of the world and of knowledge correspond to the world itself and to knowledge itself. This thesis grounds Hegel's confidence in the internal self-criticism of forms of consciousness.[36]

There is, of course, an important distinction between the actual incoherence of an inadequate form of consciousness and the recognition of that incoherence. Only persistence in elaborating and applying a pair of epistemic and ontological principles and intellectual integrity in assessing their adequacy can lead to the detection of otherwise unrecognized incoherence and error. Hegel's criterion is thus a *sine qua non* for the truth of a pair of principles, and he adopts fallibilism. However, due to the second-order level of his inquiry, and due to the systematic interrelation of the various categorial features of the objects under investigation (that is, the philosophically salient features of empirical knowledge and of empirical objects in general),[37] Hegel can reasonably contend that meeting the negative condition of the absence of detected incoherence in the long run is a very powerful criterion for the positive condition sought, namely, for the correspondence of a pair of conceptions of knowledge and its objects

Hegel's Solution to the Dilemma of the Criterion 93

with the actual structure of human knowledge and with the actual structure of the objects of human knowledge.

If Hegel's criterial inference still seems implausible, it should be noted just how complex Hegel's criterion is. First, recall that this criterion is employed by a subject that is inherently related both to the world itself and to knowledge itself. (In order for self-criticism to be possible, this claim simply needs to *be* true; no particular form of consciousness needs also to *know* that it is true in order to be self-critical.) Because of this, even when there is a discrepancy between the object according to consciousness and the object for consciousness (and hence a discrepancy between these elements and the object itself), an object's being *for* consciousness is nonetheless *the object's* being for consciousness, even if that object is misconstrued; and the object itself is an object *to* consciousness throughout.[38]

Second, there isn't just one correspondence of object and conception being sought. Consciousness must not only reconcile its conception of the world with the world for it, and its conception of knowledge with knowledge for it (with its manifest cognitive activity), this pair of reconciliations must be mutually compatible. It does not suffice to eliminate discrepancies between one's account of knowledge and one's cognitive activity only to wind up not being able to justify claims about the kinds of objects one takes oneself to have knowledge of.

Third, as an aspect of overcoming what Hegel calls merely "natural ideas" on these topics, consciousness must not only have conceptions that are adequate to its manifest cognition and objects of knowledge, it must comprehend that it has adequate conceptions and what these conceptions are. Given Hegel's concern to avoid question-begging and his notion of determinate negation, the adequacy of these conceptions can only be known through the comprehension of the proficiencies and deficiencies of less adequate conceptions.

Finally, Hegel holds that in order to be adequate, a theory of knowledge and its objects must be knowable in accordance with its own principles.

Taken together, these points form a set of five criteria:

1. No detectable discrepancy between the world for consciousness and the world according to consciousness (between elements 1 and 2).
2. No detectable discrepancy between knowledge for consciousness and knowledge according to consciousness (between elements A and B).
3. No detectable discrepancy between (1) and (2) (between the pairs of elements 1 & 2 and A & B).
4. A matched pair of accounts of the genesis and implementation of the

conceptions of knowledge and of the world indicating how they were generated through the critical rejection of less adequate alternatives.

5. An account of how the conceptions of knowledge and of the world and their implementation can be learned, comprehended, and employed on the basis of those same conceptions and applications.

These criteria, to be simultaneously satisfied, make a formidable set of criteria indeed. They will not handle the first-order problems of theory selection faced by philosophy of science because they operate at a level of generality at which different conceptions of knowledge require different conceptions of the objects of knowledge, and vice versa. But at the second-order epistemological level of inquiry pursued by Hegel, these criteria may be plenty. Indeed, it is not at all clear that any philosophy has ever satisfied them, including Hegel's.

THE PROBLEM OF COMPLETENESS

Hegel claims to present the complete series of forms of consciousness, and the success of his defense of his own views depends on critically rejecting all alternatives. Certainly he hasn't considered every logically possible position, and he hasn't provided any proof that he has. What plausibility can Hegel give to his claim to completeness? Three points may be briefly mentioned on this topic.

Perhaps Hegel's main support for his claim to completeness is his teleological philosophy of history, according to which the series of forms of consciousness he recounts is the series required to complete the principal development of the world-spirit. If Hegel could make this part of his philosophy of history independently plausible, then he could have some powerful grounds for his claim to completeness. This topic cannot be explored here, but I, for one, am doubtful.

Setting Hegel's philosophy of history aside, there is still something quite strong that Hegel can say in his defense. He claims that each form of consciousness devolves from some characteristic of human cognition. Part of the import of this claim is that the mere logical possibility of an epistemology doesn't suffice to legitimize it: an adequate epistemology must also account for what knowledge and its objects are like *for us*. This is central to Hegel's replacing epistemology with phenomenology, and it shows in his criteria as the insistence on what knowledge and its objects are like for us (elements 2 and B) in addition to our conceptions or theories of knowledge and its objects (elements 1 and A).

Even if we grant that the adequacy of an epistemology rests on its plausibly being an account of our cognitive abilities, it would be too much to say that Hegel had already treated every possible nuance within the domain of plausibly human accounts of knowledge. However, because Hegel proceeds by showing, where we are supposed to reap the philosophical benefits of those displays, the line between what is strictly speaking to be found in Hegel's text and what may only be able to be read into or out of it may simply not exist. What matters for Hegel's phenomenological enterprise is that the structures and relations he claims are there *are* to be found in the indicated form of consciousness; how fully articulated they are may be quite another matter. If we're now in a position to ask more refined questions or consider more refined views than any of the forms of consciousness present, it is incumbent on us to see whether the points Hegel makes about these less refined forms of consciousness have telling analogues in the positions that we wish he had considered. At the very least, since the instruction Hegel offers is supposed to be for "us" his readers, we need to be willing to reconstruct what he displays in terms that, on the one hand, capture what he says and does in those displays, while on the other hand, manage to address "our" (contemporary, linguistic, hermeneutic, or analytic) idioms for and approaches to the issues he discusses.[39]

Notes

1. I summarize the main points of Sextus' skepticism in *Hegel's Epistemological Realism* (Dordrecht, Netherlands: Kluwer, 1989; abbreviated *HER*), 11–16.

2. Chisholm, *The Foundations of Knowing* (Minneapolis: University of Minnesota Press, 1982), 65–66.

3. Ibid., 75; cf. 67. Robert Amico proposes to "dissolve" the dilemma of the criterion by showing that the skeptic presupposes an impossible condition for justification, namely, settling both what count as proper criteria of knowledge and what count as proper instances of knowledge before providing an account of knowledge (*The Problem of the Criterion* [Lanham, Md.: Rowman & Littlefield, 1993], 112–15). Amico is right that this is an impossible condition, but he wrongly ascribes to the Pyrrhonian skeptic a definite *position* on the nature of justification (ibid., 114). Thus he converts sophisticated, flexible, and undogmatic Pyrrhonian skepticism into dogmatic Academic skepticism. Sextus is far more subtle than that. Amico closes by noting that the interesting questions only begin once this impossible condition on justifying a theory of knowledge is rejected. Hegel's analysis begins where Amico's leaves off, with these interesting questions.

4. *Knowledge and Evidence* (Cambridge: Cambridge University Press, 1988), 260–65.

5. *Philosophy after Objectivity* (New York: Oxford University Press, 1993), 57.

6. *Philosophy after Objectivity*, 70–74, chs. 2, 3. Moser's "semantic project" specifies "in informative terms, what it means to say that something (for example, a proposition or a belief) is epistemically justified" (60). It requires answering the question "[w]hat, if anything, constitutes the correctness (at least for myself) of my semantic standards for 'epistemic justification' as an answer to the semantic project regarding what it means to say that something is epistemically justified?" (72).

7. *Philosophy after Objectivity*, 227; on Moser's conceptual relativism, see 98–99 and ch. 4.

8. *Philosophy after Objectivity*, 74–75.

9. *Philosophy after Objectivity*, 75. On Chisholm's formulations of the "problem" of the criterion, see *HER*, 217.

10. *Philosophy after Objectivity*, 41–57.

11. William Alston, "A 'Doxastic Practice' Approach to Epistemology," in *Knowledge and Skepticism*, ed. M. Clay and K. Lehrer [Boulder, Colo.: Westview, 1989], 1–29), 3; cf. *The Reliability of Sense Perception* (Ithaca, N.Y.: Cornell University Press, 1993), esp. ch. 5.

12. Alston, "A 'Doxastic Practice' Approach," 13–20. I analyze Alston's views in detail, including his comments on Sextus' dilemma, in *HER*, ch. 5.

13. Alston develops the argument for the "practical rationality" of accepting our current belief-forming practices (subject to ongoing scrutiny) in "A 'Doxastic Practice' Approach," 9–20. He recognizes the epistemic circularity facing even that modest sort of argument in "Belief-forming Practices and the Social," in *Socializing Epistemology*, ed. F. Schmitt [Lanham, Md.: Rowman & Littlefield, 1994], 29–51), 41–43. He recognizes that no one who denies the reliability of a source of belief can be justified in accepting it by an epistemically circular argument in "Epistemic Circularity" (in Alston, *Epistemic Justification* [Ithaca, N.Y.: Cornell University Press, 1989], 319–39), 328, 334.

14. *Pyrrhonian Reflections on Knowledge and Justification* (New York: Oxford University Press, 1994), 194; cf. 203. Fogelin focuses on Agrippa's "Five Modes" (133f.) and does not discuss the dilemma of the criterion. Solving the dilemma requires responding to the five modes, and also solving the level-regress and reflexive problems involved in establishing criteria.

15. This introduces an element of holism independent of considerations about conceptual meaning. Hegel is a (moderate) holist about meaning, but that doctrine cannot be appealed to in formulating a response to Sextus' dilemma without begging the question. However, Hegel's response to Sextus' dilemma is sensitive to issues raised by holistic theories of conceptual meaning and so lends itself to confronting issues about realism and relativism raised by recent analytic philosophy of language.

16. The present chapter is restricted to some core features of Hegel's method. I sketch the structure of his substantive argument in *HER*, ch. 11. I present an Hegelian argument against radical skepticism in "Transcendental Reflections on Pragmatic Realism," in *Pragmatism, Reason, and Norms: A Realistic Assessment*, ed. K. R. Westphal (New York: Fordham University Press, 1997), ch. 2.

17. See *HER*, 137–38. Hegel's solution does involve *epistemic* circularity, which is inevitable in any critique of reason, but through "determinate negation" (i.e., the internal critical rejection; see *HER*, 125–26, 135–36, 163) of alternative epistemologies he provides much more persuasive grounds to establish his epistemology than the grounds suggested by Alston.

18. Preface to the *Phenomenology of Spirit*, PG 25.16–17/PhG 27/K 46/PhS 17; cf. the introduction to the same, PG 58.13–14/PhG 70/PhS 52. Abbreviations are to the following works:

PG   *Die Phänomenologie des Geistes*. W. Bonsiepen and R. Heede, eds. *Gesammelte Werke* (Hamburg: Meiner, 1980), vol. 9.

PhG *Die Phänomenologie des Geistes*. J. Hoffmeister, ed. Hamburg: Meiner, 1952.

PhS *The Phenomenology of Spirit*. A. V. Miller, trans. Oxford: Clarendon Press, 1977.

K   The Preface to the *Phenomenology of Spirit*. W. Kaufmann, trans. In *Hegel: Texts and Commentary*. Garden City, N.Y.: Anchor, 1966.

Decimals after page references to PG refer to line numbers. Translations are my own. I provide a full translation of Hegel's introduction in *HER*, 189–96. In *HER* I place Hegel's problem and solution into the context of modern and contemporary epistemology, I reconstruct Hegel's phenomenological method for addressing that problem, and I reconstruct the structure of his epistemological argument for a socially and historically grounded realism in the *Phenomenology*.

19. Sextus Empiricus, *Outlines of Pyrrhonism*, trans. R. G. Bury (Cambridge, Mass.: Harvard University Press, 1933; abbreviated "OP"), bk. II, ch. 4, §20; cf. bk. I, ch. 14, §§116–17. Hegel briefly sketches this dilemma at the metalevel of epistemological inquiry in the middle of the introduction to the *Phenomenology of Spirit* as a problem of distinguishing between real knowledge (which he here calls "science") and merely apparent knowledge (which he calls "phenomenal knowledge"). The context makes clear the metalevel of Hegel's concern:

> [I]f this presentation [conducted in the *Phenomenology*] is viewed as a description of the way *science* is *related* to *phenomenal* knowledge, and as an *investigation* and critical *examination* into *the reality of knowledge*, it does not seem possible for it even to take place without some presupposition which will serve as the fundamental standard of measurement. For an examination consists in applying an accepted standard and in deciding, on the basis of final agreement or disagreement with the standard, whether what is being tested is correct or incorrect. Thus

the standard as such, and science too, were it the standard, is accepted as the essence or the *in itself*. But here, where science will make its first appearance, neither science nor anything else has justified itself as the *essence* or as the *in itself*; and without some such basic principle it seems that an examination cannot take place. (PG 58.12–22/PhG 70/PhS 52)

The congruence between Hegel's and Sextus' dilemmas should be no surprise, for Hegel wrote an extended analysis of classical and modern skepticisms for the *Critical Journal of Philosophy*. See "Verhältnis des Skeptismus zur Philosophie," *Kritisches Journal der Philosophie* 1.2 (*Gesammelte Werke*, 4: 197–238); translated in *Between Kant and Hegel* (G. Di Giovanni and H. S. Harris, trans. and eds. [Albany: State University of New York Press, 1985]), 311–62. However, this early piece is not a reliable guide to Hegel's use of Sextus' dilemma in the *Phenomenology*, for two years later (in 1804) Hegel radically reassesses his adherence to Schelling's philosophy and, with that, the problem of question-begging. See "Anmerkung 1. Die Philosophie" (*Gesammelte Werke*, 7: 343–47). For a discussion, see my essay "Kant, Hegel, and the Fate of 'the' Intuitive Intellect," in *The System of Transcendental Idealism in Kant, Fichte, Schelling, and Hegel*, ed. S. Sedwick (forthcoming). (Sextus' dilemma is misprinted in *HER*, 14. If your or your library's copy lacks an erratum, please request one from the press.)

20. Kant may not have stated this condition explicitly, but it is plainly an implication of his "Refutation of Idealism" (*Critique of Pure Reason*, B274–79) and so of his response to Hume.

21. Friedrich Heinrich Jacobi, one of Hegel's immediate predecessors, propounded a doctrine of "immediate knowledge" according to which there is no conceptual or inferential mediation in our knowledge. On his view, *prima facie* knowledge-claims count as knowledge, indeed, as the basic knowledge upon which any other knowledge depends. Hegel points out that Jacobi's view faces precisely this—among many other—problems (see Hegel's *Enzyklopädie*, §75). For discussion, see my "Hegel's Attitude Toward Jacobi in the 'Third Attitude of Thought Toward Objectivity,' " (*Southern Journal of Philosophy* 27. 1 (1989): 135–56.

22. In the body of the *Phenomenology* Hegel specifies a form of consciousness' principles by describing its "certainty." Part of Hegel's point in labeling this pair of conceptions a "certainty" is to argue that "certainty" is not an infallible, indubitable cognitive starting point, but rather is an end result of cognitive investigation, and a corrigible one at that; the assurance of each form of consciousness that its principles are true is time and again undermined in the course of Hegel's presentation.

23. Hegel indicates this in stating that "the moments of truth present themselves, not as abstract, pure moments, but in the peculiar determinateness of being as they are for consciousness, or as consciousness itself appears in relationship to them" (PG 61.33–36/PhG 75/PhS 56).

24. This claim may also seem to be a mere assertion about the structure of

consciousness. However, Hegel relinquishes responsibility for this claim by attributing it to common sense (see the next subsection) and by examining a form of consciousness that adopts precisely this position, namely, "sense certainty" (PG 64.15–22/PhS 58–66). Also see note 28.

25. Hegel argues for this important claim in the first chapter of the *Phenomenology*, "Sense-Certainty."

26. Michael Theunissen notes this in "Begriff und Realität," in *Dialektik in der Philosophie Hegels*, ed. R. P. Horstmann (Frankfurt: Suhrkamp, 1978), 324–59; see p. 330.

27. This simple but significant fact was pointed out to me by Professor H. F. Fulda.

28. "From this being for another, however, we distinguish the *being in itself*; that which is related to knowledge is at the same time distinguished from it and is posited as *existing* outside this relationship too. The side of this in-itself is *truth*" (PG 58.29–31/PhG 70/PhS 52).

29. PG 58.24–31/PhG 70/PhS 52–53; PG 59.8–10/PhG 71/PhS 53; PG 59.21–22/PhG 71/PhS 53; PG 59.27–28/PhG 72/PhS 54; PG 59.31–34/PhG 72/PhS 54; PG 59.38–60.3/PhG 72/PhS 54.

30. The importance of Hegel's distinction between dative and accusative cases has been insisted upon by Theunissen ("Begriff und Realität," 326–30 and note 5) and by Kenley R. Dove ("Phenomenology and Systematic Philosophy," in *Method and Speculation in Hegel's Phenomenology*, ed. M. Westphal [Atlantic Highlands, N.J.: Humanities Press, 1982], 27–40, esp. 30). However, Dove does not notice that there are two different dative objects in Hegel's analysis, he does not notice the ambiguity of the phrase "in itself," and he does not develop these distinctions into an analysis of the structure of Hegel's notion of a form of consciousness. (See the next note.) For the sake of simplicity, I have suppressed the second dative object here; it concerns how initially implicit conceptions become explicit for consciousness (see *HER*, ch. 8).

31. This fourfold distinction of aspects of consciousness (and its subsequent elaboration below) has been developed independently. However, the analysis I offer is similar to that offered by Michael Theunissen in the first section of "Begriff und Realität." He notes an ambiguity in Hegel's use of "*Ansich*" and distinguishes between the object itself and the object for consciousness (326). Furthermore, Theunissen stresses Hegel's point that the object is also an object *to* consciousness (327f.), and he emphasizes that according to Hegel consciousness declares something from within itself as the in-itself or truth (330). Thus he notices each of the four aspects that I have isolated and analyzed above, although he does not, in the confines of one short section of his essay, attempt to systematize them. Theunissen also does not analyze this "declaration" as the adoption of a conception, and he does not develop the double list of elements of knowledge that I present below.

32. Twice in the "Introduction," Hegel mentions that the fact that consciousness is reflexive, that it is self-aware, is important for his project: "But since consciousness is for itself its own *concept*, it immediately transcends what is limited, and, because this limitedness is its own, it transcends itself" (PG 57.25-26/PhG 69/PhS 51); "Consciousness is on the one hand consciousness of the object, on the other hand it is consciousness of itself" (PG 59.31-32/PhG 72/PhS 54). Cf. *Philosophische Propädeutik*, "Bewußtseinslehre für die Mittelklasse" (1809-.), §1 (*Werke in 20 Bänden* [Frankfurt-on-Main: Suhrkamp, 1968], 4:111); trans. A. V. Miller, *The Philosohical Propaedeutic* (Oxford: Blackwell, 1986), 55.

33. This is one point Hegel makes in claiming that "consciousness is for itself its own concept" (PG 57.25-26/PhG 69/PhS 51).

34. See *HER*, chs. 6-9.

35. Ernst Tugendhat rejects the attempt to understand conscious or intentional relations with "unclarified" notions of "positing" and "subject/object" relations, and he faults Hegel for doing so ("Kehraus mit Hegel I," in *Selbstbewußtsein und Selbstbestimmung* [Frankfurt: Suhrkamp, 1979], 13. Vorlesung, 303). Tugendhat misses the fact that Hegel *agrees* with him on these points. What I have argued shows that Hegel does not leave these notions undeveloped and indeed that what Hegel presents when all is told covers what Tugendhat suggests as an alternative ("Kehraus mit Hegel II" [ibid., 14. Vorlesung], 325)—and then some!

36. Hegel's criterial inference may suggest Donald Davidson's view of how "coherence generates correspondence" in "A Coherence Theory of Truth and Knowledge" (*Kant oder Hegel?*, ed. D. Henrich [Stuttgart: Klett-Cotta, 1984], 423-38), except that Hegel's project has both "externalist" elements (see note 38) and a meta-level, categorial concern with the truth of theories of knowledge, neither of which play a role in Davidson's argument. Hegel's criterial inference is closer to Susan Haack's "foundherentist" view that joint experiential anchoring and coherent integration within a comprehensive set of beliefs provides truth-conducive justification (*Evidence and Inquiry* [Oxford: Blackwell, 1993]). Hegel's criterial inference is designed to "ratify" (as Haack says) principles of justification as being truth-conducive. However, Hegel has higher aspirations for such ratification, in part because he thinks he can give an informative critique of all relevantly human kinds of theories of knowledge. (For a good critique of Davidson, see Haack, 60-72.)

37. For example, our abilities to use tokens of demonstrative terms is directly related to our ability to apply conceptions of individuation, space, and time (this point is crucial to Hegel's refutation of "sense-certainty"); the occurrant properties of things are directly related to their dispositional properties (this point is crucial to Hegel's transition from "perception" to "force and understanding"). See *HER*, ch. 11. I reconstruct Hegel's critique of concept-empiricism in *Hegel, Hume und die Identität wahrnehmbarer Dinge* (Frankfurt: Klostermann, 1997); I summarize Hegel's critique in "Hegel and Hume on Perception and Concept Empiricism," *Journal of the History of Philosophy* (forthcoming).

38. In this connection it is important to note that Hegel's criterial inference rests on several logically contingent doctrines. I have suppressed these tenets here in order to focus on the logic of his criterion. The further doctrines presupposed by his criterion need only *be* true in order for the criterion to work. If self-criticism is possible, then we can ultimately determine whether these further doctrines are true. (In a word, this is how Hegel discharges his initial assumptions.) Among the doctrines presupposed by his criterion is that memory is generally reliable, that the "K-K" thesis (knowing that x entails knowing that one knows that x) is false, and most importantly, that although there is no knowledge of objects without applying conceptions to them, our experience of those objects needn't be restricted to just those features of an object captured by the content of one's general conception of objects, where that content would be parsed by a description. In the "Introduction," Hegel's recommendation for his criterion is programmatic: accepting his criterion allows for the possibility of self-criticism and so for the possibility of responding to Sextus; rejecting his criterion is to succumb to Sextus' skepticism at the second level of epistemological inquiry. Hegel's refutation of skepticism at the first order of empirical knowledge must be a substantive result of his presentation, and not a mere corollary of his second-order criterion.

39. I thank Michael Hardimon, Maudemarie Clark, and my former colleagues at Purdue (especially William Rowe) for their discussion and recommendations. Special thanks are due to Professor Hans Friedrich Fulda for discussing and encouraging this essay's ancestor. Peter King kindly directed my attention to Sextus Empiricus. I also thank Robert Howell, whose invitation to present this paper to the philosophers at the University at Albany (SUNY), and John Kekes and especially Robert Meyers, whose discussion occasioned the new introductory section. I thank Jon Stewart for publishing this revised version here.

II

Consciousness

4

Katharina Dulckeit

Can Hegel Refer to Particulars?

Hegel introduced the *Phenomenology of the Spirit* as a work on the problem of knowledge.[1] In the first chapter, entitled "Sense-Certainty, or the This and Meaning," he concluded that knowledge cannot consist of an immediate awareness of particulars (cf. PhG 80–87; PhM 150–57; PhS 59–64). The tradition discusses sense-certainty in terms of this failure of immediate knowledge without, however, specifically addressing the problem of reference.[2] Yet reference is distinct from knowledge in the sense that while there can be no knowledge of objects without reference, there may be reference without knowledge. If that is the case, then the failure of immediate knowledge does not entitle us to conclude anything about the success or failure of reference. It is not surprising, then, that a few scholars have begun to examine sense-certainty primarily as a thesis about reference.

It has recently been argued by Ivan Soll and Gilbert Plumer[3] that Hegel denies the possibility of reference to particular objects of experience such as, for instance, trees and houses. This thesis is unacceptable, they say, not only on its own ground but because of what it implies. For if reference is a necessary condition for knowledge of objects, Hegel's view would appear to commit us to the undesirable view that such knowledge, too, is impossible—a conclusion, they readily concede, that Hegel himself would reject.

105

The argument that Soll and Plumer independently attribute to Hegel is really quite simple: Reference to particulars fails because language is universal. Soll argues further that Hegel's counterintuitive position with respect to singular reference, results from his failure to (1) appreciate the role of the *context* in demonstrative reference, and (2) to draw what are considered key distinctions in contemporary semantics and pragmatics: between meaning and reference, and type and token. It is my view that both of these allegations are simply *wrong*. I shall argue, first of all, that the validity of the argument (that reference to particulars fails because language is universal) turns on the interpretation of the term "particular." Thus it turns out that Hegel's alleged argument is either invalid or leads to a different and benign conclusion with respect to unique reference. Moreover, I intend to show that regardless of what Plumer and Soll may think, Hegel actually argues *for* the possibility of unique reference by determining precisely under what conditions it can succeed. His conclusion is that based on the conditions governing the relation between subject and object; reference, like knowledge, must be mediated. Thus, for instance, reference via description is mediated by the predicates assigned to the subject, while demonstrative reference is mediated by the context within which speaker and referent are situated. Ironically, then, Hegel not only argues precisely *for* what Soll and Plumer think he denies, but his phenomenological analysis actually constitutes an attempt to point out the very distinctions they think he overlooks.

I

Let us begin by considering the evidence which appears to support Soll's thesis.

When a speaker tries to refer to a particular by using the demonstrative *this*, he or she does so by relating its spatiotemporal position to his or her own. But Hegel points out that demonstratives such as *here* and *now* can be used correctly by the same speaker, or different speakers, at different times and places. Any point in space is a potential Here, and any point in time a possible Now with respect to someone appropriately located. Hence "This," "Here," and "Now" are universals in the sense that they are applicable to every possible place or instant. Thus Hegel writes:

> To the question *"What is the Now?"* we reply, for example, *"The Now is Night."* To test the truth of this certainty of sense a simple experiment suffices. We write down this truth. A truth cannot lose anything by being written down, nor can it lose anything through our preserving it. If we

now, this noon, look again at a truth we have written down, we shall have to say that it has become stale. (PhG 81; PhM 151; PhS 60)

And, analogously:

The Here is, for example, the *tree*. But if I turn around, then this truth has vanished.... *The Here is not a tree,* but rather a *house.* The *Here* as such does not vanish, but endures, while the house, tree, etc., vanish. The Here is indifferent to its being a house or tree. (PhG 82; PhM 152–53; PhS 60–61)

Thus the terms *Here* and *Now* remain constant, but their putative reference varies from speaker to speaker. Hence the This reveals itself as a universal.

In § 20 of the *Encyclopedia* Hegel reiterates this point: "When I say 'the *individual,*' '*this* individual,' 'here,' 'now,' all of these are universal. *Everything* and *anything* is an individual and a This."[4] Thus instead of the particular it has in mind, sense-certainty can grasp only the This-as-such which refers to anything at all, and hence to nothing in particular. Hegel considers three strategies that might salvage sense certainty's position; but none of them are successful. Briefly, the process goes like this: first, it is revealed that sense-certainty cannot pick out particular objects, second, that it cannot pick out particular objects *for consciousness,* and finally, its defeat is complete when it discovers that even the experience as a whole, the "my-knowing-this," fails to pick out a particular. What Hegel seems to be saying, then, is that despite our *intention to refer* to particulars, we cannot actually do so, because the language we must use is universal.

Perhaps the most striking passage from Hegel which supports this view is found near the end of the chapter. Speaking of the proponents of sense-certainty, Hegel says:

They speak of the existence of *external* objects which, more specifically, can be determined as *real,* absolutely *singular, entirely personal, individual* things ... this existence is to have absolute certainty and truth. They mean *this* piece of paper ... but what they mean they do not say ... it is impossible, because the sensible thing *which is meant cannot be reached* by language which belongs to consciousness, i.e., to that which is inherently universal. In the actual attempt to say it, it would therefore disintegrate. (PhG 88; PhM 159; PhS 66; emphasis mine on "which is meant")

I should like to suggest that while it is true that language, for Hegel, is universal, and while it is also true that sense-certainty fails to grasp the particulars by using demonstratives, it does not follow that reference to particulars is impossible. It merely follows that reference cannot be successful on the conditions proposed by sense-certainty.

In order to illustrate this, a discussion of Hegel's project is in order. I give this fairly substantial sketch because it raises several intrinsically interesting issues and is essential for my refutation of Hegel's critics. (At the same time it will help refresh the memory of those who have not read the *Phenomenology* lately.) I will therefore leave Soll and Plumer behind for a good while and turn my attention to Hegel.

In the *Phenomenology* Hegel undertakes a critical exposition of knowledge and follows it until it becomes philosophical knowledge or knowledge of the real. Each of the successively more adequate forms of consciousness proposes a criterion of reality which it then tests against its actual experience. The inadequacy of a given form of consciousness is revealed when consciousness finds itself in the dilemma of actually possessing a kind of knowledge which is possible *only* if its own criterion for having such knowledge is thrown over. At that point the defeated consciousness is superseded (*aufgehoben*), that is, negated yet preserved by a new, more adequate form of consciousness which makes a new proposal as to the nature of the real and the relation of consciousness to it.

What is crucial to keep in mind is that the various forms, or modes, of consciousness are just that: forms or modes. They differ *only* in what they take their object to be, *not* in how it is actually experienced. Only thus is it possible that consciousness can test what it takes to be the essence of its object against its experience of the object. This explains the unusual phrasing of the question sense-certainty asks itself: Not "What is this?" but "What is *the* This?" In answer to the first question one would of course name an individual, say, "This is a tree" or whatever. But the second question appears to be asking something like "What sort of thing is a This, or an individual?" and would presumably require an answer which would give the essential characteristics of the This, what all Thises have in common, that is, a universal.

At any rate, whenever a proposed criterion fails to correspond to the actual experience of consciousness, the conflict is resolved in favor of experience. Since the essence of each form of consciousness is constituted by the proposed criterion, abandoning that criterion engenders a different, higher form of consciousness.

The exposition proper of the *Phenomenology* begins with what Hegel considers to be the lowest form of consciousness: sense-certainty. The criterion for knowledge proposed by sense-certainty is *immediacy*. A proponent of the sense-certain attitude would see himself or herself as immediately or directly related to the object, as passively, directly, and completely receiving whatever lies before consciousness. Due to the passivity of consciousness and the directness or immediacy of the relationship, sense-certainty takes its knowledge to be the *richest* and *truest* kind of knowledge, and since nothing comes between consciousness and its object which could distort the truth—no reflection or interpretation—it takes its knowledge to be incorrigible. The certainty of sense-certainty is based on the alleged immediacy which characterizes its relation to its object.

Now sense-certainty will test its criterion of knowledge, namely immediacy, against its actual experience of the object, or—in the language of the "Introduction," it will test whether its concept corresponds with its object. Given that it experiences concrete particulars, what conditions are required to make this possible? Sense-certainty now discovers that it cannot, on its own principles, proclaim as true, that which it in fact experiences as true.[5] For the very immediacy which guarantees its certainty also compromises the quality of its knowledge. Because in order to preserve the immediacy which is supposed to be a direct pipeline to the real through which truth is straightforwardly delivered, consciousness must refrain from reflecting on its object in any way, even from comparing and contrasting it with other objects. For this would involve concepts and thus yield mediated knowledge. Admitting concepts is at the same time mediation, because they come between consciousness and its objects, so that the objects are now given to consciousness by means of, or through concepts. Hence consciousness cannot describe its object, by using words which designate qualities such as "green" or "leafy" and the like, for these predicates also apply to other objects and not *exclusively* to that of its immediate experience.

The immediate consciousness of sense-certainty, consequently, finds itself in a dilemma. True, it cannot be deprived of its certainty. Its truth is indeed indubitable and incorrigible, and by allowing nothing to intervene or mediate, it has avoided all possibility of error. This is why it is so certain. But, alas, it owes its certainty to the utter emptiness of its object, having bought it at the price of refraining from any reflection and comparison. Consequently the certainty so keenly felt is useless as *knowledge*, for all it knows about its object is *that* it is and not *what* it is. But to know nothing whatever about one's object other than that "it is," is to have hold of a trivial and worthless truth insofar as it tells us nothing about the object which could help us distinguish it from other objects. Hence on the condition of immediacy, consciousness is left with an empty being, which, since it has no inner distinction and cannot be distinguished from any other This, is no better than the empty This-as-such.

Now notice that the problem is not merely that "It is" does not qualify as knowledge proper, or that the knowledge of sense-certainty is too primitive or too abstract. The problem is rather that sense-certainty's claim to knowledge contains an inner conflict. Insofar as it presumes to have *immediate* knowledge of something radically and exclusively *individual*, it lays claim to immediacy and determinacy simultaneously, because in order to individuate its object it must determine it. But determining its object sufficiently would violate its condition of immediacy, while insisting on immediacy will leave it with an empty This-as-such; that is the crux of the matter.

The crucial point for our purposes is this: If consciousness cannot individuate or determine its object in any way, if it cannot distinguish it from other objects, it cannot pick it out from among other objects and hence cannot refer to it. The fact that consciousness actually can and does know and refer to concrete objects of experience—and this is a point Hegel takes for granted—dictates that the notion of immediacy must be abandoned.

The conflict between immediacy and determinacy illustrates how consciousness, at its most basic level, already experiences something it as yet does not fully comprehend: it cannot appropriate its object without "mediation." This crucial Hegelian notion is intimately involved with the concept of determinate negation. In fact, as Hegel puts it in a phrase inspired by Spinoza, *Omnis determinatio est negatio* or "every determination is a negation."[6] And Hegel (PhG 20; PhM 80; PhS 10) accepts the converse from which it follows that every negation is a mediation. Sense-certainty experiences this when it tries to determine what its object is. Contrary to its claim, immediacy is violated, for, true to this Spinozistic dictum, determining the object involves distinguishing it *from what it is not* by whatever qualities it has. The crucial point sense-certainty is missing is that an individual is individuated in the first place only via its negative relation to others—the mediation which distinguishes it from what it is not.

And this is true even prior to the use of language. For according to Hegel, even the silent "dumb" activity of pointing (to use Daniel Cook's phrase)[7] fails to pick out its object directly. It cannot consist of a simple and immediate pointing out of atomic instants of time and points in space. What constitutes the Here-and-Now-ness of a particular for consciousness is a function of the *context* in which both are situated.

Sense-certainty is defeated in every case in which it clings to immediacy, and since its actual experience shows that both subject and object are concrete and hence related immediately, consciousness must redescribe its relationship with the object according to the dictates of experience. In finally giving up the criterion of immediacy which is its essence, sense-certainty has been superseded by a more adequate form or attitude of consciousness: the consciousness of *perception* whose project is to take its object as it truly is.

What sense-certainty has experienced here is what consciousness will experience again and again, for it constitutes a central Hegelian doctrine: Individuality is not, as usually thought, *absolutely* opposed to universality, but first *results* from it. Hegel's main thesis is that opposites such as subject and object cannot be absolutely distinguished, absolutely identified, or related immediately, whether we are talking about the subject as knower and the object as known, about speaker and referent, or about the individuality of an object as opposed to its universal properties. Any such relationship must be *dialectical*. In their dialectic unity, each opposite takes on the determination of the other: the universal becomes determined as particular and the particular becomes determined as universal. Thus the very individuality of an individual issues from universality, which makes it a concrete particular. Conversely, the abstract universal first becomes determined through the individual which actualizes it. It is obvious, then, that language which has no existence is abstractly universal, including the empty This-Here-Now-as-such. We must now consider whether this entails, as Soll and Plumer argue, that we cannot refer to particulars.

II

Let us once again consider the argument which Soll and Plumer have independently attributed to Hegel. They allege, that since (1) demonstratives are universals, we (2) cannot use them to refer to particulars. Now, undoubtedly, Hegel accepts the premise of this argument, however, he rejects the conclusion. And since (2) does not follow from (1) anyway, as Plumer and Soll point out, it is by no means obvious why they should attribute this invalid version of the argument to Hegel in the first place. The problem apparently involves a fundamental misunderstanding on their part of how Hegel uses the terms involved, indeed of his philosophy as a whole, for they must employ considerable artifice to read Hegel in the way they do. The first problem lies in the use of the term *particular* in the conclusion. In order to make the argument valid, *particular* must be used in the sense of "*bare* particular," for if the particulars are concrete, that is, if they involve universality, then it obviously does not follow merely from the universality of language that we cannot refer to bare particulars. To preserve the validity of the argument, therefore, the sense of *particular* must be restricted to "*bare* particular." This, however, is not the conclusion drawn by Plumer and Soll, who mistakenly assume that Hegel applies the conclusion to *concrete* particulars of experience such as trees and houses. This is clear from their belief that it commits one to deny the possibility of knowledge of such entities. But to take *particular* as synonymous with "determined or concrete particular," means that the argument is *no longer valid*, because it clearly does not follow from the universality of language that reference to determined particulars is necessarily impossible. Thus Plumer and Soll offer an interpretation of Hegel which is simply indefensible as argued, because their argument is either invalid or must be restricted to bare particulars. In neither case does it follow that reference to concrete particulars is impossible. For even if we cannot, in fact, refer to *bare* particulars, in and of itself this does not imply that reference to *concrete* particulars necessarily fails, and therefore certainly does not entail that knowledge of such objects is impossible.

Ironically, Hegel himself is in complete agreement with what I have called the "benign" conclusion, that is, that we cannot refer to bare particulars. In fact, it actually constitutes part of his own argument. Knowledge, he claims. presupposes a determinate and determinable object which in turn makes reference possible. Everyone agrees that Hegel concludes that *immediate* knowledge fails, and as I interpret his argument, it fails precisely *because reference to an immediate or bare individual is impossible*, thus effectively eliminating one necessary condition for knowledge. This is the negative side of his argument. But Hegel does not stop there, for seen positively, the implication is that, if it is to be possible at all, reference can succeed only on the condition of mediation.

Why exactly does reference to bare particulars fail? In order to refer to something the subject must be able to stand in relation to its referent. And in order to relate itself to its object, consciousness must first single it out from among the field of what presents itself. But as Hegel has shown in sense-certainty, consciousness finds that it simply *cannot* do so immediately, because the very concreteness of the object involves other concepts. On *the condition of immediacy*, therefore, consciousness is *incapable* of picking out its object. This constitutes the failure of reference which entails the failure of knowledge. This failure, however, applies only to bare particulars, because it is precisely the particular lacking all universal determinations which cannot be grasped *as* particular and thus cannot be a single entity for consciousness at all.

The important point here is that being *for* consciousness, being *related to* a subject, *presupposes* determination and hence negation and mediation. Put another way, entering into a relation of reference to something demands that I be able to determine it first as *something for me*. If I cannot determine, individuate, or identify the object as particular in any way, it cannot be anything for me, and consequently I cannot refer to it. Suppose, for instance, that I experience and thus stand in some relation to X. By virtue of the condition for the possibility of a relation between consciousness and its "other," whatever I stand in relation to is *eo ipso* the result of mediation. That means X cannot be bare. For if X is bare, I cannot experience or stand in relation to it in the first place. For Hegel, then, a bare particular is an *abstraction*, something which I could not possibly come across in experience. For whatever I meet in experience is already determined at least minimally. And whatever is determined sufficiently to be something for me, is determined sufficiently to permit reference—at least minimally—even if I should do no better than point to it or grunt at it. Hegel's view in sense-certainty implies that it makes no sense to say *both* that (1) I am in relation to an entity which appears to my senses, *and* also that (2) I cannot refer to it. Either I do stand in relation to X, in which case I must also be able to refer to it—but then X is not bare. Or if X is bare I cannot stand in relation to it—but in that case I could never have any experience of X at all—it could never become my "other." And if it cannot be anything for me I certainly cannot refer to it.

In the language of sense-certainty, consciousness fails to refer to its object because in trying to grasp it as immediately given, it treats it *as if* it were bare. As a result it fails to grasp the particular *as* particular, that is, it loses the object altogether and is left holding an empty universal instead. It is important to keep in mind that this is unsatisfactory precisely because it does not correspond with consciousness' *actual experience* of particular trees and houses. This experience certainly presupposes a relationship between subject and object, but this relation simply remains inexplicable on the sense-certain criterion of immediacy.

The first, *negative, aspect* of the Hegelian argument or, more properly speaking, of the "experience" of consciousness, has thus shown that *due to the special requirements for the relationship between subject and object, it is impossible to refer to a bare particular.* But if this is Hegel's conclusion, it is only preliminary, for it hardly answers the question which is really at issue here: How it is that we *can* successfully refer to the sort of particulars given in experience?

Now, as I have said before, Hegel never really questions the possibility of reference to particular individuals *per se*, but instead wishes only to ascertain the conditions under which it is possible. Accordingly, our original question should be altered to read more properly: "*How* is reference to *particular individuals* possible?" The answer to this question constitutes the positive aspect of Hegel's argument.

Prima facie the failure of reference to bare particulars implies nothing one way or another about the conditions which must obtain when reference does succeed. However, when one considers more closely the *reasons for the failure*, it turns out that we already know a great deal about those conditions. We know, for instance, that the failure is due to the fact that consciousness *treats its object as if it were bare*, and we know that as long as it persists in this, it cannot even relate itself to it, since such a relation presupposes that it determine it *as* particular.[8] This, it seems to me, implies not only the "negative" conclusion that the referent cannot be bare, but also, expressed *positively*, that *mediation is a necessary condition for successful reference*. Consciousness itself learns the "truth" of sense-certainty, namely, that picking out one's object involves the mediation of context within which subject and object are situated. According to Hegel's argument, then, it is precisely this mediation of context which makes reference first possible. Read in this light, the argument of sense-certainty serves first and foremost to establish the context-dependency of expressions such as *this, here,* and *now*.

Soll and Plumer take Hegel to represent a view exactly opposite from what I have just presented.[9] His greatest mistake, they argue, is his total *disregard for the role of context* in demonstrative reference. According to Soll (pp. 105-6), it is Hegel's *confusion of types and tokens* which lands him in this difficulty, with the result that his criterion for the truth of a statement is that it be completely *independent of the context* in which it is uttered.

But does Hegel really *confuse* types and tokens?[10] If one and the same sentence, for example, "The rose is red," is uttered twice on two different occasions, then two tokens of the same type have been uttered. According to Soll, Hegel does not realize that only tokens, not types can be said to be true or false, and tokens, of course, are context-dependent statements. Soll thinks (mistakenly) that "Now is night"—since it changes in truth value with each utterance or token—is taken by Hegel as an example of a statement which *fails the test of truth* on the ground that its referent changes and it therefore cannot remain true. On this basis, he concludes that Hegel's criterion for the truth of a statement is that it be completely independent of the context in which it is uttered.[11] If Soll is right, it would of course be a foregone conclusion that such sense-certainty cannot conform to this criterion, as *this, here*, and *now* are expressions which most obviously depend on the context within which they are uttered, unless they are *written down*. But to write down statements such as "Now is night" frees them from their context only "illegitimately," for it changes a token into a type which simply cannot be said to be true or false. This, in turn, commits us to reject as false all context-dependent statements, according to Soll, including such unobjectionable ones as "I am happy," "The book is red," or "He is intelligent."[12] This, however, is a consequence which is simply unacceptable. Soll concludes, therefore, that if we want to grant that such statements are capable of being true (or correct), it is imperative that we make the proper distinction between tokens and types.

Soll's recommendation is hardly unpopular. Both Strawson and Quine, to whom Soll appeals, have argued for a version of the distinction mentioned above, and I agree with them wholeheartedly.[13] I strongly object, however, to Soll's claim that Hegel himself fails to make this distinction. (Although it is at least arguable that he might have responded by noting that, without mediation, reference fails for tokens as well as types, so that he would not need the distinction for his argument.)

I should like to suggest not only that Hegel does not conflate types and tokens, but also that long before writers such as Quine and Strawson, he gave a very successful argument *for* the distinction.[14] Take "Here is a tree" as an example of a type. Various tokens of this type may be either true or false depending on the context in which they are uttered. Now Soll assumes that Hegel argues that these truths cannot be "trusted" because they constantly change, and that hence he conflates types and tokens. I submit, however, that on the contrary, Hegel means precisely to point out the distinction, by showing that tokens should not be mistaken for types by *absolutizing* them. Types do not occur in context, only tokens, and only tokens are true or false. But sense-certainty does not want to recognize the mediating role of the context which ensures that a statement (token) successfully refers. It thinks it has its truth *immediately*, that is, it thinks it has hold of a *type* not a token. However, the demand to write the truth down turns it into a type, and now it is revealed that types are but empty universals which cannot be true or false because apart from a context they fail to refer to anything at all. As a matter of fact, however, sense-certainty is situated within a context; as a matter of fact, therefore, it utters only tokens, not types. And since a token is always mediated, sense-certainty's own utterance betrays its proposed criterion of immediacy by which it seeks to validate its truth.

I should note here that the same argument also demolishes a related charge by Plumer, namely that by claiming that the demonstratives "this," "here," and "now" are *universals,* Hegel confuses the *general applicability* of these terms with their actual use within a context. But their inability to refer to a specific individual in the former case, objects Plumer (pp. 84–85), certainly does not prevent them from successfully doing so in the latter case. The confusion, however, is entirely on the side of Plumer, for Hegel's whole point is to show that sense-certainty, which *does* conflate the two, cannot possibly succeed in referring to its objects unless it first accepts the crucial role of the context which mediates the reference and thereby makes it possible. Hegel's argument points out that the very distinction which, strangely, Soll and Plumer claim he overlooks could never be made in the first place except on the condition of mediation.

But we have yet to consider whether Hegel conflates *meaning and reference*. Now, on the strength of his distinction between tokens and types one might respond that he is not, in fact, guilty of such a conflation. Since a token is always an instance of the same type, and since, therefore, it *always means the same thing* while it can *refer to anything at all* depending on the context of utterance, it follows that meaning and reference must necessarily be distinguished.[15]

Suppose we take as correct the view that they must be distinguished. We will then have to say that there are at least two independent necessary conditions for knowledge: (1) successful reference, and (2) the meaning which is supplied by the predicates assigned to the subject in a proposition. Since neither condition is sufficient, the absence of either of them renders knowledge impossible. Suppose we now want to ascertain, as Hegel wishes to do in the chapter on sense-certainty, whether there is such a thing as *immediate* knowledge. Now it is quite obvious that if *either* of the two necessary conditions for knowledge required mediation, the immediacy of the resulting knowledge would be compromised. It follows, therefore, that regardless of the nature of reference, immediate knowledge is impossible on the basis of meaning alone, since meaning is supplied via predicates which are universals. If one were to conflate meaning and reference, therefore, this would be the easiest way to show that knowledge cannot be immediate.

This is *not*, however, Hegel's method, because the pointing and stammering consciousness of sense-certainty is not yet uttering propositions. Even if it were, Hegel concentrates his efforts on showing that consciousness cannot even *pick out* its object without mediation. To "pick out" the object is just what we do when we refer to it. Thus long before the possible immediacy of knowledge is spoiled by a consideration of the nature of predicates, it is rendered impossible, Hegel argues, due to the fact that reference succeeds only on the condition of mediation. Reference is mediated because it depends on the context of its use. *It is precisely because demonstratives so rigidly refer within the present context* that anything at all is a possible referent for a "this.[16] Knowing something to be a "this," consequently, is not sufficient to yield the sort of knowledge which ends up in a proposition. Accordingly, there are at least two necessary conditions for knowledge, each of which constitutes a different semantical category for Hegel: (1) successful reference mediated by the context, and (2) the meaning given by the mediation of predicates assigned to the subject of the proposition.

As always, to say that Hegel recognizes a distinction—here the one made in contemporary semantics and pragmatics we have discussed—is not to suggest that he takes it as absolute. On the contrary, no distinction is ever absolute for Hegel, but is "a distinction which is no distinction" in the sense that the terms distinguished do not lose their meaning, but merely their independence from one another. Ultimately, therefore, there is nothing which is *merely* theoretical or, to put the same thing differently, there is nothing theoretical which is not also practical. Still, this does not commit Hegel to conflating notions such as type and token in the sense that Plumer and Soll have charged. It is only to say that semantics—or the study of meaning—*by itself* is insufficient for the proper understanding of how it is that we successfully refer to objects and express knowledge about them, unless we also look at how we actually use language. For reference is a necessary condition for knowledge, and only particular *uses* of expressions can refer. And such uses clearly occur only within a particular context which mediates the reference.

III

According to sense-certainty, due to the special requirements governing the relationship between subject and object, the act of referring is necessarily mediated because it presupposes a determinate referent. *Seen from the side of the object or referent*, then, I have shown that it hardly follows from the universality of language that we cannot successfully refer to particulars, if these particulars are determinate universals or concrete particulars. However, one might still question how this reference is actually accomplished by the *subject* who uses *language* to refer, given that he or she uses a universal which, by Hegel's own admission, is merely an "abstract" universal. For even if the particular object "out there" contains universality within it, even if universality is that which first makes it particular, it may remain difficult to see how *abstractly* universal language can hook up with an individual *qua individual*, instead of merely *qua* universal. The question arises because, according to Hegel, when two opposites meet *both* must undergo a dialectical transformation in order to accomplish this. This requirement is satisfied as far as the referent goes, for it takes on meaning *qua* individual through universality. But what about language which is exclusively or abstractly universal? Must that not be "particularized" in order to hook up with the intended referent?

Once again, the answer lies in the context. For while language considered in abstraction, that is, formally or semantically, remains *abstractly universal*, in its actual *use*, within a *context*, it accomplishes precisely what otherwise would be impossible: it *determines and thus universalizes the individual*, and in this way achieves the meeting between the universal (the word) and the individual (the object) which we will call "reference." *Their meeting ground, then, is the context within which the reference takes place.* Hence, once more it does not follow that this reference to particulars must fail on the ground that language is (abstractly) universal. At most it follows that it would fail apart from the mediating context within which utterances inevitably occur. And this, I take it, is precisely Hegel's point.

We have seen, then, that Soll and Plumer are mistaken. Hegel does not deny reference to particulars on the ground that language is universal, or on any other ground. Instead, he provides us with a rich account of how such reference is possible. Overly simplistic criticisms, then, whether of the sort we have just considered, or perhaps of the sort Bertrand Russell has made, simply do not touch him. And perhaps there is a lesson to be learned here with respect to the study of Hegel. The study of any great philosopher is, of course, always of great historical interest. Hegel is no exception. But the fact that Hegel anticipated the contemporary distinctions we have discussed, the fact that he was perhaps the first philosopher who recognized what we now refer to as the context-dependency of indexicals, suggests that the study of Hegel still goes far beyond historical interest. It seems to me, then, that the contemporary philosopher—even one who does not want to accept the Hegelian philosophy as a whole—will still find the study of Hegel fruitful and enlightening.[17]

NOTES

1. All quotations are taken from Johannes Hoffmeister's edition of the *Phänomenologie des Geistes* (Hamburg: Meiner, 1952). The translations are my own, with cross references given to both J. B. Baillie's translation, *The Phenomenology of Mind* (New York: Macmillan, 1910, 1931), and A. V. Miller's *Phenomenology of Spirit* (Oxford: Clarendon, 1977). These editions are abbreviated PhG, PhM, PhS respectively.

2. The following standard works, for instance, make no mention of reference as a separate issue: Jean Hyppolite, *Genesis and Structure of Hegel's "Phenomenology of Spirit,"* trans. S. Cherniak and J. Heckman (Evanston, Ill.: Northwestern, 1974); Alexandre Kojève, *Introduction to the Reading of Hegel*, abridged trans. J. H. Nichols (New York: Basic Books, 1969); György Lukács, *The Young Hegel*, trans. R. Livingstone (London: Merlin, 1975; Cambridge, Mass.: MIT Press, 1976); Nicolai Hartmann, *Die Philosophie des deutschen Idealismus. II. Hegel* (Berlin: de Gruyter, 1923–29); John Niemeyer Findlay, *Hegel: A Re-examination* (London: George Allen and Unwin, 1958); Charles Taylor,

"The Opening Arguments of the *Phenomenology*," in *Hegel: A Collection of Critical Essays*, ed. Alasdair MacIntyre (New York: Anchor, 1972), 151–88; or Quentin Lauer, *A Reading of Hegel's "Phenomenology of Spirit"* (New York: Fordham University Press, 1976).

3. Gilbert Plumer, "Hegel on Singular Demonstrative Reference," *Philosophical Topics* 11 (1980): 71–94; Ivan Soll, *An Introduction to Hegel's Metaphysics* (Chicago: University of Chicago Press, 1969), especially 91–110. See also D. W. Hamlyn, *Sensation and Perception: A History of the Philosophy of Perception* (New York: Humanities Press, 1961), 140–46.

4. G. W. F. Hegel, *Enzyklopädie der Philosophischen Wissenschaften im Grundrisse* (1830), ed. Friedhelm Nicolin and Otto Pöggeler (Hamburg: Meiner, 1969), 56. My translation.

5. This result emerges after three aborted attempts to salvage immediacy as the criterion for knowledge of particular objects of experience. The details do not concern us here (but see PhG, 80–86; PhM, 150–57; PhS, 59–63) as the result is always the same: No matter where consciousness locates the immediacy essential to sense-certainty—in the object, the subject, or their relation—knowledge of the particulars of experience remains in every case an impossibility. Thus consciousness discovers, first, that it cannot pick out particular objects, then it is revealed that it cannot pick out particular objects *for consciousness*, and finally its defeat is complete when it finds that even the experience as a whole, the "my-knowing-this" fails to pick out a particular. Hence immediacy cannot explain how it is possible that consciousness experiences the object it *in fact* experiences.

6. G. W. F. Hegel, *Wissenschaft der Logik*, ed. Georg Lasson (Hamburg: Meiner, 1932): I:100; *Science of Logic*, trans. A. V. Miller (New York: Humanities Press, 1969), 113; cf. *Enz.* §91 Addition.

7. Daniel J. Cook, *Language in the Philosophy of Hegel* (The Hague: Nijhoff, 1973), 49. I should like to point out that this does not commit Hegel to deny the existence of contingencies, for although all bare particulars are contingent, all contingencies are not bare. By the same token, it means that merely because Hegel believes in the existence of contingencies, he is not committed to hold that bare particulars exist. As I interpret Hegel, however, reference to total contingencies would necessarily be impossible, because such reference would have to be immediate, and for Hegel reference is necessarily mediated. In addition, they would never be *actualized* or appear in experience. For Hegel, anything actual has formal possibility plus contingency. The former grounds the latter. The *wholly* contingent is an *abstraction*. It is only a logical possibility for existence, that is, it can be thought without contradiction. The *relatively* contingent exists, but it is *not bare*, because once a formal possibility becomes a fact it *appears* in *experience*. Thus *there cannot be a wholly contingent fact* because insofar as the contingent is that in which the formally possible is actually issued, it is in some rudimentary sense formally necessary. Not in the sense that it could not have been otherwise,

but only in the sense that it is thinkable—since it has occurred. We must distinguish *Denkbarkeit* from *Denknotwendigkeit* (cf. Aristotle, *Metaphysics* V, B 1019b30).

8. Of course, we must keep in mind that such determination is reciprocal since mediation runs from subject to object as well as from object to subject.

9. Given Hegel's argument, Soll's approach becomes particularly bizarre. Assuming that Hegel denies reference, and, unwilling to accept the consequences of this with regard to knowledge, he appeals to P. F. Strawson's argument in *Individuals: An Essay in Descriptive Metaphysics* (London: Methuen, 1959), 15–30, which seeks to establish that it is indeed possible to refer to a unique spatiotemporal position by assigning numerical, spatial, and temporal coordinates. Combining this position with a description, argues Strawson, enables us to refer successfully to a particular individual. (Cf. Soll, *Introduction*, 103–4). The irony of this procedure lies in the fact that each and every one of the concepts applied in this task, such as that of meridian, parallel, number, hour, second, and so forth, are *universals*. Moreover, the description combined with the reference to a unique position in space and time *necessarily* involves universals or predicates. By showing how universals can be made to apply to particulars, Soll (with a little help from Strawson) has made Hegel's point for him: Mediation of universals is a necessary condition for reference to particulars and hence for the knowledge of a truth.

10. The charge that Hegel *confuses* types and tokens, of course, presupposes that he distinguishes them first. To say he *conflates* them does not presuppose a prior distinction.

11. Soll, *Introduction*, 105. More properly, we should refer to it as Hegel's criterion for *correctness*, since elsewhere Hegel distinguishes "truth" from "correctness" (cf., e.g., Enz. §172, §172 Addition, §213 Addition, and §24 Addition 2). Accordingly, "truth" should be reserved to describe a situation in which the distinction between subject and object has been overcome. Strictly speaking, then, empirical truths are at best correct, although Hegel himself frequently and misleadingly uses the term *true* in such contexts. Reference is a necessary condition for correctness, such that "This rose is red" is correct if and only if (a) the reference succeeds and (b) the predicate assigned to the subject corresponds with the quality of the rose referred to. It should be kept in mind, therefore, that the "truth" as meant by Hegel, his critics, and myself, *must* be taken in the sense of "correctness."

12. Soll, *Introduction*, 105. Note that Soll is much too radical here. For even if one did hold that a truth, in order to *be* a truth, must be independent of all context or eternally true, this by no means entails that all context-dependent statements are *false*. Plato, for instance, makes a distinction between knowledge and true (not false) belief in *Republic* V, according to which statements of the order "the book is red" are capable of being factually correct, even though they do not constitute an eternal truth. Hegel's distinction between truth and correctness

serves a similar purpose. Apparently Soll is oblivious to this distinction, or he would have grasped that here Hegel argues simply that the statement "Now is night" becomes false *if removed from its context*, not that it is false because it fails to be independent of such context and hence fails to remain true.

13. In *Methods of Logic* (New York: Holt, 1950), Willard Van Orman Quine says on p. xi, quoted by Soll on p. 105: "Strictly speaking, what admits of truth and falsity are not statements as repeatable patterns of utterance [= statement types] but individual events of statements of utterance [= statement tokens]. For utterances that sound alike can vary in meaning with the occasion of the utterance. This is not only due to careless ambiguities, but to systematic ambiguities which are essential to the nature of language. The pronoun 'I' changes its reference with every change of speaker; 'there' changes its reference with every significant movement through space; and 'now' charges its reference every time it is uttered." In "On Referring," in *Meaning and Knowledge: Systematic Readings in Epistemology*, ed. Ernest Nagel and Richard B. Brandt (New York: Harcourt, Brace, & World, 1965), 113ff., P. F. Strawson makes a similar distinction between types and *uses* of types. Thus the expression 'I' cannot refer to a particular person; that can only be said of a particular use of the expression.

14. This is perhaps worded too strongly since Hegel never makes any distinction *absolutely*. But he does recognize the difference between "immediate" types and "mediated" tokens on the level of the understanding where it is appropriate. To say that, from the point of view of the dialectic such distinctions are never absolute, however, is not the same as to overlook them entirely.

15. Willem DeVries, in "Hegel on Reference and Knowledge," delivered at the American Philosophical Association's Pacific Division meetings, March 25, 1981, especially on p. 13 of his typed copy, also implies such a distinction. He argues that demonstratives have a minimal conceptual content which tells us "where to start looking." But since every time is a "now" and every space a "here" this small amount of meaning is not sufficient, in and of itself, to ensure reference. As in the case of all pure referring expressions, successful reference depends not only on their meaning but also on the context of their use. If DeVries is correct, the same conclusion follows: If *here* and *now* have a meaning which *always remains the same*, while the referent differs from context to context, it is not only possible, but necessary, that meaning and reference be distinguished.

16. According to DeVries, it is precisely due to this rigidity that statements such as "Now is night" can switch from correct to incorrect. In fact, the referent of *now* changes constantly; *this* never points out the same object twice. But to say that the reference *changes* makes precise sense only if the reference in each case was successful in the first place. Thus grasping the "untruth" of sense-certainty actually presupposes the possibility of reference, which consequently is necessary for the progression of consciousness toward knowledge of the real (DeVries, "Hegel on Reference and Knowledge," 4–7).

17. I should like to thank G. J. Mattey for editorial assistance.

5

Merold Westphal

Hegel's Phenomenology of Perception

The goal of Hegel's *Phenomenology of Spirit* is "Spirit's insight into what knowing is" (17/27).[1] But on his view, "The True is the whole" (11/21). This means that his philosophy can supersede other philosophies only by including them, but also that philosophy as such can validate its truth claims only by including those non-philosophical forms of experience which make a claim on truth.[2] Just as the truth of the plant is neither the bud nor the blossom, nor even the fruit, but rather the whole process in which each plays its own necessary part, thereby retaining its radical difference from the others, so the whole truth about knowledge may turn out to be quite complex (2/10). It may have to include not only the discussion of such obvious topics as sense perception and the natural sciences, but even an analysis of "the madness of Diderot's musician . . . [and the] fanaticism of Marat and Robespierre."[3]

We can at least be thankful that Hegel begins where we would expect a treatise on knowledge to begin, with sense perception and our knowledge of the external world. One way of reading the opening three chapters, collectively entitled "Consciousness," is as a retelling of Plato's *Theaetetus*. The parallel is threefold. With natural consciousness in the role of Theaetetus, Hegel's dialogue is thoroughly Socratic. At least his claim would be that, "The arguments never come out of me; they always come from the person I am talking with. I am only at a slight advantage

122

in having the skill to get some account of the matter from another's wisdom and entertain it with fair treatment.... So I will have recourse to the wisdom of Theaetetus."4 The result is as Socratic as the method. At the end of the chapters on consciousness we can say that we have learned a lot but not that we know what knowledge is, which was, of course, the goal.

A final and perhaps most fruitful parallel is that between the three answers given by Theaetetus and the three given by natural consciousness under Hegel's questioning. The most obvious link is at the level of pure sensation. What Theaetetus means when he says that knowledge is perception is what the *Phenomenology* calls "*sense-certainty.*" But careful reading shows that what Hegel calls "*perception*" and "*understanding*" are intimately connected with the second and third answers of Theaetetus, that knowledge is true opinion or judgment and that it is true judgment or opinion with the addition of an account or of reasons (*logos*). For Hegel's analysis of perception emphasizes its mediated, judgmental character, just as he finds understanding's employment of such supersensible categories as force and law to be motivated by the urge to explain the sensible world of perception.

There is another story Hegel is retelling in these chapters, the one about Kant and his Copernican revolution. The analysis of the Here, the Now, and the I in the chapter on sense-certainty can be read as another deduction of space, time, and the transcendental unity of apperception as the *a priori* conditions of the possibility of experience. The constitution of objects in space and time by and for the transcendental subject and particularly the role of the category of substance in this constitution are Kantian themes underlying the discussion of things and their properties in the chapter on perception. And the chapter on understanding restates Kant's discovery of the importance of rules and the concept of nature in general in the constitution of the objects of experience. It can thus be read as a further deduction of the categories of cause and reciprocity.

The dialogue between Hegel and natural consciousness in these chapters is not identical with either of these stories, and there are doubtless other such perspectives which throw important light on the text. Hegel's principle of totality requires that we read from all of these perspectives at once if we are to grasp the whole which is the truth about these forms of consciousness. Nor is this the only demand made by that principle. It is not loosely that Hegel's narrative is called a dialogue, for it represents both the experience of natural and the meta-experience which occurs "for us" as "we" observe the dialectical movement of natural consciousness. To see these moments both apart and together is essential to understanding this "Science of the *experience of consciousness*" (56/74). Two passages from the preface throw light on this requirement. Both contrast the movement of natural consciousness with another movement of thought which can only be that of the philosophically observant reader.

"Culture and its laborious emergence from the immediacy of substantial life must always begin by getting acquainted with *general* principles and points of view, so as at first to work up to a *general conception* of the real issue, as well as learning to support and refute the general conception with reasons; then to apprehend the rich and concrete abundance [of life] in its concrete richness; and finally to give accurate instruction and pass serious judgment upon it" (3/11–12). This movement of thought from original immediacy to the knowledge which grasps the object only through the mediation of universals, that is, in judgment, and then goes on the support its judgments with reasons, is the movement of the *Theaetetus*. Hegel stresses the abstractness of the knowledge it produces. Since thought's task is "emergence" from immediacy and "to work up" to generality, the movement of thought to the thing in general leads away from the thing itself, away from the concrete and rich fullness which it set out to think.

"From its very beginning, culture must leave room for the earnestness of life in its concrete richness; this leads the way to an experience of the real issue [*die Sache selbst*]. And even when the real issue has been penetrated to its depth by serious speculative effort, this kind of knowing and judging will still retain its appropriate place in ordinary conversation" (3/12).

Over against the thought which owes its achievements to its abstractness, there inevitably arises the appeal to concrete experience, to immediacy, to intuition, and so forth, in the name of seriousness. Enlightenment and Romanticism always go together. But there is another seriousness which distinguishes itself from both. It claims to be more serious than the seriousness of immediacy, for it recognizes the deficiencies of the first attempt to think without assuming that this exhausts the possibilities of thought. The seriousness of conceptual thinking, which is at once "strenuous effort" and a "restraint" (35–36/48), acknowledges the seriousness of the appeal to the experience of the *Sache selbst*, but it boldly claims that it is just this which it will think.

A second passage in which the same two modes of thought are contrasted gives a fuller account of what the second, the seriousness of conceptual thinking, is like. Here the abstract mode of thought is attributed to antiquity.

> The manner of study in ancient times differed from that of the modern age in that the former was the proper and complete formation of the natural consciousness. Putting itself to the test at every point of its exis-

tence, and philosophizing about everything it came across, it made itself into a universality that was active through and through. In modern times, however, the individual finds the abstract form ready-made; the effort to grasp and appropriate it is more the direct driving-forth of what is within and the truncated generation of the universal than it is the emergence of the latter from the concrete variety of existence. Hence the task nowadays consists not so much in purging the individual of an immediate, sensuous mode of apprehension, and making him into a substance that is an object of thought and that thinks, but rather in just the opposite, in freeing determinate thoughts from their fixity so as to give actuality to the universal, and impart to it spiritual life. . . . Through this movement the pure thoughts become *Concepts*, and are only now what they are in truth . . . spiritual essences. (19–20/30–31)[5]

This much is clear: If the development of natural consciousness is the movement from immediate existence to the universality of thought, the superseding of natural consciousness is the movement from pure thought to Concept, more specifically from pure thought to spirit. Hegel coins the term *begeisten* in this context. It borrows something of the sense of *begeistern* (to inspire, to fill with enthusiasm) but interprets this as be-*Geisten*. The lifeless universality of thought is overcome in the discovery that pure thoughts are spiritual essences, that they belong to spirit. The full significance of this can only come with Hegel's development of the concept of spirit, which begins in chapter four, where it is introduced as "'I' that is 'We' and 'We' that is 'I'" (110/140). But the following indications are given in the paragraph just quoted:

[F]ixed thoughts have the "I," the power of the negative, or pure actuality, for the substance and element of their existence. . . . Thoughts become fluid when pure thinking, this inner *immediacy*, recognizes itself as a moment, or when the pure certainty of self abstracts from itself—not by leaving itself out, or setting itself aside, but by giving up the *fixity* of its self-positing, by giving up not only the fixity of the pure concrete, which the "I" itself is, in contrast with its differentiated content, but also the fixity of the differentiated moments which, posited in the element of pure thinking, share the unconditioned nature of the "I." (20/30–31)

The movement is twofold. First comes the Copernican revolution, the discovery of the transcendental role of the thinking subject. The Cartesian ego, the object of thought that thinks, comes to know itself as a moment of its own knowledge, as the origin of the thought determinations which make its knowledge possible. But this is only half of what it means to *begeisten* the universal. When thought recognizes itself as a moment in the process of knowledge, it also recognizes its own relativity. In abandoning the fixed quality of its self-affirmation both as the transcendental unity of apperception and as the determinate categories by which that unity maintains itself in actual knowing, it abandons "the unconditioned nature of the I" which at first it claims for itself in the element of pure thought. Just as the transcendental turn deprives the object of its fixity by showing that it is not simply given, this second move is the discovery that the subject is not simply self-posited. Its inner immediacy is no more immediately there than the object. The road to absolute knowledge passes through the valley of the shadow of this double relativity.[6]

A full comprehension of the chapter on perception must include a grasp of its contribution to this kind of meta-experience which "we" readers are invited to share with Hegel. But the natural consciousness which we observe is itself entirely unaware of all this. It finds itself naturally at home in the world of perception. But if all our experience begins with perception, it does not therefore always stay at perception. Natural consciousness moves out of the world of perception and takes up residence in a new world which Hegel calls understanding. It does not understand why it ventures forth from its home in this way, for this movement takes place, as it were, "behind the back of consciousness" (56/74). It is the primary task of the chapter on perception to show the nature and inner dialectical necessity of this movement. This showing will be the first illustration of Hegel's claim that spirit exists "only as transcending [*aufhebend*] what it is immediately, only as stepping back therefrom."[7] Or, in more dramatic terms: "But the life of spirit is not the life that shrinks from death and keeps itself untouched by devastation, but rather the life that endures it and maintains itself in it. It wins its truth only when, in utter dismemberment, it finds itself" (19/29–30).

It may appear, however, that the movement from perception to understanding is the second rather than the first which Hegel describes in the *Phenomenology*. This is merely an appearance. For the movement of the first two chapters is not so much from sense-certainty to perception as it is the discovery that consciousness is always and inescapably at the level of perception. Sense-certainty is an unreal abstraction. Our knowledge of the external world does not begin in the rarefied atmosphere of pure sensation but in the concrete *Lebenswelt* of everyday awareness of things and their properties. It is the world of the tree here and the house over there, the world of alternating day and night, the world in which tradesman and housewife complain that it always rains at the fair and on washday, the world in which a penknife lies beside the snuffbox, and beside them both, a cube of salt with its familiar whiteness and pungency.

But natural consciousness, like the brilliant Theaetetus, is not accustomed to reflecting about its experience. When asked about its starting point, it tells where it would like to begin, namely with immediate sensible consciousness, rather than looking carefully to see where it actually begins. It is not hard to see where this wish comes from and how it is strong enough to blind perception to its real situation. Hegel subtitles the chapter on perception "The Thing and Deception." The reference to deception is a bit playful, for he wants us to see the sophistical self-deception to which perception succumbs when forced to become reflective. But the primary reference is to perceptual experience itself. "The percipient is aware of the possibility of deception" (70/93). As Socrates' conversation with Theaetetus shows, this is the first discovery perception makes on its way to self-consciousness. The inevitable result is some sort of appeal to the given. The object is there. Perceiving consciousness "has only to *take* it, to confine itself to a pure apprehension of it, and what is thus yielded is the true. If consciousness itself did anything in taking what is given, it would by such adding or subtraction alter the truth." When it begins to look as if perception is not "a simple pure apprehension" after all, it makes more explicit its appeal to the given. It "distinguishes its apprehension of the truth from the untruth of its perception" (70–72/92–95).

Just these concerns of perception underlie the appeal to immediacy as sense-certainty. Immediacy here means "we must alter nothing in the object as it presents itself. In *apprehending* it, we must refrain from trying to *com*prehend it." sense-certainty is to be the immaculate conception of the given. "For it has not yet omitted anything from the object, but has the object before it in its perfect entirety" (58/79). For the first reason it claims to be the truest knowledge, and for the second reason the richest. It becomes clear that the self-description of natural consciousness as sense-certainty is less a spontaneous and immediate response than an attempt to avoid some of the problems involved in claiming to find the truth within the world of perception.

For understanding the primacy of perception[8] in the Hegelian phenomenology of experience, however, one must grasp more than the derivative character of the appeal to sense-certainty. One must also understand that what is called by this name is not an actual form of consciousness at all. Here, as subsequently, Hegel's method is to observe the contradiction between the criterion by which consciousness seeks to validate its knowledge and the actual knowledge which it produces. Such a contradiction is already present in the claim of sense-certainty to be both the truest and the richest knowledge. Sense-certainty claims to be the truest knowledge in virtue of its immediacy. It has the object unadulterated, for it has neither taken anything from it nor added anything to it. But this criterion stands in sharpest contradiction to the richness of the actual knowledge which it takes to be its own. The knowledge which takes this criterion seriously is not the richest, but "the most abstract and poorest truth" of all. It can completely express itself by saying, "it is." Sense-certainty knows and can say that its object is, but not what it is, "and its truth contains nothing but the sheer *being* of the thing" (58/79). Any attempt to get beyond their indeterminacy runs afoul of the immediacy criterion, for every determination is a negation and every negation is a mediation.

Since Hegel seems to presuppose rather than deny that we sometimes do perceive trees, we may suppose that the "it" which "is" is a tree and is perceived as a tree. But to be a tree is to have certain qualities which distinguish one from a computer or an igloo. This is already to introduce mediation, for the tree can be a tree and not merely an "it is" only by virtue of its negative relation to other things. At the same time, to perceive the tree as a tree is to perceive it as not a computer and not an igloo. The determinate is given as such to consciousness only by the mediating act which distinguishes it from what it is not. For sense-certainty "neither I nor the thing has the significance of a complex process of mediation; the 'I' does not have the significance of a manifold imagining or thinking; nor does the 'thing' signify something that has a host of qualities. On the contrary, the thing *is*. . . . It *is*; this is the essential point for sense-knowledge, and this pure *being*, or this simple immediacy, constitutes its truth" (58–59/80). Such knowledge owes its certainty to its emptiness. As with the "knowledge is perception" thesis in the *Theaetetus*, the possibility of truth disappears with the possibility of error.[9]

This contradiction between immediacy and determinacy is fatal for sense-certainty. Hegel's merciless exposure of it in the opening chapter of the *Phenomenology* shows us not that this is an unstable form of human consciousness, but that it is not a form of human consciousness at all. The situation resembles that at the beginning of the *Logic*, as Gadamer has interpreted it, where the movement from being to nothing to becoming is not a genuine dialectical progression. "Taken as thoughts for thinking, being and nothing are not at all determinations of thought. Accordingly, Hegel states explicitly that being is empty intuition or empty thought per se and that the same holds for nothing. . . . Empty thinking is thus thinking which is not yet that which thinking is at all."[10] In an important sense becoming is the first genuine thought determination of the *Logic*, just because it has built into it the mediation which being and nothing are meant to exclude. Similarly, in the *Phenomenology*, perception is the first actual form of human consciousness because it includes the mediation which permits determination, without which it would be empty intuition or empty thought.

The principle that every determination is a negation and thus a mediation means that for an object to be given as determinate it must be taken as such, that is, mediated by the intentional act which distinguishes it from what it is not. Hegel's analysis of the Here and the Now shows the special significance of this principle for sense experience. In relation to space and time this logical principle becomes the explicitly perceptual principle—the object of perception is always distinguished within perception as a foreground against a background. In both cases the result is the same. It is only by means of the "judgmental" act of the perceiving subject which takes the object as here and not there, now and not then, tree and not computer or igloo, that the object can be determinately present to consciousness. Husserl makes the same point when he affirms the strict correlation of intentional act and intentional object, of *noesis* and *noema*. Hegel's transition to the second chapter is thus more than a pun on the term *Wahr-nehmung* (to take as true), for it succinctly locates the Achilles' heel of the appeal to sense-certainty. "I point it out *as* a 'Here,' which is a Here of other Heres. . . . I take it up then *as* it is in truth, and instead of knowing something immediate I take the truth of it [*nehme ich wahr*], or perceive it" (66/89).[11] There can be no unmediated givenness in perception, for to perceive is to take something *as* something.

Natural consciousness thus finds itself at home in the thoroughly mediated world of perception. But as we have seen, it does not stay at home; it succumbs to a wanderlust born of the desire to explain. Perception becomes understanding. Hegel's analysis of the latter differs from Kant's in two ways which are important for understanding his view of the former. First, Kant tended to equate the question, How is science possible?, with the question, How is experience possible? The result was to narrow the concept of experience, and, even more important, to blur the difference between the perceptual *Lebenswelt* and nature as conceived by the natural sciences. Consequently, when in the *Jena Logic* (1804–5) Hegel treats essentially the same materials as belong to perception and understanding in the *Phenomenology* as a discussing of the Kantian categories of relation (substance, cause, reciprocity), the same merging of natural science with the *Lebenswelt* occurs.[12] The significance of Descartes' analysis of the piece of wax in the Second Meditation is temporarily forgotten. But in the *Phenomenology* the Cartesian perspective is restored. The difference between perception and understanding is not that between the category of substance on the one hand and those of cause and reciprocity on the other, but rather between two genuinely different forms of consciousness.

Taking his cue from Descartes, but substituting a cube of salt for the piece of wax, Hegel distinguishes the sensible world of everyday perception from the supersensible world of the natural sciences. The sensible salt is the familiar salt which we sprinkle on our food and on icy sidewalks. The supersensible salt is, most simply, NaCl, an object which does not appear directly to perception.

The concept of force is one indicator of this indirect relation between consciousness and its object. When one thinks in terms of forces and their expression (whether these be Aristotelian entelechies or gravitational and magnetic forces), one takes "something not objective" or the "inner being of things" to be their truth (83/106).

> This true essence of things has now the character of not being immediately for consciousness; on the contrary, consciousness has a mediated relation to the inner being and, as the understanding, *looks through this mediating play of forces into the true background of things*. The middle term which unites the two extremes, the understanding and the inner world, is the developed being of force which, for the understanding itself, is henceforth only a vanishing. This "being" is therefore called *appearance*.... The being of this object for consciousness is mediated by the movement of *appearance*, in which the *being of perception* and the sensuously objective in general has a merely negative significance. Consciousness, therefore, reflects itself out of this movement back into itself as the true, but *qua* consciousness, converts this truth again into an objective *inner* ... an extreme over against it.... Within this *inner truth* ... there now opens up above the *sensuous* world, which is the world of *appearance*, a *supersensible* world which henceforth is the *true* world; above the vanishing *present* world there opens up a permanent *beyond*, an in itself which is the first, and therefore imperfect, appearance of reason, or only the pure element in which the truth has its essence. (86–88/110–11)[13]

Having stressed the mediated character of perception over against the claims of sense-certainty, Hegel now stresses the immediate character of perception in contrast to the mediated relation of understanding to its object. We have here a splendid example of the relativity of immediacy and mediation in Hegel's usage. In this contrast, Hegel's affirmation of the primacy of perception is enriched. It becomes clear that perception is not only the inescapable and irreducible starting point for natural consciousness, but also that when it leaves its home in the *Lebenswelt* for the new world of understanding it does not really leave the latter behind. For its presence to the supersensible world of understanding is always mediated through its immediate presence in the world of everyday perception.[14]

There is a second difference between Kant's way and Hegel's way of asking the question, How is science (in the sense of understanding) possible? It is also important for understanding Hegel's interpretation of perception. It stems from keeping the difference between the sensible and supersensible clearly in mind. One cannot ask this question without beginning on the road to transcendental philosophy. But it is possible to leave this road quite quickly. Already in Kant's transcendental dialectic the transformation of the transcendental question into the methodological question, "How does one go about doing science?," begins to take place. Neo-Kantianism and positivism are but the heirs of this tendency in Kant.

When, however, science is recognized as a radical demolition of and withdrawal from natural consciousness' home in everyday perception, the question of the possibility of science cannot be reduced to the how-to-do-it question of a methodologically oriented philosophy of science. The method question, "How does one go about doing science?," becomes less important than the motive question, "How does one come to do science?" For when the negative relation of science to ordinary perception is not forgotten, science can only be seen as a form of human behavior; and when theory is thus seen to be a form of praxis, philosophical reflection begins to ask less about method and more about the purpose and results of this activity. What is it that inspires consciousness to claim its inheritance and set out from its father's house, seeking fame and fortune in a far country? Will it turn out to be a prodigal son indeed, forced to return from the husks of the far country?[15]

To preserve the transcendental sense of the question, "How is science possible?," Hegel takes the bold step of transforming it into the question, "Why is science necessary?" Is it a mere accident that perception becomes understanding? Is there not rather a kind of internal necessity here, something about perception that drives it on to understanding? Most of the text of the chapter on perception is devoted to showing how the answer to this latter question must be affirmative.

Hegel directs our attention to a cube of salt, just as Descartes had directed it to a piece of wax. Both of these familiar objects from the world of everyday perception illustrate the movement of consciousness from that world to the world of scientific thought. It is entirely typical of Hegel that whereas Descartes generates the scientific perspective from the instability of the wax for the senses, he stresses the instability of the salt for thought. It is not the changing appearance of the salt from one moment to the next but its contradictory character at any given moment which provides the theoretical deduction of the understanding.

Beginning with the assumption that the object is the essential thing, "regardless of whether it is perceived or not," attention is directed toward its determination. First the lesson of the previous chapter is recalled. "Being, however, is a universal in virtue of its having mediation or the negative within it." This contextual definition of what Hegel means here by universality clarifies the otherwise puzzling claim that the principle of the perceptual object is "the universal, in its simplicity something mediated." As such it is *the thing with many properties* (67–68/90). To call this object a thing is to express its simplicity, while to speak of its properties is to indicate the "complex process of mediation" (58/80) through which it is given as something determinate. Both the richness of sensible content and the immediacy which sense-certainty claimed for it are present in the properties of the thing, but since this immediacy includes negation rather than excluding it, Hegel calls it "a universal immediacy" (68/90), that is, a mediated immediacy.[16]

Of course, the thing has many such properties and is thus the determinate thing it is precisely through this multiplicity. On the other hand, these determinations are properties not in virtue of their mere determinateness, but by inhering in or belonging to the one thing whose properties they are.[17] Hegel does not allow us to forget that the universal, which is the principle of perception, is "in its simplicity something mediated" (67/90). "But the simple, self-identical universality is itself in turn distinct and free from these determinate properties it has. It is pure relating of self to self, or the medium in which all these determinacies are, and in which as a simple unity they therefore interpenetrate. . . . This abstract universal medium . . . can be called simply 'thinghood.'" In order to avoid Locke's embarrassing description of the thing as "something I know not what," Hegel calls it the Here and Now, "a simple togetherness of a plurality. . . . This salt is a simple Here, and at the same time manifold; it is white and also tart, also cubical in shape, of a specific gravity, etc. All these many properties are in a single simple Here. . . . This Also is thus the pure universal itself, or the medium, the 'thinghood,' which holds them together in this way" (68–69/91).

As the initial reference to the salt indicates, the thing is simple and at the same time manifold. Hegel's reflections about the simple unity of the thing lead him, as we have just seen, to an analysis of the thing as the Also. As such it is a passive plurality rather than the active, exclusionary unity which would be a simple unity. Reflecting on the perceptual object as the One, Hegel finds himself describing it as the Also, a characteristic clearly in some sort of tension with that from which it is derived, the One (69/92).

Hegel does not hesitate to call this tension contradiction. Consciousness, he claims, actually experiences contradiction both in its object and in its conduct toward it. Its criterion for the object is self-sameness, for itself, pure apprehension. The experience which it has, however, disappoints both expectations. It is important for Hegel's method that the criteria by means of which perception is judged are not Hegel's but those inherent to the standpoint of perception itself. In that sense his critique is immanent and his method Socratic.

Perceptual consciousness begins to suspect that its conduct is not a pure apprehension when it notes the tension between the thing as the One and as the Also, as simple and as manifold (70–72/93–95). It distinguishes and separates its activity in constituting the object from its pure passive taking of the given. In order to preserve the thing as one, it takes upon itself the blame for the apparent manyness. Recalling the tradition which began with Galileo's and Descartes's view of the secondary qualities as subjective and which culminated in Berkeley's subjective idealism, Hegel reports consciousness' claim that "the thing is white only to our eyes, also tart to our tongue, also cubical to our touch, and so on. We get the entire diversity of these aspects, not from the thing, but from ourselves. . . . Through the fact, then, that we regard the characteristic of being a universal medium as our reflection, we preserve the self-identity and truth of the thing, its being a One" (72/95). But consciousness quickly realizes that the thing is the one determinate thing it is, as opposed to just something in general, only as the owner of these properties. For the sake of the thing they must be its very own properties. So consciousness reverses itself and adopts a position which might suggest motifs in Hume and Kant. "[T]he thing is the Also . . . the subsistence of the many diverse and independent properties. . . . Positing these properties as a oneness is the work of consciousness alone" (73/96). What consciousness is actually experiencing here is that the thing is both One and Also, for itself and for another, that "the truth itself, the thing, reveals itself in this twofold way . . . it contains in itself an opposite truth." It is both "doubly differentiated" and also "a One; but the oneness contradicts this diversity" (74/97). Natural consciousness suffers here from what Hegel likes to call a "tenderness" for things which will not allow them to contradict themselves.[18] So it resorts to the "insofar." Insofar as the thing is for itself or self-related oneness, it is not for an other or another related plurality. The one aspect belongs to the thing; the other comes from consciousness.

Hegel invites us who are watching the sophistical contortions of this tenderness to see what is really happening: "the object is in one and the same respect the opposite of itself: it is for itself, so far as it is for another, and it is for another, so far as it is for itself." If we ask what that respect may be, Hegel's clear answer is the determinacy which constitutes the essence of the thing. The thing can be the one determinate thing it is only by being simultaneously for itself and for an other. One must say, insofar as the thing is determinate it is for itself, and insofar as it is determinate it is for an other. "The relation, however, is the negation of its self-subsistence, and it is really the essential property of the thing that is its undoing" (76/99).

This result calls for three comments. First, this is the most explicit contribution of the entire *Phenomenology* to an understanding of Hegel's theory of contradiction. He deliberately describes the elements he takes to be contradictory as occurring at the same time and in one and the same respect, and he repeats the latter phrase to make sure we don't miss the point. Actually Hegel presents two levels of contradiction, the one within the object of perception itself and the other within perceptual consciousness, the one between its criteria and its actual experience. The former is the kind of contradiction which concerns Hegel in the *Logic*. The latter represents the contradiction of consciousness peculiar to the *Phenomenology*, previously illustrated by the contradiction between sense-certainty's criterion of immediacy and the rich determinacy of its actual knowledge.

Second, we see the need for a philosophical logic, in particular a critique of the categories of common sense which Hegel here refers to as "perceptual understanding, often called 'sound common sense.'" It despises philosophy for exerting itself to become master of what it takes to be mere thoughts, but does not see that it is itself "only the play of these abstractions." "It does not itself become conscious that it is simple essentialities of this kind that hold sway over it.... It is 'sound common sense' that is the prey of these abstractions, which spin it round and round in their whirling circle" (77–79/101–2). This is the source of the bad philosophy which grows out of reflection on perception and which Hegel here repeatedly calls sophistry.

But the *Phenomenology* is more concerned to show us the possibility of such a logic than its necessity, and as we have seen, in order to proceed it needs next to show us the necessity of understanding rather than its mere possibility. We need not only to see that the object of perception cannot sustain itself, but also that this failure of one form of consciousness is also the birth of another. In contrast to sense-certainty, the principle of perception is mediation, the universal. "[B]ut this universal, since it originates in the sensuous, is essentially conditioned by it, and hence is not truly a self-identical universality at all, but one afflicted with opposition." As such it is subject to categorial antinomies, the most encompassing of which is that we have "a 'being-for-self' that is burdened with a 'being-for-another.' Since, however, both are essentially in a single unity, what we now have is unconditioned absolute universality, and consciousness here for the first time truly enters the realm of understanding" (76–77/99–100).

Typically for Hegel the adequate statement of the problem practically provides its own solution. The trouble with the things of perception is that they can neither be nor be understood apart from their relation to other things. They are in this sense conditioned and can be fully comprehended only through grasping the whole of which they are a part. This whole is the unconditioned universal which can be and be understood in terms of itself. It is mediated and therefore real and determinate; but it is self-mediated and therefore intelligible in itself. It is Spinoza's substance. In terms of the Kantian categories of quantity, it is the totality which keeps unity and plurality from constantly warring and falling apart. It is what Kant calls the concept of nature in general.

Hegel's new task is to show now natural consciousness expresses this concept in terms of forces and laws and to observe the difficulties this new form of consciousness may experience. So far as chapter two is concerned, it is sufficient that he has tried to show that whatever the practical motivations which underlie science as instrumental reason, there is a theoretical necessity to the understanding built into the categorial structure of perception. Since his analysis begins with force, our attention is directed to Aristotle and earlier Greek speculation. But if we realize that primitive animism and dynamism are perhaps the earliest version of what Hegel discusses as force and its expression, we will realize that the necessity of which he speaks has been felt by natural consciousness for a long time without the help of speculative thinkers.[19]

Notes

1. References in the text to the *Phenomenology* have the form a/b.

   a = *Hegel's Phenomenology of Spirit*, trans. A. V. Miller (Oxford: Clarendon Press, 1977).

   b = *Phänomenologie des Geistes*, ed. J. Hoffmeister (Hamburg: Felix Meiner, 1952).

I have made minor changes in Miller's translation, substituting *Concept* for *Notion* and omitting some of Hegel's italics. But I have not inserted my own emphasis without noting it.

2. It is thus an Hegelian principle which Feuerbach directs against Hegel when he writes, "The philosopher must take into the *text* of philosophy that aspect of man which *does not* philosophize, but, rather, is *opposed* to philosophy and abstract thinking, or in other words, that which in Hegel has been reduced to a mere *footnote*." *Preliminary Theses on the Reform of Philosophy*, in *The Fiery Brook: Selected Writings of Ludwig Feuerbach*, trans. Zawar Hanfi (Garden City, N.Y.: Doubleday, 1972), 164.

3. Rudolf Haym, *Hegel und seine Zeit* (Hildesheim: Georg Olms, 1962), 241. The reference is to chapter six, section B of the *Phenomenology*.

4. *Theaetetus*, 161b–162b.

5. On this passage, see Hans-Georg Gadamer's essay, "Hegel and the Dialectic of the Ancient Philosophers," in *Hegel's Dialectic: Five Hermeneutical Studies*, trans. P. Christopher Smith (New Haven, Conn.: Yale University Press, 1976).

6. It is this thesis of the *Phenomenology* which Jürgen Habermas expresses, without realizing it, when he writes, "*The achievements of the transcendental subject have their basis in the natural history of the human species.*" *Knowledge and Human Interests*, trans. Jeremy J. Shapiro (Boston: Beacon Press, 1971), 312.

7. G. W. F. Hegel, *Jenaer Realphilosophie*, ed. Johannes Hoffmeister (Hamburg: Felix Meiner, 1967), S. 179.

8. Deliberate reference is made here to the title essay of Maurice Merleau-Ponty's *The Primacy of Perception and Other Essays*, ed. James M. Edie (Evanston, Ill.: Northwestern University Press, 1964), in which he states and defends the central thesis of his major work, *The Phenomenology of Perception*. The suggestion is that Hegel's position here in the chapters on Consciousness is very similar to Merleau-Ponty's.

9. This provides a helpful commentary on Hegel's identification of the fear of error with the fear of truth in the Introduction (47/65).

10. Hans-Georg Gadamer, "The Idea of Hegel's Logic," in *Hegel's Dialectic*, 88–89.

11. My emphasis. Cf. Kant in the *Critique of Pure Reason*: "Judgment is therefore the mediate knowledge of an object" (A68 = B93).

12. G. W. F. Hegel, *Gesammelte Werke* (Hamburg: Felix Meiner, 1971), 7:36–75.

13. Fruitful comparison can be made between Hegel's position and that of Wilfrid Sellars in "Philosophy and the Scientific Image of Man," in *Frontiers of Science and Philosophy* (Pittsburgh: University of Pittsburgh Press, 1962).

14. The importance of this dependence has been developed with great subtlety as a major theme of twentieth-century phenomenology, not only in the work of Merleau-Ponty (see note 8 above), but also in Heidegger's *Being and Time* and Husserl's *Crisis of European Sciences*.

15. It is in the preface that Hegel himself invokes the image of the prodigal son while discussing the poverty of spirit underlying the reversion to immediacy. In the following paragraph he relates this directly to the scientific revolution (4–5/13–14).

16. Cf. *Hegel's Science of Logic*, trans. A. V. Miller (New York: Humanities Press, 1969), 484ff., where Hegel examines "The Thing and Its Properties."

17. Cf. Kant's discussion of judgment in §19 of the Transcendental Deduction in the second edition of *Critique of Pure Reason*.

18. See *Science of Logic*, 423, and *The Encyclopedia Logic*, trans. Geraets, Suchting, and Harris (Indianapolis, Ind.: Hackett, 1991), Remark to §48.

19. G. van de Leeuw, *Religion in Essence and Manifestation: A Study in Phenomenology*, trans. J. E. Turner (New York: Harper & Row, 1963), part one.

6

Joseph C. Flay

Hegel's "Inverted World"

The "inverted world" occupies a most crucial position in Hegel's *Phenomenology of Spirit*: it serves to carry us forward from the phenomenological examination of appearing consciousness as a pure consciousness, that is, as pure intentional consciousness over against a pure intended world, into the examination of appearing consciousness as self-consciousness. Its importance cannot be overestimated; for such a movement in the interpretation of the meaning and structure of consciousness is central to Hegel's philosophy. We are moved from an "epistemological" and intellectualistic consideration of consciousness as a "somewhat" which is different in kind from that which is its object to an examination of consciousness as a living, internal involvement in the world such that the "knower" cannot be treated as a mere spectator. Yet it has remained for the most part one of the most obscure passages in the *Phenomenology*, a state of affairs which is usually attributed to the inherent absurdity of the position outlined in this passage. A *verkehrte Welt* is, after all, a topsy-turvy, absurd world.[1]

I shall suggest in this chapter that this "inverted world" is exactly that: an absurd position. This is not to say that it is to be ignored or condemned as "fantastic," but rather that its importance and intelligibility lay in its very absurdity, in its *appearance* as an unintelligible inversion of what previously was taken to constitute the intelligibility of the world of appearance. More precisely, I shall suggest that this inverted world is a misunderstanding and perversion of the conclusion to which we should have been brought at this point in the *Phenomenology*. It is Hegel's intention, underscored by the conditional rather than indicative construction of this section, that we see this misunderstanding as a misunderstanding. When on the other hand the inversion is correctly understood, it brings to the phenomenological "we" undergoing the *Bildungsprozess* of the *Phenomenology of Spirit* the explicit realization that consciousness is not *merely* finite intentionality, but as such is infinite. *Consciousness is self-consciousness, consciousness limited by nothing but itself.*

I

Any attempt to interpret a single section of a philosophical work is beset with difficulties. In the case of Hegel, it verges on insanity. An interpretation of the "inverted world" cannot, therefore, simply stand on its own, but must include in its structure an interpretation of the whole work of which it is a part. The limits of a short essay preclude such an interpretation of the whole. Nevertheless, I shall attempt an adumbrated version of an interpretation which hopefully will suffice as a groundwork for an interpretation of the section of the *Phenomenology* at hand.

The "inverted world" stands near the end of the examination of understanding-consciousness and its "object," force. It completes the analysis of consciousness seen as intending consciousness over against the world. This examination of consciousness as consciousness, in turn, stands at the beginning of the examination of spirit which manifests itself concretely as world history and as the true substance of the individual. The latter constitute the ultimate subject matter of the *Phenomenology of Spirit*. What is important for us, then, is to understand what part the analysis of understanding-consciousness and force plays in the whole of the articulation and analysis of spirit.

The task of the *Phenomenology* is clearly laid out both in its "Preface" and in the "Introduction" to *The Science of Logic*. It is to display the becoming of science in general, a becoming which is a journey from immediate spirit or sensible, common sense consciousness to authentic knowledge or philosophical science. The former is for-itself spiritless: it is in-itself its own substance, but is not aware of itself as substance or of this substance as subject. The latter, authentic knowledge, is for itself its own pure concept. It has come to be at home with itself, having achieved access to being, to the primordial ground of what-is as such.[2] It is necessary to display this becoming primarily because ordinary or natural consciousness is a being in the world for which philosophy makes no sense. But equally this display is required because to be science, to be the absolute grasping of absolute knowledge, the true domain of this science must be existentially embraced, casting aside the bonds of natural consciousness.[3] Philosophical science (and this is the only science of which we here speak) is an absurdity, an unnatural inversion (*ein Verkehrtes*), from the vantage point of immediate spirit or natural consciousness. Thus, the whole task of the *Phenomenology of Spirit* is to display and clarify the intelligibility of what appears at first to be an absurdity.[4] Hegel's remarks here in the preface demonstrate his view of the necessity for a discussion of inversion and inverted worlds and offer a clue to its place in the work, namely at that point at which natural consciousness is forced first to give up its "natural" world. This is at the point where the analysis of consciousness becomes the analysis of self-consciousness.

The means by which this task is to be accomplished is equally indicated. We must undertake a journey of doubt and despair[5] upon which we pass through our own substance and world spirit as it has come to be.[6] In less figurative language, we are to place our own existence (*Dasein*) before ourselves, no longer simply to undergo it but now to become explicitly aware of what this undergoing entails in both structure and content. In short, we prepare ourselves for philosophical science by becoming explicitly aware of the content and structure of what we nesciently undergo in the many modes through and in which we maintain ourselves in and toward the world. In the process of this education we become aware of the mediation and negativity entailed in any mode of being in the world. This education, then, is a journey of doubt and despair, not because we find that all modes except absolute knowing are false modes *à fond*, but rather because actuality is revealed as not immediately accessible in any one mode of being in and toward the world.

One of the many modes is that of understanding-consciousness. Understanding is a mode in which man faces what-is, not as sensuous, material being, but as categories or *Gedankendinge*. These *Gedankendinge* are intended as constituting the unconditioned universal, the absolute ground (*Urgrund*) of what appears, and to constitute it such that the distinctions which are immediately manifest in the various modes of perception and action are unconditionally grounded and united within an "objective" realm of "ideas." Understanding is to be the self-grounding knowledge of the supersensible ground of the sensible and is therefore an attempt to hold the "really real" before a knowing intentional consciousness.

The phenomenological analysis of understanding-consciousness grows out of the failure of perceptual consciousness to ground itself.

Perception and the extended world which is its "object" show themselves as a revelation of a manifold of unities, spread out in experience within the matrix of perceiver-perceived. But there is also present in this manifold a unity which is an unconditioned universal, a spatiotemporal unity which "holds together" the manifold, extended "this-here-now." When common sense (or a philosophical position based on the postulates that perception is knowledge and that the essence of what-is is extension) attempts to explicate this its own unity, it falls either into a mere positing of this unity as a "given" or as axiomatic, or into a species of deception which equivocates on the relationship between the various aspects of the one and the many experienced within the perceptual world. Perception, to be sure, has successfully grasped the "this-here-now" which eluded immediate sense awareness, and therefore has truly taken the objects of its world. But such a taking or having of what-is falls short of its own demands for knowledge; for there remains a *je ne sais quoi* which marks perceptual knowledge and empirical philosophy as abstract rather than concrete knowledge. Understanding-consciousness purports to overcome this lacuna with its explicit recognition of and attendance to *Gedankendinge* as the constituting factors of ultimate reality.

Thus the purpose of the phenomenological analysis of understanding-consciousness is to ascertain whether and to what extent such a mode of being in and toward the world is capable of being absolute, unconditioned knowledge which comprehends the absolute, unconditioned "object." The course of the inquiry will reveal the negative conclusion that understanding fails in its task to be absolute knowledge because, like the whole of the mode of pure consciousness, it presupposes the subject-object dualism and the primacy of the given. The positive conclusion, manifested by a discussion of the inverted, absurd world, will be a dialectical recognition of the truth that consciousness is self-consciousness, that is, that consciousness is an involvement in and toward the world in which subject and object mutually implicate each other as a duality *which arises out of an original unity* rather than as a pregiven dualism which then has to be unified.

With this brief outline of the problematic and thematic out of which and for which the consideration of understanding arises, we can now turn to the question of the structure of the examination of this mode of consciousness which leads to the consideration of an inverted, absurd world.

II

In the process of the examination of understanding, we find a movement embracing two fundamental stances. The first is a stance or mode of knowing and being in which the essence of what-is is to be found in a supersensible realm transcendent to the knower and constituted as a kingdom of laws which remains static and unaffected by change. This arises simply as a demand of the dialectic of perceptual appearance. Appearance itself stands "between" the knower and the intelligible reality in various ways. Ultimately appearance is constituted as extension and motion and the *mundus intelligibilis* as non-sensuous force (*Kraft*). This is the first supersensible world and entails the denial of extension and of the perceptual world as a matrix of this-here-now as ultimate reality.[7]

Now, instead of vacillating between perceiver and perceived or between the various manifestations of oneness and manyness, we attempt to hold the totality of the process of this world "as at once inseparably united in regard to the process of grasping the truth."[8] We have as our phenomenological object a stance of intentional consciousness which holds before itself the metaphysical, non-sensuous "inner of things" constituted as force.[9] We are examining a mode of consciousness which attempts to comprehend what-is as such and in totality in its *a priori*, nonsensuous ground.

This first supersensible world, however, fails to be an unconditioned, but instead involves us with a distinction between inner and outer of "things," a distinction between appearance and reality which itself calls for a ground. On the one hand, appearance is constituted by the play or manifestation of forces and consequently is a realm of change. This is in fact the same world which perceptual consciousness holds before itself. On the other hand, reality is constituted by an objective realm of law, a kingdom of laws which ground appearance and the changing, but which is itself unaffected by change.

The question arises: Wherein lies the necessity of these laws in respect to the world of appearance? If we reexamine what such a consciousness is undergoing, we find that it is involved in a process of explanation (*Erklärung*), duplicating the world of appearance, but placing this world under the rubric of unchangeable law. This first supersensible world is "the immediate and unmediated raising of the perceptual world into the element or realm of universality; it has its necessary counterpart and antitype in the perceptual world which still retains for itself the principle of alteration and succession."[10]

In short, understanding in this stance does nothing but repeat the constitution of the manifold or the world of appearance under the form of universality and necessity. It involves itself in a tautological process, and "is an explanation [*Erklärung*] which not only clarifies nothing [*nichts erklärt*], but rather is so clear [*klar*] when it prepares to say something different from that already said, it says nothing and merely repeats again the same thing."[11] The "clearing" that is made is the same as that which is to be cleared. But there is here a positive result as well: "Through the process nothing new arises in reference to the state of affairs itself, *but the process is of importance only as a process of the understanding*."[12] With this realization consciousness "has crossed over from the inner as object to the other side within understanding."[13]

The second supersensible world and the second major stance for understanding-consciousness has arisen for us. The essence of what-is is now to be found in the understanding itself, constituted such that its laws embrace change and distinction within unchanging universality. Appearance itself is taken up into this realm, or better, has already been taken up into it, since the phenomenological analysis of perception yielded the truth of perception as an indissoluble matrix of perceiver-perceived.

The "collapse into the one side" now introduces the unconditioned universal, the inner for knowledge and being, as appearance. "The supersensible is the sensible and the perceptual posited as they are in truth; the truth of the sensible and perceptual is, however, to be appearance. The supersensible is therefore appearance as appearance."[14] A distinction is here made between appearance as *Schein*, as things appearing, and, on the other hand, appearance as appearance: *Erscheinung als Erscheinung*. Hegel has articulated this distinction and its importance for us here most clearly in the preface: "Appearance is the process of arising into being and passing away, a process which itself does not arise and does not pass away, but which is in-itself and constitutes the actuality and the process of the life of truth."[15] That is to say, appearances appearing constitute the positivity of appearance itself, which in turn is their ground as process itself. Appearance, the self-containment of coming into being and passing away, is the truth which we have named the unconditioned universal. Appearance as such, then, and the second supersensible world, are one and the same.

There now follows a rather closely packed discussion of the result of the movement to this second supersensible world. From the realization that explanation is nothing but the explanation of appearances whose ground lies in understanding itself (that is to say, in being in and toward the world of appearance in this mode of consciousness), we come to the realization that the realm of law (non-change, permanence through manyness) and the realm of change (appearances, manifold occurrences) are one and the same for consciousness. Yet at the same time the distinction is maintained between that which happens (the appearing of appearances) and the laws, rules, and principles as well as the ground for that which happens.

Understanding thus learns that it is a law for the sphere of appearance for distinctions to come about which are no distinctions. In other words, it learns that what is self-same or like-named is repelled from itself; and precisely therefore that the distinctions or differences are only such that they are in truth no distinctions and are transcended yet preserved in the whole: or that what is not self-same or what is unlike-named is absorbed.[16]

It is at this point that we reach a contradictory state of affairs and the discussion of the "inverted world" arises. The law of appearance itself seemingly destroys the sought-after unity and stability which is to constitute lawfulness. Laws as well as the concept of law itself embrace an identity in difference and a difference in identity.

III

Before proceeding now to a discussion of this "inverted world," I should like to lay some groundwork with a glance toward Kant. I suggest that in the movement from the first to the second supersensible world (and their respective consciousnesses) we have undergone, by means of a dialectical critique of the first supersensible world, a phenomenological counterpart to Kant's Copernican revolution and the proofs for its necessity which are contained in the Transcendental Deduction.[17] The law expressed by the understanding is to be the law of the inner of things, that is, of the ground and essence of appearances. Insofar as consciousness is concerned, the realm of appearance as it stands for perceptual consciousness cannot ground itself. But we have also found, in the discussion of the first supersensible world (which both Kant and Hegel ascribe to Leibniz), that a supersensible beyond cannot ground appearance either, but is only the *immediate* taking up of what occurs sensuously and perceptually into an intelligible, non-sensuous world. Yet either there must be an intelligible, unconditioned realm or we are abandoned to the ungrounded "knowledge" of the perceptual world. If the latter is the case, our inquiry is at an end and, while we certainly have "natural knowledge" and can and do operate with concepts of necessity and laws, we are nonetheless condemned to the philosophical skepticism of Hume.

Kant's "transcendental turn" had arisen from the same dilemma, and he proffered his alternative to the positions of Hume and Leibniz. With the Transcendental Deduction the laid the groundwork for the ultimate principle of understanding: "Every object stands under the necessary conditions of synthetic unity of the manifold of intuition in a possible experience."[18] The pure principles of understanding then articulate the meaning of this ultimate principle and establish Kant's version of the law of appearance.

> That there should be principles at all is entirely due to pure understanding. Not only is it the faculty of rules in respect to that which happens, but is itself the source of principles according to which everything that can be presented to us as an object must conform to rules.[19]

That is to say: through the principles of the understanding the forms of the manifold as manifold and the structure and very possibility of this manifold as objective experience (empirically real and transcendentally ideal) are brought together in such a way that both the stability and the instability of the world are grounded in understanding itself. Neither necessity nor contingency, thought nor intuition, spontaneity nor givenness are prior to the other; each without the other is abstract, and it is this that the analytic of principles rectifies. Thus the unity of the spatiotemporal world and the constituting syntheses of knowledge yield the law of appearance which we must now repeat:

> The highest principle of all synthetic judgments is therefore this: every object stands under the necessary conditions of synthetic unity of the manifold of intuition in a possible experience.[20]

Kant has now established the ground for both knower and known. But in spite of the fact that "we have now not merely explored the territory of pure understanding, and carefully surveyed every part of it, but have also measured its extent, and assigned to everything in it its rightful place,"[21] Kant finds it necessary to follow with a twofold discussion: namely that of "The Ground of the Distinction of All Objects in General into Phenomena and Noumena" and "The Amphiboly of Concepts of Reflection." A question arises here as to why this analysis occurs between the "Transcendental Analytic" and the "Transcendental Dialectic." That is, why, if we have so completely articulated and established the law or appearance, can we not simply proceed to expose the nature of the misuse of pure reason and explicitly attack previous metaphysics as a "logic of illusion?"

Kant's answer to this question is the following. He argues that although we have indeed "assigned everything its rightful place," and are now prepared to "explore the sea of illusion surrounding the island of truth,"[22] in order to help strengthen our conviction we might first give a summary statement of what has been explored and *demonstrate that we are under compulsion to accept its findings*. This demonstration can reveal to us "by what title we possess even this domain, and can consider ourselves as secured against all opposing claims."[23] This is accomplished, not by an actual summary of the Transcendental Analytic, but (1) by underscoring the distinction between phenomena and noumena and marking the difference between this distinction and that offered by Leibniz between the *mundus intelligibilis et mundus sensibilis* and (2) by discussing an amphiboly which arises when understanding does not make this distinction in its own employment.[24] In other words, the reason for the insertion of these two sections is *to articulate the difference between the intelligibility of the world in Kant's own doctrine of experience and that of the* mundus intelligibilis *of Leibniz.*

Kant argues here that if the critique contained in the Transcendental Dialectic and the exposition offered in the Transcendental Doctrine of Method is to be correctly uderstood, we must comprehend how and to what extent the critical system differs from conventional metaphysics: namely that there is in critical-transcendental philosophy no external distinction between worlds or between aspects of the same world. While "Leibniz erected an *intellectual system of the world*, or rather believed that he could obtain knowledge of the inner of things by comparing all objects merely with the understanding and with the sundered, formal concepts of its thought," leaving "sensibility . . . only a confused mode of representation . . . of the *thing in itself*,"[25] Kant himself has articulated an "intelligible world" in which "the condition of the objective employment of all our concepts of understanding is merely the mode of our sensible intuition, by which objects are given to us"[26] as a manifold. Previous metaphysics were involved in "a transcendental amphiboly, that is, a confounding of an object of pure understanding with appearance."[27]

What is clarified here is that the concept as concept of the understanding is indeed the same as the inner of things; but what *inner* means here is not the same as what it meant for Leibniz and his predecessors. The distinction between inner and outer, appearance and supersensible, is no longer a distinction insofar as knowledge is concerned *in its own appearing*. My object is no longer a supersensible, merely intelligible "beyond" which is a transcendent intended by intentional consciousness; rather, understanding itself is the totality of the ground of the object as object. Understanding is not subjective, but "embraces" the subjective-objective distinction. To be sure, Kant does not offer Hegel's move from consciousness to self-consciousness, but it can be argued that he laid the ground for his move.[28]

> In dealing with appearances I shall always be obliged to compare my
> concepts, in transcendental reflection, solely under the conditions of

sensibility; and accordingly space and time will not be determinations of things-in-themselves but of appearances. What the things-in-themselves may be I do not know, nor do I need to know, since a thing can never come before me except in appearance.[29]

Given the explicit articulation of this difference Kant can now proceed to his arguments concerning the nature of the mistaken transcendent application of understanding-consciousness. The radical turn from transcendence to immanence has been made the focal point, underscoring and justifying his claim for a "Copernican revolution."

IV

I have suggested that we can gain some comprehension of Hegel's treatment of understanding by turning our attention to Kant. In particular, I have suggested that the dialectical movement from the first supersensible world to the second can be seen as Hegel's version of Kant's rejection of both Leibniz and Hume and his articulation of his own transcendental position. I have now offered an interpretation of the meaning and substance of the two sections which separate the Doctrine of Principles from the Transcendental Dialectic: namely, that it was important for Kant to underscore and argue for the difference between his own "transcendental" position and that metaphysics which constituted previous attempts to offer the unconditioned. Finally, I have suggested that this "clarification" on the part of Kant lays the ground for the argument that consciousness is self-consciousness. My purpose for discussing Kant's phenomena-noumena distinction and his discussion of the amphiboly was to allow the following further suggestion: *Hegel has made the same clarification in his discussion of the inverted world that Kant made in these last sections.*

At the point at which we left the *Phenomenology* the contradictions produced by the law of appearance were introduced. If I may repeat this passage:

> Understanding thus learns that it is a law for the sphere of appearance for distinctions to come about which are no distinctions. In other words, it learns that what is self-same or like-named is repelled from itself; and precisely therefore that the distinctions or differences are only such that they are in truth no distinctions and are transcended yet preserved in the whole; or that what is not self-same or what is unlike-named is absorbed.[30]

A second law (and second supersensible world, since understanding now gives the law of the inner world) now arises in which what was "formerly characteristic of the sphere of appearance, and lay outside the inner world, [finds] its way into the region of the supersensible itself."[31] The *mundus intelligibilis et mundus sensibilis*, the unchanging and the changing, the one and the many, the identical and the different, are now of one and the same domain. Yet this domain is identified as the inner of things, the ground of appearance itself. And this world first *appears* as a second supersensible world, with a second law of appearance which is both absurd and the inversion of the first. The reason for the inversion is that all distinction is internal distinction: the one is many and the many are one.

It is at this point that a demand is made that "thoughtlessness bring both laws together and become aware of their opposition. To be sure the second is also a law or an inner, self-like being, but a self-likeness rather of unlikeness, a constancy of inconstancy."[32] That is to say: we cannot thoughtlessly continue to interpret this second supersensible world as the first was interpreted; they are generically different. *The discussion of the second world and its law as inverted and absurd is the articulation of this distinction*, demonstrating what *would* be the case *were* this second domain of intelligibility, containing contradiction, truly a second, supersensible world standing over against either appearance or the first supersensible world. The absurdity is brought to a halt when we are reminded of the actual nature of this second law of appearance: to wit, that the "distinctions between inner and outer, appearance and the supersensible, as two *actualities*, is no longer a distinction which is here present."[33]

The task to be accomplished is the same as Kant's discussed above. The difference is that it is carried out, not by directly insisting upon the difference as such, but by drawing absurd conclusions which follow if and when the distinction between the old metaphysics (the first supersensible) and the new position (the second supersensible) is not made. Without the distinction absurd contradictions follow and the "second supersensible world," in fact, only serves to make unintelligible the world of appearance which it purports to ground and make intelligible. Sour becomes sweet, North Pole becomes South Pole, and so on, because the changing and the unchanging are of the same domain and at the same time predominantly law, that is, unchanging necessity. Insofar as the changeable perceptual world *is* this second, supersensible, lawful world, instability, change, and difference are the same as stability, changelessness, and identity. Differences and therefore identities become meaningless. The law of this second supersensible domain, as here misinterpreted, is in fact lawlessness.

When, however, the distinction is made as it really now is—namely as internal distinction—the supersensible as supersensible disappears. It is not the case that sweet *is* sour, North Pole *is* South Pole, and so forth, but rather that they determine each other, necessarily standing in a self-defining relationship. This is the law of appearance, the dialectical constitution of internal definition and determination. Law is within the realm of appearance itself and thus changing appearance is unconditioned or self-conditioned.

> Thus the supersensible world, which is the inverted, absurd world, simultaneously overreaches the other supersensible and has the other in itself; the supersensible world is for itself inverted, that is, is the inverted of itself. It is itself and its opposed world within one unity. Only thus is difference as inner difference, or difference in reference to itself: it is *infinity*.[34]

The *Gedankendinge* are within experience itself, constituting the world as it is in experience, and in particular in explanation. Understanding-consciousness is therefore infinite because it is limited by nothing but itself. That is to say: since the distinction between the manifold of perception, extended and in flux, and the lawful, ordered understanding is itself only a distinction within consciousness itself, there is no supersensible and transcendent some-thing over against consciousness itself. As Kant had also said, but Hegel now gives its strongest interpretation: "What the things-in-themselves may be I do not know, nor do I need to know, since a thing can never come before me except in appearance."[35] For Hegel, the structure and meaning of the intending (*Meinen*) and the "this" (*Dieses*) with which the analysis of consciousness began is wholly within consciousness. To say now that consciousness is aware of itself as inverted is to say that it is aware of this immanent transcendence and thus can come, phenomenologically, to the awareness of being self-awareness, self-consciousness, *Selbst-bewußt-sein*.

Thus, the inverted, absurd world remains inverted and absurd from the point of view of a pure attitude of consciousness where the knower stands over against and transcendent to the objective appearance and the supersensible which grounds this appearance. But when the limits of consciousness are explicitly brought before us, when there is awareness of an inversion of this duality and a collapse of the knowing and the knowable into experience as such, then the absurdity evaporates. With this "evaporation of the absurdity" we have made that crucial step forward toward absolute knowledge and philosophical science: we have brought into radical question the common sense, natural attitude (which, as Hegel has already pointed out in the preface, holds science to be absurd and inverted) that objects and truth are *an sich* and other than consciousness.[36] We have laid the ground for the principle of idealism which is embraced by all true philosophy.[37]

V

At this point, of course, the parallel with Kant begins to disintegrate. And well it should; for if Kant had pursued the argument further, the history of German idealism would have been different. Hegel's argument to the end of this section on understanding rounds out the transition to the announcement that consciousness is self-consciousness. We cannot follow this out here.

I hope only to have thrown some light on a difficult and obscure but crucial passage in Hegel's *Phenomenology of Spirit*. I have suggested and tried to show that this obscurity lay in its absurdity and that this absurdity is the result of a dialectical argument in which, by means of a *reductio* argument based upon the suppression of a vital difference, Hegel shows two things. (1) a misinterpretation in which the immanence of difference in a transcendental philosophy is treated as a transcendence, and (2) the correct understanding of this position from which we are led to the principle of idealism. Both are demonstrated by arguing that the distinction between appearance and a supersensible unconditioned is a mistake. I have suggested that a backward glance at Kant's distinction between phenomena and noumena and the discussion of the amphibolies of reflection would help make Hegel's intention clear.

NOTES

1. Jean Hyppolite and Hans-Georg Gadamer must be excepted here. Both have made sustained attempts to make sense of this passage, the former in a reference to Christian doctrine and the latter in a reference to Plato and Aristotle. My own attempt here to comprehend this passage in reference to Kant and Leibniz does not "disagree" with either interpretation, but rather supplements these interpretations. See Jean Hyppolite, *Genèse et structure de la Phénoménologie de l'Esprit de Hegel* (Paris, 1946), I:131–36; Hans-Georg Gadamer, "Die verkehrte Welt," *Hegel-Studien*, Beiheft3 (1966): pp. 135–54.

2. PhG 26. Cf. *Logik*, Meiner ed. (1963), 29–31, 52–53.

3. PhG 561.

4. PhG 25–26.

5. PhG 67.

6. PhG 27–28.

7. Cf. Leibniz's "New System of Nature and of the Communication of Substances," sect. 2 and 3. That Hegel is here calling on Leibniz as an example of this stance of understanding could be shown by a careful analysis of the argument in the beginning of this section on extension and force. See also Hegel's remarks on Leibniz in *Geschichte der Philosophie*. As will be seen below, I am attempting to understand this chapter in the *Phenomenology* as a discussion between Kant and Leibniz.

8. PhG 106. Cf. Leibniz's discussion of perception and apperception in the *Monadology* and *New Essays on the Understanding*, bk. IV, chs. 1–4.

9. PhG 106.

10. PhG 121. Cf. Kant, *Kritik der reinen Vernunft* (KrV), A271, B327. There is here strong evidence for indicating Leibniz and Kant as paradigms for Hegel's analysis.

11. PhG 119–20.

12. PhG 120. Italics mine.

13. *Ibid.*

14. PhG 113.

15. PhG 39.

16. PhG 120.

17. It might be added here further that such a suggestion is possible as attested to by Hegel himself in the preface, namely that we are to retraverse the path already taken by world spirit in such a way that we make it our own. See PhG 26–28. Leibniz and Kant play a major role in the introductory chapters of the *Encyclopedia* where, in more didactic form, a preparation for the *Logic* is made. My suggestion that it is Leibniz and Kant that are here being "repossessed" can be established only by evidence which I hope will become manifest in the remainder of this paper.

18. KrV A158, B197.

19. KrV A158–59, B197–98.

20. KrV A158, B197.

21. KrV A235, B294.

22. KrV A235–36, B295.

23. KrV A236, B295.

24. In both sections it is Leibniz to whom Kant opposes himself.

25. KrV A270, B326.

26. KrV A286, B342

27. KrV A270, B326

28. See his discussion of self-consciousness at B139. Hegel, at any rate saw Kant in this way. See his *Geschichte der Philosophie*.

29. KrV A276–77, B332–33.

30. PhG 120.

31. *Ibid.*

32. PhG 121.

33. PhG 123. Italics mine.

34. PhG 124.

35. KrV A276–77, B332–33.

36. PhG 133.

37. *Logik*, I:145–46.

III

Self-Consciousness

7

Howard Adelman

Of Human Bondage

Labor, Bondage, and Freedom in the *Phenomenology*

> *The easiest thing of all is to pass judgements on what has a solid substantial content; it is more difficult to grasp it, and most of all difficult to do both together and produce the systematic exposition of it.*
>
> —Hegel, Phenomenology of Mind

It is easy to become absorbed in judging Hegel and his interpreters. It is harder to grasp the development of non-rational self-consciousness. This paper concentrates on "grasping" that development rather than the even harder task of providing a systematic exposition of it.[1] The later is facilitated by translating the language of religious myth into thought. In order to grasp that thought in the fullness of living, in the specific acts of individuals it is appropriate in dealing with the middle section of the *Phenomenology* to translate thought back into myth. This is particularly true since the non-rational development discussed is, for Hegel, archetypically Jewish and Hegel realized how little of that "Jewish" spirit could be rendered by an intellectual analysis.[2]

These three aspects: (1) classifying and judging, (2) grasping the material at hand and expressing it, and (3) producing a systematic exposition are also ways of differentiating the three different aspects of the spirit depicted in the most basic divisions of the *Phenomenology*: consciousness (naming, classifying, and subsuming under general laws), self-consciousness (which leaves the lifeless universals for the fullness of experience), and the third section of rational self-consciousness including reason, spirit, religion, and absolute knowledge. Since our subject matter falls within the middle section in the fullness of living experience and not its abstract corpse, it is appropriate to plunge directly in and dwell within the section.

But before we dive, note the lifeless corpse which is our diving board. What began as a world full of sensations of which consciousness was certain, a dynamic world of flux and change in which one sought stability, ends up in understanding as a stable system of mechanical forces in equilibrium in which, instead of certainty, everything is the opposite of what it appears and things are defined by what they lack. Life has been reduced to a system of forces in equilibrium within a self-moving world system. Life has become lifeless without movement and development.[3] Man has become master of the knowledge of nature, subsuming everything under his laws and categories, but he has not grasped life in the living of it for he has not faced the fact their life ends in the experience of death. The world is a projection of man's categories and laws and thereby his self has become other; man cannot find himself in that otherness. He cannot say who he is in what is projected. He is a lonely, empty "I." Adam in the Garden of Eden with all his powers of naming everything in nature is alone and needs a helpmate.

The Truth of Self-Certainty

Desire

To be conscious of himself as a self, there must be another self-consciousness. This is generally agreed. However, it is also generally believed that the other self-consciousness does not appear in Hegel until the "Lordship and Bondage" section. What Hegel says, however, is that an independent self-consciousness does not appear as a *fact* for self-consciousness until then. But it does appear before this as an object which is not yet recognized as an independent self-consciousness. A helpmate appears as *a physical* projection of myself, as "bone of my bone and flesh of my flesh." The other self-consciousness at this state is not an intellectual projection. It has the physical shape of an independent self-consciousness but it has not yet expressed the essential independent spirit. As Hegel says, "When for self-consciousness the distinction does not also have the shape of *being*, it is *not* self-consciousness" (PhM 219). Of course, everything is the opposite of what it appears, as has-been learned from consciousness, and this fantasy is in reality the fact that I am born as a projection of another body into the world and project this in my isolated dream world as if everything out there were merely a projection of my own body.

If the infant thinks he is the center of the world, he feels he is nothing, that he is merely an extension of the mother. But he doesn't yet recognize that feeling. The consciousness of that feeling as the first stage of self-consciousness, of consciousness as an inward state, emerges in an inverted way distorted by the prism of consciousness which experiences the world as a projection of self. The mother is an extension of self, but not merely any extension. The mother is a physical extension with whom one desires to be physically reunited.

The three moments of desire remain an abstraction. Desire has not yet become a vital experience. Adam is conscious of himself as the center of the universe. His consciousness tells him that he is not allowed to eat of the Tree of Knowledge of Good and Evil, that is, to eat of that which will destroy that consciousness of himself as the center of the world, and his consciousness as the essence of that self. Knowledge of his bodily self will destroy both the illusion that the self is the center of a self-moving cosmic system and the illusion that the essence of that system is simply thought. At this stage, however, Adam merely knows himself as one who names objects in nature and does not know his own body or govern its conduct. Adam is defined by what he lacks *in knowledge*, the knowledge of his body. Further, Adam is alone; he has no body in the world with whom he can be. It is a duality in which Adam has a body which he cannot know and has no body with whom he can be.

In the second moment, unknown to Adam's conscious experience, while Adam is sleeping another body appears which in consciousness must necessarily be a projection of his own body. Eve is made as a projection of Adam's flesh. Further, there is something in the ego, which is other than thought, which is rooted in the body, and which, when raised into thought, is interpreted as a projection of the body. One might say that, for Hegel, the superego is conscious thought when it addresses itself toward the body; responsibility for the body is reciprocally projected onto the thought of the world. The unconscious is in turn the body as a thing which makes other things; when raised into consciousness the responsibility for making things is projected onto the world as a unity of thought.

But if consciousness is this refusal to take responsibility for the body while at the same time insisting that the self is the center of a self-moving world, then it is imperative for consciousness that the self reincorporate that physical projection of itself as part of itself, even if again the responsibility for this instruction is also projected into the thought of the world as a whole. In the third moment of desire, God *tells* Adam and Eve that they shall be one flesh. What was actualized without reflection in the second moment is now posited as a unity in consciousness without actualization. What was a mere abstraction without realization becomes in the third moment a recognition of a duality, internal and external, with an imperative to achieve unity.

Life

Nevertheless, desire, as the first moment of learning the truth about oneself, is still an abstraction. It has not yet been experienced in life. In the first moment of self-recognition, the meaning that the self is not-other has been given substantive meaning, but only in thought. The meaning of the self as that which identifies objects has not yet been dealt with. Since that self already exists in consciousness, what it needs is actualization in life.

If desire is the inversion of consciousness of self as a non-other, a bare ego, so that one becomes conscious that one is ignorant of one's own identity at the same time as the other is experienced, although only in the abstract, life is the inversion of the other aspect of consciousness, the consciousness of the object which receives its identity from the I. In the inversion, the object becomes an object for experience rather than for consciousness and thereby loses *its* identity. The only unity is the unity of the self in contrast to desire in general in which a duality exists in the ego between one's ignorance of who the self is and one's self as a concrete other; from an infantile perspective, we feel the mother is our self as other while we are curious about our own body as if it were another of which we are ignorant.

In the first moment of life, the self is experienced as extension. Thus there is a negation in experience, as it appears to the self, of the negativity of the first moment as we reach out to make the other part of the self. There are objects independent of the self but the subject does not regard objects as having any continuity independent of the self. When an infant watches an adult come in one door and leave through another, it looks back to the first door to see that adult reappear. There is no extension except as a projection from the subject; there is no continuity in time except as a continuity within that spatial extension. The existence of *independent* objects in experience is not yet recognized.

> The essential element (*Wesen*) is infinitude as the supersession of all distinctions, the pure rotation on its own axis, itself at rest while being

absolutely restless infinitude, the very self-dependence in which the differences brought out in the process are all dissolved, the simple reality of time, which in this self-identity has the solid form and shape of space. (PhM 221)

This is, of course, life as the self-moving world system described at the end of consciousness, but the solar system is no longer an object for consciousness here; rather, I experience myself as a solar system. Life, which, in general, is the *experience* of unity of the self, in its first moment is a duality in the unity, for though independence of all objects is sublated in the existence of the self, the objects are still sublated as independent objects. The independence of objects is itself broken up in the second moment of life when there are no objects, as such, but only an infinitude of distinctions in experience. For the first moment is but an abstraction; its actualization in experience results in the immediate grabbing for the infinite number of objects presented among which no distinctions can be made. The mother's breast and the corner of the child's blanket are sucked as if they were the same.

In the third moment of life, the self posits itself by separating out objects as extensions of the self and then denying the separateness of the object by consuming it. In the process, stability is consumed. At the same time the self experiences objects as food for the body; the self is posited as a body to consume objects, as the continuity of the self in relationship to an undifferentiated continuity.

Life as living has become the process of defining oneself as the eater of fruit in a Garden of Eden in which no distinctions are made. There is no evaluation of what is good or bad for the body. Life, the reunion of the object world and the subject, is no longer a mere idea. Nor is it a natural instinct to guide us to the breast which provides sustenance. It has become universalized.

In life as spirit, *all* things are seen to exist for consumption by man's body. Man lives obsessed with the Tree of Life in the Garden of Eden. In the first moment of life, objects exist for man but are not yet in man. In the second moment, the existence of objects themselves is negated in favour of undifferentiated experience. In the final moment, the mother, Eve, is opposed to the self since she is not simply an object which exists only for consumption by the self; the individual, Adam, in turn exists, but only lives to feed his body. "Life as such is partly the means of spirit, and as such opposed to it; and partly it is the living individual, and life is its body."[4] Note that it is Eve who is the means of spirit. Adam has become his body, has become the solar system, and he ignores his body as other.

Desire in Life

The third stage following desire and life is the experience of desire in life. It is not an abstraction of which we learn. Nor is it experience without consciousness. It is desire directed toward the Consciousness for which we hunger, the lack of knowledge of our own bodies both in ourselves and as other.

In desire in general one is torn between the feeling of one's body projecting into the world as an object, and the consciousness of ignorance of one's body. In desire in life, an inversion takes place. The self wants to "make" an object in the world, that body which is already projected in the world as ourselves, while at the same time being an independent life, a self which exists in its own right, which experiences all the fruit of the Garden as objects to be consumed. The self wants both to consume that object and be consumed by it.

However, Eve wants to be one flesh with Adam, not just as an idea but as a concrete reality. It is Eve, the second moment in human creation, consciousness which maintains itself as an immediate unity, who gives substance and acts out her will through her feelings as a concrete individual. Adam is hung up on his own duality—as the one given dominion over all of nature but who has no dominion or command over his own body, as the one who knows that he shall be one flesh with Eve but who knows he must not eat of the Tree of Knowledge of Good and Evil. His thoughts and feelings are internally torn apart.

> Thus one sex is mind in its self-diremption into explicit personal self-subsistence and the knowledge and volition of free universality, that is, the self-consciousness of conceptual thought and the volition of the objective final end. The other sex is mind maintaining itself in unity as knowledge and volition of the substantive, but knowledge and volition in the form of concrete individuality and feeling. In relation to externality, the former is powerful and active, the latter passive and subjective.[5]

Adam and Eve ate of the Tree of Knowledge of Good and Evil, and Adam knew Eve and Eve knew Adam.

> And self-consciousness is thus only assured of itself through sublating this other, which is presented to self-consciousness as an independent life; self-consciousness is *desire*. Convinced of the nothingness of this other, it definitely affirms this nothingness to be for itself the truth of this other, negates the independent object, and thereby acquires the certainty of its own self, as *true* certainty, a certainty which it has become aware of in objective form.

In this state of satisfaction, however, it has experience of the independence of its object. Desire and the certainty of its self obtained in the gratification of desire, are conditioned by the object; for the certainty exists through cancelling this other; in order that this cancelling may be effected there must be this other. Self-consciousness is thus unable by its negative relation to the object to abolish it; because of that relation it rather produces it again, as well as the desire. (PhM 225)

But, of course, this whole section leading to desire in life is itself an abstraction *in feeling*, a fantasy which is not yet recognized as such by the self-conscious individual. Because these feelings are filtered through the prism of consciousness, where the child is the self-moving center of a world he controls, and since the child does not yet know who he himself is and cannot yet make distinctions between feelings, thoughts, and actions, he thinks that what he feels is real. In experience the other is an independent self-consciousness which is nor sublated into the self. They do not become one flesh. The child comes to the shocking recognition of a truth, that the other is an *independent* object.

But if the self only knows and recognizes itself as the center of the *whole* world excluding nothing, then it experiences frustration. The self finds new satisfaction only when it projects onto the other the desire to negate itself, to become one with the first self; this is seen as the essence of the other. It is Eve who seduces Adam, who negates herself as other, who is seduced by "force" of desire which Adam "*controls.*"

On account of the independence of the object, therefore, it can only attain satisfaction when this object itself effectually brings about negation within itself. The object must *per se* effect this negation of itself, for it is inherently (*an sich*) something negative, and must be for the other what it is. (PhM 225–26)

To ensure *satisfaction*, self-consciousness has had to come to recognize another self-consciousness who is not merely oneself objectified, while retaining the illusion that it is oneself "subjectified," as it were, oneself out there but as an independent source of action.

When God discovers that Adam and Eve have eaten of the fruit of the Tree of Knowledge of Good and Evil and have become conscious of their mortality, consciousness, which saw the world out there as the objectification of self, now must take account of the self as an actor. Man has set out on the path of history; thought operates through that which is acted out by passion. Emotions and thoughts are sundered so that feeling ignores thought and thought distorts feeling.

Lordship and Bondage

> *"Self-consciousness exists in itself and for itself, in that, and by the fact that it exists for another self-consciousness, that is to say that it is only by being acknowledged or "recognized."*
> *(PhM 229)*

This is how the section "Lordship and Bondage" begins. And Hegel warns us immediately after making this assertion that in the distinction of the moments of self-consciousness, these moments must be taken as *not* distinguished. They must always be understood and accepted in their *opposite* sense. To interpret the above to mean that a self-consciousness is truly other takes Hegel's meaning in the introduction not in its *opposite* sense but in its literal sense. The latter self-consciousness is not a self-consciousness which also is said to exist in and for itself.

Hegel is *not* simply talking about two self-conscious beings in relationship to one another. He is talking about the *nature* of self-consciousness itself where double meaning is rooted, it is the nature of self-consciousness to see double meaning even when reflecting on its own nature. Self-consciousness at this stage is still narcissistic, seeing the other as the extension of self at the same time as it experiences the self as other than itself, and, as such, wanting the same reunion with itself as it wants with the other.

Seeking recognition by another self-consciousness is *acting out* the process of self-recognition. How does narcissistic thought, which considers the world as an extension of itself, come to recognize the self, which experiences the world as alien and other?

Self-Consciousness Doubled

To understand this question we must clarify the sense in which one self-consciousness appears to itself as another self-consciousness outside itself. Hegel says that self-consciousness has "outered itself," has come outside itself when self-consciousness has before it another self-consciousness. To see this simply as a depiction of two selves in relationship makes no sense of how one self-consciousness is outered. At the end of "Truth of self-certainty" we were left with a self which had not abandoned thought, which had taken the other self as an extension of its own body; feeling, however, reveals the self as other, as a subject with an independent source of will. The development is now carried forward but on the level of the immediacy of feeling, and, since we are dealing with the phenomenology of experience, we are concerned with feelings as they first appear in development. And when they first appear they are still accompanied by thought. The rest of the middle section of the *Phenomenology* has as one of its themes the increasing effort of feeling to jettison thought.

The first moment (of Lordship and Bondage) is concerned with sexual feelings as an experience (not the experience of sex), and the first moment of that moment is concerned with the thoughts that accompany these sexual feelings. In the negative moment (particularly if masculine imagery is utilized) the self experiences itself as split. The self is *not* itself but is lost in the other. On the other hand, the self is not other, since that self was projected into the other. This moment of negation is itself negated; in the immediacy of feeling, the self experiences itself as a unity (since the self experiences itself by sublating the other, an other which is itself, and therefore the self sublates itself). Sublating itself and sublating the other are then one and the same experience. But, upon reflection on this experience, the self recognizes itself as only one with itself by cancelling itself as other and cancelling being in the other. The other goes free; the pair split.

The second moment of the development of sexual feeling negates the consciousness, negates thought, and considers the relationship strictly as an *act*. As consciousness, one self-consciousness is active and the other merely passive, continuing the subject-object dichotomy. But as an action, it is mutual. Therefore, the consciousness of the first moment is reflected in the mutual immediate feelings of the partners in the second moment.

As a result, in the third moment, when recognition comes, one begins with a double consciousness both in relationship to oneself and to the other. One is conscious of restrictions at the same time as one has risked oneself by projection outward toward the other. One also assumes that, in one sense, one is the other; but one is also not the other. No wonder lovers are all mixed up. Unity can only be experienced by repetition, by cancelling itself as existing for itself, which is identical with experiencing one's self-existence only in the self-existence of the other. Upon reflection, "they recognize themselves as mutually recognizing one another" (PhM 231). "And the eyes of them both were opened, and they knew that they were naked" (Genesis 3:7). Each recognizes his own body and the body of the other; each also recognizes that the other recognizes both his own body and the body of the other.

The Battle

In the first moment of "Lordship and Bondage," the sexual appetite, the desire to be one flesh, is acted out in fantasy, and thereby experienced, but only in consciousness as the enactment of the living desire. In the second moment of "Lordship and Bondage," two bodies, self-conscious of themselves as bodies, experience the body itself *in actuality*.

Each individual now experiences himself as the unity of his own body.

> Self-consciousness is primarily simple existence for self, self-identity by exclusion of every other from itself. It takes its essential nature and absolute object to be Ego; and in this immediacy, in this bare fact of its self-existence, it is individual. (PhM 231)

The second moment of the "Lordship and Bondage" section is the antithesis of two individuals as bodies and not spirits; for each the other is only an unessential object. Each is *not* thought and *not* other. Each tries to be only his or her body. This is the battle.

Each experiences itself as a body and not as other. Then each acts out that experience. For Eve, in the immediate unity of feeling, Adam becomes unessential, although she is servant to him and he is her master. Her essence is the experience of her body as a mode of reproduction. In the bringing forth of children, she suffers in pain and *labor*. Eve is enslaved within her body; she is an object over which her husband has mastery; she is a slave to natural reproduction. Both are experienced as one and the same. Sex is experienced merely as reproduction. Adam at this time *names* her Eve for she no longer lives in herself but is the mother of all that lives.

Adam experiences his body in his labor on the soil and becomes a slave to that soil. Eve experiences her body in the labor to bring forth future life and, therefore, as the means for life's continuity. But Adam experiences the unity of his body as a duality. For the body not only performs, but Adam recognizes that it will cease performing. Adam becomes conscious that he will die.

In this, each achieves an *abstraction* of existence, Eve as the mother of all living, and Adam as the bare struggle for survival, *knowing* that he will die. This is the first moment of the struggle (which is the second moment in the development of "Lordship and Bondage"). Lordship has appeared in Adam's mastery over Eve, and in death's mastery over Adam, and bondage is experienced in Eve's labor pains and Adam's labor and toil, but neither lordship nor bondage have been brought into reflection, into *self*-consciousness.

In the second moment of the struggle the battle is acted out. For Adam and Eve experience their submission only in consciousness which has nor yet become actualized (the precondition of its becoming self-conscious).

And it is acted out by that which embodies the first moment as a unity of feeling. Their unity is embodied in their children—Cain and Abel.

Adam and Eve are conscious of their individuality as a body, but their bodies are fettered to one another, and to life, Eve as the mother of all living and Adam as the one who earns a living and knows he will die. The acting out of the independence of the body is left to their children.

Cain, as the first born, is akin to his father and tills the ground. Abel, as the second born, is akin to his mother and is a keeper of sheep just as his mother tended her babes. They express their independence from the objects produced by their labor, by the "pure negation of its objective form"—Cain sacrifices some of his produce and Abel one of his lambs. Action entailed the death of the objects of their own labor, thereby risking that which is their own life objectified. They are prepared to alienate the products of their labor, for their bodies as laboring devices are still felt to be alien. The immediacy of feeling follows this split in consciousness. Only the animal offering receives recognition as a sacrifice. Cain becomes *angry* and *crestfallen*, for he had *not* been *recognized* as an individual independent of the objects of his labor. Cain kills Abel.

In the second moment of the struggle (Cain and Abel) a *second* action is involved in the attempt to bring to recognition the body as individual and independent of that on which it labors. In the action of the other, Abel, the shepherd, gains recognition from God (the world as thought), and not Cain. Yet, in fact, shepherding becomes obsolete and is succeeded by agriculture. Only one economic form of life can survive as primary; one must die. Though each economic form of life aspires to primacy and the death of the other, the one that dies both projects responsibility for its death onto the subsequent form and views the succeeding form as living everafter, but as empty meaningless existence. There is thus a double action and death involved, the death of one's body in an objective form as the sacrifice of the products of one's labor, and the death of a competing form of economic life.

> The process of bringing all this out involves a twofold action—action on the part of the other and action on the part of itself. Insofar as it is the other's action, each aims at the destruction and death of the other. But in this there is implicated also the second kind of action, self-activity; for the former implies that it risks its own life. (PhM 232)

The life and death struggle involved is *not* one between two warriors but between two embodiments of different forms of economic life. The struggle is to gain recognition for their bodily independence. In so doing, they "risk life," their own life objectified into otherness through labor, though this has not yet come into consciousness. They literally "stake their life"; one sacrifices his agricultural produce and the other an animal. Each takes the risk in order to be recognized as unfettered to themselves as other.

> The individual who has not staked his life, may, no doubt, be recognized as a person; but he has not attained the truth of this recognition as an independent self-consciousness. In the same way each must aim at the death of the other, as it risks its own life thereby. (PhM 233)

In the second moment of the struggle (which is the second moment in the development of "Lordship and Bondage"), Cain, who fails to gain recognition for his independence, slays Abel. The truth of the independence of the self as a body is cancelled. "Death is the natural 'negation' of consciousness, negation without independence, which thus remains without the requisite significance of actual recognition" (PhM 233).

The lack of independence is itself negated as a fact; the negation is negated. Abel is dead. Cain is evicted from the soil and loses his source of sustenance. He becomes a fugitive and wanderer, one of the living dead who cannot even be put to death. In the second moment of the struggle, unity and independence of the self is realized but as a "lifeless existence," "merely existent and not opposed."

And the meaning must be taken in its opposite sense, for it is Abel's feeling projected into Cain. This is how consciousness translates the feelings engendered by the experience of being suckled as an infant and shepherded about. The self projects itself as the shepherd, but in order to grow into independence the shepherd must be killed off. But, of course, there is a double inversion. Since in consciousness the other is a projection of the self, the thought of killing the other is also projected onto otherness. It is the other that wants to snuff out the life of the self. The mother becomes the monster of the crib who wants to devour her own children.

But after destroying itself in fantasy, the self feels itself as not only alone but cut off from its own body as well. For feeling projected into fantasy through the prism of consciousness, which insists that the self exist in and for itself, reveals again that in the struggle between feeling and thought thought is victorious and cuts feeling off from the body and the reality of death. If the first stage in the acceptance of death is total denial (Eve), the second stage involves denying that consciousness will die while accepting the death of the body. But *I* don't die; the real I lives on. But in being cut off from the body and feelings, its living is lifeless.

Independence and Dependence of Self-Consciousness

In the first moment of "Lordship and Bondage," the moment of immediate self-consciousness, the self becomes conscious of itself as having substantial bodily independence. In the experience of the second moment, the consciousness of oneself as an independent body seems to dissolve, for survival seems to depend on thought in general. In the third moment the negation of the negation is inverted, and self-consciousness is posited as existing not only for itself but for another, which at this stage is regarded as a thing. The third moment entails the inversion of lifeless existence in the recognition that life is essential to existence and is not to be sacrificed.

In the first moment of this third moment, self-consciousness for itself and for another exists as a duality without unity, but for the first time they exist *in consciousness* as master or lord, thought in general, which is independent, and the essential nature of which is to be for itself, and as bondsman, as a body which is dependent for its *existence* on another and whose essence is life for another.

Noah is an artisan, unlike Cain, the agriculturalist, or Abel the shepherd.[6] He designs a boat. Noah is the descendant of Seth, the third-born son of Adam and Eve, through whom the third moment could be realized. And it is only when Seth's son is born that man began "to call upon the name of the Lord" (Genesis IV:26). The lordship of God emerges only at this stage. God is the only one who is independent and whose *essential* nature is to be for itself. Noah is dependent for his existence on the soil which the Lord hath cursed. Further, the essence of Noah's existence is to live for another; his name means comforter, from the Hebrew *na ben*, "to comfort."

Now God as the Lord exists for itself in *consciousness* but not in actuality. Actualization is mediated through another, man as a body—or Noah in particular—whose existence is bound up with the existence of all things. For it is upon Noah's shoulders that his own salvation and the salvation of everything else depends. Further, Noah's existence is to live for an other—God; Noah walks with God. Feeling for another is ultimately in the service of thought which is for itself.

In the description following the introduction of the master or lord and the bondsman, what is depicted is not primarily the relationship of the master to the slave but of the master (a) to self-existence, to existing in and for himself, and (b) to the fact that the realization of self-existence requires that the master's existence be experienced through that which is other, through an existence which is an object in the world. As a projection in the physical world, the master is related to his self-existence only through mediation in a twofold sense. The master has a relationship to an independent self-existing being only because he controls the life of the bondsman and has power over that self-existence; that is, it is the self-existence as other over which the master has control. Second, the master has a relationship to his self-existence only because the bondsman obeys the master, believing that what he too wants, independent self-existence, is possessed by the master. The body feeling as filtered through the prism of consciousness comes to think that only the mind or thought possesses independence.

If the master is related to his self-existence mediately in a twofold sense, in the bondsman (*a*) seen as an existence independent of the master, and (*b*) seen as cognizing the master as possessing an independent self-existence, there is also a twofold sense in which the master is related to himself as other, as a thing in the world. Insofar as it is through the bondsman's work on the things in the world that the master relates to otherness, his immediate relationship to the external world is mediated by the bondsman. Insofar as he alone has the pure enjoyment of the thing, he is immediately related to self-existence as other, and mediation is negated. The master, since he dosen't work on the world, is indifferent to the independence of the object.

The relationship must now be considered from the point of view of the bondsman. Noah does not work in forced labor for the Lord. He freely gives himself in the service of the Lord. Slaves and bondsmen have a common characteristic in that both give service without pay, but only the servant of the Lord gives it freely. As opposed to forced slavery, the bondsman is also one who is bound, in the sense that he gives security for the other. Noah is the archetypal bondsman freely giving himself in the service of the Lord doing all that God commands.[7] "We have thus here the moment of recognition, viz. that the other consciousness cancels itself as self-existent, and, *ipso facto*, itself does what the first does to it" (PhM 236). In a second sense of bondsman, Noah is the one who builds the ark and provides security for *all* that is other. But giving security to the world is properly God's role.

> In the same way we have the other moment, that this action on the part of the second is the action proper of the first; for what is done by the bondsman is properly an action on the part of the master. The latter exists only for himself, that is his essential nature; he is the negative power without qualification, a power to which the thing is naught. And he is thus the absolutely essential act in the situation, while the bondsman is not so, he is an unessential activity. But for recognition proper

there is needed the moment that what the master does to the other he should also do to himself, and what the bondsman does to himself, he should do to the other also. On that account a form of recognition has arisen that is one sided and unequal. (PhM 236)

What does the Lord do to the other that he should also do to himself? He commands the other who is good but does not command himself. He destroys that which he considers evil but does not yet self-destruct. What does the bondsman do to himself that he should do to the other as well? He gives himself freely but he should get others (including his Lord) to give freely without *quid pro quo*'s. The bondsman must bind the other to give security for himself.

God as master is again Lord and master of all he surveys and returns to Noah the dominion that he took away from Adam, a dominion over the birds and the beasts and all life on earth; but Noah does not have dominion over man. Noah does not appear to have the power to do to others what he does to himself. God as Lord and Master does have the power to do to himself what he does to others. The Lord commands himself neither to curse the ground anymore nor to smite everything living, and in so doing voluntarily begins to self-destruct, to destroy his own power.

Noah not only lacks the power to do to others what he does to himself, he is also, even though made in the image of God, not a very good representation of the Lord. This is true in a double sense. For considered from the "thought-side," from the point of view of consciousness, the bondsman is totally dependent on the Lord to tell him what to do. He is dependent on the Lord for his consciousness as practical reason, as conscience. The truth of God is found only in an unessential consciousness which needs to reveal itself as an independent self-consciousness.

The external, however, is only the acting out of the internal, and the inner side of Noah as the archetypal bondsman is the reflection of the external bondage to the Lord and must be unveiled. God as Master and Lord is taken to be an independent consciousness, but this is an illusion of thought, for the Lord depends on man for his realization. The mind depends on the body for expression. But if this is an illusion of feeling reflected in thought, the truth exists in feeling itself. For Noah felt the fear of death, of total destruction, fear for the entire being of the world, and as such knew in his gut that death was the sovereign master, that the Lord and Master was absolute negativity. The illusory thought which takes the Lord to be the embodiment of all independent self-consciousness and the feeling that the Lord is absolute negativity come together *in* Noah, in his work. For, in work, self-sacrifice rather than sacrifice of the other, he cancels out his dependence and attachment to natural existence, thereby establishing himself as an independent consciousness, and at the same time negates that existence through work. But they have not yet come together in his self-consciousness.

Thus, labor makes man free but man has still to come to the recognition of this. For it is the worker who experiences natural existence and his body as essential and does not suffer the illusion of consciousness desiring to be freed from external existence. Instead of the world existing as objects which are projections of the self, the self projects itself into the world with its labor to create a world of objects. The desire to negate the object and assert the independence of the self becomes the negation of the self as consciousnessness detached from feelings to create and fabricate a world of independent objects. In giving form to objects, the freedom is made substantive and given permanence. It is when the self works in voluntary bondage in labor that the self first externalizes itself as an objectified individual self-consciousness. And it must be work impelled by the fear of death, not simply of the death of one's own self, for that would only mean working in the anxiety of loss of contingent existence, but in the fear of the death of existence in general. Further, that work must express itself not merely in contingent forms but in forms which are permanent and therefore resist death, forms in which the sacrifice of the body expresses the spirit in a true objective immortality.

NOTES

Epigraph of section I is from *Phenomenology of Mind*, trans. J. B. Baillie (London, New York, 1931), 69–70. Hereinafter cited as PhM.

1. Cf. Howard Adelman, "Labour and Freedom" in *Hegel's Dialectic of Desire and Recognition: Texts and Commentary*, ed. John O'Neill (Albany: State University of New York Press, 1996), pp. 171–86.

2. Cf. H. S. Harris, *Hegel's Development: Toward the Sunlight 1770–1781* (Oxford: Clarendon Press, 1972), 278.

3. Piaget has noted in child development as well that "the elimination of life leads to a mechanization of force." *The Child's Conception of Physical Causality* (Totowa, N.J.: Littlefield, Adams), 246.

4. Hegel's *Science of Logic*, vol. II (London, 1929), 403.

5. Hegel's *Philosophy of Right*, trans. T. M. Knox (Oxford, 1942), 114.

6. Cf. Harris, *Hegel's Development*, 273–79, for a clear discussion of Hegel's earlier explicit references to Noah.

7. Lawrence of Arabia captured the essence of the experience of giving oneself freely into bondage in service of an idea.

> Willy-nilly it [the ideal] became a faith. We had sold ourselves into its slavery, manacled ourselves together in its chain-gang, bowed ourselves to serve its holiness with all our good and ill content. The mentality of ordinary human slaves is terrible—they have lost the world—and we had surrendered, not body alone, but soul to the overmastering greed of victory. By our own act we were drained of mortality, of volition, of responsibility, like dead leaves in the wind.

T. E. Lawrence, *Seven Pillars of Wisdom* (New York: Doubleday, 1926, 1962), 28.

8

George Armstrong Kelly

Notes on Hegel's "Lordship and Bondage"

What is living in Hegel? The mid-twentieth century is prone to answer: his sense of the collective, his notion of a politically structured people as the unit of historical meaning, his grounding of right in intersubjective purpose, his penetrating explorations of psychological and sociological conflict. Both admirers and hostile critics fasten on these categories, because, as issues of debate, they are not only living in Hegel, but living in our time.

Thus Hegel's philosophy did not, as it were, merely paint "gray on gray." Not surprisingly, however, contemporary interest in this "ultimate philosophy" is due chiefly to the suggestive expansion of its insights, rather than to any desire for systematic reconstruction. In a discretionary way, Hegelian problems and patterns have gained a new lease in the fields of social and religious thought and among those for whom classical political theory is not a dead exercise. One might say that Hegel remains vital because he continues to raise polemical questions. When a giant structure of human speculation is superseded—a fate which some feel, wrongly I think, that Hegel tacitly acknowledged for his own philosophy—but survives *in membris disjectis*, anthologies tend to be compiled for partisan purposes. Karl Löwith reminds us that this was the destiny of the fragile Hegelian balance in the hands of the philosopher's immediate disciples.[1] The last generation has seen a renewal of this *Kulturkampf*, but now on the far side of total war, Marxism, and religious crisis. The opposition of "What did Hegel mean?" and "What does Hegel mean for us?" is posed and reposed. I personally feel—as a historian of ideas—that some intellectual mischief is caused by the failure to raise the two questions in mutual rapport.

An important case in point would be the characteristic modern treatment of Hegel's famous scenario of "Lordship and Bondage," the account of liberation through work which so deeply affected the young Karl Marx in his 1844 manuscripts.[2] This tableau is most fully developed in the *Phänomenologie des Geistes* of 1807, but is also covered more tersely in the *Propädeutik* (1808–16) and the *Enzyklopädie der philosophischen Wissenschaften* (editions 1817, 1827, 1830, and 1840–45), essayed in rudimentary form in both series of Jena lectures on the philosophy of spirit (1803–4 and 1805–6), alluded to in the *Grundlinien der Philosophie des Rechts* (1821), and, according to some interpreters, foreshadowed in the discussion of Hebrew religion in the so-called early theological essays.[3] As a form of consciousness, lordship and bondage was continuously indispensable to Hegel's dialectical deduction of the formation of subjective mind and had occupied him from his earliest attempts to construct a system. Since there can be no quarrel about the centrality of this philosophical "moment," it becomes essential to grasp its precise meaning and content.

A full *précis* of this much admired passage will be dispensed with here. I have no particular dispute with, for example, Hyppolite's treatment, as far as it goes.[4] However, many modern readings—inspired by Kojève's artful exegesis in his *Introduction à la lecture de Hegel*[5]—tend to distort lordship and bondage in the total Hegelian structure. Though every student of Hegel is deeply enriched by Kojève, this experience is not without its dangers. In the present case, the difficulty seems to me chiefly twofold: the subjectivity of the scenario is largely ignored, and the master-slave relationship is made an unqualified device for clarifying the progress of human history. The one tendency leads to a unilaterally "social" interpretation of the *Phenomenology*, particularly the section on "*Selbstbewußtsein*";[6] the other easily gathers in anachronistic overtones of the Marxian class struggle.

The regulative idea of lordship and bondage runs like a golden thread through much of Kojève's analysis. His general introduction stresses the point: "The slave alone is able to transcend the world as it is (in thrall to the master) and not perish. The slave alone is able to transform the world that forms him and fixes him in bondage, and to create a world of his own making where he will be free."[7] In a later passage, Kojève asserts that he has given an "anthropological" reading of the *Phenomenology*, and that

Hegel intends a "metaphysical" dimension as well, the two currents being necessarily syncretized in the final chapter on absolute knowledge.[8] A footnote here seems to clarify Kojève's resolve to treat equally of the interior and exterior relations of the consciousness (as was surely Hegel's purpose) under the anthropological notion. But, in fact, although both exterior (political) and interior (psychological) consequences are acknowledged, he sees the master-slave relationship purely as an external confrontation. For Kojève this *motif* persists in various ascending forms until the Hegelian end of time. Thus: Work and Struggle = Freedom = Time = History = Transience = Nothing = Man. In more humble language, the future belongs to the once-terrorized producer, progressively liberated by the spiritualized quality of his own labor, not to the seemingly omnipotent consumer, who treats both the servant and his product as mere dead things. Effectively, the slave releases history from nature, and it is the slave's satisfaction that will bring history to a close. Thus, while retaining the Hegelian primacy of ideas over things, Kojève, like Marx, tends to regard forms of servitude as epiphenomena of the relations of production.

As students of the career of philosophical ideas know, Kojève's lectures on Hegel have had an enormous impact. To take a recent example, the British scholar John Plamenatz, in his two volumes on European political thought, has, with full acknowledgment, provided a Kojève-Hyppolite reading in his chapter on the *Phenomenology*. He casts lordship and bondage entirely at the interpersonal level, and his conclusion reflects the familiar line of argument: "the future is with the slave. It is his destiny to create the community in which everyone accords recognition to everyone else, the community in which spirit attains its end and achieves satisfaction."[9] But where did Hegel ever say this? Plamenatz's criticisms of Hegel (via the French commentaries) are grounded in the same analysis. How, he inquires, can one explore the possibilities of community in terms of one master and one slave, as Hegel appears to do? How can one refuse to see that manual toil is not the exclusively dignified form of labor; is there not also managerial toil?[10] Although Hegel is sometimes no easier to vindicate than he is to understand, this type of question will not seem so pressing if lordship and bondage is given a more balanced, more "phenomenological" interpretation. By "phenomenological" I mean that Hegel's ego must be seen here as an ideal type, collective only in the sense of exemplary, subject to a genetic onslaught of existential moods (*Gestalten*), each of which will be cancelled but also retained as a moment of eternal significance.

I am not proposing some legerdemain that will take the "social" out of Hegel. Clearly he argues that the true ethical life (*Sittlichkeit*) of man is "concrete" and "objective," grounded in collective experience according to the immanent harmonies of a rational community where liberty and order coalesce. "The experience of what spirit," according to the *Phenomenology*, is "the ego that is 'we,' a plurality of ego, and 'we' that is a single ego."[11] Although the pages that introduce the discussion of self-consciousness announce this principle, collective mind does not become a reality until reason (*Vernunft*) achieves intersubjectivity and passes into spirit (*Geist*).[12] Lordship and bondage is a "moment" of *Selbstbewußtsein* that foreshadows society and has explicit historical ramifications. However, the view that the scenario represents a purely social phenomenon is one-sided and needs correction.

What I am about to argue is that lordship and bondage is properly seen from three angles that are equally valid and interpenetrable. One of these angles is necessarily the social, of which Kojève has given such a dazzling reading. Another regards the shifting pattern of psychological domination and servitude within the individual ego. The third then becomes a fusion of the other two processes: the interior consequences wrought by the external confrontation of the self and the other, the other and the self, which has commenced in the struggle for recognition (*Kampf des Anerkennens*). On the overtly social plane there are, at a given point in history, slaves and masters. In the interior of consciousness, each man possesses faculties of slavery and mastery in his own regard that he struggles to bring into harmony; the question arises whenever the will encounters a resistant "otherness" that goes beyond mere physical opposition to its activity. In turn, the social and personal oppositions are mediated by the fact that man has the capacity to enslave others and be enslaved by them. Because of the omnipresence of spirit, the continuum is not broken by the distinction between world and self.

In brief, man remits the tensions of his being upon the world of fellow beings and is himself changed in the process. This relationship should be stressed since it furnishes the bridge between psychology and history. Let it be added here also that Hegel's psychology is moral, not analytical: this is why experience continually causes it to shift its ground and why it is, in the deepest sense, historical, a psychology of development, a *Bildungsroman*.

On the one hand, Hegel is showing that mere political mastery or subjection cannot inaugurate the long adventure of history and freedom unless faculties of the subjective mind, necessarily present in all men, create the possibility and condition the result. On the other hand, it is clear that none of this is conceivable in a solipsistic universe. "*Es ist ein Selbstbewußtsein für ein Selbstbewußtsein*"[13] is the abrupt and dramatic prelude to the struggle for recognition out of which mastery and slavery will arise. The possibility of philosophy, morality, and right depends on the postulation of a second finite ego and, ultimately, on the assumption of a plurality of egos. Much in the same way that Fichte produces a second ego in order to ground his doctrine of natural right,[14] Hegel posits society at the dawn of self-consciousness for a still more profound purpose: the analysis of the broken ego striving to restore itself. But if the self and the other are, to speak bluntly, men, they also dwell within each man. They are original principles of the ego, awakened to combat by the appearance of another ego in which they are reduplicated, and thenceforward transformed by history. Without this shock, there would be no history, only desire (*Begierde*), man's link with the animal world, and the unproductive and repetitive cycles of biological nature.

Hegel is, to be sure, much less explicit about the internal aspects of lordship and bondage than he is about the interpersonal and historical dimensions. The most casual reading of the *Phenomenology* and other texts makes clear that Hegel intends the analysis of relations among men and a reflection on the rise of historical communities through conquest. But my elucidation in no way denies this obvious fact.

Certain other contingencies obscure the reading I am suggesting. In the first place, the "social" implications of the tableau are even more emphatic in the Jena sketches, to which a scholar will wisely refer if he wants to understand the evolution of Hegel's thought. In many passages of this early and experimental "philosophy of the spirit" Hegel is deeply concerned with the concrete formation of society, the nature of work and its elevation to spiritual substantiality, and the creation of a scheme of dialectical development. Different sequences of unfolding and different terminologies—some derivative (mainly Schellingian) and some original—are essayed in these lectures. What will later have discrete places in the treatment of subjective and objective spirit—desire, labor, love, family, *Volksgeist*, and so on—are seen struggling for systematic deployment. And admittedly in the "recognition" scenario the emphasis is on the concrete and social. In the 1803–4 lectures, the deduction of the family precedes the struggle for recognition, indicating that Hegel is here concerned with anthropohistorical development rather than the presentation of "facts of consciousness."[15] But in the 1805–6 lectures, in a passage corresponding to what Hegel will later call "anthropology" (the forms of the human soul before the awakening of consciousness), the other is evoked as a Schellingian "dark principle": "The other [is] evil, a being-in-itself, the subterranean principle, the thing which knows what lies in daylight and witnesses how it purposively [brings about] its own decline, or is in such active opposition that, on the contrary, it substitutes negativity for its own being, for its own self-preservation."[16] The *Encyclopedia* will clarify for us how the preconscious being is bifurcated even before it gains awareness of its own selfhood, and how lordship and bondage will display an analogous autoalienation at the higher conscious level.

A second factor which might mislead is the characteristic Hegelian insistence, against Kant, that the properties of the mind are integral and not the derivations of separate faculties or principles, like theoretical and practical reason (cognition and will),[17] or like the Fichtean dichotomy of finite ego and pure ego resolved only by an *ought*.[18] Of course, this is the "standpoint of reason," the goal of the Hegelian philosophy. But one obviously cannot jump from here to the conclusion that lower forms of consciousness apprehend themselves monistically. In fact, the opposite is true, whether the other is felt as impulse, as a hostile stranger, or as a transcendent God. Since Hegelian philosophy is process, even though its apotheosis is unity, it has mostly to do with the logical, genetic, or historical oppositions that have come about in the progress of the spirit.

G. R. G. Mure in his excellent study of Hegel's *Logic*, has called particular attention to the dualistic tread of "higher" and "lower" principles in Hegel and has doubted their effective resolution.[19] I share this feeling. One cannot of course gather in the depths of the *Phenomenology* by looking at it through post-Enlightenment spectacles alone. In the background always and at the surface much of the time Hegel is wrestling with the problems of Greek antiquity and seeking both to overcome and to eternalize them in an alien climate. The Platonic parallel between the struggles in the state and the struggles in the soul is never far distant. I will permit myself the liberty of saying that the great figures of Aristotle, Plato, and Sophocles bestride, respectively, the sections on *Bewußtsein*, *Selbstbewußtsein*, and *Geist*. The problem of lordship and bondage is essentially Platonic in foundation, because the primal cleavage in both the history of society and the history of the ego is at stake. The two primordial egos in the struggle that will lead to mastery and slavery are also locked in battle with themselves.

A third deterrent to a balanced reading of lordship and bondage is the temptation to treat the *Phenomenology* as an enigmatic philosophy of history. Sometimes this is done so that its "progressive" implications can be favorably compared with the conclusions of Hegel's later lectures. But the schematic arrangement of Hegel's finished system, given by the *Encyclopedia* should warn us away from this adventure: history belongs to objective spirit and phenomenology to subjective, even though the experience of objective spirit is a fact of consciousness. Although the *Phenomenology* must necessarily utilize history to illustrate forms of consciousness, it is not to be inferred that the two genealogies are integrally parallel. Hegel's conscious avoidance of proper names is the best clue to his design.

This point can become confused since Hegel in both instances is dealing with temporal process and since historical time is the condition for human thought. The evolution of mind runs along the same time scale as the fate of nations. Thus, philosophical analyses that are conceptually independent must be joined in communicative discourse and must plunder the same treasury of empirical materials. Mind as *Geist* is the integrative operator, just as temporality makes the operation possible. But the *Phenomenology* is not primarily a disquisition on political philosophy; it is the record of the spirit's efforts to attain peace in the knowledge that there is nothing outside itself.

One may question, as I do, the prestidigitatory feats of Hegel in keeping these two lines of philosophical inquiry discrete and correlative at the same time. There is more than *animus* in Haym's famous complaint that "*etwas Anderes ist die Geschichte, und etwas Anderes ist die Psychologie.*"[20] In fact, we all do read the *Phenomenology* as historical and political commentary quite legitimately, since it is concerned with the external relations of mind amid a plurality of egos. But the transformations of mind within itself are equally important. Both destinies, according to Hegel, will be identical in the last analysis.

Finally, if we hypothesize that mastery and slavery contains both developments, we shall not be greatly disturbed by Hegel's leaps between the social and the solitary in his deduction of *Selbstbewußtsein*, as he delineates the forms of "otherness" (*Anderssein*) in stoicism, skepticism, and the "unhappy consciousness."

The clue to the whole matter is, I think, given in the following passage from the *Phenomenology*:

> The conception of this its [of self-consciousness] unity in its duplication, of infinitude realizing itself in self-consciousness, has many sides to it and encloses within it elements of varied significance. Thus its moments must on the one hand be strictly kept apart in detailed distinctiveness, and, on the other, in this distinction must, at the same time, also be taken as not distinguished, or must always be accepted and understood in their opposite sense.[21]

If Hegel means what I think, he is encouraging us to draw the plenitude of associations from the Self-Other confrontation. Thus although Hegel can be only imperfectly conveyed by static formulas: Self = Other; Self = Self + Other; Self (Other) <> Other (Self); and Self + Other in Self = Self +

Other in Other, and so on. I regard the final formulation as most complete. In the following discussion, Hegel expands this idea:

> This process of self-consciousness in relation to another self-consciousness has ... been represented as the action of one alone. But this action on the part of the one has itself the double significance of being at once its own action and the action of that other as well. ... The action has then a *double entente* not only in the sense that it is an act done to itself as well as to the other, but also in the sense that the act *simpliciter* is the act of the one as well as of the other regardless of their distinction.[22]

A corresponding passage from the *Propädeutik*, being simpler (prepared for the instruction of pre-university students), has perhaps greater clarity:

> A self-consciousness which is for another self-consciousness is not only for it as a pure object, but *as its other self*. The ego is not an abstract universality which, as such, contains no distinction or determination. The ego being thus object for the ego, it is for it, in this view, like the same ego which it itself is. In the other, it intuits itself.[23]

One difficulty in following Hegel lies in the fact that he often tries to convey the experience of the consciousness both from its own point of view and from the high ground of the philosopher. Another is in the perpetual passage from inner to outer which is the motor of the consciousness' experience that will be dissolved in ultimate knowledge. But the awakening of opposed faculties in the ego proposed by the fact of society is the principle on which self-consciousness would seem to depend. First, the spiritualization of desire will create the basis for selfhood. Then recognition will be demanded for its authentication. The faculties of the ego must contend in order to act, since a single comprehensive faculty, in however many egos, would render them either totally static or totally destructive (which amounts to the same thing).

Correspondingly, the pattern unfolds in social life. The mutual awareness of two persons, their reciprocal need for recognition, their struggle to obtain it, and the final subjection of the one to the other—these stages idealize the primitive sources of human history, seen this time from the angle of society but still rooted in the problem of the developing consciousness. Plamenatz should have no difficulty with the fact that there are only two protagonists. For, from this angle, when the struggle concludes in mastery and slavery, the master will perceive but a single slave-machine that does his bidding and the slave but a single source of oppression. Hegel's formulation here establishes the mediating link between consciousness and society, serving somewhat the same purpose as the analogous device of the *homo economicus*. Indeed, it is to the famous tale of Robinson and Friday that Hegel refers us in the *Propädeutik*.[24]

Just as the Hegelian analysis demands the postulation of two egos (one man as spirit would be God, or would possess no spirit),[25] so at each of its ascending stages the consciousness must apprehend itself as two estranged principles until its goal is reached. This is most clearly seen in the *Encyclopedia*, where we can delve behind the stirrings of subjective mind or "phenomenology" proper into "anthropology," which has as its focus the notion of the "natural soul." Here spirit has emerged out of nature but not yet awakened to consciousness. In this relatively little-studied part of Hegel's work, the soul corresponds roughly to what psychoanalysis will later label the "preconscious"; here are contained many perceptive insights into neurotic anxiety, undoubtedly based on the philosopher's personal experience and the tragic deterioration of his friend Hölderlin.[26]

In *Encyclopedia*, §§318–19 (1817),[27] Hegel makes it clear that the soul is life on the margin of consciousness, that it primitively feels its bifurcation, its antagonism with otherness. It is subjectively anchored to its future self-conscious career and yet mired in the blind universality of nature. On the other hand (§323),[28] the opposition is productive and necessary. Here is the primary internal opposition in the genesis of the human condition.

Consciousness arises when the natural soul, by setting its instinct against nature, can affirm itself as an ego (§327).[29] The relationship to otherness is now a dichotomy between self and natural soul (§329).[30] Self-consciousness, on the other hand, will require the affirmation by the ego of its own identity, taking the immediate form of desire (§§344–46).[31] Here the "*Selbstbewußtsein*" section of the *Phenomenology* properly commences, with the inadequacy of repetitive desire, the application of desire to another ego, the struggle for recognition, and the dialectical resolution in lordship and bondage. The internal struggle which expressed itself first in the natural soul, then in the consciousness, has not been resolved or abandoned. Rather, personality can emerge only because of its need for self-recognition, a consequence of ceasing to direct desire merely upon the objects of sheer natural appetition (§351).[32] A higher, resistant otherness has been encountered; it expresses itself externally as a second ego, internally as primitive reason or self-mastery, and reciprocally as the capacity for will and freedom. But, like the original assertion of self-consciousness through the ego's becoming aware of itself, this new stage of being must in turn be authenticated. This will happen in the struggle for recognition, where appetition and spiritual self-regard contend. They can no more destroy each other than can the social antagonists: the career of man is the proof. Thus mastery and slavery ensue, both within the ego and, as Hegel makes abundantly clear (§355), in the history of society.[33]

The parallel explanations are necessary. For, taken from a purely social point of view, there is no good reason why two identical egos, locked in combat, should not struggle to a static stalemate. To say that Hegel's resolution is good dialectics answers nothing. Instead we should discern the idea that natural inequalities arise in consequence of internal imbalances, not through the absence or presence of pure principles in single individuals. I shall return to this point in connection with theories of history.

"Where did Hegel's ideas on the relation of lord and servant originate?" inquires Dirk J. Struik in his edition of Marx's 1844 manuscripts.[34] This interesting question has a considerable bearing on the subject at hand. We can help to clarify the significance of Hegel's passage by referring to the intellectual milieu in which his philosophy took shape.

It is important to understand that this is still a world where normative psychology is seen as dominating the forms of society. Despite primitive stirrings of a social science, one still asks the question "What is a man?" in order to understand the social order man has created. The strife within man's nature is a commonplace; as Montesquieu put it: "man ... is composed of the two substances, each of which, in its flux and reflux, imposes and suffers domination [empire]."[35] On the psychological plane we should recall Hume's striking dictum that "reason is the slave of the passions" and the consequent attempts of German idealism to restore the primacy of reason by enlarging its content. We should notice also that the reason-passion relationship gathers in a metaphorical content, which is precisely that of mastery and servitude. In essence, Kant's philosophy, grounded in the ideal of personal autonomy, is a theorization both of how the individual can acquire mastery over his content-directed interests through the exercise of morality or "pure practical reason" and of the conditions by which a legitimate social order can make this possible. The famous aphorism "man needs a master"[36] carries both public and private overtones. In fact, according to Kant, man *ought* to be his own master. But, in the words of Richard Kroner, "because he ought to master himself, man is not really free but divided against himself, half-free and half-slave. At best, he is his own slave, enslaved by his master, reason."[37]

Behind this urgent question, which burst out of speculation and into history with the coming of the French Revolution, lies the dual preoccupation of Rousseau: his assertion that there is no "right of conquest" in society, and his profound research into the warring sides of the human personality which the shock of social relations has induced. "A man thinks he is master of others, whereas he is actually more of a slave than they," writes Rousseau in *Contrat social* (I.i);[38] in his eighth *Lettre de la Montagne* he repeats: "He who is a master cannot be free."[39] As we know from the second discourse, *Émile*, and the autobiographical writings, a struggle of the human faculties underlies the social dilemma.[40]

Not only for Hegel, but for his great predecessors and his age as a whole, mastery and slavery was a multi-dimensional problem—and a paradoxical one. The paradox is this. Antiquity, which had sanctioned the institution of slavery, had nevertheless intensely researched the dilemma of man's enslavement of himself. The Enlightenment, by contrast, progressively attacked social bondage as abusive and immoral, while scratching only at the surface of its spiritual dimensions. And yet the Enlightenment, taken generally, viewed the social order from individualistic premises. Descartes had founded the ego and, from the time of Hobbes on, the empirical school had constructed a mechanistic psychology which purported to explain the nature of society by way of its members. The revival of antiquity, in substance as well as form, by Rousseau on the one hand and the German idealists on the other—even when the battle of ancients and moderns had been seemingly won by the latter—is in part a response to this perplexity. The Enlightenment had furnished a sense of progress; it had not restored the conviction of harmony. Both the mind and the social order were implicated. If society was in process, then the mind could not be explored statically as the rationalists had taught. With Hegel there is the recognition that both elements of explanation are necessary and that they must be mediated. This becomes possible only when mind is seen to have a history of its own. The tensions that propel social history are correspondingly translated to the development of the ego (a procedure in which the works of Rousseau and Kant are way stations). Here the profundities of Greek thought find their place and their role. The problem of mastery and slavery lies along this axis. For Hegel, however, the resolution can be only tragic or unbearably smug (one takes one's pick) because history, the carrier of *Geist* and freedom, is also the perfect warrant of man's fate.

A passage from Fichte's *Contributions to the Rectification of Public Opinion Concerning the French Revolution* (1793) further illustrates the currency of the lordship-bondage metaphor. Here the youthful Fichte employs the figure of the warring personality in a coinage borrowed from the French historian Marmontel.[41] Reason (i.e., the principle of the Revolution) rhetorizes against conventional self-interest (hereditary privilege):

> From our birth, he [reason] invited us to a long and terrible duel where liberty and slavery were at stake. If you are stronger, he told us, I will be

your slave. I will be a very useful servant for you; but will always be a restless servant, and as soon as there is some slack in my yoke, I will defeat my master and conqueror. And once I throw you down, I will insult you, dishonor you, trample you under. Since you can be of no use to me, I will profit by my right of conquest to seek your total destruction.[42]

We do not know whether Hegel read Fichte's incendiary tract against the German Burkeans, but it seems likely that he did, since it was, to say the least, hot copy among young intellectuals. In any case, the contemporary associations of lordship and bondage are not to be understood without the illustrations from across the Rhine.

However, when Hegel came to formulate his mature system, he was, as we know, not an unqualified admirer of the French Revolution or of the autocracy of abstract reason with its "bad infinity." The new "right of conquest" had no more appeal than the old. Like all stages of human struggle, the oppositions of the ego had to be reconciled, not concluded in a new unilateral domination.[43] In the primitive scenario of the *Phenomenology* the resolution of lordship and bondage is in "stoicism," and it is probably no accident that there are resemblances between this form of consciousness and Kant's transcendental idealism, the ideal posed by the French Revolution.[44] Though I do not want to draw parallels out of context in Hegel's system, it may not be amiss to call attention to the climate of ideas in which his thoughts about lordship and bondage developed. Undoubtedly the split-personality view of contemporary European philosophy counts for much.

Another brief excursion into German intellectual history can provide a different illustration. When Hegel was developing the rudiments of the master-slave dialectic, he was associated, though not uncritically, with the philosophical ideas of his younger but more precocious friend Schelling. By the time he published the *Phenomenology* in 1807, he had struck his own highly original posture. In the meantime, the split between the philosophies of Schelling and Fichte (which Hegel himself attempted to mediate in his *Differenz des Fichte'schen und Schelling'schen Systems* of 1801) had become irreconcilable and had led to vituperative exchange. The same half-decade saw the rise of the Romantic movement, under the aegis of Novalis and the Schlegels, and the efflorescence of interest in philosophy of history, which had been heralded by Lessing and Herder in the previous century.

Schelling's philosophy, which began from the premise of the identity of the absolute, required a theory of history by which the descent of the absolute into the plurality of creation and the return of created things to the absolute could be explained. The key to this movement was to be discovered in the principle of human freedom. Schelling traced the idea grandiosely and abstractly in the *System des transzendentalen Idealismus* (1800), in the *Vorlesungen über die Methode des akademischen Studiums* (1802), and in some later writings. In reply to Schelling and, more especially, the Romantics, Fichte entered the lists with his public lectures, the *Grundzüge des gegenwärtigen Zeitalters*, delivered in 1804 and published in 1806. Fichte's scheme of philosophical history, built on purely deductive foundations and in some ways indebted to Kant, challenged his opponents on a variety of issues that do not concern this essay.[45] What is of interest is a fundamental assumption that Fichte and Schelling shared and which could scarcely have failed to draw Hegel's attention.[46]

The speculative histories of Fichte and Schelling were phased and developmental; both in effect sought to deduce the pattern whereby original man, innocent but instinctual in nature, mounted to his goal of rationality in freedom, or achieved what Schelling described as a "second nature." In order to do this, the principle of reason had to be explained at its origin. Schelling was the first to postulate that at the dawn of humanity there had been creatures of pure instinctual reason and simple barbarians. Fichte borrowed this explanation (which is not without its obvious indebtedness to mythology): "out of nothing, nothing can arise; and thus unreason can never become reason. Hence, in one point of its existence at least, the human race must have been purely reasonable in its primitive form, without either constraint or freedom."[47] However, this "*Normalvolk*" had no history; for them, one day was like the next, and "religion alone adorned their existence."[48] It was thus necessary to postulate a race of barbarians. The union of the two races was what made history and society possible. In the "*Normalvolk*" there was no tension to activate the spring of progress; on the other hand, they embodied the principle of human destiny. The savages, on their part, lacked this principle utterly, but they contained the force of historical propulsion. Consequently, after an interlude when Cartesian paradise and Darwinian brutishness presumably coexisted, society took form with the dispersion of the races, the subjection of the savages to "*Normalvolk*" kings, intermarriage, and the tortuous ascent of miscegenated man to freedom. Apparently, Asia was the historical location for this event; the Old Testament was a "myth of the normal people."[49]

The parallel between this historical hypothesis of Schelling and Fichte and Hegel's lordship and bondage is much more than coincidental. Either the idea was in the air, or there was direct cross-fertilization from Schelling. However, Hegel does not accept this solution.[50] He nowhere endorses any speculation concerning original "rational" men and original "savage" men. Reason is not a natural principle in his anthropology, any more than it is for Rousseau. In Hegel, as we have seen, the appearance of self and self-awareness will succeed the primitive efforts of the preconscious soul to wrest its being from nature. Consequently, although a social event, mastery and slavery will result necessarily from struggles of awareness and recognition within the ego and not from the absolute opposition of racial principles embodied in discrete, historical individuals. Hegel is defending a doctrine of original equality which is curiously and dangerously denied by Fichte.[51]

Thus I believe that the passage in the *Phenomenology* and in other works can be justifiably interpreted, *inter alia*, as an attempt to explain inequality at the foundation of society without resorting to the dual-nature hypothesis. The alternative is to explain it from within the ego. Here, precisely, is the "phenomenological" dimension that we lack in Kojève.

Let us attempt to restore this dimension. The "master" who emerges from the struggle for recognition can be identified with the primitive notion of control or decision. Hegel tells us specifically that this act of victory is the birth of freedom (*Encyclopedia*, §355).[52] Man is the only creature which, under certain "non-natural" pressures, is willing to stake its life. This is, so to speak, the first creative act of the human personality: the slave will invent history, but only after the master has made humanity possible. The master's solution, however, is without issue. Hegel has already (in *Encyclopedia*, §323 and elsewhere)[53] pointed out the danger of imbalance between higher and lower principles. One cannot abandon nature, nor should one drown himself in it. In the master-slave situation, there is neither education, nor progress, nor history—only the repetitive fulfilment of the master's wants.

In this impasse, the master-principle—courage, decisiveness, idealism—is seen to pass into its opposite, becoming, as Kojève points out,[54] a new form of *Begierde*. Higher development can come only from the slave-principle, which has itself been transformed through the experience of subjection and terror into the activities of labor, conservation, and memory: the conditions of human advance. Here are manifold historical overtones which it is not difficult to exploit. I think, though, that two points must be argued against Kojève: (1) the slave-master dialectic is appropriate only to a certain stage of consciousness for Hegel, even though it is still cancelled and retained (*aufgehoben*); succeeding history will be a record of more subtle and comprehensive forms of estrangement; (2) both principles are equally vital in the progress of the spirit toward its destiny: if Marx developed one side of this dichotomy, Nietzsche seized upon the other.

This is decisively clarified by Hegel himself in the *Philosophy of Right*:

The position of the free will, with which right and the science of right begin, is already in advance of the false position at which man, as a natural entity and only the concept implicit, is for that reason capable of being enslaved. This false, *comparatively primitive* [my italics], phenomenon of slavery is one which befalls mind when mind is only at the level of consciousness. The dialectic of the concept and of the purely immediate consciousness of freedom brings about at that point the fight for recognition and the relationship of master and slave.[55]

In a corresponding Addition, Hegel adds: "if a man is a slave, his own will is responsible for his slavery, just as it is its will which is responsible if a people is subjugated. Hence the wrong of slavery lies at the door not simply of enslavers or conquerors but of the slaves and the conquered themselves."[56]

This should be sufficient to show that "the future belongs to the slave" is an unwarranted and romanticized refraction of Hegel's thought. Slavery cannot found the right of political communities any more than it can account for the free personality. But it is necessary for history as well as for the development of mind: both right and free personality appear in history and do not repose above it. In the *Encyclopedia* of 1845 (§435, Addition) Hegel describes the subjection of the servant as "a necessary moment in the education (*Bildung*) of every man."[57] "No man," he adds, "can, without this will-breaking discipline, become free and worthy to command." As for nations, "bondage and tyranny are necessary things in the history of peoples." This could be adapted to the Marxian view of the proletariat. But as we recall from the *Phenomenology*, the dialectical outcome is not a transhistorical class struggle but the temporary refuge of stoicism, where emperor and slave see the world with the same eyes. Even though "only through the slave's becoming free can the master be completely free,"[58] the Hegelian future will unfold out of their joint endeavors. They can no more be incessantly opposed than can the organic faculties of the ego itself.

My conclusion is foreshadowed. Although inner and outer, higher and lower, reason and passion are undoubtedly intended to be dissolved at the ultimate Hegelian apex, the internality of the ego cannot be disregarded in understanding the development of *Selbstbewußtsein*. The social reading, taken alone, can encourage sharp distortions. Nor is history for Hegel simply a record of the millenial efforts of the slave to overthrow the master, just as the development of spirit is not the continuous attempt of a single faculty to triumph in the ego. In both cases, the aspiration is harmony and self-knowing identity, the sense of "being at home" (*zuhause sein*) so frequently evoked in Hegel, the assimilation of freedom and fate. The failure to read Hegel's texts (especially those leading up to "lordship and bondage") with close attention to levels of discourse can beget social hypotheses that do not square with Hegel's known conclusions. We can further profit by exploring the philosophical and historical issues of Hegel's own time, instead of superimposing those of an industrial epoch which he only narrowly, if shrewdly, glimpsed. That the character of the rational Hegelian society is much more Platonic than it is Marxian is already clear from the Jena lectures which antedate the *Phenomenology*.[59] Kojève's original exegesis of Hegelian themes is a profound work for our own times. But from the standpoint of historical understanding a "Marxian" *Phenomenology* does not make very good sense. This view ignores the depth and passion of Hegel's Greek attachments; it ignores, too, the complicated range of his struggle with the Kantian split vision. These are the two combatants wrestling on the soil of Christian Europe for the possession of Hegel's own ego.[60] It is to be questioned whether he resolved this struggle of the old world and the new in his higher *Sittlichkeit* of the nation-state and in his "Christianity without pictures."

NOTES

1. See Karl Löwith, *From Hegel to Nietzsche*, trans. David E. Green (New York, 1964), 65–135.

2. Karl Marx, *The Economic and Philosophical Manuscripts of 1844*, ed. Dirk J. Struik (New York, 1964), esp. 170–93 ("Critique of the Hegelian Dialectic and Philosophy as a Whole"). Marx writes (p. 177): "The outstanding achievement of Hegel's *Phenomenology* and of its final outcome . . . is thus first that Hegel conceives the self-creation of man as a process, conceives objectification as loss of the object, as alienation and as transcendence of this alienation; that he thus grasps the essence of *labor* and comprehends objective man . . . as the outcome of man's *own labor*." It would be appropriate here to mention that, like Hegel, I assign no particular significance of nuance to the synonyms "slavery," "bondage," and "servitude." I have also chosen to avoid taxing the patience of the reader with unnecessary dialectical vocabulary.

3. Cf. Jean Hyppolite, *Genèse et structure de la Phénoménologie de l'Esprit de Hegel* (Paris, 1946), I:166; and T. M. Knox (trans.), *Hegel's Early Theological Writings* (Chicago, 1948), intro. by R. Kröner, p. 13.

4. Hyppolite, I:161–71.

5. This remarkable study is a compilation of Alexandre Kojève's courses on the *Phenomenology* (ed. Raymond Queneau [Paris, 1947]), given at the Sorbonne

in the years 1933–39, which exerted a powerful influence on Sartre and French Hegelianism in general.

6. "Awareness" is conceivably a better translation of *Bewußtsein* than is "consciousness," but there are problems with each. I have reluctantly chosen the traditional term because in Hegel's language *Bewußtsein* is an agent as well as a condition or capacity.

7. Kojève, *Introduction*, 34.

8. Ibid., 308–9 and 308n. A comment on the perspective of the *Phenomenology* imposes itself at this point. I tend to agree with those who hold that the sequence and development of the *Phenomenology* are *sui generis* and related to the intention of the work, as juxtaposed, especially, to the *Encyclopedia*. Thus these differences alone do not allow us to conclude that Hegel changed his philosophical viewpoint between 1807 and 1817. In cases of disagreement between a "philosophy of mind" and a "phenomenology of mind'" caution of interpretation is advised. This reservation does not seem applicable to the case of "lordship and bondage."

9. John Plamenatz, *Man and Society*, 2 vols. (New York–San Francisco, 1963), II:155.

10. Ibid., II:190–92. However, neither Kojève nor, especially, Karl Marx would ask Plamenatz's second question. Cf. Marx, *Manuscripts of 1844*, 177: "The only labor which Hegel knows and recognizes is *abstractly mental labor.*"

11. G. W. F. Hegel, *Phänomenologie des Geistes* (PhG), ed J. Hoffmeister (Hamburg, 1952), 140; *Phenomenology of Mind* (PhM), trans. J. Baillie (London, 1927), 227. I have furnished Baillie's translation throughout.

12. PhG 313 ff.; PhM 455ff.

13. Hegel, *Enzyklopädie und Schriften aus der Heidelberger Zeit, Sämtliche Werke*, VI, ed. H. Glockner (Stuttgart, 1927), §352, p. 253.

14. J. G. Fichte, *Grundlage des Naturrechts, Sämmelte Werke*, III (Berlin, 1845), 30ff.; *The Science of Right*, trans. A. E. Kroeger (Philadelphia, 1869), 48ff.

15. Hegel, *Jenenser Realphilosophie*, I, ed. J. Hoffmeister (Leipzig, 1932), 223ff.

16. Ibid., I:200.

17. See for example, Hegel, *Philosophy of Right*, trans. and ed. T. M. Knox (Oxford, 1945), Addition to §4, p. 227; the paragraph citation will enable the reader to locate the passage readily in the German edition.

18. *Enzyklopädie*, in Glockner, VI, §332, p. 246.

19. G. R. G. Mure, *A Study of Hegel's Logic* (Oxford, 1950), 367–68.

20. Rudolf Haym, *Hegel und seine Zeit* (orig. ed. 1857; photostatic reproduction, Hildesheim, 1962), 241.

21. PhG 141; PhM, 229.

22. PhG 142; PhM 230.

23. *Philosophische Propädeutik*, Glockner, III, §30, p. 108.

24. Ibid., §35, p. 110.

25. Cf. PhM 226–27: "A self-consciousness has before it a self-consciousness. Only so and only then *is* it self-consciousness in actual fact; for here first of all it comes to have the unity of itself in its otherness."

26. See Johannes Hoffmeister, *Hölderlin und Hegel in Frankfurt* (Tübingen, 1931).

27. Glockner, VI, pp. 236–37.

28. Ibid., p. 242.

29. Ibid., p. 244.

30. Ibid., p. 245.

31. Ibid., pp. 251–52.

32. Glockner, VI, p. 253.

33. Ibid., p. 255.

34. Marx, *Manuscripts of 1844*, 232.

35. Charles, Baron de Montesquieu et de la Brède, *Pensées, Oeuvres complètes* (Paris, 1949), I:1015.

36. Immanuel Kant, "Idea for a Universal History from a Cosmopolitan Point of View," *Kant on History*, ed. L. W. Beck (New York, 1963), 17.

37. Kroner, introduction to Knox (trans.), *Hegel's Early Theological Writings*, 11.

38. C. E. Vaughan, *The Political Writings of Jean-Jacques Rousseau*, 2 vols. (New York, 1962), II:23.

39. Ibid., II:234.

40. *Émile ou l'Éducation* (Paris, 1961), Bk. 404: "O my friend, my protector, my master . . . prevent me from being the slave of my passions, and force me to be my own master by obeying my reason and not my senses."

41. Jean-François Marmontel, contributor to the *Encyclopédie*, replaced Duclos in 1771 as historiographer of France. He was elected to the *Conseil des*

Anciens in 1797, but was retired from public life by the *coup d'état* of 18 Fructidor. Fichte cites one of his poems.

42. J. G. Fichte, *Beiträge zur Berichtigung der Urteile des Publikums über die Französische Revolution*, ed. Stecker (Leipzig, 1922), 51.

43. See *Enzyklopädie*, Glockner, VI, §393, pp. 276–78.

44. See especially *Philosophy of Right*, introduction, §§19–21, pp. 28–30. Cf. Hegel's early (1797) attack on Kant (re: *Religion within the Limits of Mere Reason*, IV, 2, §3) in his essay "Der Geist des Christentums und sein Schicksal," *Hegels theologische Jugendschriften*, ed. Herman Nohl (Tübingen, 1907), 265–66: "between the Tungusian Shaman, the European prelate governing Church and State, or the Mogul or Puritan, and the man obedient to the commandment of duty, [the Kantian], the distinction is not to be made that the one enslaves himself while the other is free, but that the one is dominated from without, while the other, having his master within, is by that token his own slave.

45. For a full clarification of these issues, see Xavier Léon, *Fichte et son temps*, 3 vols. (Paris, 12924), II:394–463.

46. We know that Hegel read Fichte's excursus on philosophical history and thought little of it, as well as of the "popular philosophy" in which Fichte indulged; see Hegel's letter to Schelling, dated Jena, January 3, 1807, no. 82, *Briefe von und an Hegel*, ed. J. Hoffmeister (Hamburg, 1952), I:131. His knowledge of the *Grundzüge* was probably too late to affect the *Phenomenology*; however, he was perfectly familiar with all Schelling's ideas antecedent to 1804 because of their close collaboration at Jena.

47. J. G. Fichte, *Grundzüge des gegenwärtigen Zeitalters*, lecture IX (Hamburg, 1956), 138; *Characteristics of the Present Age, The Popular Works of Johann Gottlieb Fichte*, trans. William Smith (London, 1884), II:147. See also F. W. J. Schelling, *Vorlesungen, Sämmtliche Werke* (Stuttgart and Augsburg, 1854–60), V:224–25.

48. *Grundzüge*, 139; Smith, 148.

49. *Grundzüge*, 143; Smith, 152.

50. See Hegel, *Die Vernunft in der Geschichte* (Hamburg, 1955), 31.

51. Fichte is, of course, the German philosopher who, *par excellence*, stressed equality and was often attacked as a Jacobin. However, there is a nervous resemblance, across all human history, between the "*Normalvolk*" of the *Grundzüge* and the "*Urvolk*" of the *Addresses to the German Nation* (1808).

52. Glockner, VI, p. 254.

53. Ibid., p. 242.

54. *Introduction*, 52.

55. Knox (trans.), §57, p. 48.

56. Ibid., 239.

57. Glockner, X (*System der Philosophie*, III), p. 288.

58. Ibid., Addition to §436, p. 290.

59. *Jenenser Realphilosophie*, II:253–63. We must not ignore, however, that Hegel carefully draws the distinction between the Platonic (Lacedemonian) and the modern polity (p. 251).

60. The Greeks for Hegel, as for Schiller, Hölderlin, and others, have developed the perfect harmony and proportion of humanity; Kant's morality, on the other hand, represents the infinity of striving and is framed not for man but for "all rational beings." In one of his most electrifying and brilliant passages, Hegel describes the impact of the infinite and the finite, always in the same metaphor of struggle and comprehension: "I am the struggle [between the extremes of infinity and finitude], for this struggle is a conflict defined not by the indifference of the two sides in their distinction, but by their being bound together in one entity. I am not one of the fighters locked in battle, but both, and I am the struggle itself. I am fire and water" (*Vorlesungen über die Philosophie der Religion*, Glockner, XV, p. 80).

9

John W. Burbidge

"Unhappy Consciousness" in Hegel

An Analysis of Medieval Catholicism?

Hegel's *Phenomenology of Mind* does not fit easily into the traditional categories of philosophical literature. On the one hand, it does not appear to be epistemology, outlining the universal conditions necessary for any knowledge at all; for it explores stages of development that fit into some historical periods and not others. On the other hand, it is not a philosophy of history, for it does not trace a linear historical sequence from stage to stage. The advanced achievements of understanding precede the elemental desires of the man who has virtually no self-consciousness, for example, and the discussion of primitive, totemistic religions follows the liberation of the Enlightenment and the French Revolution.

This difficulty of categorization has presented a challenge to scholars. As they move from section to section in the *Phenomenology*, they have looked for the concrete historical situations to which Hegel refers. Or they have sought those analyses of the human condition which would make each stage a part of the universal structure of consciousness. The first tendency has been particularly strong with the section on unhappy consciousness. Enlightened moderns have disdained any thought that such practices as thoughtless devotion, ascetic self-denial, and the reliance on another to mediate truth could be a universal condition of personal development. Therefore they are taken to be descriptions of medieval Catholicism, a stage totally transcended and left behind.

The explanatory footnotes in this section of the first English translation point the reader in this direction. For example, the three forms of the unchangeable are said to be "God as Judge," "Christ," and "The religious communion."[1] Elsewhere reference is made to "the historic Christ as worshipped, e.g. in the medieval church," the Crusades, asceticism, the priesthood, and the use of Latin in church services.[2] The unwary can be excused for imagining that these notes stem from the hand of Hegel himself, and that the original intention of the text was to refer explicitly to medieval Catholicism.

The footnotes, however, are not in the original German. Indeed, a first reading of the text would give no immediate occasion for supposing that it is describing Christian phenomena. The vocabulary includes terms like "the changeable" and "the unchangeable," or "particularity" and "individuality" contrasted with "universality." Such abstract philosophical terms do not indicate any specific historical referent for the discussion.

In his prefatory comment on the section, Baillie, the English translator, expands on the point made in his footnotes: "The background of historical material for this type of mind is found in the religious life of the Middle Ages and the mental attitude assumed under the dominion of the Roman Catholic Church and the Feudal Hierarchy." Even though Baillie admits that "these are merely instances of an experience found in all mankind," he goes on to affirm that "Hegel selects forms assumed in European history, and has these in mind throughout the succeeding analysis."[3]

To what extent is Baillie's claim justified? Does this section of the *Phenomenology* analyze one particular epoch, or does it represent a universal characteristic of human nature?

To answer this question, we need a criterion for distinguishing a unique historical period from an experience that is found more generally—what we shall call a "universal experience." Two related characteristics will serve. In the first place, a historical period is unique because it is, in some sense, unrepeatable. When it has become part of cultural memory, it endures as a component within a more complex development, and as such cannot be recreated in its pristine innocence. In contrast, a universal experience is common to different periods and can be generalized by disregarding the specific conditions.

In the second place, it is the total set of historical conditions which renders one stage concrete and unrepeatable. Only in light of the complete context can it be understood logically. In contrast, a universal experience is abstract and can be examined in isolation. To be sure, each concrete setting will affect the way in which that experience appears. But the analysis is concerned, not with these specific (and in some sense accidental) factors, but with a structure which is logically independent of the various situations. It does not require concrete reference and can be expressed abstractly.

Our question has now been defined more precisely. Is the analysis of unhappy consciousness *abstracted* from particular settings, or does it require reference to concrete conditions to be logically complete? Alternatively, is the stage of unhappy consciousness *repeatable*, and in fact repeated, within the development of history, or is it simply a seldom-recalled moment within a cultural memory.

I

On first glance, the text itself seems to justify Baillie's suggestion that Hegel has "the forms assumed in European history... in mind." Unhappy consciousness develops from stoicism and skepticism and these movements were current in Imperial Rome. Indeed, Hegel uses the term "stoicism" because that was what the freedom of consciousness was called when it "appeared as a phenomenon conscious of itself in the course of the history of man's spirit." In conscious allusion to both Marcus Aurelius and Epictetus, he says that "the essence of this consciousness is to be free, on the throne as well as in fetters, throughout all the dependence that attaches to its individual existence." He locates the phenomenon even more specifically within history when he writes: "It is a freedom which can come on the scene as a general form of the world's spirit only in a time of universal fear and bondage, a time, too, when mental cultivation is universal, and has elevated culture to the level of thought."[4] Much later, in his lectures on the history of philosophy, Hegel said that, along with Platonists, Aristotelians, and Epicureans, there can no longer be any stoics.[5]

This suggests that stoicism occurs only when a number of conditions are present. In addition to the "universal fear and bondage" of the slave, there is "universal mental cultivation" which "has elevated culture to the level of thought."[6] It appears that this concrete historical phenomenon can never be repeated in its original simplicity.

> To reawaken [it] would be to try to bring back to an earlier stage the mind of a deeper culture and self-penetration.... It would be an impossibility and as great folly as were a man to wish to expend his energies in attaining the standpoint of youth, the youth in endeavouring to be the boy or child again.[7]

The phenomena analyzed in this section of the *Phenomenology* seem to be neither abstract nor repeatable.

Further evidence to support this interpretation can be found in Hegel's lectures on the *Encyclopaedia*. While the small chapter entitled "Phenomenology of Mind" in that schema does not pretend to encompass the broad scale of his earlier work, Hegel does discuss consciousness and self-consciousness, and in particular the life-and-death struggle and lordship and bondage.[8] The original text is brief and condensed. Of more direct interest to us are the comments made in Hegel's lectures which the editor has added as "*Zusätze*" or Additions to the various sections.

When referring to the life and death struggle, Hegel says:

> To prevent any possible misunderstanding with regard to the standpoint just outlined, we must here remark that the fight for recognition pushed to the extreme here indicated *can only occur in the natural state*, where men exist only as single, separate individuals; but it is absent in civil society and the state because here the recognition for which the combatants fought already exists.[9]

This stage, Hegel affirms, is unrepeatable. While it may have been found under different conditions in different parts of the world in the early stages of human development, it is not an instance "of an experience that is strictly found in all mankind."[10]

His comments on "Lordship and Bondage," however, point in a different direction. To be sure, the specific historical references are to Pisistratus in Athens and the strict rule of the kings in Rome. But his comments are more general: "This subjugation of the slave's egotism forms the *beginning* of true human freedom. This quaking of the single, isolated will, the feeling of the worthlessness of egotism, the habit of obedience, is a necessary moment in the education of all men."[11] The moment analyzed in "Lordship and Bondage" is abstract, independent of any particular historical context, and is, hence, explicitly repeatable.

This suggestion of the universal possibility of subjugation is supported when we look elsewhere in the *Phenomenology*. The religion of God as pure light "includes within it the form which we found in the case of immediate self-consciousness, the form of lord and master, in regard to the self-consciousness of spirit which retreats from its object."[12] Slave-consciousness, then, is not found simply as a secular response to a political power[13] or to the individual slave-owner but as a religious response to a transcendental Lord.

Baillie's footnote to the passage just quoted refers to Judaism and Mohammedanism. A phrase in the discussion of the slave seems to point in the same direction: "Albeit the fear of the Lord is the beginning of wisdom," Hegel writes, "consciousness is not therein aware of being self-existent."[14]

The subordinate clause is an explicit quotation from Hebrew scriptures.[15] We should not be surprised, then, to discover that, in his *Lectures on the Philosophy of Religion*, Hegel develops the motif of slave-consciousness in his discussion of Judaism.[16]

The evidence suggests that the stage analyzed by Hegel as lordship and bondage can be abstracted from any one particular historical context. It is a facet of human experience to be found repeated under distinctly different conditions. Indeed, Hegel has gone so far as to suggest in the *Encyclopaedia* that anyone who has not had his egoistic will broken by the discipline of a fearful master cannot discover the genuine freedom of human maturity. This subjugation of the will must be experienced by each one personally; it cannot be simply relived as a moment of cultural memory.

Considerations so far seem to lead to contrary conclusions. On the one hand, stoicism and the life-and-death struggle seem to be unrepeatable and unique. By analogy they would support Baillie's suggestion that medieval Christianity is the specific locus of unhappy consciousness. On the other hand, the results of our discussion of lordship and bondage lead to the inference that unhappy consciousness may be the analysis of a phenomenon abstracted from a number of distinct historical settings. Can we resolve this apparent dilemma through a second look at the section on stoicism?

That discussion does not include all facets of stoic theory. While it refers to the calm assurance of self-consciousness, which reduces the diversity of natural existence to the simplicity of a single thought, it ignores the whole area of stoic political philosophy. This is picked up explicitly later in the *Phenomenology* in the section "Legal Status": "What in Stoicism was implicit merely in an abstract way is not an explicit *concrete* world."[17] Is stoical self-consciousness but an abstracted moment of a concrete historical situation after all?

The introduction to Hegel's chapter "Spirit" provides an answer to that question. In this section Hegel considers spirit as a concrete historical totality, constituted by the interaction of individuals within a society. Only within the social context, where the individual contributes by thought and action to the well-being of others, and in turn benefits from their activity, does self-sufficiency become possible. Hegel writes:

> Spirit is . . . the self-supporting, absolutely real ultimate being. All the previous modes of consciousness are abstractions from it: they are constituted by the fact that spirit analyses itself, distinguishes its moments, and halts at each individual mode in turn. The isolating of such moments presupposes spirit itself and requires spirit for its subsistence, in

other words, this isolation of modes only exists within spirit, which is existence.[18]

The "previous mode" called self-consciousness (which explores desire, struggle, lordship and bondage, stoicism, skepticism, and the unhappy consciousness) does not treat complete historical phenomena. Rather, it isolates the self-conscious efforts of individuals to understand themselves.[19] As such it abstracts from the total context of relations, which define and determine individuals in their real existence.

It is in the search for unquestionable and assured knowledge that the *Phenomenology of Spirit* analyzes its sequence of stages. Each claim to certainty is tested against its implicit truth. When they do not correspond, that claim collapses and becomes transformed into a subsequent, more inclusive one.[20] At the level of spirit, certainty claims that the social context must be understood before knowledge is possible. In contrast, at the level of self-consciousness, the individual claims that truth will be attained if one focuses simply on oneself. The truth claim of the natural order is ignored, as well as the truth claim of any other person.[21] From the broader perspective of spirit we can recognize this as but an isolated and abstract moment within the total picture. The individual's eyes, however, are closed to that broader perspective.

Thus the discussion of stoicism examines that type of consciousness which seeks truth about itself in pure, simple thought, isolated from its relations to the legal and political world. But stoicism as an historical movement covered more than this individualistic concern. It made political claims which set the individual in a larger context. This broader setting is considered in the section "Legal Status."[22]

We turn back to unhappy consciousness with a clearer picture of its role in the *Phenomenology*. Baillie's suggestion that its background is the "mental attitude assumed under the dominion of the Roman Catholic Church and the Feudal Hierarchy" is too strong. The ecclesiastical and social structures of the Middle Ages make up the total cultural setting of an historical period. They cover far more than the individual, abstracted from his social context, who seeks truth simply about himself. The section on self-consciousness is concerned only with the latter, more limited, phenomenon.[23]

II

A question still remains. We noted earlier that the life and death struggle for recognition cannot recur in developed societies. There is a sense in which it is unrepeatable, even though it is abstract. Is this also true for unhappy consciousness? Does it specifically refer to the psychology of medieval Catholicism? Or is it a phenomenon which is found at different times, and is in principle repeatable like that of slave-consciousness? For we have suggested that both abstractness *and* repeatability are conditions for a universal characteristic of human experience. To answer the question of repeatability specifically we need to know the basic structure of unhappy consciousness' experience.

In Hegel's analysis,[24] this stage arises out of skepticism. The skeptical distrust of any truth claim acknowledges universal denial to be its implicit truth. The universality of that claim comes to consciousness, however, only when skepticism is left behind. Even then it is present, not as fully achieved, but as yet to be attained. On the one hand, unhappy consciousness retains the experience of skepticism, aware of itself as changing and inconstant, fluctuating with every new thought or event. But on the other hand, unlike skepticism, it is certain that thereby it has missed the essential moment of truth. The unchanging and secure essence lies beyond—present in consciousness only as a yearning for that which it lacks.

Hegel explores the experience of individuals who seek to appropriate unchanging truth by transcending their own changing inconstancy. Since they are aware of themselves simply as changing, the reconciliation only becomes possible if the initiative comes from beyond—from the unchanging. For the unhappy consciousness, the unchanging essence takes on distinct forms—forms which provide a bridge over the ugly, broad ditch between time and eternity. Not only does the unchanging stand absolutely opposed to the individual's fluctuating consciousness, but it also assumes on its own the particular structure of individuality—a structure which it shares with the yearning seeker. This specific union of individual particularity with the unchanging only *represents* the desired integration. In its third form the unchanging allows the changing consciousness itself to be taken into a reconciled life. As external beyond, as changing individual, and as achieved reconciliation the unchanging appears to the unhappy consciousness. But the *appearance* as a form of the unchanging is not yet its fully realized *experience* within the alienated consciousness. To appropriate that promise the individual selves, on their part, have to overcome the changeable and insecure character of their own lives. Since the experienced reconciliation is yet to be achieved, it is the second, individual, form of the unchanging which becomes the focus of their attention. For it is the agent by means of which the culminating experience is to become manifest.

Hegel outlines three progressive stages of the quest. The first incorporates the response of devotion. Self-consciousness turns directly toward the individual form of the unchanging and absorbs that awareness into its own intellect. Disdaining any effort to comprehend by reflective thought, it surrenders itself to the immediacy of intellectual feeling or intuition.

The attitude of devotion, however, does not overcome the alienation. On the one hand, the unchanging as individual still lies beyond and outside of the devotee. The only concrete evidence available is a grave, empty of the living essence of eternal truth. On the other hand, the changing self has achieved only its own immediate feeling of devotion which, it discovers, is condemned to fluctuate and vanish. It has not transcended change.

The second stage of unhappy consciousness, then, turns not outward toward an objective embodiment of the unchanging, but inward into its own awareness of itself. Its own desire and labor are to be the means of reconciliation. Earlier in the *Phenomenology*, primitive self-consciousness through desire and the servant through labor, achieved positive certainty about themselves. At this stage, however, those who desire and labor are alienated from themselves. As a result, these two ways of functioning share in their alienation and reflect their fundamental lack of self-certainty. Desire is not for that which will immediately satisfy the senses, but rather consumes the natural world to appropriate thereby the unchanging. Labor does not reproduce an objective expression of the self's activity, but rather seeks to reproduce that which will escape decay.

Desire and labor can achieve the desired reconciliation only if the unchanging allows itself to be appropriated and embodied through them. For the alienated individuals, then, the reality which is desired and the actions to be performed already participate in the unchanging essence of all things. Indeed, their own instincts and capacities are effective only because they too have been made powerful through the initiative of the unchanging. When this comes fully to consciousness, the individuals can only give thanks. For both the material, desired and worked upon, and the ability, to appropriate and embody, have been received from beyond.

The culminating act of thanksgiving, however, has been undertaken as their own personal response. They are thrown back once again into their remaining independence, still condemned to be alienated from the truth. In the third stage of unhappy consciousness, they seek to divest themselves completely of any remaining self-conscious initiative.

At this point everything the changing selves do consciously is valueless. Instead of rejoicing in their own activity—even in their animal functions—they mourn, for such actions condemn them to their separate, changing existence. All initiative must come from elsewhere. The individualized form of the unchanging essence, which started as the object of devotion and became the sacramental world of desire and labor, is now the mediator who alone can act with positive effect and accomplish the reconciliation. The changing individuals self-consciously transfer the guilt of their own acts, as changing, to the mediator. And in return they receive from the mediator direction concerning what they are to do. In total obedience the individuals surrender the positive value of self-determination. Even their own satisfaction in achievement must be sacrificed. They are told to use meaningless formulae, to confiscate the products of their own labor, to abstain from eating, and to mutilate their bodies. The determinate content of their action, together with the satisfaction of achievement belong not to the changing self-consciousness, but to the unchanging.

In this third stage of self-mortification, the unhappy consciousness finally transcends its changing, isolated individuality. Its deeds are but an instance of the universal activity of the unchanging mediator. As far as it is aware, this universal act is still that of a beyond, not of itself. If it were to become fully conscious of the unchanging universal as the truth of its own activity, it would have transcended the isolation of its self-concerned individuality and recognized that reason is common to both self and world. Reason, then, is the stage which Hegel will examine next in the *Phenomenology*.

III

Unhappy consciousness has as its object the three forms of the unchanging: external beyond, changing individual, and achieved reconciliation. Its subjective life is characterized by the three attitudes of devotion, of sacramental desire and labor, and of self-mortification. This double triad provides the schema for this stage of human development.

As Baillie suggests, individual Catholics in the Middle Ages may have embodied this pattern in their personal faith—the devotion directed toward the saints, the Virgin, or Jesus himself; the sacramental sacrifice and communion of the Eucharist;[25] and the self-mortification of the ascetic hermits. Is this, however, the full range of application for Hegel's analysis? Are the three experiential stages repeated elsewhere, or are they retained only as part of our cultural memory?

Hegel himself provides a reminiscence of this structure within the section on "Belief and Pure Insight" later in the *Phenomenology*—a discussion that recalls both the medieval period and the age of Enlightenment.[26] And he makes explicit reference to unhappy consciousness as a necessary condition for the appearance of revealed religion.[27] However, both passages consider the Christian tradition: one, within a social context that includes its cultural counterpart; the other, as it provides the locus for the revelation of absolute truth.

If the absolute, when revealed, can be known by individuals they must have within their own consciousness and life a capacity to comprehend which corresponds to that which is to be comprehended.[28] This capacity, Hegel suggests, is centered in "the yearning agony of the unhappy despairing self-consciousness."[29] If the truth to be known is absolute and complete, the capacity to know must also be universal—implicit in all conscious individuals. We might, then, expect to find manifestations of unhappy consciousness in historical contexts other than those which are specifically Christian.

We have already noticed that Jewish religion, the economic structure of the ancient world, and the political pattern of oriental despotism provided concrete historical settings for the type of consciousness analyzed in lordship and bondage. By analogy we may infer that unhappy consciousness will be found in contexts which, though roughly contemporary with the appearance of Christianity, are yet distinct from it. The influx of oriental religions into Rome during the second and third centuries in fact does provide such an alternative setting.

While there is little literary documentation for the religious psychology underlying that movement,[30] there is evidence to suggest that the devotee of these religions, yearning for immortality, is an instance of changing consciousness seeking reconciliation with the unchangeable. In Attis or Osiris, the unchangeable takes on the form of a man or god, who in dying manifests its identity with the changeable.[31] The cult of the dying and rising god becomes the context for the joy of experienced reconciliation. There are, then, clear parallels to the three forms of the unchanging essence.

From Cumont's description we can reconstruct some elements of the second-century Roman's personal experience. In the first place, the initiates may devote their individual attention to the divinity in pure adoration: "During the entire forenoon, from the moment that a noisy acclamation had greeted the rising of the sun, the images of the gods [Isis and Osiris/Serapis] were exposed to the silent adoration of the initiates."[32]

Secondly, they may eat a cultic meal, or purify themselves by means of ritual baths. "Frequent sacred repasts maintained a spirit of fellowship among the mystics of Cybele, Mithra or the Baals." And "a series of ablutions and lustrations [were] supposed to restore original innocence to the mystic."[33]

> In the third place, purgation of the soul was not effected solely by liturgic acts but also by self-denial and suffering. . . . Macerations, laborious pilgrimages, public confessions, sometimes flagellations and mutilations, in fact all forms of penance and mortifications uplifted the fallen man and brought him nearer to the gods.[34]

In addition,

> it was the priest's prerogative to judge the misdeeds and to impose the penalties. . . . The priest was no longer simply the guardian of sacred traditions, the intermediary between man or the state and the gods, but also a spiritual guide. He taught his flock the long series of obligations and restrictions for shielding their weakness from the attacks of evil spirits. He knew how to quiet remorse and scruples, and to restore the sinner to spiritual calm. Being versed in sacred knowledge, he had the power of reconciling the gods.[35]

Initiates into Syrian cults learned the magic incantations by which they might satisfy the divinity. And in the more enthusiastic religions of Asia Minor devotees would mouth ecstatic utterances, unintelligible even to themselves.

When one places Hegel's analysis of religious psychology beside the detailed account of oriental religions in second-century Rome provided by Cumont, one suspects that historians might well consider the dynamics of unhappy consciousness in their efforts to explain those developments. Indeed, one may infer that Hegel is directly concerned with this period of Roman history, disenchanted with stoicism, threatened by skepticism, entranced by Oriental religions, and infiltrated by Christianity; not with that later, medieval church, which shared in the stability of the feudal order.

In the doctrine and practice of Buddhism we find a second historical instance of unhappy consciousness. Nirvana, not immortality, is the unchanging for the Buddhist:

> We may have, O priests, the case of one who, himself subject to birth, perceives the wretchedness of what is subject to birth, and craves the incomparable security of a Nirvana free from birth; himself subject to old age . . . , disease . . . , death . . . , sorrow . . . , corruption, perceives the wretchedness of what is subject to corruption, and craves the incomparable security of a Nirvana free from corruption.[36]

In Mahayana thought, this unchangeable essence takes on concrete forms: "The Body of Essence, the Body of Bliss, the Transformation Body—these are the bodies of the Buddhas." The Body of Essence, "uniform and subtle," corresponds to the pure unchanging, the Transformation Body, which "displays with skill birth, enlightenment, and Nirvana, for it possesses much magic power to lead men to enlightenment," is the individual form of the unchanging as agent of reconciliation. The Body of Bliss, which "varies in all the planes of the Universe according to region, in name, in form, and in experience of phenomena," represents the ecstatic union of the individual consciousness with eternal truth.[37]

Hegel's three levels of religious experience fit, although awkwardly, with the eightfold path. The first two steps, right belief and right resolve, introduce a preliminary focusing of the mind and will on the eternal truth.[38] Often this is nurtured through silent meditation in a temple, responding to the pervasive influence of a statue of Buddha immersed in inner contemplation. Right speech, right behavior, and right occupation take up the pattern of the sacramental life in which desire and labor are given transcendental significance. The middle way of moderation and the discipline of the Sangha (or order of monks) are concrete embodiments of this stage.[39] Finally, the culminating stages of right effort, right contemplation, and right concentration direct the initiates to divest their minds of all concrete desires, and all concrete thoughts:

> Whenever, O priests, a priest, having isolated himself from sensual pleasures, having isolated himself from demeritorious traits, and still exercising reasoning, still exercises reflection, enters upon the first trance which is produced by isolation and characterized by joy and happiness; when, through the subsidence of reasoning and reflection, and still retaining joy and happiness, he enters upon the second trance, which is an interior tranquilization and intentness of the thoughts and is produced by concentration; when, through the paling of joy, indifferent, contemplative, conscious, and in the experience of bodily happiness—that state which eminent men describe when they say, "Indifferent, contemplative, and living happily"—he enters upon the third trance; when through the abandonment of misery, through the disappearance of all antecedent gladness and grief, he enters upon the fourth trance, which has neither misery nor happiness, but is contemplation as refined by indifference, this, O priests, is called "right concentration."[40]

These words of direction and advice come from the Lord, Gautama Buddha himself, who thus takes the initiative for the content of the believer's individual actions.[41]

The abstract terms used in the chapter on unhappy consciousness seem to apply not only to the quest for immortality in second-century Rome, but also to the yearning for Nirvana in traditional Buddhism.[42] Hegel has avoided specific historical reference lest he direct the reader's attention away from the more universal relevance of his analysis. In our third example, we suggest that the individual psychology of unhappy consciousness is not simply a cultural memory from the past, but is a recent phenomenon.[43]

The skepticism of the 1970s stemmed from our knowledge of historical change and diversity. Claims to certainty were taken to be but the expression of a psychological need or the result of sociological conditioning, lacking truth. In this context young people turned to religious perspectives which promised personal security and a way of transcending the world of change, doubt, and cosmic despair. Hindu cults and Buddhist literature vie with Christian premillennial sects for the individual's attention and commitment. The alienation of the unhappy consciousness, however, also pervaded the realm of political concern and action,[44] and there are those who took up Marxism, not as a scientific theory of explanation, but as a way of transcending the agony of contemporary insecurity and despair.

We can only sketch the parallels. The necessity of the historical dialectic was the eternal unchanging which stood over against the fluctuating dynamic of rapid social change. The necessity was present concretely in the theoretical analyses of Karl Marx, in the achievements of Communist China, or in the potential of the exploited proletariat. The individual would finally be reconciled with dialectical necessity in the classless society.

Devotion appeared when individuals contemplated the various embodiments of the unchanging truth with an intellectual attitude that accepted without critical reflection. It came to grief in the realization that there were significant events in the world which could not be explained directly from the texts, that China was not a paradise on earth, and that the proletariat manifested characteristics far more complex and ambiguous than pure theory suggested.

Consciousness could then claim that the universality of the historical dialectic was immanent within the total dynamic of social and political life, and could be appropriated only through specific desires and actions. Life in a commune anticipated the classless society. Political action in one's place of work sought to reproduce dialectical necessity. These acts, however, could reconcile individuals with what is ultimately significant in history only if the implacable dialectic so determined it. They had thought themselves to be participants in the classless society through their own initiatives. Experience taught them that they were totally insignificant, and their initiatives had no determining effect on the course of events.

So, finally, individuals were prepared to sacrifice themselves to this ultimate goal, even if that sacrifice was completely useless. They sought to initiate violent revolution, though they were aware that the result might well be their own deaths and a despotic regime of reactionary repression. They followed blindly the one who, professing to know Marxist theory, directed the action of the revolutionary cell. And they mouthed the cant phrases of propaganda which had lost any value as informative speech.[45]

Marxism, like Christianity and Buddhism, included much more than this one dimension of individual psychology. It may be, as Hegel suggests, that this quest for reconciliation with ultimate security anticipates within the individual psyche the structure of universal truth. Despite Hegel, however, we are not certain that absolute knowledge is attainable. Therefore such a possibility can only be proposed, not established as the truth.

Our more limited goal, however, has been attained. The parallels suggested between unhappy consciousness and the phenomena of Oriental religions in the Roman Empire, of Buddhism, and of contemporary Marxism provide some support for the conclusion that Hegel, in this section of the *Phenomenology*, is not simply concentrating on medieval Catholicism. He uses an abstract vocabulary and analyzes the individual self-consciousness, isolated from its historical context, because the experience of the unhappy consciousness is universal. It is a perennial possibility in human nature, reappearing in the lives of individuals even in our day.

We can conclude, then, that Baillie's suggestions and footnotes are misleading. Hegel does not have in mind "the forms assumed in European history." He is consciously analyzing "an experience that is strictly found in all mankind."[46] Indeed, from this limited study we are encouraged to make a stronger claim. The *Phenomenology* is not primarily a philosophy of history. Despite its analysis of developmental stages, it more closely approximates traditional epistemology. For it seeks to outline the universal conditions necessary for any knowledge whatsoever. Despite the confident assumptions of the Enlightenment and its heirs, the alienation of unhappy consciousness is, for Hegel, one of those conditions.

Notes

1. *The Phenomenology of Mind* (PhM), trans. J. B. Baillie, 2nd ed. (London and New York, 1955), 253.

2. PhM 255, 258, 263, 265.

3. PhM 241.

4. HGW 9:117–18; PhG 121; PhM 243–45.

5. G. W. F. Hegel, *Sämmtliche Werke*, ed. Glockner (Stuttgart-Bad Canstatt, 1965), XVII:76: *Hegel's Lectures on the History of Philosophy*, trans. E. S. Haldane and F. H. Simpson (London, 1892), I:47.

6. Only the slave has appeared in the immediately preceding analysis. Universal mental cultivation presupposes the level of understanding, but it is not clear why the enlightened slave should appropriate it. The contingency of historical concreteness seems to have been introduced.

7. *Sämmtliche Werke*, XVII:76; *History of Philosophy*, I:47.

8. He does not handle stoicism, skepticism, and the unhappy consciousness in the section on self-consciousness. This poses interesting questions which deserve separate examination. How essential are these steps for attaining the level of reason? What is the systematic relation between the discussion in the *Encyclopaedia* and that in the *Phenomenology*?

9. *Enz.* (*Philosophy of Mind*) §432, Addition. My italics.

10. PhM 241.

11. *Enz.* §435, Addition. Hegel stresses the universality of "all" in the next sentence: "Without having experienced the discipline which breaks self-will, no one becomes free, rational, and capable of command. To become free, to acquire the capacity for self-control, all nations must therefore undergo the severe discipline of subjection to a master."

12. HGW 9:371; PhG 419f.; PhM 699.

13. "Now finitude of the will characterizes the Orientals, because with them the will has not yet grasped itself as universal, for thought is not yet free for itself. Hence there can but be the relation of lord and slave, and in this despotic sphere fear constitutes the ruling category." From the *Lectures on the History of Philosophy* (I:96); *Sämmtliche Werke*, XVII:131. In the next paragraph Hegel refers to the Oriental religious attitude as well.

14. HGW 9:114; PhG 117f.; PhM 238.

15. Psalms 111:10; Proverbs 1:7; 9:10. See also Job 28:28: "The fear of the Lord, that is wisdom." The expression is also used in §435 of the *Philosophy of Mind*.

16. HGW 17:131–37; see G. W. F. Hegel, *Vorlesungen* (Hamburg: Meiner, 1985), 4a.58–66 and 356ff. The new edition makes it clear that the reference to the slave is in the lecture notes of 1821 but is not retained in either the lectures of 1824 or those of 1827. E. L. Fackenheim, in *Encounters between Judaism and Modern Philosophy* (New York, 1973), documents the inadequacy of Hegel's understanding of Judaism. "Abstract lordship" is found in Roman religion as it culminates in emperor worship, although Hegel makes no mention of slave-consciousness in this context. See HGW 9:262–64; PhG 292–94; PhM 504–6,

and *Vorlesungen*, 4a. 584–86, 589ff.; Hegel, *Lectures on the Philosophy of Religion*, ed. P. G. Hodgson (Berkeley: University of California Press, 1988), 381ff.

17. HGW 9:261; PhG 290; PhM 502. My italics.

18. HGW 9:239; PhG 264; PhM 459.

19. "When again [Spirit] holds fast by the other abstract moment produced by analysis, the fact that its object is its own self become objective to itself—is its self-existence—then it is *Self-consciousness*." HGW 9:239; PhG 264; PhM 459.

20. See the "Introduction" to the *Phenomenology*, HGW 9:53–62; PhG 46–57; PhM 131–45.

21. Both the master and the slave treat the other simply as a means to their own self-knowledge.

22. Similarly Hegel's comment in the *History of Philosophy*, cited above, that there can be no Stoics today refers to the total context and not simply to the moment of individualistic self-concern.

23. Elsewhere, in "Virtue and the Course of the World," Hegel explores the motivation of the knight of virtue. And "Spirit in Self-Estrangement" considers aspects of faith and culture embodied in the medieval world.

24. HGW 9:122–31; PhG 126–38; PhM 251–67.

25. The reader is reminded that *eucharist* is derived from the Greek verb for "to give thanks."

26. Compare especially the analysis of consciousness in estrangement in HGW 9:288; PhG 323; PhM 551.

27. HGW 9:403; PhG 456f.; PhM 755.

28. Kierkegaard presented a radical challenge to this presupposition in *Philosophical Fragments*.

29. HGW 9:403; PhG 456f.; PhM 755.

30. See the comment by E. R. Dodds, *Pagan and Christian in an Age of Anxiety* (Cambridge, 1968), 3: "The evidence for them is chiefly inscriptional and inscriptions seldom tell us much about the underlying religious experience." The source used in the present discussion is Franz Cumont, *Oriental Religions in Roman Paganism* (New York, 1956, originally published in 1906).

31. Cumont, *Oriental Religions*, 56ff., 98.

32. Ibid., 96.

33. Ibid., 41, 39. See also the description of the taurobolium on p. 66.

34. Ibid., 40.

35. Ibid., 41.

36. Quoted in H. C. Warren, ed., *Buddhism in Translation* (New York, 1963), 333. This work, A. K. Coomaraswamy, *Buddha and the Gospel of Buddhism* (New York, 1964), and *The Buddhist Tradition in India China and Japan*, ed. W. T. de Bary (New York, 1972) are the sources used in this discussion.

The concentration on individual salvation and the refusal of the Buddha to answer questions concerning the cosmic order (see Warren, *Buddhism in Translation*, 117ff.) correspond to the isolated individualism of the section on self-consciousness. We might note as well that the age in which Siddartha Gautama was born was one of skepticism and doubt: "Siddatha experienced the intellectual and spiritual unrest of his age. . . . We know, for example, that many groups of wandering ascetics were engaged in the same quest, and that they were largely recruited from an intellectual and social aristocracy to whom the pretensions of Brahmanical priestcraft were no longer acceptable, and who were no less out of sympathy with the multitudinous cults of popular animism." (Coomaraswamy, *Buddha*, 9–11).

37. De Bary, *Buddhist Tradition*, 94.

38. "The knowledge of misery, O priests, the knowledge of the origin of misery, the knowledge of the cessation of misery, and the knowledge of the path leading to the cessation of misery, this, O priests, is called 'right belief.'

"The resolve to renounce sensual pleasures, the resolve to have malice towards none, and the resolve to harm no living creature, this, O priests, is called 'right resolve'" (Warren, *Buddhism in Translation*, 373).

39. "But by charity, goodness, restraint, and self-control man and woman alike can store up a well-hidden treasure which cannot be given to others and which robbers cannot steal" (de Bary, *Buddhist Tradition*, 36). "Your majesty, he that is not free from passion experiences both the taste of that food and also passion due to that taste; while he who is free from passion experiences the taste of that food, but no passion due to that taste" (Warren, *Buddhism in Translation*, 421).

40. Warren, *Buddhism in Translation*, 374.

41. "The speaking of what has no sense or meaning" (HGW 9:130; PhG 137; PhM 265) may find its embodiment in the Ceylonese monk reciting in Pali the virtually infinite permutations on the Buddha's counsel, or in the cryptic incomprehensibility of the Zen koan.

42. It is interesting to compare Hegel's somewhat inadequate discussion of the cult of Buddhism in *Vorlesungen* 4a.211–18, 458–75; *Philosophy of Religion*, 250–67.

43. E. R. Dodds draws a parallel between second- and third-century Rome and our day: "In calling it 'an Age of Anxiety' I have in mind both its material and its moral insecurity; the phrase was coined by my friend W. H. Auden, who applied it to our own time, I suppose with a similar dual reference" (*Pagan and Christian*, 3). A passage in Cumont, written in 1906, sounds like a prophecy of

the sixties and seventies: "Let us suppose that in modern Europe the faithful had deserted the Christian churches to worship Allah or Brahma, to follow the precepts of Confucius or Buddha, or to adopt the maxims of Shinto; let us imagine a great confusion of all the races of the world in which Arabian mullahs, Chinese scholars, Japanese bonzes, Tibetan lamas and Hindu pundits would be preaching fatalism and predestination, ancestor worship and devotion to a deified sovereign, pessimism and deliverance through annihilation—a confusion in which all those priests would erect temples of exotic architecture in our cities and celebrate their disparate rites therein. Such a dream, which the future may perhaps realize, would offer a pretty accurate picture of the religious chaos in which the ancient world was struggling before the reign of Constantine" (196ff.).

44. The liberal assurance of immanent progress had given away to despair of ever attaining a just society by means of our present social structures and political constitutions.

45. My colleague, Michael Neumann, recently provided a trenchant analysis of the New Left movement of the sixties and seventies. See *What's Left? Radical Politics and the Radical Psyche* (Peterborough, Ontario: Broadview, 1987).

46. PhM 241.

IV

Reason

10

Alasdair MacIntyre

Hegel on Faces and Skulls

The Phenomenology of Spirit was written hastily. It is notorious that one outcome of this is that arguments are compressed, that the relation of one argument to another is often unclear, and that paragraphs of almost impenetrable obscurity recur. The commentator is therefore liable to feel a certain liberty in reconstructing Hegel's intentions; and the exercise of this liberty may always be a source of misrepresentation, perhaps especially when Hegel's arguments are relevant to present-day controversies. Nonetheless, the risk is sometimes worth taking, for although it is true that to be ignorant of the history of philosophy is to be doomed to repeat it, the joke is that we are doomed to repeat it in some measure anyway, if only because the sources of so many philosophical problems lie so close to permanent characteristics of human nature and human language. It is in this light that I want to consider Hegel's arguments about two bad sciences—physiognomy and phrenology—and their claims to lay bare and to explain human character and behavior, and the relevance of those arguments to certain contemporary issues.

I

Physiognomy was an ancient science that in the eighteenth century enjoyed a mild revival, especially in the writings of Johann Kaspar Lavater

(1741–1801). The central claim of physiognomy was that character was systematically revealed in the features of the face. Character consists of a set of determinate traits; and the face, of a set of determinate features. In some cases the cause of the face's being as it is, is the character's being as it is; but in other cases certain experiences, such as the experiences incurred in certain occupations, may leave their marks both on the character and on the face. In this latter type of case the features of the face are not effects of the traits of character, but remain revelatory of character.

In his discussion of physiognony, Hegel begins by noting that its adherents assert that their science makes a different type of claim from that made, for example, by the adherents of astrology. Astrologers assert that types of planetary movements and types of human actions are correlated in certain regular ways; the connection is purely contingent and external. But the face is an *expression* of human character; what a man is, appears in his face. Hegel next notes the difference between this claim as it is made by the physiognomist and this claim as it is made in everyday life. Part of our ordinary human relationships is to read off from each other's faces thoughts, moods, and reactions. But we do not treat the facial expression simply as a sign of something else, the outer as a sign of something inner, any more than we treat the movement of the hand in a human action as a sign of something else, the inner meaning of what is done, the intention. We treat the expression of the face and the movement of the hand as themselves actions, or parts or aspects of actions. In this connection Hegel makes four points.

It is not what the face is, its bone structure or the way the eyes are set, that is the expression of character or action; it is what the face does that is such an expression. We are therefore not concerned with mere physical shapes, but with movements that are already interpreted. This leads on to Hegel's second point. A man's character is not something independent of his actions and accessible independently of his actions. There is nothing more to his character than the sum total of what he does. Hegel here sides with Ryle in *The Concept of Mind* in his enmity to the notion of dispositions as causes of the actions that manifest them. The conjoint force of these two points is as follows:

When we see someone with a sad expression on his face, we do not infer to an inner sadness he feels on the basis of an observed correlation between such a physical arrangement of the facial features and inner states of sadness. We read or interpret the expression as one of sadness in the light of the conventions in our culture for interpreting facial expressions. Notice that we have to learn how to do this in alien cultures, and that no amount of correlating one observable characteristic with another in the search for regularities would assist us in the task of such learning. There is thus a difference between seeing a set of physical features and seeing that set as a face and as a face with a particular expression, just as there is a difference between seeing a string of physical shapes and seeing that string as an English sentence and as a sentence with a particular meaning. To learn how to read a face or a sentence is not to follow rules justified by observation that embody a correlation between two sets of items, one of which is the physical features or shapes.

What Hegel's argument has done so far is to show that the physiognomist's treatment of the face as expressive of character, and the physiognomist's treatment of the face as (at least sometimes) the effect of character, cannot be combined without damaging inconsistency. Hegel's two next points are still more damaging to the claim of physiognomy to go beyond the prescientific understanding of facial expression to a scientific knowledge of the causal relations allegedly underlying that expression. He points out sharply how the rules that we use in everyday life in interpreting facial expression are highly fallible. We can express Hegel's point in this way: if someone is apparently glaring at me and I accuse him of being angry with me, he has only to retort that he was thinking of something quite different and I shall have no way to rebut him by appeal to some set of rules for interpreting facial expression. Hegel quotes Lichtenberg: "If anyone said, 'Certainly you behave like an honest man, but I can see from your face that you are compelling yourself to do so and are a villain underneath,' there is no doubt that every brave fellow so greeted will reply with a box on the ear."

Finally—although Hegel makes this point earlier in the discussion—our dispositions of character, as expressed in our actions, speech, and facial expressions, are not simply given as physical features are given. My bone structure can be altered by surgery or violence, but at any given moment it is simply what it is. But my character is not determinate in the same way as my bone structure, and this in two respects: First, a disposition to behave in a particular way always has to be actualized in some particular context, and the nature and meaning of the action that manifests the disposition is in many cases unspecifiable apart from that context. If I strike a man dead when he attacks me murderously, my action does not have the same nature and meaning as when I strike a man dead in a fit of bad-tempered gratuitous aggression. Dispositions that are actualized independently of context are like tendencies to sneeze or to produce compulsive movements; their manifestations will be happenings that in virtue of their independence of context cannot be viewed as intelligible behavior, except perhaps as nervous habits. But about my action produced in a context, we can ask if it is appropriate or inappropriate in the light of the norms defining intelligible behavior in such a context;

indeed this is a question that any agent can ask about his own actions. In asking this, he has to characterize his actions in such a way that he becomes self-conscious about what he is doing.

An agent, for example (my example, not Hegel's), may find himself performing a set of multifarious individual actions. Becoming conscious of the character of these, he becomes aware that his overall conduct is jealous, let us say, or cowardly. But now he is able to place, indeed cannot but place, his conduct *qua* jealous or *qua* cowardly in relation to what Hegel calls "the given circumstances, situations, habits, customs, religion, and so forth," that is, in relation to the relevant norms and responses of his culture. But to do this is to provide himself with reasons, perhaps decisive reasons, for altering his conduct in the light of those norms and responses and of his own goals. It is of the nature of the character traits of a rational agent that they are never simply fixed and determinate, but that for the agent to discover what they are in relation to his unity as a self-conscious agent—that is, what they are in his personal and social context—is to open up to the agent the possibility of exchanging what he is, for what he is not.

Moreover, the agent who does not change his traits may change their manifestations. Indeed, for him to become conscious that he manifests certain traits and so appears in a certain light, is to invite him to do just this. The relation of external appearance, including the facial appearance, to character is such that the discovery that any external appearance is taken to be a sign of a certain type of character is a discovery that the agent may then exploit to conceal his character. Hence, another saying of Lichtenberg, in *Über Physiognomik*, which Hegel also quotes: "Suppose the physiognomist ever did have a man in his grasp; it would merely require a courageous resolution on the man's part to make himself again incomprehensible for centuries."

II

But who now is likely to be impressed by the claims of physiognomy? Reading Lavater's *Physiognomische Fragmente zur Beförderung der Menschenkenntniss und Menschenliebe*, with all its romantic whimsy—Lavater on the basis of a youthful acquaintance associated piercing eyes with power of memory, for instance—one might well ask, ought anyone ever to have been impressed by such claims? Part of the answer is that we ought in any case to be interested in bad sciences if only in order to illuminate the contrast with good ones. The study of astrology, physiognomy, or phrenology is justified in so far as it helps us to understand the character of chemistry and physiology. But part of the answer concerns the way in which certain issues may be raised in precisely the same way by bad sciences such as phrenology and physiognomy as by good ones such as genetics or neurophysiology.

In the case of phrenology some of the central theses actually survive in the history of physiology into the present day. It was, for instance, a central thesis of phrenology that different features of the brain were localized in different areas of the brain. This thesis is still controversial, of course, but the empirical neurophysiological and neuroanatomical evidence seems to be against it, especially if localization is understood in anything like the terms in which the phrenologists understood it. There is secondly the thesis, distinctively phrenological, that the different areas of the brain correspond to different areas of the cranial bone, and that the shapes of these areas, the famous bumps of the phrenologists, reveal the different degrees of development of each area of the brain. It is scarcely necessary to remark that this empirical contention is false. There is finally the thesis that the local activity of the brain is the sufficient cause and explanation of behavior, and that therefore the shape of the cranium allows us to predict behavior.

Buried in these dubious contentions is one that is less obviously dubious, that is indeed familiar and widely accepted. I mean of course the thesis that there are biochemical or neural states of affairs, processes, and events, the occurrence and the nature of which are the sufficient causes of human actions. This thesis wore phrenological clothing in 1807; today its clothing is as fashionable as it was then, only the fashions are not what they were. Moreover, when Hegel attempted to rebut the claims of physiognomy and phrenology, he did so in such a way that if his rebuttal is successful it would hold against the thesis that I have just stated whatever its scientific clothing.

At this point, someone may object to my metaphor. The thesis, so it may be protested, does not merely wear scientific clothing, it is itself part of science; and, being a scientific thesis, it is an empirical question, and purely an empirical question, whether it is true or false. My reply to his point, and what I take to be Hegel's reply to this point, occupies a large part of the rest of the paper. But it is worth noting initially that the thesis *has* survived the most remarkable changes in our empirically founded beliefs about the anatomy, physiology, and chemistry of the human body, and that if it is a thesis in natural science, it is certainly not a thesis at the same level as the contention that the shape of the brain is partly the same as that of the cranium or that the nucleic acids play a specific part in reproduction.

In the debate about phrenology in the early nineteenth century, the attempt to challenge the thesis was undertaken by a number of writers very different from Hegel, and his project deserves to be sharply distinguished from theirs. The standard statement of the phrenological position was taken from the writings and lectures of Franz Joseph Gall (1758–1828) and his pupil J. C. Spurzheim, who developed Gall's doctrine, later claiming both that he had in fact originated some of the basic ideas and also that his doctrine was very different from that of Gall. Gall and Spurzheim drew maps of the cranium locating not only character traits but abilities in different parts of the brain, and their manifestations in what they took to be the corresponding parts of the skull. Examples of traits are secretiveness, combativeness, and acquisitiveness; examples of abilities are the power of speech and the power of imagination. Gall was charged by his critics with determinism, materialism, and consequently atheism. Both Gall and Spurzheim denied these charges, Spurzheim seeking to show that they held of Gall's version of phrenology but not of his. The critics in question, notably Francis Jeffrey, the editor, and Brougham, the lawyer, fastened all their attention on the alleged causes, seeking to show that the mental cannot have a physical, or more specifically a physiological, cause. To show this, they rely on a simple dualism of matter and mind, and the vapid naiveté of Gall's and Spurzheim's science is matched only by the vapid naiveté of Jeffrey's and Brougham's philosophy.

The spirit of their attack on phrenology is as alien to the spirit of Hegel's attack as any could be. Hegel's opposition to Cartesian dualism is of so thoroughgoing a kind that he would have to reject all the premises of Jeffrey's and Brougham's attacks. Nor is Hegel interested in showing that there cannot be physiological causes of the type cited by the phrenologists. His whole attention is focused not on the existence or non-existence of the alleged causes, but on the character of their alleged effects.

Hegel deploys a number of arguments that are closely allied to his arguments against physiognomy in the interests of his conclusion that "it must be regarded as a thoroughgoing denial of reason to treat a skull bone as the actuality of conscious life." What Hegel means by this is indicated by his further contention that "It is no use to say we merely draw an inference from the outer as to the inner, which is something different." Hegel wants to say that if we regard the traits of a rational agent as belonging to the type of item that can stand in a genuinely causal relation to anatomical or physiological or chemical states, then we are misconceiving the traits of a rational agent. Why does Hegel think this? We can usefully begin from a point that Hegel did not make in his discussion of physiognomy.

Traits are neither determinate nor fixed. What does it mean to say that they are not determinate? "Just as, e.g., many people complain of feeling a painful tension in the head when thinking intensely, or even when thinking at all, so it might be that stealing, committing murder, writing poetry, and so on, could each be accompanied with its own proper feeling, which would over and above be bound to have its peculiar localization." Hegel's discussion in terms of the localization of feeling has of course a specific reference to contemporary phrenology; but what he goes on to say about local feelings can easily be translated into a thesis about particular dispositions. "Feeling in general is something indeterminate, and that feeling in the head as the center might well be the general feeling that accompanies all suffering; so that mixed up with the thief's, murderer's, poet's tickling or pain in the head there would be other feelings, too, and they would permit of being distinguished from one another, or from those we may call mere bodily feelings, as little as an illness can be determined from the symptom of headache if we restrict its meaning merely to the bodily element."

What would the corresponding theses about dispositions be? Let us consider points from two of Hegel's examples—those of the murderer and of the poet. A given murderer, for instance, commits his crime because he fears his own humiliation by losing his beloved. If we are to look at the traits and other qualities manifested in his action, they do not include a disposition to commit murder, but such things perhaps as a general intolerance of suffering, a disposition to avoid specific kinds of humiliation, his love for the girl, and so on. The same dispositions might explain to precisely the same extent the same person's outbidding others in giving to a deserving cause in order to impress the same girl. But just this fact puts in question the use of the word "explain." Hegel makes this point in relation to phrenology: "And again his murderous propensity can be referred to any bump or hollow, and this in turn to any mental quality; for the murderer is not the abstraction of a murderer."

Suppose that to this the reply is made that the same given set of dispositions may well produce quite different actions, but that this is because the agent is responding to quite different situations (although in some sense, in my example, the situations are certainly the same). So that we explain the particular action by reference to a conjunction of the set of dispositions and some feature of the situation. We then explain the acts in an entirely familiar and unproblematic way by appealing to a generalization of the form "Whenever such and such a set of dispositions and such and such a type of situation are ignored, such and such an action will occur." To cite human traits in such an explanation would be precisely parallel to citing the dispositional properties of physical objects in explaining physical events.

But this is to suppose that what the agent is responding to is some conjunction of properties and not the specific historical situation. An empiricist would generally not be prepared to draw this contrast; for him, there is nothing to any specific historical situation but a set of properties, the conjunction of which may as a matter of contingent fact be unrepeated, but which is in fact repeatable. Why, then, does Hegel insist on the contrast and deny this characteristic empiricist contention?

A particular historical situation cannot on Hegel's view be dissolved into a set of properties. One reason for this is that such a situation has to be characterized in terms of relations to earlier specific events and situations. There is an internal reference to the events and situations that constitute its history. So the English revolt against Charles I not only has as key properties specific reactions to particular acts of Charles I, but responses to events and situations in the past as recent as acts of Elizabeth and as far off as the Magna Charta and the Norman Conquest. Now, to respond to a particular situation, event, or state of affairs is not to respond to any situation, event, or state of affairs with the same or similar properties in some respect; it is to respond to *that* situation conceived by both the agents who respond to it and those whose actions constitute it as particular.

Suppose that to this position some empiricist were to respond as follows: that the agents treat the situation as particular and that the situation is partially constituted and defined by reference to the particular events and situations, does not show that everything relevant to explanation cannot be expressed in terms of repeatable properties. But this reply fails to notice one key point. Hegel would be the last to assert the ultimacy of unanalyzed and unanalyzable particulars (such as Russell's logical atoms). But he does assert what we may call the ultimacy of concreteness. What the ultimacy of concreteness amounts to is this: just as there are good conceptual reasons for holding that existence is not a property, so there are good conceptual reasons for holding that occurrence at some specific time and place is not a property.

By a property I mean that kind of attribute which a subject of the appropriate type (appropriate for that type of attribute) may or may not possess, which a given subject may possess at one time but not at another, and which may (although it need not) be possessed by more than one subject. On such an account of properties, existence fails to count as a property, because the appropriate type of subject cannot either possess it or fail to possess it and because the appropriate type of subject cannot possess it at one time but not at another. On the same account of properties, occurrence at some specific time and place (e.g., at 3 P.M. in the year 1776 at the point where the Greenwich meridian crosses the south bank of the Thames) fails to count as a property, because any subject of the appropriate type (events, situations, states of affairs) cannot possess any particular example of this attribute at one time but not at another and because any particular example of this type of attribute cannot be possessed by more than one subject.

It is properties about which we construct genuine empirical generalizations of such forms as (x) $(\phi x \supset \psi x)$ and (x) $(\phi x \supset \psi y)$, in which the values of variables of the type of ϕ and ψ are property-ascribing predicates. But it is on Hegel's view universals particularized in their concrete occurrence to which we respond in our actions—both those concrete particulars which we actually encounter and those which are the counterpart in the actual world to the intentional objects of our belief, attitudes, and emotions. A poet does not take pride in his having written some poem that has properties of such and such a kind, but in his having written *this* poem. A murderer did not strike out at anyone who happened to have such and such properties but at *this* person. Just because this concreteness is not constituted by a mere collection of properties, it evades causal generalizations and so makes causal explanation, whether phrenological or neurophysiological, inapplicable.

Note what Hegel is *not* saying. Hegel is not asserting that the movements of the murderer's hand or the poet's hand do not have causal explanations. Nor is he asserting that it is impossible that there should be agents with responses only to the abstract universal and not to the concrete. It is just that in so far as someone did respond to presentations of properties with the degree of uniformity that would warrant the construction of causal generalizations, he would not be at all like characteristic human agents as we actually know them and they actually exist. It is a contingent empirical fact about human beings that they are as they are and not otherwise, but in Hegel's philosophy there is no objection to taking notice of such contingent empirical facts. Nonetheless, Hegel is not denying that it is logically possible for some human actions to have causes, and he is not denying that some human actions do or may have physiological causes. Let me draw a parallel with another type of case.

Some Africans who believe in witchcraft point out that to explain the onset of a disease by referring to bacterial or virus infection leaves unexplained such facts as that Jones should have been afflicted by such an infection immediately after quarreling with Smith. "What is the cause of that conjunction?" they inquire, pointing out that Western science gives no answer. Now, if indeed it were true that every event had a cause, that event which is Jones-going-down-with-measles-on-the-day-after-he-quarreled-with-Smith would presumably have a cause. But no champion of natural science feels affronted by the assertion that this is not an event with a cause or an explanation, although the event that is Jones-going-down-with-measles certainly has a cause and an explanation. So also, when Hegel allows that a certain kind of causal explanation will not give us the understanding that we require of self-conscious rational activity, his argument does not require him to deny that many properties of the agents engaged in such activities will have such explanations.

I now return to Hegel's point that traits are not determinate or fixed. I have argued that the indeterminacy of traits is an indeterminacy *vis-à-vis* any action or given set of actions. From the fact that an agent has a given trait, we cannot *deduce* what he will do in any given situation, and the trait cannot itself be specified in terms of some determinate set of actions that it will produce. What does it mean to say that traits are not fixed? Let me reiterate the crucial fact about self-consciousness, already brought out in Hegel's discussion of physiognomy; that is, its self-negating quality: being aware of what I am is conceptually inseparable from confronting what I am not but could become. Hence, for a self-conscious agent to have a trait is for that agent to be confronted by an indefinitely large set of possibilities of developing, modifying, or abolishing that trait. Action springs not from fixed and determinate dispositions, but from the confrontation in consciousness of what I am by what I am not.

It is a failure to notice this, that on Hegel's view most of all underlies those would-be sciences that aspire to give to observation the same role in the study of human beings that it has in inquiries into nature. For what we can observe in nature is, so to speak, all that there is to discover; but what we can observe in human beings is the expression of rational activity, which cannot be understood as merely the sum of the movements that we observe. (For a Hegelian, Hume's failure to discover the character of personal identity is the result of his fidelity to the methods and criteria of observation.) From Hegel's position, a radical thesis about experimental psychology would follow.

For a large class of psychological experiments, a necessary condition for experimental success is that the stimulus that is administered or the situation with which the agent is confronted shall have its effect independently of the agent's reflection on the situation. The situation or the stimulus must be the same for all experimental subjects; so one subject's envisaging the situation in a particular way must not constitute that situation as a different one from that which it is for a subject who envisages that situation in some quite different way. Now, there is a real question as to whether this requirement can ever in fact be satisfied except in experiments in which the stimulus is purely physical (for example, a variation in intensity of light) and the response purely physiological (for example, a constriction of the pupil). But this question I shall put on one side. What Hegel would assert is that even if such experiments are possible, they are so different from the key situations in which rational agents operate, that any inferences from the behavior of such experimental subjects to behavior outside the experimental situation will be liable to lead us into error.

III

Whatever else the arguments in this chapter may or may not establish, they do seem to show that between the Hegelian mode of understanding human action and the mode that has dominated modern thinking about the relevance of such sciences as neurophysiology and genetics, there is a basic incompatibility. Hence, the refutation of Hegelianism in the relevant respects would be a prerequisite for that mode of thought and not merely that frivolous, positivistic refutation to which Hegel has so often been subjected and that he himself adequately characterized. Whether a more adequate refutation is possible, I shall not discuss here. What I do want to do, in conclusion, is to try to characterize Hegel's alternative mode of understanding inquiry into human action.

Three features of Hegel's account stand out: The first is the way in which each stage in the progress of rational agents is seen as moving toward goals that are only articulated in the course of the movement itself. Human action is characteristically neither blind and goalless nor the mere implementation of means to an already decided end. Acting that is the bringing about of such an end by a calculated means certainly has a place, but a subordinate place, in human activity. That it is only in the course of the movement that the goals of the movement are articulated is the reason why we can understand human affairs only after the event. The Owl of Minerva, as Hegel was later to put it, flies only at dusk. The understanding of human beings is not predictive in the way that natural science is.

The second feature of Hegel's account is the role of rational criticism of the present in the emergence of the future. Hegel did not believe that the future followed from the present simply as its rational sequel; this he denies as strongly as Voltaire does. But it is in the working out of the failure of the present to satisfy the canons of reason that the future is made. It is this which involves Hegel in seeing history as composed of sequences in which the actions that constitute later stages of the sequence involve reference to, and thus presuppose the occurrence of, actions that constituted earlier stages of the same sequences. The sequences that constitute history are themselves discrete and can stand in the same logical relation to each other as can the stages of a single sequence. But the doctrine that all the sequences of history constitute a single movement toward the goal of a consciousness of the whole that is absolute spirit and that by its consciousness of the whole of history constitutes that whole into a single rational totality, is a thesis certainly held by Hegel to be the key to his whole doctrine; yet Hegel's other doctrines as to human history do not seem in any way to entail his doctrine about the absolute, and to be willing to admit the truth of that doctrine ought not to be a source of prejudice against Hegel's other doctrines.

The third feature of Hegel's account relates closely to his criticism of physiognomy and phrenology. Historical narratives are for Hegel not a source of data to be cast into theoretical form by such would-be sciences. Instead, Hegel sees our understanding of contingent regularities as being always contributory to the construction of a certain kind of historical narrative. History, informed by philosophical understanding, provides a more ultimate kind of knowledge of human beings than inquiries whose theoretical structure is modeled on that of the natural sciences. It is outside the scope of this paper to develop or to assess Hegel's view on this matter, but a concluding remark may be in place.

It concerns the question: if history is not a matter of general laws and of theories, in what sense does it give us understanding at all? The Hegelian reply is that the self-knowledge of a self-conscious rational agent has always to be cast in a historical form. The past is present in the self in so many and so important ways that, lacking historical knowledge, our self-knowledge will be fatally limited. Moreover, this type of self-knowledge could never be yielded by theoretical sciences that aspire to explain behavior in terms of physiological structures and processes. It is in fact just because our history constitutes us as what we are to so great an extent, that any explanation that omits reference to that history, as did and do the explanations of phrenology and neurophysiology, may explain the aptitudes and conditions of the human body, but not those of the human spirit.

11

Gary Shapiro

Notes on the Animal Kingdom of the Spirit

> Were I still capable of taking seriously that naive conception of the unity of the "ego" that's presupposed by the concept of insult, I suppose I'd be insulted by your apology for not, as you put it, "being able to compensate me for my contribution." I would be, that is, if it mattered to me in the slightest that—as I've heard recently—you promised to pay Bob Alter something in the ball park of $500 for his contribution. That Alter should get five C's (which I should think he hardly needs) while I get zip is one of those Hegelian ironies of history that to me are so profoundly meaningless that the very propositions in which I attempt to formulate them seem nonsensical.
> —Gerald Graff, in Tri Quarterly (Spring 1978)

> Amongst all the celebrated Germans none possessed more esprit than Hegel, but he also had that peculiar German dread of it which brought about his peculiar and defective style. For the nature of this style resembles a kernel, which is wrapped up so many times in an outer covering that it can scarcely peep through, now and then glancing forth bashfully and inquisitively, like "young women peeping through their veils," to use the words of the old woman-hater Aeschylus. The kernel, however, is a witty though often impertinent joke on intellectual subjects, a subtle and daring combination of words, such as is necessary in a society of thinkers as gilding for a scientific pill—but, enveloped as it is in an almost impenetrable cover, it exhibits itself as the most abstruse science, and likewise as the worst possible moral tediousness.
> —Friedrich Nietzsche, The Dawn (aphorism 193)

One of the more neglected chapters of Hegel's *Phenomenology*, which contains neither the obvious drama of the master and slave dialectic nor the deep enigmas of the final pages on absolute knowledge, carries the somewhat puzzling title "Das geistige Tierreich und der Bertrug oder die Sache selbst." Of the major commentators on Hegel only Lukács has suggested its central place in the design of the whole; Kojève and Lowenberg (following Royce) have suggested vivid readings of it as an analysis of the conflicts and jealousies of intellectual, artistic, and professional work. What follows is a series of remarks and variations on Hegel's text which agrees in the main with Lukác's notion of its importance and with Kojève's and Lowenberg's account of what is important in it. To begin with an expression of indebtedness to one's intellectual sources is an important gesture, for part of the point of Hegel's chapter is to trace the illusions of ownership and sole responsibility to which intellectuals are liable. Just as the sheer *meinen* of sense-certainty (my attempt to really *mean* that which is truly *mine*—my present sensation) collapses into the most abstract and universal language, so *my* work, the more rigidly I insist that it is mine, turns out to be one more minor variation on the texts, commentaries, thematics, and traditions of one school of thought or another.

How should we translate Hegel's title? Baillie's version is clumsy enough: "Self-contained individuals associated as a community of animals and the deception thence arising: the real fact." It may be useful to point out that the agents whom Hegel is describing take themselves to be self-contained individuals, although (as so often) Baillie's instructions to the reader are confusingly intermingled with the text. And his "real fact" fails to capture the sense of a goal or cause in terms of which the agents justify their work. Miller's more recent and literal title is "The Spiritual Animal Kingdom and Deceit, or the 'Matter in Hand' Itself." This has the merit of suggesting that we are dealing with an animalized or degenerate form of *Geist*—which is Hegel's ultimate subject in this work in more senses than one. Hyppolite's is even more succinct: "La règne animal de l'esprit et la tromperie ou la chose même."

The choice of a title is both a symptom and a statement of hermeneutic decisions which have more far-reaching consequences in terms of how one understands paragraphs, chapters, indeed the whole work. Baillie's pedagogic incursions into and additions to the text show how he situates *his* work in relation to Hegel's. Although he usually is at great pains to tell us that it is now the Middle Ages, or Antigone, or Aristophanes which is the subject of Hegel's analysis (in notes that might be taken for Hegel's own), he has played down the colorful hints of this title; perhaps the chapter raises painful questions about the mediating role of translators who might very well be among those rushing to a work started by another "like flies to fresh milk." And it is just the incursive translator for whom the question of whether it is "*my* work" or "my *work*" (to use Lowenberg's helpful phrases) ought to loom largest. The modest translator simply lets the emphasis fall on "my *work*." But if we were to suggest some of the force and relevance of Hegel's title we might try "The Spiritual Jungle and the Lie or Where It's Really At," so updating Royce's "The Intellectual Animals and Their Humbug, or the Service of the Cause." "Spiritual Zoo" (Findlay) is not right; first because it's simply not a standard meaning of *Tierreich* and second because a zoo is a place where animals are exhibited and displayed rather than being free to engage in animal activity. (If Hegel had meant zoo, he would have said *Tiergarten*, which suggests placidity even more than does our word.) The "jungle" is well-established colloquial English for a place in which humans behave like animals. To describe an academic department as a zoo would suggest a collection of relatively tame specimens from a wide array of species; to call it a jungle would emphasize both the similarities of the members and their activity.

Yet the most straightforward translation of *Tierreich* would be "animal kingdom," conceived as one of the three kingdoms of nature: mineral, plant, and animal. To speak of a *geistige Tierreich*, then, turns out to be a deliberate crossing of Hegelian categories, since *Logik*, *Natur*, and *Geist* are the three great Hegelian realms. "Kingdom" or "realm" would then be better than "jungle" to suggest the play of categories. It would also allow the possible reference to Kant's *Reich der Zwecke*. The *geistige Tierreich* is clearly not a *Reich der Zwecke* because its members do not obey universalizable rules; yet it contains something of a parody of that realm. As in the *Reich der Zwecke* each member of the *geistige Tierreich* thinks of him or herself as autonomous and as working in a structure which supports the autonomous activity of other agents like him or herself. That the intellectual activity which seems to bring us asymptotically close to the kingdom of ends may very well leave us in the animal kingdom is certainly part of the kernel of Hegel's humor.

Perhaps something should be said about the argument of *das geistige Tierreich*, so as to show that Hegel is doing more than taking a parting shot at some contemporary forms of individual consciousness before passing on to *Geist* (see Charles Taylor's *Hegel*, 167, for such a view). But let me first construe Hegel's analysis as a narrative before asking how rigorous the arguments are. Certain kinds of work appeal to us because they offer the possibility of doing at the same time that which is our very own thing (the particular) while being a part of or contributing to something of general meaning and importance (the universal). To think of ourselves as part of a community of workers, each of whom puts his or her talents to work in the service of some general goal, is appealing; and even more appealing if we are aware of the difficulties encountered in observational reason or individual adventure in bringing those aspects together. So, as usual, Hegel proceeds by first showing the attractions of the form of consciousness to be examined and then demonstrating the unhappy experience which comes from really assuming the attitude involved. Here the attractions are many: being part of a community but having a unique identity and interest of one's own, developing one's own talents while contributing to an impersonal good, combining theory and practice in a work which is intelligible and articulated. Yet the disappointments are also many. For suppose that I throw myself into intellectual, artistic, or professional work of some kind (for the time being, consider these only as examples of the work Hegel has in mind, although I will show that they are paradigms). My first disappointment (let us remember how high and naive my initial expectations were) is the discovery that it doesn't come easy, that there's no simple and spontaneous gesture which does the whole thing and effectively completes a work that embodies both my activities and a general cultural or intellectual meaning. The writing is awkward, the drawing is wooden, I have little feeling for the guitar, and so on. So I must work on myself as well, but since I now seem to be more amorphous and untalented than in my earlier fantasies, where do I begin?

The problem of the beginning is of course dear to Hegel's heart; here Meno's paradox is overcome (as in the *Meno*) by simply jumping in and doing things. Given my commitment to meaningful work I'll find *something* to do, even if it's public relations work for hospital management or grantsmanship for the anthropology department. Suppose that I do manage to produce some result, some work (in the sense of a finished product). As a self-conscious person I can't help but realize that the finished work is not me; it is determinate and closed while I see new possibilities in it and beyond it. And anyone else who should come along will see it as even more of an alien reality than I do. So finished works are vanishing moments, ephemeral fulfillments at best. If I thought to realize myself in such a work, I can be thrown into a profound self-doubt, for I see that I've not only misunderstood the character of work but must have had a faulty conception of myself to have expected completion and reconciliation from writing that paper or producing that devastating legal argument. If work is still to offer fulfillment I must find a way of overcoming the vanishing character of the particular work, and I find this in the *principle* of work itself, *die Sache selbst*. Where it's really at is not in the work-object but in the work-activity. My particular work may be a vanishing moment but scientific research, the advance of art, scholarship, the profession, or the discipline—these can all be conceived as embracing and worthwhile ends to which I can devote my activities. But now the cause cannot be mine alone; the good of the profession, for example, can't be (just) my work. So just as self-consciousness destroyed the illusory stability of the work-object, the dialectic of recognition, already encountered between master and slave, will guarantee the impossibility of any simple identification of myself with *die Sache selbst.*

A social aspect has been implicit in *das geistige Tierreich* all along, for as an intellectual animal with a sense of my own identity, I had to be capable of at least acknowledging the possibility of others who would be formally if not materially similar to me. Since I now see that I will never realize myself in a single determinate work—or in any number or sequence of such works—I will want to be recognized by others (or at least by my own reflective self) as genuinely committed to the cause. So I think of myself as *ehrlich*, honest (or "integral," in Miller's translation) to the extent that I really do concern myself seriously with the cause. The problem now will be to maintain any substantial sense of this honesty or integrity in the face of the infinite malleability and dissolution of my work. For I have set the game up so well that *everything* counts as serious devotion to *die Sache selbst.* We have already seen that given the primacy of the larger goal, such as the state of the art or the health of the profession, every individual piece of work appears with the seeds of its own destruction built into it. Each painting or article or book is simply one of its kind and so demands to be answered, modified, criticized, parodied, or refuted. "It has incited the others to do this, and in the vanishing of its reality, still finds satisfaction, just like naughty boys who enjoy *themselves* when they get their ears boxed because *they* are the cause of its being done" (Miller's translation—which from now on I shall designate "PhS"—§413).

If *everything* counts (and Hegel's list of the ruses which the intellectual worker can use to make everything count is ingenious), then my honesty must consist in ignoring this wild vacillation among my pursuits and their justifications. In other words I must be absentminded, so caught up in what I'm doing that I don't know what I'm doing. Yet all along it's been supposed that the consciousness in question is self-conscious; it must really be (or have an essential tendency to become) aware of its contradictory character. Sincere and absentminded devotion to the cause is no longer a possible pose. If this doesn't become apparent to me within the internal structure of recognition which I've rigged up to certify my own honesty, it will become painfully clear from my encounters with others. For all are still separate individuals, and none has been more successful than I have in fusing myself with the cause. When we respond to one another's work, we all are aware of our own investment and interest, despite our attempts to justify ourselves by appealing to *die Sache selbst.* "It is, then, equally a deception of oneself and of others if it is pretended that what one is concerned with is the *'matter in hand'* alone. A consciousness that opens up a subject-matter soon learns that others hurry along like flies to freshly poured-out milk, and want to busy themselves with it; and they learn about that individual that he, too, is concerned with the subject-matter, not as an *object,* but as his *own* affair" (PhS §418). But this is typical of all, and this is why Hegel says that "each and all find themselves both deceiving and deceived" (PhS §416). We discover ourselves, then, to be much more alike than was originally supposed: none is realized or satisfied, all are hungry for recognition, each is willing to justify his or her incursions, attacks, and neglect by a lofty appeal to the cause.

To see the argumentative, dialectical structure of this narrative is to see why the project it depicts is necessarily a failure and so just one more stage on that "highway of despair" Hegel calls the path terminating in absolute knowledge. What is aimed at is the reconciliation of the particular and the universal, but the particular is still a single individual competing with others while the universal is left so indeterminate that it cannot be concretely united with any particular agents. All of part V of the *Phenomenology* is concerned with the ways in which consciousness, having played out the permutations of dependence and independence to their unhappy conclusion, "discovers the world as *its* new real world . . . the *existence* of the world becomes for self-consciousness its own *truth* and *presence;* it is certain of experiencing only itself therein" (PhS §232). The world appears to reflect back the image of the individual consciousness. But in observation it finds at the end only its own dead skull, while in the search for individual pleasure, adventure, or virtue it finally confronts the way of the world—the objective order of society.

In *das geistige Tierreich* it finds a more lively version of itself, but one whose predatory character is hardly flattering. Its own other turns out to be nothing but all those who are alert to take up any task, to pounce on their rival, to deceive and be deceived for the sake of an elusive satisfaction. Where the theoretical mode of reason leads to death in the form of the skull and the practical mode leads to the metaphorical death of the fixed way of the world, the attempt to combine theory and practice through spiritually significant work leads to the constant threat of death so familiar from the struggle for recognition. If it is not actual death that is now at stake but the annihilation of one's work and individuality by all the others who are seeking whatever I am seeking, the situation is all the more hellish. For the life-and-death struggle terminates in death or the relatively settled condition of master and slave; but for Hegel (who did not believe in evolution within the animal kingdom), the spiritual animals may prey upon one another indefinitely.

Perhaps this is the place to gloss once more the irony of Hegel's title. Originally those who toil in the animal kingdom of the spirit are called animalistic for a fairly straightforward reason. Like animals they simply accept their given proclivities and environment and seek their own survival. In doing so they are of course untrue to their spiritual nature, which should give them a greater awareness of themselves and of others. So the self-consciousness that has been suppressed tends to make their struggles both more constant, deceptive, and cruel than the occasional, but quick and clean, combats of the genuine animal kingdom. What was implicit animality in the original terms of the whole attitude thus becomes explicit animality—although only in that metaphorical sense in which, when we say that a man is an animal, we mean that he is far worse than one.

Yet why should we follow Kojève in identifying (more or less) the agent of *das geistige Tierreich* with the man of letters? Let us postpone for just a bit the vexed question of whether the whole *Phenomenology* is basically a disguised historical commentary. Adorno has suggested that intellectuals are tempted by an error of perspective to think the worst of their own kind: "The circumstance that intellectuals mostly have to do with intellectuals, should not deceive them into believing their own kind still more base then the rest of mankind. For they get to know each other in the most shameful and degrading of all situations, that of competing supplicants, and are thus virtually compelled to show each other their most repulsive sides.... Intellectuals, who alone write about intellectuals and give them their bad name in that of honesty, reinforce the lie" (*Minima Moralia,* para. 7). Adorno makes no reference to Hegel's chapter, yet the higher level of irony that can be detected in deceiving oneself and others into thinking that one's kind is worse than they really are—all in the name of honesty—is one that Hegel would probably have relished. But the point might be put this way: In the elementary struggle for recognition, Hegel has already depicted all human consciousness as prone to such struggles for survival and glory. Yet *even here,* among the articulate ones with training and culture, one finds a more refined version of the same thing. *Et in Arcadia ego.* And it is just such training, linguistic skill, and the resources for apparent justification contained in the possibility of appeal to notions like the good of the profession or the state of the art that render this version of the life-and-death struggle both more cerebral and more deceptive. Royce's observation is acute: "of such is the kingdom of those who have no justification for their life task except that it is a life task." This suggests that we are not dealing with all intellectuals or only with intellectuals, but with intellectuals who lack something essential.

René Girard claims that a devouring envy is typical of intellectuals in the modern age because their work now lacks either a transcendent religious goal or obvious social supervision and pressure. Therefore they must fall back upon what others of their own kind *think* of their work; consequently they are caught up in an infinitely reduplicated play of mirrors in which each must envy the others, but can assert him or herself only at the risk of incurring a greater share of their envy. Girard convincingly cites Nietzsche's envy of Wagner as such a case and finds Dostoyevsky's narratives of doubles an important analysis of the whole phenomenon (see *Modern Language Notes*, December 1976).

Marx and Lukács read the chapter as a description of the *bellum omnium contra omnes* of bourgeois society. Unlike Hobbes, Hegel does not see this total individualistic conflict as a permanent possibility of degradation which can be activated by any lapse of authority; rather he sees it as something that has *come about* and which assumes different forms in different social conditions. More specifically Kojève reads the section as a commentary on the activities of the bourgeois intellectual. I've already suggested some reasons for favoring the more determinate interpretation. But this all supposes that something like a historical reading of the *Phenomenology* has been established. Of course Hegel will say, later, that "philosophy is its own time comprehended in thought" and will describe the *Phenomenology* as a unique early work with a special relation to the time when it was written. Yet to identify the various attitudes of consciousness with particular historical developments would rob the work of both philosophical necessity and relevance to the present. In fact, Hegel, in exhibiting the spirit's passage to self-knowledge, is tracing one necessary path that has actually been taken. Despite the fact that the path has already been traversed by the race in general, there is reason to suppose that a good many individuals may never succeed in retracing it themselves and simply get stuck in one of the many waystations which Hegel had charted in 1806.

Those who do not learn from the past may be destined to repeat it, but even those who do learn from the past may be condemned to repetition if history does come to an end. If Hegel is right and if a major phase of our history did reach a conclusion of sorts in 1806 or 1831, then the alternatives seem to be either a radically new beginning or some sort of a repetition of what we have already been through. Yet since historical awareness has become a common possession of intellectuals, the absent-mindedness involved in honestly proceeding as if this is not so or does not matter is reminiscent of the false absent-mindedness of Hegel's "honest" consciousness.

Being intellectuals and professionals, where else should we begin in considering what the end of history would mean than in seeing whether or not we have managed to work our way through the many impasses Hegel described to some new attitude toward our work? The force of Hegel's analysis, the Socratic element in the system (to which Kierkegaard is unfortunately so blind), is his biting analysis of our day-to-day activity, our desires and our fears. Although the *Phenomenology* was conceived as a vehicle of self-education to the level of philosophy for the cultured class of a whole generation, one of the indications of the fragmentation of cultural life (sometimes anticipated by Hegel) is the dissolution of a general audience for philosophical writing. Yet despite the dissolution of such an audience *we* are still here to consider Hegel's analysis.

Surely there is much in Hegel's account that cuts close to the bone of contemporary intellectual life. There is the cult of productivity, for example, in which it is not enough to have completed a body of work, but a demand that each scholar or artist be producing something *now*. The work, billed at first as one's *raison d'être*, quickly proves to be ephemeral; the only way of escaping from the bad infinite of continually seeking fulfillment in the product only to find it criticized or outdated is just the allegiance to the cause which Hegel analyzes. Indeed, this is one of the more endurable stages of the development which Hegel traces—certainly more endurable than the pervasive envy and hypocrisy which he discloses among the intellectual animals. It may be thought that these are accidental features of intellectual life, or features which it has simply because those involved in it are also human beings with their specific passions and ambitions. As such they should be regarded as extraneous to serious intellectual activity; to take them more seriously is to overlook the efforts which various professions, institutes, and academies valiantly make toward minimizing and neutralizing the presence of such factors. Even more, it seems scandalous to talk about these matters. A studied silence about such things—at least in our more serious and professional performances—is not only more dignified but necessary so that we don't give encouragement to the very envy and *ressentiment* of which we would be speaking. Briefly, it is supposed that there is a clear distinction, both morally and conceptually, between intellectual work and intellectual gossip. Now of course it is Hegel's claim that the insistence on such a distinction within *das geistige Tierreich* is just the symptom of its *Betrug*. From the standpoint of philosophy it is necessary to know the dialectical structure of the entire phenomenon and especially to be suspicious of any attempt to dismiss apparently inconsistent aspects of same attitude or practice as irrelevant. The gossip in which intellectuals indulge is the *truth* of their enterprise rather than its idle accompaniment. This is pointed out even more perspicuously in the *Phenomenology* when Hegel comes to analyze the witty and disintegrating consciousness of *Rameau's Nephew*.

The temptation persists to suppose that Hegel is speaking of a degraded form of intellectual life. Of course there is much truth in this. What I want to insist on is that this spiritually degraded form of intellectual life can be overcome only by a rather difficult spiritual movement. Hegel himself, even in the *Phenomenology,* portrays forms of artistic and intellectual life (in chapters VII and VIII) which have managed to avoid the traps of the *geistige Tierreich.* But it must be noted that these forms are distinguished from the normal, degraded form of intellectual life in civil society by their commitment to an overriding religious or philosophical quest—one which not only fills the place assigned to *die Sache selbst* in the degraded form, but which is capable of taking on sufficient concreteness and determinacy so that the strictly individual self can indeed find satisfaction in working for it. In fact, the free market model which is often proposed for the life of the artist and intellectual is close to the framework described in the *geistige Tierreich.* It's often been pointed out that the last of the classical entrepreneurs are to be found among artists and intellectuals who have succeeded in staking out a new stylistic nuance or a novel area of scholarship. Of course the presence of the successful entrepreneur is a symptom that many more are unsuccessful and that the structure which breeds such success must involve envy and deception. Since the prevailing tendency—despite corporate and socialist drift in the rest of society—is to propose something like the laissez-faire structure of civil society for the realm of the spirit, it can be seen how intellectual life could be capable of a systematic regression and self-degradation from the Hegelian perspective.

Hegel is of course not alone in his awareness of the dangers. The whole Hegelian school has a tendency to speak a bit more candidly than do philosophers of some different persuasions about the prevalence of market-like conditions in the spiritual world. The brilliant if somewhat heavy sarcasm of the opening pages of the *German Ideology* is in this vein:

> When the last spark of [Hegelianism's] life had failed, the various components of this *caput mortuum* began to decompose, entered on new combinations and formed new substances. The industrialists of philosophy, who till then had lived on the exploitation of the absolute spirit, now seized upon the new combinations. Each with all possible zeal set about retailing his apportioned share. This naturally gave rise to competition, which, to start with, was carried on in moderately staid bourgeois fashion. Later when the German market was glutted, and the commodity in spite of all efforts found no response in the world-market, the business was spoiled in the usual German manner by fake and shoddy production, deterioration in quality, adulteration of the raw materials,

falsification of labels, fake purchases, bill-jobbing and a credit-system devoid of any real basis.

Now Marx, who was fond of the *geistige Tierreich* chapter (letter to Engels, June 18, 1862) has in this passage, written with Engels, a quite different purpose than Hegel, even if they do employ similar metaphors. Given the primacy of material conditions for Marx, one expects to find intellectual life reproducing the social relations of production, whereas Hegel sees the competition of the phase as transitional; for Hegel, bourgeois society can continue to exist while intellectual life escapes from the constraints of civil society.

This miraculous escape from the terrors of civil society through philosophy (and via religion) is just where Lukács sees the argument of the *Phenomenology* going wrong. What neither Hegel nor Marx envisioned was the continuation of bourgeois relations with the artistic and intellectual classes within an increasingly collectivist society. Such continuation is overdetermined. It is to be attributed, paradoxically, both to the apparent determination of bourgeois society to leave its intellectuals alone and its need that they reflect the society's own ideal notion of itself. A secular and liberal society, in professing to leave its artists and intellectuals on their own, opens up the possibility Girard has described of their increasing dependency on the opinions of their own kind and their consequent envy. Yet, in fact, this leaving them on their own is not so neglectful as it appears for it involves a complex network of support which provides for a degree of insulation from the wider society. Within that insulation the intellectual classes can act out that animal kingdom and of the spirit which is rapidly disappearing from the wider society but whose image that society requires. Given the relative publicity of what artists and intellectuals do (contrary to their own frequent impression that they are neglected), their animal behavior will enact that which society in general is less and less able to do. As Sartre said in *Search for a Method*, the bourgeoisie is the class which as soon as it discovers the fact of history wishes to bring it to an end.

Let us consider a self-confessed Hegelian of another stripe, and a strong advocate of scientific objectivity, Charles Peirce. Peirce, so it seems, saw the commitment to eventual agreement and a willingness (or, better, eagerness) to put one's own results and hypotheses to the test as the minimal conditions of scientific practice. In doing so, Peirce seems not to be prescribing for a scientific utopia but describing the presuppositions of any scientific work—and Peirce's broad sense of science, it should be remembered, includes philosophy and such of its branches as aesthetics and phenomenology. Yet Peirce believed that these minimal prerequisites for scientific work were identical with the theological virtue of faith, hope, and charity (given a suitably broad and non-sectarian yet still "Buddho-Christian" interpretation of those virtues). And in what seems to be a logical examination of the problems of probability he characteristically states that "He who would not sacrifice his own soul to save the whole world, is, as it seems to me, illogical in all his inferences, collectively" (*Selected Writings*, ed. Buchler, 162). Within the systematic framework of Peirce's philosophy, this is not surprising, since he holds logic (including scientific inquiry) to be a normative science subordinate to the normative science of ethics. Like Hegel, he believed in a marriage of science and religion and recoiled even more strongly from the suggestion that the individualistic political economy of the nineteenth century could furnish a model for any admirable intellectual or moral achievement. There's no doubt that this pragmatist would be appalled by the suggestion that the intellectual community could operate on the basis of a widespread moral and cognitive relativism. Without faith in the truth, the scientific community is on the verge of falling back into the animal kingdom.

There are some interesting points of contact between Hegel's account of *das geistige Tierreich* and Nietzsche's analysis of scientific praxis. Both are attempts to describe concretely what the life of science amounts to and to disclose the instinctive or egoistic drives which alternately give force to or undermine the impersonal scientific ideal. In *The Genealogy of Morals* Nietzsche attempts to turn science on itself by proposing to analyze the true heritage of the scientific way of life. It is an Oedipal inquiry which begins with the recognition that "We are unknown to ourselves, we men of knowledge," and proceeds to argue that the values implicit in scientific work are subtle and refined forms of the ascetic ideal that is generated by the weak, through *ressentiment*, in response to the powerful. The scientist takes over the form of this ascetic ideal by accepting the necessity of subordinating his individuality to the goal of truth. Like Peirce's scientist, he has faith not in his own results but in the process of science itself and its presumed asymptotic approach to the truth. He must be willing to sacrifice pleasure and honor in order to add just a bit—even in the form of a refuted hypothesis—to the accumulating edifice of the scientific enterprise. At this point, however, Nietzsche's analysis becomes a bit fuzzy. The ascetic ideals which he had interpreted earlier were all said to stem from *ressentiment* toward fairly identifiable others: slave morality is directed against the masters and Christian morality against all that which is healthy and well turned out. Now there are hints in Nietzsche's account that suggest it could be either the strong and healthy man in general or the adventurous artist, in particular, unconstrained by the tyranny of the facts, who is the object of the scientist's *ressentiment*.

Hegel's phenomenology of scientific praxis is more radical and perspicuous at this point. The envy which is at work in science (keeping the broad sense of *Wissenschaft* in mind) is a mutual envy among the members of what Nietzsche would call the scientific herd. Here, of course, there is a suggestive distinction to be made between the two animal metaphors: the herd, with at least an internal peacefulness, and the mutual voracity in *das geistige Tierreich*. Hegel, with his analysis of the generality of the struggle for recognition, would be able to see the possibility of intellectual envy being minimized or suppressed by being directed toward same outside group—philistines, laymen, administrators, and so on. This suppression will probably occur more frequently when the intellectual animals are forced by the threat of outside intervention to assume the attitude of the herd; but where they are more numerous and their status not in great danger, they will again focus their envy on their own kind. *Die Sache selbst* is broad enough to accommodate both possibilities.

Of course it should be remembered that the Hegelian and Nietzschean dialectics move in essentially different directions. Hegel's moves toward a concrete synthesis of particularity and universality which does promise the possibility of spiritual life free from the struggle for recognition. Nietzsche's drive is toward an increasingly deeper and more intense conception of the individual (and so he is interested in the *body*, which classically individuates the individual) until that point is reached (as Zarathustra reaches it in his realization of the eternal recurrence) in which the ultimate dissolution of the individual must be confronted. This, I take it, is the philosophical background of Gruff's speaking of "that naive conception of the unity of the 'ego' that's presupposed by the concept of insult."

It should be clear that the kind of conflict which occurs in the *geistige Tierreich* is not a struggle for survival or for scarce goods of any material sort. As even Hobbes observes, the human war of all against all is not for those alone but also for "glory." Now whatever Humpty-Dumpty may have to say about the meaning of that word, it designates a recognition which cannot be granted to all for it consists in one being recognized by others as having attained a marked superiority of same sort. Yet it might be thought that a human community could—as in an ideal aristocratic society—rest on a basis of mutual recognition of the remarkable achievements of its members. Whether in fact this is possible, and to what extent, is not my present concern; Hegel is widely interpreted as believing that the modern state of the form described in his *Rechtsphilosophie* does achieve such mutuality of recognition. However, it should also be remembered that this is not a recognition of great achievement but of citizenship, and so hardly satisfies the urge for glory. Although Hegel implies that the service of absolute spirit will help us transcend the problem of envy and Marx suggests the same about a society free of class divisions, both are disappointingly vague as to *how* this is supposed to happen.

In this respect some of the anarchist theorists of the nineteenth century may have had a deeper intuition of the radical change that such a dissolution of envy would require in all social values and structures, even if they had no real sense of how such a change could be brought about. When Proudhon says that work is the most private and sacred of human activities, he is suggesting a transvaluation of our standards of judging ourselves and others and of the divisions which we draw between the public and the private. The private and sacred is that which is beyond evaluation and comparison. The original alienation of labor in this perspective is not its control or use for the sake of another but its entry into the circle of mutual observation that constitutes civil society. The use of religious language is, of course, an indication that the moral change desired is not one which is intelligible from a Hegelian or Marxist perspective; like the more recent calls to do your own thing, it is not likely to be effective in a world in which the dialectics of recognition seem destined to cover more and more areas of life. The anarchist ideal is in fact a reversion to the attitudes which Hegel takes up just before the *geistige Tierreich* in the *Phenomenology* in which "the law of the heart" or the faith in one's own virtue are destined to run up against "the way of the world."

It may seem as if envy is a topic for literature and psychology rather than for philosophy. This is indicated by Aristotle who treats envy not in his *Ethics* but in the more literary context of his *Rhetoric*. (There Aristotle makes a useful distinction between emulation and envy. The former is the desire to be honored as others are for their value or accomplishments, while the latter is the desire for a recognition which will exclude others. Since Aristotle's *Rhetoric* is based upon what it seems plausible to say within the *polis*, the distinction may be weakened considerably when it is recalled that both forms of the desire for glory occur within a social structure which depends on the recognition of the master by the slave. Hegel's account is arguably more inclusive because it takes this context into account.) But the easy relegation of problems to non-philosophical fields may itself be a refusal of the kind of self-knowledge that Hegel's analysis invites. It may in fact be true, as René Girard says in *Mensonge romantique et verité romanesque*, that the most penetrating accounts of envy and even a close structural analysis of the same are to be found in the novels of Stendhal, Dostoyevsky, and Proust. A critic might turn this against Hegel by suggesting that it simply shows once more his tendency to tell stories, to write an idealized *Bildungsroman* of world history, rather than to provide solid conceptual analysis. Now, while Hegel is in many respects what Schelling called a "narrative philosopher," it is just the ability of this philosophical narrative to include such uncomfortable facts that makes it a model of philosophical achievement. Dismissing such narrative philosophy excludes any *philosophical* analysis of the kinds of questions which Hegel raises about intellectual work, although it may allow us to demonstrate once more our honest consciousness and our allegiance to the good cause, *die Sache selbst*, or philosophy. But what audience (*in foro interno* or *externo*) would we be trying to convince? And what would be the source of our passion?

V

Spirit

12

Patricia Jagentowicz Mills

Hegel's Antigone

> *The Antigone [is] one of the most sublime and in every respect most excellent works of art of all time.*
> —G. W. F. Hegel, Aesthetics

Hegel's interpretation of Sophocles' play *Antigone* is central to an understanding of woman's role in the Hegelian system. Hegel was fascinated by this play and used it in both the *Phenomenology* and the *Philosophy of Right* to demonstrate that familial ethical life is woman's unique responsibility. Antigone is revealed as the paradigmatic figure of womanhood and family life in both the ancient and modern worlds, although there are fundamental differences between these two worlds for Hegel. In order to situate the interpretation of this play within its wider context, I use Seyla Benhabib's understanding of the "doubled vision" of feminist theory, a method that takes traditional issues into account but does so by simultaneously focusing on gender issues that have been "traditionally" marginalized.[1] Thus, my analysis of Hegel's *Antigone* proceeds through an internal or immanent critique of the *Phenomenology*, then turns to an immanent critique of the *Philosophy of Right*.

In the *Phenomenology* we learn that history can be understood as a dialectic of particular and universal: man seeks recognition of his own particular self from all men; he seeks universal recognition of his particularity.[2] And universality, as the overcoming, reconciliation, or *Aufhebung* of the opposition between particular and universal, is "concrete" or universal individuality. However, in the pagan world, which is a specific historical moment in the movement of spirit toward self-realization, the dialectical opposition between the particular and the universal cannot be overcome in life because the *polis* or city-state only recognizes or realizes the universal aspect of human action and risk, while the particular remains embedded in the family.

Man is necessarily a member of a family and the family is the sphere of the particularity of the pagan male's existence. Within the family, man is *this* particular father, *this* husband, *this* son, and not simply *a* father, *a* husband, *a* son. But the family is the sphere of "merely natural existence," "mere particularity"; as such its supreme value is essentially inactive biological existence or animal life. While man has particularity inside the family circle, it is an unconscious particularity because, within this circle, there is no negating action—no risk of life for recognition. Within the family man cannot achieve self-consciousness or truly human satisfaction because, according to Hegel, in the pagan world the truly human demands the conscious risk of life.[3]

While neither male nor female can achieve self-consciousness within the family in Hegel's schema, the pagan male moves out to become a citizen. He does so "because it is only as a citizen that he is actual and substantial; the individual, so far as he is not a citizen but belongs to the family, is only an unreal insubstantial shadow."[4] Hegel writes that within the *polis* "the community is that substance conscious of what it actually does," which is in opposition to the family as "the other side" whose form is that of "immediate substance or substance that simply is" (PhS §450, 268). The community draws man away from the family: By subduing his "merely natural existence," and his "mere particularity," it induces him to live "in and for the universal." What is achieved in the *polis*, through action and risk, is "the manhood of the community." But while the universal aspect of a man's existence is recognized here, this existence is not truly *his*: it is not *he* as a particular who is recognized by the *polis*. Acting on behalf of the *polis*, man achieves universality at the expense of his particularity. The *Aufhebung* of the familial particular and the political universal that results in concrete or universal individuality is possible only in death in the pagan world.[5]

In that world the transcendence of death in and by historical memory is achieved through the family. The ethical relation between the members of the family is not that of sentiment or love but duty in connection with burying and remembering the dead — as well as avenging them if need be. Through these obligations to the dead the "powerless, simply isolated individual has been raised to universal individuality" (PhS §452, 271). Since familial life does not depend on the activity of the members but simply on their being—their inaction—death changes nothing in the value attributed to and by the family.[6] And by burying and remembering the family members, the family maintains the continuity of the human community through time.

In the pagan world the family and the *polis*, the particular and universal spheres of man's existence, are mutually exclusive: the family represents life and the *polis* represents the risk of life. The conflict between these two spheres is inescapable and unalterable. Man cannot renounce the family since he cannot renounce the particularity of his existence, nor can he renounce the universality of his action in and for the *polis*. This conflict between the familial and the political makes for the tragic character of pagan life and creates a fundamental antinomy between family life, as the natural ground of ethical life, and ethical life in its social universality, or "second nature," in the *polis*.[7]

For Hegel the conflict between family and *polis*, particular and universal, is also a conflict between divine law and human law as represented in the conflict between woman and man. Nature, according to Hegel, assigns woman to divine law and man to human law. Thus while the political life of the city-state represents the manhood of the community, the family is the sphere of womanhood. The two are opposed such that when they come into open conflict woman, as the representative of divine law, sees human law as "only the violence of human caprice," while man, as the representative of human law, sees only "the self-will and disobedience of the individual" in obedience to the divine (PhS §466, 280).

In the section on the pagan or Greek ethical world in the *Phenomenology* where the interpretation of the *Antigone* appears, and where we find the only discussion of woman, Hegel is in search of the ideal relationship between a man and a woman as a relation of identity-in-difference. He begins with an analysis of heterosexual marriage and says that there is reciprocal recognition between husband and wife in the pagan world, but that this recognition is "natural self-knowledge," not realized ethical life. That is, it is a process of recognition rooted in the immediacy of desire or affective understanding, not in conscious ethical intention.

Hegel claims that the wife's desire for the husband always has a universal significance, while for the husband desire and universality are separate. Here Hegel accepts the traditional view that there is a separation of morality and desire in man's relation to woman, but that morality and desire are united in woman's relation to man, and, therefore, that woman is ethically "purer" in her love relations. That is, a wife's ethical relation to her husband is not to feeling or the sentiment of love but, rather, is a relation to the universal (PhS §457, 274–75). What creates the separation of morality or universality and desire or particularity in man is the bifurcation of his life into the public and private spheres. While woman remains confined to, and defined by, the family, man lives within the *polis* as well as within the family. In this way Hegel distinguishes the family for-itself from the family in-itself. That is, woman represents the family as immediately universal for-itself while, from the perspective of the man, she represents the family in-itself as the sphere of particularity. Thus, central to the relationship between particularity and universality in the family is the split between desire and morality in the pagan male's existence.

For Hegel, the husband acquires the *rights* of desire over his wife precisely because he has the rights of a citizen. The husband's authority and position in the *polis* allow him to have sexual domination over the wife in the family and simultaneously keep him "detached" from his desire for her: man rules woman in the private sphere because he rules in the public world. And as he rules in the public world and in the family he rules himself.

What is most significant in this analysis of desire in marriage is that for Hegel it is *male* desire that taints the purity of the male-female relationship: the husband's desire for the wife is expressed as merely particular desire such that a moment of indifference and ethical contingency is introduced into the relationship. However, insofar as this relationship *is* ethical, the wife is without the moment of knowing herself as *this* particular self in and through an other.[8] Thus, in the ethical family of the pagan world the husband gains an unconscious particularity, as *this* husband, through the wife's exercise of universal recognition of him as *a* husband, while his recognition of her is such that she never achieves particularity. He is particularized but she is not. Man, says Hegel, achieves particularity in the pagan family, through the wife's recognition of him, precisely because he leaves this sphere to attain universal recognition in the political sphere. But woman never enters the political sphere; she is caught and bound within the immediacy of the family circle.

For Hegel, the relationship between husband and wife in the pagan world is a mixed and transitive one in which male desire infects the process of recognition between a man and a woman so that each maintains a knowledge of dissimilarity or "independent being-for self." Husband and wife are separated as male and female. Because the husband and the wife each retain a moment of independence—a being-for-self—the "return-into-itself" of the relationship cannot take place. Rather, the relationship is necessarily externalized through the child. Thus, the husband-wife relationship is not complete in itself; it needs the child to complete it, and the child changes the relationship (PhS §456, 273). Given this, the husband-wife relationship is not the ideal relationship of identity-in-difference between man and woman.

However, Hegel believes he has found this ideal in the relationship between a brother and a sister because he believes that this relationship is without desire and therefore without the separation and ethical uncertainty that male desire entails:

> The relationship [between man and woman] in its unmixed form is found, however, in that between brother and sister. They are the same blood which has, however, in them reached a state of rest and equilibrium. Therefore, they do not desire one another, nor have they given to, or received from, one another this independent being-for-self; on the contrary, they are free individualities in regard to each other. (PhS §457, 274)

Brother and sister are not independent of one another because they are united through the blood tie. Thus, the brother-sister relationship is a unity of male and female that is not recognition as separation, distinctiveness, or dissimilarity: it is a relationship of identity-in-difference. Their recognition is that of "free individualities in regard to each other" which transcends the indifference or ethical contingency characteristic of the husband-wife relationship. Whereas mere particularity is implicated in the husband-wife relationship through male desire, "The brother . . . is for the sister a passive similar being" and the recognition of the sister in the brother "is pure and unmixed with any natural desire" (PhS §457, 275). The brother's nature is ethically like the sister's—that is, directly universal—which allows for the realization of self in and through an other. The sister's recognition of herself in the brother is therefore pure and complete, as is his recognition of himself in her, and "the moment of the individual self, recognizing and being recognized, can here assert its right" (PhS §457, 275). Thus, Hegel makes a distinction between, on the one hand, the process of recognition between man and woman based on an immediate unity (an immediate universality grounded in blood) that is transcended through the process of recognition into a unity or identity-in-difference (brother-sister); and, on the other hand, recognition grounded in desire, the mere particularity of male desire, that necessarily retains separation and dissimilarity in such a way that a unity of male and female cannot be fully realized (husband-wife).

While Freud's theories and anthropological studies of incest taboos would seem to make the assertion that "brother and sister . . . do not desire one another" at least dubious if not altogether untenable, it is significant that Hegel believes that this lack of desire offers woman, as sister, the possibility of truly mutual recognition. The death of a brother thus becomes an irreparable loss for the sister since with his death she loses the ideal relationship with a man. And the nature of this relationship is such that the sister's familial duty to the brother is the highest in terms of honoring and remembering him after his death.

Woman as sister in the pagan world is the paradigmatic foreshadowing of ethical life, precisely because she represents familial duty to man which is "purely" spiritual. But the brother-sister relationship is not one of *conscious* ethical life; rather, the law of the family is the sister's immediate, unconscious nature. The sister in the pagan world cannot realize or actualize this life completely because, according to Hegel, the dualism of the pagan world resists the possibility of transcendence or the realization in consciousness of ethical life:

> [T]he feminine, in the form of the sister, has the highest *intuitive* awareness of what is ethical. She does not attain to *consciousness* of it, or to the objective existence of it, because the law of the Family is an implicit, inner essence which is not exposed to the daylight of consciousness, but remains an inner feeling and the divine element that is exempt from an existence in the real world. The woman is associated with these household gods [Penates] and beholds in them both her universal substance and her particular individuality, yet in such a way that this relation of her individuality to them is at the same time not the natural one of desire. (PhS §457, 274)

Hegel retains his understanding of the ethical purity of the brother-sister relationship being tied to sexual purity in his *Philosophy of History* where he describes Apollo as "pure" precisely because "he has no wife, but only a sister [Artemis, the virgin goddess of the hunt], and is not involved in various disgusting adventures, like Zeus."[9]

The unity of the brother-sister relationship necessarily "passes beyond itself" when the brother "leaves this immediate, elemental, and therefore, strictly speaking, negative ethical life of the Family, in order to acquire and produce the ethical life that is conscious of itself and actual" (PhS §458, 275). The sister merely moves into another family situation by marrying and becoming a wife: she moves from the family of origin to the family of procreation. Thus, the brother passes from divine to human law, while the sister continues to maintain divine law as wife. In this way, according to Hegel, natural sexual difference comes to have an ethical determination.

At this point it is important to note several problems in the brother-sister relationship which Hegel does not address. In the first place, this relationship takes place *within* the family of origin before the brother has entered the sphere of the city-state and accepted the claims made on him by that sphere. Woman is said to realize herself within the family, but insofar as the brother is still only part of the family, he is an adolescent, not part of the manhood of the community and therefore not an adult male in Hegelian terms. The fact that the brother is in this way only a *potential* man, not a realized one, undermines Hegel's claim that brother and sister represent the ideal relationship between man and woman. Certainly such a relationship requires, at the very least, that there *be* a man and a woman. Second, the brother-sister relationship does not entail equal responsibility. Since the brother's vocation is to accept the bifurcation of life, and with it the separation of desire and morality, he leaves the family of origin and does not look back. The sister assumes the familial obligations of divine law, which require that she bury and remember her brother when he dies, but there is no mention of any responsibility the brother has to his sister in terms of human or political law. Thus woman, as sister, assumes a responsibility for the brother, as a member of the family of origin, that the brother does not reciprocate. This unequal responsibility mitigates the sense in which the brother-sister relationship can be seen as ideal. And third, Hegel is in search of the self-complete relationship between man and woman that is an identity-in-difference: it must be a "natural" relationship that is dialectically transcended through consciousness (recognition/history). But there is no guarantee that a woman will *have* a brother. Insofar as Hegel attempts to institutionalize forms of consciousness, this means that a woman without a brother can never achieve even a glimmer of an unconscious self that might be the equal of man's.

Setting aside these objections for the moment, we find that in Sophocles' *Antigone* Hegel finds the superiority of the sister-brother relationship demonstrated in a way that reveals the profound ethical conflict inherent in the pagan world between family and *polis*, woman and man, particular and universal, divine law and human law. Thus, while the central *conflict* for Hegel is between Antigone and Creon (as woman and man who represent the conflict between the family, as the natural ground of ethical life, and ethical life itself in its social universality in the *polis*), the central *relationship* in this drama is, for him, that between Antigone and Polyneices: Antigone's enduring sense of duty to her dead brother is explained in terms of the ideal male-female relationship of mutual recognition.[10] Antigone "premonizes and foreshadows" most completely the nature of familial ethical life precisely because she represents the relation between man and woman not as wife but as sister. She is the paradigm of the law of the family as she carries out her "highest duty" toward her brother in attempting to bury and honor him.

While it is true that Antigone's burial of Polyneices represents familial duty (and in particular that between sister and brother), Hegel does not consider the play in its entirety. His references to the *Antigone* are scattered throughout his discussion of the ethical world and ethical action in the *Phenomenology* as "evidence" for his claims regarding the relationship between male/human law and female/divine law in the Greek pagan world. But Hegel's interpretation of this play, and in particular the conflict between Creon and Antigone, is an oversimplification made to fit his view of the tragic character of pagan life as a conflict between equal and contrary values.

Hegel considers the situation that precedes the action in the *Antigone*: the struggle between the two brothers, Eteocles and Polyneices, for control of the city of Thebes. "Nature" has provided two potential rulers where only one can rule. In the pagan world the ruler is the community as individual soul: two cannot share power. Hegel claims that the two brothers each have an equal right to rule and that the inequality of the natural order of birth can have no importance when they enter the ethical community of the *polis*. Thus, the right of primogeniture is denied here. However, the equal right of the brothers to rule destroys them both, since in their conflict over power they are both wrong.

In human law or political terms, it is the right of possession that is most important. Thus, because Eteocles was in power when Polyneices attacked the city, Eteocles is given a formal burial by Creon, who has become the ruler of the war-torn city-state. But Creon's edict, which forbids anyone to bury Polyneices on pain of death, is a denial of sacred claims: without burial Polyneices' soul cannot safely enter Hades. By honoring one brother and dishonoring the other, human law and divine law are set in opposition. And the "right" of human law is revealed as "wrong" through the vengeance of war waged on Thebes by Argos (PhS §§473-74, 285-87).

Through his elliptical discussion of the *Antigone*, Hegel reveals the way in which the tragic conflict in pagan society between the universalistic *polis* and the particularistic family ends in the destruction of the pagan world such that it becomes one "soulless and dead" bare universal community. But, according to Hegel, it is not only external forces that destroy the community. Rather, there is within the community the seeds of its own destruction in the family. The family, for Hegel, is "the rebellious principle of pure individuality" (PhS §474, 286), which, in its universality, is inner divine law; and this law, as he claims again and again, is the law of woman. Here, woman is the agent of destruction of the pagan world. Since particularity is not *included* in the *polis*, it destroys the *polis*. Woman, as the representative of the family principle, the principle of particularity which the *polis* represses, is the internal cause of the downfall of the pagan world:

> Since the community only gets an existence through its interference with the happiness of the family, and by dissolving [individual] self-consciousness into the universal, it creates for itself in what it suppresses and what

is at the same time essential to it an internal enemy—womankind in general. Womankind—the everlasting irony [in the life] of the community—changes by intrigue the universal end of the government into a private end, transforms its universal activity into a work of some particular individual, and perverts the universal property of the state into a possession and ornament for the family. (PhS §475, 288)

Woman, as the representative of both the immediacy of family life and the principle of particularity, represents the spirit of individualism as subversive. She revolts and destroys the community in the pagan world by acting on the young man who has not yet completely detached himself from the family of origin and therefore has not yet subordinated his particular existence to the universality of the *polis*. She persuades him to exercise his power for the family dynasty rather than for public welfare. According to Hegel, woman does this by asserting the power of youthful male authority, as the power of the son, the brother, or the husband.[11]

The question of exactly how woman can represent the sphere of particularity while never knowing herself as this particular self is a question never addressed by Hegel. In *Negative Dialectics* T. W. Adorno challenges Hegel on precisely this transformation of the particular into particularity. For Adorno, "the particular would not be definable without the universal that identifies it, according to current logic; but neither is it identical with the universal."[12] Thus, for Adorno the concept of the particular is a concept of the dialectics of non-identity, whereas the concept of particularity eliminates the particular *as* particular in order to absorb it into a philosophy of identity dominated by the universal. The transformation of the analysis away from a concern with the particular to a concern with particularity in relation to woman is the paradigm case of what Adorno points to. That is, Adorno shows that Hegel's identity philosophy necessarily excludes forms of human experience, and it is my contention that it is primarily forms of *female* experience, which Antigone symbolizes, that are excluded.[13]

While Antigone, as the paradigm of the ethical family, does not, in the *Phenomenology*, represent woman as the principle of particularity destroying the *polis* through intrigue and perversion, nevertheless Hegel misses what is most significant: that Antigone must *enter* the political realm, the realm of second nature, in order to defy it on behalf of the realm of the family, the realm of first nature. In doing this, as we shall see, Antigone transcends Hegel's analysis of "the law of woman" as "natural ethical life," and becomes *this* particular self.

Sophocles presents a situation in which Antigone must reconcile her obligations to the family and its gods with the demands of the political sphere represented by Creon. Her tragedy is that no matter which course of action she chooses she cannot be saved. If she defies the law of the *polis* and buries Polyneices, she will die; if she fails in her familial duty to her brother, she will suffer divine retribution and loss of honor. She defies Creon and in so doing brings divine law into the human community in opposition to the authority of the *polis*.

According to Hegel, in the pagan world the two forms of law, human and divine, as represented by man and woman, exclude and oppose each other; their separation means the loss of certainty of immediate truth and creates the possibility of crime and guilt. Crime is defined here as the adherence to one of the two laws over and against the other. Thus, there is no *Aufhebung* of the two laws, but only opposition. For Hegel, "essential reality" is the unity or identity-in-difference of both human law and divine law; that is, there can be no justice without revelation (PhS §460, 276). But such an *Aufhebung* is only possible in the *modern* world, after the advent of Christianity. It is the revelation of God in Christ that allows man to acquire the knowledge necessary to make the transition to an ethical life that is self-conscious and therefore truly universal. In the pagan world conflict is always "resolved" on one side or the other, but the two laws are inextricably bound up with each other such that the fulfillment of one calls forth the other's revenge. The purer ethical consciousness acknowledges the other law but interprets it as wrong and acts as it deems necessary because "what is *ethical* must be *actual*" (PhS §460, 276). In this sense Antigone wittingly commits a "crime," according to Hegel. However, by acknowledging the other law, ethical consciousness must acknowledge that it has committed a crime against this law, and it must admit guilt. It is here, in the analysis of the relation between crime and guilt, that we begin to see the inadequacy of Hegel's interpretation of the *Antigone*.

Against Hegel's interpretation, Sophocles does not create Antigone and Creon as ethical equals. Antigone alone is the ultimate defender of the good; one sees this revealed in the fate meted out to Creon and in Antigone's *refusal* to admit guilt. In Hegel's attempt to fit the *Antigone* into his view of the tragic character of pagan life in terms of crime and guilt, he has to "interpret" this play in the *Phenomenology* to the extent of changing Antigone's final words. In the section on ethical action Hegel makes it seem as if she acknowledges her "guilt" for the "crime" of burying her brother. What she actually says is:

> I have done no wrong,
> I have not sinned before the gods. Or if I have,
> I shall know the truth in death. But if the guilt

> Lies upon Creon who judged me, then, I pray,
> May his punishment equal my own.[14]

With her death she believes that she will enter the world of the gods and that *they* will determine whether her act was right or wrong. In a dialectical turn, Creon ends up living the fate he has tried to inflict on Antigone by entombing her alive: he must endure the solitude of a "living death," for his actions lead to the suicides of his son, Haemon, and his wife, Eurydice. In the end he declares: "I alone am guilty" (32).

While Antigone chooses to obey the gods, or divine law, nevertheless she does not admit guilt concerning human law.[15] From Hegel's point of view Antigone's admission of guilt is necessary for her ethical consciousness to be equal to that of Creon and for the play to represent the tragic conflict of pagan life. When we adhere to what actually happens in the play and put it within Hegel's interpretative framework, we find that Creon's admission of guilt actually makes *him* the hero of the play since it gives him a *higher* ethical consciousness. Thus, there are not two equal and contrary values in opposition in the conflict between Antigone and Creon, as Hegel tries to claim, but rather a "higher" political consciousness of the male and a "lower" familial consciousness of the female. From this perspective the play should have been called *Creon* since only Creon has the self-recognition made possible through the admission of guilt. While the action of the play transforms Creon from a criminal to a tragic figure for both Sophocles and Hegel, within Hegel's framework Antigone remains "criminal" in that she upholds only the law of the family and does not recognize the law of the *polis* as legitimate. Thus, Hegel *wants* Antigone to be a tragic character but he cannot show her as such without misrepresenting and "adapting" what she says to make it look as if she admits guilt.

In his interpretation of the *Antigone*, with its emphasis on crime and guilt, Hegel misses several critical components of the play that are central to an understanding of female experience. To begin with, Antigone retains a steadfast devotion to what is noble and just that goes far beyond the mere intuition of natural ethical life and the consciousness that comes from burying and remembering the dead. Antigone has a moral courage that allows her to *choose* a course of action even though it condemns her to death. Whereas Hegel claims that the sister's intuition of ethical life is not open to the daylight of consciousness, the chorus in Sophocles' play cries out to Antigone: "Your death is the doing of your conscious hand" (21). Sophocles shows Antigone choosing to carry out her duty to her brother and choosing to disobey Creon's edict. While she claims to owe a stronger allegiance to the dead, to her brother and to the gods, it is not an unreflective position she takes. It is not an unconscious intuition of her ethical duty as Hegel would have us believe. Rather, it is a noble stance, consciously taken.[16]

According to Hegel, the woman who remained in her place never felt the tragic character of pagan life, never felt the conflict between particular and universal because she never entered the *polis*, the sphere of universality. Thus, it is Ismene, Antigone's sister, rather than Antigone herself, who maintains the traditional place of woman. Curiously, Hegel fails even to mention Ismene in his references to the play. This is probably because Ismene's "instinctive" reaction is contrary to her supposed "natural ethical orientation": she explicitly sides with the political authority of the *polis* over the divine law. And in siding with the law of the *polis* Ismene bows to "the law of woman" as male domination. When Antigone asks Ismene if she wishes to help bury their brother, Ismene cries out:

> Think how much more terrible than these
> Our own death would be if we should go against Creon
> And do what he has forbidden! We are only women,
> We cannot fight with men, Antigone!
> The law is strong, we must give in to the law
> In this thing, and in worse. (2)

However, Ismene, motivated by feelings of sisterhood, overcomes her initial fears and attempts to share the responsibility for burying Polyneices. Antigone protests that there is no need for both of them to die for something she alone has done. To this Ismene replies:

> What do I care for life when you are dead? (14)

While Antigone rejects Ismene's offer of sisterly solidarity, what we see here in Ismene is a second, more traditional woman, a woman representing conventional womanhood, created in human rather than heroic proportions, choosing an honorable death over the continuation of an ignoble life.[17] Thus, Ismene wavers in her commitment to the good but her decision to do what is right is rooted in the familial devotion between sisters, not in the sister-brother relationship. Hegel completely disregards this aspect of the play.

Unlike Ismene, Antigone *acts* on behalf of the family, the sphere of inaction. She moves outside the sphere of the family and as a consequence becomes different *within* the family. As we saw earlier, the brother-sister relationship of mutual recognition, in which the sister is said to realize herself, necessarily ends when the brother leaves the family of origin. And Hegel asserts that it makes no difference to woman that she is not *this* particular self within the family of procreation. He claims that there is reciprocal recognition between husband and wife, but when we examine this claim carefully we find that it contradicts his claim concerning what one is to *gain* from the process of recognition within the family of procreation, that is, particularity. Thus, man gains an unconscious particularity through woman's relation to the universal, but man's relation to the universal is separate from his relation to woman so that she is never *this* particular self. While the husband cannot renounce the particularity of his being in the pagan world, the wife never achieves it. She cannot achieve an unconscious particularity as *this* wife within the immediacy of the ethical family and she is not allowed out into any other sphere of life.

In the Hegelian schema woman cannot even achieve the self-consciousness of the slave since she does not experience the two central elements of slave-consciousness. That is, she experiences neither the ubiquitous personal fear of death as "the absolute Lord," nor the "service" or work on nature as thinghood, the work of objectification that recreates the world to create history.[18] Woman's response to death is said to be resignation, while her primary responsibility is to memorialize the dead in order to raise them to living memory (PhS §457, 274–75). And woman is represented as someone that does not *do* anything and therefore can have no universal recognition of her action or humanity in the *polis*; she is not seen as someone who *acts* but merely as someone who *is*.

Since woman remains confined inside the family she must remain the walking dead of "unreal insubstantial shadow." Thus, if Antigone were to proceed as a "normal" woman she would marry Haemon, her betrothed and Creon's son, move from the family of origin to the family of procreation, and never know herself as *this* particular self. But Antigone, like the male, leaves the family to risk her life in the *polis*. While it is true that she is in the *polis* on behalf of the family, nevertheless she experiences the duality of pagan life and has the potential to become *this* particular self. Through the conscious risk of life in the sphere of the polis, Antigone transcends the limitations of womanhood set down by Hegel.

If we accept Hegel's interpretation of pagan life as a tragic conflict between the familial particular and the political universal that cannot be overcome in life, then Antigone's decision to commit suicide, which Hegel does not discuss, is of paramount importance. That is, unlike the male, Antigone cannot *live* out the contradiction of pagan life. Man is able to endure the duality of pagan life through his relation to woman— she maintains the family as the sphere of his particularity while he acts in the *polis*, the sphere of universality. But woman's relation to man does not offer her a way to make this duality tolerable. His desire for her is such that she is never a particular self in relation to him nor does she experience the universality of the *polis* through him. When woman leaves the family to experience the universality of the *polis* and to achieve particularity her relation to man cannot sustain her. Thus, man lives the tragic conflict of pagan life but woman dies from it. By violating the norms of womanhood set down by Hegel, Antigone comes to embody the tragic conflict that he finds inherent in Greek life. Her suicide expresses the inability to be both particular and universal in the pagan world. It expresses the fact that there can be no reconciliation, no *Aufhebung*, of particular and universal in that world. Against Hegel's focus on crime and guilt, which misrepresents Antigone, a consideration of the play itself, and most notably, a consideration of Antigone's *actions* on behalf of the sphere of inaction, reveals her tragedy as the tragedy of Greek life in Hegelian terms.

In addition, we can see Antigone's suicide as a form of defiance against patriarchal domination. By choosing to kill herself Antigone does not allow Creon to have the ultimate power over her fate which he seeks: she takes her own life to refute the power of the male, as the power of the universal, over her. In Greek society death was seen as preferable to slavery: it was more noble to kill oneself than to have one's fate controlled by another. Hegel himself writes of the liberating aspects of suicide, although not in regard to Antigone's tragedy. In his essay on "Natural Law" (*Naturrecht*) Hegel claims that voluntary death is a manifestation of freedom because it reveals one's independence from the life situation. He qualifies this by saying that this is not a realization of freedom, since it ends in nothingness rather than in free existence.[19] However, in Antigone's situation a manifestation of freedom is all that is possible since her choices are only death or submission to the male principle as the principle of universality, which decrees that she remain confined to the family in subjugation to man. If we extrapolate from Hegel's theory of desire, we can also see Antigone's suicide as maintaining her purity since she never marries and therefore never has a husband whose desire can overreach her ability to become this particular self. Antigone's suicide is an honorable alternative which shows that she prefers honor and *areté* to male domination.

In the *Phenomenology* "action is the principle by which distinction in unity is carried out in social life. Therefore the consideration of its significance is an essential problem of the social mind."[20] Yet Hegel chooses to emphasize only Antigone's burial of Polyneices and misrepresents her "confession." When one considers *all* of Antigone's actions, we see first that her burial of Polyneices was a moral imperative that goes beyond the mere intuition of ethical life and that she confesses no guilt in terms of the human law; second, that her action in the sphere of the *polis* allows her to transcend the Hegelian framework (which confines her to the family) so that she becomes a particular self; and third, that her suicide may be seen as the ultimate expression of the tragic character of pagan life as well as a refutation of male domination. Thus, through her actions Antigone goes far beyond what Hegel attributes to her.

For Sophocles it is because Antigone and Creon come upon the limits of their respective spheres that they both are transformed from criminal to tragic figures. Hegel also wants to show this, but he misrepresents Antigone and Creon. That is, where Hegel does not consider the consequences that result from the fact that Antigone must leave the family in order to protect it, must *act* on behalf of the sphere of inaction, he also does not consider that Creon's behavior must *necessarily* be unjust. Hegel's interpretation of Creon as the just representative of the law of the *polis* is as radical a departure from Sophocles' tragedy as is his portrayal of Antigone. The conflict between the just moral law and the unjust political law that is central to Sophocles' *Antigone* is muted in Hegel's interpretation. For Sophocles, Creon's rule is *not* that of reasoned arguments and the rational order of the city-state; nor is Creon the community as an individual soul. Rather, Sophocles shows Creon to be a misogynist and a tyrant who requires unquestioned obedience.

Creon is forever fearful that man shall be "done in" by woman, yet he expects a man to bury Polyneices; he finds it unthinkable that a woman, even as the necessary defender of the divine law, would act in the public realm to transgress the laws of the *polis*. When he finds out that Antigone has committed the "crime," he exclaims: "If we must lose, let's lose to a man, at least! Is a woman stronger than we?" (17). And when Haemon challenges Creon's decision condemning Antigone to death, Creon rebukes him saying "Fool, adolescent fool! Taken in by a woman!"[21] Finally, when the *polis*, in the form of the chorus, sides with Antigone, Creon declares:

> Whoever is chosen to govern should be obeyed—
> Must be obeyed, in all things, great and small,
> Just and unjust! . . .
> My voice is the one voice giving orders in this City! . . .
> The State is the King!
>   (16, 18)

Confronted with the inexorable force of Antigone acting on behalf of the family, Creon becomes irrational precisely because he cannot incorporate the claims of the family within the political sphere that he rules. In a world divided between family and *polis*, particular and universal, Antigone becomes tragic when she must leave the family to protect it, and Creon becomes tragic when, to protect the *polis*, he must become an irrational and unjust ruler.

In summary, what we find are four aspects of Sophocles' *Antigone* that are overlooked by Hegel in the *Phenomenology* in his attempt to use the play to reveal the pagan world as a world defined by tragic conflict between particular and universal, family and *polis*, divine law and human law, woman and man. First, Hegel completely disregards the sister-sister relationship in his search for the ideal relationship as a male-female relationship of identity-in-difference. Thus, Hegel describes the family as the sphere of womankind without showing any curiosity about the relations *between* women. This is like describing the sphere of pagan political life as "the manhood of the community" without ever discussing the relations between men! While Antigone rejects Ismene's show of solidarity, nevertheless, it is important to note the attempt at sisterhood and to recognize that Ismene does not display the "natural ethical orientation" required of her sex: she instinctively sides with male political authority rather than with the divine law of the family.

Second, Hegel disregards the conscious choice involved in Antigone's actions. Sophocles creates a conflict in which Antigone represents not only eternal familial values but individual moral choice, in opposition to Creon who represents not only temporal legal authority but dictatorial rule.[22] Hegel fails to see Antigone's action as anything more than the result of her intuition of the natural ethical law of the family, just as Creon fails to see it as anything more than the result of female rebellion against his absolute, patriarchal authority. But Antigone's tragedy is the result of strength and moral courage—the so-called "masculine" virtues—not simply a response to "feminine" intuition. (One wonders if Hegel would have "reduced" Socrates' *daimon*—which is a private intuition unrecognized and persecuted by the *polis*—to the level of "feminine intuition" if Socrates had been a woman.)[23]

Third, Antigone transcends woman's place in Hegel's framework because she breaks out of the limitation to the familial, which he requires of her sex. She represents the ethical family and as such she must relate to the universal as immediate, but, according to Hegel, she is not to know herself as this particular self. When we look carefully we find that woman is bound to immediacy as wife within the family through male desire, which overreaches her ability to become this particular self in and through her relationship with her brother. The brother-sister relationship as a relationship of mutual recognition, is transitory and ends when he enters the *polis*. The sister does not act in the *polis* but merely moves into another family to become the wife—the object of male desire. And the husband's life in the pagan city-state overreaches the wife's familial life as she remains confined to first nature. Woman has no contradiction to negate between herself and "first nature"; she lacks negativity because she remains confined within the sphere of "mere animal life" and thus remains "unreal insubstantial shadow." But Antigone moves into the political sphere on behalf of the sphere of the family and becomes, like man, a participant in both spheres. She does not represent "the irony of the community," the principle of particularity that changes the community through intrigue, but openly insists on the rights of the family, the rights of "first nature," within the *polis*.[24] Unlike other women, it becomes possible for Antigone, subordinating herself to the universal, to know herself as *this* particular self and thus to epitomize the tragic conflict between particular and universal which Hegel claims characterizes the ancient Greek, pagan world.

And finally, Hegel fails to discuss Antigone's suicide. When the chorus declares: "What woman has ever found your way to death?" (20) it reveals Antigone as unique, as the exception to female behavior, and therefore as a transitional character, not the paradigm of pagan divine law as represented by woman. While embodying the tragic conflict between particular and universal, Antigone represents the history of the revolt of women who act in the public sphere on behalf of the private sphere, the sphere of inaction. She is the precursor of the women who, in the recent past, proclaimed the personal as political.[25] Antigone rebels against Creon's claim to the right of the universal *over* the particular; in so doing she refuses to fit neatly into the Hegelian enterprise in which universality ultimately dominates. In criticizing Hegel's interpretation of the *Antigone* we begin to see another story in Western philosophy, one other than that of Hegelian reconciliation: the revolt of the particular against subsumption under a universal schema.

In the analysis of Hegel's interpretation of the *Antigone* in the *Phenomenology*, I have focused on Hegel's understanding of the pagan world as suffering from a dualism in which particularity, as represented by woman in the family, is in conflict with universality, as represented by man in the *polis*. I have shown that his understanding of this conflict causes him to systematically misrepresent or ignore crucial aspects of female experience that Sophocles' play actually reveals.[26] Given the inadequacy of the account of the *Antigone* in the *Phenomenology*, it is not surprising to find that Hegel's use of the play in the *Philosophy of Right* is also partial, and therefore "false." This indicates that Hegel's own philosophy of the modern world cannot reconcile the opposition between particular and universal in the context of sexual difference any more than the ancient world could. I will argue in the following pages that the modern world described by Hegel, like the pagan world, is made at woman's expense and that Antigone is misused to represent woman in the family in transhistorical terms.

In the *Philosophy of Right* we learn that the bifurcation of reason in the pagan world is *aufgehoben* in spirit's movement toward universal self-knowledge with the development of the modern Christian world into a triad consisting of the family, civil society, and the state. The bourgeois family is the sphere of the universal as undifferentiated unity or immediacy;[27] civil society represents the moment of particularity; and the state is the sphere of universality in which the universal and particular are reconciled. The aim of the *Philosophy of Right* is to resolve the relationship of desire to morality and ethical life; the analysis begins with a discussion of sexual desire within marriage, shifts to a focus on the generalized desire of civil society and the abstract morality of that sphere, and ends with a consideration of the concrete ethical life or *Sittlichkeit* of the state.

The reference to the *Antigone* and the only discussion of woman in the *Philosophy of Right*, as in the *Phenomenology*, appears within the discussion of the ethical life of the family. And, as in the *Phenomenology*, the *Antigone* is used as a paradigm to justify woman's confinement to the family. But, significantly, here the play does not represent the relationship between brother and sister as a relationship untainted by male desire; nor does the play represent the relationship between crime and guilt. Rather, it represents the opposition between man and woman as the opposition between divine law and human law within the context of a discussion of the relationship between husband and wife. In the *Philosophy of Right* Hegel is not concerned with finding the ideal relationship between man and woman that is *free* from desire, but with showing how the relation *of* desire itself can be transcended.

Hegel claims that the husband-wife relationship is the ideal ethical relationship between man and woman in the modern world because the secret moment of desire, the moment of physical passion, is transformed into self-conscious love through marriage. Physical desire is a moment that vanishes when satisfied, while the spiritual bond of Christian marriage is above the contingency of desire. Here Hegel distinguishes the marriage ceremony from the marriage contract. The ceremony, as a public proclamation of the ethical intention to take responsibility for family life, puts sensual desire into the background while the marriage contract is said to be a contract to transcend the standpoint of contract.[28] That is, a contract is a relation of civil society between atomic individuals, while the ethical family is a unity bound together by love in such a way that one exists in it not as an atomic individual but as a member of the group. Through a relation of civil society the family transcends the familial problem of desire: the marriage contract eliminates the capricious subjectivism of love as sentiment, an "immediate form of reason," and makes love the ethical or self-conscious moment in marriage.

This is quite a different situation from the one we encountered in the *Phenomenology*, where love in the pagan world was not self-conscious and where male desire infected the relationship between husband and wife so that it could not be the ideal relationship between man and woman. The bifurcation of man's life in the pagan world into public and private spheres caused a split between desire and morality that introduced a moment of ethical contingency into the marriage. Only the brother-sister relationship, which was supposedly free from desire and took place before the brother entered the *polis* and experienced the bifurcation of his life, could be seen as ideal. According to Hegel, the modern Christian world has radically transformed the situation so that male desire is no longer a problem. The tripartite structure of this world is seen as overcoming the dualism of the pagan world and allowing for the reconciliation of desire and morality through the marriage ceremony, which is both a contractual relation (a relation of civil society) and a religious (familial) one.

Thus, in the *Philosophy of Right* there is a significant shift away from the brother-sister relationship as the ideal relation of recognition between man and woman, as a relationship *free* from desire, to a consideration of the husband-wife relationship as a relationship that *transcends* desire. This shift is characteristic of the claim of the Hegelian philosophy as a whole to overcome the externality of Greek philosophy and society with the realization of philosophy in historical life. Significantly, the shift changes the site of the paradigm of male-female relations from the family of origin to the family of procreation. Here Hegel wants to distinguish the "natural" feeling of love, which binds family members through an original blood tie, from a later, deeper, self-conscious tie of love in marriage.[29] He defends the nuclear family against the rights of the extended family of origin. In the modern world any conflict of claims regarding duties and obligations between the family of origin and the family of procreation is always resolved in favor of the higher ethical family, the family of procreation; that which comes later is a more mature form of reason. The shift to the focus on the family of procreation also replaces the contingency noted earlier. That is, while only some women may have brothers in the family of origin, all women may potentially have husbands.

In the *Philosophy of Right* love is subordinated to the claims of marriage and reproduction, which in turn are subordinated to the claims of property. Thus, the relation of husband and wife in the modern world is no more inherently self-complete than it was in the pagan world. The husband and wife still need the child as an externalization of the unity of their love (PR § 173, Addition, 264–65). Marriage is for procreation and woman must remain confined to the family as "mother" so that the family may achieve its objective, explicit unity. As I have argued more comprehensively elsewhere, it is not really a question of man and woman coming together in love that is at issue here, but rather the inheritance of family property.[30] For Hegel, property is the manifestation of ethical self-consciousness in the material and public world. Man expresses his freedom and gains historical continuity by effectively appropriating and transmitting property through his family. Woman, on the other hand, is allowed to own property in her lifetime, but she cannot bequeath it to others. Thus, woman's relation to the family property leaves her deprived of the experiences of freedom and historical continuity. Hegel's complicated schema, which attempts to give woman, as person, equal rights in terms of the family property, is ultimately overreached by his conception of woman as mother, tied to immediacy.

According to Hegel, woman, as wife and mother in the modern world, like her sister in the pagan world, is a passive and subjective being who has knowledge only as feeling or intuition. She never leaves the family but "has her substantive destiny in the family, and to be imbued with family piety is her ethical frame of mind." Here Hegel refers to the *Antigone* as "one of the most sublime presentations" of family piety as the law of woman (PR §166, 114). However, the reference to the *Antigone* in the *Philosophy of Right* is within a context that puts the claims of the family of procreation over and above the claims of the family of origin, whereas Hegel's interpretation of the *Antigone* in the *Phenomenology* concerns the highest claim of duty and obligation within the family of origin: the duty of the sister to bury and honor her brother. Given Hegel's original interpretation of Antigone as the paradigm of ethical family life *precisely because* she represents the relationship between man and woman *not* as wife but as *sister*, this new appropriation of the play within the context of a discussion of marriage in the modern world seems quite untenable. While Hegel believes that the modern world has transformed the relation of desire between man and woman through the Christian marriage tie, and consequently has solved the problem of male desire, nevertheless, since Antigone represents "holy sisterly love" (a love free from desire according to the *Phenomenology*) *and* since she never marries, it is hard to see how she can serve as a model for wifely piety in the modern world. Hegel's attempt to use the play to reinforce his assumption that woman must remain confined to the family in the modern world is without a historical or conceptual analysis that would justify such a use. Most significant, Hegel posits Antigone as a *transhistorical* paradigm of ethical family life and the role of woman: the play has lost its historical reference to the pagan world in the *Philosophy of Right* in order to justify the confinement of woman within the family in the modern world. While Hegel's system is meant to be an historical account of the development of humanity, woman is presented as outside history.

For Hegel, as we have seen, particularity must necessarily be incorporated into political life in order for that life to be truly rather than abstractly universal. But this does not mean that woman *qua* woman needs incorporation into the political sphere. Rather, Hegel develops a philosophical system in the *Philosophy of Right* in which he conceives of particularity without the impediment of immediacy. Where woman was confined to the family in the pagan world as the representative of particularity, in the modern world she is confined to the family as the representative of immediacy; particularity and immediacy are separated, and particularity is taken up into the male realm of civil society while woman remains trapped in the ahistorical immediacy of the family. Thus, the *Philosophy of Right* details man's progressive movement into a world that reconciles particular and universal, but woman is forced to take a step backward: she now represents immediacy—a moment that *precedes* particularity and is therefore a less developed form of reason.

Hegel wants to claim that freedom is realized in the modern world; at the same time, he excludes woman from the spheres of civil society and the state, the spheres in which man manifests his freedom. Woman's exclusion from these spheres is made necessary by the dialectical structure which requires that the sphere of the family be maintained or preserved, as well as negated, in the process of development toward the universality of the state. Modern man leaves the family in order to move into the realm of civil society, where he emerges as a particular; but the sphere of undifferentiated universality or immediacy must be maintained. Therefore, modern woman is forced to do the family "maintenance" work required by the Hegelian dialectic: woman stays home to preserve the family. Only man "dirempts" himself; only he struggles for recognition in the universal sense. Fortunately, he can come home after a hard day of self-diremption to the wife who offers him "a tranquil intuition of . . . unity" (PR §166, 114). In this way man achieves a wholeness through woman, while woman remains confined to the family, where only an abstract or undifferentiated identity can be achieved. Confined to the family as the sphere of immediacy in the modern world, woman still lacks the negativity that results from the initial sundering from nature; therefore she never achieves an independent self-consciousness. In preserving the sphere of the family woman is again forced to sacrifice her claim to self-consciousness. Thus, modern man's realization of himself and the dialectical structure are at modern woman's expense.

Given Hegel's schema in which woman must necessarily remain confined to the family, he must systematically misrepresent Antigone, especially her movement out of the family. His failure in the *Phenomenology* to analyze Antigone's actions comprehensively means that he cannot bring an analysis of these actions into the discussion of Antigone in the *Philosophy of Right*. Rather, he misuses her as a transhistorical ideal of woman as wife confined to the family as the sphere of animal life, the sphere of inaction.

Examining the *Philosophy of Right* via Hegel's discussion of Antigone raises two crucial issues: the problem of female desire and the question of whether or not the sphere to which woman has been assigned can *be* taken up and dialectically *aufgehoben* in Hegel's sense if woman is to be allowed her freedom.

In the *Philosophy of Right*, as in the *Phenomenology*, Hegel tries to solve the problem of the division of man's life by leaving woman in the position of not experiencing the division. Marriage to woman is said to resolve the bifurcation of modern man's life between family and civil society by mediating two forms of desire: (1) desire as familial, heterosexual union, and (2) desire as general and differentiated in civil society. Woman remains confined to one sphere, the sphere of the family, precisely for the purpose of giving man an intuition of unity. In Hegel's schema, if woman lived in two spheres she could not offer man the access to wholeness he seeks. However, Hegel does not address the fact that *because* she lives in only one sphere woman has no internal motive for seeking marriage as mediation. That is, there is no necessity for the institutional mediation of two forms of desire in woman's life since she does not experience two forms. Therefore, woman does not need marriage as ceremony and contract. From her perspective, marriage is the result of external coercion: out of *his* need for marriage man forces her to accept it. Given this conceptual framework, what emerges is that woman's confinement to the family as the sphere of immediacy indicates that she can represent desire only as capricious and contingent. Just as woman has no internal motive for marriage, she also has no internal motive for desiring one man over another. Female desire itself, if it is to focus on a stable object (one husband rather than many lovers), must be coerced. Thus, when we look carefully, we find that in Hegel's schema of the modern world the problem of male desire is "solved" only by creating a problem of female desire.

In terms of the dialectical structure, Antigone can be seen as the representative of woman as actor who refuses to fit neatly into Hegel's system, a system that requires her to stay home to preserve the family. Her move out of the family transforms her so that she has the potential to be a particular self. However, when woman in the modern world follows in Antigone's footsteps by participating in civil society and the state, the spheres of particularity and universality, then the family is not preserved or maintained as well as transcended in the Hegelian sense. Once woman lives in more than one sphere she cannot offer man the intuition of unity he seeks and the dialectical structure necessarily breaks down.[31]

Hegel's philosophic formulation of the relation between woman and man in the modern world is important because it reveals the problem of how to achieve unity in a world in which each one seeks satisfaction of particular needs and desires. But through an examination of Antigone in the *Philosophy of Right* we find that his solution, which separates particularity and immediacy so that the family remains the sphere of immediacy in which woman is confined and coerced, is not an adequate formulation of the required mediation. And, for Hegel, it is precisely the *Aufhebung* or reconciliation of the modern world that reveals the dualistic conflict of the ancient world. Given the inadequacy of Hegel's formulation of the modern reconciliation in the context of sexual difference, he must necessarily misrepresent this conflict in his interpretation of the *Antigone* in the *Phenomenology*.

By confining woman to the family in the *Phenomenology* and the *Philosophy of Right*, Hegel prevents the progressive movement of spirit toward universal self-consciousness from being recapitulated in woman. The development of human consciousness outside the family is sex-specific, limited to man. Woman can never aspire to "concrete" universality or individuality; she cannot attain particularity much less universality.

With the limitation of woman there is a limitation of the Hegelian system. Hegel's universal is necessarily male, and male is *not* universal. Humanity is both male and female, and the claim to encompass the universality of human experience must allow for woman's experience and participation outside the sphere of the family; it must allow for a more comprehensive account of the *Antigone* than Hegel can provide.

My immanent critique of Hegel's *Antigone*, done through the lens of a feminist doubled vision, uses the force of Hegel's premises against his own conclusions. It reveals that Hegel's attempt to include dialectically all oppositional "moments" presents us with an abstract negation in which woman, defined as an ontological principle of otherness, represents the "difference" that cannot be fully comprehended in the logical idea. As a result, Hegel's dialectical theory becomes a closed system, a system that is the quintessential form of identity logic in which difference is ultimately dominated and denied rather than reconciled. Hegel's concept of reconciliation—the idea that latent in contradictions is an ultimate unity or identity-in-difference of subject and object, mind and matter, universal and particular, history and nature, man and woman—has always meant domination: of the subject over the object, mind over matter, universal over particular, history over nature, man over woman.[32]

However, my critique should not be understood as a dismissive stance that claims that Hegel has "nothing to say to feminists." Rather, I believe Hegel's philosophy is significant because the Hegelian problem of the relation between identity and difference that is central to his phenomenology is at the heart of the feminist project to create a free and equal society. That is, Hegel *articulates* the fundamental problem of contemporary society with which feminists are concerned even though his analysis fails when sexual difference is "essentialized" and all that woman represents is confined to the family and "overreached." But it is precisely this "failure" to "overcome" or "reconcile" sexual difference that moves us to reconceive dialectical thinking. The contradictions in Hegel's philosophy thus lead us in the direction of Adorno's *negative* dialectics, a form of dialectical thinking that refutes Hegel's identity logic.

For Adorno it is the *non*-identity of nature and history, subject and object, particular and universal, that is required of a dialectical theory motivated by a concern for freedom. Thus, negative dialectics seeks to realize the goal of Hegel's philosophy, the goal of intersubjective recognition without recourse to domination, by refuting the moment of Hegelian reconciliation in which the negation of the negation becomes a positive moment of domination. Adorno writes: "The reconciled condition would not be the philosophical imperialism of annexing the alien [the Other]. Instead, its happiness would lie in the fact that the alien, in the proximity it is granted, remains what is distant and different, beyond the heterogeneous and beyond that which is one's own."[33] Adorno's critique of Hegel keeps dialectical thought open to the negativity that motivates it and in so doing allows for the emergence of Antigone as the particular, the representation of difference, beyond the domination of a logic of identity.

Notes

This article is a reprint of the revised and updated essay included in my anthology on *Feminist Interpretations of G. W. F. Hegel* (Pennsylvania State University Press, 1996); the original version appeared in *The Owl of Minerva* 17. 2 (Spring 1986). The article is reprinted here with the permission of *The Owl of Minerva* and the Pennsylvania State University Press. A slightly different version was incorporated into chapter 1 of my book *Woman, Nature, and Psyche* (New Haven, Conn.: Yale University Press, 1987). © Patricia Jagentowicz Mills.

1. Seyla Benhabib, "On Contemporary Feminist Theory" in *Dissent* 36 (Summer 1989): 366–70. Joan Kelly-Gadol was the first to formulate a concept of a feminist "doubled vision" in "The Social Relations of the Sexes: Methodological Implications of Women's History," *Signs: Journal of Women in Culture and Society* 1. 4 (Summer 1976): 809–23; reprinted in *Women, History and Theory* (Chicago: University of Chicago Press, 1984), 1–18.

2. Throughout this essay the term *man* is used to refer to adult males and never as a generic or universal term. This is done to illuminate the problems of sexual difference and sexual domination that are obscured by the use of "man" and "mankind" to refer to the human species.

3. Alexandre Kojève, *Introduction to the Reading of Hegel*, trans. James H. Nichols Jr. (New York: Basic Books, 1969), 58–61.

4. G. W. F. Hegel, *Phenomenology of Spirit*, trans. A. V. Miller (Oxford: Clarendon Press, 1977), §451, 270 (amended translation); hereafter cited as PhS, with paragraph number (§) followed by page number. Miller's translation of *marklose* as "impotent" is not to be confused with Hegel's term *Ohnmacht*, used to describe nature as "impotent" or "unconscious." Many of Hegel's ontological insights are rooted in Aristotle's philosophy. The bifurcation between familial and political life which Hegel subscribes to here can be found in Aristotle's *Politics*.

5. J. N. Findlay, *Hegel: A Re-Examination* (London: Allen and Unwin, 1958), 116–17; Kojève, *Introduction*, 60–61, 296–98; Charles Taylor, *Hegel* (Cambridge: Cambridge University Press, 1975), 172–77.

6. Kojève, *Introduction*, 61.

7. Ibid., 61, 298.

8. PhS §457, 274–75; cf. G. W. F. Hegel, *The Phenomenology of Mind*, trans. J. B. Baillie (New York: Harper Torchbooks, 1967), 477; hereafter cited as PhM. In both the Miller and the [1910, 1931] Baillie translations of this passage, the word "particular" is added in several places to reveal Hegel's meaning. Hegel sometimes underscores the word for "this" (*dieser*) instead of using the word *Einzelheit* to refer to the "particular" individual.

9. G. W. F. Hegel, *The Philosophy of History*, trans. J. Sibree (New York: Dover, 1956), 245–46.

10. The speech in which Antigone defends her decision to bury her brother, saying she would not make the same sacrifice for a husband or son, is omitted from many modern translations. This speech is reprinted in *Ten Greek Plays in Contemporary Translations*, ed. L. R. Lind (Boston: Riverside, 1957), 100. For a

discussion of the history of the inclusion/exclusion of this speech, see Costas Douzinas, "Law's Birth and Antigone's Death: On Ontological and Psychoanalytical Ethics," *Cardozo Law Review* 16. 3-4 (January 1995): 1353-54.

It is worth noting that this paradigm of mutual recognition between sister and brother, which is supposed to be devoid of desire, is rooted in the incestuous origins of the house of Thebes. Antigone's father, Oedipus, is also her brother, making Polyneices her uncle as well as her brother and she his aunt as well as his sister. In choosing this seemingly atypical family to represent the family as natural ethical life, Hegel gives significance to the Oedipus myth long before Freud.

It is also important to note here that the figure of Antigone in the ancient Greek tragedy is not quintessentially European or Aryan. As Martin Bernal has persuasively argued, the culture of ancient Greece emerged out of the colonization of Europeans by Egyptians and Phoenicians (Africans and Semites). See his *Black Athena: The Afroasiatic Roots of Classical Civilization*, vol. 1 (New Brunswick: Rutgers University Press, 1987).

11. PhS §475, 288. By claiming that woman shows man the power of his authority, especially that as son he is master of his mother, Hegel suggests that woman conspires to realize male domination.

12. Theodor W. Adorno, *Negative Dialectics*, trans. E. B. Ashton (New York: Seabury Press, 1973), 173.

13. I understand experience not as something fixed and unalterable, grounding an "essentialism," but rather as a continuous process of engagement with and in the world through which subjectivity is created, re-created, and understood.

14. Sophocles, *Antigone*, in *Drama: An Introductory Anthology*, alternate edition, ed. Otto R. Reinhert (Boston: Little Brown & Company, 1964), 22 (amended translation); all subsequent references to *Antigone* are to this edition. See also PhS §470, 284; and PhM 491.

15. One might want to argue that these gods are the divine representatives of male authority to which Antigone bows. Nevertheless, she does not accept male domination in its more obvious human guise.

16. Later, in his *Aesthetics*, Hegel himself describes Antigone as choosing her course of action: insofar as she has pathos, she has free will. Here, Hegel describes Antigone's pathos as less than that of Creon's because she worships the underworld gods of Hades while Creon worships the daylight gods of self-conscious political life. However, the argument concerning the conscious, deliberate choice involved in Antigone's actions undermines the claim in the *Phenomenology* that the sister's ethical life is not conscious or actualized. See *Aesthetics: Lectures on Fine Art*, trans. T. M. Knox (Oxford: Clarendon Press, 1975), 232, 464.

17. Joyce Nower, "A Feminist View of Antigone," in *The Longest Revolution* (February/March 1983), 6. Why Antigone rejects Ismene's offer of sisterly solidarity is an enigma that can perhaps be illuminated by the fact that patriarchal society

attempts to set women against each other so that they learn to see themselves primarily in relation to men.

18. It is important to note the fact that in Hegel's analysis of the master-slave dialectic there is no mention of woman: master and slave are both seen as males even though historically many slaves were women. This means that the difference between "free" and slave women is necessarily overlooked. For an important discussion of how the man-woman distinction ignores class and race divisions in the ancient world, see Elizabeth V. Spelman's discussion of Aristotle in "Who's Who in the Polis," ch. 2 of Inessential Woman (Boston: Beacon, 1988).

Several authors have attempted to present gender relations as an instance of the master-slave dialectic in which woman's consciousness is equated with slave consciousness. One of the earliest feminist attempts was that done by Simone de Beauvoir in The Second Sex, trans. and ed. H. M. Parshley (New York: Vintage Books, 1974), 73. The inadequacy of Beauvoir's account is examined by Mary O'Brien in her book The Politics of Reproduction (Boston: Routledge and Kegan Paul, 1981), 67–73.

More recently Stuart Swindle has tried to make the case in a rhetorical attack on my own analysis of Hegel. In a detailed response to Swindle I show that it is delusive to argue that we can simply "recall" the master-slave dialectic to explain gender relations. There is no textual evidence in the Phenomenology for such a claim. To argue as Swindle does is to misconstrue Hegel's analysis of the master-slave dialectic while subverting the analysis of woman's unique consciousness. See Stuart Swindle, "Why Feminists Should Take the Phenomenology of Spirit Seriously" and my response, "'Feminist' Sympathy and Other Serious Crimes: A Reply to Swindle" (The Owl of Minerva 24. 1 [Fall 1992]: 41–62).

19. G. W. F. Hegel, Natural Law, trans. T. M. Knox (Philadelphia: University of Pennsylvania Press, 1975), 90–92. See also Kojève, Introduction, 247–48.

20. PhM §483. These are Baillie's words, not Hegel's.

21. Page 18. Creon's reproach to Haemon underscores Hegel's contention that woman acts on the adolescent male in her effort to destroy the pagan world. In Let's Spit on Hegel, Carla Lonzi extrapolates from this relation to argue for the revolutionary potential of political solidarity between women and young men in bringing down the modern world of the patriarchs. See chapter 12, Feminist Interpretations of G. W. F. Hegel, ed. Patricia J. Mills (Pennsylvania State University Press, 1996), 275–97. The psychological basis of Creon's fear of womankind is explored by Eli Sagan in The Lust to Annihilate: A Psychoanalytic Study of Violence in Ancient Greek Culture (New York: Psychohistory Press, 1979), 95–101.

22. In their play The Island, Athol Fugard, John Kani, and Winston Ntshona present the Antigone as a play within a play to reveal the ancient drama's relevance to the situation of South African prisoners. In both plays moral laws are juxtaposed to state laws to demonstrate that justice and the law are not necessarily the same thing. This point, as we have seen, is lost in Hegel's interpretation.

23. My intent here is not to demean "feminine intuition" but rather to reveal the sexist implications in Hegel's account, which does demean it.

24. According to Hegel it is because Polyneices offered Antigone the ideal relationship of mutual recognition between woman and man in life that Polyneices makes the greatest claim on Antigone with his death. I have argued that within the family of origin Polyneices was only a *potential* man and becomes a man at the same time that he severs his relationship to his sister, thus challenging the sense in which this relationship can be seen as the ideal one between woman and man. According to Sophocles, it is not the relationship of recognition based on blood ties, but the *uterine* relationship, that exerts the primary claim on Antigone: it is the fact that Polyneices and Antigone are of the same womb, the same mother, that is most significant. Antigone says: "if I had suffered him who was born of my mother to lie in death an unburied corpse, in that case I would have sorrowed . . . it is nothing shameful to revere those . . . from the same womb" (lines 465–511). Here the ancient womb/tomb imagery, the association of women with life and death, is revealed as an integral part of the play. Creon shifts the discussion away from the uterine relationship to a discussion of the more general concept of blood ties (lines 512–13). This shift and the emphasis on the uterine relationship in the Greek text are revealed in the Oxford translation of the *Antigone* (1880).

25. Antigone may also be seen as the precursor of the suffragists of the late nineteenth and early twentieth centuries and the women involved in the temperance movement insofar as those women were trying to achieve familial goals in the public realm. For an interesting analysis of this process, see Jean Bethke Elshtain, "Moral Woman and Immoral Man: A Consideration of the Public-Private Split and Its Political Ramifications," *Politics and Society* 4. 4 (1974): 453–73.

26. To be sure, Hegel believes that the real historical conflict of the pagan world would be visible only after the Christian revelation had introduced the possibility of its *Aufhebung*. Nevertheless, since Hegel sees the tragic conflict of the pagan world revealed through the great Greek tragedians, all significant aspects of the plays of these ancient authors would have to be taken up in the *Aufhebung*.

27. Hegel's philosophy is ideological in its lack of an analysis of the difference between the working class and the bourgeois family as well as in its patriarchal assumptions. It is difficult to know how the working-class woman, confined to a subsistence level of existence within her own family which is *not* based on property and capital, or confined to the bourgeois family as a domestic servant, fits Hegel's schema. The working-class woman produces and reproduces laborers, not heirs to family property.

28. G. W. F. Hegel, *Philosophy of Right*, trans. T. M. Knox (London: Oxford University Press, 1967), §§161–64, 111–14; hereafter cited as PR, with paragraph (§) number followed by page number.

29. PR §172, 116; Hegel also maintains this understanding of the relation

between the family of origin and the family of procreation in the *Aesthetics*, 463–64.

30. Patricia Jagentowicz Mills, "Hegel and 'The Woman Question': Recognition and Intersubjectivity," in *The Sexism of Social and Political Theory: Women and Reproduction from Plato to Nietzsche*, ed. Lorenne M. G. Clark and Lynda Lange (Toronto: University of Toronto Press, 1979), 74–98; see also ch. 1 of my *Woman, Nature, and Psyche* (New Haven, Conn.: Yale University Press, 1987), 39–43.

31. My analysis of Hegel is part of a larger project which focuses on the relation between the domination of nature and the domination of woman in the dialectical tradition that includes Hegel, Marx, Marcuse, Horkheimer, and Adorno. See Mills, *Woman, Nature, and Psyche*.

32. Adorno, *Negative Dialectics*, 3–8.

33. Ibid., 191.

13

David W. Price

Hegel's Intertextual Dialectic

Diderot's *Le Neveu de Rameau* in the *Phenomenology of Spirit*

The strangest intertextual incursion in Hegel's *Phenomenology of Spirit* occurs in the section on Self-alienated Spirit and Culture where we, as readers, come across lines taken from Denis Diderot's story, *Le neveu de Rameau*. Hegel does not attribute these quotations to Diderot; rather, the editors of the various editions of the *Phenomenology* indicate that these lines are taken from Diderot's dialogue, or more precisely, from Goethe's 1805 translation, *Rameaus Neffe*. Diderot constructs a dialogue in which a philosopher, "*Moi*," and the nephew, "*Lui*," discuss art and politics in late eighteenth-century French culture. The nephew is a bit of a charlatan, a sycophantic swindler who entertains the rich and lives off of their wealth. For the nephew, a human being "spends his life taking up positions and carrying them out."[1] Culture, he insists, consists of a dance, a vile pantomime in which each individual person adopts a specific role. Unlike his fellow Frenchmen, including his philosophic interlocutor, the Nephew recognizes the nature of the social game; he adapts to each situation, transforms his voice and body with Protean skill, and "speak(s) as occasion requires" (82).

Why Hegel chooses to incorporate some of Diderot's dialogue at this particular point in the *Phenomenology* makes perfect sense to Jean Hyppolite, who sees the nephew as the matchless illustration of the lacerated consciousness at a specific moment in European cultural history.[2]

"Diderot's description offered Hegel the satire of a world," writes Hyppolite, "a concrete example of human self-consciousness, and, with regard to the dialectical development under discussion, the result of the culture in which the I is always alien to itself" (412–13). I agree with Hyppolite's explanation, but I would add that his is a partial explanation, and it only holds if we conceive of Hegel using Diderot solely for illustrating the historical development of consciousness.

I wish to examine Hegel's use of Diderot from a different perspective. Diderot's is but one of several texts that appears (often in an altered form) in the *Phenomenology*. I want to explore what it means for Hegel to re-inscribe literary texts into his own speculative, philosophical text: (1) What does Hegel's specific choice of quotations from Diderot's text reveal? and (2) How does Hegel's incorporation of Diderot's dialogue relate to his use of other literary texts (e.g., the poetry of Goethe and Schiller, *Antigone, Oedipus Rex*, et al.)? My intent is to show how Hegel's use of literature within the *Phenomenology* relates to the notion of recollection or inwardization (*Erinnerung*).

Diderot's translated words make their first appearance in the *Phenomenology* when Hegel discusses how the individual becomes actualized through culture. Hegel writes that "only that which externalizes itself . . . obtains an actual existence."[3] Hegel then quotes the nephew's condemnation of the *espèce*, or type, in order to refute those who believe that individuality inheres in a particularized nature. Such an individuality for Hegel exists only in the mind; it is "an imaginary existence" (298). Hegel chooses this passage from Diderot for two related reasons. First, in Diderot's dialogue, the notion of the "type" occurs during an exchange in which the *Moi* asks the nephew how he will instruct his son. The nephew argues that he will not teach his son because he does not want to interfere with the natural inclination of his child. If he were to do so, Diderot informs us, "he would be torn between two opposing forces" (108). It is precisely this image of the individual drawn or pulled in contrary directions which must have attracted Hegel's eye to this particular passage in Diderot because it characterizes the idea of the dirempted consciousness. I am not suggesting that Hegel derived the notion of the Unhappy Consciousness from his reading of *Rameaus Neffe*, nor am I saying that the nephew in any way describes the Unhappy Consciousness. Rather, I believe that Hegel and Diderot share a similar repertoire of images, and that many of these images appear in Diderot passages that Hegel chooses not to quote. If, as Hegel argues, the Unhappy Consciousness is "dual-natured" and an "inwardly disrupted consciousness" (126), then Diderot's text offers Hegel another expression of this lacerated consciousness. Diderot's lines, in retrospect, are a retelling of the Hegelian tale of the

Unhappy Consciousness, and, although not quoted by Hegel, are simultaneously absent and present in the quoted lines, because the trace of their context accompanies them in the Hegelian text.

Although my first point may appear to be an amplification of Hyppolite's position, I want to stress the imagistic element provided by Diderot's text. Hegel seizes upon *Le neveu de Rameau* not only because it illustrates a particular stage of consciousness in European history, but also because it offers specific images patterned and shaped by Diderot's imaginative consciousness which are in turn disseminated through Goethe's translation and flow into the current of Hegel's philosophical text. In other words, just as Hegel argues that individuality does not inhere in a particularized nature, his own text demonstrates how individual images do not inhere in particularized texts.

To my mind, Hegel also quotes these lines on *espèce* for a second and more important reason. Hegel uses the French term *espèce* in his 1807 essay, "Who Thinks Abstractly?", in order to characterize a mode of thinking that wants to appear exalted, noble, and special. Hegel rejects this exalted way of thinking—the type of thinking which will reduce a murderer to "the abstract fact that he is a murderer" and will at the same time "annul all other human essence in him with this simple quality."[4] In the context of the *Phenomenology*, Diderot's words provide an apt retort to those who, through a process of abstract thinking, cling to the notion of an individuality "rooted in the particularity of nature" (298). As John H. Smith points out, both Hegel and the nephew despise a "type" (*espèce*) because such a person "falsely thinks [*meinen*] he has an individual personality and thereby fails to recognize that he, like everyone else, must take his personality from the social roles at his disposal."[5] Hegel rejects the notion of an autonomous, reason-centered subjectivity *à la* Descartes in favor of an interactive or dialectically produced individuality that achieves actualization only by being "moulded" by culture (298). The Hegelian text itself instantiates this philosophy by taking on the language of Diderot. In other words, Diderot's text molds the Hegelian text and effects the transition from "thought-form" into actuality.

The second instance of Hegel quoting Diderot occurs when Hegel describes the "content of what spirit says about itself" (317). Hegel lashes together quotations taken from two different moments in Diderot's dialogue. As an illustration of what the talking spirit sounds like, Hegel offers the description of the nephew at his greatest moment of triumph when he gives the *Moi* a virtuoso performance of thirty arias. Hegel then describes what such talking would sound like to the tranquil consciousness by quoting lines taken from a scene in which the *Moi* narrator relates his reactions to the nephew acting out a scene between a pimp and a young girl. The last phrase—"but blended with the latter will be a tinge of ridicule which spoils them" (318)—however, comes from the description of the nephew's triumphant performance.⁶ In other words, Hegel inserts a quotation from the pimp scene in between lines that describe the scene of triumph.

Why does Hegel do this? At the beginning of the paragraph in which these quotations appear in the *Phenomenology*, Hegel characterizes the content of spirit's utterances as "the perversion [*Verkehrung*] of every Notion and reality" which in turn expresses "the greatest truth" (317). In the pimp scene in *Le neveu de Rameau*, the *Moi* narrator is bewildered by the nephew's combination of shrewdness and depravity, a combination which he describes as an "absolute perversion of feeling and utter turpitude" (51). Goethe's translation renders this phrase, "*einer so völligen Verkehrtheit der Empfindung*" (948). It is the word *Verkehrtheit*, which resonates with the notions of a state of perversion, inversion, being upside down, or topsy-turvy, that establishes the associative link between the Diderot dialogue and Hegel's *Phenomenology*. Hegel finds in Goethe's translation of Diderot's dialogue the very word that expresses his key concept of the inverted world. But it is not just that Hegel simply finds a reference to *Verkehrung* and cites it in his own text. On the contrary, Hegel selects this passage and inserts it in the middle of another passage thereby inverting the context of that passage. In other words, the description of the pimp scene inverts the description of the scene of operatic triumph and both together constitute the truth of the Nephew.

Hegel's handling of Diderot's text performs the very philosophic argument he makes; the construction of the Hegelian text enacts the Hegelian philosophy. This act of intertextual dialectic draws attention to Diderot's description of the nephew who, as he imitates an operatic performance, intertwines the vocal and instrumental parts "so as to preserve the connecting links and the unity of the whole" (103). Although not quoted in the *Phenomenology*, these lines appear in *Rameaus Neffe*⁷ just before the phrase Hegel chooses to close off his quoted material in the *Phenomenology*, and they accurately describe Hegel's paratactic maneuver which grafts two scenes together in order to preserve a new unity of the whole which includes the idea as well as the textual act of inversion.

The third and final Diderot quotation appears during Hegel's discussion of the struggle between the Enlightenment and superstition. Hegel states that the "pure insight" of the Enlightenment spreads like the diffusion "of a perfume in the unresisting atmosphere," and possesses all the qualities of a "penetrating infection" (331). Hegel then quotes the nephew's description of how the foreign gods of an invading culture topple the religious idols of the indigenous culture: "That, they say, is how the Jesuits planted Christianity in China and the Indies," declares the nephew (101).

Once again the unquoted language of the context from which the quotation is taken contains the key to Hegel's choice of quoted material. The irony of using a passage that describes Christianity's triumph over sections of the Far East in order to recount the triumph of Enlightenment rationality over the Christianity of the West should be readily apparent. In this case the importance of Hegel's choice of quoted material lies beyond his own ingenious inversion of contexts. Hegel chooses a passage describing the smashing of idols because this is exactly what the entire project of the *Phenomenology* is meant to be. During the march along the highway of despair, Hegel presents his readers with one idol after another—the stoic, the skeptic, the phrenologist, the toiling workers in the spiritual animal kingdom, the beautiful soul, and so on—each of which is examined and rejected for failing to provide its adherents with absolute knowledge.

In this regard, it is quite clear why Hegel privileges Diderot's text to such a degree in the *Phenomenology*. The nephew is himself a *Galerie von Bildern*, a picture gallery—the very metaphor Hegel uses in the last paragraph of the *Phenomenology* to characterize the structure of his own text. As the narrator, *Moi* describes him in one scene, the nephew becomes "a one-man show featuring dancers, male and female, singers of both sexes, a whole orchestra, a complete opera-house," and he is capable of "dividing himself into twenty different stage parts" (103). Thus I disagree with critics James Hulbert and Hans Robert Jauss, who criticize Hegel's use of Diderot's dialogue. For Hulbert, Hegel fails to grant the philosopher *Moi* equal time. Hulbert argues that Hegel cannot "afford even to quote a passage in which Diderot's philosopher embraces the disruption of continuity and sees in that a possible access to truth, for this would cut across the *Phenomenology*'s individual characterizations of philosopher and nephew."[8] Jauss, in a similar fashion, criticizes Hegel's method of quoting material which he claims "supremely disregards the rules of the game of citation."[9] For Jauss, "the dialogical principle disappears as soon as it enters into the monologic discourse of a dialectical philosophy" (170). Hegel's dialectical narrative dissolves the dialogical form of Diderot's text, he argues, and in doing so, "destroys not only the equilibrium of antagonist voices; it puts an end to the freedom of investigation and to the unforeseen discoveries that the dialogical form offers" (176).

Both critics, in a sense, fault Hegel for not being Diderot. Both contend that if Hegel chooses to quote material from Diderot then he must reproduce the dialogue. This assumes, of course, that Diderot's text yields to *one* interpretive strategy to which both Hulbert and Jauss have access. In addition, both critics read the *Phenomenology* as a closed work. For Jauss, the *Phenomenology* is monological, and for Hulbert it has a telos, whereas for these two critics respectively, *Le neveu de Rameau* is dialogical and endless.

But such criticisms fail to account for the dialectical relationship between the two works. As I hope I have shown, Hegel initiates an intertextual dialectic when he inserts, and at times subverts, quotations taken from Diderot. The very method he uses to construct the *Phenomenology* in language, his own and Diderot's, instantiates the very argument he presents in the section "Culture." In this section, Hegel discusses the process by which "the individuality moulds itself by culture." "The power of the individual," writes Hegel, "consists in conforming itself to that substance, that is, in externalizing its own self (*seines Selbsts entäußert*) and thus establishing itself as substance that has an objective existence" (299). As Smith points out, "the substance mediating self and other is written tradition" (21). The externalizing or alienating process (*Entäußerung*) only occurs when the individuals attempt to express themselves through language. On the textual level of the *Phenomenology*, Hegel engages in much the same process. Hegel's method of narrative construction performs this alienating or externalizing process by taking on and re-inscribing the text of Diderot. Hegel establishes an intertextual dialectic through which the already written words of Diderot mold and give voice to Hegel's own writing.

How then does Hegel's incorporation of passages taken from *Le neveu de Rameau* relate to his use of other texts in the *Phenomenology*? All of the attention I have directed toward Diderot's dialogue should not obscure the fact that the *Phenomenology* is replete with references to and quotations from other works of literature. Readers cannot fail to notice lines from the poetry of Schiller and references to *Antigone, Hamlet, The Robbers*, and *Macbeth*. Donald Verene points out that the very term *verkehrte Welt*, which Hegel uses and makes famous, comes from a 1797 Ludwig Tieck play of the same name, and that this theme of the inverted world can be traced back in German literature to the *Narrenschiff*, a work written in 1494 by Sebastian Brant, and *Der Ackermann aus Böhmen*, written by Johannes van Saaz in 1401.[10] Undoubtedly these literary texts provide Hegel with examples, turns of phrase, and images. But I want to focus briefly on what it means for Hegel to engage in this activity of re-inscribing literary texts and how it relates to his philosophy.

The *Phenomenology* is indeed a book of images, and the various *Bilder* provide us with a means of grasping the concept "*Begriff.*" Perhaps Smith puts it best when he writes, "The *Bild*, according to Hegel, has the general form of an 'extended metaphor' [*ausführliche Metapher*]. It is therefore implicitly related to the classical conception of allegory" (177). The *Bild* as extended metaphor relates to allegory in the following manner: the *Bildern* constitute a group of already written texts, and in the case of the *Phenomenology*, Hegel re-inscribes these already written texts into his own text. In order to examine the allegorical dimensions of the *Phenomenology* in greater detail, the views of allegory of Walter Benjamin and Paul de Man are helpful.

In his pathbreaking work, *The Origins of German Tragic Drama*, Walter Benjamin argues that the popular notion that characterizes allegory as being inferior to symbol stems from the Romantic conceptualizations of these two terms. For the Romantics (e.g., Coleridge, Goethe, et al.), the symbol achieves a perfect unity of form and content; like the Eucharist, the symbol participates in that which it symbolizes. "As a symbolic construct," writes Benjamin, "the beautiful is supposed to merge with the divine in an unbroken whole." In contradistinction to the Romantic mode of conceptualization, Benjamin offers the Baroque mode, which he claims achieves a dialectical apotheosis and constitutes a speculative activity. Quoting Friedrich Creutzer, Benjamin notes that symbol offers a "momentary totality, " whereas allegory provides a "progression in a series of moments. And for this reason it is allegory, and not symbol, which embraces myth."[11] For Paul de Man, the allegorical sign can only refer to an antecedent sign, one "with which it can never coincide." De Man contends that, "whereas the symbol postulates the possibility of an identity or identification, allegory designates primarily a distance in relation to its own origin." "In doing so," de Man continues, "it prevents the self from an illusory identification with the non-self."[12]

The allegorical mode generates an endless progression of signs that can never reduce the gap that separates sign and meaning. The symbolic mode, on the other hand, effects a unity, a unity which Benjamin and de Man characterize as false, and one which, I might add, Hegel would consider false too. As Verene argues, "Hegel's notion of unity is completely process-like"; it "is just the notion of a twoness that can never be compressed into a oneness" (107). For Verene, this notion of twoness consists of the struggle between the concept and the image, the *Begriff* and the *Bild*. Hegel's science of consciousness consists of the act of recollection in language, but this act can never achieve complete unity because "language never speaks the whole" (111).

This recourse to language, the medium that always fails, is what de Man calls the *dédoublement*—"activity of a consciousness by which a man differentiates himself from the non-human world." The "reflective disjunction" of consciousness, says de Man, occurs in language—a language that consciousness "finds in the world like one entity among others, but that remains unique in being the only entity by means of which it can differentiate itself from the world" (213). But the type of *dédoublement* that concerns Hegel is not mere representation (*Vorstellung*); rather, it is what Verene characterizes as *bildhaftes Denken* (xii) or image thinking, a type of thinking strictly associated with metaphoric structuration.

In order to enact imagistic thinking, the individual consciousness must engage in a process of externalization or alienation (*Entäußerung*) through language and construct a *Bild* that designates the *Begriff*. But the metaphor, by its very nature, will never achieve a unity. The two dissimilar objects joined together through metaphoric structuration will always preserve their separateness. The rose will remain *in-itself* a rose, whereas *for consciousness*, the rose is the beloved. Thus, when Verene associates absolute knowing with the preservation of the "and" in the in-and-for-itself (*An-und-Fürsichsein*: 106–8), he touches upon the very method by which Hegel performs his philosophy through the actual construction of the *Phenomenology*. At the textual level, Hegel must externalize his own thought and construct various *Bildern*, and this necessitates his use of the images, literary fragments, the poems and plays: in short, the other texts that make up the reservoir of cultural language.

Consider for a moment the closing lines of the *Phenomenology*. Hegel does not offer a summary statement. Instead, he offers two slightly altered lines from Schiller's poem, "Die Freundschaft." Note the last word—*Unendlichkeit*—which Miller translates as "infinitude" but which also means endlessness. Just like the "Yes" that closes *Ulysses* and the "le-Temps" at the close of *À la recherche du temps perdu*, Hegel's last word, *Unendlichkeit*, carries tremendous weight. I think the endlessness to which Hegel refers is the infinitude of allegorization. Schiller's poem depicts a God who, feeling lonely, creates spirits (*Geistes*) which the poem describes as the "blessed mirror of his happiness" (*"Sel'ge Spiegel seiner Seligkeit"*).[13] Nevertheless, even with his mirror, God can find no likeness (*Gleiches*). The key image here is the mirror that fails to provide an exact replica. Even God, the supreme artist, cannot, through the creative act of representation, reproduce experience. Similarly, the myriad representations available to the travelers on Hegel's highway of despair will never reproduce the experience represented. For the writers of texts, be it Hegel the philosopher or Schiller the poet, the expression through language will always constitute a failure. But each of these writers repeats the whole by means of a re-collection or a re-ordering of the already written which always points beyond itself.

Hegel's act of recollection or inwardization (*Erinnerung*) constitutes an aesthetic act of allegorization by which he re-inscribes other texts—what many would describe as literary texts—into the *Phenomenology*. At the textual level, each re-inscription is an inwardization, an incorporation of the already written into the body of the Hegelian text, a re-expression of the irreducible gap between language and experience, between the sign and its meaning. The inscribed material provides Hegel with the extended metaphors, the *Bildern* of his *Galerie*. Like Rameau's nephew, Hegel, the virtuoso writer, incorporates other texts into his own written work and combines and alters them in various ways, and in so doing constructs a text that enacts his philosophy.

I offer this brief digression into the notion of allegory in order to stress a point. The popular notion of Hegel's *Phenomenology*, particularly among literary scholars, is that it expresses an aesthetic form of totalization through which Hegel stresses the whole and achieves a unity not unlike that which is described by the Romantic advocates of the symbol. For this reason many literary critics label the *Phenomenology* a closed work, a monologic text that denies pluralities of meaning. But as Benjamin points out, the Romantic method of representing the individual's encounter with the symbolic consists of placing the individual through a "progression of events which is, it is true, infinite but is nevertheless redemption, even sacred." Such an individual has a heart "lost in the beautiful soul" (160). Readers of the *Phenomenology* know that Hegel offers no redemption of that soul; absolute knowing is Golgotha, and the beautiful soul "vanishes like a shapeless vapour that dissolves into thin air" (400). The Hegelian metaphor will never collapse into a false unity of the symbol. Instead, Hegel offers the allegorical mode, the interplay of texts that invert, pervert, and illumine one another while at the same time preserving their separateness.

The Hegel of the *Phenomenology of Spirit*, therefore, instantiates an intertextual dialectic in which his philosophic discourse, by re-inscribing antecedent literary texts, performs the very philosophical point he argues. The appearance of passages from Diderot's *Le neveu de Rameau* provides the most striking example of this. Just as Hegel argues that the individual must be molded by culture in order to achieve actualization, his own text is molded by Diderot's dialogue. In the *Phenomenology* as a whole, the works of literature form the *Bildern* of Hegel's textual *Galerie*. The literary works signal Hegel's recognition of the necessity of metaphoric structuration through which philosophy must speak. Thus the act of re-collection that Hegel describes in the closing paragraph of the *Phenomenology*, when viewed from a textual level, is an act of allegorization.

Notes

1. Denis Diderot, *Rameau's Nephew and D'Alembert's Dream*, trans. Leonard Tancock (London: Penguin, 1966), 120. All further quotations of Diderot are taken from this translation.

2. Jean Hyppolite, *Genesis and Structure of Hegel's "Phenomenology of Spirit,"* trans. Samuel Cherniak and John Heckman (Evanston, Ill.: Northwestern University Press, 1974), 410–15.

3. G. W. F. Hegel, *Phenomenology of Spirit* (PhS), trans. A. V. Miller (Oxford: Oxford University Press, 1977), 298.

4. G. W. F. Hegel, "Who Thinks Abstractly?," in Walter Kaufmann, *Hegel: Reinterpretation, Texts, and Commentary* (New York: Doubleday, 1965), 463.

5. John H. Smith, *The Spirit and Its Letter: Traces of Rhetoric in Hegel's Philosophy of Bildung* (Ithaca, N.Y.: Cornell University Press, 1988), 210.

6. See J. W. Goethe, *Rameaus Neffe, Johann Wolfgang Goethe: Gedenkausgabe der Werke, Briefe und Gespräche*, ed. Ernst Beutler, 24 vols. (Zurich: Artemis-Verlag, 1953), 15:1001. All quotations from the Goethe translation are from this volume.

7. Goethe renders this: *"die Einheit des Ganzen erhalten wurde,"* Rameaus Neffe, 1001.

8. James Hulbert, "Diderot in the Text of Hegel: A Question of Intertextuality," *Studies in Romanticism* 22 (1983): 284.

9. Hans Robert Jauss, *"Le neveu de Rameau:* dialogique et dialectique," *Revue Métaphysique et Morale* 89 (1984): 173. All quotations from this work are my translations.

10. Donald Phillip Verene, *Hegel's Recollection: A Study of Images in the "Phenomenology of Spirit"* (Albany: State University of New York Press, 1985), 50–55.

11. Walter Benjamin, *The Origin of German Tragic Drama*, trans. John Osborne (London: NLB, 1977), 160–61, 165.

12. Paul de Man, "The Rhetoric of Temporality," *Blindness and Insight: Essays in the Rhetoric of Contemporary Criticism*, 2d ed. (Minneapolis: University of Minnesota Press, 1983), 207.

13. Friedrich Schiller, "Die Freundschaft," *Schillers Werke: Nationalausgabe*, vol. 1, ed. Julius Petersen and Friedrich Beissner (Weimar: Hermann Böhlaus Nachfolger, 1943), 111. My translation.

14

Translated by Jon Stewart

Karlheinz Nusser

The French Revolution and Hegel's Phenomenology of Spirit

The revelation of the depth of the universe, of the absolute notion, is the goal of Hegel's *Phenomenology of Spirit* which the self-knowing spirit attains. The "French Revolution" is one stage along this way, the contents of which must be experienced and endured by human self-consciousness and by the subject of history. In his excellent study, *Hegel and the French Revolution*,[1] Joachim Ritter makes clear the central meaning of the French Revolution for Hegel: "there is no other philosophy that is a philosophy of revolution to such a degree and so profoundly in its innermost drive as that of Hegel."[2] Every Romantic philosophy of subjectivity is in agreement in positing the discontinuity of history with the abstract theories which want the "revolutionary denial of the present." Since Hegel recognizes "that the historical essence of the Revolution and of the entire age and all its problems is the emergence of the modern industrial civil society of labor," it is clear to him, according to Ritter, that in emancipation, society limits itself to "the natural sphere of human existence" in order to liberate the "true determinations of freedom."[3] The dialectic which informs this rests on the coordination of natural needs, which are not historical, and on the historical existence which they necessarily imply—a coordination which makes possible "reason presently existing" in the form of division. Therefore, for Hegel the historicity of modern society rests on the fact that "it sets free in the form of dichotomy the substance preserved in subjectivity and thereby contains it as the living content of the freedom it has posited."[4]

Ritter is entirely right to have seen that Hegel accepted the civil economy of his time (Locke, Stewart, Smith, Ricardo, Say)[5] as an economic law of the present economic society, while he took up a critical position vis-à-vis the contemporary political theories of the French Enlightenment.[6] These differing evaluations on Hegel's part, however, are in my view conditioned by a context which just as much encompasses both sides simultaneously as it issues forth from them. The metaphysical being of man presupposes just as much the fulfillment of the necessities of "material" natural needs as these needs for their part have their goal in the realization of the existence of freedom. Hegel sees the chance for success in political life in the free, historical acceptance of this context and not in the interpretation of actuality as something produced or appropriated by work. The definition of "revolution" as a process of work which emancipates civil society[7] made it possible for Ritter to set forth Hegel's approval of the French Revolution with emphasis: "Nevertheless, neither the experience of the Terror nor the critical insight into the Revolution's inability to come to any positive and stable political solutions was able to turn Hegel into its opponent. . . . Hegel always affirmatively accepted the French Revolution; there is nothing more unambiguous than this affirmation."[8]

In contrast to this, I would like to ask if there is not in fact a serious "no" to the French Revolution in Hegel, which calls it, *qua* individual thing, into question insofar as it is taken for itself, and which justifies it only on the basis of and for the preservation of the rationality of the actual and of politics in order not to fall back into the "standpoint of division," into the absolute as night.[9]

Hegel's efforts to reach a sensible philosophical and historical understanding of the French Revolution is criticized by Jürgen Habermas on the basis of the ethos of an actualization of philosophy.[10] Hegel purportedly fears the Revolution and therefore "elevates the revolution to the primary principle of philosophy for the sake of a philosophy which is to overcome the revolution."[11] His ambivalent relation to the French Revolution is, on this view, summarized as follows: "Hegel desires the revolutionizing of reality, without any revolutionaries."[12] The picture of Hegel celebrating the Revolution with raised glass which Habermas brings to the fore in his essay is, however, just as transparent as it is one-sided.[13] This picture makes us forget that Hegel at that time in his life was struggling, in the midst of an immeasurable confusion of opinions, with the problem of a stabile, just, political order. Habermas relieves himself of the problem of treating the intellectual sources of Hegel's position by taking up the view, overemphasized by Ritter, of the philosophical and historical march of emancipation through the working individual—which in Hegel implies "mere" Enlightenment in the universal sense of intellectual history. But then Habermas radicalizes this event in the sphere of the claim to totality of a theory of society with a practical intention. With the twofold Habermasian presupposition that the essential forces of man are economic and species-historical and from the nevertheless asserted historical supersession of the ancient Christian understanding of man inside of society by the process of socialization (*Vergesellschaftung*) and its reflection, there arises the discontent with Hegel's rescuing of individual personal freedom from itself.[14] The main burden of his interpretation is carried by the corresponding passages in the young Hegel, which the mature Hegel revised since he saw them as overly enthusiastic and dangerous.

Our recourse to the *Phenomenology of Spirit* has the advantage of being a safe text edited by Hegel himself[15] which, as "the darkest and deepest work of Hegel,"[16] sufficiently makes possible a speculative, metaphysical understanding of his political philosophy and—as will be shown—anticipates the basic thought of the later *Philosophy of Right*.

The discussion over the last several years about the relation of the *Phenomenology* to Hegel's system as a whole[17] has produced among others two problematic aspects which must be maintained and kept together for our undertaking: (1) the *Phenomenology* is the introduction to the system, and (2) it is the system itself under its phenomenological aspect.

While Otto Pöggeler suggests that we take the *Phenomenology* as a mental road in which both motifs overlap and develop in different directions,[18] Hans Friedrich Fulda claims that "a line of questioning directed at the method of the *Phenomenology* in its structure must seek a truth which is not necessarily that of the self-thinking Notion and perhaps therefore admits of a rational understanding."[19] From the standpoint of the *Phenomenology* it can be said that the work is itself science since it leads to "spirit," which is the "self-supporting absolute, real being" (PhG 314; PhS §440) and which therefore "displays its existence and movement in this ether of its life and is *science*" (PhG 562; PhS §805). The experience which consciousness of the *Phenomenology* has on the strength of its own reaching out to the natural and historical world is right from the start not only "conceived from the whole and therefore stronger and stronger from the result of experience"[20] but rather is also *determined* by the necessity of the externalization of spirit which itself is science.[21] History in its reciprocal relation of continuity and change does not create the condition for the emergence of an "absolute knowing" but rather the context completed in the historical experience of consciousness that the truth can only be there where it makes itself its result, that is, absolute knowing is the sole condition of its emergence. The necessity of the phenomenological return of the subject to itself is thus tied to the measure to which it understands how to bring in its historical externalization. The demand of the knowledge of what are for Hegel the essential "moments" of European history—the Greek World, the birth, death and resurrection of Christ, the Roman Empire, the Middle Ages, absolutism, and the French Revolution—corresponds to the *original* situation of Hegel's philosophy. Hegel tries to be fair to the special meaning of Christ in that He does not represent simply one "figure" among others but rather is introduced in a special extension beyond the history of religions as the founder of "the absolute religion."

Now we must now address the questions of the why and the how of the development of these "figures" which precede the French Revolution come about. Is there an overarching connection on the strength of which they lead to the Revolution? Finally, we ask about the immediate ground of the dialectical structure and possible historical and metaphysical consequences of the French Revolution.

A LORD AND BONDSMAN AS INDIVIDUAL EVENT OF CULTURE (*BILDUNG*)

In the *Phenomenology* the Revolution is a figure of spirit. It forms the end of the section "Self-Alienated Spirit. Culture." Hegel treats it under the title "Absolute Freedom and Terror."[22] Even at first glance, there are words there which seem above all to refer to a portrayal of the Terror of the French Revolution: "The sole work and deed of universal freedom is therefore *death*.... It is thus the coldest and meanest of all deaths, with no more significance than cutting off a head of cabbage or swallowing a mouthful of water" (PhG 418f.; PhS §590). The following passage brings to mind Robespierre's struggle against hypocrisy: "*Being suspected*, therefore, takes the place, or has the significance and effect, of *being guilty*" (PhG 419; PhS §591). On the other hand, the fact that this section appears inside of the section "Self-Alienated Spirit. Culture," makes us suspect that there is something more at issue than a memory of "the dangers and terrors" of the French Revolution.[23]

Before we begin the treatment of those sections which deal with the Revolution, we must first test the much acclaimed section "Lordship and Bondage" against the points of departure of a theory of revolution. At its level of the *Phenomenology*, the lord-bondsman relation constitutes self-consciousness in the dialectical unity of reciprocal dependence of its members, the lord and the bondsman. This relation is the result of the life and death struggle which self-consciousness fell into after it had previously failed to find the necessary opposition—and thus the possibility of being recognized—in a substantive object. As soon as consciousness comes upon another self in this quest to be recognized, the life and death struggle takes place. This is for the philosophical self-consciousness objectifiable (cf. PhG 145), only if one of the struggling parties yields, that is, if the struggle is resolved peacefully. The defeated party comes into a relation of dependency and must work for the victor. The work on the one hand shapes and fashions the worked object and on the other hand, however, objectifies the for-itself of the worker as a worker, that is, a bondsman. While the lord emanates his being-for-itself as lord in the unhindered satisfaction of his desires, the bondsman reaches his "own meaning." Thus, a sort of satisfaction is reached, namely, an inner independence as presupposition for the stoic self-consciousness which hardens itself in the thought of itself.

Culture (*Bildung*) here still has, however, a very limited meaning: "Just as little as the pure form can become essential being for it [i.e., self-consciousness], just as little is that form regarded as extended to the particular, a universal formative activity, an absolute notion; rather it is a skill which is master over some things, but not over the universal power and the whole of objective being"(PhG 150; PhS §196).

Here at this level the self as temporary whole is not yet with itself. The figure as whole does not reflect itself into itself in order to set free another one from it. In the whole there is always only a part which is self-moved and since the part—even if also inside of the whole—determines the movement, a new self-sameness of the whole is in no way reached. And the question of whether a "metaphysical" theory of revolution can be appended here, is completely clear, when one hears what Hegel says later in the *Phenomenology* in his general definition of spirit: "All previous shapes of consciousness are abstract forms of it [spirit]. They result from spirit analyzing itself, distinguishing its moments, and dwelling for a while with each. . . . In this isolation they have the appearance of reality existing as such; but that they are only moments . . . is shown by their advance and retreat into the ground and essence; and this essence is just this movement and resolution of these moments"(PhG 314f.; PhS §440).

At the same time, however, there is a positive similarity to the chapter on "Culture." Here in the figure of the bondsman, the same thing happens in the particular and in individuals as happens there in the "Culture" chapter as a movement of the world: the externalization in the object as a necessary condition of the coming to itself.

However, before we continue along the way of the *Phenomenology*, it is necessary to make some further remarks explaining the context and the task of the *Phenomenology*. Hegel's *Phenomenology* arose from the knowledge that the absolute was at hand, although the dominant schools of thought—the systems of Jacobi and Fichte which in the one case used Kant as a starting point and in the other criticized him—had not recognized it. The absolute, substance which is conditioned by nothing, does not exclude consciousness, even if it has already passed over into the wanting-to-know-the-truth. Whatever is present as knowing in knowing of the self is reconciled with the self of the absolute. Even if naive consciousness is ignorant of the absolute, the *Phenomenology* can give him the ladder to true knowing.

The *Phenomenology* begins with what is closest to naive consciousness—sense-certainty. From these simple elements of experience it climbs to ever more complicated spheres until a first fundamental unity of the knowing self with the known takes place. Not that now the roles of knower and known are switched; the knower knows rather the known as an incipient reconciliation of the object with the self as knowing, and this taking home of the self is the existence of spirit and is only possible in the remembering (*Er-innern*) of history. While man truly knows the past in its meaning, he knows also his own past in the truth of the object, and it is in this movement that what Hegel calls "spirit" is present. Or in Hegel's words: "But essence is *in* and *for itself*, and which is at the same time actual as consciousness and aware of itself, this is spirit" (PhG 314; PhS §438). In the course of history from the Greek world to the present, to the treatment of the *Phenomenology*, the absolute was there to be recognized. It is truly present and recognizable to the "courage of knowing" even inside of the greatest disruption as it is for instance in the French Revolution. The deepest and highest to which the *Phenomenology* leads is the spirit as the "self-supporting absolute, real being" (PhG 314; PhS §440). The movement of the truth of the object is therefore a movement of truth itself and its history. Since Hegel directs our view to the essential self-portrayals of history in antiquity, the Middle Ages, and modernity,[24] he avoids and overcomes any sort of culturally or historically relevant restriction of the event under the aspect of the production and reification of modern subjectivity.

THE HARMONY OF THE ETHICAL WORLD AND ITS DESTRUCTION AS THE IMMEDIATE PRELIMINARY STAGE OF DISSOLUTION

Spirit begins its particularization as a world figure in the ethical life of a people. The laws of the community are the power appointed to it, laws which constitute the self-consciousness of this spirit since they can be recognized by the citizens of this order. Here Hegel has the Greek *polis* in mind. Law and the life of the community bring about the unfolding of what is at issue in it, what is valid as the handed-down order of the fathers, namely, the substance of spirit. The unfolding of the order, the judgment and governance, is ascribed to human beings in the form of male and citizen. Man's attitude realizes what the previous stage of the *Phenomenology*—"Reason as Testing Laws"—has missed: "By acknowledging the *absoluteness* of the right, I am with the ethical substance" (PhG 312; PhS §437). When seen from the side of the man, this means that he sees his essence in the ethical substance. His self-consciousness is thus "the implicit unity of itself and substance" (PhG 317; PhS §444). Hegel summarizes the thought as follows: "As *actual substance*, it [spirit] is a nation, as *actual consciousness*, it is the citizens of that nation"(PhG 319; PhS §447).

The goal and the movement of this figure is now the becoming-for-itself as bond between the universal essence and the individualized realities. This becoming-for-itself is, however, problematic in a fundamental sense.[25] The becoming-for-itself was now possible only in a previous isolation of spirit. Such a movement corresponds, however, to the dissolution of the being-with-itself; the latter differentiated itself in itself, and thus this event must also find its difference in spirit's becoming-for-itself. Here the world is ordered in a twofold ethical essence in accordance with the being-for-itself, an essence which is the whole spirit but which has an accessible form and a hidden one: the human and the divine law (cf. PhG 317f.) Just as the civil power is present in the ethical world as conscious action, so also a simple and immediate side belongs to ethical life, which is just as universal as any other power but still has not yet found its reflection in an existing other, that is, the family; therefore, Hegel calls it the "unconscious, still inner notion" (PhG 320; PhS §450). Since only work for the public good is valid as ethical activity, and the male wholly devotes himself during his lifetime to this task, only the care of the dead is left over for the spirit of the family and its appointed individualities, the woman. This care, the burial of the dead, is therefore an activity which is just as universal and related to the substance of ethical life, since the dead family member cannot simply be destroyed or decay, but rather remains alive in the honorable remembrance of the family and of the community: "Through this it comes about that the dead, the universal being, becomes a being that has returned into itself, a being-for-itself, or, the powerless, simply isolated individual has been raised to universal individuality" (PhG 322; PhS §452). All other relations of the divine law in the family, that of love, of sibling friendship, of deferential behavior of the children toward the parents represent a more or less similar picture to spirit (cf. PhG 323–28; PhS §§ 453–57) but are not ethical in the actual sense.

Now we concern ourselves with the collapse of this beautiful ethical life without treating further its wealth and the self-complementing movements of the human and divine law, the person and his aspect as citizen. The collapse of this figure of spirit comes about through the fact that its actual being-for-itself, as it develops into the representatives of the community—man in the case of government and woman in the case of family—no longer has unity in the division as was the case at the beginning. The external occasion is easily produced. Hegel chooses examples from Greek mythology and poetry. The natural, undifferentiated understanding of God through man is the real cause of the collapse. The acting individuals behave just like nature and hold fast to their respective laws as the real unmediated and immediate. They become "character" (PhG 332; PhS §466) and pass into the unreality of conviction since the being-for-itself which contains them is itself *only* for them, without their still presenting themselves for the side of the public universal. What happens in the realm of the subjective, particular individuality is also valid generally for the individual peoples, the Greek city-states, which will develop into the "simple," "cold and dead universality" of the Roman world hegemony.

Hegel calls his new conception of the individual and the universal order "Legal Status." It is the one-sided continuation of the "divine law" of ethical life. The individual has his being-for-itself only so that he is brought into universal equality with all his fellow citizens. To this bringing together corresponds the self-dissolving of the spiritual substance into the tense unity of particular, atomic individuals. Hegel calls these individual points "persons," borrowing from the use of this word in jurisprudence. The unity of the person is tense since the individual, as immediate unity with the universal spirit, at once strives for all being outside of him, but at the same time must radically strive against this self-dissolving. In Hegel's words,"Because the ethical substance is only the *true* spirit, the individual therefore withdraws into the *certainty* of his own self; he is that substance as the *positive* universal, but his actuality consists in his being a *negative* universal self" (PhG 343; PhS §477).

At this level the necessity of the particularizing of the whole relationship corresponds to the substantial relation of spirit portrayed above. Each person is valid as such and also demands this absolutely from all others. Since spirit as positive unifier is no longer present and since the person in itself understands its spirit immediately as an ownership claim to land and other natural goods (one might compare the dialectical disappearance of the "This" of "Sense-Certainty" in intending [*Meinen*]), therefore there arises a "general confusion and reciprocal dissolution" (cf. PhG 344f.; PhS §480).

This dissolution can only be steered if a center is found which guarantees to every individual his right: the master of the world, who does not hesitate to destroy the meaningless and artificial reality of persons, to make them subordinates in order thus to reach godlike power. In possession of this "omnipotence," he has, however, no longer any similar opposing figure, in which and through which he can have his self-consciousness. Having become immoderate in this way, he is destroyed in dissipation.

An overview of the movement of the world of "ethical life" and of the condition of right arises insofar as a possibility of revolutionary development cannot be won again as the intact figure of Greek ethical life. The fact that these figures are anticipatory is characterized by the immediacy of their unity with their essence. Inside of this immediacy there is no movement of figure in the sense of a gradual, perpetual self-transformation. The figures exist, or they are dissolved.

Their rudimentary, immediate and unspiritual self-understanding, however, experiences a mediation in the destruction of the legal status. This arises in the fact that the realization of its universal self is no longer sought in the real, yet object-like external sphere of representation, but rather in an objective realm of agreement of all, which as the true universality and objectivity is the level of validity, of culture. Here in this dimension, which is at once fictitious and real, room will also be found for a continuity in self-change, for development, decay, revolutionary escalation and the breaking out of revolution.

The Alienation of the World and the Revolutionary Break

The attempt of an individual self-consciousness to reach an immediate and lasting reflection of himself in the universality of substance fails, and the two worlds, that of the individual and that of the state, stand opposite one another, separated now as before. But they *stand* opposite one another and the *particular* manner of their unity is the self-alienating spirit. The individual tries to reach his recognition in the universally validating power of culture.

The new existence begins with the "unnatural" alienation of already existing institutions and cultural products. This doubled real world, however, finds its justification in an otherworldly God of pietism—and his representatives on earth—who wanted this world as to be divided and who thus holds it together in His consciousness. This is the side of the "pure consciousness" or of "essence"' (PhG 348; PhS §485). Hegel understands what has been described so far as follows: "The *present* actual world has its antithesis directly in its *beyond*, which is both the thinking of it and its thought-form, just as the beyond has in the present world its actuality, but an actuality alienated from it" (PhG 348; PhS §485). And "consequently, this spirit constructs for itself not merely *a* world, but a world that is double, divided and self-opposed" (PhS §486).

Hegel begins the adventurous course of this section with an extensive explanation of the now present wealth of the world from the real view of the consciousness having honestly worked through from this world. The consciousness in the beyond knows this as existing. According to its conception, the individual educates himself to what he is in himself, to the universal.

Hegel employs a comparison from Schelling's philosophy of nature in order to explain the universal structure of culture. Just as nature arises from elements and unfolds itself into them and in their forms, so also does culture. This basic picture which is similar to nature is valid for all concrete figures of culture, but upon further examination it brings no conclusions for our theme. Next the "pure insight," that is, the medieval philosophy of the state, asserts its thoughts, which we will now summarize.

Just as good and evil are set opposite one another without any middle term, so also the civil power and wealth are placed side by side, in accordance with their "dividing" thinking, and a good and bad side is found in both. Then consciousness recalls and finds that it also has two sides, an in-itself and a for-itself; this arises for both opposing realities and the two opposing predicates good and evil.

Thus, it depends upon consciousness which side makes itself a criterion; it is itself thus good or evil, "and the distinction between them falls solely within its own *essence*, viz. in the relation of itself to the actual" (PhG 358; PhS §499). Consciousness, which finds civil power just like wealth good and equal to itself, is the noble consciousness. The other, which finds in the governing power a fetter, in wealth its fleeting side, is the base consciousness.

The noble consciousness gives up all its own interests and dedicates itself exclusively to public service. It alienates itself as in-itself, but demands only respect for itself and for others. Only the self is the true reality. The civil power becomes through its sacrifice the "True which is acknowledged as such" (PhG 360; PhS §507). It does not reach only the true existing power, and it cannot reflect itself in a particular will, for the serving self-consciousness has not yet given up its representations of the beyond, its being-in-itself, in order to transfer it to the civil power. The haughty vassal is active through his giving advice for what is generally best for the well-being of the civil power. All other members of the people who have unified themselves in classes demand this same honor and are not ready "to make this chatter about the general good a substitute for action" (PhG 361; PhS §506). It maintains its particular will against the civil power and stands "always on the point of revolt" (PhG 361; PhS §506). This prerevolutionary condition, to which both the classes as well as the vassal belong, is dissolved in the following manner (which recalls the condition of ethical life): the man stands as ethical whole in the service of the "state." As individual "This" he was comprehensible to the universality of the family consciousness in the form of the departed spirit, as dead. Precisely in this way he fulfills the divine law and the ethical order. Also the vassal and the individual classes have used their life in the service of the state. They died in the defense of the medieval empire and the holy graves. It is only the sacrificial death, the self-maintaining—and thus coming-to-itself—of the self in universal consciousness which is no longer possible here since consciousness is alienated: "This contradiction which being-for-self [cf. base consciousness] must resolve . . . is at the same time present in the following form. That renunciation of existence, when it is complete, as it is in death, is simply a renunciation; it does not return into consciousness; consciousness does not survive the renunciation, is not *in and for itself*, but merely passes over into its unreconciled opposite" (PhG 361f.; PhS §507).

Hegel sees in this fact the accompanying cause—we here go back to the theological aspect of the event—of the collapse of this empire in the misunderstanding of the Christian secret of resurrection whose *linguistic announcement* has already ceased to be accepted with belief and mastered with thought. There is only nominalistic talk and preaching. "Consequently, the true sacrifice of *being-for-itself* is solely that in which it surrenders itself as completely as in death and yet in this renunciation no less preserves itself" (PhS §507). One no longer believes in the actual death and the fact of resurrection.

The major political cause of the collapse is the stubbornness of the egoism of the particular powers of the princes, classes, and cities. The very character of language, which makes possible lies and hypocrisy, creates the conditions for this. Hegel's forthcoming comments on language, which come as a surprise to the modern observer, point out language's ability to represent and wholly contain the individual. It is in language that the universality of those who are politically active during this age promises their sacrifice for the goals of the empire but without carrying them out. Language, the art of speaking and dissembling thus becomes a new power: "For here it has for its content the form itself, the form which language itself is and is authoritative as *language*. It is the power of speech, as that which performs what has to be performed" (PhG 362; PhS §508).

Language is thus the fruit of the progressive alienation and the new medium of self-escalating revolutionary power, which was only pushed into the trap. The further development of language rises again to a trial of the task of the self. The service for the civil power becomes a "heroism of flattery." The "noble consciousness" rejects his personal self and raises the civil power to the absolute self. Wealth, the reward which one receives for it, is, however, the only motivating factor. The state becomes *appearance* and its power an empty *word*: "wealth already contains within it the moment of being-for-self. It is not the self-less universal of state power" (PhG 367; PhS §515).

This corrupt world of French absolutism creates dependency which is much more humiliating to people than the dictatorship of the Roman world. The noble consciousness, the admired prototype of an epoch, sees its life goal in something wholly external, in the acquiring of wealth, and externalizes itself through this in the will of the sovereign. What the man of the court should receive stands at the discretion of this sovereign. "Self-consciousness can make abstraction from every particular aspect, and for that reason, even when it is tied to one of them, it retains the recognition and *intrinsic validity* of itself as an independent being. Here, however, as regards the aspect of that pure *actuality* which is its very own, viz. its own 'I,' it finds that it is outside of itself and belongs to another, finds its *personality* as such dependent on the contingent personality of another, on the accident of a moment, on a caprice, or some other utterly unimportant circumstance" (PhG 368; PhS §517). The rulership of the base empire brings all social relations of dependency in a likewise tense relationship, as is already the case between the king and his nobles. It leads to that arrogance which assumes that, on account of alms given, it has a claim on the person of the recipient. Hegel illustrates the justified reaction of these deeply injured people with Diderot's *Rameau's Nephew*. The nephew cannot help admitting that he is base to the same extent as his patron and the rest of society. Angry but yet happy about his effluence of words, the nephew tries to characterize this condition. His language, however, no longer forms a valid judgment since to him everything appears just as bad as good. The "language of this disrupted consciousness is, however, the perfect language and the authentic existent spirit of this entire world of culture" (PhG 370; PhS §520). The goal of this speech, of the spiritual critique of the French moralists is, however, not positive criticism but rather noble joy in the art of criticizing: "The content of what spirit says about itself is thus the perversion of every notion and reality, the universal deception of itself and others; and the shamelessness which gives utterance to this deception is just for that reason the greatest truth" (PhG 372; PhS §522). Unmoved by the failure of this noble disinterestedness, the Enlightenment and the religious world take up the problems of the age and try to solve them each in its own way.

The common interest of both the Enlightenment and belief[26] in a change in the condition of this inverted world leads first, since both have different remedies in mind, to a confrontation between them in the realm of spirit.[27] The Enlightenment is from the beginning superior to this sort of belief. As we have already seen, belief makes way for a thinking spiritual understanding of the secret of the resurrection and has transferred Christ, the resurrected, and with him the present to a heaven in the beyond. The empirical "Now" of belief thus becomes powerless and alienated from itself. The Enlightenment denies the existence of the beyond with the assertion that it is a reification of the difference between the object and self-consciousness, and it is successful in convincing belief that one can only maintain oneself in itself, and only consider one's own reality as the truth. "This pure insight is thus the spirit that calls to *every* consciousness: *be for yourselves what you are in yourselves*—reasonable" (PhG 383; PhS §537).

But what specifically should belief accept in order to be rational? First, it must recognize that its object, the "absolute essence," is produced from itself.[28] Trust and the feeling of security in the "absolute" are nothing, asserts the Enlightenment, as the effect of the accustomed obedience and service opposite the "absolute being" (PhG 402f.; PhS §562). The sensible object of the cult and the cult celebrations of belief now and then occasion the Enlightenment to point to the material condition of the "honored object." The Enlightenment asserts that reality is spiritless, which belief must finally admit since its cult object can only express the existence of a reality in the beyond. In like manner, the Enlightenment deals with the grounding of the written transmission and the asceticism of belief. Everything external, to which belief is attached, is tainted by the irresistible sophistry of the Enlightenment, and belief robs itself of its dynamic. "As a result, faith has lost the content which filled its element, and collapses into a state in which it moves listlessly to and fro within itself" (PhG 406; PhS §573).

The Enlightenment's satisfaction with its victory does not last long. Indeed, it takes over the spiritual leadership of the world of culture, but also with it the unsatisfied longing of an unfulfilled religiosity. In the conflict with belief, the Enlightenment, for its part, experienced a radicalizing: its "idealistic" assertions that everything valid in itself is only the essence of self-consciousness are reduced to their true materialistic core. No object has more than one actual determination, but rather everything is valued according to its utility. The material world is now posited as "being other" in the enlightened consciousness itself. This consciousness, in its reaching out in the world perceives only what belongs to it and the object, that is, the civil power and the wealth of the *ancien régime*, appears under the claim of these plausible arguments to be nothing more and nothing else than this. The Enlightenment "*qua* absolute notion, is a distinguishing of differences, of abstractions or pure notions which are no longer self-supporting, but are supported and distinguished only by the *movement as a whole*" (PhG 407; PhS §574).

The "movement as a whole," which is constituted by the Enlightenment and used up in it, is the principle of utility. The useful thing at all times awakens the desire for it. It is in no way merely an empty thing or a beyond like the object of belief. The employment of the useful thing nevertheless points out a structure unknown to the Enlightenment. While it earlier constituted the object of hope and of difference, every consciousness consuming difference disappeared in the moment of fulfillment, for example in the consumption, and the hollow longing, which is still present in the enlightened consciousness, collapses with the possibility of a return of the subject into itself; for the "*being-in-itself*" of the Enlightenment and its object "is therefore not an enduring *being*, but in its difference immediately ceases to be something; such a being, however, that is immediately without support is not an *intrinsic* being, but is essentially for *an other* which is the power that absorbs it" (PhG 411; PhS §580).

However, as long as the Enlightenment does not have all goods in its possession, it cannot fully unfold. The dissatisfaction which the use of an individual thing calls forth, is always easy to explain when other goods exist which belong to the Enlightenment on the basis of its principal claim, but factically they are in the hands of others. The model of reality of the Enlightenment can only be verified according to its own presuppositions when everything stands under its hegemony. This experiment is carried out in the French Revolution.

All "world material" heretofore, all development and cultivating means an increasing subjectivization and heightening of the situation without the individual being able to be reflected in the universality since this would have meant the true being-with-itself of the individual. The only way out of this historically concrete situation is the breaking of the band drawn too tight, the Revolution. The Revolution is the final phase of culture and thus of self-alienated spirit. The thought at this level has its presupposition in utility, for on the basis of this principle the Enlightenment makes everything into its own property and pleasure and is real consciousness (cf. PhG 413). At the same time, this principle is the dissolution of itself, that is, it has alienation immediately in itself and sublates it.

An overview of the formal structure of Hegel's interpretation of the Revolution will help us to ascertain the course of the three levels of consciousness. The first level is the increasing acceptance of the immediate consciousness. The second stage is the reflecting of consciousness in the otherness of itself, which in this way ceases to be a foreign other. However, since the otherness stands inside of an historical phase of alienation, the becoming one of consciousness with it is not a "This-like," subjectivistic encapsulation, but rather a becoming and a growing of the self in its opposite, in its negation. The third level, as the aggregate dissolution of the first and the second, leads immediately to a new point of departure.

The Revolution begins silently—in representation. An appearance of objectivity is still present—that is, there still exist the differences of the civil classes and the corresponding privileges—which separate the consciousness of *egalité* from its actual possession. As soon as this appearance of objectivity has disappeared, self-consciousness moves only in itself, and the "pertinence" and relation to interests which had been present in the principle of utility yields to a blind dogmatism. Hegel portrays the movement of this spirit in the figure of the general will of Rousseau and of the terror of Robespierre. The unity of this movement is the "spirit of absolute freedom" (PhG 415; PhS §584). The word "spirit" should be understood here no differently than in the previous course of our treatment, as a real and ideal reflecting of a whole into itself, which strives for a further, more comprehensive unity. We will come back to what is still a hidden unity for it at this phase.

Every particular, individual will must be brought under the general will. Since the general will becomes actual, it also becomes every individual will. No power can stop "this undivided substance of absolute freedom" from ruling. The general will is the self-understanding of the state which collapses into itself: "for since, in truth, consciousness alone is the element in which the spiritual beings or powers have their substance, their entire system which is organized and maintained by division into 'masses' or spheres has collapsed" (PhG 415; PhS §585). The world, particularly the order of the state, loses the meaning of a foreign being for consciousness, and consciousness "sees through" (*durchschaut*)—also in the sense of looking away or overlooking—the opposition of individual and general will which still exists.[29] Hegel speaks therefore of a "gazing of the self into the self"—whereby the looking is intended in the sense of projecting into—and of "absolute seeing of *itself* doubled" (PhG 414f.; PhS §583). Consciousness *is* this "gazing" and therefore is an individual will. Its unity seen in "gazing" of universality and particularity can only bring forth such works, which are likewise abstract and general: the laws and acts of the state. "This movement is thus the interaction of consciousness with itself in which it lets nothing break loose to become a *free object* standing against it. It follows from this that it cannot achieve anything positive . . . either of laws and general institutions or *conscious* freedom, or of deeds and works of a freedom that *wills* them" (PhS §588).[30] The way out would be the particularization Montesquieu had suggested: "This otherness would be the moment of difference in it whereby it divided itself into stable spiritual 'masses' or spheres and into the members of various powers" (PhG 417; PhS §588). The enlightened self-consciousness can, however, tolerate nothing intermediary in the unity of particularity and universality: "For where the self is merely *represented* and is present only as an idea, it is not *actual*; where it is represented by proxy, it *is not*" (PhG 417; PhS §588). The way out of the new governmental order (*Staatlichkeit*) is not yet possible. There remains only the possibility that it treat itself as an individual. The actual deed itself becomes particularity, of which all other individuals have only a limited part or none at all. The aforementioned unity of the world which is fanatically sought after as unity of particularity and universality would be in danger: "it remaining . . . only the negative action," "the fury of disappearance." "The only work and deed of the universal freedom is therefore death," which the unity necessarily prepares for other individuals. The general will must for once come to the insight in the true reality of the act of government which is a particularity, and punish the government as an individual for its guilt. The actuality of the general will is not deceived by this "abstract" universality about its claim for a "concrete" universality. The "abstract" universality in the madness of its pure state of virtue fails to see the actual, threatening liquidation until, having become powerless, it actually suffers it. "The universal will, *qua* absolutely *positive*,[31] actual self-consciousness, because it is this self-conscious reality heightened to the level of *pure* thought or of *abstract* matter,[32] changes round into its negative nature and shows itself to be equally that which *puts an end to the thinking of oneself*, or to self-consciousness" (PhG 420; PhS §592). According to Hegel's interpretation, the collapse of the dictatorship of Robespierre as a result of his own political principle has world-historical and spirit-historical meaning. Hegel sees in it the collapse of two principles which cannot support each other since they, existing in isolation, are not true: the cult of reason of the *être suprême* and materialism: "Here, however, this self-consciousness [i.e. the consciousness recognizing this time or the spirit of the epoch as the true self-consciousness] which, as pure insight, completely separates its positive and its negative nature—completely separates the predicateless absolute as pure *thought* and as pure *matter*—is confronted with the absolute *transition* of the one into the other as a present reality" (PhG 420;

PhS §592). The change of "pure thinking" into its collapse means the failure of the philosophically grounded, purposive action of the revolutionaries in precisely the realm which it seeks: realization of theory as theory. Real knowledge has from itself that effect of changing society whose "ontological" possibility is what is meant by the famous dictum of Hegel's preface: "What is rational is actual; and what is actual is rational."[33]

Spirit, absolute freedom—and thus we come to the other side of absolute freedom which was mentioned above—recognizes in the observation of this event the negation as belonging to the pure self-likeness. The unity of both is for it now the meaning of culture. Culture does not grow mature without alienation, and simple remaining-with-self (*Beisichbleiben*) is death. In this knowledge, spirit has run back and prefigured its absolute form, whose action is the possibility of particularity. Spirit as absolute freedom has two history-making forms, whose "logical" aspect Hegel analyzed in the Nürnberg *Logic* as first and second negativity. As revolutionary negation it is abstract and thus negates what exists, but this action brings the deeper side of reality into appearance, which negates the first negation on its side and makes room for the particular, the concrete.[34]

This is the foundation of the apparently backward movement in the external world: "insofar as this substance has shown itself to be the negative element for the individual consciousness, the organization of spiritual 'masses' or spheres to which the plurality of individual consciousnesses are assigned thus takes shape once more. These individuals who have felt the fear of death, of their absolute master, again submit to negation and distinctions, arrange themselves in the various spheres and return to an apportioned and limited task, but thereby to their substantial reality" (PhG 420; PhS §593). This final sentence contains Hegel's definitive statement in the *Phenomenology* on the governmental order (*Staatlichkeit*) and the society of the division of labor of the "new" man. In contrast to Kojève,[35] we assume that Hegel means a universal foundation of the essence of classes and of representation. Seen politically, it concerns the interim government of the Directory—Napoleon is thus not an immediate result, but rather an "offshoot" of the Revolution. Hegel's text does not expressly specify the new governmental form. That it concerns a constitutional monarchy, as Rosenzweig thinks, can nowhere be deduced from the text.[36] Napoleon is likewise not meant. He is only mentioned after the thinking to the end of all results of "Culture," and there he is unambiguously understood only as a brief transitory appearance. In contrast to the later *Philosophy of Right*, Hegel in the *Phenomenology* does not think that a fixed grounding of the head of state is necessary or possible. He ventures straightaway the question about the necessity of a renewed running through of this "road to culture" (*Bildungsweg*), which he rejects by reference to the thoroughness of the penetration of particularity and universality (cf. PhG 420). A good decade after the French Revolution, Hegel thus thought that the civic and social forms reached by it are sound and possess a certain atemporality. But what should belong to what is left over as an unconditional presupposition of every form of state in every case is the division of society. To the "externality" of the absolutely valid order of classes of society corresponds—seen metaphysically—the securing of true innerness and freedom of the self-consciousness reached at this level of the *Phenomenology*.

After the social, political effects of the Revolution (and before the hint of the political hegemony of Napoleon), Hegel comes, in the context of the larger aspect of the "Culture" chapter and its playing itself out, to speak of the fruits of the Revolution. He points out the specifically new character of the change which represents its apex *vis-à-vis* earlier modifications of the spirit of culture: "The culture to which it attains in interaction with that essence is, therefore, the grandest and the last, is that of seeing its pure, simple reality vanish and pass away into empty nothingness" (PhG 421; PhS §594). Since revolutionary reason which is empty of reality negates itself in itself, it likewise sublates the fiction of a theory passing over into unlimited practice of human essence, as it posits its emptiness in relation to reality in the unity of limitation and openness of the universal will. That "interaction" of self-consciousness and substance is, as the return of history into itself, a way back to reason and therefore not to either the "fulfilled negation" of "honor" or "wealth" or to the language of the "disrupted consciousness" or of all disintegrating "Enlightenment." Insofar as historical consciousness is in reason, it has, since is it nothing except reason, all conditions for the formation of its political and civil future in itself and is "pure knowing," and insofar as it is legitimate, it is "universal will." It is thus the interaction of pure knowing with itself; pure *knowing qua essential being* is the universal will" (PhG 422; PhS §594).[37]

Napoleon as brief appearance constitutes the conclusion of our chapter (Napoleon as "the determinate," "insubstantial point" in "universal will" [cf. PhG 421f.; PhS §594]). Napoleon cannot touch the reality of absolute inner freedom of the "new" men but nevertheless pushes this stage further. In the up and down through the antinomies of reality and duty, this innerness becomes also real for the self as self in reconciliation of conscience: "It is the actual 'I,' the universal knowledge *of itself* in its *absolute opposite*, in the knowledge which remains *internal*, and which on account of the purity of its separated being-within-self, is itself completely universal" (PhG 472; PhS §671).

The reflecting and reflected self thus enters the realm of all concluding knowing. By *recalling again* its figures as the historical course of the world which is essentially temporal but incomplete, it finds the contents for its form to be actualized as notion: "This last shape of spirit—the spirit which at the same time gives its complete and true content the form of the self and thereby realizes its notion as remaining in its notion in this realization—this is absolute knowing" (PhG 556; PhS §798).

The development which happened in time was necessary for self-knowing: "Time, therefore, appears as the destiny and necessity of spirit that is not yet complete within itself" (PhG 558; PhS §801) and it is only the difference of the development with itself. "The movement is the circle that returns into itself, the circle that presupposes its beginning and reaches it only at the end" (PhG 559; PhS §802).

Looking back, we can say by way of summary that the French Revolution means political freedom as emancipation of the individual from the old order of the *ancien régime*, but that it is at the same time the presence of spirit as absolute freedom. However, this freedom does not remain in empty formulas about simply being able to vote but rather opens up, as the further development of the *Phenomenology* shows, into the dimension of moral, religious, and philosophical innerness. Hegel ends the interpretation of the profane history with the phenomenon of Napoleon only because at the time of the composition of the *Phenomenology* in 1807 the events had not advanced any further. The further course of the *Phenomenology* does not intend a final form of history, but rather completes the absolute and personal freedom in its innerness, without falling into the idea of a technological perfection or of a governance by a police state.

Contrary to all misunderstandings that Hegel connects progress ultimately with philosophical reflection, Hegel really thought that any progress—even social-political—is possible only on the condition of a society with a division of labor and the present institutions. Habermas' assertion that Hegel contradicts himself since he justifies the Revolution and condemns revolutionaries[38] must thus be corrected in light of the fact that for Hegel the historical, philosophical justification of the Revolution is in no other way possible than by a criticism of revolutionaries; for after the chasm which has separated the state, society, and individual for millennia ever since the destruction of Greek ethical life, the revolutionaries create the insight that the negation of the concrete universal in the political sphere means *eo ipso* collapse. Since they themselves complete and suffer this, at the same time they document the necessity of the particular and of compromise in politics and are thus just as world-historically justified as the French Revolution.

Notes

1. First Edition Cologne, Opladen, 1957; I cite from the Suhrkamp edition, Frankfurt 1965, now in the collection *Metaphysik und Politik. Studien zu Aristoteles und Hegel* (Frankfurt, 1969), 183–255.

2. Joachim Ritter, *Hegel und die Französische Revolution*, 18. [Cf. the English edition *Hegel and the French Revolution*, trans. Richard Dien Winfield (Cambridge, Mass., and London: MIT Press, 1982), 43—TR.]

3. Ritter, *Hegel und die Französische Revolution*, 52, 65, 66 (English translation, 68, 77, 78.)

4. Ritter, *Hegel und die Französische Revolution*, 71 (English translation, 82.)

5. Ritter mentions Locke in another essay, "Person und Eigentum, zu Hegels *Grundlinien der Philosophie des Rechts*," in *Marxismus-Studien*, ed. I. Fetscher, 4. Folge. (Tübingen, 1962), 196–218, esp. 205.

6. Ritter, *Hegel und die Französische Revolution*, 53f. (English translation, 68ff.).

7. This is the view of Ritter: "Thus in all its forms this revolution of emancipation ultimately has its source for Hegel in civil society; in reality this is itself the revolution" (*Hegel und die Französische Revolution*, 64; English translation, 76). However, it seems to me that according to Hegel's concept of civil society this can in no way be the ground of the possibility of division. Nowhere does Hegel speak of society as of the "characteristic and true ground in which freedom has existence" (cf. Ritter's "Person und Eigentum," 213), rather "civil society," as the mutual play of the satisfaction of desires of individuals, is the phase of "abstract" freedom and thus of "freedom" which is still ethically indifferent (Hegel, *Grundlinien der Philosophie des Rechts* (RP), ed. J. Hoffmeister [Hamburg, 1962] §208, 181). For this reason only an original "is" or a "formal liberation" comes to the personality in the phase of "abstract right" and "civil society" (RP §104, §195 respectively). Ethical life, lost inside "civil society" in "its extremes"(RP §184), is now won again with the positing of the goal and the determination of tasks of the state: "The state in and by itself is the ethical whole, the actualization of freedom. . . . The essence of the modern state is that the universal be bound up with the complete freedom if its particular members and with private well-being, that thus the interests of family and civil society must concentrate themselves on the state" RP, ed. Addition to §258 and §260). [I cite from the standard English edition, *Hegel's Philosophy of Right*, trans. T. M. Knox (Oxford: Clarendon Press, 1952), 279, 280—TR.] Revolution as split is thus a "complete" (*ganzheitliches*) phenomenon. It threatens according to Hegel only when the satisfaction, the right of the individual, is taken away from him in the fulfillment of his duty to the state. We can agree with what Ritter, in the determination of the relationship of contract, claims for a specific determination of society: "thus is the relation, to give existence to the self in the person in objects" (Ritter, "Person und Eigentum," 211).

For civil society, therefore, Ritter's interpretation is valid: "the externality of civil society, in which it offers on the one hand the show of dissipation and of misery, is on the other hand for Hegel the existence of individual freedom" (ibid., 214). Hegel, on the other hand, places the aspect of the inevitability and the necessity of civil society at the forefront. The bourgeois subject is supposed to be led by this to the recognition of the "substantiality of ethical life," to a greater commonality beyond the economic society. Insofar as the bourgeois society isolates itself and only reflects itself, it does not agree with this compulsion: "the interest of the Idea—*an interest of which these members of civil society are as such unconscious*—lies in the process whereby their singularity and their natural condition are raised as a result of the necessities imposed by nature as well as of arbitrary needs, to formal freedom and formal universality of knowing and willing—the process whereby their particularity is educated up to subjectivity" (RP §187, my emphasis; cf. also RP §186; English translation, 124–25).

8. Ritter, *Hegel und die Französische Revolution*, 21f. (English translation, 46).

9. *Gesammelte Werke*, ed. H. Glockner (Stuttgart, 1941), 49.

10. "Hegels Kritik der Französischen Revolution," in *Theorie und Praxis, Sozialphilosophische Studien* (Neuwied, 1963, 2nd ed., 1967), 83–107. [In English as "Hegel's Critique of the French Revolution," in his *Theory and Practice*, trans. John Viertel (Boston: Beacon Press, 1973), 121–41—TR.]

11. Ibid., 89–103 (English translation, 121).

12. Ibid., 105 (English translation, 139).

13. Ibid., 89 (English translation, 121).

14. When Habermas (in his book *Erkenntnisse und Interesse* [Frankfurt, 1968]) asserts that "a transcendental subject is replaced by a *species* that reproduces itself under cultural conditions, that is, *that constitutes itself* in a self-formative process" (240; English translation, 95), and the self-enlightening of the individual leads to the standpoint "from which the identity of reason with the will to reason freely arises" (244; English translation, 197). [I cite from the English edition: Jürgen Habermas, *Knowledge and Human Interests*, trans. J. Shapiro (Boston: Beacon Press, 1971)—TR.]

15. I cite from the edition by Johannes Hoffmeister, 1952 (6th ed.), abbreviated as "PhG" followed by the page number. [In order to facilitate matters for the English reader, I have included the corresponding paragraph numbers of the Miller translation of the *Phenomenology* (*Phenomenology of Spirit*, trans. A.V. Miller [Oxford: Clarendon Press, 1977], hereafter PhS)—TR.]

16. Ernst Bloch, *Subjekt—Objekt. Erläuterungen zu Hegel* (Frankfurt, 1962), 59 (1st ed. 1951).

17. Otto Pöggeler, "Zur Deutung der *Phänomenologie des Geistes*," *Hegel-Studien*, ed. F. Nicolin and Otto Pöggeler, Bd. 1 (Bonn, 1961), 255–94; Karl-Heinz

Volkmann-Schluck, "Metaphysik und Geschichte," *Die Philosophie und die Frage nach dem Fortschritt. Verhandlungen des Siebten Deutschen Kongresses für Philosophie* (Munich, 1964), 292–302; Hans Friedrich Fulda, *Das Problem einer Einleitung in Hegels Wissenschaft der Logik* (Frankfurt, 1965); Reinhart Klemens Maurer, *Hegel und das Ende der Geschichte* (Stuttgart, 1965), 26–41; Otto Pöggeler, "Die Komposition der *Phänomenologie des Geistes*," *Hegel-Studien*, Beiheft 3, ed. Hans-Georg Gadamer (Bonn, 1966), 27–74; H. F. Fulda, "Zur Logik der *Phänomenologie* von 1807," ibid., 75–101.

18. Pöggeler, "Zur Deutung der *Phänomenologie des Geistes*," esp. 288ff.; and his "Die Komposition der *Phänomenologie des Geistes*," 33–45, 64f.

19. Fulda, "Zur Logik der *Phänomenologie* von 1807," 84. If one asserts this "rational understanding" which is not supposed to be "the self-thinking notion," then the question arises of what is meant when Fulda at the same time asserts "that under the truth of spirit the logic is to be understood" (ibid., 79). Precisely this fact, that Hegel at the end of the introduction of the *Phenomenology of Spirit* speaks of the experience, which comprehends "the entire realm of the truth of spirit" (PhG 75; PhS §89), indicates that any content in itself of spirit cannot be adequately formulated through the concept of the "logical." Moreover, the "logical" constitutes only the universal determination, the realm of the notion in spirit.

20. O. Pöggeler, "Die Komposition der *Phänomenologie des Geistes*," 51.

21. "Science contains within itself this necessity of externalizing the form of the notion, and it contains the passage of the notion into *consciousness*" (PhG 563; PhS §806). The previously outlined structure shows itself to be likewise in the doubled constitution of the "naive consciousness" which must first have the experience of the *Phenomenology*. It "finds" itself in the "element" of "science," but it does not recognize it; it stands foreign opposite it. (cf. PhG 24ff.)

22. The relevant passage covers PhG 414–22.

23. *Sämtliche Werke*, Jubiläumsausgabe, ed. H. Glockner (Stuttgart, 1956, 3rd ed.), VI: 354 ("Über die Verhandlungen der württembergischen Landstände").

24. Cf. Justus Schwarz, "Die Vorbereitung der *Phänomenologie des Geistes* in Hegels Jenenser Systementwürfen," *Zeitschrift für Deutsche Kulturphilosophie* 2 (1936): 127–59; Raimar Kakuschke, "*Geschichlichkeit und Christentum in Hegels Phänomenologie*," dissertation (Bonn, 1955), esp. §6, no. 3 ("Der Weg zur *Phänomenologie des Geistes*").

25. The previous stages have already led us—the philosophical consciousness—to knowing, that the absolute is absolutely different from itself, and it is this which the historical figure is still unaware of. And therefore the absolute is not only substance according to Spinoza's understanding, but also subject, which freely externalizes itself and in this externalization is absolutely different

from itself. Thus, it is immediately possible that the absolute appears in a doubled being-for-itself as is the case in Sophocles' *Antigone*. Hegel therefore tries to let the moment of difference—in the sense of foreignness and distance from itself—come up for decision. The Greek is compelled by the obedience against the absolute understood in a one-sided manner—he does not recognize the in-itself of the difference of the absolute—to split up the unity of action and of the tragedy that stems from it into the contradictory dualism of blind fate and naked reduction to one's own action: "Because we suffer we acknowledge that we have erred" (PhG 336; PhS §470).

26. Hyppolite remarks correctly that Hegel nowhere in the *Phenomenology* speaks explicitly of the world-historical meaning of the Reformation (J. Hyppolite, *Genèse et structure de la Phénoménologie de l'Esprit de Hegel* [Paris, 1946], 2:411). By "belief," in our context, the French Catholicism is meant. The relative truth, that the Enlightenment possesses in refuting this alienated religion, formulates the positions of Lutheran religion as Hegel understood it. Thus, Hegel's later assertion from his lectures on the philosophy of history that in Germany "in view of the worldliness already everything had become better by the Reformation" is already present, so that the effect of the Enlightenment on the state and the Church in Germany could no longer be so great as in France (*Vorlesung über Philosophie der Weltgeschichte*, Bd. IV, ed. Georg Lasson, 1923, 915ff.).

27. Cf. PhG 376–85.

28. Jean Hyppolite (*Genèse et structure*, 2:425) has already pointed out Hegel's anticipation of Feuerbach's anthropological reduction. At the same time Hegel showed the essential lack of enlightened argumentation which we will later come across in the course of our interpretation.

29. Hegel by this fictitious gazing in fact means the republican form of government, which wants to strive for a complete justice in the form of equality. This assumption is sharpened through the fact that the utility "was still object for knowing"(PhG 415; PhS §583), since here we are concerned with a material object different from man, while there the object is posited entirely by the revolutionary consciousness. The emancipatory aspect, which Ritter overemphasizes in Hegel's understanding of the French Revolution, is thus for Hegel a self-deception on the part of the revolutionaries. Revolutionary action is therefore not merely a process of development in the sense of a becoming valid of a historical principle, but also—and in the phase of the French Revolution the sole and only—spontaneous "setting free" of individual subjects and the constituting of a *fictitious, artificial* relation to nature, which is not limited to a policy which is pertinent or economically relevant, but rather it is ensnared in the *aporia* of subjectivity. Hegel justifies the French Revolution seen as a whole only through the fact that he accepts it as a dialectical stage of development in history. Its positive effect consists in the fact that it does away with the injustice which the entire governmental system represents (cf. *Vorlesungen über die Philosophie der Weltgeschichte*, 4:925). Ritter posits his basic thesis that the French Revolution for Hegel essentially

means the emerging of civil society, and this is justified insofar as it can and should no longer be resolved theoretically as the existing split (Ritter, *Hegel und die Französische Revolution*, 70f.). Even if Hegel is led beyond the form of the inner, Romantic, subjective reconciliation by the theory of civil society (p. 61), it would have to be shown that according to Hegel the split already has its negation in itself. If Ritter presupposes with Hegel that the whole historical existence, the reciprocal expulsion of subjectivity and objectivity guarantees subjective freedom in society (p. 49), then the possibility of an enduring split in the historical actuality is inconceivable.

30. PhG 417; PhS §588: the "interaction of consciousness with itself" brings to mind the movement of the wandering of the stars, which was characteristic of the literal sense of the German word *"Revolution"* from the fifteenth to the seventeenth centuries; cf. Franz Wilhelm Seidler, *"Die Geschichte des Wortes Revolution. Ein Beitrag zur Revolutionsforschung,"* dissertation (Munich, 1955); Karl Griewank, *Der neuzeitliche Revolutionsbegriff. Entstehung und Entwicklung* (Weimar, 1955; 2nd ed., Frankfurt, 1969).

31. The word "positive" here has entirely the meaning of a no longer legitimate, antiquated reality, as in the meaning of "positivity" in the young Hegel.

32. The ideology of revolution exists only as a proclamation which is dead to reality, or as a practice of government, which kills every dissident.

33. *Grundlinien der Philosophie des Rechts*, ed. J. Hoffmeister, Vorrede, p. 14.

34. Robespierre is thus in no way the world spirit, as Habermas ("Hegels Kritik der Französischen Revolution," 104) believes, but rather only a negating moment in it.

35. With his unproven assertion that Napoleon is the one who completes the French Revolution, Kojève creates the political basis for his doctrine of the final state. Alexandre Kojève, *Hegel. Eine Vergegenwärtigung seines Denkens*, ed. I. Fetscher (Stuttgart, 1958), 37, 45f., 65. The "integral human being" of this final condition which has been created by Napoleon is then so anticipatory that he must "be completed by a third, indeed very short historical period" (ibid., p. 68). Reinhardt Klemens Maurer gives an extensive analysis of Kojève's book, in his *Hegel und das Ende der Geschichte. Interpretationen zur Phänomenologie des Geistes* (Stuttgart, 1965), 139–56. Also, Günter Rohrmoser, *Subjektivität und Verdinglichung* (Güterloh, 1961), 102–5.

36. Cf. Franz Rosenzweig, *Hegel und der Staat* (Munich and Berlin, 1920; rpt. Aalen, 1962), 1:217. In contrast to Hyppolite, who in this context draws on M. Busse (cf. Hyppolite, *Genèse et structure*, 1:75; 2:316ff., 446f.; Martin Busse, *Hegels Phänomenologie des Geistes und der Staat* [Berlin, 1931]), Rosenzweig correctly sees that for Hegel in the *Phenomenology* it is less of a question of the governmental form of the ethical (Rosenzweig, *Hegel und der Staat*, 218). On the other hand, he reduces the renewing of society, which Hegel principally meant as postrevolutionary, too much to a profane historical—and here the already

emphasized restoration—aspect, since he speaks of the "monarchy of Napoleon" and of the existing societal "Restoration" (p. 219).

37. The result reached here is the core of the theory of the state in the *Philosophy of Right*. The further course of the *Phenomenology* makes valid the foundation of human freedom.

38. J. Habermas, "Hegel Kritik der Französischen Revolution," 89, 94, 103, 105 (English translation, 121, 126, 137, 139).

15

Moltke S. Gram

Moral and Literary Ideals in Hegel's Critique of "The Moral World-View"

> *Hubert Meessen zum Gedenken*
> Kein ding sei
> wo das wort
> gebricht.
> —Stefan George

In this chapter I argue that the section in Hegel's *Phenomenology of Spirit* extending from "The Moral World-View" to "Religion" can be read as a criticism of themes and ideas to be found in the literature of the German *Sturm und Drang* and early German Romanticism. If I am able to establish this thesis, I shall use my conclusions to illuminate the logical character of the transitions from one form of consciousness to another in this section. But my primary concern will be the relevance of Hegel's phenomenology to literature. To have shown that Hegel was influenced by notions that were current in his time is to pay lip service to a commonplace of Hegel scholarship. What has yet to be shown is the place such notions have in the economy of Hegel's phenomenology and the importance of his treatment for our understanding of them. Hence, I shall not stop at offering evidence to show that Hegel was influenced by the literary activity of his time. I shall go on to point out the sense in which he offered trenchant criticism of this activity.

Before I can even ask about the literary relations of the *Phenomenology*, I must make clear what I am and what I am not asking about. The purpose of my argument cannot be to establish which authors or which works Hegel had in mind when he wrote the section I am about to examine. I cannot do this because Hegel does not intend to criticize any given author or work but treats forms of consciousness which admit of an indefinite number of embodiments. Still, it is legitimate to ask about the resources upon which Hegel drew in finding the forms he criticizes. Our ability to find some clearly recognizable embodiments or paradigms of these forms of consciousness will help redeem Hegel's claim to be criticizing the manifestations of mind and not manufacturing them from the machinery of the dialectic. We must find paradigms of the forms of consciousness outside the *Phenomenology*, if Hegel's claim to be doing phenomenology (i.e., description rather than invention) is to be made good. Within this framework, the specific aim of this paper is clear: by ferreting out the references to literature implicit in one section of the book, I hope to show that Hegel's phenomenology is a phenomenology of consciousness. In all cases, my argument will demonstrate that Hegel could reasonably be expected to have read the works in question in virtue of his relation to their authors and the attitudes toward them found in his other works. The probability of these historical connections will, I think, be increased by their ability to make the text intelligible.

That the Moral World-View is a critique of Kantian ethics is too well known to warrant a repetition of the proof. I treat it in this context only because Hegel's criticism of Kantian ethics sets the problem for the forms of consciousness that are to follow. His main objection to the Moral World-View is that it separates the universal and the particular elements of moral experience so as to give an inadequate account of the relation between duties and inclinations in ethical deliberation. For in Kant moral consciousness is the consciousness of universal *duty* to the exclusion of *inclinations* peculiar to the individual moral agent. There are thus two ways to view a specific moral decision. As an act of a moral agent, it is just an event in his life history and a realization of intentions and purposes governing his action. As a morally significant act, it is the expression of duty done for duty's sake and, as such, is universal. Insofar as an act is done out of duty, it is not inclination or the realization of particular ends. But implicit in this account of moral action is the view that ethical decision consists in the antagonism between pure duty on the one hand and inclination on the other. I take this to be Hegel's point when he says:

> For the universality that does not allow itself to develop into the reality of organic structure, and seeks to preserve itself in undivided continuity, in itself immediately distinguishes itself because it is generally movement or consciousness. And in fact it divides itself for the sake of its own abstraction into equally abstract extremes: into simple, inflexible, cold universality and into the discrete, absolute, hard obstinacy and stubborn punctuality of actual self-consciousness.[1]

That Kant has in fact separated two elements of moral action that cannot be separated is for Hegel shown by the fact that the moral law gives us no grounds to decide on any particular occasion between two conflicting duties save the purely formal test of universalizability.[2] Hegel's point here is that our ethical deliberation is never between pure inclination and pure duty but rather between two *prima facie* duties, each of which is certified by the criterion of universalizability. More particularly, what contradicts one duty is not pure duty but rather other specific and limited social and legal institutions, each of which, if taken alone, would be compatible with the purely formal demands of the moral law.

From this it follows that my reason for acting morally is much more specific than the consistency of my proposed action with the categorical imperative. Willing duty for duty's sake is for Hegel a fiction just because it is an abstraction from what happens in moral deliberation. Really important cases of moral perplexity are perplexities about conflicting duties, not about something which is either wholly universal or wholly particular.[3] Hegel has already discussed cases of this kind of deliberation in the section on "Guilt and Destiny,"[4] where he makes constant reference to the tragic hero who is forced to decide between two conflicting duties. And here he turns the same point against Kantian ethics in order to show that the account of moral action it gives not only leaves out the most characteristic mark of moral experience but even argues for its inconceivability. From this, Hegel concludes that Kant has put the particularity of moral action in the wrong place. He is not denying the presence of a distinction between universal and particular in moral action. All he is arguing is that, once Kant has separated the universal from its particular embodiments, the universal becomes another particular. Hegel insists that a moral agent wills a particular action even in willing duty for duty's sake. In fact, for Hegel, duty is nothing but an aspect of particular actions. Yet the action as dutiful is neither mere inclination nor pure duty. It is not the former because it is an action which is commanded by the complex of moral commitments in which the agent finds himself. It is not the latter since, in most cases, any of a number of opposing courses of action could qualify as one's duty. And the rejected ones do not cease to be (*prima facie*) duties once they are rejected. Even if we are tempted to suppose that there are acts which we can describe as expressions of pure moral will (e.g., as in the sacrifice of one's life for the community), the issue here is the existence in most moral situations of a number of duties not all of which can be actualized simultaneously. (This is to be strictly separated from the quite different issue, which Hegel also discusses, concerning the intelligibility of acting from the motive of duty as such in abstraction from any inclinations.)

There are, of course, various rescue efforts made by proponents of the Moral World-View. Hegel considers the two principal ones under the heading of "Dissemblance."[5] If inclination and duty be reconciled in the notion of a holy will, morality is lost. A holy will would be one in which there would be no inclinations opposed to duty. For it the categorical imperative would not be an imperative at all. But this way out of the dilemma of the Moral World-View fails because, as Hegel argues, creatures having holy wills are not moral agents at all. Whatever else it may be, practical reason is at least the ability to deliberate, to give answers to the question "What shall I do?" And where there are no desires or no conflicting duties, there can be no deliberation, no weighing of alternatives, since there would be no alternatives at all for a holy will. So, if the separation between pure duty and inclination is ever overcome in such a holy will, it would be the undoing of practical reason.[6] But the Moral World-View dissembles in an even subtler manner. The reconciliation of duty and inclination is posited as an end, and moral action is held to be valuable only as a means to that end. Yet since any given moral act is, *qua* moral, pure duty, it must be valued as an end. The particular moral act must exhibit the reconciliation of duty and inclination. But, if this is so, the conclusion of the dissemblance of the holy will applies with equal force to this second dissemblance.[7] Hegel argues this way when he says:

> pure morality completely removed from actuality, so that it would equally lack any positive relation to it, would be an unconscious, unreal abstraction in which the concept of morality, being a contemplation of pure duty and a will and activity, would be completely abolished. Such a purely moral being is, therefore, another distortion of the matter and is to be rejected.[8]

I cannot decide here whether Hegel has given an accurate account of Kant's ethical theory. But if we grant there is a difference between ethical theory and a phenomenology of moral experience, we may be reluctant to accept Hegel's criticisms. It is crucial to understand that Hegel is not purporting to criticize answers to the question "What are the conditions of moral experience?" but rather answers to the question "What is the character of moral action?" To ask about the character of moral action is not to set about justifying moral experience but only to give an account of what we are doing in moral action. That these activities are distinct is shown by the fact, frequent in the history of ethics, that the moral experience we justify may not be the moral experience we have. And this distinction, I hold, animates Hegel's criticism of Kant.

The form of moral consciousness called "Conscience" (*Das Gewissen*) is another attempt to answer the question about the character of moral action. It is an attempt to solve the problem of explaining how actions can be both particular and universal without running afoul of the difficulties of the Moral World-View. Here we are told that these difficulties are overcome by having practical reason act from individual conviction. Hegel states this alternative in the following way: "Only as conscience does it [i.e., moral self-consciousness] have in the *certitude of itself* the *content* of the previously empty duty as well as of the empty general will, for this certitude of itself is at once *immediate*, existence itself."[9] The moral law as it appeared in the preceding sections is no longer an empty formula which could fit any of two opposed duties. It has become the expression through conscience of the moral agent's rational desires. But it is not merely particular for that reason. Since it is the expression of the universal will common to all rational agents, it has the universality required for the moral law. Thus, conscience is "simple, dutiful conduct that knows and does, not this or that duty, but rather what is concretely right."[10]

This conception of conscience as the universal will in the individual agent is to be found in Fichte's *System der Sittenlehre*.[11] The form of consciousness Hegel introduces at this point in the *Phenomenology* is identical with the position which he attributes to Fichte in *Die Wissenschaftlichen Behandlungsarten des Naturrechts* (1805), which was Hegel's final contribution to *Das Kritische Journal der Philosophie*. The same position was linked with Fichte's system as early in Hegel's career as 1802, when he wrote his *System der Sittlichkeit*. Fichte had argued that Kant's difficulties about conflicts of duties had resulted from Kant's definition of conscience in terms of duty. Thus conscience could never arbitrate between opposed duties. The improvement in Kant's ethical theory which Fichte hopes to achieve is to make the deliverances of conscience the touchstone of duty. This is evident in the *System der Sittenlehre* where Fichte argues: "Do what you can consider with conviction to be duty, and do it solely because you have convinced yourself that it is duty."[12] For Fichte this meant that a moral agent cannot be involved in the situation of hesitating about what his duty is. For although the moral law governs conscience, it is conscience that tells us what the law is: "Conscience can never err; for it is the immediate consciousness of our pure, original self which no other consciousness transcends.... To want to transcend it is to want to transcend oneself, dividing the self from itself."[13]

The ethics of conscience offers a twofold solution to the problem of the Moral World-View. The rift between universal and particular elements in moral action is allegedly overcome by replacing the conception of the moral law as being imposed from without by the conception of the moral law as being the deliverances of the conscience of the particular agent. Moral acts are still not merely particular because conscience is the expression of the noumenal self, which like the moral law of Kantian ethics, legislates for the community.[14]

The transition from the Moral World-View to conscience has not come about by a formal deduction of one from the other. For it was only because the latter form of consciousness lacked any notion of conscience that it collapsed as an account of moral action. Still less does Hegel let Kant's position "grow" into Fichte's. For he is concerned to show that Fichte is offering a new start, even though he accepts Kant's problem. What has in fact happened is that the position of conscience owes its presence in the *Phenomenology* to the historical fact that the theory of the moral law developed as it did.

Just how are we to connect a criticism of Kant's theory of the moral law deductively to the introduction of a theory of morals based on the deliverances of conscience when Hegel does not argue that the former implies the latter and in fact acknowledges the introduction of a theory of conscience as a new beginning to remedy the defects of Kant's notion of the moral law? What is puzzling is how an apparently discredited theory can have any deductive connection with a theory that is formally incompatible with it and which no available account of dialectical reasoning can coherently map. Thus the appeal to purely historical rather than deductive or dialectical connections of the two passages.

But conscience is now exposed as being as impoverished as the theory of pure duty. Just as the moral law could sanction either of two opposed duties, so also conscience can sanction either of two conflicting courses of action, so long as each carries with it the stamp of conviction. What we have been given is another word for the problem of the Moral World-View, not a solution of it.[15] So conscience fails just where the moral law failed: both purported to specify the sense in which a particular moral action is performed out of principle. The moral law gave only a negative answer to this question by means of universalizability. But action was seen to be no less moral for being a choice between two maxims each of which is universalizable. The doctrine of conscience tries to resolve this difficulty by making the law a function of conviction. But we can feel the same amount of conviction toward two conflicting courses of action. Furthermore, if we accept this view of duty, there is no way to distinguish between the dictates of duty and the lures of conviction. The ethics of conscience started out to reconcile the moral law with specific inclinations and duties. It ends by reducing the former to the latter.

At this point there is an abrupt swerve in Hegel's argument. Having destroyed one view of conscience, Hegel then takes up a theory according to which conscience no longer *expresses* the moral law as it did in Fichte's position; it *is* the moral law. Hegel says of this view: "In the majesty of its aloofness to the determinate law and every content of duty, conscience thus places an arbitrary content in its knowledge and volition; it is moral geniality, which knows the inner voice of its immediate knowledge as a divine voice."[16] Conscience now has "the absolutely autonomous majesty to charge and to discharge."[17] This theory of conscience differs from the one Hegel has just criticized in two ways. First, unlike Fichte's theory, this theory posits a distinction between the moral order of conscience and a moral order, dictated by a theory of natural law, which opposes the validity of conscience. Secondly, there is an open opposition between these two orders, each of which claims to be the touchstone of morality.

I propose to account for this turn in Hegel's argument by arguing that this new form of consciousness finds its expression in the *Kraftgenie* and the creative personality of the *Sturm und Drang*. There is, further, strong evidence that Hegel is drawing upon this type as it is depicted in Friedrich Heinrich Jacobi's two early novels, *Woldemar* (1777) and *Allwills Briefsammlung* (1775). Hegel was well acquainted with Jacobi's writings, various discussions of which are to be found in Hegel's contributions to *Das Kritische Journal der Philosophie*. Jacobi's ethics of conscience was discussed in one of Hegel's early essays entitled *Glauben und Wissen*, published in *Das Kritische Journal* in 1802.[18] In 1813 and 1817 Hegel published critical reviews of Jacobi's complete works in the *Heidelberger Jahrbücher der Literatur*, where many of the criticisms made of the form of conscience found at this point in the *Phenomenology* are repeated with reference to Jacobi.

Both *Woldemar* and *Allwill* are extended discussions of the moral experience of a consciousness whose deliverances are at variance with the established moral order. The main tenet of both novels is that men should obey the impulse of the heart (a metaphor occurring frequently in both), and that both morality and religion should derive from an intuitive certainty that is very much like the immediacy of self-knowledge.

Now, Jacobi was hardly original in the choice of this kind of character. He was merely giving literary expression to a notion of genius that had captured the imagination of most of his most eminent contemporaries. Herder, calling the genius a man whose activity was governed by inspiration as opposed to reason, identified this notion with that of the poet when he wrote in his letters "Über die neuere deutsche Literatur" in 1767 that "Passion and Activity are the soul of poetry."[19] Goethe, too, had declared the artist free from rules imposed from without when he wrote in *Kunst und Altertum*:

Everyone constructs his work out of elements that some can, to be sure, weave together more organically than others. Then, too, the presiding maxim greatly depends on the observer. But when the artist takes hold of an object, it thereby ceases to belong to nature. Indeed, it may be said that it is in this moment that the artist creates, that he extracts from the object what is meaningful, characteristic, interesting, or rather for the first time lends it a higher value.[20]

Yet even though Jacobi is indeed depicting this sort of poetic genius in his novels, what he adds to this notion is the element of moral genius. Thus, both of his characters view the relation of rules and laws to moral action as they view the relation between rules and aesthetic creation: the moral agent is self-legislative, not in the sense that he freely chooses the rule of his action, but that he rejects all externally available rules, relying on the inspiration of his conscience for his ethical knowledge. Moreover, what distinguishes this conception of conscience from Fichte's is that the moral genius here sees himself in opposition to a standard of morality that he condemns. Accordingly, Jacobi has Woldemar exclaim that "atrophy of feeling, confusion of the heart, is the universal affliction."[21] This opposition between the conscience of the moral genius and the moral law is to be found in both of Jacobi's novels. The character, Hornich, who appears in *Woldemar* as a wealthy merchant, argues throughout the novel that ordinary conscience is inculcated by the moral order of the community.[22] Similarly, Sylli, a character in *Allwill*, refers to the moral genius when she writes that "the driving force of morality is as good as dead in them."[23]

The moral point of both novels is set forth clearly in *Woldemar* in a scene that occurs during a conversation between Woldemar and Carl Sidney, an Englishman who is a student of Ferguson and Reid. Woldemar, during his conversation with Sidney, says: "The science of the good, like that of the beautiful, falls under the province of taste, without which it cannot even be *begun* and beyond which it cannot be led. . . . Both are free art forms and do not subject themselves to guild laws."[24] The argument of conscience, then, comes to this: the activity of moral deliberation is like that of artistic creation in that both are subject, not to laws or rules, but to the free activity of the agent. A conscience that imposes its own rules on its action is creative of moral experience in just the way that an artist creates a work of art.

Hegel does not criticize this form of consciousness as he criticizes the Moral World-View. There he exposed the position as an inadequate account of moral experience and then introduced the ethics of conscience as a fresh start on the same problem. Here, on the other hand, he introduces the beautiful soul as the outcome of a consequent moral genius. His point here is that the position of the moral genius is unstable in that, once its consequences are developed, it will coincide with another position in the history of ethical theory: that of the beautiful soul.

The consciousness of the beautiful soul, as Hegel points out several times, is merely knowledge of itself and what it creates, which is "its *talk* that is at once immediately heard, and whose echo returns only to him."[25] While the moral genius acted in opposition to the moral order which threatened to destroy its freedom, the beautiful soul regards all morality, not merely its own, as a free creation of the ego. And this is not, I submit, an unfair conclusion to draw from the position of moral geniality. For if the moral genius were consistent in his ethical position, he would see that what he opposes is really only the free creation of an ego and that opposition to it is as immoral as its opposition to him. If this position were seriously held, ethical action would disintegrate into the contemplation of the products of the artistic consciousness. That is, to adopt the position of the beautiful soul is to remove the mainspring of all ethical deliberation: the conflict of duties or the opposition of duty and inclination constituting moral choice. If there are no conflicts, no alternative courses of action, then there can be no deliberation, no choosing between opposed courses of action; for there would be no opposed courses of action, only alternative deliverances of the freely creating aesthetic consciousness. And to hold a position like this would be to abstain altogether from moral commitment. I suggest that Hegel is criticizing this kind of position when he says of the beautiful soul:

> It lacks the power of externalization [*Entaüßerung*], the power to make itself into an object and endure existence. It lives in the fear of marring the splendor of its interiority by action and existence. And in order to preserve the purity of its heart, it flees from contact with reality and perseveres in the stubborn incapacity to renounce an ego lifted to the extreme of abstraction and give itself substantially or to transform its thought into existence and entrust itself to the absolute difference.[26]

The fate of the beautiful soul is either that it "disappears as a formless vapor that dissolves into air" or that it is "unhinged to the point of madness and flows apart in yearning consumption."[27]

My argument, however, is open to an apparent objection. If one accepts my argument, the notion of the *Kraftgenie* implies the notion of the *schöne Seele*. The former is rooted in the assumption that what we ordinarily call duty is the free creation of the self which acts independently of moral rules or laws making the deliverances of its creativity be morally right or wrong. But the *schöne Seele*—and this is the thrust of the present objection—does not act in a *morally* significant way at all. Hegel tells us that the *schöne Seele* does nothing ("It lacks the capacity of renunciation") while the *Kraftgenie*, so far from being actionally impotent, at least acts and as such presents us with an implied theory of morally significant action.

The objection, however, misses the critical point of Hegel's text. True, the *schöne Seele* does nothing but merely promulgate while the *Kraftgenie* acts. But what makes a *Kraftgenie* into a *schöne Seele* is that it lacks a criterion for moral judgment. An appeal to free creation is not so much an appeal to a criterion—and this is Hegel's main criticism here—as it is the abdication of moral responsibility. This is what makes the *Kraftgenie*, however active it might be, as morally bankrupt as the *schöne Seele*. The issue, then, does not turn on who does or does not act but instead on whether the performance of or forbearance from an action has any independent *moral* sanction at all. And, after all, promulgation is an act itself—only a morally empty one in the same way as the acts which a *Kraftgenie* touts as self certifyingly moral. That is the connection between the two apparently quite different forms of moral consciousness.

Although the beautiful soul is a consequence of the view of moral decision taken by the *Kraftgenie*, it is nonetheless meant to be a separate form of consciousness in the economy of the *Phenomenology*. And, if this state of Hegel's argument is not to be written off as a *Hirngespenst* of Hegel's dialectic, there must be some historical foundation for it. Many commentators, hoping to save Hegel from the notoriety of *Hirngespenster*, have taken him to be criticizing Schiller's conception of the beautiful soul, arguing that Schiller was, after all, the main literary proponent of such a notion. Jean Hyppolite[28] is chiefly, though not completely, responsible for reading Schiller's notion of the beautiful soul into Hegel's text—a poor fit for Schiller and, as I hope to show, an injustice to Hegel's text. Some commentators have had the eminent, if belated, good sense to see that Schiller's beautiful soul and the beautiful soul discussed here have only the name in common. They, then infer that Hegel misunderstood Schiller and either used this inference as a ground to denounce Hegel's architectonic or spend pages machining excuses for Hegel's outlandish inaccuracy. I, however, suggest that Hegel was not criticizing Schiller at all in this section but rather a notion of the beautiful soul which was developed by Novalis in his *Heinrich von Ofterdingen* (1799–1800). This hypothesis is enhanced by the fact that Hegel refers directly to Novalis in other works, where he calls Novalis a beautiful soul and links the notion of a beautiful soul with Novalis's writings. One such reference occurs in Hegel's Berlin essays.[29] Here he refers to Novalis as a beautiful soul that was doomed to die of intellectual consumption. The reference to consumption is introduced in the *Phenomenology* as the fate of the beautiful soul.[30] Another reference is to be found in the *Aesthetik*,[31] and yet another in the *Geschichte der Philosophie*.[32] In both places Hegel characterizes Novalis' work as that of a beautiful soul.

I propose to strengthen my thesis by discriminating briefly between two independent notions of the beautiful soul that were current in the literary tradition of Hegel's Jena period. Having distinguished between those divergent notions, I can better show how Hegel's criticism does in fact have historical foundation.

The idea of the beautiful soul, although it was an offspring of the identification of the beautiful and the good found both in Plato[33] and in Plotinus,[34] was introduced into German literature through Shaftesbury. To be sure, Shaftesbury talks of a virtuoso instead of a beautiful soul; but it is in the virtuoso that the harmony of art and the harmony of virtue are the same:

> Harmony is Harmony by Nature, let Men judge ever so ridiculously of Musick. So is Symmetry and Proportion founded still in Nature, let Men's Fancy prove ever so barbarous.... 'Tis the same case, where Life and Manners are concerned. Virtue has the same fix'd standard. The same Numbers, Harmony, and Proportion will have place in Morals.[35]

It is in the concept of harmony that the virtuoso combines ethical and aesthetic qualities. Shaftesbury conceived ethical action as a harmony of different affections; virtue, for example, consisted in the balance or harmony of egoistic and social affections. Similarly, harmony governed the composition of a work of art both in its internal organization and in our appreciation of it. Thus, for Shaftesbury morality and virtue are beautiful in that they are governed by the same proportions (what he calls "inward numbers") as artistic creation. And both the beautiful and the moral are judged by an emotional response of the moral sense. For Shaftesbury, then, the judgment of a character or a moral situation is at least in part like an aesthetic judgment. The virtuoso is for him one who, as a result of direct acquaintance with "that consummate grace, that beauty of Nature and that perfection of numbers of which the rest of mankind ... feel ... only the effect whilst ignorant of the cause," can unerringly appreciate the harmony of art and the harmony of morals.[36] Elsewhere he says of the virtuoso:

> The sense of inward numbers, the knowledge and practice of the social virtues, the familiarity and favor of the moral graces are essential to the

character of a deserving artist. . . . Thus are the arts and virtues mutually friends, and thus the science of *virtuosi* and that of virtues itself becomes in a manner one and the same.[37]

The most characteristic feature of the virtuoso—and the feature that sharply distinguished Shaftesbury's virtuoso from Schiller's beautiful soul—is that the macrocosmic harmony which is reflected in him and exhibited in his moral-cum-aesthetic judgments is innate and not acquired. The harmony of sensibility and reason in aesthetic and moral appreciation is not treated as an ideal of education just because the two are not separated to begin with.

Wieland, who directly borrowed the idea of the virtuoso from Shaftesbury around 1756 (in *Araspers und Panthea*, 1756–60), repeats most of Shaftesbury's doctrine while underscoring the instinctiveness of the moral beauty of the beautiful soul. This borrowing is so well known that exhaustive references to the sources is hardly necessary.[38]

Schiller gives us, however, a new account of the concept of beautiful soul, coming as he did from a prolonged study of Kantian ethics. Kant had maintained that actions are moral only if they are performed out of respect for duty. If duty and inclination coincide, then no moral goodness attaches to this. Schiller, accepting the distinction between duty and inclination, nonetheless held that the coincidence between duty and inclination has an aesthetic value. A beautiful soul is the harmony of duty and inclination understood as form and matter (which Schiller calls *Stofftrieb* and *Formtrieb*) in an ethical context:

> We are in the presence of what is called a "beautiful soul" when the moral sentiment of all of man's sensations is finally assured to the degree that it can give the direction of the will over to affect without fear and run the risk of contradicting decisions. With a beautiful soul, therefore, it is not really the individual actions but rather the entire character which is moral. . . . Thus in a beautiful soul sensibility and reason, duty and inclination, harmonize; such a soul is expressed phenomenally as grace.[39]

If we understand by "beautiful soul" a moral agent that exhibits the harmony of Schiller's distinction between *Stofftrieb* and *Formtrieb*, we are faced with a notion that is erected on a presupposition running directly counter to Shaftesbury and Wieland: namely, the difference in kind between sensibility and moral reason. The harmony which figures in the argument of Shaftesbury and Wieland is based on the Leibnizian theory that moral reason and sensibility are two aspects of the same faculty. The only difference lies in clarity and distinctness with which the object is grasped by the intellect. It was for this reason that both Shaftesbury and Wieland could hold that the harmony of the beautiful soul is innate and not acquired; for there are not, on their theory, two opposed elements such as *Stafftrieb* and *Formtrieb* to be reconciled with each other. This distinction, fundamental to Schiller's understanding of the beautiful soul, also explains the place of aesthetic education in Schiller's theory of the education leading to the harmony of freedom and law. Schiller never conceded any but a regulative status to the beautiful soul in moral theory. Thus, for him the notion is an ideal not realized in particular cases of moral action.

Nor does Goethe's treatment of the *schöne Seele* in his *Wilhelm Meisters Lehrjahre*[40] shed any light on the notion that Hegel's *Phenomenology* critically discusses under that name. This exegetical mischief is to be found, for example, in J. B. Baillie's introduction to the relevant section of the text in his translation of *The Phenomenology of Mind.*[41] The facts of that chapter of *Wilhelm Meister*, thrust into the continuity of the novel without any preparation and concluded just as abruptly without any transition to what follows, are basically these. The context is a series of love relations—first with a certain Narziss and later with Philo—which dramatize the increased rejection of reliance on anything but the momentary deliverances of one's sensitivity to define relations to others. The case is pathological: the woman cannot face the fact that she could not alter a society in which she must live according to her dictates and withdraws to a communion with God and the absolute freedom of the deliverances of her sensitivity. This chronic disorder—same call it *Empfindsamkeit*—finds its resolution in what she believes to be an immediate and inviolate relation to God[42] supplemented by the conviction that "I hardly remember an obligation. Nothing appears to me in the form of a law. It is instinct that leads me and always guides me aright. I follow freely my inclinations and know as little of restraint as of remorse."[43] This, however, is as alien to what Schiller discusses as the *schöne Seele* as it is to what the Hegel of the *Phenomenology* criticizes under the same name. Two points should clarify this superficially complicated hermeneutical issue. Let me take them in turn.

In the first place, Schiller uses the notion of a beautiful soul to designate a moral agent whose inclinations invariably coincide with his action according to duty. The notion as Goethe uses it in *Wilhelm Meister* records the complete collapse of the distinction between acting from duty and acting from inclination. Goethe's beautiful soul rejects the notion of duty, while Schiller's recognizes a harmony between duty and inclination. This is what makes them totally different concepts even though they wear the same semantical clothing.

What is more important for my present purpose, however, is that the Hegel of the *Phenomenology* cannot be addressing himself to Goethe's description of the beautiful soul. Hegel criticizes a kind of moral consciousness that takes the creation of an imaginary world to be itself just like performing an action in a world that is not imaginary. But the beautiful soul Goethe describes, so far from making this kind of substitution, acts in the real world, not claiming it to be imaginary, but saying, rather, that the only grounds for action in a world, be it real or imaginary, are the deliverances of instinct. There are, then, two confusions here, only one of which fits Hegel's text. There is, first, the claim that talking about actions in an imaginary world is no different from performing actions in the real world. And there is the different claim that the deliverances of instinct cannot be judged by moral rules. Hegel argues here against the former, not the latter. *He has already disposed of the issues which surround the latter claim in his critique of Fichte.*

We are now ready for a discussion of a theory of the beautiful soul found in Novalis' *Heinrich van Ofterdingen*. It is this notion, not Schiller's, which is the historical foundation of Hegel's treatment of the concept in the *Phenomenology*. There is, however, a difficulty which complicates efforts to establish such a connection: Novalis himself does not explicitly use the designation "beautiful soul." But this difficulty can, I submit, be overcome, once it is seen that the theory Novalis adumbrates concerns the *concept*, if not the *word*, we are discussing.

We are told by Tieck in his *Nachwort to Heinrich von Ofterdingen* that the novel is meant to state Novalis' views about the relation between poetry and society. Of interest to us is the theory of conscience as the source of poetic creation as it is presented in the second part of the novel (*Die Erfüllung*). Here Heinrich appears as a pilgrim whom Mathilde, the girl he has met in the first part of the novel, takes to a man, Sylvester. His conversation with Sylvester concerns the relation of what is called conscience to artistic creation:

> I know only that phantasy is for me the entire instrument of my present world. Even conscience—this power that produces sense and the world, this seed of all personality—appears to me as the spirit of the cosmic poem, the accident of the eternal romantic coincidence of the infinitely changing totality of life.[44]

Sylvester's reply to this is significant for us in that it characterizes the change that the notion of conscience has undergone in the history of moral and aesthetic theory from Fichte to Novalis:

> All education leads to what cannot be called anything but freedom despite the fact that the creative ground of all existence and not a mere concept is to be designated by it. Such freedom is mastery. The master exercises free power according to intention and in definite and considered sequence. The objects of his art are his and accord to his wish, and he is not chained or limited by them. And just this all-encompassing freedom, this mastery or lordship is the essence, the drive of conscience.[45]

The ego of the moral agent is no longer above the law, as in Jacobi's doctrine of conscience. It is literally creative of its own deliverances. And it regards its creations as existing for its own contemplation. In this sense Novalis fuses moral with aesthetic activity. Both moral action and artistic creation may be conceived as acts of decision in which certain alternatives are elected and others rejected. Even if we hold that conscience is the voice of the moral law, we may still talk about obligations and duties which provide a matrix for the agent's decision and which are not created by the agent. Accordingly, what is produced in moral action is a decision in accordance with a law. Even the notion of conscience that Jacobi formulated did not deny this. What was denied was that the moral law must be always something outside the deliberating consciousness. Here this notion is developed in an entirely different way. What artistic deliberation produces is not given by any matrix of institutions or rules but, according to Novalis, is generated by consciousness according to the lights of conscience. In calling this moral, Novalis has made practical action impossible. For in envisioning a compresence of possibilities in the act of artistic creation or aesthetic enjoyment, the agent has not acted—only contemplated. To regard this as a kind of action leads to an abandonment of action altogether.

This consequence was, in fact, openly embraced by Novalis:

> The idle conscience in a smooth unresisting world becomes a captivating conversation, a phantasy recounting all. The poet lives in the halls and corridors of this primal world.... Enthusiasm is to the doctrine of phantasy as religion to virtue; and if histories are preserved in the holy books for revelation, the life of a higher world depicts itself multifariously according to the teachings of phantasy in wonderfully generated poeticizations.[46]

The notion of action as taking place within social institutions has been replaced by artistic activity, where there is no *moral* choice at all. Action has melted into aesthetic enjoyment.

It is, I think, clear that such a notion of the beautiful soul has little in common with Schiller's. For Schiller always held a strict separation between duty and inclination. In his beautiful soul, duty becomes an inclination, but it is no less a duty for that reason. And Schiller's position, unlike that of Novalis', does not stem from regarding ethical deliberation as a poetic creation of conscience but only as a motive governing action. Thus, what Novalis is propounding is not related to Schiller and fits Hegel's criticism of the life of the beautiful soul, while Schiller's notion does not.

So, we are confronted with a choice in our interpretation of Hegel. We can attribute the error in interpretation to Hegel's commentators or we can attribute it to Hegel. I urge that we adopt the former alternative because

1. Commentators holding the view that Schiller, not Novalis, is being criticized marshall no evidence for it other than the naive assumption that Hegel could not but be referring to Schiller if both used the same word.
2. Hegel's references to the beautiful soul in other parts of his *corpus* are always linked with Novalis and never with Schiller.
3. Such a choice would make an otherwise perverse and opaque text into a keen and accurate account of a form of consciousness having important relations with the foregoing discussions in the *Phenomenology*.

The third reason does, of course, rest upon the general assumption that Hegel is not purposely turgid. But, if we cannot accept this assumption, it is difficult to understand why people would want to write commentaries about him in the first place.

Having exposed the beautiful soul as an inadequate form of moral consciousness, Hegel goes on to argue that such a form must resort to irony when it sees that the object it creates is only imaginary and, as such, hardly a substitute for the reality of action. This, at any rate, is how I propose to interpret the passage in which he says: "Its activity is a longing that only loses itself in this becoming directed toward an insubstantial object and, beyond this loss and falling back upon itself, finds itself only as lost."[47] What Hegel is attempting here is to relate the notion of the beautiful soul to that of romantic irony. Now, those authors in the history of ideas in whose works those concepts figure did not try to make any connection between them. So, here of all places we must be quite sure that Hegel is trying to do so. This is made more explicit by a passage in his *Rechtsphilosophie*, where the position of the beautiful soul is said to commit it to doubt even the objects it creates. But, finding that it is only as real as its action, it is forced to irony to preserve the reality of its own ego. (This is to be found in *Rechtsphilosophie*, §140.)

But, even though we can establish that such is Hegel's intention, we must ask what foundation such a connection has in the history of ideas. If this view of irony is meant to be a criticism of Friedrich Schlegel, it is flagrantly unfounded. And most commentators have not neglected to point this out. What they *have* neglected to point out is that this section deals with a notion of irony quite different from that of Schlegel. I suggest that this section. is nothing more than a criticism of Novalis' doctrine of the creativity of conscience, by which Hegel is drawing a conclusion to which that doctrine commits Novalis. If I can distinguish the notion of irony as it appears in Schlegel from the notion of Novalis, I will be able to show that Hegel's criticism has an historical foundation.

Schlegel's view of irony, although it is propounded in a distressingly sybilline manner, is at least a theory about the relation between the organization of a work of art and the freedom of the artist in the act of creation. In what sense, he asks, is the artist limited by his creation? If we conceive the problem of irony in this way, we will not find Hegel's discussion of certain solutions of it so arbitrary and perverse. For the kind of problem to which irony was offered as a solution is closely related to that of the beautiful soul. In admitting that the ego expresses itself in what it creates, Schlegel then asks whether it is subject to the laws it imposes on the object of its creation. If it is, then the conclusion for him is that the ego is not free in its expression. Schlegel could not accept this conclusion because, if it were true, there would be little sense in talking about artistic creation. And this was a fact of aesthetic activity too patent to him to be argued out of existence.

Taking the notion from Fichte that the artist prescribes his own law to himself, Schlegel talks about the relation between the ego and its object as that of the unconditioned to the conditioned. In the *Lyceums-Fragment 108* he says: "It [irony] contains and excites a feeling of the irreducible opposition between the unconditioned and the conditioned."[48] The unconditioned is here taken as the creative activity of the ego, while the conditioned is its production. And the point Schlegel is developing by means of Fichte's conceptual framework is that the artist cannot identify himself with his creation because, as conditioned, it cannot be an adequate expression of the ego. For the ego, according to this theory, is *ex hypothesi* unconditioned. No particular creation can exhaust its resources. And the ability of the artist to distance himself from his creation, to recognize the inadequacy of the object to the ego, is what Schlegel means by irony. Schlegel argues in this fashion when he says elsewhere in the *Lyceums-Fragment*: "It is the most free of all licenses, for by means of it one transcends oneself; and nonetheless it is also the most lawful because it is unconditionally necessary."[49] This contrast always presupposes the existence of something beyond the work which is not articulated in it but in terms of which the work is measured and found inadequate.

What is important about Schlegel's position for our understanding of its relation to Novalis' is that Schlegel, unlike Novalis, introduces the notion of irony into artistic creation in order to show that the artist does not attribute to his creation—the work of his imagination—a reality that it does not have. He shows that there is a difference between the product of the productive imagination and that of which it is a product. The former does not condition the latter and thus the self-expression of aesthetic activity is not confused with the self-expression of moral and social activity. In recognizing the imaginary character of aesthetic self-expression. the artist is not committed to a position like that of the beautiful soul. In showing irony toward his work, the poet is not subject to the object he creates.

Novalis is also concerned with this problem even though he rarely, if ever, uses the word "irony" to designate his solution. There are several passages in which he speaks of the productive imagination as a unity in diversity characteristic of poetic creation. Two of these passages are relevant to our concern.

> *Harmony* is the condition of its activity—a *hovering* between opposites. ... *Hovering* between *extremes* that are necessarily to be combined and separated. All reality streams from this luminous point of hovering—everything is contained in it—Object and subject exist through it, not it through them. ... But the genius says so arrogantly and assuredly what he observes occurring in himself because he is not caught up in his presentation and therefore the presentation is not caught up in him. Rather, his observation and what is observed seem freely to harmonize, to combine freely in *one* work. When we speak of the external world, when we really depict objects, we proceed like the genius. ... Thus genius is this capacity to treat of imaginary and real objects alike.[50]

For Schlegel, it will be remembered, both the ego of the artist and his creation are distinct, although they are somehow related in irony. Artistic creation is a harmony of opposites, the ego of the artist and the object which is produced. Neither of those elements loses its individual character in the harmony. Novalis, relying upon his conception of the productive imagination, simply equates the object with the self-expression of the ego; the creative act itself produces the extremes that it mediates. The conception of irony destroys that distinction between the imaginary and the real, which Schlegel still preserves. If the act of self-expression does not distinguish between the object it creates and the ego whose self-expression it is, then the ego can no longer recognize the reality of anything outside its own creation. And this is because it can no longer distinguish between aesthetic activity or self-expression and any other kind of self-expression. Thus, whereas Schlegel introduced irony into artistic creation to avoid confusing the work of art with other expressions of the artistic self, Novalis uses the same notion to destroy this distinction.

I will, perhaps, be reminded that there is same evidence to suggest that Hegel himself was not aware of this distinction between types of irony that I have just tried to draw. In his review of Solger's *Nachgelassene Schriften*, for example, he discusses the concept of irony, calls Friedrich Schlegel its father, and attacks it as a rejection of the reality of those very relations and activities which are for Hegel part of what constitutes the moral and social activity of mind. Many of the commentators who maintain that Hegel misunderstood Schlegel draw their evidence for this position from Hegel's review of Solger's works. If one looks into Hegel's *Aesthetik* (*Werke* [Berlin, 1842], X:80ff.), however, one will find a discussion of two kinds of irony. The first is accompanied by the criticism Hegel makes of Schlegel in his review of Solger. Schlegel is held to have argued that no object can be real save insofar as it has been posited by the transcendental ego. Thus, no object can be viewed as real apart from the activity of the ego. And, in morality, the consequence of this view is that no moral obligation or social institution is objectively binding on such an ego. This is, according to my interpretation, a mistaken view of Schlegel's theory of irony. But Hegel goes on to distinguish this from another view, which he associates with the beautiful soul. He characterizes the second view as follows:

> The insatiability of this quietude and impotence that cannot act and cannot touch anything in order not to sacrifice inner harmony, and that remains with its yearning inactual and empty even though pure in itself, allows morbidly beautiful bliss and longing to arise. For a genuinely beautiful soul acts and is actual.[51]

This helps to establish my point that Hegel was aware of a distinction between two kinds of irony. Whatever the difficulties that attend his interpretation of Schlegel, Hegel offers here an outline of the doctrine of irony that he relates to the beautiful soul in the *Phenomenology*. I conclude, then, that he must be taken to criticize, not Schlegel, but Novalis in the *Phenomenology*.

The transition from the beautiful soul to the next form of consciousness introduces a position about ethical action that is in no way deducible from the position taken by the beautiful soul. There, it will be remembered, the individual consciousness claimed a universal validity. This claim was seen to be destructive of the notion of the individual in a social context. Now two positions follow upon the wreckage of the beautiful soul: "The Bad" and "The Judgment." *The Bad* is a particular agent who regards himself as more important than the social order of which he is a part, which is presented in the form of *The Judgment*. The Judgment unmasks the moral pretensions of the Bad as hypocrisy:

> When the former [the Bad] renounces its opposition to the consciousness of duty and upholds what this consciousness holds to be bad [to be absolutely incommensurable with the universal] as an action according to inner law and conscience, there remains in this one-sided assurance of commensurability its incommensurability with the universal.[52]

The criticism Hegel is making of the Bad run like this. If the Bad really were the spokesman of a moral order which it opposes to the existing moral order, then its maxims would be universal and not merely particular. In this way Hegel hopes to show the self-refuting character of the Bad. But the claims of the Judgment are not less impeachable. For it is hypocritical in that it fails to act at all. While condemning the Bad as purely particular in that its moral claims are merely the mask of actions done out of personal interest, the Judgment separates pure duty from all particular action. In this sense it substitutes moral condemnation for action. "It remains in the universality of thought, conducts itself passively, and mere judgment is its primary action."[53] The Bad acts out of a personal interest that it asserts to be moral purpose. The Judgment condemns this as hypocrisy; but, in doing nothing else, the Judgment cannot claim to be representative of the moral order either. For what is *morally* significant is a kind of action; and the Judgment does not act at all. This is *its* hypocrisy.

The historical foundation for this stage in Hegel's argument is given by Friedrich Schlegel's attempts to expose existing morality as a fraud and to erect a kind of immorality as the only rightful morality. His novel *Lucinde* (1799) is the vehicle of this new morality, which he had promised in his *Oeffentlicher Brief über die Philosophie* (1798). Within this novel, the Bad is represented by Julius, an artist who sets forth the Schlegelian morality in opposition to the established moral order. This tension between the artist and society finds examples in many parts of the work. Julius' description of the young Wilhelmine, a child whose freedom from convention he takes to be the ideal of morality, is a case in point.[54] Another such reference occurs in Julius' discussion of the education of his child, who is to be saved from the harness of morality.[55] The disjointed series of scenes that record episodes in the demoralization of Julius and Lucinde is repeated in an allegory entitled *Die Allegorie der Frechheit*, where the figure of Impertinence appears as the spirit of the new morality. She opposes the young girl's modesty, beautiful soul, decency, and delicacy, threatening to expose their hypocrisy.[56] Throughout the allegory and other parts of the novel, public opinion appears as an effete monster capable only of condemnation of impertinence but otherwise incapable of acting and accepting moral responsibility. If I am right in saying that Hegel is criticizing *Lucinde* in the form of the Bad and the Judgment, then his argument becomes very significant. While apparently accepting Schlegel's judgment of conventional morality in the form of the Judgment, Hegel goes on to condemn the hypocrisy of the Bad for the same reasons that he condemned the one-sided account of moral responsibility found in the ethics of conscience earlier in this section.

The evidence that Hegel was in fact criticizing Schlegel's moral theory is strong. Hegel was long acquainted with Schlegel; and his immediate dislike for the author of *Lucinde* can be found expressed in Hegel's correspondence from his Jena period.[57] Schlegel's novel caused such universal outrage within the literary community of his day that Hegel could hardly have avoided contact with it. In his *Aesthetik*,[58] Hegel discusses the novel with regard to its moral and aesthetic notions, and his criticism there runs parallel to his treatment of the Bad and the Judgment in the *Phenomenology*.

The Bad and the Judgment now give way to what Hegel picturesquely calls "The Hard Heart" (*Das harte Herz*), a form of consciousness which is the particular agent purporting to represent the moral order while condemning the universal evil of the age. The Hard Heart, like the Bad, maintains a position in opposition to the prevailing moral climate of its time. Yet, unlike the Bad, the Hard Heart ceases to be the voice of the *de facto* moral order and becomes instead the isolated opponent of an order that it is powerless to overcome. This is, I take it, the reason why Hegel calls the Hard Heart a beautiful soul.[59] For the Hard Heart, like the beautiful soul, claims to be the source of the moral order which is found unacceptable by its contemporaries. But here, as in the case of the beautiful soul, the moral order of which it is the advocate is not the source of action but only of imagination. The only action the Hard Heart undertakes is condemnation.

The form of consciousness which Hegel describes as the Hard Heart is, I submit, found in Hölderlin's *Hyperion* (first published in Schiller's

Thalia in 1796) and the *Tod des Empedocles*, the first version of which was written while Hölderlin was in close association with Hegel in Homburg from 1798 to 1800. Hegel's close attachment to Hölderlin is well documented and the evidence for it is too well known to need further presentation. They were both students of the Tübingen-Stift in 1788, when Hölderlin started work on *Hyperion*. Although Hegel explicitly refers to Hölderlin only once by name in his works,[60] the probability that Hegel is dealing with Hölderlin in this section is nonetheless high. A reference to another section of the *Phenomenology* shows the influence of Hölderlin directly. The section entitled "*Das geistige Tierreich*" is a criticism of a kind of moral attitude which Hölderlin condemns in almost the same words when he has Hyperion say: "As I wandered among those scholars, I occasionally felt as if human nature had been dissolved into the multitude of the animal kingdom."[61]

An examination of the contents of *Hyperion* reveals the connection even more forcefully. Despising the life around him as alien to his cultural ideal, Hyperion, like Julius in *Lucinde*, albeit for very different reasons, was dissatisfied with the moral climate of his time. Returning to his native Greece after a visit in Germany, Hyperion sees only a country enslaved by a foreign power which has caused it to abandon its cultural ideal. Thus Hölderlin can have Hyperion say:

> I contemplated more quietly my fate, my belief in the world, my desperate experiences. I considered man as I had sensed and recognized him from early youth in many kinds of education and everywhere found dull or shrill cacophony. I found genuine melodies only in childlike, simple restraint.[62]

Hölderlin recognizes the pact, both here and later in *Empedocles*, as the law-giver and the source of art and nature. This ideal, which is found embodied in Diotima and is championed vainly by both Hyperion and Empedocles, is set forth in Hölderlin's essays, "*Grand zum Empedocles*" and "*Über die Religion*," in both of which poetry, being the harmony of the sensibility and the intellect, is held to unify nature and spirit. The *vollendete Menschennatur* which is the achievement of such a harmony is found only in poetic creation, where Hölderlin sees a unification of what he calls the ordering and the receptive processes of the intellect. It is in this sense, I suggest, that we are to understand Hegel's remark that the Hard Heart is a Beautiful Soul. The Hard Heart is the source of the moral values in it because it, like the Beautiful Soul, claims to be the source of the moral order.

On the other hand, although both Hyperion and Empedocles acknowledge this ideal, they are not quite like the Beautiful Soul of the previous section just because they see themselves in opposition to the existing order, represented in *Hyperion* by the conquering nation and the *Bund der Nemesis*, a secret society of the revolution whose victory will, in Hyperion's judgment, establish only another dictatorship. This same theme appears in *Empedocles*, where the priest Hermocrates represents the alien order. Both of these oppositions are to be seen in the light of Hölderlin's letter to his brother of June 4, 1799, which is a plea of the Hard Heart complaining of the barbarousness of the age which only destroys those pursuing the ideal of the *vollendete Menschennatur*. And this opposition between the artist and the society around him is paralleled exactly by Hegel's discussion of the Hard Heart and the Bad in the *Phenomenology*.

The evidence I have introduced gives support to these conclusions. The *Phenomenology* can no longer be excluded from any serious consideration of the literary-cum-critical movements from the *Sturm und Drang* through early Romanticism in German literature. Even if we consider the section of the *Phenomenology* I have tried to interpret as a study of certain literary themes with the *apparatus criticus* left out, the interrelations Hegel has pointed out are very illuminating. For, in point of fact, Jacobi's notion of the moral genius can be treated as the alternative to the Kantian conception of self-legislation just as Novalis' notion of conscience, which Hegel calls the Beautiful Soul, can be seen as the consequence of Jacobi's position when it is argued to its logical conclusion. Further, the relation between irony and the Beautiful Soul is a suggestive commentary on the dire straights into which the Beautiful Soul gets when it acknowledges the inadequacy of its notion of ethical responsibility. Further, the ethical import of both Schlegel's and Hölderlin's works can be more clearly seen when they are weighed in terms of the tension between the individual agent and a social order to which he cannot give his assent as moments in a phenomenology of moral experience in literature. And, quite apart from the possible suggestiveness of these analyses for historical study, we must not forget that we are being presented with the first phenomenological study of literary themes in the history of German literature.

If my hypothesis about the character of those analyses is right, philosophers will realize that I have succeeded in offering a position about the character of certain transitions in the *Phenomenology* and the evidence for the justification of the individual *Bewußtseinsgestalten*. I hope to have pointed out that the so-called deductive model of understanding the *Phenomenology* in some clear cases fails to show just how the later forms are to be coaxed out of the foregoing ones. Hegel must here be understood, if I am right, as grouping several forms around one theme while not imposing a set rule on the relations among these forms. Some present alternatives to the ones preceding them. Others, however, present only a refutation. And there are still others, in isolated cases, which are literally inferred from the ones preceding them. My point has been to show that the very use of all three of these relations is proof enough that Hegel was not uniformly following any kind of deductive model.

One final cautionary qualification: nothing in my argument implies that the Hegel of the *Phenomenology* repudiates what we commonly call deductive proof as a method of philosophical demonstration. He frequently demonstrates the inadequacy of a form of consciousness by using indirect proof. He also shows that one form of consciousness straightforwardly *implies* the one that follows it in the text. But there are large stretches of the *Phenomenology* that cannot be ordered by an appeal to these techniques of deductive argumentation. Granted, then, that Hegel uses such techniques within the context, say, of one form of consciousness or the other, he does not invariably use them in moving from one such form to another. My examination of the foregoing sections of the *Phenomenology* is intended to make it intelligible on historical grounds why Hegel could have grouped the forms of consciousness as he does here without denying that he admittedly uses deductive methods to reject one or another of them.

What I have said here shows only the magnitude of the problem facing historians of ideas without offering a page-by-page solution of it. If I have been successful in showing that the Hegel of the *Phenomenology* is not trying to generate the world from his own ratiocinative processes, then our understanding of this great work must be systematically revised by a study of its foundation in the history of ideas. It has been my purpose here to adumbrate the beginnings of such a study.

Notes

1. G. W. F. Hegel, *Phänomenologie des Geistes* (PhG), ed. J. Hoffmeister (Hamburg: Meiner, 1952), 418; trans. A. V. Miller, *Hegel's Phenomenology of Spirit* (PhS) (Oxford: Clarendon Press, 1977), 359. The translations are my own.

2. PhG 430; PhS 370.

3. PhG 429; PhS 369–70.

4. PhG 335ff.; PhS 283ff.

5. PhG 434–44; PhS 374–75.

6. PhG 437–38; PhS 377–78.

7. PhG 438–39; PhS 378–79.

8. PhG 442; PhS 381.

9. PhG 446; PhS 384–85.

10. PhG 447, 448, 455; PhS 386, 392.

11. J. G. Fichte, *Sämtliche Werke*, ed. Fritz Medicus (Leipzig: Meiner, 1922), II, sections 15 and 16. Hereafter cited as Fichte.

12. Fichte, II:167.

13. Fichte, II:178.

14. Fichte, II:238–39.

15. PhG 454; PhS 391–92.

16. PhG 460; PhS 397.

17. PhG 456; PhS 393.

18. See *Hegels Erste Druckschriften*, ed. G. Lasson (Leipzig: Meiner, 1928), 306ff.

19. J. G. Herder, *Werke*, ed. Bernard Suphan (Berlin: Weidmann, 1889), XXXII, 122.

20. J. W. Goethe, *Werke*, ed. Sophie von Sachens (Weimar: H. Böhlar, 1887), XVII:110.

21. F. H. Jacobi, *Werke*, ed. Friedrich Roth (Leipzig: Fleischer, 1812), V:47. Hereafter cited as Jacobi.

22. *Woldemar*, in Jacobi, V:103.

23. Allwill, in Jacobi, I:181.

24. Jacobi, V:78.

25. PhG 462; PhS 369.

26. PhG 462–63; PhS 399–400.

27. PhG 463, 470; PhS 400, 407.

28. Jean Hyppolite, *Genesis and Structure of Hegel's Phenomenology* (Evanston, Ill.: Northwestern University Press, 1974), 512ff.

29. G. W. F. Hegel, *Sämtliche Werke*, ed. Hermann Glockner (Stuttgart: Fromman, 1927), XX:196. Hereafter cited as Hegel.

30. PhG 470; PhS 407.

31. *Vorlesungen über die Aesthetik*, in Hegel, XII:221; trans. T. M. Knox, *Hegel's Aesthetics* (Oxford: Clarendon Press, 1975), I:158-59.

32. *Geschichte der Philosophie*, in Hegel, XIX:644ff.; trans. E. S. Haldane and Frances H. Simson, *Lectures on the History of Philosophy* (New York: Humanities Press, 1974), III:507ff.

33. Plato, *Philebus* 64c; *Symposium* 201c.

34. Plotinus, *Enneads*, trans. Stephan MacKenna and Bertrand S. Page (London: Faber ad Faber, 1962), I:2; I:6; V:8.

35. Shaftesbury, "Advice to an Author," in Shaftesbury, *Characteristics of Men, Manners, Opinions, Times* (London: Darby, 1723), I, part III, section 3.

36. Ibid., I:214.

37. Ibid., I:216-17.

38. See C. M. Wieland, *Abhandlung vom Naiven* (Berlin: Akademie Ausgabe, 1753), IV:17, for the first occurrence of this notion in his thought.

39. J. C. F. Schiller, *Anmut und Würde in Schillers sämtliche Schriften*, ed. Karl Goedeke (Stuttgart: J. G. Cotta, 1871), X:103-4.

40. J. W. Goethe, *Wilhelm Meisters Lehrjahre* in *Goethes Werke*, ed. Erich Trunz (Hamburg: Ch. Wegner, 1959), VII, chapter 6, passim. Hereafter cited as Goethe.

41. G. W. F. Hegel, *Phenomenology of Mind*, trans. J. B. Baillie (London: Allen and Unwin, 1964), pp. 642-43.

42. Goethe, 387, 391.

43. Goethe, 420.

44. Novalis, pseud., Friedrich von Hardenburg, *Gesammelte Werke*, ed. Carl Seelig (Zurich: Bühl-Verlag, 1945), I:321. Hereafter cited as Novalis.

45. Novalis, I:321-22.

46. Novalis, I:323.

47. PhG 463; PhS 400.

48. F. Schlegel, *Lyceums-Fragment 108* in *Friedrich von Schlegel, 1794-1802: seine prosaische Jugendschriften*, ed. J. Minor (Wien: C. Konegen, 1882), II:195.

49. Schlegel, II:198.

50. Novalis, II:178, 37-38.

51. *Vorlesungen über die Aesthetik*, X:84-85; Knox, I:66-67.

52. PhG 465; PhS 402.

53. PhG 466; PhS 403.

54. F. Schlegel, *Lucinde* in *Deutsche Literatur*, ed. Paul Kluckhohn (Leipzig: Wissenschaftliche Buchgesellschaft, 1931), IV:163.

55. *Lucinde*, IV:215.

56. *Lucinde*, IV:164.

57. *Briefe von und an Hegel*, ed. J. Hoffmeister (Hamburg: Meiner, 1977), II:98.

58. *Vorlesungen über die Aesthetik*, XIII:108; Knox, I:507-8.

59. PhG 469-70; PhS 407.

60. *Geschichte der Philosophie*, XIX:644ff; Haldane and Simson, 507ff.

61. F. Hölderlin, *Hyperion*, ed. Marie Joachimi-Dege (Berlin: Deutsches Verlagshaus, 1908), II, book I, letter 6, 47.

62. *Hyperion*, II:130.

16

Daniel P. Jamros, S.J.

"The Appearing God" in Hegel's Phenomenology of Spirit

My title comes from a significant passage in Hegel's *Phenomenology of Spirit*,[1] at the very end of his analysis of conscience, in a section called "Evil and Its Pardon." There we find the following statement: "the reconciling YES... is[2] the appearing God[3] among those who know themselves as pure knowing" (362.25, 28–29) or universal thinking. A divine appearance at such a moment in the *Phenomenology* is quite plausible: both conscience and pardon can be considered human effects of divine power and action; while pure universal knowing can be interpreted as ultimately leading to a knowledge of God. Hegel then seems to be relying on conventional themes for his theophany: God appears through the pure knowing of conscience which pardons its enemy. This theophany is then used as the basis for a new chapter called "Religion" (PhG VII) which immediately follows the analysis of conscience (PhG VI-C:c). When it pardons evil, conscience discovers a new object of consciousness—namely the appearing God—which religion then develops further.

Yet the familiarity of Hegel's themes—conscience and religion, pardon and pure knowing—should not mislead us into interpreting him in a conventional way. One must pay careful attention to the peculiarly Hegelian meaning of these topics. For example, Hegel does not mean that all religion depends on conscience, for in the course of the *Phenomenol-*

ogy many other instances of religion (such as the unhappy consciousness in PhG IV-B or the Greek religion of the underworld in PhG VI-A) precede conscience (PhG VII-C:c). Conscience rather leads to religion in a precise way: it provides the concept of spirit[4] on which certain types of religion depend. These are the incarnational religions described in the chapter called "Die Religion." Chronologically their historical counterparts all precede the appearance of conscience; but conceptually they surpass it, since with conscience God appears only in pure intellectual knowing, while incarnational religion puts God in the whole person, body and mind. Common to both of them however is the concept of spirit as the appearance of God in human form.[5]

How this concept emerges during Hegel's analysis of conscience will now be examined, in three steps: (1) a survey of "Conscience," with special emphasis on "Evil and Its Pardon"; (2) an attempt to identify the real persons Hegel alludes to as embodiments of conscience; (3) a discussion of the meaning of conscience and its contribution to religion.

The Movement of Conscience

A helpful guide to its phases is provided by Hegel's title: "[VI-C:]c. Conscience, the Beautiful Soul, Evil and Its Pardon" (340.26–29). From the title alone, one might think that conscience is only the first member of a series continued by different shapes of spirit, namely the beautiful soul and then evil and its pardon. In fact however the last three shapes all derive from conscience and are variant forms of it rather than distinct shapes in their own right. When the beautiful soul pardons evil, one type of conscience pardons another.

What then does Hegel mean by conscience? It refers to a post-Kantian development in German thought. Conscience in general unifies in the real self two elements which Kant claimed could not be unified in this life, namely pure duty and immediate sensual existence (341.8–10, 15–16); the self of conscience therefore is the harmony which Kant postulated beyond the self. This identification of rational duty with immediate being is Fichte's theory of conscience, in which "duty... is immediately *actual* [consciousness and] no longer merely abstract pure consciousness" (344.28–29) as it was for Kant.[6] The link between abstract universal duty and determinate individual duty is made internally by individual conviction (347.19–20; 351.33), whose linking of the two is somewhat arbitrary.[7]

Conscience therefore has two sides, individual action and universal duty, joined arbitrarily by individual conviction and by words expressing this conviction. Since the two sides are not connected by any rational necessity, they soon slip apart into two distinct shapes of consciousness, both of them aware of the distance between universal duty and individual action. Both shapes must correspond to real types of conscience found in Germany after Fichte. The first shape is the "beautiful soul" which remains universal by avoiding action, while the second is "evil" which acts for selfish aims while continuing to speak about its universal duty. The reconciliation of the beautiful soul with evil comes about in "pardon," which ends Hegel's discussion of morality and furnishes the transition to incarnational religion.

How does this reconciliation come about? First of all, the so-called evil conscience rightly sees its antagonist, the beautiful soul, as itself evil. Since the beautiful soul refuses to act, and since its condemnation of action separates action from duty, it is no longer faithful to the original concept of conscience, according to which universal duty combines with singular existence in one's immediate conviction of specific duties. Consequently both types of conscience are evil, since both of them separate universal duty from real singular existence.

Seeing the similarity between itself and its critic (359.10–11), active evil conscience confesses (359.14, 24) its guilt of separating universal from singular.[8] In this confession active conscience is therefore "*pronouncing. . . its equality*" (359.14, 13) with the beautiful soul[9] and "views itself... in the other" (359.34–35). By its confession active conscience "renounced [its] *isolated being-for-itself* and posited itself as [a] surmounted particularity and hereby as continuity with the other, as universal" (360.2–4).[10] Through its confession it seeks the mutually "recognizing existence" (359.16) of "community" (359.26) with the beautiful soul. And when the evil, singular, active conscience portrays itself as universal, it is accepted by the beautiful soul (361.13–16) which all along has tried to remain a consciousness of the universal. This acceptance entails the pardon of evil. The beautiful soul, hearing its own universal thinking echoed in the confession of active conscience,[11] pardons its antagonist (361.16) and "recognizes as good" what it formerly called "evil" (361.19). Pardon is granted because the evil singular conscience is now recognized as a universal thinking. Thus in confession and pardon there is "a mutual recognizing" (361.25) of each by the other. The so-called evil conscience discovers a like evil in the beautiful soul, while the beautiful soul discovers a congenial universal-mindedness in the evil conscience.

Hegel attaches great importance to this "mutual recognizing." He calls it *"absolute spirit"* (361.25) and then "the appearing God among those who know themselves as pure knowing" (362.18–19). Therefore we need to understand as accurately as possible the "reconciliation" (361.22) that has taken place.

Both know themselves in the other only because "they know themselves as pure knowing" (362.29), a term which needs explanation. The beautiful soul obviously knows itself as pure universal knowing; but what about the active evil consciousness? Although its activity brings it into the world of singular material existence, its inner knowing of itself as a singular self has also become universal (witness its confession) and therefore "pure." In other words thinking is both a singular knowing of one's own subjectivity and a universal knowing of objectivity. Both aspects converge in the reconciliation of these opposing types of consciousness. Even though both kinds are "different" (362.2), so different in fact that Hegel calls their opposition "absolute" (361.28) and their knowing of one another a *"consciousness"* (362.15) of something other than oneself, "the movement of this opposition" (362.16–17) nevertheless turns this consciousness of the other into *"self-consciousness"* (362.16) or a knowing of one's *self* in the other. By knowing its resemblance to other selves, an individual recognizes that its own selfhood is both singular and universal. In this way singular subjectivity and universal objectivity converge.

This convergence has its greatest importance in the pardon itself, whereby the beautiful soul's universal knowing acknowledges goodness in singular subjectivity.[12] Through such a pardon, human subjectivity is identified with universal objectivity.

But what exactly is this universal? According to Hegel's *Logik*, divine essence is the underlying universal substance producing human essence and existence. Thus the essence known by the beautiful soul must be ultimately divine;[13] and this is the universal which its *pure* knowing knows. And since this universal has been identified with the singular subjectivity of the active conscience, the "reconciling YES" (362.25) of confession and pardon becomes "the appearing God among those who know themselves as pure knowing" (362.28–29). The universal object of consciousness is now identified with a singular subjectivity which thinks universally;[14] through individual thinking universal divine essence appears in singular human existence.[15] The object of the beautiful soul then is no longer the pure God of universal thinking but rather God as the universal thinking of the singular active conscience.

This concludes the movement of "Evil and Its Pardon," the first part of this chapter. I pass now to the second part, a consideration of the historical characters Hegel had in mind.

Identifying Hegel's Allusions

Three different interpretations have been proposed, as far as I am aware: Jesus; Napoleon; and German Romanticism.

Solomon suggests that the beautiful soul which forgives evil is Jesus himself, who taught forgiveness and who provides the easiest explanation for Hegel's reference to the "appearing God."[16] Solomon also appeals to Hegel's unpublished essay called "The Spirit of Christianity and Its Fate," which described Jesus as a beautiful soul.[17] But such arguments are not convincing. The term "beautiful soul" comes from Hegel's own day, when it described a certain type of literary figure, and was used by numerous authors, including Goethe and Hegel himself.[18] The beautiful soul which forgives evil in the *Phenomenology* belongs to post-Kantian thought,[19] and Hegel's rigor in following historical sequence *within* each of his chapters (though not in the book as a whole, where the sequence is according to a dialectical development which does not imitate actual chronology) is preserved if the beautiful soul of "Evil and Its Pardon" is a "beautiful soul" (or souls) from the early 1800s. Forgiveness is expected from any follower of Jesus; and so there is no difficulty in supposing that a beautiful soul following its conscience in Hegel's time could also be forgiving.

Moreover, the "appearing God" at this point in the *Phenomenology* is not a single person like Jesus but an intersubjective reality which appears "among those who know themselves as pure knowing" (362.29). A more careful analysis would link the "appearing God" to the *meeting* of two people rather than to a single person. In Hegel's text, the evil conscience which confesses its evil belongs to the "appearing God" no less than does the beautiful soul which pardons it. This brings us to the second interpretation, that of Kojève, who thinks the active conscience is Napoleon, while the forgiving conscience is Hegel himself, the philosopher who understands the universal significance of Napoleon.[20] Thus Kojève writes: "the *appearing God* is the *reality* of Napoleon *revealed* by Hegel."[21] Kojève does respect Hegel's historical coherence, both in time and in place: Napoleon and Hegel appear after Kant, and in Germany. But there does not seem to be much positive evidence for identifying Hegel's analysis of the active conscience with Napoleon.[22] And even if Hegel can be imagined to have assumed the role of the beautiful soul and then to have "forgiven" Napoleon (all of which seems to suppose a great deal), did the emperor ever confess his likeness to the beautiful soul's wicked side? Kojève does not offer enough precise evidence to be truly convincing.

Best of all is the third interpretation, proposed in 1924 by Emanuel

Hirsch, linking "Evil and Its Pardon" to writers belonging to the Romantic movement in Germany.[23] Unfortunately, his article does not seem to be well known outside Germany; the standard English commentaries on the *Phenomenology* make no reference to it. According to Hirsch,[24] the evil conscience is Friedrich Schlegel. One of evil's traits, hypocrisy (356.10), is attributed by Hegel's *Lectures on the History of Philosophy*[25] to Schlegel; and in his *Aesthetics*,[26] Hegel refers to the "depravity" of Schlegel's novel *Lucinde*. In this autobiographical novel, published in 1799 and based on Schlegel's affair with Dorothea Veit, Hirsch finds the historical counterpart of evil's confession in the *Phenomenology*.[27] Hirsch then identifies the forgiving consciousness as Hegel himself, whose "highest philosophical thought unifies the Romantic consciousness [that has been] torn apart within itself."[28] This may be correct; no other contemporary figure has been proposed, as far as I know. And despite leaving some questions unanswered, Hirsch's interpretation has much to commend it.

It obviously deals with a group of writers connected with the historical situation Hegel had in mind. Conscience clearly refers to Fichte, and its development in the *Phenomenology* must allude to people connected with him. Now in Hegel's *Lectures on the History of Philosophy*, Schlegel and Novalis are explicitly mentioned as connected with Fichtean thought, while Hölderlin is undoubtedly alluded to in Hegel's mention of "madness."[29] Similarly, the *Phenomenology*'s analysis of conscience makes clear allusions to Novalis (355.5; 360.28–30) and to Hölderlin (360.28). Chronologically, both would fit: Novalis died of tuberculosis in 1801; Hölderlin's madness began in 1802; and the *Phenomenology* was written in 1806–7.

Nevertheless I have some reservations about Hirsch's identification of "Evil and Its Pardon" with the historical Schlegel and Hegel, even though I have little knowledge of German literary history. Schlegel may well be the evil conscience Hegel had in mind; if so, the confession must be Schlegel's too. But two points about the confession make it hard for me to accept *Lucinde* as its historical counterpart. First, in the *Phenomenology*, confession is due to a likeness between the evil conscience and the beautiful soul; but *Lucinde* seems rather to be a declaration of difference. And second, the *Phenomenology*'s confession admits to evil, whereas *Lucinde* appears to be a shameless description of unconventional behavior.[30] Likewise, one should be cautious about identifying Hegel with pardon at this point in the *Phenomenology*. In his *Aesthetics*[31] and also in his *Lectures on the History of Philosophy*,[32] Hegel hardly sounds like someone who has forgiven Schlegel's confession.[33] Of course it remains possible that when he wrote the *Phenomenology*, Hegel felt more kindly toward Friedrich von Schlegel than he did later on. But Hegel's later antipathy toward Schlegel, as well as the difficulty of calling *Lucinde* a confession of evil, means that Hirsch's interpretation has not answered all possible questions.

Conscience and Religion

Even if we leave the historical situation of "Evil and Its Pardon" with less than complete clarity, we can still independently appreciate the significance of its movement. Completing Hegel's analysis of conscience, "Evil and Its Pardon" leads into a study of incarnational religion.

In pardon the beautiful soul's consciousness of universality identified itself with the singular subjectivity of human action, because the latter's "confession" shows it to be a universal thinking too. Pardon brings about an incarnational insight, evident in Hegel's mention of "the appearing God" (362.28–29) and also in his later (in PhG VII-C) explanation of the incarnation: the "*universal* itself" (406.2) is the hidden God, while through the incarnation "*this pure universal* is however revealed as *self*" (406.3).[34] This dialectical identity of the universal God and human selfhood is established by the reconciliation of universal and singular consciousness in "Evil and Its Pardon." The thinking of the singular consciousness is also universal, and so the beautiful soul interprets it as the appearance of the universal God.

Thus incarnational religion begins in the following way in *Phenomenology* (VII): thanks to "conscience" (364.21) and its concluding reconciliation, where *thinking* is the existence of divine thought,[35] individual human being is considered to be

> universal spirit ... which contains within itself all essence and all actuality, but is not in the form of free actuality or of independently appearing nature ... the actuality which it contains ... is the universal actuality [that is] *thought*. (364.24, 25–26, 30, 32)

Because spirit is able to *think* universal reality, its *thinking* is acknowledged as the appearance of the universal God; its godlike "essence [is] the *self-consciousness* which is all truth to itself and [which] in this [truth] contains all actuality" (367.28–29). In other words, thinking is absolute, and the distance between itself and its divine object seems to have been "surmounted." Before conscience, God was viewed as a transcendent object; but after conscience, as immanent in human thinking.

That seems to be the reason why religion is treated in *Phenomenology* (VII) as the "self-consciousness of spirit" (363.8), rather than as simply "the consciousness of *absolute essence*" (363.5) or of God as an object distinct from human subjectivity. The self is now seen to be the expression and existence of divine essence, which acquires a self or self-consciousness in human thinking. In self-conscious religion the self gradually comes to know itself as the real existence of divine essence. The transition to this type of religion comes through evil and its pardon, where the universal (or divine) object of thinking is identified with singular human subjectivity. Thus conscience makes an essential contribution to the development of religion in Hegel's *Phenomenology*. It produces "the appearing God" which makes religion incarnational.

At the same time the existence of religion shows the limits of conscience, as Hegel understood it. In conscience God appears through "pure knowing,"[36] but in religion God appears as incarnate, and fully so in the singular person of Jesus. In conscience only the singular human existence of *thinking* is identified as divine, for thinking is what led to pardon; while human existence itself, in its bodily and material aspect, is not explicitly included in the reconciliation that has been described. This further development belongs to religion.[37]

Thus religion too makes an essential contribution to Hegel's *Phenomenology*. Conscience leads only to a "pure knowing" (362.10, 24, 29) that excludes the material side of human being. But this is the side which gives existence to human thinking. Spirit is reality's universal meaning—thought, substance, essence, deity, or whatever else it might be called—appearing as individual human *existence*. Therefore the pure thinking of conscience needs to be improved by showing that it leads to real human existence. In religion this goal is finally reached by Christianity. Pre-Christian religions put the universal meaning of reality into individual shapes of gods that resemble and yet remain separate from empirical human being. The divine shapes of pre-Christian religions begin the movement towards full incarnation; they are incomplete attempts at a divine incarnation in human being.[38]

But even Christianity fails at a complete incarnation. Both Son and Spirit remain "in the form of objectivity" (368.34) distinct from all the human subjects they may be related to. As objects of consciousness they have a "*shape*" in "*presentation*" (368.32, 33), which always imagines a divine object as distinct from a human subject. They are not yet the "*concept*" (368.34) which completely unifies abstract thought and empirical human existence by comprehending the divine object as an essence which differentiates itself into existing human subjectivity.

Thus religion fails to complete the identification of universal divine essence with individual human subjectivity. Two specific deficiencies may be mentioned: the lack of universality and the lack of necessity.

In conscience the identification of divine and human was not limited to one person, for any instance of conscience could provide it; thus the "appearing God" should be universal. Christianity however limits God's appearance in the flesh to the singular person of Jesus; and when it universalizes divine appearance through the spirit, the appearance is no longer God appearing in the flesh but a God hidden in the human heart. Furthermore, the appearances of God in Christianity are considered "fitting"[39] means of bringing about human salvation, but not strictly necessary ones. In Hegel's terminology, Christianity views its mysteries of salvation as "contingent."[40] The movement of conscience thus needs a completion beyond Christianity. This task Hegel reserves for his own philosophy, where the concept of God includes nature and spirit. Unlike religion, Hegelian thought can think of human existence as the universal and necessary appearance of God.

Conclusions

If my analysis of Hegel's text is correct, at least two conclusions can be drawn for the further interpretation of Hegel's thought. First, his *Lectures on the Philosophy of Religion* can undoubtedly be understood more clearly in light of the incarnational meaning found in the *Phenomenology*, where "the appearing God" is the human self insofar as it thinks universally, for then the universal God appears as human being. This position implies that God's incarnation should not be singular, as in Christianity, but universal in principle. Since every self is capable of universal thinking, every self can be viewed as a divine incarnation. The vexing question of whether Hegel means to say just that in his *Lectures* on religion receives an affirmative answer from the *Phenomenology*. By isolating the origin of the incarnational principle in conscience, thereby separating it from any traditional religion, we obtain a good clue to Hegel's own thought. If "the appearing God" is found in every conscience, then Hegel must intend us to view divine incarnation as universal to human being rather than as a singular event.

A second conclusion cautions against enthusiastic applications of this principle. Even though conscience appears to call for a general type of divine incarnation, certain restrictions seem to apply. "The appearing God" presupposes a universal thinking, which means that such thinking is necessary for any incarnation. A self-centered thinking, or an overly particular one, could not be considered as "the appearing God." Excluded from the concept are the usual categories of human wickedness: greed, racism, homicide, and the like. One often hears the remark that

"The Appearing God" in Hegel's Phenomenology of Spirit 343

genocide and war disprove Hegelian philosophy; but such catastrophes are better understood as the failure of human being to be "the appearing God." They do not fall under the incarnation of God because they do not illustrate universal thinking. The movement of conscience in the *Phenomenology* shows that God appears only under precise conditions, namely as a universal thinking aware of human likeness. Thus "the appearing God" has to be a highly moral human being, respectful of everyone and hating no one. Grounded in conscience, the incarnation may be universal in principle, but its real actualization is not so easy. Hegel's description of "the appearing God" indicates that its occurrence may not include every feature of human life.

NOTES

1. Georg Wilhelm Friedrich Hegel, *Phänomenologie* in *Gesammelte Werke* vol. 9, ed. Wolfgang Bonsiepen and Reinhard Hedde (Hamburg: Felix Meiner, 1980). Hereafter this edition cited as PhG by page and line numbers, e.g. 420.16–19 means page 420 lines 16–19. It may be referred also as GW 9, with page and line numbers following. Translations from this edition (and from other non-English works) are my own, unless otherwise indicated.

2. In Hegel's "*es ist der erscheinende Gott*, etc." (362.28-29), I understand "*es*" to refer to "JA" (362.25) rather than to "Ich" (362.27); the word of the "I" is "the appearing of God." If, however, "*es*" refers to no neuter noun (like "JA" or "Ich") but simply introduces its clause, the meaning remains the same. Hegel would then be saying that "the appearing of God is among those who know themselves as pure knowing" (363.29). The precise appearance of God would then consist of what those people have "among" (362.29) themselves, namely the "reconciling YES" (362.25) of mutual acceptance.

3. Or "God appearing," as the standard translations render the passage. In G. W. F. Hegel, *The Phenomenology of Mind*, trans. J. B. Baillie, 2nd ed. (London: Macmillan, 1931; rpt. New York: Harper & Row, 1967), 679: "it is God appearing in the midst of those who know themselves in the form of pure knowledge." In Hegel's *Phenomenology of Spirit*, trans. A. V. Miller (New York: Oxford University Press, 1977), 409 (§671): "it is God manifested in the midst of those who know themselves in the form of pure knowledge." In Hegel, *La phénoménologie de l'esprit*, trans. Jean Hyppolite (Paris: Aubier, Editions Montaigne, 1941), 2:200: "*il est le Dieu se manifestant au milieu d'eux qui se savent comme le pur savoir.*"

4. See 419.39–420.1: "the concept of spirit came to be for us as we entered into religion, namely as the movement of the self-certain spirit which pardons evil." Hegel's phrase, "self-certain spirit" refers to "Morality" in general, to which "Conscience" belongs; the title of PhG VI-C is "Der seiner selbst gewisse Geist: Die Moralität," whose third section is "Das Gewissen," or "Conscience."

5. For Hegel spirit is divine *"essence . . .* which *essentially* assumes human shape" (387.26-27), or divine "essence which essentially is [human] *self-consciousness"* (405.25). The first passage explains the second; the self-consciousness of spirit is human.

6. Yet it is not only Fichte whom has in mind here. According to Jean Hyppolite (*Genèse et Structure de la Phénoménologie de l'Esprit de Hegel* [1946; rpt. Paris: Aubier, Editions Montaigne, 1974], 488) and *GW* 9:517 (note to 344.17-18), the paragraph we have just quoted from also contains a clear allusion to Jacobi.

7. Hegel's analysis clearly suggests that conscience raises individual bias into a universal norm, and therefore deludes itself about its moral worth. Lauer's explanation (Quentin Lauer, S.J., *A Reading of Hegel's Phenomenology of Spirit* [New York: Fordham University Press, 1976, 1982], 222-25) of Hegel's critique is especially clear. So is the one by Robert C. Solomon, *In the Spirit of Hegel: A Study of G. W. F. Hegel's "Phenomenology of Spirit"* (New York: Oxford University Press, 1983), 566-67.

8. By proclaiming universal ideals while acting selfishly.

9. Which also separated universal from singular by refusing to act and by condemning action in principle.

10. See also 361.13-14.

11. The content of confession, according to Hegel's text, is a simple acknowledgment of individual guilt: *"Ich bins"* (359.24), and hardly seems to carry the universal meaning Hegel ascribes to it. But this meaning may be contained in the *motive* for confession, if not in its literal content.

12. Evil conscience sees itself in the beautiful soul's evil. Such knowing is a universal knowing of two singular selves; but the object need not be explicitly universal. Evil may not clearly advert to the universal presupposed by its confession. But the beautiful soul's pardon of evil does discern evil's universal knowing. Thus the real synthesis of singular and universal belongs to the beautiful soul.

13. Hegel presupposes a loose equivalance between deity and the universal object of consciousness. The text does not argue for such an equivalence; it moves toward another goal, namely, the identification of that universal object with singular human subjectivity. Hegel always assumes that the universal (broadly understood) corresponds to divine essence, and singularity to real existence. When this universal becomes identified with a singular human being (as in our text), it becomes "the appearing God," or universal divine essence appearing as real (or singular) existence. In all beings the universal appears in singular form; but only in human thinking does it also appear as universal. Therefore God can appear only, as a thinking existence, or as human being. Christianity presents this idea to religion, and Hegel's concept of spirit (see above, n.5) comprehends it for philosophy.

14. In my interpretation, the precise universal thought by evil consciousness is not God (the universal essence of all reality) but only the lesser universality of a

"human nature" common to different people. Such universal thinking indicates that the universal does appear in real experience as individual human thinking. But who equates this thinking universal with God? The beautiful soul, whose consciousness appreciates the universal, seems a more likely candidate than the evil conscience (see above, n.12). On the other hand, the divinizing of the thinking (or human) universal at this point in the PhG may well be the work of the phenomenologist who sees the real significance of all the shapes of consciousness that appear in the PhG. In that case "the appearing God" appears to Hegel, but not to the beautiful soul who pardons evil. Hegel would then be comprehending the episode more deeply than does the beautiful soul.

15. Nevertheless, Hegel's argument (if indeed there is an argument) is not very clear on this point. Identifying the exact event (historical or fictional) Hegel is thinking of here would help immeasurably. The appearance of God at this point in his text is not a total surprise, however, since conscience by definition identifies its singular human experience with universal essence. A similar identification occurred in Hegel's earlier (and half-satirical) description of a religion of conscience (352.35–353.35).

16. Solomon, *In the Spirit of Hegel*, 578, 622–25.

17. Ibid., 624; see (cited by Solomon, 624n94) Hegel's *Early Theological Manuscripts*, trans. T. M. Knox (Chicago: University of Chicago Press, 1948), 236, 239, or (what I used to verify these references) *Early Theological Writings*, trans. T. M. Knox (rpt. Philadelphia: University of Pennsylvania Press, 1970), 236, 239.

18. Book VI of Goethe's *Wilhelm Meisters Lehrjahre* [*Wilhelm Meister's Apprenticeship*] is entitled *Bekenntnisse einer schönen Seele* [*Confessions of a Beautiful Soul*]. Hegel in his *Aesthetik* refers to the beautiful soul in Jacobi's *Woldemar*; see Hegel's *Aesthetics*, trans. T. M. Knox (New York: Oxford University Press, 1975), 1:241–42. Hirsch (520; see below, n.23) points out that Hegel in his *Lectures on the History of Philosophy*) SW. 15:644) refers to Novalis as a "beautiful soul" (see Hegel's *Werke*, Theorie-Werkausgabe, ed. Eva Moldenhauer and Karl Markus Michel [Frankfurt: Suhrkamp Verlag, 1969–1971], 20:418).

19. Kant himself was analyzed by the *Phenomenology* in the two sections preceding "Conscience"; the section on "Conscience" begins with Fichte.

20. Alexandre Kojève, *Introduction à la lecture de Hegel* (Leçons sur la *Phénoménologie de l'Esprit* professées de 1933 à 1939 à l'Ecole des Hautes Etudes), ed. Raymond Queneau (1947; rpt. Paris: Editions Gallimard, 1979), 95, 147, 152–53, 157, 195.

21. Ibid., 157: "*C'est la réalité de Napoleon révélée par Hegel qui est le erscheinender Gott.*"

22. The only textual connection between Napoleon and Hegel's discussion of conscience is the French saying, "no man is a hero to his valet" (see PhG

358.32–359.2; and the corresponding note, GW 9:518), which Napoleon may have made famous (Hyppolite, 504, calls it a *"parole de Napoléon"*; but according to Bartlett it was known a century earlier).

23. Emanuel Hirsch, "Die Beisetzung der Romantiker in Hegels Phänomenologie: Ein Kommentar zu dem Abschnitte über die Moralität" ["The Burial of the Romantics in Hegel's *Phenomenology*: A Commentary on the Section about Morality"], *Deutsche Vierteljahrschrift für Literaturwissenschaft und Geistesgeschichte* 2 (1924): 510–32. A brief summary of Hirsch's identifications may be found in Ernst Behler, "Friedrich Schlegel und Hegel," *Hegel-Studien* 2 (1963): 205.

24. Hirsch, *"Beisetzung der Romantiker,"* 522. Behler (208) agrees with Hirsch's identification, but also thinks that Hegel's interpretation of Schlegel as an evil consiousness has little support in Schlegel's own texts.

25. Hirsch (522) cites SW 15:642; the passage may be found also in TWA (my abbreviation for the Theorie-Werkausgabe cited above n.18), 20:416.

26. Trans. T. M. Knox, 1:508.

27. Schlegel's novel must have seemed improper to respectable moral standards in 1800. It rejected the chaste love portrayed by the beautiful soul of Jacobi's *Woldemar*; see *Friedrich Schlegel's Lucinde and the Fragments*, trans. with an introduction by Peter Firchow (Minneapolis: University of Minnesota Press, 1971), 21, 24. According to Gordon A. Craig, *The Germans* (1982; rpt. New York: Penguin, 1984), "Schlegel's novel *Lucinde* . . . titillated the prurient and shocked the sober-minded by the frankness with which it discussed intimate relations between the sexes" (151).

28. Hirsch, *"Beisetzung der Romantiker,"* 525.

29. TWA, 20:415–16 (Schlegel), 418 (Novalis and Hölderlin, though the latter is not named).

30. Such appears to be Hegel's estimate of it in his *Aesthetics*. In reference to another work, Hegel says that in it "moral depravity was not made into something sacred and of the highest excellence as it was at the time of Friedrich von Schlegel's *Lucinde*" (trans. Knox, 1:508).

31. See previous note.

32. See above, n.25.

33. Another good reason for caution is found in the structure of the *Phenomenology*. Evil's confession and its pardon occur through a "pure knowing" (362.29) that will be surmounted by incarnational religion in PhG VII, which in turn will be surpassed by the "Absolute Knowing" of Hegel's philosophy in PhG VIII. The reconciliation found in this pardon is therefore a limited figure of consciousness; it is not the "highest philosophical thought" (see above, n.28) of Hegelian dialectic at the time of the *Phenomenology*.

"The Appearing God" in Hegel's Phenomenology of Spirit   347

34. He also likens the appearance of God in this reconciliation to the presence of the Holy Spirit in the Christian church. See 419.38–420.8.

35. Divine essence is not only a human thought, for logic seems prior to thinking, which is the final differentiation of divine essence in Hegel's *Logik*. See also PhG 123.31–34; 298.20–24; 363.7–8.

36. Such was its development in German idealism or (if we follow Hirsch's identifications) Romanticism. Hegel has not analyzed all possible types of conscience, but only those he was familiar with.

37. In PhG VII self-consciousness is empirical as well as thoughtful. The term "self-consciousness" is itself ambiguous because it can refer to abstract thinking (as in 364.17–36) or to the actual sensual self (as in 369.23–29). However, the full meaning of "self-consciousness" is obviously both sides of it together, and this synthesis is the aim of PhG VII (see 364.36–365.5).

38. Insofar as the gods are not yet identified with individual existent human being, they remain objects separated from human subjectivity. But when human being is understood as the existence of divine essence, divine objectivity can be identified with human existence; and this identification seems to be how divine substance is also a subject.

39. See, e.g., Thomas Aquinas, *Summa theologica*, III, q. 1, a. 2; q. 50, a. 1.

40. See, for example, 412.31–35; 418.19–25.

VI

Religion

17

Translated by Jon Stewart

Jean-Louis Vieillard-Baron

Natural Religion

An Investigation of Hegel's *Phenomenology of Spirit*

The pages which Hegel dedicates to "Natural Religion" in the *Phenomenology of Spirit* do not seem heretofore to have aroused much attention among commentators. The historian of religion sees there only an outdated theory, while the philosopher finds in these pages only a supplemental application of an interesting analysis of the relations of religion in general to specific religions in particular. But when we consider Hegel's work itself and the progressive elaboration of the philosopher's thought, these pages present themselves as a *terra ignota*, a virgin forest which asks to be entered in order to reveal some of its secrets.

I

The introduction which Hegel gives to "Natural Religion" begins with a dialectic of religion and religions, a theme reached a little earlier in the general introduction to the "Religion" chapter. Here "Natural Religion" presents itself as a particular religious figure. What then is its relationship to religion in general? If Hegel insists so much on this question, it is as Labarrière has shown,[1] because the general economy of the *Phenomenology* transforms itself radically beginning with the "Religion" chapter. The progression among the different figures which compose the different moments of the "Religion" chapter is not merely linear. The profound reason for this is that it is first in the "Religion" chapter that absolute spirit appears. The relation of each religious figure to the totality of spirit is no longer comparable to the relation of the preceding figures to their sections. Spirit is actual in each figure, but there is a temporal succession among these figures such that, historically, the representation of the totality of spirit becomes more and more adequate. The figures of religion are situated in the form of objectivity, and here we are in the presence of an organization infinitely more complex than the chapters where spirit is not posited in self-consciousness; therefore, it is not astonishing to find precise correspondences among the moments of religion. With respect to this, Hegel was careful to indicate earlier, "it is the depth of spirit that is certain of itself, which does not allow the principle of each individual moment to become isolated" (PhS §681).[2] This indicates that the individuality of the religious figures has nothing of the absolute, and "all its [the spirit's] particular moments take and receive into themselves the like determinateness" (PhS §681).

"Natural Religion" is the first figure of this temporal trilogy which constitutes the "Religion" chapter; the others are "Religion in the Form of Art" and "The Revealed Religion." The idea that religion is a trilogy which is played out in three dramas had already appeared in 1799 in Schleiermacher's *On Religion: Speeches to Its Cultured Despisers*.[3] This work indicates distinctly three directions of religious consciousness: toward the self, toward the indeterminacy of the intuition of the world, and finally toward art and its works.[4] Kroner has correctly noted Hegel's debt to Schleiermacher on this subject: in these texts "Hegel perfects the thoughts of Schleiermacher and Schelling. In his *Speeches*, Schleiermacher had separated natural religion coming from the 'intuition of the world' and 'oriental mysticism' established 'on the most abstract road of introspection,' and he had said that these two kinds of religion have been ennobled by the artistic sense. Schleiermacher was the first to use the expression the 'religion of art' in this context, although at the same time expressing a doubt about its existence" (cf. *Reden*, Pünjer, p.172).[5] However, Hegel diverges from Schleiermacher when he says that he wants to consider only the "actualities of spirit," that is, the religions which declare themselves as such. Thus, he is not concerned with religious conscience but rather with religion as an institution, so to speak. From this fact, the direction of the religious conscience toward itself is rejected for a study of religions. This was already made the object of Hegel's earlier criticism in the form of the impotent interiority of the beautiful soul. Moreover, the relationship of religion to its forms is not envisioned by everyone in the same way; for Schleiermacher, these are simultaneous directions arising from the same common, subjective, and rather vague aspiration—religion. For Hegel, the succession of religious figures is objective and temporal, submitted to an extremely complex dialectic of refraction of the determinations of the in-itself, the for-itself and the in-and-for-itself "across the prism of their assumption in spirit."[6] Thus, Hegel's own originality appears even more clearly once one has discerned his debt to his contemporaries. The rupture with the thought of Romanticism proclaimed in the preface to the *Phenomenology* is well confirmed by his study of religion, but his study nonetheless strongly carries with it the mark of the spiritual climate in Germany during the first decade of the nineteenth century.

Studying Hegel's religious thought beginning with the texts of the *Lectures on the Philosophy of Religion* and dwelling on the dialectic of religion and of religions, which constitutes the very subject matter of the introduction to "Natural Religion" in the *Phenomenology*, Monsieur Vancourt believes that we can affirm that among the formulas of Schleiermacher and those of Hegel "there are incontestable analogies; however, these are to be differentiated, as one distinguishes a 'sentimentalist' interpretation from a 'rationalist' one."[7] Certainly, it appears quite difficult to have an exact opinion on this matter which concerns the Berlin lectures, the text of which still remains poorly established;[8] but it is certainly impossible to adopt the opinion of M. Vancourt if one wants to apply it to the text of the *Phenomenology*. An evolution in Hegel's thought between the two texts is quite possible, but this is not the object of our present study. However, the problem posed by the thesis of M. Vancourt must be resolved for an interpretation of the pages of the *Phenomenology* which we wish to examine. For Hegel, there is a diversity (*Verschiedenheit*) of religions in the sense that one is always concerned with particular religions. The singularity of religions can be overcome only in absolute spirit. The singularity, in fact, holds insofar as religion has still not reached the real self, but it rests at the level of representation or picture thinking: the diversity of religions is the diversity of representations. Let us say "diversity" and not "difference" (*Unterschied*)—this is one of the new aspects of the progression between the figures of the "Religion" chapter and the figures of the preceding chapters. "The ideas which seem to distinguish one actual religion from another occur in each one" (PhS §684),[9] and each individual religion has points in common with the other religions. But if one considers not just the relationships of the one individual religion to the another individual religion, but rather to the collection of religions, then religion appears to us as a real totality, with respect to which each religion maintains a determinate relationship. Here we see that the lecture which Schleiermacher gave in his "Fifth Speech" has been understood. "If you want to consider," says Schleiermacher, "these manifestations themselves [the singular religions, as manifestations of religion in general] in a religious spirit, as a work of the spirit of the world which this pursues to infinity; if it is thus, then it is necessary that you renounce as sterile and vain the desire that there be only one religion, you must abandon your repugnance in the face of the plurality of religions, and in a state of the soul as disabused of prejudices as possible, you must come to consider alongside those religions which have already been developed those that, in movement and under the changing and thus progressive aspects of the evolution of humanity, spring forth from the rich eternal breast of the universe."[10] It is thus in the religious spirit, with the rational effort that this spirit demands, that Hegel examines the relationship of religions to the religion. The diverse religions are taken seriously in so far as they are manifestations of the religion. The hypothesis of a unique religion is at the same time rejected as a vague and futile aspiration. Certainly, there is a progression among the religions but not under the eye of an observing consciousness and critic such as that of the master who in Rousseau's *Émile* observes the progress of his student,[11] and the truth of a figure is from now on no longer to be found in the figure that comes after it. In the same Speech, Schleiermacher already indicated clearly what role a singular religion plays: "A particular institution . . . the institutionalized central point of all religion."[12] Expanding on this idea, Hegel remarks that all religions have the same representations, but that each organizes these representations in a specific manner and that the philosophical analysis should attach itself uniquely to the representation that each religion takes for the essential and central religion. Finally, the inspiration which guides Hegel's thought is, as in Schleiermacher, against the skepticism of the *Aufklärung*. They both want to show that the plurality of religions is not at all the proof of the uselessness or the falsity of any one of them, but rather of the manifestation of the progressive development of spirit. Schleiermacher doubtless justified this plurality in a manner that was too individualistic in Hegel's eyes since when Schleiermacher shows that the essential is the individual fervent religious experience, then the result is that there are, so to speak, as many religions as individuals. Without a doubt Hegel's account in *Faith and Knowledge* in 1801 remained more cursory than Schleiermacher's due to the fact that it neglected the various lower forms of religious life. Be that as it may, the *Phenomenology* shows us a similarity of thought between them which extends further than a simple similarity in their ways of speaking. The profoundly religious inspiration in Hegel's philosophy is revealed in this relation to Schleiermacher.

In fact, it is more than the idea of an originary "pure religion" in the thought of Schleiermacher that Hegel wants to oppose. This Romantic conception did not wait until the Romantic movement to be expressed. As early as 1772 Herder exclaimed, "Light, magnificence, radiance, beatitude, this eternal image of the orientals . . . we have lost it!"[13] For Hegel, on the contrary, the development of religions is progressive and verifies the law announced by Fichte in his *Lectures on the Vocation of the Scholar* (1794):[14] "It is *in front of* us that is placed that which Rousseau under the name the state of nature and the poets under the title the Golden Age have situated *behind* us."[15] Hegel thus underlines the progressive elements of religions; there are in each region lower determinations and higher determinations, and a religion is more or less evolved according to the place, higher or lower, that it accords to the latter.[16] The idea of a history of religions becoming aware of the progressive revelation of spirit can clearly be found in the *Phenomenology of Spirit*, and it is not a coincidence that during the same year, 1807, the first part of the great unfinished work by Görres, *Wachstum der Historie, Religion in der Geschichte*, originally appeared, a Romantic work with much information relevant to this question. In that study, the author clearly distinguishes *Historie*, that is, reflective history from the point of view of the scholar, and *Geschichte*, that is, history which human beings make or lived history,[17] and finally religion, which, accomplishing its metamorphoses in history, alone produces the growth of history. He claims that religion's historical becoming corresponds to a law of spiritualization which is the law of progress. Consequently, the first forms of religion have a positive interest and cannot simply be lumped together under the global and negative name of "paganism." From Görres, Hegel borrows the idea of a temporal succession of different religions and the correspondence of different religious figures to the stages of consciousness on the way to its education. But if, on the one hand, the analogy drawn by Görres between the first forms of religious life and the unconscious or semiconscious phenomena of individual life finds a structurally organized and rationalized echo in Hegel, then, on the other hand, the myth of a unique religion venerable at its origin is radically rejected. Görres, in fact, was wrong to seek to reduce religion to a unity without seeing the particularity of the individual religious figures: "*One sole* duty and *one sole* myth existed in the ancient epoch. There was *only one* Church and likewise *only one* state and *only one* sole language."[18]

II

It is only when one has situated Hegel's thought in the context of his epoch that one can appreciate to what degree the title of this first stage of the "Religion" chapter is paradoxical. In his lectures in Berlin, Hegel will speak of natural religion and will characterize it by its immediacy.[19] But in 1807 it is the title "Natural Religion" which he adopts, according to all evidence, intentionally. Employing the same terms as the *philosophes* of the eighteenth century, that is, as the *Aufklärung*, and giving them an entirely different content, Hegel marks concretely in his style itself the absolute and definitive character of his break with the thought of the preceding century. It is not that he revels in ambiguity; in fact, the eighteenth century saw in natural religion an instinctive and vaguely deist aspiration that it preferred to faith in religious revelation. Now at first Hegel distinguishes religion insofar as it was a determinate figure "in which it [the spirit] appears to itself and knows itself" (PhS §684) from the religiosity not informed by religion or "its unembodied essence" (PhS §684) of which he spoke in the preceding chapters. Thus, when he speaks of natural religion, what is at issue is clearly not what Schleiermacher criticized as an "indeterminate idea, indigent and miserable, which can have no existence on its own and for itself," which "is ordinarily so watered down and has such a philosophical and moral slant that it hardly lets the particular character of the religion shine through."[20]

But, by a typically Hegelian dialectical inversion, Hegel's natural religion is likewise opposed to the Romantic conception of a religion of nature such as that expressed by Rousseau in his *Reveries of a Solitary Walker*,[21] or that of Hülsen, a follower of Fichte. Hülsen had published in Friedrich Schlegel's *Athenäum* an article, "Reflections on Nature at the Time of a Trip to Switzerland," where a truly religious veneration of nature is revealed which parallels in some measure the *Herzreligion*, that is, the religion of the heart, of Schleiermacher. There, Hülsen writes as follows: "I know of nothing greater than this meaning of nature. Not a branch does not grow green, not a stem does not flourish; they are the loving sign that it is in the light of nature that our eyes should find themselves and our spirits know each other."[22] This Romanticism appears to Hegel to be of the most vague sort, and he rejects it as he will reject the Christian mysticism of nature analyzed by Solger in the latter's *Lectures on Aesthetics* held in Berlin in 1819.[23]

Hegel's reticence with respect to a Romantic religion of nature is grounded in his criticism of the very notion of pantheism. It is this that the historian of religion, Friedrich Christian Baur, noticed some years later. On this view, the Hegelian concept of *Naturreligion* is much too narrow because God is supposed to correspond to a particular natural reality and not to nature as a whole. This restrictive analysis excludes pantheism from the start, but it is wrong thus to miss what in Baur's eyes is essential in natural religion. "Why can't the concept of natural religion also be valid where it is nature in its collectivity which determines the contexts of religious consciousness?" asks Baur, and he goes on to show that the Hegelian concept is too narrow to correspond to any real religion. Moreover, Hegel did not see that natural religion, which he defines as the form of religion for a spirit fettered by nature, subsists under different forms for as long a time as religious consciousness needs the mediation of nature. In fact, what Hegel has missed is the relation between the image and the idea: "In the visible phenomena of nature one intuits the divine power which reigns among them, and with as much diversity as the image is represented in its two principal forms, the symbol and the myth, nature makes itself divine in diverse ways in natural religion."[24] It is in Hegel's *Lectures on Aesthetics* that one finds the clearest explication of his point of view and the anticipatory response to Baur's criticisms. Evoking the pantheism of art regarding the symbolism of the sublime, Hegel declares,

> In employing the term *pantheism* one is today exposed to numerous misunderstandings. Because, on the one hand, *all* means in our modern sense everything entirely empirical in its particularity. . . . The whole in what one calls pantheism is not this or that particular thing but rather the whole in the sense of the whole (*das All*), that is, of a unique substance which is to be sure immanent to particular things, but in abstraction from their particularity and their empirical reality, in such a way that it is not the particular as such, but the universal soul, or in accordance with a more popular expression, the true and the perfect which are present in this particular thing are placed in relief and seen.

This equivocation has provoked scorn among contemporary theologians who accuse Hegel's philosophy of being wrong for having admitted for God absolutely everything, which amounts to saying nothing at all. But "such a representation of pantheism can rise up only in crazy heads and can be found in no religion . . . or in any philosophy."[25]

Therefore, it is probably out of prudence that Hegel does not envision pantheism as a figure of natural religion, prudence with respect to the inherent equivocation in the word itself, prudence also with respect to the exalted interpretations of the Romantic circle. Not that Friedrich Schlegel had failed to criticize pantheism severely on repeated occasions, saying in his course at Cologne, for example, in 1804–5 that the God of pantheism rests on the empty principle of identity, which is expressed with the formula "God is all."[26] But Hegel himself, as well as Schelling and Hölderlin, was enthused by the ξν και παν which Herder had formulated so masterfully.[27] In 1807 this enthusiasm of his youth inspired in him only mistrust. Studying particular religions, he was very careful to avoid any reference to the passionate discussions of his youth, all the more since the very idea of pantheism, considered as atheism by the traditional thought of the eighteenth century, did not seem to be incarnated in a precise form of religion.[28] In 1835 these problems were long since forgotten, and the criticism addressed by Baur to Hegel is understandable. The dispute about pantheism does not appear in Rosenkranz's strictly Hegelian work devoted to *Naturreligion* in 1831.

III

The first figure of natural religion is the essential light (*Lichtwesen*), to which Hegel dedicates two pages of his grandest style, pages that contain a flurry of formulas, evoking a density of thought and a richness of problems. The structure of the text is simple, but it has not been sufficiently explicated because commentators have too quickly reduced Hegel's thought to a unitary whole without seeing that it is deployed here in four instances which are distinct: (1) the creative secret of the birth of spirit, (2) the essential light strictly speaking, (3) the indeterminacy represented by light, and (4) the dissolution and the holocaust of the essential light.

Self-conscious spirit first runs afoul with the creative secret of its birth. It is, so to speak, by an absence of figure that the *Lichtwesen* begins. Self-conscious spirit knows that all reality is only itself. As a result, the creative secret of its birth is nothing other than the secret of creation. Here it is important to understand the text in all its generality and not to let ourselves be guided too quickly by the assimilation of the *Lichtwesen* with the Parsi religion or the religion of light which was historically the religion of Iran, reformed by Zarathustra (or Zoroaster) and then having become the religion of the *Avesta*.[29]

In this birth, spirit which knows itself is only its own notion, "and this notion is, as contrasted with the daylight of this explicit development, the night of its essence; as contrasted with the outer existence [*Dasein*] of its moments as independent shapes, it is the creative secret of its birth" (PhS §685). The daylight symbolizes here the presence of the moments as independent figures and evokes the "spiritual day of the present" which attains consciousness in becoming conscious of itself and in living without being aware of the concept of spirit.[30] But these two days are not opposed to the same night, although they both have an equally mystical resonance. The first night is situated at the level of consciousness; it is the night of ignorance which brings it about that instead of considering reality, consciousness takes refuge in the emptiness of the supersensible beyond.

The second, on the contrary, is the night of mystery, not that of obscurantism or of scorn of knowing. As we have already seen, Hegel's analysis at the level of religion cannot be a critique; instead, it is observing reason which is the figure that refuses all mystery *a priori*, but it is supposed to have already been sublated. Certainly, if the language is good, "the perfect element in which inwardness is just as external as externality is inward" (PhS §726).[31] The stage of mystery is supposed to be overcome, but it is necessary to begin by analyzing it carefully. From the first Jena system, Hegel indicated the sense of this creative night: "There is certainly an opaque intermediary between the *sentiment* and *science*, a speculative sentiment or the Idea which cannot free itself from the imagination and from the sentiment and which, however, is no longer uniquely a sentiment or imagination. I allude to the *mysticism* or rather the *oriental* search as much as that of *Jakob Boehme* as representing the Idea."[32] In order to understand the nocturnal secret of the birth of spirit, just as in order to understand the creation and the essential light in general, the triple reference to mysticism, the Orient, and Jakob Boehme show themselves to be absolutely essential. Moreover, there is nothing either strange or extravagant in this association, especially if one recalls that Friedrich Christian Baur was able to speak very reasonably of Hegel's Gnosticism.[33] Now even if mysticism has nothing of the specific character of Gnostic thought, nevertheless the thought of the Orient and that of Jakob Boehme can also be called Gnostic.

The secret of the birth of spirit is creative, says Hegel. It is enigmatic creation which elucidates the following sentence: "This secret has its revelation within itself; for the existence of its moments has its necessity in this Notion, because this notion is self-knowing spirit and therefore has in its essence the moment of being consciousness, and of presenting itself objectively" (PhS §685).[34] If the spirit which we are concerned with here is God, then one can limit the creation which Hegel tells us about to the question of the origin of God, and, evoking the text of the *Vedas*, we can ask, "Who knows, in truth, who could announce it here,/ from where does it arise, from where comes all creation?/ Are the gods less than all creation?"[35]

But it would, in fact, be an error to separate the creation of God from the creation of the world by God; indeed, self-conscious spirit knows that all true reality is itself. Hegel takes up the terms from Jakob Boehme in the *Mysterium Magnum*: "It is precisely there that the great mystery of the creative act resides, to know that the interior, God, is therefore revealed with his Word eternally speaking, which is nothing other than he himself: the exterior is a symbol of the interior. God is not at all a stranger; all things live and act in him, each according to its own principle and in its own degree."³⁶ Rather than as a free decision of God, the creation appears here, whether in Hegel or in Boehme, as a simultaneous genesis of God and the world. According to all evidence, Hegel knew the text of Boehme if not directly at least through the intermediary Oetinger, whose *Theosophy* took up the notion of creation from the Gnostics and the Cabala. Spirit becomes an other for itself; it creates a world and thus enters into existence by a contradiction which has been posited and then overcome. Having arrived at the stage of the in-and-for-itself, spirit recognizes itself in the world, and interior and exterior are no longer separated. God reveals himself. The creative secret of his birth is no longer so much explained, but its revelation becomes the essential object of thought. In fact, Hegel's thought here is in agreement with that of Oetinger, for whom "the being of God is in the *manifestatio sui*," and he understands this manifestation or revelation as the consequence of the very essence of spirit.³⁷

IV

This mysterious creation finds its philosophical explanation in the following sentence from Hegel, which is clearly separated from the preceding development by a dash, a sign that we pass through to an elucidation which in itself does not belong to natural religion but rather to the philosophical reflection: "—This is the pure 'I,' which in its externalization (*Entäußerung*) has within itself as *universal object* the certainty of its own self, or, in other words, this object is for the 'I' the penetration of all thought and all reality" (PhS §685). It is no accident here that Hegel uses the Fichtean concept of the pure "I"; in fact, it calls to mind, it seems, the first lesson in the *Lectures on the Vocation of the Scholar* where Fichte says, "It is certainly not true that the pure 'I' is a product of the Not-I ... but it is certainly true that the 'I' is never, nor can ever be, conscious of itself only in its empirical determinations, and that these empirical determinations necessarily presuppose a something outside the 'I'."³⁸ To be sure, Hegel, saying that self-conscious spirit recognizes itself in the world, eliminates the practical and infinite aspect of the task assigned to the "I" in order that it recognize itself in the not-I and attain the pure "I"; but it is significant that he returns to the Fichtean concept and shows that the problem of the object is posed there, because it is the equivalent or the analogue of the creation of the world on the philosophical plane. The composition of the "I" and the not-I by analogy throws light on the co-creation of God and the world. Self-conscious spirit—the term which indicates the relation of the pure "I" to itself in so far as the universal object is that of *Entäußerung*, which has a precise meaning since it explains the status of religious representation—will first be honored under the objective form in a representation, the light. Albert Chapelle remarks on this subject that "the religious representation articulates the dialectic of the free externalization and of the substantial abandonment of the absolute self, the more of the necessary externalization and ideal abandonment of the finite consciousness. This is why religious consciousness never affirms its truth or its certitudes except through an *Entäußerung*."[39] The complexity of the "Religion" chapter as a whole and of the *Lichtwesen* in particular comes from the fact that the representation is always the convergence of these two forms of externalization, even if, as is the case in the passage cited, it is only spoken of at the start. The objectivization of the pure "I" can therefore not be understood as a dissolution in nature, which is what pantheism is, but it is the "penetration of all thought and all reality" (PhS §685 cited above). The very notion of reality is not irrelevant here since in 1813 in the *Logic* it will likewise be in this context that Hegel will pose the problem of creation. Eugène Fleischmann remarks that the actual reality has the characteristic of manifesting itself by its own forces and that it is "a totality of which the essence consists in its creative power."[40] In the *Phenomenology*, the problem of actuality appears in religion for the first time as that which will be deployed in absolute knowing.

In the abandonment of itself, absolute spirit, which knows itself, divides itself: it is "the immediate, first diremption [*Entzweiung*]" the result of which takes the form of the *Lichtwesen*. The French translation[41] cannot render the structural analogy between the word *Entäußerung*, the meaning and scope of which we have just analyzed, and the word *Entzweiung* (division, split in two),[42] with which the second paragraph of the Hegelian study of the *Lichtwesen* begins. It is more than a question of a mere analogy of words here. Hegel marks by it the logical connection between the two paragraphs. The poetic density of his style presupposes that the reader recognizes immediately that this first immediate division is the first externalization of absolute spirit assimilated in the preceding sentence into the pure "I." This spirit posits itself in opposing itself, and the first figure of the movement is the essential light. From the conceptual point of view, this first division evokes the last division, which Hegel speaks of in a magnificent passage from the *Lectures on the Philosophy of Religion* of 1821: the life of Christ is "in its development the progress of the divine idea until the supreme *division*, until the opposition of the pain of death, a progress which is the absolute conversion, the supreme love of the negative of the negative in itself, the absolute *reconciliation*."[43] Taken in its true scope, the concept of *Entzweiung* shows that externalization is necessary in order to open to the other and to reconcile itself with it.⁴⁴

Before examining the *Lichtwesen* on its own, Hegel examines the determination of this figure issuing from the first division of absolute spirit. The first part of the second paragraph (PhS §686) is dedicated to this examination. Hegel situates the figure of essential light in relation to the chapters "Consciousness" and "Self-Consciousness" of the *Phenomenology*. In fact, if one cuts off the figure here from its religious significance, it is a sensible entity given to immediate consciousness or sense-certainty. But this perspective is not tenable; essential light cannot be considered as a sensation of contingent determinations, if one wants to respect its religious meaning. In it being intuits itself not under the form of uniquely sensible being, but rather as being "full of spirit." Thus, Hegel recalls also the figure of "Lordship and Bondage," which is at issue in the "Self-Consciousness" chapter. On this subject, we can do no better than to take up the explication given by Labarrière. It is the immediate character of the essential light which makes it similar to the certitude and the immediate intuitions from the here and now but also to the figure in which immediate self-consciousness expresses itself, the figure of "Lordship and Bondage."⁴⁵ Hegel writes, "It [spirit] also includes the form which appeared in immediate *self-consciousness*, the form of *lord and master* over against the self-consciousness that retreats from its object" (PhS §686).⁴⁶ Essential light evokes the figure of the lord, not that of the bondsman; in fact, it shares with the lord the character of primary immediacy which the bondsman overcomes. Otherwise, how else can one explain the opposition that Hegel raises here between the figure of the lord and that of self-consciousness of spirit which withdraws itself from its object? In the figure of essential light, spirit posits itself in a sensible reality and becomes one with it; thus, it becomes intimately united with its object, far from detaching itself from it. The entire first paragraph of the text, as we have seen, shows the creative movement by which self-conscious spirit makes itself objective without losing itself in the objectivity. Essential light is the first immediate figure, by which spirit becomes an object and gives to itself an actuality in which it clearly recognizes itself. Essential light is the aspect of the externalization, of the abandonment, not that of a retreat beyond the object, or that of the reconciliation. Adhering entirely to objective reality, spirit is no longer free in the figure of the essential light except as self-consciousness in the figure of the master.

With this figure having been located in the text, it is by a word play that Hegel introduces essential light: "This being which is filled up with the notion of spirit is, then, the 'shape' of the *simple* relation of spirit to itself, or the 'shape' of the 'shapelessness'" (PhS §686).⁴⁷ The term that

Hegel plays on here is the word *Gestalt* or figure, a term that he uses in a precise technical sense throughout the *Phenomenology* to refer to the fundamental mediating units in the process of the experience of consciousness.[48] This term in its banal sense means "silhouette" or "form." Hegel thus presents the essential light of the dawn as the figure—in the "phenomenological" sense of the term—of the absence of figure since it does not have the form, which contains and fills all without having its own contours. Hegel begins his development of the symbolism of the sublime in the *Lectures on Aesthetics* with a similar word play. With respect to the representations of the art of the sublime, he says, "Sublimity is this figure (*dieses Gestalten*) which is itself negated for its part by that which it makes explicit, such that the explication (*Auslegung*) of the contents shows itself at the same time as a sublation of this explication."[49] It is the term for explication, *Auslegung*, here which is taken in two different senses. In a first sense, it is the act by which the artist renders a content manifest, the act by which the implicit absolute becomes explicit; in addition, the word *Auslegung* is employed in the technical sense which Hegel gives to it in the *Logic* to indicate the imperfect deployment of the absolute in the figures.[50] The second meaning is static, designating the result of the preceding act. One can thus say that in the art of the sublime which wants to represent the absolute, the explanation is the overcoming or the sublation of the explanation; in fact, the act of making explicit sublates the result which it reaches, because it is judged to be perpetually inadequate to the absolute itself. The similarity of the plays on words in the *Phenomenology* and in the *Lectures on Aesthetics* corresponds to a similarity of situation. At the analogous stage of development, whether in religion or art, the absolute posits itself as unseizable.

After the word play that we have just examined, Hegel writes, "In virtue this determination, this 'shape' is the pure, all-embracing and all-pervading *essential light* of sunrise which preserves itself in its formless substantiality" (PhS §686). The immediate character of the *Lichtwesen* is at first underlined by the fact that it concerns the dawn, that is, the birth of the day, not of the day itself. But for the twentieth-century reader, this notion is at the very least bizarre. Are we concerned here with poetry, pseudo-anthropology in the manner of the Incas of Marmontel, of the *Indes galantes* of Rameau, or the religion of the Parsis? There is no search for exoticism in the Hegelian text. Thus, let us exclude these hypotheses and simplistic approaches which are not in harmony with the deep and sometimes hidden development of Hegel's thought. In fact, the religion of the essential light is not so much a *primitive* religion as an *originary* one. Now what do we find at its origin? Jakob Boehme, with his *Aurora* and his *Mysterium Magnum*. Schelling and Hegel knew his works, and both of them used the notion of essential light. Certainly, this idea does not belong to Boehme alone, and it is in harmony with the mysticism and Orientalism of the epoch. But we think that we can show that it is truly Jakob Boehme who is the primary source here. The expression "essential light" itself comes from the Cabala, where it refers to an entire meditation on the problem of the luminous and fiery origin. There is nothing strange in the fact that it finds a place in the Hegelian reflection on originary religion. Even today, analyzing the problem of the beginning, a philosopher such as Robert Misrahi can write, "A consciousness can begin to know by beginning to see."[51] The doctrine of *Zohar*, the study of which led Misrahi to Jacob Boehme, seems to him to manifest the deep link between the light and the fire: "If the origin is the shining point, or the supreme point, the origin of the origin, the mysterious *en sof* is nothing other than a dark fire or the original source from where the fire is born. It is thus in any case that a metaphysical imagination nourishes everything that the Cabala can perceive on the occasion, the beginning of being and the foundation of things."[52]

After having said that the first figure of "Natural Religion" is the essential light, Hegel explains in a passage which is only entirely meaningful by an appreciation of its similarity to Boehme's thought: "Its otherness is the equally simple negative *darkness*. The movements of its own externalization, its creations in the unresisting element of its otherness, are torrents of light; in their simplicity, they are at the same time the genesis of its being-for-self and the return from the existence [of its moments], streams of fire destructive of structured form" (PhS §686).[53] Certainly, the opposition between the light and the darkness is most current in all the works of Romantic philosophy, and it is not necessary to recall the twelfth chapter of the *Mysterium Magnum* where Boehme begins with the mystery of creation of the world and, with respect to the divine words, "Let there be light!" declares, "These words contain everything that there is to understand; because the beginning is the first movement."[54] In this way, he makes the separation of the light from the darkness, so to speak, the "unique text" of his theosophy. But what is specifically Boehmist in the text of Hegel is the idea that the creations of essential light in contact of the darkness should be at once the rays of light and at the same time the torrents of fire which reduce all visible configuration to nothing. In Boehme, in fact, the fire is at once the source of light as well as its result. The light will be the positive and creative aspect of it, the fire on the contrary the destructive and negative side, the symbol of negativity, the negation of the negation because it negates the simple negative that there is darkness. At the same time, the fire hinders the essential light from reifying itself in the objects with visible colors and preserves its unseizable and formless character. Here the inspiration of Hegelian thought meets Boehme even more profoundly. We are not concerned with describing the static opposition of the light and the darkness but rather with the birth of the light, its dynamic conflict with the darkness, especially its brightness and its radiance. We are not concerned with the light of midday but with the shining dawn, with the birth of the day. It is therefore impossible not to think of the Boehmist assimilation of God with the tendency toward the light, that is, toward the fire, toward desire. Essential light symbolizes the "eruptive effulgence" of this God-desire.[55]

V

One could, however, say that it is incoherent to see here allusions to the thought of Jacob Boehme since in the pages we are studying it is not the Christian religion that is at issue but rather natural religion, and, moreover, the Boehmist theory of the anger of God, which is evil, will be clearly evoked in the pages dedicated to revealed religion. However, in reality, Boehme is present in the pages on good and evil in "The Revealed Religion" and also in the pages that Hegel devotes to "The Living Work of Art" in the section, "Religion in the Form of Art," and finally in the pages of "Natural Religion" that we are studying.[56] Hegel took great care right from the beginning of the text on natural religion to make clear that "the ideas which seem to distinguish one actual religion from another occur in each one" (PhS §689).[57] Now precisely the principal characteristic of the allusions which he makes to Boehme is that they are situated at the level of representation under an imagined form. For Hegel, Boehme's effort seems especially interesting because it shows the fullness of the representation which tries to attain the absolute without the help of the concept. This is a specifically religious attitude, remarkable yet destined to fail, which, according to the text of the project of the Jena system already cited, Boehme shares with mysticism and Oriental thought.

When, in his courses at Berlin, Hegel takes up again the study of the religion of light, he insists on the contribution of the Orient doubtless because his information on the subject had grown during the interim. The opposition between the light and the darkness symbolizes an immediate dualism. In 1813 in the *Logic*, Hegel again took up the idea expressed in the *Phenomenology* with respect to the *Lichtwesen* in a remark on the subject of the Spinozist absolute: "In the *Oriental* representation of the *emanation*, the absolute is also the light which is itself illuminated. Only it is not satisfied with illuminating itself and flows out [*ausströmen*] as well. Its flowing out [*Ausströmungen*] is the removal of its undefiled clarity; the emanations which succeed each other become less and less perfect. The flowing out is taken only as an *event*, and becoming as a progressive loss. Thus, being ceaselessly becomes obscure, and the night, the negative, is the end of the line which does not return at the onset in the first light."[58] Here we find again all the essential themes of the analysis from the *Phenomenology*, the opposition of the light and its negative, the night, the rivers which flow from the light, but in the *Logic* Hegel is more critical with respect to this emanationism because it represents a stiff dualism lacking negativity, whereas in the *Phenomenology* the rivers of shining fire are the negativity in action. In "The Doctrine of Essence" [*Wesenslogik*] the Oriental emanationism is the dualism of the straight line, the opposition between light and night which remains insoluble, a straight line to which Hegel opposes "the line of scientific progression . . . the circle."[59] In the introduction to the *Lectures on the History of Philosophy* and in the *Lectures on Aesthetics*, the religion of light is clearly designated as the religion of Zoroaster.[60] It seems that Hegel progressively finds an ever richer meaning in the dualism of light and darkness. "I remark on this subject," he says, "that from the sole point of view of philosophy this dualism is remarkable. It renders the concept necessary. In this dualism the concept is immediately the contrary of itself; it is in the other a unity of itself with itself." Although the religion of light is situated without a doubt at the level of picture thinking, the opposition between light and night, once in the modality of religion, no longer appears as a chance but as a necessity. This is understood better if we keep in mind the originary character of this religion. The religion of light is, due to its dualism, the first religion because it posits the contradiction in the element of picture thinking. Now the contradiction is the first element of thought. In the interval of around ten years from the *Phenomenology* to the courses in Berlin, the Hegelian meditation on the religion of light became more precise in a more "archaeological sense" (in the both historical and the strict sense of the term) and not in the Boehmist sense. Let us not forget that it was, in fact, in 1808 that F. Schlegel published his celebrated work, *On the Language and the Wisdom of the Indians*,[61] the fourth chapter of which treats the dualism of the religion of light.

Finally, let us note that in 1807 the reader of the *Phenomenology* could hardly have been more surprised than we in the face of the notion of essential light because Schelling had made use of it in the "Essay on the Relation of the Real and the Ideal in Nature," which appeared as the introduction in the new 1806 edition of *On the World Soul*, and the subtitle of which is "An Extension of the First Principles of the Philosophy of Nature to the Principles of the Weights and Light." Our purpose is not to study these pages for their own sake as such, but to note how much

Schelling reveals himself there as a heir of Jakob Boehme and of Otinger. "This essential light is present everywhere, in which the totality of things is dissolved. This Jupiter by which everything is filled in all directions," he characterizes as "the view of life in the center which is present everywhere in nature."[62] This "symbolism of a center," as Mahnke has called it, had likewise been used by Boehme for whom the center of God is desire,[63] ardent life. Schelling here makes two images of the mystic origin coincide: that of the essential light and that of the center everywhere present in nature. But Boehme already assimilated the fiery center and the luminous center of God to the center of nature, passing from the divine center, which is desire, to the center, the source of nature, which is itself only that of realized desire, in order to arrive at the center of nature, the materialization of the magic desire.[64]

Hegel then pursues his analysis: "The difference which it gives itself does, it is true, proliferate unchecked in the substance of existence and shapes itself to the forms of nature; yet the essential simplicity of its thought moves aimlessly about in it without stability or intelligence, enlarges its bounds to the measureless, and its beauty, heightened to splendor, is dissolved in it sublimity" (PhS §686).[65] Luminous essence therefore appears as an absolute without genuine difference in the same manner as its unseizable, omnipresent character, which it cannot renounce without negating itself again. The natural forms are too limited for it to be able to be incarnated in them, and that is why it dissolves them in sublimity. Let us note here again the aesthetic terms used by Hegel. The categories of the beautiful and of the sublime are those of Kant's *Critique of Judgment,* to which Hegel has acknowledged his debt. The sublimity tied to the immensity of nature, which goes beyond all limits and which refuses all measure, is a manifest memory of the Kantian analysis of the sublime of nature.[66] Was it not Kant who wrote, "Nature is thus sublime in those of its phenomena of which the intuition gives rise to the idea of its infinity"? The sublime is presented by Hegel as a dynamic and negative notion. Like the rivers of fire, it shows the impossibility of essential light satisfying itself with a particular empirical existence in a natural form. In his *Lectures on Aesthetics,* Hegel will designate the sublime as "that which raises the absolute above all immediate existence," that which is "incapable, by its very nature, of finding its true expression in finite manifestations."[67] Thus, one can say that essential light itself calls forth its own sublation.

In the third paragraph of his analysis of the *Lichtwesen* (PhS §687), Hegel takes up again this representation by insisting on the negative aspect of the notion of essential light: "The contents developed by this pure being, or the activity of its perceiving, is, therefore, an essenceless by-play in this substance which merely *ascends*, without *descending* into its depths to become a subject and through the self to consolidate its distinct moments" (PhS §687). Hegel there explains further that the light of dawn is only a beginning. It is not the sun and thus cannot complete a cycle; it is pure upheaval. From this fact itself it is interiority without difference. The *Logic* explains quite well the relation between the measureless (*Maßlos*) and indifference. It is impossible that there be a substance or a genuine substrate, that is, a substance which is at the same time subject, as much as it remains "that which escapes measure."[68] In essential light, self-conscious spirit is represented as an inert substance without depth or consistency since its omnipresence is in reality only indifference, indetermination. In fact, it is there the absolute that the celebrated passage from the preface criticizes as the night in which all cows are black.[69] And Hegel continues, "The determinations of this substance are only the attributes which do not attain to self-subsistence, but remain merely names of the many-named One" (PhS §687). It is there the mechanism of the litany in which the impossibility of names of adequately expressing the absolute engenders an infinite series of names. Each is sublated from itself, thus rendering necessary the passage to an other. What characterizes the determinations, which are attributes with relation to the One, is their exteriority. The multiplicity has only a secondary and evanescent role with respect to the absolute One. The movement of externalization, of division, which gives a place to the essential light is thus an aborted attempt since it remains a beginning without continuation. Likewise, in the *Logic*, the attribute is itself suppressed by the dissolution in the absolute because it is inconsistent, deprived of genuine differentiation.[70] Hegel then takes up again this idea under imagined form: "This One is clothed with the manifold powers of existence [*Dasein*] and with the 'shapes' of reality as with an adornment that lacks a self; they are merely messengers of its might, visions of its glory, voices in its praise" (PhS §687). The mere presence or the being-there[71] of the One is not satisfactory. Here we recall the analyses that the *Lectures on Aesthetics* will give of the poetry of the Psalms as indefinite praise of God which is also negative because all finite existence is insignificant, impotent, and evanescent in face of God. However, in these lectures, Hegel, again taking up the same terms from the *Phenomenology*, is careful to note that there is in fact a difference in level. Certainly, he again uses the term "the One" to designate God in order to make clear that we are not still at the stage of an achieved revelation and that as a result the notion of God, in the strong sense that he gives it, would still be premature. Moreover, he recalls the Boehmist distinction between the absolute, the One, and God, according to which God alone is perfectly personal. But he declares, "According to its general determination, the substance is intuited at this level as immanent to all its created accidents, which however are not still rejected as servants and as a simple ornament to the glory of the absolute."⁷² With respect to the *Lichtwesen*, on the contrary, the images of the splendor, of the glory, are synonyms with dissolution. Doubtless Hegel's opinion was that these notions are as empty as they are striking such that they do not take a new sense by Christ's climbing to Golgotha.

Finally, the last paragraph of the Hegelian analysis (PhS §688) shows us the holocaust of the essential light. Just as the figure of the master leads to its own sublation, so also the glory of the *Lichtwesen* is the very sign of its precariousness. Moreover, let us note the similarity between the German words *Herr* and *Herrlichkeit*, which cannot be rendered in the French translation.⁷³ Hegel writes, "However, this reeling, unconstrained life must determine itself as being-for-self and endow its vanishing 'shapes' with an enduring subsistence. The *immediate being* in which it stands in antithesis to its consciousness is itself the *negative* power which dissolves its distinctions" (PhS §688). There is nothing astonishing here if it is true that without mediation the beginning, the immediacy are nothing. Here again, the *Logic* will supply all the necessary conceptual adjustments in the introductory text of "The Doctrine of Being" (*Seinslogik*), which treats the point of departure of science. The beginning is "pure being," "immediate being," expressions which apply perfectly to the *Lichtwesen*.⁷⁴

Hegel again insists on the necessity of a transformation of spirit: "It is thus in truth the Self; and spirit therefore passes on to know itself in the form of self" (PhS §688). As we have seen from the beginning of the text, spirit knows itself in religion, but it does not at first find an adequate form. The form of pure and immediate being which is the essential light needs mediation in order to acquire determinations which are not vanishing. And Hegel concludes the study of the essential light by passing once again to the concrete style, to actual realities of which the preceding abstractions were only the explication: "Pure light disperses its unitary nature into an infinity of forms, and offers up itself as a sacrifice to being-for-self, so that from its substance, the individual may take an enduring existence for itself" (PhS §688). It is there the final sacrifice that one will find again in "The Revealed Religion," but then it will be lacking the seal of reconciliation. Here on the contrary, it prepares the scattering of the Absolute into particular realities, and there is still a long road ahead before the final reconciliation. Thus, is terminated in defeat this effort which, in the text prior to the *Phenomenology* already cited, Hegel characterizes as follows: "The orientalism is raised above the simple beauty or the limited configuration. It is the infinite without form which it strives to conceive in the imagination of its images, but pushed without respite from the infinite towards the image, orientalism sublates [*aufhebt*] without cease its image, and *it* looks for itself in an other, which it makes disappear once again in the same way. It is therefore only a *powerful rhetoric* which is always aware of the *danger of the intermediary* which knows the images and which represents the essence."[75]

But the essential light has not finished its career. It will reappear in the section, "The Living Work of Art," where Hegel intentionally takes up again the terms of the final pages that we have just studied: "The moving impulse is, however, nothing but the many-named divine light of the risen sun and its undisciplined tumultuous life which, similarly let go from its [merely] abstract being, at first enters into the objective existence of the fruit, and then, surrendering itself to self-consciousness, in it attains to genuine reality—and now roams about as a crowd of frenzied females, the untamed revelry of nature in self-conscious form" (PhS §723).[76] Is not this image of the frantic dance and of the drunkenness of the Bacchants—the second manifestation of the essential light, but in the higher form that is the human form—the sign of the essential importance of the notion of the Cabala in Hegel's philosophy of religion?

Notes

1. P.-J., Labarrière, *Structures et mouvement dialectique dans la Phénoménologie de l'Esprit de Hegel* (Paris: Aubier, 1968), 156–61.

2. *Phänomenologie des Geistes* (hereafter PhG), ed. Hoffmeister, 478. [In order to facilitate matters for the English reader, I have used the Miller translation (*Hegel's Phenomenology of Spirit*, [Oxford: Clarendon Press, 1977]) for all of Vieillard-Baron's quotations of the *Phenomenology*. I have then inserted Miller's paragraph numbers with the abbreviation "PhS" in the text for easy reference—TR.]

3. *Über die Religion. Reden an die Gebildeten unter ihren Verächtern*. English translation (under the title *On Religion: Speeches to Its Cultured Despisers*) by Richard Crouter (Cambridge University Press, 1988)—TR.

4. Schleiermacher, *Über die Religion. Reden an die Gebildeten unter ihrer Verächter*, edited by G. C. Bernhard Puenjer (Braunschweig, 1879).

5. Cf. Hyppolite's translation, II:222n.26: "*L'idée d'une religion esthétique, ou d'un moment de la religion qui corresponde proprement à l'art, est indiquée dans Schleiermacher, Reden*, Prüyer (sic) 172. *Schleiermacher parle d'une religion de la nature et d'un mysticisme oriental qui se rattacherait à la religion chrétienne par l'intermediaire d'une religion de l'art (Kunst-religion); il doute d'ailleurs de l'existence de cette religion.*"

6. P.-J. Labarrière, *Structures et mouvement*, 155, n.31.

7. R. Vancourt, *La pensée religieuse de Hegel* (Paris: P.U.F., 1965), 117.

8. A. Chapelle, *Hegel et la religion* (Paris: Éditions Universitaires, 1964–67), I:229–32, and III.

9. PhG 481, lines 25–27.

10. Schleiermacher, *Reden*, Pünjer, 242.

11. Cf. A. Philonenko, *La liberté humaine dans la philosophie de Fichte* (Paris: Vrin, 1966), 307 and *passim*.

12. Schleiermacher, *Reden*, Pünjer, 259–60.

13. Herder, *Dialogue avec un Brahmane*, ed. Suphan, VI:138–40; cited in Gérard, *L'Orient et la pensée romantique allemande* (Paris: Didier, 1963).

14. *Einige Vorlesungen über die Bestimmung des Gelehrten*—TR.

15. Fichte, SW, VI:343.

16. Cf. PhG 482, line 11 to 483, line 2; the term "lower" reappears four times, the term "higher" three times. [PhS §684—TR.]

17. Cf. Michel de Certeau (*Annales: économies, sociétés, civilisations*, May/June 1970, p. 654): "This commonplace has the merit of indicating among two meanings the space of a work and of a mutation."

18. Görres, *Mythengeschichte der asiatischen Welt*, in *Romantische Wissenschaft* (Leipzig, 1940; Darmstadt, 1966).

19. *Vorlesungen über die Philosophie der Religion*, ed. Lasson, II: 22–38. Let us note that Hegel's manuscript (1821) is extremely cursory on this question.

20. Hegel, PhG 481, lines 6–11. Schleiermacher, *Reden*, 243, 248.

21. *Rêveries d'un promeneur solitaire*—TR.

22. Cited in Haym, *Die romantische Schule*, 452.

23. Solger, *Vorlesungen über Ästhetik* (Leipzig, 1829; Darmstadt, 1970), 151–52: "Among the ancients the laws of nature had become symbols . . . one never finds among them a particular sentiment for nature beyond the symbolic significance of the divine. . . . In a fashion contrary to the Christian manner of thinking, there is always attached a nostalgia for nature. . . . There was therefore a mysticism of nature by which nature is personified."

24. Fr. Chr. Baur, *Die christliche Gnosis, oder die christliche Religionsphilosophie in ihrer geschichtlichen Entwicklung* (Tübingen, 1835; Darmstadt, 1967), 722–23.

25. *Ästhetik*, ed. Bassenge, I:355. Hegel uses transitively the term "pantheism"

with respect to the religion of plants and animals in the text of the *Phenomenology* on the natural religion.

26. F. Schlegel, *Kritische Ausgabe*, XII:164; it is necessary to remark that the author nevertheless accords great importance to this doctrine, for example, in 1808 in *Über die Sprache und Weisheit der Indier* (SW, VIII:344): "Pantheism is the system of pure reason, and in this measure it already accompanies the passage of oriental philosophy to European philosophy."

27. Hölderlin wrote for example: "In the particular as in the whole grows and lives infinitely a spirit which maintains all, a spirit of peace and of order which intervenes in the combat, the suffering and death in order to lead absolutely everything to a higher harmony through the contradictions of life." Cited from Hoffmeister, *Hölderlin und Hegel* (Tübingen: Mohr, 1931), 28. It is likewise under the sign of the ἓν καὶ πᾶν that Tilliette (*Schelling, une philosophie en devenir* [Paris: Vrin, 1970], I:381–407) examines the second philosophy of nature of Schelling, which extends from 1803 to around 1806. See especially 398n.65.

28. Cf. Ayrault, *La genèse du romantisme allemand* (Paris: Aubier, 1961), 511–29.

29. Cf. *Vorlesungen über die Philosophie der Religion*, ed. Lasson, II:195. The religion of the Parsis was known at the time from the works of Anquetil-Duperron.

30. PhG 140, *in fine*.

31. PhG 505, I.30–33.

32. Cited from Rosenkranz, *Hegels Leben*, 182. [Karl Rosenkranz, *Georg Wilhelm Friedrich Hegels Leben* (Berlin, 1844; reprint, Darmstadt: Wissenschaftliche Buchgesellschaft, 1963)—TR.]

33. Baur, *Die christliche Gnosis*, on the subject of the relationship of Gnosticism to the Oriental religions, 36–48; on the subject of the relationship of Hegel's thought to Gnosticism, 670–75.

34. PhG 483, I.18–22; French translation, II:214.

35. Cited from Marie-Françoise Cassiau in *L'Arc* 38 (1969), special issue on Hegel, p. 59.

36. Chapter 11: "Caractère secret de l'acte créateur," 33.

37. Cf. Ernst Benz, *Les Sources mystiques de la philosophie romantique allemande*. (Paris: Vrin, 1967), 46.

38. SW, VI:294–95.

39. *Hegel et la religion*, annexes, p. 116.

40. *La science universelle ou la logique de Hegel* (Paris: Plon, 1968), 215.

41. Likewise for the English translation—TR.

42. *Entzweiung* is rendered in the English translation by Miller rather unhappily here as "diremption."—TR.

43. Hegel *Sämmtliche Werke*, ed. George Lasson (Leipzig: Felix Meiner, 1920–60), vol. 14, *Vortesungen über die Philosophie der Religion*: Teil 3, Die absolute Religion, p. 163.

44. Boehme says very well that the One is not God. God should be two in order to know himself; cf. A. Koyré, *La philosophie de Jacob Boehme* (Paris: Vrin, 1929), 325n.3.

45. *Structures et mouvement*, 162–64.

46. PhG 483, I.34.

47. PhG 484, lines 1ff.

48. Cf. Labarrière, *Structures et mouvement*, 41–44.

49. *Ästhetik*, ed. Bassenge, I:354.

50. Lasson ed., II:157.

51. Robert Misrahi, *Lumière, commencement, liberté* (Paris: Plon, 1969), 29.

52. Ibid., 43.

53. PhG 484, lines 5–11.

54. *Mysterium Magnum*, I:138.

55. Cf. A. Koyré, *Jacob Boehme*, 284ff.

56. PhG 539, 503, 484.

57. PhG 481.

58. Hegel, *Sämmtliche werke*, ed. George Lassen (Leipizig: Felix Meiner, 1920–60), vol. 4, *Wissencahft der Logik* II:167.

59. *Logik*, I:57.

60. *Ästhetik*, ed. Bassenge, I:319ff.; *Vorlesungen über die Philosophie der Weltgeschichte*, ed. Glockner, XVII:114–15.

61. *Über die Sprache und Weisheit der Indier: Ein Beitrag zur Begrundung der Altertumskunde*—TR.

62. *Werke*, ed. Cotta, II:368–69.

63. Mahnke, *Unendliche Sphäre und Allmittelpunkt* (Halle, 1937), 222–23. Koyré, *Jacob Bochme*, 362; cf. likewise pp. 331, 338.

64. Koyré, *Jacob Boehme*, 383.

65. PhG 84, lines 11–17.

66. Kant, *Kritik der Urteilskraft*, §26, ed. Weischefedl, VIII:342. Hegel (*Ästhetik*, ed. Bassenge, I:353) cites a similar passage of Kant (ibid., 330). The authentic sublime cannot be contained in any sensible form; it concerns only the ideas of reason, which although no representation of them is possible, are nevertheless recalled in the spirit and revived by this very inadequacy, of which a sensible representation is possible."

67. *Ästhetik*, I:353.

68. Lasson, ed. I:384–87.

69. PhS §16—TR.

70. *Logik*, ed. Lasson, II:161–62.

71. In the passage Miller translates *Dasein* as "existence," whereas Vieillard-Baron here underscores the literal meaning "being-there"—TR.

72. *Ästhetik*, ed. Bassenge, I:354.

73. Vieillard-Baron points out the etymological connection between the German word *Herr*, here meaning the "Lord" in the religious sense (instead of its usual meaning "man" or "gentleman"), and *Herrlichkeit*, which means "greatness" or "magnificence." An interesting and bizarre disanalogy can be found in the corresponding feminine forms. While the abstract noun that corresponds to man means "magnificence" or "greatness," the corresponding abstract form of *Dame* or woman is *Dämlichkeit* meaning "stupidity" or "silliness."—TR.

74. *Logik*, ed. Lasson, I:54.

75. Karl Rosenkranz, *Hegels Leben*, p. 182.

76. PhG 504.

18

Translated by Jon Stewart

Harald Schöndorf, S.J.

The Othering (Becoming Other) and Reconciliation of God in Hegel's Phenomenology of Spirit

Hegel attempts to make Christian doctrine comprehensible in its inner context, starting with the internal trinitarian life of God and working through the entire biblical and secular world history. According to the widely accepted view, it is God's becoming-human (incarnation) that for him plays the central role in this account. However, Hegel's compact exposition of his theological interpretation in the overall philosophical concept of his *Phenomenology of Spirit* shows unambiguously that it is the death and resurrection of Christ that for him stand at the focal point of the theological and Christological events.

Our analysis of the text, which refers to the corresponding pages and lines of the sixth printing of the Hoffmeister edition (Hamburg, 1952; hereafter PhG),[1] skips over Hegel's accounts of the form, value, and place of "Revealed Religion" and starts at the point where Hegel begins to observe "this content . . . as it exists in its consciousness" (PhS §766; PhG 532.24) This chapter offers an aid to reading and understanding the second part of chapter "Revealed Religion" (which begins here and stretches from PhG 532.24 to 548 inclusive [i.e., PhS §§766–87]). It tries to make accessible the meaning of Hegel's statements individually as well as to bring to light the inner structure and theological meaning of the text. Although there is generally a lack of detailed explanations of Hegel's text in the manner of this study, the question of whether and to what extent Hegel's conception can be interpreted in such a way that it is consonant with Christian doctrine has been the subject of numerous interpretations and discussions. For this reason, an extensive criticism of Hegel's line of thought from a theological point of view would require a study in itself. However, since the decisive points of criticism are well known, although some of them may be disputed, we can limit ourselves in the context of this study to a concise critical reflection at the end of our account.

Sketch of the Point of Departure

God: From Substance to Subject

God envelops the totality of the objective. This means that the different dialectical movements of unity and plurality have already been overcome in the objective sphere. In God, consciousness grasps the whole in its self-sameness and thus in its true essence. God is absolute essence; He is all reality as simple totality. As this absolute essence (*Wesen*), He is, on the one hand, the essential (*Wesentliche*) of consciousness, that is, what consciousness actually is and should be; on the other hand, He nevertheless stands opposite consciousness as the absolute beyond. For this reason, the conflicting situation arises in the unhappy consciousness, which is unable to negate the infinite distance and reach an identity with God without losing its own identity in the process. This is, in fact, only possible when the movement of reconciliation is brought about from both sides. Religion represents this movement from the side of God; however, here this movement must ultimately prove and effectively does prove itself to be the movement of consciousness in its highest form. The section "Revealed Religion" describes this movement of reconciliation which leads to the identity of consciousness and God. With this the shortcomings are eliminated which characterized the concept of God in the various forms of religion, which Hegel has treated in the previous chapters. Just as consciousness must be both self and essence simultaneously, so also God must unite essence and self in Himself. First, God is essence, absolute essence, and that means substance. In order to be also spirit, it is necessary that God also become subject or self. Therefore, we can characterize the entire chapter as the justification of the sentence, "God is spirit." What is at issue is that "absolute spirit" be "in the shape of its truth" (PhS §766; PhG 532.25). The movement thus goes from the "pure substance" (PhS §767; PhG 533.10) to the self-knowing and actual spirit (PhS §786; PhG 546.32, 37). This spirit is self-knowing as subject or as self. However, it must at the same time remain the "true, absolute content" (PhS §786; PhG 546.34). In the transition from the "in-itself" to the "for-itself," the "in-itself" cannot be allowed to be lost entirely, but rather at the end of the dialectic it must be preserved in the sublated form of the "in-and-for-itself."

The Three Elements:
Pure Thought, Picture-Thinking, Universal Self-Consciousness

Religion, according to Hegel, is characterized by the fact that it consists in "picture-thinking" [*Vorstellung*],[2] which is an intermediate stage between pure thought and the concept as concept. Picture thinking is a way in which content and form are separated for consciousness. While the content is already true and real, the form still exhibits a defect. Picture thinking is the intermediary stage between the pure in-itself of pure thought (cf. also the pure abstraction of the "This" of sense perception) and the for-itself of self-consciousness. One could perhaps say that with respect to content what is at issue is a for-itself which is comprehended in the manner of the in-itself. What is typical of picture thinking is its "synthetic" character: it is only an "externally" related coexistence *Nebeneinander*, the "Also." Thus, it is the element of space and time, of history, of immediate sensible existence and therefore of actuality *Wirklichkeit*, which is conceived only in its naturalness and not yet in its concept, only in its particulars and not yet in its universality.

The characteristic feature of picture thinking in this chapter at this stage consists in the fact that it, as "the middle term between pure thought and self-consciousness as such" (PhS §767; PhG 533.25–27), is one of three different elements and at the same time the element which encompasses the three. How is this possible? In picture thinking both immediacy as well as universality are present. Therefore, all the elements in which immediacy (determinacy) or universality come up can be presented in picture thinking. In anticipation of the text to be analyzed, we can say that in so far as othering (*Anderswerden*) is already carried out in pure thought, what is at issue here is picture thinking, specifically in the form of the juxtaposing of two opposites. Then when spirit climbs up into the determinate individuality of existence (PhS §767; PhG 533.11), we reach the realm of picture thinking in the strict sense of the word, that is, as existing actuality. Here we stand, so to speak, on the cutting edge, where, on the one hand, substance has already become subject, but, on the other hand, this subject has at first only immediate existence. Here once again the dialectic is applied so that this self-consciousness becomes universal. As long as it is still understood here in the sense of othering as coexistence (*Nebeneinander*) and separation (*Auseinander*), we are still at the level of picture thinking, until conceptual thought as such is reached in absolute knowing. As long as we are still concerned with othering, we are still in the realm of picture thinking, even if this othering—as in the case of the universal self-consciousness—is already in another respect a return from picture thinking. Only when this return has been completed in every aspect, have we reached absolute knowing, which is no longer characterized by the synthetic connection of the picture thinking.

The Othering and Reconciliation of God

The Othering of God in Pure Thought

The first form of the othering of God occurs in the element of pure thought (PhS §769; PhG 534.5). The point of departure or the concept at the beginning is God as an "immediately simple and self-identical, eternal essence" (PhS §769; PhG 534.6). But this implies pure abstraction since it corresponds to the level of pure thought, that is, abstract, unchangeable universality. But now God is spirit, and since the community calls God "spirit," it expresses the fact that God is not merely abstract universality. Spirit implies specifically the unity or the unification of substance (= absolute essence) and subject. Already in the fact that the community understands God, on the one hand, as simple eternal essence and, on the other hand, as spirit, there is a contradiction, and negation is present. In the course of the further development, Hegel shows to what degree the community is hereby right. Negativity lies, however, not in the simultaneous assertion of the absolute essence and spirit in juxtaposition, but rather the simple essence as such has negativity in itself. Simplicity is established in the abstraction, but this abstraction is posited opposite the concretely changing. In order to refer to God as the eternally unchangeable, I make him, so to speak, into the "entirely other," not merely with regard to me but rather in general. He is the negative in-itself. Put differently, precisely due to the fact that God is entirely in-itself, this otherness does not exist in the opposition to the thinking consciousness, but rather it must be otherness in-itself. It is otherness which characterizes knowing and thinking in general: the eternal essence is the otherness, the negativity of thought (PhS §769; PhG 534.16). Therefore, it is shown that it is thinking itself. First, "essence" implies only the side of the in-itself in thought. In this dialectic, however, it is shown that the absolute in-itself is not only an extreme in thought but also is thought itself. God is thus not only in-itself—and that means at the same time "for us," but he is also for-itself, that is, he is self, thought, and concept (PhS §769; PhG 534.20).

Thought is, however, duality, otherness, and difference. If God is thought, he distinguishes himself from himself and becomes an object. He thinks himself, conceives himself, that is, he seizes himself as object. Put in human terms, this means His "I" comes about for Him in the form of the "not-I." Thus, the transition to the second moment in God, to His otherness, has been effected. In the form of picture thinking this is presented as a juxtaposition in the succession: the eternal essence produces an other to itself (PhS §769; PhG 534.24). The inner necessity is not understood here, but is recast in terms of an actual event. At this point it may be indicated that Hegel writes that the simple essence is the negative in itself. This does not mean that the other of the simple essence is the negative. If, in the othering of God, one wanted to ascribe simplicity to the Father and negativity to the Son, then one would be at the level of picture thinking. Only because of the fact that the otherness, that is, negativity, must be predicated of the not other, does the other arise. The fact that the contradictory, that is, the radical negativity, must be asserted of the one constitutes its "doubling." The necessity of othering is found in this. However, according to Hegel, this is understood only when the necessity is comprehended. When this does not happen, we are concerned only with an external othering, that is, picture thinking.

It was shown that God, in so far as He is pure essence, is othering. But, this now means that He is only an other for Himself. The difference remains a pure in-itself, a pure essence: God is only distinguished from Himself (PhS §769; PhG 534.27). He is only an other in so far as he thinks himself. But He is thus at the same time identical with Himself. He is, as Hegel says, the unity returned into itself. At the same time, He is only other in so far as He thinks Himself: the opposition has its existence only in the immediate unity which has returned into itself. This means that the othering of God remains in the element of pure thought. It is thus a being other, which remains on the side of essence; with respect to essence, no opposition takes place (PhS §772; PhG 536.15). The two sides are not posited freely in existence, but rather only by becoming perceived does the word have existence (PhS §770; PhG 534.39), and only in the return does the externalization have existence. If God is other in Himself, He is also not only an object of knowing, but rather is Himself knowing. He is thus self, for-itself and in principle also being-within-itself (PhS §780; PhG 541.18). This being-in-itself, however, does not come about here as such in appearance, but rather first of all God constitutes Himself as knowing by an externalization, by the positing of an opposite in God Himself. This externalization is radical. To put it in religious terms, only when the Father Himself wholly externalizes Himself in the Son, can He wholly recognize Himself again in the Son. The fact that God recognizes Himself fully in this way presupposes that the Word, the Son, leaves the speaker of the utterance behind as empty. God recognizes Himself only in so far as He becomes other. In absolute externalization, God comes entirely to Himself in the moment of perception, of the self-knowing in the other (PhS §770; PhG 534.40, 33). But since God sees Himself in the other only as He sees Himself, this relationship of the Father to the Son (the Holy Ghost) is simple and immediate: the difference is immediately no difference. A kind of recognition comes about, but not that of another for-itself. Therefore, this recognition is mediated not by a struggle or labor but rather by love (PhS §772; PhG 536.14). This form of recognition does not stand at the end of a process, but rather it is the process itself. For otherness in God in general exists only in so far as it is loved.

As restless concepts, as moments of the constant movement, the Father, Son, and the Holy Ghost (essence, for-itself, for-itself in the other: PhS §770; PhG 534.30–33) represent God as spirit and not only as an abstract void (PhS §771; PhG 535.6). But this spirituality remains incomplete and defective since it has not gotten beyond the abstract level of pure thought.

The Othering of God in Picture Thinking (Actuality)

At the end of the previous dialectic, it turned out that the trinitarian God has not abandoned the sphere of pure thought. Now, however, pure thought is pure thought only by virtue of the fact that it distinguishes itself from actuality. The other of pure thought is, therefore, the transition into actuality in the element of picture thinking. Reality is the spatiotemporal, existent event, which is comprehensible not (only) in the realm of thought but also in the realm of sense. Reality is there where the other can be encountered free and existing independently of our abstract thought.

The opposition in the element of pure thought did not lead to a reflecting of being-for-itself into itself. The otherness in God was only "for-itself" in view of the opposition. Put differently, the Son existed only as other in view of the Father and vice versa. Whereas in the element of picture thinking the othering of God will lead to a being-other which is reflected into itself, that is, to a human being, who carries the difference, that is, the otherness in himself, and exhibits this not merely *vis-à-vis* God. The doubling then exists not only in the opposing of God and other, but also again in this other itself. This is the meaning of the paragraph in which

Hegel discusses the fact that in the element of picture thinking the moments of the pure concept are subjects (PhS §773; PhG 536.21–29). What is essential is that the moments possess being-for-itself in itself, and that they thus come to an opposition in their self-affirmation, that is, that they contain substantial existence *vis-à-vis* one another (PhS §773; PhG 536.25). This is grounded in itself and not only in opposition. The element of picture thinking fulfills this demand since it contains the meaning of historical existence, which is, so to speak, objectively at hand independently of whether it is thought as an opposition or not. Of course, to understand this assertion correctly we must be clear that, as the unfolding of this dialectic shows, it is not an issue of an ultimate or final independence. But we are now concerned with objectivity, with facts in the usual sense of the word, and no longer with a realm that is only accessible to thought. Now there thus takes place a doubling in the other itself, specifically into the world and man in the first instance. The other (which is opposite God) divides itself into two other opposed moments of which it can again be said that the one (the world) can be set free dialectically from out of the other (man). The latter, man, is thus both the other of God as well as the other of the world. But this must still be shown in its details.

The World

Pure thought is itself negative and thus is self-opposed or other. Hegel has already shown in the inner-trinitarian dialectic how this inner opposing is to be understood, and thus he need not repeat it here in detail. In so far as essence in pure thought is immediacy, its "first" form of othering is accordingly represented as immediacy in the transition to the element of picture thinking. What is at issue is the becoming of an immediate existence, an immediate, sensibly comprehensible actuality. Specifically, one can regard this reality, the world, as the othering of God, insofar as He is (only) essence, thus as the othering of the Father since it has no self. This time negativity does not imply the becoming of the self as in the transition from the Father to the Son, but rather only an externalization, unfolding apart. Therefore, this othering contains the moment of the "for" since othering or becoming other is always a "becoming for." (But the absolute essence apprehended in pure thought as a pure concept at the beginning knows no "for.") But it does not come to any self. The world is not for-itself but for-another. If in the previous dialectic what was at issue was the opposing of essence and the knowledge of essence, then here we are likewise concerned with the opposition of abstract simple universality (substance) and its unfolding into the determinate existing actual plurality (particularity). As separation (*Auseinander*), the world is the fundamental level of picture thinking (actuality). It is the unfolding of everything that is contained in substance.

Human Beings

Determinate plurality is only possible in relation to unity. Moreover, the self belongs essentially to spirit, just as the othering is essentially the becoming of the self. Therefore, the determinate self is also necessary in the element of picture thinking. The positing of this self is at first clearly only immediate: the human being is in itself spirit or self; he is in itself a for-itself, but he must become this for itself. However, let us leave to the side for the moment this new series of dialectical movements, which begins here. First, let us consider the level of othering at which we now find ourselves. The first level was the othering of God in the element of pure thought, that is, the Trinity. Othering means here now only the transition to pure for-itself in knowing, whereby all other characteristics of the eternal essence, like abstraction, immediacy, simplicity, remain the same. Only externalization took place, which was again immediately taken back in the withdrawal-into-itself (*Insichgehen*). At the present second level what is at issue is that abstraction is overcome since it is shown that actuality belongs to essence (PhS §780; PhG 541.20). This happens in a doubled form: on the one hand, in the pure externalization into the particulars (world), and, on the other hand, as othering in the form of the existent spirit (man). In picture thinking these two forms of othering, the second of which can simultaneously be understood as the othering of the first, appear as an external, successively executed event of creation, which remains absolutely free *vis-à-vis* God. Hegel expresses this with the word, that the in-itself assumes the form of the indifferent being. This is, so to speak, still less than an inessential being, since an inessential being must be sublated, while the indifferent being is purely external. There can no longer be something like this at the level of the concept since it would be something incomprehensible there.

While the world, in so far as it expresses the material of the substance, is the conceptual analogue to the Father, mankind, in which the self is manifested, corresponds rather to the Son. For the world, this interpretation is confirmed by the fact that all further levels of othering can also be read as levels of othering of the world (so to speak from below) and by the fact that the completed reconciliation means the final reconciliation of God with the world. The association of man with the Son is supported by the dialectic of man's withdrawal-into-himself to which we must now turn.

The Division of Man into Good and Evil

By way of introduction to this paragraph, we might recall the statement from the book of Genesis that man is made in the image of God. For we stand here at first before the same point of departure: man is posited as immediately existing, and he should be spirit. But there is also right from the beginning a fundamental difference between God and man. The in-itself, that is, absolute substance, totality collected in the unity, stands in God at the start. The othering into actuality in the case of God means the abandoning of all moments collected in him in their concrete determination and particularity. This is the result of the fact that God at first is objectivity or essence. With man, on the other hand, it is exactly the opposite. He is originally subjectivity due to his essence. But at the immediate stage of the in-itself, precisely the stage of objectivity is given, that is, the stage of consciousness. Man is thus not collected into the totality but rather is dispersed out into the manifold of consciousness (PhS §775; PhG 537.20); he is worldly. Common to both God and man at this initial stage is the selflessness, which must be overcome since otherwise God and man would be without spirit. Since in God the collection stands at the beginning, His othering is at first and above all externalization; since in man the dispersion stands at the beginning, his othering is at first and above all a withdrawal-into-itself. Clearly it is valid in each case, that each othering, insofar as it means a positing of a second, is externalization, and, insofar as it means knowing and being-for-itself, represents a withdrawal-into-itself.

Since with man we are not concerned with the othering of a pure abstract thought, the other is thus not a pure abstract universality like the son of God. The negation as negation of a determinate, conditioned (PhS §775; PhG 537.26) consciousness is rather a determinate, conditioned negation. As such, it manifests its particularity through the fact that it is again opposed in itself. This doubling is not possible for abstract universality since for this a second othering would be necessary. However, the thought which comes from the immediacy and the worldliness simultaneously completes its division again in the single movement of the othering. At the level of the pure concept this othering does not mean multiplying; and this also holds true when the movement is one of reconciliation since then othering implies reduction, as we will see later. At the present level of picture thinking as picture thinking (of actuality), we are, however, concerned with a mixture, with determinacy, particularity, and conditionedness. We find ourselves as coexistence (*Nebeneinander*) and separation (*Auseinander*) of the Also of the spatiotemporal, of sensibly accessible history, of the unity of which man only glimpses in pure thought, but which must be worked out in its concrete existence and then finally in philosophy.

Hegel refers to the spirit, which is now spirit in-itself but not yet for-itself, as "innocent" (PhS §775; PhG 537.15). He has in mind here presumably the innocence of a child who has not yet reached the age of reflection. However, spirit cannot remain at this level of innocence. As long as the condition of paradise lasts, man has not yet reached thought. The innocence of paradise and of the child must be overcome if man truly wants to become man. The two sides of othering which arise when spirit comes to itself are good and evil. Good and evil are opposites, which are not immediately sublated in the taking back. The discussion is not about immediate recognition in love; instead, it is about work, which refers us to the lordship-bondage dialectic (PhS §775; PhG 537.34). We are here not concerned with absolute opposites which like the different persons in God can be immediately sublated. There is rather good and evil only at the level of picture thinking since what is at issue here is essentially a putting together of unlike things, of contradictories. Such a putting together is in fact impossible at the level of pure thought, and for this reason the creation and fall of the angels can be for Hegel only a backward projection from picture thinking into the element of pure thought, as we will see.

The split into good and evil comes about through the fact that the othering of man means the transition to reflection. Thus, man becomes aware of himself, of his self: the for-itself is reached and becomes at the same time the object of consciousness. In other words, the for-itself occupies the position of the in-itself. Thus, a conflict arises between the for-itself and the in-itself. Since this movement is at the same time the becoming of thought or changing into thought (PhS §775; PhG 537.23), this means that man, in the very act of thinking, becomes conscious of the subject-object split. He recognizes the difference between essence and self, which he had not yet known in the innocent state of paradise, since there he had been abandoned as still purely worldly and dispersed on objects. With this knowledge of the difference of essence and self, he knows that the one is the negation of the other, but simultaneously posits the self in the place of essence. Man knows that his essence exists in the fact that it is essence and for-itself which is contradictory. Since this othering is the becoming of thought, good and evil arise as differences of thought. Since on the other side this othering concerns the existing spirit itself, the good man and the evil man come on the scene. Both times good and evil are the in principle incompatible juxtaposing of essence and self which have not yet reached the true sublation of the one in the other in the reconciliation of God and man, but rather they stand unsublated beside one another. A contradictory relation has been entered into, which has as its result the fact that one of the two alternately is declared as the essential and the other as the unessential. Instead of the true sublation through the completed negation, only an unreal sublation takes place through the suppression of the other element. If it remains in this state of tension in the mode of picture thinking, then a constant swinging back and forth between essence and self takes place, which never arrives at reconciliation but rather, like the unhappy consciousness, endures in perpetual self-destruction.

When, in the juxtaposition of essence and self, the side of the self is declared to be the essential, we have evil before us. When, on the other hand, the essence is essential, the good is present. Where there is only essence in general as in pure thought, we are therefore nearer to the good. The movement, which brings about the division of good and evil, namely the withdrawal-into-itself, thus produces evil first and foremost. If also good and evil are thus characterized by their opposition in connection (synthetic picture-thinking) and show themselves thus by their dissimilarities, so also this dissimilarity is stronger and is presented, so to speak, essentially and immediately with that which declares the in-itself unessential and the for-itself the essential in the relation (PhS §776; PhG 537.37–40). Evil is constituted immediately by the withdrawal-into-itself of spirit, and it is only in contrast to it that good appears (PhS §777; PhG 539.18–22).

The dual nature of the existence of good and evil, on the one hand, as thought and, on the other hand, as existing man, indicates that in every man there takes place a struggle between good and evil, and moreover the first man (Adam) together with Christ represent the embodiment of good and evil in every human being. Insofar as good and evil are represented as the essence of thought in pictures, they can also be projected back in the element of pure thought. This means that man has no essence since the struggle, in which his essence actually consists, takes place in him. But since good and evil, on the other hand, are embodied by two kinds of existences, namely in one case by man in general, who is synonymous with the first man but is represented in every man, and in the other case by Christ, they therefore possess free autonomy *vis-à-vis* one another. Good and evil stand here entirely at the level of picture thinking, that is, they are mixtures of thoughts and independent existence as actually existing humans. As such, they carry the opposition in themselves, and for this reason the movement of the dissolution of the opposition begins in them. Only when good and evil are posited merely as thoughts (as is the case in the backward projection in the world of angels and likewise as is the case in the consciousness of every human being), the dissolution of the opposition is only possible through the struggle of the one against the other (Michael against Lucifer; good and evil inside man), since both in general have existence only in the opposition (cf. the opposition of God the Father and the Son) and no longer as freely posited and existing in actuality (PhS §779; PhG 540.11–16).

The Projection of Good and Evil into Pure Thought

Since finally everything is contained in absolute essence (PhS §780; PhG 541.16–18) and since every othering as becoming-for-itself is at the same time a withdrawal-into-itself and also a becoming evil, the entire dialectic of good and evil can also be returned to the element of pure thought. The reason why we are concerned here only with a returning and why the arising of good and evil must take place at first in the element of picture thinking was explained above. Thus, at first one can in the realm of pure thought make a doubling out of the othering of God, as is the case in the othering of man, so that there are two Sons of God, an evil one (the Son of Light, or Lucifer) and then a good one. Then one can still go a further step, and the moment of othering which comes to expression above all in the world, namely the plurality, can be put into the element of pure thought since one distinguishes between the one Son of God and the many angels. Through this distinction between the simple Son, on the one hand, and the plurality of angels, on the other hand, the otherness is ordered, it concerns a determinate plurality. The withdrawal-into-itself, the becoming evil, then is not put into the Son as in the first case, which was just discussed, but rather in the angels. First, it must be said that the division into the one Son and the many angels means also a division of what was attributed to the Son in the dialectic of the Trinity. Insofar as the otherness of God means specifically knowledge, it is attributed to the Son; on the other hand, the aspect of the externalization is attributed to the angels. Insofar as the Son only has existence in the simultaneous taking back of the othering, as Hegel explained in the inner trinitarian dialectic, he belongs here, so to speak, to the side of essence; he is the self-knowing essence. But if now, on the other hand, in the angels the otherness assumes the form of externalization without immediately being taken back, then a dual object is produced. Since we find ourselves in the realm of pure thought, we are not concerned with a freely existing existence, but instead the existence of the angels is only possible in relation to God. The angels thus live only in the praise of essence, as Hegel says (PhS §776; PhG 538.28). On the other hand, the possibility therefore exists for them (in contrast to the Son) of a further othering, namely a kind of opposite movement, which is not, however, as in the case of the Son, the being taken back to the Father, but rather it is, as in the case of humans, the withdrawal-into-itself of evil. It seems to me that the text is not entirely clear about whether this withdrawal-into-itself of evil is assumed by Hegel for all angels or, in correspondence to the classical Christian doctrine, only for a part of them. This is, however, not important since the entire backward projection of the movement of becoming evil and good in the realm of pure thought represents merely a sort of digression. For an account of the different lines of the othering of God and the dialectical sublation of these levels of otherness of God in the movement of reconciliation, the world of angels need not be taken into consideration.

Good and Evil as the Ways of Othering of God

With the unfolding of good and evil, the movement of the othering of God has reached its highest stage in so far as it represents an unfolding from itself, an alienation, and a multiplication. The exposition is now completed, and the dialectic of dissolution, which at the same time is the dialectic of the transition into a new element, can and must begin. But the central point of this transition, the death of Christ, is only briefly indicated in order to be treated again later. First, Hegel undertakes a kind of recapitulation. Until now the dialectical development had been represented from one stage to the next. Now it must be shown in what relation and in what context the unfolding, which has now been reached, stands with respect to the point of departure.

Whereas in the course of things so far the split into good and evil has been developed out of the being of man, now Hegel adds expressly what was already implicitly obvious, namely, that all these levels are levels of othering of God. In itself all of these moments are contained from the beginning in the eternal essence, and all otherness is only conceivable as already founded in the totality of substance (PhS §780; PhG 541.12–18). This is not only expressed in the fact that picture thinking knows the thoughts of the one-becoming-human, which implicitly implies that evil is contained in the divine essence, as is indicated in the aforementioned passage. Even picture thinking does not remain there to grasp evil as "an event foreign to the divine essence"(PhS §777; PhG 539.29), but rather it tries at the same time to express it as the wrath of God himself—clearly a representation, which stands on the threshold of contradiction. A double alienation of God takes place: first the positing out of itself of the two moments "self" and "simple thought" and, subsequently, the juxtaposition of these two moments in existence, that is, in concrete actual human beings (at the level of picture thinking) but in the way that one of the two moments (that is, either the self or the simple thought, or put differently, either the for-itself or the essence) is essential *vis-à-vis* the other. Thus, there exists a dissimilarity in this juxtaposition, as we have already seen above in the description of the split into good and evil. The first alienation, the unfolding of God into "the self" and "simple thought," takes place already at the level of the Trinity since one can interpret the self as the Son and the simple thought as the Holy Ghost (or perhaps also as the Father), whose absolute unity is the movement of the three moments in God Himself (or, according to the other interpretive option, the Holy Ghost), which constitutes His spirituality (PhS §778; PhG 539.33–36). (The assigning of references is difficult here and was perhaps made so intentionally by Hegel in order that things might remain somewhat ambiguous.) The two moments of the self and simple thought are thus to be constituted by their juxtaposition of good and evil, in which it is shown that here with good and evil, we are concerned with a further level of the othering of God.

But this is only one side of the consideration. Good and evil in their dualism represent the double alienation of the divine essence. Yet inside of this dualism good in special manner must be called a form of othering of God. For if we follow through with the othering of God from the realm of pure thought so that we hang on to the divinity, then we see in the good the level of the othering of God, which connects human beings with the essentiality of essence and therefore connects the property of existing self-consciousness with the divinity (PhS §777; PhG 539.22; PhS §778; PhG 539.41–540.1). This form can therefore be called the realization of the othering of God in the Trinity in the form of becoming-human and thus at the level of picture thinking. With respect to the othering of the Son, what is at issue is no longer an othering of God, which at the same time means a transition from abstraction into concreteness and thus from unreality into reality. Hegel characterizes this transition with the classical concepts "self-abasement" and "renunciation." Certainly, the divine essence with this form of othering climbs down from a level which only apparently or at least only in one respect means an abundance or a higher level (in so far as level of thought is at issue), whereas in another respect (insofar as the abstract non-actuality is at issue) it is more incomplete (PhS §778; PhG 539.22–27).

The Becoming-Human (Incarnation) of the Son of God

In the last section we already began the description of the becoming-human of the Son of God. Good arises, as a dialectical countermovement to the arising of evil, and it is identified with the becoming-human of the Son of God in the section just discussed. For the consciousness of picture thinking in religion what is at issue is an incomprehensible event which is not necessarily but freely executed by God, that is, the second person of God assumes human existence foreign to Him in itself and to which he does not stand in a necessary relation (PhS §780; PhG 541.23–25: God freely creates man). But the fact that God assumes human nature, which according to the religious interpretation is not necessary to Him, means precisely that this human nature is only a moment of the absolute essence in its unfolding of itself. Divinity and humanity are only apparently opposites which flee from one another. Clearly for picture thinking, the independence of God *vis-à-vis* the world and man in the picture of creation as well as the assigning of roles to both in the picture of the incarnation remain without being understood.

In the exposition, that precedes the passages treated here, Hegel expressly underscored the actuality of the becoming-human of God and the two-sided externalization of substance and of self-consciousness expressed in it. In our section, the weight lies more on showing why and to what degree becoming-human is a figure which carries the movement further. Hegel indicates that the situation of the one-having-become-human is not durable. The one-having-become-human is being-in-itself, but only in opposition to evil; he is self-consciousness, but he strives to negate a side of himself (PhS §779; PhG 540.24–27; PhS §778; PhG 540.1–2). From the side of the being-for-itself as from the side of essence, we are concerned here with alienation and externalization. Put pictorially, one could say Christ, having become man, is certainly the embodiment of the eternal divine substance, but precisely in this substantiality he has almost entirely disappeared and become incomprehensible. On the other hand, he is certainly a human being, but he lacks the real being-in-itself of human beings; he lacks the aspect of evil as a necessary consequence of self-reflection. From the side of substance and of pure thought as from the side of being-for-itself and from the level of picture thinking, the God-having-become-man represents a borderline case. He is the mediator (PhS §785; PhG 546.1, 7) since it is through him that the mediation of the reconciliation between God and humans takes place, as must still be shown. But indeed one can also say he is the mediator since he is the middle term between God and man. And precisely because of the fact that he stands in the middle—externalized God and externalized man—at the middle level of picture thinking, he can also mediate and represent the necessary transition to the reconciliation of essence and self to spirit in its complete form. This transition completes itself in the externalization of the God-man in his death, which at the same time means the opposite movement of reconciliation.

The Death of Christ—Center and Key Point of the Dialectic of Othering and Reconciliation

The Meaning of the Death of Christ for Christ Himself

For the religious consciousness, the death of Christ, just as the creation and becoming-human, represents an autonomous act of a free will. But to declare something in this way as not necessary means, for Hegel, simply to place it alongside other facts and to apprehend no inner line of development in it; this is the procedure typical of picture thinking in religion. To apprehend the death of God means to perceive its necessity, from which it follows that the figure of the God-having-become-man has no duration. Since the two figures of man, the evil and the good (= Christ), each carry its opposite in itself, their othering and their dissolving results not on the basis of a confrontation of the evil with the good, but rather Christ begins this movement from out of himself. But at the same time the necessity of this movement is produced from the instability of the one-having-become-man, which results from that fact that he is only in opposition to another being-in-itself. We thus reach the realization that Christ is independent essence in the mixture of thought and existence; in other words, he is really man since he is characterized in the same way as evil. Yet he is also characterized as one who is being-in-itself only by way of contrast, as we have already seen. Therefore, he is precisely characterized as the different aspects inside the Trinity which exist as distinct aspects only in their opposition (PhS §770; PhG 534.40–535.3). In this account of Hegel, the next foothold for the continuation of the dialectic is provided with the determination of divinity since here it is immediately implied that the movement must go on. When we observe the statement that Christ is he to whom divine essence is essential (PhS §778; PhG 539.41–540.1), we see actual divinity expressed together with actual humanity. However, when we also take into account the description of the arising of evil and good, then we see that properly speaking only evil is "in fact self" (537.16). On the other hand, he is described as actual God and actual man; on the other hand, he is not yet true God or true man. Since he is determined specifically only in opposition as being-in-itself, the withdrawal-into-itself of knowing has not yet been executed, and his divinity as well as his humanity must first prove themselves to be true in negation.

Without death, Christ remains only externalization or alienation: he must reflect himself into himself (PhS §780; PhG 541.36) in order to become true spirit. The becoming-human of God is only truly completed in the death of Christ. Only the sacrifice of the immediate existence of Jesus leads to the actual reconciliation of self and essence. Only this movement, which is externalization and reconciliation all in one, frees the figure of the one-having-become-man from its one-sidedness and dissimilarity (PhS §785; PhG 546.10–15). Only through the death of Christ is the still existing opposition to actuality sublated. Only in this death has God, to put it pictorially, actually left heaven and come to earth. Only now is humanity no longer external for God, but rather now Christ through his death has become spirit. But therefore divine essence and human nature are in him no longer in opposition but rather "as they are in truth"(PhS §780; PhG 542.39); since the becoming-human is sublated, it is at the same time completed. In the complete sense of the word, Christ is thus the God-man only in his death; only the death of the mediator represents the mediation. This mediation is the transition to a new level; for Christ himself it is the resurrection as spirit in the community. He himself reconciles himself with the divine essence and at the same time with self-consciousness in general. One can, it seems to me, summarize this as follows: the God + man (in picture thinking) dies in order that God = man (spirit) can be resurrected.

The Death of Jesus Christ as Transition to the Universal Self-Consciousness of the Community

The death of Jesus is at the same time resurrection, but resurrection at a new level. It is the death of the individual in his particular individuality in the sensible present of physicality, and therefore at the same time it is the resurrection in the universality of spirit. This sublation of the individual self means simultaneously the abandoning of the element of picture thinking and the introduction of the third element, the universal self-consciousness. If we remain at the level of picture thinking, and if we regard the death of Christ only as death, then it represents the negation of a concrete individual and consequently the transition from particularity to universality, but this would then be a merely natural universality, and the negation would remain merely abstract, as Hegel himself says (PhS §784; PhG 545.14–17). We found ourselves in a similar situation as with the death of the individual in the chapter "Ethical Action, Human and Divine Knowledge, Guilt and Destiny." But in our case, the sublation of the particular being-for-itself is apprehended positively by the community and raised to a higher level; there takes place a procedure of integration. To put it in religious terms, it does not remain at the level of the death of Christ, but rather Christ is resurrected since his death is apprehended by the self of the community, and therefore a reconciliation or a return takes place. Universality and self become unified, and the community is spirit.

The Reconciliation of All the Aspects in the Universal Self-Consciousness

The death of Jesus Christ and his resurrection, that is, his becoming spirit in the universal self-consciousness of the community, means the return of the whole, the reconciliation of all self-unfolding and alienation. In the death of Christ, at the level of reality the whole movement of reconciliation in itself has taken place. The fact that through the event of the death the reconciliation is already present, must be understood by the community and finally must be grasped conceptually in absolute knowing in order that it not remain an incompletely understood in-itself, but rather that it become a fully realized for-itself.

The Withdrawal-into-Itself of the Community

The death of Jesus is understood by the community and here is completed in its double aspect as death and resurrection. But we find ourselves here no longer at the level of picture thinking, that is, of the spatiotemporal actuality, but rather in the universality of spirit, which clearly does not yet represent the completed level of spirit. The death which is understood by the community is, therefore, no longer completed as a real death, but rather what is at issue is a spiritual or conceptual death and resurrection, a death and resurrection in consciousness (PhS §784; PhG 545.19–22).

Hegel turns back to the dialectic of good and evil. The self-becoming of man was a withdrawal-into-itself or reflection into the for-itself. In the case of evil, this withdrawal-into-itself means at the same time a moment of alienation, so to speak, an othering in the direction away from the eternal essence. In the case of the good, however, that is, in the case of the God-having-become-man, two accents flow together into one and the same act of negation, namely, the negativity of the othering which corresponds to the withdrawal-into-self, and the reconciliation of the self with the eternal essence. This reconciliation, which is at first produced in itself from the mediator, must now be carried through at the various other levels. At the level of the universal self-consciousness, evil or the community must now appropriate the reconciliation. This happens in a second movement of the withdrawal-into-self, which at this stage—in the element of the universal self-consciousness and no longer in the element of picture thinking—obtains the second part of what was completed in-itself in the death of Christ. In opposition to the good, for which the divine essence is essential, human nature is essential for evil. To this degree, Hegel can call the community simply the "natural spirit" (PhS §782; PhG 543.30) which has to withdraw into itself out of this naturalness. At the level of the transition from the worldly consciousness to reflection, which is turned purely to the object, this means becoming evil in general. Put differently, the arising of self-consciousness (the spiritual becoming-human, so to speak) was synonymous with becoming evil. However, at the same time this was the arising of self-consciousness in actuality at the level of picture thinking. Here we are now one stage further along; what is at issue is no longer to become "I" in general, but rather the in-itself-having-become-self already becomes conscious of itself as evil, which is already in-itself (PhS §782; PhG 543.30–34).

If the first reflection (the becoming evil) was the apprehending of selfhood in general, so also the present reflection is a reflection on the character of this selfhood, the knowing and the conviction of the evil of this natural self (PhS §782; PhG 543.33, 39). This knowing is an action of consciousness since it is the apprehension and comprehension of the negativity of the death of the mediator. Therefore, it is itself negativity and a return from natural evil into the thought of evil. In this return what is at issue is a form of othering, which means a withdrawal-into-self and is an aspect of reconciliation on account of the transition into the element of universal self-consciousness. It is the dying away of sin, which had meant opposing the for-itself and essence, and now implies a step toward the essence whereby the character of the for-itself, nevertheless, is not given up since this step is completed precisely by a movement of the for-itself, specifically a withdrawal-into-self (PhS §783; PhG 544.18–26). Thus, we stand before the paradox that the parallel movement is at one time the actual becoming evil (*Bösewerden*) and yet at another time a "becoming" or "development of evil" (*Bösewerden*) (PhS §783; PhG 544.19), which means an abandoning of evil. The movement of the withdrawal-into-self, which nature has completed in-itself, is evil and as such is the ground for the second movement of the withdrawal-into-self in the element of the universal self-consciousness, which is a becoming of thought of evil, and to this degree once again it represents a becoming of evil (PhS §783; PhG 544.26–32). Certainly, this second movement is mediated by the death of the mediator at the level of picture thinking and therefore means the abandoning of sin. One could say that through the insertion of the death of the mediator this same movement receives a qualification; at the level of universal self-consciousness something like an inverted world arises at the level of picture thinking. To put it in religious terms, one could say the recognition of sin means at the same time regret and thus a turning away from sin. This completes the first step of the turning back to God. It is, therefore, at the same time self-renunciation, a turning away from self-assertion which wants to oppose itself to God; however, the self cannot be allowed to go by the wayside as in the unhappy consciousness, but rather it must remain contained in the unity with God.

The Reconciliation of Substance with Self on the Basis of the Death of Christ

The death of Christ thus completes in itself the reconciliation of the divine essence with the other in general, with all levels of othering of God, and *in concreto* with evil, the thought of the other (PhS §780; PhG 541.37–40). We have just seen how the community makes this latter aspect of reconciliation its own. Before we explain to what degree this reconciliation of the community with God still remains incomplete, it is worthwhile first to see in general what dimensions the event of reconciliation takes on. The transition to the element of universal self-consciousness represents a return (PhS §780; PhG 533.15–17; PhS§785; PhG 545.39).

We find ourselves again in a mental-spiritual element which, however, is now no longer non-actual or abstract as pure thought was, but rather which has taken up the concrete particularity—transformed into the universality—into itself. Picture thinking, extended in coexistence, succession, and the Also, is collected in the unity of the self and sublated. The only actual existent in this element has become subject. At the same time, the first element, pure thought, is sublated in universal self-consciousness since in it both totality (by the mediation of picture thinking) as well as the figure of thought (on the basis of its own character) are unified. All aspects are thus contained in this element. But it follows from this that not only the figures of picture thinking of good and evil but also the figure of pure thought or the eternal God in the beyond must be brought into the movement of negation and othering. The "pure or nonactual spirit of mere thinking" (PhS §785; PhG 546.5), in which form God represented himself in the element of pure thought, comes over to the side of universal self-consciousness. Thus, God loses his abstractness and gains life and actuality; substance becomes subject (PhS §785; PhG 546.28–31) and therefore truly becomes actual spirit. This transition of abstract divine substance to the unification of substance and subject and therefore to the actual living spirit completes the death of the mediator for the community; therefore, before the level of reconciliation which we have reached is described as the completion of the entire dialectical movement, it should first be shown how it accounts for Jesus Christ and his death and how it emerges from the side of the community.

The Death of Christ as the Death of God

The death of Christ means the definitive negation of God as He is represented in the element of pure thought. In Christ God dies not only in so far as He has become man, that is, it is not only a form of othering of God which dies, but rather it is at the same time the beyond, eternal, abstract, universal God Himself who dies (PhS §785; PhG 546.6–10). What dies in Christ is not an abstraction of the abstract God, that is, not merely an apparent God. It is not an external figure which, although having come forth out of God, nevertheless still only lifeless and without content, points to him while he has long since slipped away from it (PhS §785; PhG 546.9: "the already dead husk stripped of its essential Being"); no, the God of the beyond is actually afflicted by this death of Christ: God actually dies in Jesus Christ. In this is shown that this Christ is not a figure of the othering of God in the sense of an opposite but rather represents at least, and above all in his death, a God who has become other in his entirety. We are no longer concerned with the creation and unfolding, but rather with the dialectical overturning which closes into itself the collapse of the source of the dialectical movement so that everything can be raised into a new sphere. God is dead insofar as he is not posited as self. The selfless, abstract God has died: God himself has died. One could expand on this sentence and say he has died unto himself. The pure selfless abstract substance is negated so that it can become self. As substance in opposition to and opposite the subject, God no longer exists (PhS §785; PhG 546.18, 23–25).

The Death of God in the Consciousness of the Community

If there is no longer substance as the opposite of the self, what does this mean for the subject? First, the sentence "God is dead" implies that there is no longer an outside of the subject. The self has been thrown back absolutely and uniquely onto itself; the totality of the substance, which was thought to be "outside," has been lost (PhS §785; PhG 546.23–25). This phenomenon has many levels. First, the experience of the unhappy consciousness, the pain of the loss of essence, can be found here again. It is like the absolute failure of the attempt to unify subject and substance. In the chapter on the unhappy consciousness this is expressed in the pain of the radical division of consciousness and the positive essence of the beyond. The being thrown back onto oneself which results from this is finally the same situation as the result of the "de-deification" which the consciousness of comedy has brought about, the complete loss which expresses itself with the hard word that God is dead (PhS §752; PhG 523.24; PhS §785, PhG 546.18–20).

Secondly, the flip side of this negative experience clearly exists in the knowledge that all truth is found in the self. This self-certainty of all truth disguises itself in the formula of idealism: I = I (PhS §785; PhG 546.22). In this abstract, at first empty, formulation, this means the coming together of all aspects in the indistinguishability of the radical self-ownership which forgets everything outside of itself. It is the apprehension of the self as of the totality of reality, an apprehension, however, that remains abstract in this indistinguishable collection of everything, which is like a bud which must break out in order to prove the truth of the fact that the self contains all reality in the unfolding and distinguishing of this reality. As long as this step has not yet been taken, consciousness finds itself in the "depths of the night"(PhS §785; PhG 546.26) which must break out from the day of distinct knowing. These two aspects belong together, as is shown in the transition from the unhappy consciousness to the "Certainty and Truth of Reason." Hegel also underscores their belonging together in the section treated here since he shows that the "loss of substance" is at the same time "the pure subjectivity of substance" (PhS §785; PhG 546.23–28).

As we have just seen, Hegel here refers back to earlier sections of the *Phenomenology*. The dialectic set into motion by the death of Jesus reaches beyond the chapter in which it takes place. The movement of reconciliation, of integration, of dialectical sublation takes on the dimension of the entire work. It attaches itself to what immediately precedes the chapter "Revealed Religion," namely the consciousness of comedy, for whom the gods disappear. And it refers also once again back to the first appearance of the tension between the individual self and the eternal substance in the figure of the unhappy consciousness. Thirdly, we find ourselves here at a transition, which refers back to the decisive caesurae of the *Phenomenology*, where consciousness becomes conscious of itself as the certainty of all reality (cf. the first lines of "Reason" as well as "spirit," and the introduction to "Self-Consciousness"). In order to complete the chain, it must now be shown that, with the death of Christ, the point of the movement is taken up again, which spirit had reached when Hegel moved to the treatment of religion. Hegel develops this since he formulates the reference clearly and unambiguously, and expresses the parallelism of the two points. Spirit has now reached from the side of God the point which it had reached in the development preceding religion from the side of world spirit: the coincidence takes place here. Since both times the absolute opposition recognizes itself as the same, world spirit recognizes itself as identical with the spirit of God; the two-sided movement toward each other dissolves into *one* (PhS §786; PhG 547.3–15). The I = I has in both cases not (only) remained the mere referring back to the self, but rather has become raised up through the externalization (through the forgiving reconciliation in the case of the spirit certain of itself and through the death of the God-man in the case of revealed religion) in the mutual reconciliation. Knowing has come about in which substance and subject, God and existence have become one (PhS §785; PhG 546.28–31). Substance has now truly become spirit, for which reason Hegel speaks of the "spiritualization" (*Begeistung*) (PhS §785; PhG 546.28).

The Completion of the Movement of Spirit

The Absolute Spirit In-Itself

The movement of the absolute essence through the three elements is completed. Spirit has become actual spirit; it is not only the pure object of consciousness as the eternal essence of pure thought was. Likewise, it has not merely become subjectivity which has lost everything else. In running its course through the three stages, through the "three elements of its nature," it has come to itself: substance and subject, in-itself and for-itself, movement and self-movement have become one (PhS §§786; PhG 546.35–547.2). The movement of God as that of spirit is thus at an end. God has now truly become spirit not only at the abstract level of pure thought but also in the course of the three elements. We can now say that God, who was at first abstract essence, alienated Himself—as Son—in the element of picture thinking, in order to come back to Himself—as spirit—in the element of universal self-consciousness, thus sublating the moment of alienation (PhS §779; PhG 540.29–39). God has now realized for-itself what He is in-itself, namely spirit; He now knows Himself as spirit on the basis of this experience (PhS §786; PhG 546.32–37).

Absolute Spirit in the Form of Picture Thinking

What is from the side of God completion remains from the side of the community still incomplete. Religious consciousness looks at this coming-to-itself of spirit and it does still more; it sublates the distinction between this spirit and itself and identifies itself with it (PhS §786; PhG 547.10–15). However, so writes Hegel a few lines later, the whole thing remains for the community in the form of picture thinking. How can these two apparently opposed statements be reconciled? Hegel wants to make clear in what aspect the particular feature of the universal self-consciousness exists, which is beyond the element of picture thinking as such (i.e., picture thinking in the strict sense as actuality), but has not yet become absolute knowing, and rather remains still religious and thus picture-thinking consciousness.

Picture thinking in the strict sense, the appearance of independent existence in space and time, in history and concrete instantiation, is overcome. For Jesus has died and not only into a natural universality, into a pure negation of his particularity, but rather he has been resurrected, that is, the community has taken up his death in its own movement of withdrawal-into-self and thus has let it become a positive universality, an arising of spirit. Thus, the community has made its own the reconciliation of substance and subject which happened in itself in the death and resurrection of Jesus Christ: it is itself spirit (PhS §786; PhG 547.10–15). But it does not yet know itself as spirit. Indeed, it knows that it has come in as the result of the movement, that it is one with God; seen thus, it therefore knows that it is spirit. However, what is does not know is that it is itself which completes this same movement in a fashion parallel to the eternal essence. For the consciousness of the community, the unification of itself with God remains the gift gained in subsequent understanding. There remains for it the difference between the reconciliation between God and man effected by Christ and its own comprehension. It sees itself split insofar as it knows itself as the object of its knowing as one with God, but this unity is not brought forth by its knowing itself. Since it itself becomes the object of its knowing, it has overcome picture thinking in the strict sense; however, since it fails to apprehend this as a necessary consequence of its withdrawal-into-self, of the action of its knowing, it remains at the level of juxtaposition, or picture thinking. What goes to its credit is merely the negative side of the process: the externalization of natural existence, the mental dying with and resurrection with Christ. However, what the community fails to understand is that it at the same time itself completes its identity with God, that in Hegel's words the "pure inwardness of knowledge is just as much the self-identical essence [= God]" (PhS §787; PhG 547.31–33). This side remains for the community something external, foreign, and other which it adds simply to its own action, whose ground it nevertheless sees in an "alien satisfaction" instead of recognizing that the unity of substance and self necessarily comes about on the basis of its own knowing and not only on the basis of the reconciling death of Jesus.

This incompleteness of the self-consciousness of the community must have as a result that the movement of reconciliation also is not yet entirely finished. In itself at the level of picture thinking, in feeling, in the heart, in love, the reconciliation of the community with God is finished and complete. At the level of knowing, however, this reconciliation is still broken (PhS §787; PhG 548.24–26). There remains an opposition; in the existing actuality, there remains a character of the beyond in the reconciliation. The coexistence, separation, and the Also of picture thinking which remained for the community bring with them the fact that at this level of picture thinking in the strict sense, in the spatiotemporal sphere, the reconciliation has not yet been reached. The beyond seems to be interpreted also very generally as a beyond in opposition to the world; first and foremost what is at issue with it is the beyond of the still-to-come eschatological completion. The fulfillment of reconciliation is postponed in the distance of the future, while the reconciliation in-itself once and for all realized by the one remains in the past (PhS §787; PhG 548.14–18). The present community thus stands in the still unreconciled middle ground between the two extremes of a not yet sublated temporal line. The reconciliation of Christ and the reconciliation of all creation are still kept apart by the distance of time. Thus, the reconciliation of the figure, which appeared as the first form of othering of God in the element of picture thinking, namely, the world, has not yet come about. The distance between this first form of othering of God and the last form, namely, of the Son of God having-become-human, is not yet sublated. The self-consciousness of the community still remains constantly referred back to the mediation at the level of picture thinking; it has not yet completed the decisive dialectical jump to a new immediacy. There is still a step missing; the overcoming of religious consciousness in general, the absolute in-itself's becoming absolute for-itself. Certainly all the lines of the earlier forms of the *Phenomenology* are already united, but the gaping split of past and future must still be overcome. Only in absolute knowing is the entire world reality reconciled with the absolute spirit, and history reaches its goal, namely the absolute concept.

HEGEL'S THEOLOGY AND CHRISTOLOGY

As we already mentioned at the beginning of the chapter, only a few positive and critical remarks on Hegel's theological and Christological sketch are to be suggested. Hegel's great achievement exists doubtless in the fact that he wants to make the Christian message comprehensible in its entirety from a single inner principle. This is indeed the task of any theology: to demonstrate the unity and inner connection of the different elements of the Christian doctrine, so that belief does not become merely the agreement to a more or less arbitrary set of propositions. Hegel shows that a single great circle spans from the "immanent" Trinity over the becoming-human of Christ, his death, and his resurrection until the present. He conceives of the doctrine of God and Christology so that both the unity of the "immanent" and "economical" Trinity as well as the connection of incarnation and resurrection mystery become clear. The central figure in the process described by Hegel is Christ, who externalizes himself in order to become man as the Son of God and thus to represent the opposite figure to the evil embodied in Adam and in every other human. He springs from a divine (= in-itself existing) father and a human (actual) mother (PhS §787; PhG 548.19). From the person of Jesus, of the "God + man" as we called him, his work follows: since the good has the being-in-itself opposite the for-itself as its essence, it must give its life. Thus, the death of Jesus becomes his own action, which has no other cause. Jesus' giving of his life is initiated by himself and does not come forth out of a struggle between good and evil (PhS §779; PhG 540.9–14).

Only in the death of Jesus, the incarnation is completed. The death is certainly still a negation opposite the becoming-human, but only in death is the unity of the "God = man" completely attained. Thus, Hegel brings the incarnation and death/resurrection together into a relation, which makes the death the central event without denying the becoming-human as the ontological presupposition. Even if through becoming-human and death can be called out simultaneously (PhS §784; PhG 545.7–10), it comes about from the ensuing complete structure that the death represents the crux of the whole.

Hegel's understanding of the resurrection as sublation in the community, whereby it reaches an identity of God and man, shows the dubiousness which is also contained in this conception. It is no longer possible to speak of a further life of the risen Christ according to all appearances in the actual sense. Therefore, it also appears as if the historically contingent individuality of this Jesus were ultimately unimportant; it appears as if it only depended upon the fact that through some figure of the dialectical process that point is reached where the reconciliation and identification of everything in spirit takes place. Thus, we come upon what is probably the fundamental problem of the Hegelian view of Christianity, namely, the all-encompassing dialectic which proceeds from an inner necessity. The gratuitous action of freedom and underivable contingent individuality seem here still just as little possible as a reconciliation and unification, which can preserve in the unity of all the remaining difference in kind according to level between God and man. We do not want to explicate these critical considerations further. It only still appears noteworthy that Hegel understands the death of Christ as the death of God, and in a way that one has the impression that in the death of Jesus the Father also dies. Hegel probably did not count on the fact that the further history of the thought of the "death of God" would lead rather in the direction of an unhappy consciousness instead of necessarily to a resurrection and reconciliation since to us today the night of the I = I seems more abysmal than we would sometimes like. But perhaps this is only a confirmation of the fact that redemption is not the result of a necessary process but rather can only be the free act of a God standing over the world.

Notes

1. In order to facilitate matters for the English reader, I have included the corresponding paragraph numbers of the Miller translation of the *Phenomenology*. (*Phenomenology of Spirit*, trans. A. V. Miller [Oxford: Clarendon Press, 1977]. Hereafter PhS.)—TR.

2. I have consistently followed Miller's rendering of *Vorstellung* in this religious context as "picture thinking" instead of employing the obvious alternative "representation."—TR.

19

Martin J. De Nys

Mediation and Negativity in Hegel's Phenomenology of Christian Consciousness

Central to Hegel's philosophy of religion are two claims. First, Hegel claims as a philosopher to succeed in "the task of taking all religious existence as it takes itself,"[1] avoiding the pitfalls involved in interpreting religious existence and consciousness through an extrareligious rationality, be that rationality aesthetic, moral, or whatever. Second, Hegel claims to show that even the consummate form of religious consciousness, in its most developed moment, is the necessary object of a speculative appropriation. The thinking that makes this appropriation somehow "surpasses" religious consciousness. Any philosophy of religion must deal with religion speculatively in order to be, for Hegel, truly philosophical.

What is most characteristic of Hegel's philosophy of religion is the belief that connects these two claims. This is the belief that religious consciousness as it takes itself, as it builds up its own self-understanding, is precisely that which calls for a self-surpassing philosophical appropriation. Hegel exhibits this belief in the several discussions of religion that appear in his systematic writings. He also attempts to show the warranted nature of this belief from the standpoint of religious consciousness in the dense and difficult penultimate chapter of the *Phenomenology of Spirit*. It is this which makes Hegel's *Phenomenology* an indispensable source for all considerations of his philosophy of religion as a whole. In that work, Hegel as a phenomenologist observes the process of self-examination that comprises the experience of religious consciousness.[2] He shows religious consciousness to detect in its own self-assessment exigencies that call forth a speculative appropriation of itself.[3] This is especially the case insofar as religious consciousness, phenomenologically observed, builds up and examines its own contents through processes of mediation and through a negativity that overcomes otherness and duality. These notions link Hegel's phenomenology of religion to his earlier religious writings and to his later writings on religion undertaken from an achieved speculative standpoint.

I want in this chapter to consider Hegel's phenomenology of religious consciousness, especially with reference to the difficult notions of mediation and negation at work therein. Two intimately related questions will focus my considerations. In just what manner, according to Hegel, does religious consciousness present to itself and build up within itself its own self-understanding, through its own self-interpretation and assessment? In what way do the mediations and negations that come to belong to religious consciousness through its own self-interpretation and assessment point that consciousness beyond itself to speculative thinking? In dealing with these questions I shall treat in detail not the whole of Hegel's phenomenology of religious consciousness but the concluding phase of that phenomenology, which describes what for Hegel is the consummate form of the experience of religious consciousness, namely, Christian consciousness. It is in the experience of Christian consciousness, Hegel believes, that the process of self-examination that belongs to religious consciousness generally reaches its most complete form. This completeness involves the most extreme developments of mediation and negativity of which religious consciousness is capable.[4]

The focus of my considerations herein is historical and textual. Their import, I believe, is more broadly philosophical and theological. In recent scholarship, writers such as Albert Chapelle, Emil Fackenheim, Michael Theunissen, and, more proximately, Quentin Lauer and James Yerkes have opposed the view that, for Hegel, the speculative thinking that surpasses religious self-understanding overcomes the religious standpoint *qua* religious, interpreting that standpoint as a stage on the way to a transreligious, philosophical truth. Especially, Lauer and Yerkes have retrieved Hegel in a way that takes the thinking he determines as philosophically necessary to be a thinking that exhibits the truthfulness of religious self-understanding *qua* religious by reinstating its truthfulness in speculative concepts. But others would argue that, in 1807 at least, Hegel's phenomenology of religious consciousness and his account of the way in which religious consciousness gives rise to speculative thinking involve mediation and negativity in a way that so thoroughly overcomes the dualities proper to religious self-understanding as to annul the latter.[5] One might proceed from such an argument to the judgment that Hegelian speculative thinking, because it is a response to necessities ingredient in the prespeculative shapes of consciousness that give rise to it, overcomes the religious standpoint not only in the *Phenomenology*, but in principle. A defense of the sort of retrieve of Hegel that Lauer, Yerkes, and others support calls for a careful consideration of the dialectic of religious consciousness observed by Hegelian phenomenology. Moreover, an account of the precise manner in which, according to Hegel, religious consciousness brings forth its own speculative appropriation would contribute to the beginning of a discussion of the degree, if any, to which Hegelian philosophical thinking requires that religious understanding be expressed in properly religious as well as in properly philosophical terms. This issue is distinct from the issue just mentioned with reference to Lauer, Yerkes, and others. It is important on its own terms. The positions one takes on both these issues affect the manner in which one supposes Hegelian thought to be appropriable for current theology and philosophy of religion. Both issues call for careful consideration of Hegel's *Phenomenology*.

I

Religious consciousness emerges in Hegel's *Phenomenology* as that consciousness in which finite, self-active subjectivity, or finite spirit, depicts its relation to an other which is absolute, infinite, and divine. Religious consciousness in fact holds distinguishable attitudes together. It takes itself to be consciousness of a divine other, knowledge of which is an essential feature of religious consciousness.[6] It supposes itself to know that divine other in its relation to its own finite selfhood. And religious consciousness claims that its relationship with its divine other is radically constitutive of its own selfhood. It claims its knowledge of the divine to be knowledge of its own finitude as genuinely finite and as self-transcending, because defined by a relationship with an infinite other. Finite religious consciousness claims, in other words, that its consciousness of the divine is at once a real and a radical self-consciousness.[7]

The unity of consciousness and self-consciousness is, for Hegel, the crowning and distinguishing feature of religious consciousness as it presents itself to the "science of the experience of consciousness," to phenomenology.[8] Religious consciousness is not simply human self-consciousness, defined by whatever privacy or profundity one might mention. It is directed to an other represented as infinite and divine. At the same time, religious consciousness is not simply consciousness of a divine other, defined by whatever tremendous and overwhelming qualities one might mention. It is consciousness of a divine other as that to which finite selfhood is fundamentally and constitutively related, and thus self-consciousness along with consciousness. This unity of consciousness and self-consciousness determines the intentionality of religious consciousness. It must be articulated in the phenomenologically observed experience of that consciousness. That articulation occurs as religious consciousness passes through a number of distinct representations of the divine and achieves different modalities of consciousness and self-consciousness with reference to those representations.

Through its experience, religious consciousness makes two discoveries. It discovers, first, that it cannot represent its divine other as that to which it simply finds itself related. This is because even finding is an *activity*, in which the self-active subjectivity of religious consciousness is implicated. Therefore, religious consciousness must represent the divine other to which it is related as a term in a relationship brought about in part by the action of human subjectivity.[9] But second, religious consciousness discovers that it cannot reduce the divine-human relationship to that aspect of that relationship which human action brings about. Phenomenologically pre-Christian consciousness, at least, learns to its unhappiness[10] that the attempt to define the human-divine relationship exclusively with reference to the dimension of that relationship brought about by human activity brings about the loss of the otherness of the divine from the human, and thus the loss of an ingredient essential to religious consciousness itself.[11]

These discoveries prepare religious consciousness for an understanding of the divine as that which, precisely as other than the human, reveals itself in human selfhood. It is this understanding, of course, that the Incarnation represents. Christian consciousness is just that form of religious consciousness that centers its understanding of the divine upon a belief in the Incarnation.

The "experience" of Christian consciousness, the process of self-examination which belongs to that consciousness, proceeds from the belief upon which it centers itself. That experience occupies three phases, the first of which sets the stage for the remaining two. The first task of Christian consciousness is simply to present itself with reference to the several characteristics that define it as a form of religious consciousness.

The very fact that Christian consciousness recognizes the divine in its manifestation in human selfhood determines it as a recognition of the divine in terms of its relatedness to that which is finite and human. Simultaneously, and in its own particular terms, Christian consciousness acknowledges the divine as other. It "does not start from *its* inner life, from thought, and unite within itself the thought of God with existence; on the contrary, it starts from an existence that is immediately present and recognizes God therein."[12] Moreover, that consciousness which primordially belongs to the Christian religion acknowledges that "in this religion, the divine being is *revealed*," and therefore "that what it is, is known."[13] It is consciousness not simply of predicates attributable to the divine being, but more fully of the divine self of which those predicates are determinations.[14] Finally, Christian consciousness determines itself as human consciousness of the divine, which is at the same time self-consciousness. This is the case for Christian consciousness in principle because of its Incarnational center. It becomes the case in fact as "this individual man," whom Christian consciousness recognizes as the incarnate revelation of the divine, "passes over into 'having been,'" with the consequence that "just as formerly he rose up for consciousness as a *sensuous existence*, now he has arisen in the spirit,"[15] in the community that remembers him and finds in this remembering its own self-recognition.

The preceding comments show, for Hegel, how Christian consciousness, from the start in its own particular terms, determines itself with respect to the features of religious consciousness in general. In its own particular way, Christian consciousness initially contains along with its thought of the divine its own self-recognition. But it contains these as a form of representational consciousness. The manner in which Christian consciousness is representational, and the exigencies which follow from this, bring on the next phase of its development.

II

Hegel states concerning Christian consciousness that "Representational thinking constitutes the middle term between pure thought and self-consciousness as such, and is only *one* of the specific or determinate forms; at the same time, however, as we have seen, its character—that of being a synthetic connection—is diffused throughout these elements and is their common determinateness."[16] Christian consciousness is the thought of the divine, just because the divine is available only to thinking consciousness. And Christian consciousness is self-consciousness; it finds self-recognition in its recollection of the Incarnate revelation of the divine "risen up" in the community. But its thinking and its self-consciousness proceed of necessity from images: of the recollected deeds of a individual, of his death, of his being raised, and so forth. These are by no means "mere" images: they are reflected upon and ordered by the consciousness that recollects them toward knowledge of its divine object, and toward self-knowledge.[17] Still, that knowledge of the divine and that self-knowledge that constitute Christian consciousness are suffused with the images from which they proceed. The thinking of Christian consciousness, then, is "representational thinking," a form that if "diffused throughout" the knowing and self-knowing that belong to Christian consciousness, a form "which is their common determinateness."

Christian consciousness, just because it is representational thinking, endows its products, representations (*Vorstellungen*), with four basic characteristics. I have already alluded to the first of these. The representations of Christian consciousness[18] are orderings of and reflections upon images, brought about by consciousness for the sake of placing before it that which it knows.[19] As Yerkes points out, "thought is 'mixed' with sensuous recollection in the production of a *Vorstellung*."[20] Second, these representations, because they are thoughtful orderings and analytical reflections of images, preserve the discrete character of their bases and appear "as completely independent sides which are externally connected with each other."[21] Third, the mutual externality that belongs to the products of Christian representational thinking splits the recognitions of Christian consciousness into recognitions of "a Here and a Beyond."[22] That same mutual externality, finally, splits objective consciousness and self-consciousness.[23]

Again, though, the body of representations that belong to Christian consciousness is a "middle term" between its (pure) thought of the divine and its self-consciousness, just because that body of representations "is diffused throughout all those elements and is their common determinateness." For this reason, Christian consciousness is the project of articulating its thought and its self-awareness in the mode of this determinateness. It makes explicit what is implicit within, relates and distinguishes what is to be related and distinguished within, the body of representations that belong to it, while remaining on the level of representational thinking.[24] These processes involve, not a looking back on the part of Christian consciousness to its origins, but its pressing forward toward an articulation of its representational contents in terms of their proper ideality.[25]

Thus, the God known by Christian consciousness in the Incarnation is known, precisely therein but at first implicitly, as a self possessed of its own inner life. This inner life is trinitarian insofar as the divine self reveals itself both in the "individual man," the mundane person of Christ, and in that person "risen up" in the consciousness of the community.[26]

The inner life that Christian consciousness represents to itself, because it is divine, is further represented by this consciousness as self-diffusive.[27] "Accordingly it *creates* a world," which world is both the other of its divine principle, and dependent thereupon because created.[28] But finite and self-determining persons, parts of the created world that reflects its divine source, assert their autonomy by denying dependence upon the divine in favor of otherness from the divine. This "withdrawal into . . . self-centeredness" and denial of creatureliness ruptures the relation of the human with the divine; it is a "fall" from that relation which constitutes the finite self as "evil."[29] The rupture, though, is to be healed and evil overcome. This occurs as the divine unites itself with that which has alienated itself from the divine, such that, "actuality has ceased to be something alien and external"[30] to the divine, even with respect to death, the extreme consequence of that alienation.

Christian consciousness, then, as these brief remarks indicate, builds up its content by bringing forth, from its initial center and through its self-examination, a cycle of representations, implicit in its beginning and/or in each other. This cycle ultimately terminates in doctrines: Trinity, Creation, Fall, Incarnation, Redemption. The cycle exhibits the beginning from which it proceeds as both *"immediate"* and as characterized by an "immediacy" that is "equally pure mediation or thought" and that "must therefore exhibit this in its own sphere as such."[31] The thinking that belongs to Christian consciousness realizes the mediations that belong to its constitutive center and starting point by mediating that starting point through the cycle of representations which it builds up within itself. In this mediating process, Christian consciousness both remains on the level of representational thinking and points beyond itself to the necessity of a thinking that supersedes representations.

Hegel emphasizes the second of these points in the *Phenomenology*. For just this reason it is valuable to linger for a while with the first, so that the nature of the connection between the two, and eventually the character of the second, may become clear. As Christian consciousness, on the level of representational thinking, reflects upon recollected images, articulates what is implicit in them, and recognizes relations between and distinctions among its reflections, it brings forth diverse representations that have two features discussed as one in my previous remarks about the characteristics of *Vorstellungen*, and now in need of independent treatment. First, the diverse representations brought forth by Christian consciousness are severally connected. They form a whole in which each contributes to the intelligibility of the others. But second, their relatedness or connectedness is *external*. Each is discrete and distinct from the others. Insofar as the representations in question are others of each other, their relations are negative. Insofar as the representational thinking that articulates those representations constitutes them as being in such relations, that thinking is itself a negative power.

Negativity is present in Christian consciousness from the start. In fact, the representation that initially determines it, the Incarnation, represents the divine as self-revealing in an individual and thus represents the divine as related to itself in "the negativity of itself."[32] In dealing with its initial content, Christian consciousness incorporates this negativity into its own thinking processes. Those processes, as already seen, bring about mediation in the content of Christian consciousness. Those processes bring that mediation about insofar as the content in question is reflected in a network of relations that are, in part at least, negative relations.

I dwell on these comments because it is important to note that, as Hegel performs his phenomenological analyses of Christian consciousness, the claim that underlies those analyses is *not* a claim to the effect that the contents and processes of Christian consciousness call for mediation and negation, capacities for which belong to speculative thinking exclusively. His claim is rather, in the first place at least, that mediations and negations belong to the contents of Christian consciousness *themselves*, and that the powers of mediating and negating are constitutive of the consciousness' own processes. Hegel's views about Christian consciousness are, in this regard, continuous with his overall treatment of different "shapes" of consciousness in the *Phenomenology*. Each "shape" of consciousness that phenomenology observes detects differences in an object previously thought simply to be self-identical and then defines the relations among those differences as external and in that sense negative. This is the case for Christian consciousness as well. This point is important for an adequate understanding of the manner in which, for Hegel, Christian consciousness, the consummate form of religious consciousness, simultaneously develops its own rationality and on its own terms calls for speculative comprehension of itself. I shall return to this below.

But before that, yet a further stage of the experience of Christian consciousness needs discussion. It follows from what has preceded. Christian consciousness now deals with representations mediated by being externally, and in that sense negatively, related. But those external, negative relations are also *connections*. The connectedness of these representations needs to be made explicit. If this is to occur, the thinking processes of Christian consciousness must again express the power of negativity, but now in a new way. Previously, those powers expressed this power by mediating discrete representations through explicit distinctions, by, as it were, making explicit the externality of the connections among them. Now these processes must make connectedness explicit. This involves overcoming externality; it in some sense involves negating discreteness previously identified and distinctions previously made. Some advance the position that Christian consciousness discloses the necessity of this overcoming but cannot accomplish it on its own terms. Then, the speculative *Begriff* comes on the scene. The *Begriff* deals with the contents of Christian consciousness as that consciousness cannot. It negates external relations among those contents, and in so doing annuls the differences among terms externally related.[33] This position is quite other from the one I am taking herein. Crucial to my view is the observation that Christian consciousness can and does, on its own level, turn to the project of overcoming external relations among its contents. It makes this turn, however, not with reference to abstract ideas like the ones I have just mentioned but from the standpoint of its own experience. That standpoint reveals in just what sense Christian consciousness realizes itself in a new way as a mediating process and negative power.

III

As already indicated, Christian consciousness represents the phenomena that stand before it—the divine reality and the human world—as other, but not *simply* as others to each other. Christian consciousness understands divine reality both as other than the human world, and as that which, "*from the beginning* externalizes itself,"[34] in creation and again uniquely in the Incarnation, such that its otherness from the human world is simultaneously its relatedness thereto. Christian consciousness must now deal with this aspect of its representational content.

This occurs as Christian consciousness internalizes the revelation inaugurated in the Incarnation and articulated through its own mediations. The Incarnation reveals the unity of the divine and human natures. Finite consciousness, in the face of this revelation, recognizes both this unity and its own "fallen" self-centeredness, its own self-asserted independence from the divine. The withdrawal of the finite into itself has rendered it evil. Now, finite consciousness withdraws into itself again in self-recognition. But this "withdrawal consists, therefore, in *convincing itself* that natural existence is evil."[35] Self-centered consciousness, Hegel says, recognizes in "the propitiation of the absolute being"[36] its own self-centeredness, and the evil with which it is endowed in virtue of the same.

This recognition simultaneously involves finite consciousness' incorporating into its self-awareness the content of that which prompts self-recognition. That content depicts divine reality as having emptied itself by uniting itself with that which is other than and alien to itself, even to the uttermost extremes of that alienation. It therefore depicts human reality as a reality whose alienation from the divine is overcome, and whose otherness from the divine is defined in terms of and in the context of relatedness thereto, insofar as, "by bringing to pass its own externalization, in its historical incarnation and death, the divine being has been reconciled [versöhnt ist] with its (natural) existence."[37]

The process described here is a process that Christian consciousness undergoes on the level of representational thinking. That thinking, however, has now articulated and extended its mediating capacities from its "pure thought" of divine reality to its own self-consciousness. It has explicitly focused on the second of the two elements between which "Vorstellung" stands as a middle term, while also being "diffused" throughout both. Christian consciousness, Hegel holds, ineluctably "passes over from the second element constituting it, i.e., from representational thinking [Vorstellen], into the third element, self-consciousness as such."[38] It accomplishes this transition, however, initially but genuinely in terms of itself as representational thinking. In dealing with its own representations, it determines its self-recognition.

But, of course, in this further reflection Christian consciousness does not only focus its thinking on itself; it focuses on itself just by pressing forward in its examinations of its representations of divine reality in relation to itself. Its focus on itself follows from renewed attention to its representation of the kenotic nature of the divine. From this two things result. The divine is understood both as other and as from its innermost self united with its other, and this in both a general way, as the idea of creation represents, and in a way that extends to the most extreme moments of the otherness of its other, as the idea of the Incarnation now represents. With this Christian consciousness grasps the death of "the *abstraction* of the divine being."[39] It overcomes on its own terms that understanding which depicts the divine as being unattainably beyond the human world, while nevertheless being the principle of its existence and incarnation therein. It attains on its own terms an understanding of the divine as that which, in the innermost otherness of its self from the human world, unites itself most intimately with that world, in a way that requires that otherness be thought of in terms of union, that transcendence and immanence be thought of together.

At the same time, Christian consciousness, the culminating form of finite, religious subjectivity, overcomes an abstract and attains a concrete understanding of itself. It now depicts "the nature of spirit in its (natural) existence" as an existence that "preserves itself in its otherness."[40] It now, that is to say, understands its own otherness from the divine as an other-directed otherness, an otherness determined from the standpoint of its own existence as a union of others, due in principle to the nature of creation and due concretely to the divinely initiated reconciliation of the human with itself. The final moment of the experience of

Christian consciousness is a dialectic of the conviction of evil and confession, of forgiveness and reconciliation. The upshot of this dialectic is an understanding of the divine-human relationship as "the movement in which what is an abstract antithesis recognizes itself as the same as its opposite, this recognition bursting forth as the *affirmative* between these extremes."[41] Christian consciousness knows its own existence to be directed out of itself toward a union in otherness with the divine, just as it knows the divine to be that which directs itself out from itself toward its union in otherness with the human. And it knows itself in this way by knowing itself in its other, which knowledge is made possible by the divine other having made itself known in the way that the Incarnation represents.

These remarks provide a context for being explicit as to how the representational thinking of Christian consciousness has achieved mediating capacities and expressed the power of negation in a new way, different from, albeit consequent upon, the way described above. Before, that thinking distinguished and articulated discrete representations. Those representations were interconnected, but the connections among them were external. Now Christian consciousness has, as it were, internalized those connections. In fact, it is perhaps no longer proper to speak of "connections" at all. For what Christian consciousness has done is to overcome while preserving the discreteness of its representational contents. It has defined otherness in terms of sameness, through seeing itself in its others, insofar as its divine other is self-same in its human incarnation. It has defined identity in terms of difference by understanding the differences between the divine and the human in terms of the specific kinds of identities each enjoys with that which is different from itself. It has defined the non-union of the divine and the human as a nonunion of each term with the other in its union with the other. Representational thinking has mediated its contents a second time, not as an activity of making implicit distinctions explicit through reflection but as an activity of relating distinctions already made through inwardizing the same. This activity expresses the "power of the negative," now in a way that involves overcoming distinctions while at the same time retaining them.

It is important to note, again, that representational thinking realizes itself, now in two ways, as a mediating capacity and a "power of the negative," while remaining itself, from within its own possibilities as representational.[42] Christian consciousness begins by defining itself as a specific form of religious consciousness. It then builds up the initial content that determines it, by realizing the mediations and negations that belong to that content, in two different, albeit intimately interrelated, ways. But the point to note is that even in the final way in which it expresses the "power of the negative," that thinking continues to dwell with representations.

And while it finally defines otherness in terms of sameness and difference in terms of identity, it also defines sameness in terms of otherness and identity in terms of difference. It overcomes dualities while at the same time retaining them in the way that is necessary (Hegel claims at least) if Christian consciousness is to be Christian. The way in which representational thinking exercises the "power of the negative" a second time must be emphasized in an account of the transitions from representational to speculative thinking in Hegel's phenomenology of Christian consciousness. On one reading, representational thinking begins to negate external relations but cannot complete this process just because, *qua* representational, it is thinking that "places" its contents "before" itself and does not finally comprehend them. Then, speculative thinking calls upon the speculative *Begriff* to complete the process that it begins but cannot complete. The *Begriff* does fully comprehend the contents of representational thinking. It thereby overcomes the externalities which that thinking cannot overcome, annulling them through its radical, negative power.[43]

In important respects this view is correct. Speculation does comprehend representational thinking in a way in which the latter cannot comprehend itself. Speculation does complete a process that representational thinking begins but cannot complete. But the process that representational thinking begins is the process of negating and overcoming external relations among its contents in unities that preserve differences, not in abstract identities that abolish them. Representational thinking has shown itself as a negative power by determining that God and the community of finite spirits are self-same in their union with each *other.* One needs to ask, What precisely about this exercise of negativity on the level of representational thinking calls forth speculative thought? What does that thinking achieve?

IV

Hegel writes, "This *form of representational thinking* [*Form des Vorstellens*] . . . is not yet spirit's self-consciousness that has advanced to its notion *qua* notion: the mediation is still incomplete."[44] Representational thinking points beyond itself due to its inability to complete its mediations from within itself. Given all that is indicated by the preceding discussion, what is missing?

The thinking that belongs to Christian consciousness has doubly mediated its contents by doubly expressing its own negative power. This thinking has determined the otherness of its representations of the divine and the human as an otherness in which each term is self-same in its union with its other. Or, it has determined the difference between its representations of the divine and the human as a difference between terms, each of which is self-identical in its union with that which is different from itself.

Representational thinking has achieved these determinations. But it has achieved them with reference to and while dwelling with representations. It has paid attention to and dealt with those representations themselves. It has not paid attention to and dealt with the ideas of otherness and sameness, difference and identity, non-union and union *themselves*. It has not thematized these and brought these forward as explicit focuses of its own considerations. It has mediated its representational contents in terms of these ideas but has not explicitly considered the ideas with reference to which it brings about mediations.

Representational thinking has not done this. It cannot do this as long as it remains representational thinking. That thinking is constrained by the necessity of ordering, reflecting upon, distinguishing, and interrelating ideas that proceed from images and that preserve in themselves the "sensuous content" of images as essential to their definitions. But as long as representational thinking fails to do this, there remains in the content of its thinking something unthought. That content, for this reason, continues to "stand before" it as a content that it has not fully comprehended and therefore as a content present in thinking that opposes itself to thinking. Likewise, representational thinking fails to know itself as thinking, to achieve a full comprehension of thinking's own capacities, so long as there remains in the content of its thinking a dimension that is radical, can be thought, and is unthought. So long as this situation remains, there belong to thinking itself capacities which it has not brought before itself by exercising them, and which therefore remain unthought.

These defects belong necessarily to representational thinking. They indicate that representational thinking cannot on its own terms fully overcome the externality of its contents from each other, because it cannot explicitly consider the ideas ingredient in overcoming these externalities. Nor, on these terms, can Christian consciousness fully recover itself as self-consciousness. It cannot be fully conscious of itself as a mode of thinking as long as it remains representational thinking.

In order to overcome these defects, Christian consciousness must, in its thinking, surpass its own representational character. It must give rise to a thinking that does explicitly deal with the ideas of otherness and sameness, difference and identity, non-union and union. It must give rise, in short, to speculative thinking. The nature of this speculative thinking needs to be carefully understood. It does overcome the "external connections" among the contents of Christian representational thinking. But it does this by thematizing and comprehending the ideas with reference to which that thinking itself overcomes those externalities on its own level, which ideas, however, it does not thematize and consider. For this reason, the speculative thinking that emerges from the consummate form of religious representational thinking continues to be a thinking of that which concerns religious consciousness: the relation of the divine and the human.[45] The same objects that concern religious consciousness are comprehended by speculative thinking, but in a way that supersedes the capacities of representational thinking, just because speculation thematizes a dimension ingredient in, but unavailable to, that thinking that deals with representations. Thus, Hegel writes, "God is attainable in pure speculative knowledge alone and is only in that knowledge ... for He is spirit; and this speculative knowledge is the knowledge of the *revealed* religion."[46] Speculative knowing makes explicit that which is ingredient in but not acknowledged in representational thinking's considerations of the divine and thus knows the divine in a way unavailable to representational thinking. But it is still a knowing of the divine. Similarly, representational thinking is a "spiritual self-consciousness which is not an object to itself as this self-consciousness."[47] It is a human understanding of the selfhood that belongs to being human in its relationship with the divine. That self-consciousness is not fully present to itself as long as it is representational thinking. Speculative thinking explicitly deals with what's operative in but not present to representational thinking, thus bringing about human self-knowing in a new, more radical and comprehensive way. But it is still a knowing of the human.

Finally, speculative thinking expresses the "power of negativity" in a new and more radical way. It comprehends the difference between or otherness of the terms that it considers by way of the specific modes in which these different terms are self-identical or self-same in union with each other. It achieves this comprehension by considering specific ways in which "difference" and "identity," "otherness" and "sameness," give themselves over to each other. In so doing speculative thought explicitly considers negativity itself. It explicitly thematizes and grasps the negativity ingredient in "difference" and "identity," "otherness" and "sameness," that allows and requires each term to other itself in its other while remaining itself. It simultaneously thematizes and grasps the "pure negativity" which it is as a "pure knowing"[48] and which allows it to think mediations among these categories.[49] This double thematizing of negativity is a new exercise of the negative power of thinking. Through it, thinking turns from representational contents to itself as a capacity for dealing with "pure" ideas and mediates those ideas with reference to the reciprocity that severally defines them.

But the mediations brought about among these ideas by speculative thought do not fail to reflect the dialectical nuances of the mediations already achieved by representational thinking. The former mediations effect a reconciliation among the different contents of religious consciousness with reference to pure ideas. But, Hegel remarks,

> If this reconciliation is *notionally* expressed by saying that evil is in *itself* the same as goodness, or again that the divine being is the *same* as nature in its whole extent, or that nature separated from the divine being is simply nothing—we must regard this as an unspiritual way of talking and one that is necessarily bound to give rise to misunderstanding.... When expressed in terms of their notion, their unity is at once evident ... it must also no less emphatically be asserted that they are *not* the same, but are utterly different, for simple being-for-self, or pure knowing, is each in its own self equally pure negatively or absolute difference. The whole is only complete when the two propositions are made together, and when the first is asserted and maintained, it must be countered by clinging to the other with invincible stubbornness.[50]

I have already remarked that Christian representational thinking, itself a negative, mediating power in Hegel's *Phenomenology*, defines the differences among the contents it considers in terms of the precise way in which those different terms find their self-identity in each other. It does not thematize ideas such as "difference" and "identity." Speculative thinking does thematize these ideas. It thinks the contents of concern to Christian consciousness with reference to these ideas. It mediates those contents in terms of the ways in which those ideas allow for negative mediations. But just for this reason it does not collapse identity into difference, or otherness into sameness. Or, I submit, it does not collapse the difference between divine reality and human (inter-) subjectivity into identity, even though it surely does, in its own way, think the self-sameness of each of these terms in its *other*. Hegel claims at least to present a phenomenology of Christian consciousness that achieves, at the finale of its self-examination, an understanding of the identity-in-*difference* of the human and the divine.[51] The speculative thinking that emerges from Christian representational thinking in Hegel's argument retains that understanding and reinstates it in its own conceptuality. It defines difference and otherness through identity and sameness but also defines the latter pair of terms through the former because of the negativity that it detects and exercises. This is, of course, the case in Hegel's overall position regarding the nature of speculative thinking. Such thinking is, for Hegel, in principle thinking that comprehends what is of concern to it by determining the way in which differences play into each other, forming unities that negate external relations among differences just as they preserve those same differences. Writers such as Quentin Lauer and James Yerkes recognize this very important feature of Hegelian speculative thought. In the light of it, they argue that that thought, far from annulling religious self-understanding, reinstates the truthfulness of the same in speculative concepts. My argument shows, I believe, that this thesis holds good even in relation to the text that seems most stoutly to challenge it, the *Phenomenology of Spirit*.

V

I have now dealt with the questions that animate this essay. I shall conclude with a remark about the issue of whether speculative thinking, as Hegel conceives of it in the *Phenomenology*, requires that the truthfulness of religious self-understanding continue to be expressed in properly religious as well as in properly philosophical terms.

Religious self-understanding is, for Hegel, the self-understanding of finite, self-active subjectivity, finite spirit, in the face of its relatedness with that which is absolute and infinite. It is a self-understanding that holds together feeling and knowing, ideally allowing each to find itself in and determine the other. Through the expressions proper to it—representations—religious consciousness places before itself its knowledge of infinite selfhood, of its own finite selfhood, and of the relatedness that binds these together.

A unique feature of religious representations is that they depict the relatedness of the finite with the infinite from the standpoint of the finite. As previously noted, religious representations result from a series of orderings of and reflections upon images drawn from the finite, experienced world. Representations retain those images in themselves even as they "mix" them with thought. The thinking that mediates representations by distinguishing and interrelating them is a rational power; which in its dealings with its contents realizes the rationality intrinsic to those contents.

That thinking, Hegel argues, discovers in itself the possibility and necessity of superseding itself, of allowing its representational form to give way to speculative activity. This is because it deals with representations in terms of determinations that it cannot recover, thematize and justify, determinations that remain for it presuppositions. Speculative activity does thematize those determinations in categories. The very terms that must be presuppositions for representational thinking are recovered and justified speculatively. Just this, however, points thinking back to the religious representation. To show the warranted nature of terms which, on the level of the representation, are only presuppositions, is to redirect attention to the particular significance of the representations in which those terms are ingredient. A particular significance does belong to religious representations. This is the case, again, because representations express the relatedness of the finite and the infinite *from the standpoint of the finite*. Their rootedness in retained images drawn from the experienced world enables them to exhibit the abilities of that world itself to point beyond itself to absolute infinity. This is the case even though the meanings of finitude and infinity cannot be fully comprehended with reference to representations alone. Likewise, the thinking that deals with representations continues to possess a particular purpose of its own, even though this thinking also supersedes itself in speculation. It is a thinking that does mediate and express the intelligibility of its contents. It cannot do this fully or adequately. It can and does interpret the complex, meaningful ways in which dimensions of the finite world stand as symbols of that world's relatedness to the infinite and divine, even if it cannot probe those mediations with reference to which the intelligibility of those symbols finally needs to be understood.[52] And in so doing this thinking progressively educates that feeling which integrally belongs to religious consciousness by exploring the meaningfulness of the "sensuous content" through which feeling is molded.

I would argue, then, that Hegel's phenomenological claims about the way in which the representational thinking of Christian consciousness supersedes itself in speculation entails the claim that speculation points back to the continuing integrity of thinking that deals with representations. Speculative thought radically probes the intelligibility belonging to the contents of religious knowing. Hermeneutical thinking progressively examines the meaningfulness which those contents possess as symbols for religious existence. The former activity provides a context of understandings made possible by, and for Hegel, indispensably necessary for, the latter. The latter activity interprets symbolic contents from within that context. This is still a further way in which Hegelian speculative thinking may preserve the standpoint of religious self-understanding.

Notes

1. Emil Fackenheim, "Demythologizing and Remythologizing in Jewish Experience: Reflections Inspired by Hegel's Philosophy," in *Myth and Philosophy: Proceedings of the ACPA* (Washington, D.C.: Office of the National Secretary of the ACPA, 1971), 45:18.

2. Hegel discusses his concept of phenomenology as observation of the process of self-examination proper to the experience of determinable shapes of consciousness in his introduction to the *Phenomenology* (see G. W. F. Hegel, *Phänomenologie des Geistes*, ed. J. Hoffmeister [Hamburg Felix Meiner, 1952], 67–74; *Hegel's Phenomenology of Spirit*, trans. A. V. Miller [Oxford: Clarendon Press, 1977], 49–57 [hereafter cited as PhG, PhS]) Kenley Dove shows the descriptive nature of Hegelian phenomenology in this volume. Ardis B. Collins ("Hegel's Redefinition of the Critical Project," in *Method and Speculation in Hegel's Phenomenology*, ed. Merold Westphal [Atlantic Highlands, N.J.: Humanities Press, 1982], 1–13) comments most helpfully on the nature of the phenomenologically observed processes of self-examination through which distinct shapes of consciousness give rise to others. Werner Marx (*Hegel's Phenomenology of Spirit*, trans. Peter Heath [New York: Harper & Row, 1975], 50–77) demonstrates continuity between the later and the earlier sections of the *Phenomenology* with reference to the method that Hegel defines for the latter.

3. Emil Fackenheim (*The Religious Dimension of Hegel's Thought* [Bloomington: Indiana University Press, 1967], 117–18) holds that "the Hegelian texts treat religious and Christian realities extensively. They never give an account of them which is severely confined to the standpoint of religious self-understanding. ... Hegel's own central writings on the subject—the *Phenomenology*, the *Encyclopedia*, the *Philosophy of Religion*—all treat religion *as it is already reenacted and transfigured by philosophical thought: they give no sustained description of religion from the representational—i.e., philosophically unreenacted and untransfigured—standpoints of religion itself.*" This statement, even though not false regarding the *Phenomenology*, needs to be qualified. Hegelian phenomenology indeed does consider religious consciousness with reference to that consciousness' examination of its own most basic presuppositions, an examination that religious consciousness *fully* performs not in its "natural" state but only when phenomenologically assisted. In this sense religious consciousness, as it appears in the *Phenomenology*, is philosophically mediated. Still, the content if not the occurrence of that full self-examination is determined, Hegel claims at least, wholly from the standpoint of religious consciousness, and is in this sense "confined to the standpoint of religious self-understanding." One of Hegel's claims about his phenomenology of religious consciousness, then, is that phenomenology shows religious consciousness to find in its own standpoint the necessity of superseding itself in speculative thinking. And this claim is made plausible by the obvious fact that, in thinking historically prior to the *Phenomenology*, religious self-understanding has already attempted ascents to speculative self-comprehension, if for Hegel with only partial success.

4. It is common to discuss Hegel's understanding of religious consciousness by analyzing Hegel's views concerning the religious *Vorstellung*, the mode of expression peculiar to religious consciousness, and then to raise the question of whether or not speculative thinking somehow preserves the religious *Vorstellung* in surpassing it. Paul Ricoeur, for example, in "The Status of *Vorstellung* in Hegel's Philosophy of Religion" (in *Meaning, Truth, and God*, ed. Leroy Rouner

[Notre Dame, Ind.: University of Notre Dame Press, 1982], 70–88) presents a most helpful version of this discussion in an essay that pays careful attention to the *Phenomenology*. But the characteristics belonging to the religious *Vorstellung* in the *Phenomenology* are determined by the experience of that religious consciousness which (necessarily) adopts this mode of expression. An analysis of this experience, then, provides a needed framework for understanding those characteristics, as I will in part show below. And, with reference to Hegel's *Phenomenology* at least, the question as to whether or not speculative thinking somehow preserves the standpoint of religious self-understanding while also surpassing it needs to be discussed with reference to the process of self-examination through which religious consciousness points beyond itself to speculative thought.

5. For example, Merold Westphal (*History and Truth in Hegel's Phenomenology* [Atlantic Highlands, N.J.: Humanities Press, 1978], 192) states that "Hegel's trinitarian speculation suggests that the overcoming of contradictions which torment Unhappy Consciousness is to be found in the church, insofar as it comes to a proper kind of self-consciousness, not in a transcendent personal deity," the "power of the negative" being of course precisely that through which contradictions are overcome. See also Stephen Crites ("Dialectics and Apologetics in Yerkes's Interpretatation of Hegel," *Journal of Religion* 60 [April 1980]: 210–17, 216), who argues that the negativity of the Hegelian *Begriff*, anticipated by religious consciousness, "negates all religious *Vorstellung*[*en*], negates the entire representational sphere of the religious consciousness from within."

6. PhG 473; PhS 410. Hegel insists that even the most attenuated form of religious consciousness is essentially a "consciousness of *absolute being* as such."

7. PhG 475; PhS 412 ("in religion consciousness is posited essentially in the determination of *self*-consciousness").

8. Quentin Lauer, *A Reading of Hegel's Phenomenology of Spirit* (New York: Fordham University Press, 1976), 231. "For Hegel, then, religious consciousness is indispensable in the march towards adequate self-consciousness; it is at once consciousness of the divine and consciousness that to be adequately consciousness of the self is to be of the divine—without the self's consciousness ceasing to be human." In recent scholarship, Lauer has most especially emphasized the unity of consciousness and self-consciousness in Hegel's account of religious consciousness (see also Lauer, *Hegel's Concept of God* [Albany: State University of New York Press, 1982], 43–46, 154–58, 188, 220–23).

9. PhG 481–89; PhS 416–24. These remarks state, in very general terms, the conclusion of the dialectic of "Natural Religion."

10. See PhG 523, PhS 455.

11. PhG 490–520; PhS 424–53. These remarks state, in very general terms, the conclusion of the dialectic of the "Religion of Art."

12. PhG 527; PhS 458. James Yerkes (*The Christology of Hegel* [Missoula,

Mont.: Scholars Press, 1978], 173) emphasizes that, for Hegel, knowing in general and religious knowing in particular proceed from, "in the *ordo cognoscendi*, something objective for consciousness as mediated by sensuous intuition in perception." The author of the *Phenomenology of Spirit* certainly identifies Christian consciousness with reference to such a starting point. It is the consciousness of "the believer" who "*sees, feels*, and *hears* this divinity."

13. PhG 528; PhS 459.

14. See PhG 528–29; PhS 459–60.

15. PhG 531; PhS 462. Paul Ricoeur ("Status of *Vorstellung*," 79) notes that, for the Hegel of the *Phenomenology*, "Ecclesiology, then, absorbs Christology." These remarks indicate in what manner this is the case for Hegel and in what manner, for Hegel, Christology not only is absorbed by ecclesiology but also points beyond itself to ecclesiology. They are reinforced by a statement that follows them in the text cited: "Not the individual by himself, but together with the consciousness of the community and of what he is for the community, is the complete whole of the individual as spirit."

16. PhG 533; PhS 464. A. V. Miller translates *Vorstellung* as "picture thinking." But Yerkes (pp. 91–95) offers strong reasons for translating *Vorstellung* as "representation" or "representational thinking." Lauer (*Hegel's Concept of God*, 34–35) endorses this translation. I shall modify Miller's translations of Hegel along these lines in the remainder of this essay.

17. Thus, while I say that the knowing and self-knowing of Christian consciousness proceed from images, I agree fully with Quentin Lauer (*Hegel's Concept of God*, 34) when he states that "it should be obvious . . . that the term (i.e., *Vorstellung*) cannot be translated by 'image'; it belongs fully to the realm of thought and not to that of sensibility or imagination (unless, of course, the meaning of the latter term is broadened considerably)."

18. My brief remarks are limited to these and, moreover, to Hegel's discussion of these in the *Phenomenology*.

19. These orderings and reflections can proceed from the images upon which they base themselves in complex and far-reaching ways. Thus Ricoeur ("Status of *Vorstellung*," 70) is quite correct in noting that, for Hegel, "*Vorstellung* covers not only stories and symbols—images, if you will—but also such highly defined conceptualized expressions as Trinity, Creation, Fall, Incarnation, and Salvation, not only in religious but also in theological discourse." I shall allude to the significance of this below.

20. Yerkes, *Christology of Hegel*, 93.

21. PhG 532; PhS 463.

22. Ibid.

23. Ibid. Westphal (*History and Truth*, 204) offers an analysis of the charac-

teristics belonging to the products of Christian representational thinking similar to the one given here. I am in substantial agreement with Westphal regarding this analysis but disagree with him as to Hegel's views of the transition that Christian consciousness, in the *Phenomenology*, makes from *Vorstellung* to *Begriff*, as subsequent remarks will show.

24. Stephen Crites (*In the Twilight of Christendom: Hegel vs. Kierkegaard on Faith and History* [Chambersburg, Pa.: American Academy of Religion, 1972], 44) writes that, for Hegel, "with respect to any sphere of spirit, i.e., politics, art, religion, or its own history, philosophy must treat not only what is positively given but also the intermediate efforts of consciousness within that sphere to come to terms with its own positive material." The part of Hegel's phenomenology of Christian consciousness now under consideration observes, Hegel claims, the efforts of Christian consciousness, from within its own sphere, to come to terms with the material (i.e., positive) products of its own initial self-determination.

25. Hegel indicates his impatience with historical theology, as he construes it, in this part of the *Phenomenology* (see PhG 766-67; PhS 463). In this connection, Robert Williams ("Hegel and Schleiermacher on Theological Truth," in *Meaning, Truth, and God*, ed. Leroy Rouner [Notre Dame, Ind.: University of Notre Dame Press, 1982], 65) is correct in stating that "Hegel tends to identify Christianity with its historic doctrines." Hegel would add that the identification follows from the necessary formulations of doctrines that Christian consciousness makes in its efforts to deal with those representational contents that are its initial determinations.

26. See PhG 534; PhS 465. In this passage, Hegel makes use both of the representational language of Christian consciousness itself and of the notional conceptuality toward which, Hegel wants to show, Christian consciousness is groping. This is typical of this section of Hegel's phenomenology of Christian consciousness.

27. This use of this bit of medieval terminology is mine, not Hegel's, but it is quite in accord both with his account of Christian consciousness on its own terms and with the notional language that he integrates into that account (see PhG 535-37; PhS 466-67). And it is suggested, from the point of view of a problem slightly different from the one with which I am dealing in this essay, by Anselm Min, "Hegel's Absolute: Transcendent of Immanent?" *Journal of Religion* 56 (January 1976): 61-87, 81.

28. PhG 536-37; PhS 467.

29. PhG 537-38; PhS 468-69.

30. PhG 540; PhS 471.

31. PhG 530; PhS 461.

32. Ibid.

33. See, e.g., Westphal, *History and Truth*, 201-7.
34. PhG 541; PhS 471.
35. PhG 543; PhS 475.
36. Ibid.
37. PhG 545; PhS 475.
38. PhG 541; PhS 471.
39. PhG 546; PhS 476.
40. PhG 545; PhS 475.
41. PhG 547; PhS 477.

42. Ricoeur ("Status of *Vorstellung*," 80) notes that "the *Phenomenology* does not conceal the impatience of Hegel with the resistance of figurative thought to its 'sublation' in and by conceptual thought." This is true, and is indicated in part by Hegel's practice of always associating developments in the representational thinking of Christian consciousness with the notional terms that they prefigure, as I note above. But I hope my remarks have shown that, even in the *Phenomenology*, Hegel is patient enough with representational thinking to observe the ways in which, according to his phenomenology, it realizes from *within itself* mediating capacities and the power of the negative in its dealings with its own representational contents. This is the case even though the reader of the last section of the penultimate chapter of the *Phenomenology* needs laboriously to distinguish Hegel's (putative) observations of the processes of Christian representational thinking taken on their own terms from his notional comments about those processes.

43. See, e.g., Crites, "The Golgothia of Absolute Spirit," in *Method and Speculation*, ed. Westphal, 47-56.

44. PhG 532; PhS 463. This remark occurs relatively early in Hegel's phenomenology of the dialectic of Christian consciousness, but it anticipates the conclusion of that dialectic.

45. Ultimately, speculative thinking, for Hegel, must extend itself beyond the limits set for it in its emergence from religion. This extension occurs, in the phenomenology, as speculative thinking reconciles its transfigured comprehension of religious self-consciousness with the final moment of moral consciousness that gives rise to religion in the *Phenomenology*. Hegel treats this issue in the chapter on "Absolute Knowing," and it is an issue of critical importance, but also beyond the scope of this chapter.

46. PhG 530; PhS 461. The words omitted from this citation are: "and is only that knowledge itself." They may seem to challenge the interpretation of the emergence of speculative thinking in Hegel's phenomenology of religious consciousness toward which I am building. But they do not. For what this statement

says is that God is pure knowledge of himself in his union with that which is other than himself, and thus pure knowledge itself.

47. PhG 547; PhS 477.

48. PhG 542; PhS 472.

49. Perhaps one can claim, with reference to Hegel's *Logic*, that Christian representational thinking deals with the terms that it considers belonging to the domains of "Being" and "Essence," whereas the speculative thinking now under discussion deals with its terms in an explicitly notional way. Representational thinking displays its terms as discrete determinations and then considers them as consequences emergent from a ground and with reference to their reciprocity. Speculative thinking comprehends its terms explicitly with reference to the intrinsic negativity that enables the self-identity of each to other itself and to recover itself in differences. This claim is somehow hazardous. Neither Christian representational thinking nor the speculative thinking to which it gives rise in the *Phenomenology* is conscious of the categories of "Being," "Essence," and the "Notion," as is that thinking which develops in Hegel's *Logic*. Nevertheless, this speculative thinking is notional and proceeds from the intimate phenomenological gestalt that allows absolute knowing to appear.

50. PhG 542; PhS 472.

51. This, I propose, is Hegel's claim at least, and a claim that he makes good. Whether the claim is finally adequate—whether this way of thinking of the difference between the human and the divine sufficiently preserves the understanding of divine transcendence essential to Christian thought—is another question. But one most ask whether a position less dialectically nuanced than Hegel's adequately holds together the understandings of divine transcendence and divine immanence upon whose togetherness much thought in the Christian tradition seems to insist.

52. See n.41 above. The correctness of Ricoeur's observation regarding Hegel's "impatience" with the resistance of representational thinking to its own speculative reenactment is here perhaps most apparent. Hegel labors to show how the processes of representational thinking ultimately lead that thinking to supersede itself in speculation. He does not labor in the *Phenomenology* over a discussion of the integrity that continues to belong to representational thinking and to representations after the emergence of speculation. But, I claim, the position I espouse here is ingredient in what Hegel does say about representational thinking. I discuss this issue briefly and with regard to another problem in "The Cosmological Argument and Hegel's Doctrine of God," *New Scholasticism* 52 (Summer 1978): 364–66.

VII

Absolute Knowing and the Structure of the Phenomenology

20

Mitchell H. Miller Jr.

The Attainment of the Absolute Standpoint in Hegel's Phenomenology

In Hegel's *Phenomenology of Spirit*, immediate sensory consciousness passes to absolute self-consciousness. In each of the many and substantially diverse intermediate transitions, essentially the same rhythm of passage occurs: a certain standpoint or "shape" (*Gestalt*) of consciousness grasps reality as such-and-such, only to find that this grasp is one-sided and cannot be maintained except by the further accepting of what it excludes. Implicit in this finding is a twofold insight fundamental to the *Phenomenology* as a whole. First, every finite standpoint exists only as a determinate aspect or part of a higher, relatively whole standpoint; and second, inasmuch as each finite standpoint, by thus pointing beyond itself, shows itself as a stage or moment in a process of consciousness toward wholeness, this wholeness itself—that standpoint which knows reality as a whole—must in some sense exist as this process itself of determination of itself into various moments or finite standpoints. But this is to say that the arrival of consciousness at the absolute standpoint, the completion of phenomenology, will be the actual recognition by consciousness itself of itself as this process of self-determination—a process that has, as its own culminating moment, precisely the appearance of consciousness to itself as this very self-consciousness of itself as process.

In what follows, we want to explicate and examine this very complex recognition, the culmination of the *Phenomenology*, as it is characterized by Hegel in the dense, sometimes seemingly chaotic closing chapter of that work. Our discussion is divided into three main sections, in correspondence with the internal structure of chapter VIII itself. First, we want to discuss in detail the attainment of the absolute standpoint, as this is the focus for Hegel in paragraphs 788–97.[1] Second, we want to consider several important discoveries about the temporality and historical aspect of consciousness which emerge in the course of that attainment; and we want to observe Hegel's own characterization of the place of his philosophy—that is, of the absolute standpoint—in the history of philosophy and culture. Those are the basic concerns of paragraphs 798–804. Finally, since the culmination of the *Phenomenology* is the beginning of Hegel's "system" according to his excruciatingly compact remarks in paragraphs 805–8, we will attempt an elucidation of the relation of the absolute standpoint, as it is attained in chapter VIII, to its explication in the "system."

Attaining the Absolute Standpoint

The task of paragraphs 788–97 is to execute the transition from "Revealed Religion" (VII. C) to "Absolute Knowledge." The method of execution involves a gathering up of various moments of all that has preceded; by disclosing what these moments, set in light of "Revealed Religion," essentially *imply*, Hegel generates a shape of consciousness radically different from what they initially and explicitly were. Our procedure shall be to consider first the task, then its execution, and, finally, the character of the emergent absolute standpoint.

In the Hegelian version of phenomenology, as we have already observed, each finite standpoint of consciousness involves a conception of reality which, as its own experience shows, is one-sided. And this means that consciousness, to preserve the "side" which it asserts, must also accept the "side" which it unknowingly at first excludes. But, by this acceptance of both sides at once, consciousness transcends its earlier shape, knowing now a whole where before it was the knowing of only a part. What, then, we may begin by asking, is the one-sidedness of "Revealed Religion"?

"Revealed Religion," as the last part of chapter VII, is the last stage in the development of that shape of consciousness wherein absolute or world-constituting spirit beholds itself through various shapes of human religious consciousness. The obvious tension here arises between absolute spirit's, or God's, knowledge of himself and man's knowledge of God. The remarkable achievement of "Revealed Religion," or consciousness as it takes final shape in Christian Communion and the church, is that this tension is healed. God here makes himself man, a natural being, and reveals himself as man to men; as man, God assumes the form of consciousness, and as conscious of himself as God who has made himself man, he reveals himself as the action of universal being, in which it opposes itself, as particular natural self, to itself as universal being; this opposition is only a moment, however; because the opposition is internal to God, the opposites must each contain the other; this mutual containment is played out as the event of Resurrection, in which, on the one hand, universal being, God, takes on natural particularity completely and dies, whereas, on the other hand, the natural particular self, in dying, takes on the character of universal being and survives its death as a universal self which knows itself as such, that is, as God's knowing himself to be this whole process of simple unity, self-opposition, and self-conscious reunification. Now, *all this* is the *object* for Christian consciousness; but this means that God, by making himself man and then raising himself as man to the status of divine self-consciousness, has permitted men, by participating in religious knowledge, to know themselves as raised to divine being; or, through God's knowing of himself as man, man may come to know himself as God, as the whole process of simple unity, self-opposition, and self-conscious reunification. *All the same,* Christian consciousness is not absolute, for the process is known as God's, rather than man's own; or, the knowledge of the process is viewed as a gift from God, an alien source; this is reflected by *the form* which Christian consciousness takes: it is a pure thinking of God, representative imagining of Christ, and feeling for the reunification of these opposites in the Resurrection; of these specific modes, feeling most of all overcomes the otherness of God from man, for it least of all presents its object to itself as other—and yet, by contrast, feeling is the most receptive of the modes and hence that in which man, as celebrant, least of all feels his autonomy; yet *what* man feels, his union with God as process of absolute spirit, requires that here most of all he should know himself as autonomous. Thus there is a contradiction: the subject as religious knower remains opposed to what, through religious knowledge, he knows himself to be. The union of God and man which is accomplished in the object of religious knowing is denied by the subject's mode of knowing.

It is this contradiction to which Hegel refers in arguing that the truth of the content of Christianity requires the overcoming of its religious form. The meaning of the Incarnation and Resurrection itself requires a mode of knowing which—by itself overcoming the separation of subject from object—will be adequate to the unity of God and man which is its object.

Hegel discovers the new form or mode of consciousness—which he will call the concept (*Begriff*)—through a complex reflection. The task, first of all, is to move from object-oriented consciousness to self-consciousness, that is, to a knowing which knows itself, as knowing, as the truth of its object. Now, key to this movement is the revelation that the object of object-oriented consciousness, present to it as other, is really the self of consciousness. Since this revelation has already occurred, in stages, in the course of the *Phenomenology*, the new form or mode of consciousness may be generated by recollection of the relevant earlier moments in the development of consciousness. But that is not all. First, in order for the recollected transformation from object to self-consciousness to relate properly to the transformation of religious consciousness, the object first present as other in the process to be recollected must be shown to coincide in nature and structure with the object of religious consciousness. And secondly, the self which, as a result of the process to be recollected, knows itself to be the reality of its object, must also be shown to include within itself all of what is known in the object of religious consciousness. Hence the whole reflection which generates the new mode of knowing has three basic parts:

1. Hegel begins by showing how the mode of object-oriented consciousness generated by the unity of chapters I–III has a total object whose nature and structure is identical with that of Christian religious consciousness.
2. He then gathers together key moments from chapters V–VI, showing them as moments in a process wherein the truth of the object known in chapters I–III is recognized as the self which does the knowing—and the recognizing of this truth itself.
3. Finally, by setting the last stage of this self-recognition in light of chapter VII, he shows it to be that form or mode of knowing which overcomes the inner contradiction and fulfills the truth of religious consciousness.

Let us retrace these steps.
1. The first step might be understood as a demythologization of the object of religious consciousness. In chapters I–III, or "Consciousness," natural consciousness knew being, first, as a "this" or universal thing, accessible to immediate apprehension; second, as—in its thinghood—essentially determinate and, thus, divided between its isolated being for itself and its relational being for another, in its presence for perception; and, third, as—in that very dividedness—the self-expression of a supersensible inner, a universal concept known to understanding. Collecting those moments, we see that the object for object-oriented consciousness is, in its totality, the purely thought universal that, opposing itself as a being for

itself to itself as a being for another in perception, is immediately apprehended or felt as a universal individual. Now this total structure is precisely that of the object—regarded formally, apart from its mythic contentual character—which Christian religious consciousness knows: God, as the purely thought, supersensible universal, expresses "it"-self as an object of perception or, for second and later generation Christians, an object imaginatively represented which, in the immediate consciousness or feeling of the rite of Communion, is felt as a universal thing, a being with which all others can identify or in which they can be subsumed.

2. Given this disclosure, namely, that object-oriented consciousness of chapters I–III is a consciousness of—formally speaking—the same object as that of religious consciousness, it becomes all the more remarkable to watch the experiential sequence by which consciousness discovers that its complex object is, at its core, itself. Of course, in one sense this has already happened; when in chapter III consciousness regards the real as, in its ultimacy, a universal concept which expresses itself in the realm of what may be perceived, it essentially takes the real as ego, or as the universal rationality of the phenomenal. But this is not at all to say that consciousness, in its knowing what the real thus understood is, recognizes that knowing itself as real in any substantial sense; and it is this recognition which is necessary for the transformation of object-oriented consciousness to self-consciousness, that is, to consciousness of the self itself, in its consciousness of its object, as the reality of that object. For this transformation, Hegel recalls three key moments from earlier in the *Phenomenology*: "observation" (chapter V. A), in which the things of nature are apprehended as the external expression of ego or (since this is the shape of ego in observational science) rational categorical structure; the development of a basic utilitarianism ("the truth of enlightenment," chapter VI. B. IIb), in which all things, precisely as appreciated by observational science, and including human persons, are treated as useful, hence as partly natural or self-subsistent and as partly cultural or "for another" in that sense; and, finally, the absolute freedom achieved by, or as, "conscience" (chapter VI. Cc), wherein ego, as pure knowledge of what is universally good, knows itself as the "inner" reality of everything, hence as the ultimate basis for any utilization of things. In these three moments, of course, we see the three basic structures of determinateness which came to light in chapters I–III. Here, however, they have a basically new meaning. Already at the outset of chapter V. A the object has the whole complex of structures worked out in chapters I–III. Here, then, the three basic structures of determinateness, in their distinct appearances in V. A, VI. B IIb, and VI. Cc, mark out not the object as such but rather stages in the subject's recognition of itself in its object. In "observation,"

the passive disposition towards the object expresses the subject's non-self-recognition; even while nature is externalized ego, it is not ego as knowing this—rather it is a universally rational order essentially indifferent to its being known, hence other than the individual ego which, as scientific consciousness, knows it. "Utilization," by contrast, appropriates as well as observes; in this posture consciousness, by its assertion that the object is partly for itself (natural) and partly for another (for use, cultural), knows its own action as use of the object to be in part the reality of the object. In "conscience," finally, this self-recognition is radicalized: as the knowledge of universal good which is the basis of and expresses itself in the "utilization" of things, "conscience" is that posture which knows itself, *as knowledge of the good*, to be the basic reality of its object. It is here, therefore, that the movement from object-oriented consciousness to self-consciousness appears to be completed; the individual self knows its own knowing to constitute reality.

3. But there is still recollective work to be done. To begin with, there is the question of how a form of moral self-consciousness, which belongs to finite spirit, can correlate with the content of religious consciousness, that is, with infinite spirit represented as God. Hegel responds to this problem by singling out, as the particular form of "conscience" necessary for the transition into absolute spirit, the "beautiful soul." The "beautiful soul" is an extreme form of "conscience"; the moral self, secure in its knowledge that its own knowledge of the good makes up the "inner" reality of everything, preserves and holds to this knowledge in its purity. This has two consequences, the first of which appears to solve the problem of the relation of finite and infinite spirit. The "beautiful soul" knows the *universal* good, and it knows this good prior to its specification in terms of particular things, acts, and interests. But this is to say, the "beautiful soul" is, as a universal knowing which has not yet taken any finite form, an infinite knowing. Hegel already indicated this in VI. Cc when he said of the "beautiful soul," "it is true that God is *immediately* present in its mind and heart, in its self," and then added that "the *immediate* relation, however, means in fact nothing else but the unity of the terms."[2] In chapter VIII, however, he goes beyond talk of "relation" and "unity of terms"—language which suggests objective identity—and declares,

> the "beautiful soul" is its own knowledge of itself in its pure, transparent unity— . . . not only the intuition of the divine but the divine's intuition of itself.[3]

Thus, through the purity and unmediatedness of its knowing of the good, consciousness as "beautiful soul" appears to be the existence, as subject, of the universal knowing which is only objectively known as God in religion. But this is not the culmination of the phenomenological movement to the absolute on account of the *second* consequence of the purity of the "beautiful soul." Precisely in order to preserve its purity, consciousness as "beautiful soul" must abstain, withhold itself from all action; for action is determinate and so involves reducing the universal good to some particular and finite significance. Action, however, is the mark of existence and reality,[4] and thus consciousness as "beautiful soul" is in a remarkable double bind: either it can preserve its status as infinite knowing at the cost of its own existence, or it can give itself over to action and so surrender its claim to infinitude. This impasse and its dialectical overcoming are, of course, not new; as Hegel remarks, the "beautiful soul" is "the one-sided shape we saw before [in VI. Cc] vanish into thin air, but also positively externalize itself and move onward."[5]

This further advance was the process of "forgiveness" wherein the extremes—universal knowing of the good and particularizing, hence selfish, action—are reconciled, and Hegel will now repeat this process. What is new, however, and what makes this more than mere repetition is the newly revealed status of the "beautiful soul." As the existing, as subject, of "the divine's intuition of itself," the "beautiful soul" is now more than a moral structure; it is the fully appropriated life of God in man. On the other hand, insofar as this appropriation is full, that is, insofar as this man is fully consciousness of the life he lives as *his own*, the structure of consciousness which emerges from the process of "forgiveness" is more than religious. The new structure is rather that of philosophical self-consciousness or, in Hegel's terminology, "absolute knowledge."

Consider first the process of "forgiveness," then the form of consciousness emergent from it. The process has three phases. To begin with, to encompass the whole good, the "beautiful soul" must keep himself from all action, for action would, even while objectifying his knowledge, make it partial, set it against the objectified knowledge or action of others; and that, because it would contradict the "beautiful soul's" claim to knowledge of the universal good, the good for all, would set it against itself; hence the "beautiful soul" has a knowledge which must remain inert, unenacted, or in simple unity, in order that its claim to universality be preserved. But—secondly—this means that this knowledge is in itself opposed to particularizing or determining action; that is, the arising of his opposite, the selfish acting self, over against him is itself necessary to his own existence, is itself implied by what he, insofar as he is real, really is; hence, the "beautiful soul" himself opposes to his own knowledge, as simple substantial unity, the particularizing action of the selfish, acting self. Now—thirdly—the internality of this opposition is itself the key to its resolution. Because the particularizing actor represents the "beautiful soul's" own otherness or opposition to itself, he needs only to recognize himself in, or as, this other, and the double bind we noted earlier is overcome. The "beautiful soul's" acceptance of the necessity of action—the "forgiveness" of selfishness which consummates chapter VI. Cc—now takes on the status of the infinite's recognition of itself in, or as, the finite. The "beautiful soul" ceases to be merely "beautiful," standing aloof from and in contrast to the other, and comes to know himself as that which comprises both—action which determines and objectifies knowledge and knowledge which is determined and objectified through action.

The form of consciousness which emerges from this recollected process is, in Hegel's terms, absolute knowledge or the "concept." On the one hand, the unity which this consciousness knows itself to be unites the same fundamental moments within itself as did the unity known by religious consciousness: simple substance, the self-opposition of this substance, as universal, to itself as particular finite self, and the reunification of these as aspects of one another within this three-phase process. This contentual identity of the two unities is to be expected, of course, since the "beautiful soul," in its uttermost withdrawal from finitude is, according to Hegel, God himself. On the other hand, the new unity also overcomes the fundamental self-alienation of religious consciousness. Not only is it known, but it is also that which consciousness knows *itself to be*: it is thereby the object of religious consciousness *become subject for itself*, and thereby transcending the object-subject separation itself. As such, it is all that 'is,' but existing *as self-knowing*. This is not to say— and the *Encyclopedia* goes on to show this—that substance/subject, God/man, universal/particular, object/subject, being/consciousness become meaningless or illusory polarities. On the contrary, their significance as polarities, that is, as polarizations or differentiations of unity, is only first secured with the disclosure of this unity; and this unity, in turn, exists and explicates itself only through such self-differentiation. In this sense, as the irreducible one which is through self-differentiation, this unity is "absolute," and the knowing or grasping of it which *it itself is and knows itself to be* is "absolute knowledge."

Temporality and History

Temporality and Absolute Knowledge

Hegel's remarks on temporality in chapter VIII must remain obscure so long as they are not appreciated within the context of the fundamental thesis of the *Phenomenology* as a whole. That thesis, which the work itself is intended to demonstrate, is that consciousness, *qua* object-oriented, necessarily transcends itself and shows itself to be the movement of becoming the concept, that is, of taking within itself the otherness which, regarded naively, appears as the ultimacy of the subject-object separation. In traditional terms, consciousness is the dialectical unity of the four Aristotelian causes. Whereas, on the one hand, in its object-oriented modes it is itself the *matter* that has, as its potentiality and innermost *goal*, to be subject to the *form* of object-subject unity, it is also, on the other hand, both the *agency* for the formative process that achieves this goal and, in this achievement, the actuality of object-subject unity. And if, on the first count, it always has an other external to it that it must take within its thereby ever-expanding self, on the second count it is that fully self-sufficient being that, containing all otherness within itself, must also preserve it in its externality as a pervasive feature of its genesis. In this dialectical unity of the four causes, two characters of the Aristotelian world-view—or, more precisely, of a naive appropriation of that worldview—are overcome. First, as already implied, the object-realm has been grasped as, in its very existence as *object*-realm, a moment of the subject's own being—with the result, however, being not a subjectivism (a one-way subordination of object to subject) but, rather, a grasp of object-subject unity which transcends both traditional objectivism and modern subjectivism. Secondly, any naive conception of maturity as a stage *following* genesis becomes impossible. Though, on the one hand, the standpoint of absolute knowledge or the concept follows and presupposes all of the preceding shapes, it involves, on the other hand, the insight that it itself has been present all along, present as that inherent goal the actual attaining of which is the motion through the preceding shapes to itself. But this is to say: the *presence* of the concept *in* the preceding shapes has the form, in each case, of that shape's *need*—in order that it be validated—to be transformed, to be converted into a higher shape, that shape, in particular, which saves the first shape's truth from that shape's own one-sidedness and partiality. Now, that need, the necessity to become other, is what Hegel means by "time." When Hegel writes,

> [Time] is the *outer*, intuited pure self which is *not grasped* by the self, the merely intuited concept,[6]

he gives a characterization, from the standpoint of absolute knowledge, of the appearance of time insofar as it is grasped from a non-absolute standpoint. The need to become other, or the need which consciousness has of proceeding beyond each of its particular object-oriented shapes, as moments, presents itself to the self—as it exists *qua* one of these shapes—as external. Each shape initially takes itself to be the ultimate shape, that is, the self *in* each non-absolute shape mistakes itself as ultimate, so that the need to become other appears to it to arise *from the outside*, from a source external to consciousness as such. Likewise, the whole sequence must appear as a collection externally linked or in a medium—sequentia*lity*, seria*lity*, or "time," as such—external to what lies *in* this medium. But, says Hegel, this externality is only a function of the *self*'s having not yet achieved full self-consciousness, that is, of consciousness' failure to have grasped *as its own* the necessity of actually becoming what it ultimately is, namely, the concept or absolute self-consciousness as such. Of course, once this "last" standpoint is actually achieved, consciousness will recognize the necessity as its own, will be the very grasping of otherness as internal to it; having actually *become*, through the process of its development, what it ultimately *is*, it will recognize that it *is*, essentially, this very *becoming* or process. It is here, however, that the naive view of maturity as the "last" stage in genesis becomes most deeply problematic. Precisely because this "last" stage entails consciousness' recognition of itself as the process culminating in this stage and of the necessity of this proceeding or becoming-other as its own necessity, this stage transcends the process-character itself. It cannot be grasped merely as "last," for this implies that it exists *in* time, *in* the medium of sequentiality, whereas, in truth, this very medium, namely, the otherness of process or sequence, exists in it as a function of its own self-relation. Or, more strictly put, to grasp absolute knowledge as the "last" stage is one-sided. Rather, it is *both* true that, as Hegel says, "spirit necessarily appears in time" *and* true that, as he also says, "when [the concept] grasps itself, it sets aside its time-form."[7] From a non-absolute standpoint, spirit exists in time—but from the standpoint of absolute knowledge, time or temporality is only the form of spirit's existence for itself as non-absolute, the pervasive mode which, as a *proceeding toward* full self-consciousness, it assumes in its own eyes *before* the completion of this process, *before* its vision has become fully reflexive.

This radical reflection does not, however, make time meaningless, non-existent, mere illusion, and so on. For, as Hegel continues, the process toward self-consciousness is nothing else than the task which constitutes *actual history*.[8] Hegel's philosophy of history is too large an issue to treat frontally here. Nonetheless, it should be observed that, even while consciousness as the concept or absolute knowledge knows its process as an *internal* necessity, this very insight entails the reflexive recognition, in turn, that it itself presupposes this process. Except as a culmination of historical process, the insight which "transcends"—in the sense of "grasps as its own and as a whole"—this very process is impossible.[9] Consciousness, then, relativizes itself to history at the same time that it relativizes history to itself, grasps historicity as its own essential character at the same time that, in this very grasp, it transcends this character.[10]

The History of Philosophy and Culture

In paragraphs 803–4 Hegel gives content—both positive and exemplary in function—to his claim that actual history is the process toward self-consciousness. These paragraphs are terse and obscure, but essentially they trace the movement from the posture of consciousness culminative for the Middle Ages, the feeling of Communion, to that which is culminative for the Enlightenment, Hegel's own grasp of the movement of spirit. These paragraphs are interesting not only because Hegel reveals his own conception of the historical place of his own philosophical orientation but also because they both gather together preceding moments of the *Phenomenology* itself and illustrate one of Hegel's fundamental contentions about historical process.

The initial step Hegel notes is the turn from the "alien manner" of self-consciousness represented by Christianity—"alien" because, as noted earlier, feeling implies radical heteronomy, dependence of man on an alien, unworldly power (what Schleiermacher calls *"das schlechthinnige Abhängigkeitsgefühl,"* "the feeling of utter dependence," which is the feeling of God's power)—back into the actual and present world; this is the movement which occurs in the Renaissance and which, as part of the emergence of "insight" out of "belief" (cf. chapter VI. B. I. b, II. a), first takes the form of "observation of nature" (cf. V. A). From this beginning of post-medieval culture, consciousness proceeds through

1. Descartes' rationalist discovery of the unity of thought (*res cogitans*) and existence as extension (*res extensa*), a unity initially formulated in Spinoza's doctrine of the unitary substance,
2. Through the recoiling, opposite assertion—formulated in Leibniz's doctrine of monadic substances—of the primacy of individuality,
3. Through, further, the actual cultural development of individuality which passes from Enlightenment utilitarianism (cf. chapter VI. B. II. b) through the "absolute freedom" of the French Revolution and Terror (cf. chapter VI. B. III) to the explicit assertion of the primacy of "Individual Will" in the moral philosophy of, especially, Kant and post-Kantian Romanticism (cf. chapter VI. C) into, finally,
4. The philosophical revelation of the underlying thought of this movement,

the $I = I$ as articulated first by Fichte (cf. PhS §803), then antithetically by Schelling (cf. PhS §803), and, finally, in a way which both integrates and surpasses these, by Hegel himself (cf. PhS §804).

Of this reconstruction, terse as it is, two interpretive remarks might be made.

(i) Hegel's division of postmedieval history into these four stages reflects, first, what he will say both in the concluding paragraph and in the preface about historical development as "recollective" or a process of "inwardization," within the thematic unity of an epoch, of the self-consciousness achieved in previous epochs. The theme which constitutes the unity of postmedieval Enlightenment culture is this-worldly thinking, the rejection of the "alien manner" of Christianity for the self-responsible rationality which begins in Renaissance "observation." But this rejection and reorientation, a determinate negation of medieval Christian otherworldliness, signifies not a simple rejection of the past but rather the establishment of a new general orientation within which the past will be reappropriated. Hegel explicitly points out that "(a)"—the doctrine, articulated by Spinoza, of the unity of thought and extension as modes of the one substance—marks an "inwardization" and "revival" of the "substance" of the Oriental religion of "Light" (cf. chapter VII.A, especially a); "(b)," in turn, the opposing assertion by Leibniz (himself a Grecophile) of the primacy of the individual, would seem to mark a reappropriation of the individualism which is the underlying theme of the Greek ethical world (cf. chapter VI. A. a, b), expressed in the culmination of its religious art (cf. chapter VII. B, especially c); "(c)"—the primacy of the individual will as conscience—we have already seen to be an "inwardization" of Christianity, first in the social-political (chapter VI. B. III), then in the individual-moral sphere (chapter VI. C, especially b); "(d)," finally, is the rising to explicitness of that which, as the result of the movement which passes through these stages, marks the development of modern consciousness beyond them: the recognition of $I = I$. Seen in this way, modern consciousness represents the culmination of preceding history, a culmination which, as such, presupposes and results from a reappropriation of preceding history.

(ii) The fourth stage, or "(d)," within the interior development of the modern epoch is that which is articulated by Fichte, Schelling, and Hegel. Hegel's remarks on this triad are obscure in their detail, but their general line of thought is visible. $I = I$, firstly, is the philosophical thematization of the essence of reality as this emerges in the assertion of the primacy of individual will in "(c)"; Fichte is the first, and Schelling the second, to bring to light the seminal truth of Kantian philosophy. This truth might be generally expressed in several ways; for example, the external (extension) is a function of the internal (time), or reality is constituted by the active self-identity of consciousness. But, from Hegel's point of view, the articulations given by Fichte and Schelling to this principle are each one-sided. The absolute self-identity of consciousness, or of the self in consciousness, is, says Hegel, "the movement which reflects itself into itself";[11] by this phrase Hegel recalls the dialectical action of self-consciousness; the self-identity of the self in self-consciousness consists in its double action of distinguishing itself from itself (so that it is present to itself as other from itself) and cancelling or negating this distinction (so that it grasps this other as itself, or grasps itself as the unity of itself and the other). Fichte's conception of this process, Hegel's remarks suggest, one-sidedly emphasizes the moment of self-distinction and thus sets ego over against itself as other, emphasizing its character as self or subject constantly confronting itself as other than itself (the Fichtean "non-ego"); the categorical expression of this constant otherness, an otherness constantly "to be" overcome, is the temporality (and, more specifically, the future-orientedness) of experience. (See the preceding remarks on "time.") Schelling, by contrast with Fichte, one-sidedly emphasizes the cancelledness of this distinction, the "absolute unity" of self with itself—to the exclusion of its otherness; hence, for Schelling, the self appears not only as subject but also as substance, or rather as absolutely undifferentiated substance; by consequence, the diversity or otherness of experience must appear as merely contingent and, indeed, must disappear in the "empty abyss of the absolute"—this is the famous "night in which all cows are black." For Hegel, the reciprocal one-sidedness of the two articulations of self needs to be overcome in the recognition of both sides within the context of the whole movement of "spirit." In paragraph 804 he expresses synoptically the insight which underlies the movement of the whole *Phenomenology,* that selfless substance and insubstantial self are abstractions and express themselves as such, each by calling forth the other in a relationship which, precisely because it precedes either moment alone, expresses itself as the overcoming of their distinction in the emergence of a substantial self.

The Threefold Beginning

This emergence, the concluding achievement of the *Phenomenology,* is at the same time a threefold beginning. Hegel devotes his closing paragraphs (805–8) to the explication of this.

First, in having arrived at the concept—that shape of consciousness which, transcending the distinction of object from subject, is substance become totally self-conscious or (in terms which, should we forget what the *Phenomenology* has brought us to, must sound absurd) being which is the thinking of itself—we are ready for an absolute ontology. In terms of the rhythm of transition and recommencement from chapter to chapter in the *Phenomenology*, we have come to a new shape of consciousness and must let it set forth its conception of reality. What distinguishes this new shape, however, is that, as substance or being become totally self-conscious, its conception of reality will be immediately the same as its self-conception; for the concept is consciousness existing as the very knowing which knows itself to be that which reality is and which is reality. We have arrived, then, at the unity of being and thinking which exists as the thinking which thinks itself and knows what it is. This thinking is the content of the first moment of the "system," the *Logic*. As thinking, it presents itself in a process through moments; in fact, in its motion from "Being" through "Essence" to "Concept" it presents precisely the motion of God as presented in chapter VII—with the crucial qualification, however, that now there can be no estrangement of consciousness from its object, any inadequacy which will give rise to a new standpoint. Rather, the divine process is presented in its purely conceptual, dialectical necessity, a necessity which, because it derives from the object-subject unity itself and nothing external to it, is equally its freedom or self-determination. The key structural character of the *Logic* is that, in the presentation of each moment of the process of being thinking itself, the process as a whole is apparent and present-to-mind. There is no tension but rather a pure translucence which relates each moment to the process as a whole, such that the latter is fully contained and expressed in the former.

This purely conceptual motion, however, implies its own impurity as well. Or, to put this another way, precisely the unity of object and subject entails their disunity not only as aspects of explicit unity (as in the *Logic*) but also as actually torn apart from one another, as alien or abstract moments in non-philosophical life. That alienness, as the negation of the unity of the moments as moments, is precisely what is negated—and so, as we have seen, also preserved—in the attainment of absolute knowledge. For this reason, the *Logic* points both backward to the *Phenomenology* and forward to the second and third parts of the "system," the *Philosophy of Nature* and the *Philosophy of Spirit*.

The *Logic* points back to the *Phenomenology*, first of all, in that the alienness of object from subject will be the *hiddenness* from the subject of the identity it has with itself as object, or with the object which is itself. The result of this hiddenness is that reality appears, to the subject, solely as object. But just insofar as reality *appears to the subject* solely as object, this very appearance entails the reality of the subject as well. This situation is, of course, that of sense-certainty, which takes being itself as its object and regards itself as a merely contingent, inessential moment. The *Logic*, then, returns us to the beginning of the *Phenomenology*; or, what is the same point, the standpoint of absolute knowledge or self-consciousness preserves within it, as that standpoint whose truth it is, the un-self-consciousness of immediate experience.

At the same time, Hegel also points out that this circle is not broad enough. Being is still, in immediate experience, related to consciousness as its object. But their absolute union for the concept (the last shape of consciousness) entails, as well, the absolute negation of their union, that is, the self utterly externalized. The utter externalization of the self, or of the unity of object-subject, is utter selflessness, and this Hegel identifies as, on the one hand, "nature," wherein the self is outside of itself in the double sense of existing spread out in space and in continual development, and, on the other hand, "history," wherein the self is outside of itself in the double sense of existing as a "free contingent happening" and, again, in continual development.

Now, these modes of non-union must, like the very union of which each is the negation, be *for the concept*; that is, the concept must, as the standpoint of *absolute* knowledge, know itself in its own selflessness, its own utter otherness. Precisely this being for itself completes the sense in which the concept *is* the standpoint of absolute knowledge. Hence the *Logic* fits together with the *Philosophy of Nature* and the *Philosophy of Spirit*, the three together comprising the complete "system" of absolute knowledge.

This system, finally, is circular in form. This is the logical result of the double sense of selflessness or externality with regard both to space and to time. The concept or self in space, existing as natural being, is not only selfless but in continual abandonment of itself in its very selflessness—but this means: out of nature arises, as initially a natural being, conscious life or subject. Likewise, the concept or self in time, existing historically as "free contingent happening," is not only selfless but in continual abandonment of its very selflessness—and this means: history is the process toward self-consciousness, the series of epochs or world-forms wherein, through each successive world's "recollection" or "inwardization," *Er-innerung*, of the preceding, consciousness gradually becomes self-conscious of itself as spirit and, in culmination of this becoming, attains the shape of the concept. Thus, the *Philosophy of Nature* points, through the *Philosophy of Spirit*, toward the *Logic*.

Our entryway into this systematic circle is, finally and to begin with, the *Phenomenology*, the propaedeutic to absolute knowledge.

NOTES

This essay was first published in the *Graduate Faculty Philosophy Journal* 7.2 (Winter 1978): 195–219. It is republished here with only minor revisions for the sake of clarity.

1. All the paragraph numbers (§) and quotations in this chapter refer to the translation by A. V. Miller, *Hegel's Phenomenology of Spirit* (Oxford: Oxford University Press, 1977).

2. § 656, p. 398.

3. Ibid.

4. See especially chapter V. Ca for Hegel's argument for this.

5. § 795, p. 483.

6. § 801, p. 487.

7. Ibid.

8. § 803, p. 488

9. Culmination of history does not, of course, mean its end (in the sense of absolute *terminus*). The trivial point to be observed here is that the achievement of absolute knowledge preserves, as its own medium, time; so time must be ongoing. More interestingly, Hegel's doctrine of epochs suggests that there may be a number of culminations and (as the corresponding forms of self-consciousness) relative absolutes. Does this open the way to the possibility that the achievement of absolute knowledge, or the concept, whereas absolute in the sense that it relativizes to itself all that precedes it, may also be partial in relation to a still more comprehensive standpoint that is yet to reveal itself? In pondering this question, it should be noted from the outset that its very language belongs to the history of consciousness of which the achievement of absolute knowledge is the culmination. If Hegel's doctrine of epochs is right, this is inescapable. Whether this implies the negation of the possibility or—what is quite different and may point to its affirmation—to the negation of our present ability to adequately entertain it is another question.

10. It is important to stress that Hegel's grasp of time does not produce a vision of man as atemporal. Though the grasp itself, self-consciously understood as the self-*qua*-concept's grasp of itself as such, transcends time, what it grasps is the fundamentality of time as the character of man-*qua*-consciousness in the process of self-development. What, however, is the specific structure of time? Four remarks might be made here. (1) Hegel does not *focally* address this question in the *Phenomenology*. (2) But, since the process of self-development is the processive reformation of man's relation to himself in experience, and since experience is, phenomenologically conceived, the appearance of this very relation to man himself, time will itself, though not necessarily *as such*, be given to man-*qua*-con-

sciousness. (3) The character of time as itself apparent will depend on the stage of self-development which man has attained. Hence, to construct an example, Oriental man (chapter VII. A) will experience time differently, have a different sense of temporality, than Enlightenment man (chapter VI. B); to make a rough characterization, a man who knows the self as divine nature will experience reality as cyclically repeating itself, whereas a man who knows the self as human fabricator will experience reality as open-endedly progressive. (4) The consciousness that knows itself as concept, finally, that is, as the unity of the process of self-distinction and self-reunion, will know time not only as the mode of the appearance of the self to itself *qua* subject *in* this process but, moreover, will, *as* that subject *in* process, experience reality as the movement of appropriation of substance. As *appropriating*, this subject will be *ongoing* and future-oriented; as appropriating *of substance*, it will be directed toward what it *already* is: thus time will have the structure of a revitalization, in the future, of the past, this itself being the whole character of the present. Notice here the unification of the characters of linear and cyclic motion, that is, of "advancing beyond . . ." and "returning to. . . ."

11. § 803, p. 489.

21

Jon Stewart

The Architectonic of Hegel's Phenomenology of Spirit

After the virulent criticisms of Nietzsche, Kierkegaard, and much of the analytic tradition, systematic philosophy has for the most part gone into eclipse in contemporary European thought.[1] The main target of these criticisms was often the daunting edifice of the Hegelian system which dominated so much of nineteenth-century philosophy. Despite a small handful of scholars who try with might and main to salvage this edifice,[2] the general belief among scholars today is that at bottom Hegel's philosophical project as a system is simply bankrupt and indefensible all around.[3] Of all the texts in the Hegelian *corpus*, the *Phenomenology of Spirit* with it plethora of themes and troubled composition has been in particular singled out for criticism as a disunified and unsystematic text.[4] Typical of this general belief is Kaufmann's characterization: "the *Phenomenology* is certainty *unwissenschaftlich*, undisciplined, arbitrary, full of digressions, not a monument to the austerity of the intellectual conscience and to carefulness and precision but a wild, bold, unprecedented book."[5] The *Phenomenology* is thus seen simply as an eclectic and at times bizarre collection of atomic analyses on sundry topics. This preconception of the *Phenomenology* as a disunified text then leads to a predetermined and, in my view, erroneous interpretive approach.

The strategy of a number of specialists, who have found Hegel's system so impenetrable in its overall architectonic and so problematic at its particular transitions, has been simply to give up entirely on his project as a system and to approach his philosophy in an episodic manner. With this interpretive method one tries to understand individual sections of the *Phenomenology* in abstraction from the systematic contexts in which they appear. This seems intuitive enough since the contexts of Hegel's analyses are so varied that it is often difficult to imagine what could be the schematic connection between them in any case. This leads many scholars to try to exploit the isolated sections and analyses of the *Phenomenology* for their own purposes. Pöggeler expresses this tendency with the following rhetorical questions: "Should we not simply keep to the things that the *Phenomenology* offers as positive results—for example, concerning physiognomy or the Roman world? Should we not, when possible, exploit Hegel's work as was done in the Middle Ages when people went to ancient buildings in search of construction materials for their own structures without any regard or consideration given to their disparate forms?"[6] In this way the commentator can make Hegel topical by showing how the individual issues that the philosopher treats are similar to contemporary problem constellations, thus emphasizing, for example, Hegel's philosophy of action,[7] his philosophy of language,[8] or his account of demonstratives.[9] Scholars of this persuasion try to explicate these sections out of context as containing interesting and relevant issues in themselves. In this way, it appears these commentators can save Hegel from himself, given that his system appears so hopeless. However, this strategy of selection and omission, although attractive to modern scholars bent ever more toward specialization, is seriously misguided since Hegel himself, like the rest of the German idealists before him,[10] expressly insisted on the systematic nature of philosophy as an intellectual enterprise.

Hegel believed that truth could only be expressed in terms of a system, and he explains this in numerous places, insisting that the particular parts of the system are meaningful only inside the systematic context in which they appear. "Apart from their interdependence and organic union," he writes, "the truths of philosophy are valueless, and must then be treated as baseless hypotheses, or personal convictions" (EL §14; Enz. 41).[11] A truth in a philosophical system has its truth value only in relation to the other members of the system, and an atomic thesis asserted without relation to a wider system cannot rely on such a system to provide a context and thus to support it since apart from such a system it stands without relation to other concepts and theories which give it meaning in the first place.[12] For example, a tile in a mosaic seen on its own in abstraction from the other tiles of which the mosaic is composed is in a sense meaningless, that is, one could not divine the picture of the mosaic as a whole with knowledge of the single tile alone. The tile has its true meaning only in its relation to the rest of the tiles and to the mosaic as a whole. Likewise in philosophy, according to Hegel, the truth and meaning of the individual propositions depend upon the context in which they are found in the system as a whole. I take this to be the point of the well-known passage in the preface of the *Phenomenology* where Hegel claims, "The True is the whole" (PhS §20; PG 19).[13] In other words, whatever truth there is in the individual claims of a system lies in the organic or systematic relation of those claims to one another inside the whole of the system. In the *Encyclopaedia Logic*, Hegel says of the absolute Idea, "The science of this Idea must form a system.... Truth, then, is only possible as a universe or totality of thought.... Unless it is a system, a philosophy is not a scientific production" (EL §14; Enz. 41).[14] As we can see from these passages, Hegel is quite forthcoming with respect to the relation of truth to a systematic philosophy. The notion of a philosophical system is not something that one aspires to attain merely for the sake of some mild aesthetic pleasure gained from a certain order or symmetry or from the satisfaction won by being able to pigeonhole sundry concepts under orderly headings, but rather it is, according to Hegel's holism, essentially bound up with the very notion of truth itself.

If truth can only be expressed in the form of a philosophical system, then we do Hegel a disservice by randomly excerpting parts of his system which we find interesting and relevant to our contemporary philosophical agenda while ignoring the role they play in the system as a whole. This approach misunderstands the spirit of Hegel's systematic enterprise and dismisses his own clear statements of explanation and intention in this regard. By excerpting individual analyses out of their systematic context, we lose the very meaning of those analyses. If we are going to talk about Hegel at all, we must also talk about the Hegelian system. Although perhaps we will not be able to understand the most opaque parts of the Hegelian architectonic, it is more advisable, given Hegel's conception of philosophy, simply to admit this up front than to give up on it, and Hegel with it, altogether.[15]

One of the central interpretive challenges of the book as a whole is in a sense posed by what Hegel says about the *Phenomenology* in a letter to Schelling. There he claims that the work contains an intricate "interlacing of cross-references back and forth"[16] that he unfortunately was unable to make as clear as he would have liked. It seems to me then that one of the appropriate tasks of the secondary literature on the *Phenomenology* is to try to uncover these cross-references and by so doing to uncover the hidden structure of the work as a whole. In this essay, I would like to attempt to reconstruct the systematic structure of Hegel's *Phenomenology of Spirit* with respect to its formal unity. Of course, in an investigation of this kind, this can amount to little more than a sketch since a full-length commentary would be required to demonstrate the systematic connections one by one. However, although this analysis will serve only as a general outline, this is in itself not a negligible service since, as I have indicated, Hegel's systematic pretensions, especially in the *Phenomenology*, have long been subject to attack, and thus a study which could indicate how this part of his system might be at least plausible would be valuable in its own right. Since my principal aim is to demonstrate the unity of form in the *Phenomenology*, I will not be able in my discussion to offer more than the most cursory account of the unitary movement of the *contents* of the individual sections and chapters. Moreover, I will not treat the biographical questions concerning the turbulent composition of the *Phenomenology* since this too would require a study in itself. In order to establish the unity of form, some scholars have attempted to read the *Phenomenology* by transposing the structure of Hegel's *Logic* onto it.[17] These attempts, however, blur the systematic relation between the two works by collapsing them into a single project. Instead, my strategy for establishing the unity of the text will be to take as a model the revised version of the table of contents that Hegel wrote after the completion of the work and then to test this organizational scheme against a number of passages throughout the *Phenomenology* that serve as indicators for the systematic structure as a whole. These passages, I wish to argue, when pursued consistently, will lead us to a picture of the general economy of the text which contains parallel chapters and sections as Hegel indicated in his letter to Schelling. In my account, I will linger somewhat on the "Reason" chapter since it, in my view, holds the key to the structure of the work as a whole. An understanding of this hitherto neglected structure, it is hoped, will in turn help us better to understand this difficult text as it was originally intended to be understood by allowing us to place the individual analyses in their proper context. By uncovering this structure, we will also be in a position to criticize the "patchwork" interpretations that are so inimical to Hegel's own expressed methodology and conception of philosophy.

The Table of Contents

The first major difficulty with respect to the systematic unity of the work concerns the table of contents. When one critically examines the outline indicated there, one will notice straightaway the rather confusing mixture of Latin letters and Roman numerals, sufficient to discourage the most intrepid interpreter who wishes to insist on the systematicity of the work. The story of how this confused table of contents came about is not a simple one. When Hegel first wrote the *Phenomenology*, he used the Roman numerals for the sections "Sense-Certainty," "Perception," "Force and the Understanding," "The Truth of Self-Certainty," "The Certainty and Truth of Reason," "spirit," "Religion" and finally "Absolute Knowing." This first scheme can thus be represented as follows:

The First Scheme

I. Sense-Certainty
II. Perception
III. Force and the Understanding
IV. The Truth of Self-Certainty
   A. Lordship and Bondage
   B. Freedom of Self-Consciousness
V. The Certainty and Truth of Reason
   A. Observing Reason
   B. The Actualization of Rational Self-Consciousness Through its own Activity
   C. Individuality which takes itself to be Real in and for itself
VI. Spirit
   A. The True Spirit. The Ethical Order
   B. Self-Alienated Spirit. Culture
   C. Spirit that is Certain of Itself. Morality
VII. Religion
   A. Natural Religion
   B. Religion in the Form of Art
   C. The Revealed Religion
VIII. Absolute Knowing

This organizational scheme has caused a great deal of confusion concerning the disproportionate lengths of these sections, some of which include as few as nine pages in the English translation (i.e., "Sense-Certainty") while others contain as many as 146 (i.e., spirit"). Hegel, however, revised this table of contents in a very illuminating way when he was reading the proofs for the book.[18] In the second scheme he used the Latin letters A, B, and C for the "Consciousness," "Self-Consciousness," and "Reason" chapters respectively (and thus, it is due to this change that the argument arises that the original plan for the work consisted of only three chapters). At that time he also affixed the double letters AA, BB, CC, and DD to "Reason," "spirit," "Religion," and "Absolute Knowing" respectively. Thus, the second plan for the work appears as follows:

The Second Scheme
A. Consciousness
B. Self-Consciousness
C. (AA.) Reason
  A. Observing Reason
  B. The Actualization of Rational Self-Consciousness Through its own Activity
  C. Individuality which takes itself to be Real in and for itself
(BB.) Spirit
A. The True Spirit. The Ethical Order
B. Self-Alienated Spirit. Culture
C. Spirit that is Certain of Itself. Morality
(CC.) Religion
A. Natural Religion
B. Religion in the Form of Art
C. The Revealed Religion
(DD.) Absolute Knowing

The confusion about the table of contents stems from the fact that the various editions of the *Phenomenology* in German, as well as the English translations, have combined these two organizational schemes instead of opting for the one or the other.[19] The result is an extremely confusing mixture of Latin letters, both single and double, and Roman numerals. This, however, is simply a problem with the editing of Hegel's text and not with its intrinsic structure.

The key argument that this change gives rise to is that Hegel changed his mind about the structure of the work during its composition and was compelled to revise the table of contents as a result of the change.[20] Thus, according to this view the text must be disunified since it compresses two different organizational schemes into one. This argument is perhaps valid enough when applied to the editors of the *Phenomenology* who combined the two versions of the table of contents into one, but it amounts to a simple *non sequitur* when it is applied to Hegel's text itself. Simply from the fact the Hegel changed his mind about the structure of the text and subsequently revised the table of contents in accordance with that change, it does not follow that the text itself is disunified. Nothing here necessarily excludes the possibility that he was able to incorporate the first scheme adequately into the second, which he then represented in the revised table of contents. The most this argument can establish is that due to the perceived need for revision in the table of contents on Hegel's part, there *may be reason to suspect* that there is a discontinuity in the text, but in order ultimately to prove this, one must examine the arguments of the text itself.

In my view, the changes that Hegel made in his revised version of the table of contents are in fact quite helpful. When we regard the ultimate organizational scheme as authoritative, since after all it represents his considered opinion, then we have a fairly clear outline of the structure of the work itself which corresponds to its internal argumentation. What then makes this simple change so illuminating? As I will argue below in more detail, what Hegel means to indicate with the single letters of the second version is a set of parallel structures; thus, "Consciousness" and "Self-Consciousness" are meant to run their course in a fashion parallel to one another. On the other hand, what he indicates with the double letters is that the dialectic is to return to the beginning; thus, "Reason," "spirit," and "Religion" return to the same starting point that we saw in "Consciousness" and work through the same material again under different aspects in accordance with the sphere that each governs. The important point for our purposes is that Hegel's revision of the table of contents is a welcome aid to those searching for a key to the systematic unity of the work. In the following, I wish to test this thesis in a very general way against the actual analyses of the *Phenomenology* and in a more detailed fashion against Hegel's own explicit statements about the systematic structure of the work. I will thus briefly work through the text of the *Phenomenology* section by section with an eye toward the nature of the relationships of the various chapters and sections to one another.

CONSCIOUSNESS

Hegel begins the *Phenomenology* with his account of "Consciousness," which consists of three discrete conceptions of objectivity, all sharing the fundamental realist belief in an independently existing external world of objects which are ontologically prior to human subjects and their capacity to know. The analyses of "Sense-Certainty," "Perception," and "Force and the Understanding" represent attempts to demonstrate that objects are simply given as predetermined entities. The "Consciousness" chapter thus concerns above all the object sphere or what Hegel refers to as the "in-itself." The challenge in the "Consciousness" chapter is to give a complete account of the determination of objectivity with reference to the object sphere alone; however, in the course of the dialectic this conception proves to be inadequate and collapses under the weight of its own internal contradictions. What consciousness learns is that even in its most basic attempts to conceive of an object as, for example, a thing with properties or an unseen force behind the appearances, there are certain universal concepts involved which are not, strictly speaking, to be found in the empirical manifold or in the object sphere. These concepts can only be accounted for by an appeal to the human capacity for thought, and thus the human subject is drawn into what was originally an attempt to think the object as an independent ontological entity. As a necessary presupposition for the determination of objectivity, the subject sphere must be taken into account as well. This then leads us to the "for-itself" sphere of "Self-Consciousness," where the categories are reversed and the self-conscious subject is given ontological priority, with the world of objects thought to be dependent on it. These two units "Consciousness" and "Self-Consciousness" run parallel to one another in their respective spheres of in-itself and for-itself. The analyses in the "Consciousness" chapter that are given with respect to individual objects are then in "Self-Consciousness" reapplied to the self-conscious subject.

Self-Consciousness

The structure of the "Self-Consciousness" chapter is somewhat problematic. Its appearance in the table of contents displays straightaway a certain asymmetry. Whereas Hegel in the rest of the book orders his chapters into three sections, here we seem to have only two, "A. Lordship and Bondage" and "B. Freedom of Self-Consciousness," both of which apparently fall under the heading of "IV. The Truth of Self-Certainty." Because of this asymmetry, there is some confusion about the status of the section "The Truth of Self-Certainty." Does it encompass the entire "Self-Consciousness" chapter since it is the only heading with Roman numerals or is it a simple introduction to the chapter which officially begins with "Lordship and Bondage"? This typical understanding of the problem, however, once again rests upon an interpretation that combines the two versions of the table of contents. But when we concentrate only on the second version, the problem becomes less acute. First the "Self-Consciousness" chapter, referred to with the letter B, seems unproblematically to follow the "Consciousness" chapter, which bears the letter A, without any further commentary about the organization or division of the contents of the chapter. Now what are we to make of the question of the structure of "Self-Consciousness"? My thesis is that the material that precedes the "Lordship and Bondage" section,[21] which according to some interpretations is only introductory,[22] is in fact expected to do philosophical work and thus is not merely intended as an introduction. Specifically, I wish to argue that this section, in fact, forms the first argumentative step in the "Self-Consciousness" chapter and that it represents the first of a three-step argument that is complemented by "Lordship and Bondage" and "Freedom of Self-Consciousness."[23] I will refer to this material for the sake of simplicity as the "The Truth of Self-Certainty," although originally this title was apparently intended to cover the dialectical movements of "Lordship and Bondage" and the "Freedom of Self-Consciousness" as well. Thus, I propose to read the "Self-Consciousness" chapter as containing the following structure: "1. The Truth of Self-Certainty" (PhS §§166–77), "2. Lordship and Bondage" (PhS §§178–96), and "3. Freedom of Self-Consciousness" (PhS §§197–230).

There are three important arguments that speak in favor of this view and against the thesis that "The Truth of Self-Certainty" constitutes only introductory material or forms something distinct from the course of the argumentation of the rest of the "Self-Consciousness" chapter. First, when Hegel reworked the same material in the *Encyclopaedia*, he removed the apparent asymmetry in the "Self-Consciousness" chapter and used the material that I am calling "The Truth of Self-Certainty" as the first part of a three-step argument in precisely the way I have indicated above. In the *Philosophy of Mind*,[24] which constitutes part three of the *Encyclopaedia*, the "Self-Consciousness" chapter is organized as follows:

> B. Self-Consciousness
> α. Appetite
> β. Self-Consciousness Recognitive
> γ. Universal Self-Consciousness

From the contents of this chapter it is clear that "α. Appetite" corresponds to "The Truth of Self-Certainty," where the key term is "desire." It is likewise obvious that "β. Self-Consciousness Recognitive" corresponds to "Lordship and Bondage," where the key category is recognition (*Anerkennung*), and finally that "γ. Universal Self-Consciousness" corresponds to "Freedom of Self-Consciousness."

Second, in addition to Hegel's account of "Self-Consciousness" in the *Encyclopaedia*, we also have his analysis from *The Philosophical Propaedeutic*, written during Hegel's Nuremberg period from 1808 to 1811, shortly after the *Phenomenology*. "Self-Consciousness," according to the discussion there, likewise contains three different moments:

Self-Consciousness has, in its formative development or movement, three stages:
1. Of *Desire* in so far as it is directed to other things;
2. Of the relation of *Master and Slave* in so far as it is directed to another self-consciousness unlike itself;
3. Of the *Universal Self-Consciousness* which recognizes itself in other self-consciousnesses and is identical with them as they are identical with it.[25]

The course of his discussion there likewise leaves no ambiguity about the fact that the material preceding the "Lordship and Bondage" dialectic in the *Phenomenology* corresponds to the first stage, that is, that of "desire," in the *Propaedeutic*.

The third argument that speaks against the thesis that the material preceding "Lordship and Bondage" forms only an introductory section concerns the subject matter of the section itself. When we examine the text closely, we see that the argument here parallels the argument that was given in "Sense-Certainty," the first section of the "Consciousness" chapter. In "Sense-Certainty" we are concerned with the pure being of the object, which at the beginning of "Self-Consciousness" becomes reinterpreted as the pure being of the subject. Moreover, "Lordship and Bondage" parallels the "Perception" section in a similar fashion. In "Perception" a second object is introduced, and the categories of identity and difference become relevant for the determination of objectivity. So also in "Lordship and Bondage" we see a second self-consciousness introduced for the first time which forms a standard for comparison and contrast for the other, and it is this standard which then serves to determine the self-conscious subject. Finally, the "Freedom of Self-Consciousness" parallels the "Force and Understanding" section.[26] Instead of forces operating behind the scenes causing the world of experience to appear as in "Force and the Understanding," in the "Unhappy Consciousness" section it is a self-conscious other, God or what Hegel calls "the Unchangeable,"[27] which constitutes the otherworldly reality which is responsible for the mutable mundane sphere. This structural parallelism between the two chapters indicates that this material at the beginning of "Self-Consciousness" is intended as an independent argument in its own right just as "Sense-Certainty" was an independent argument at the earlier stage.

The task of the "Self-Consciousness" chapter is to fulfill the original goal—to give a complete account of objectivity—but this time with reference to the subject sphere. This too proves to be inadequate since, as we learn in the dialectic of the "Unhappy Consciousness," the self-conscious subject there operates with the conception that it is an isolated atomic entity. The dialectic, however, shows that self-consciousness is in fact ontologically bound up with other self-conscious subjects. Thus, an account of the interaction of one self-consciousness with other self-conscious subjects must be given in a way that demonstrates how the social whole serves to shape the determination of objectivity in the course of this dialectical interaction among self-conscious subjects. This is the task of the "Reason" chapter.

Reason

The structure of "Reason" is somewhat problematic due to its inordinate length, which seems to set it apart from the "Consciousness" and "Self-Consciousness" chapters.[28] However, this length is only troublesome if we consider the "Reason" chapter as a whole to correspond to "Consciousness" and "Self-Consciousness" respectively as seems to be indicated by Hegel's first table of contents. If, on the other hand, we see "Reason" as going back to the beginning of the dialectic and working through the same material as "Consciousness" and "Self-Consciousness" at a higher conceptual level, then the problem disappears since "Reason" would then correspond to "Consciousness" and "Self-Consciousness" *taken together* and not as individual units. Evidence for this interpretation of the structure of the work can be seen in the double letters AA which precede "Reason" in the second version of the table of contents. The key question here is what the single and the double letters in the revised version are supposed to indicate about the structure of the text. In my view, which I think is supported by the text internally by virtue of the corresponding arguments in the relevant chapters, the single and double letters are meant to indicate the parallelisms among the various parts of the text. "Consciousness" and "Self-Consciousness" are meant to form independent units that build upon one another (hence the A and B). Then comes "Reason," which also forms a substantive independent unit (hence the C), but yet here something is different. By inserting the AA in front of the "Reason" chapter, Hegel means to indicate that the dialectic at this point goes back to the original position in the "Consciousness" chapter (represented by A) and works through the same forms of consciousness again but at a different level. Likewise "spirit" and "Religion," which are also represented with double letters (BB and CC), return to the beginning of the cycle as well and work through each of the figures again under their own aspect. Thus, we see that "Reason" is meant to return to the beginning of the so-called highway of despair, that is, to "Consciousness."

The three sections of the "Reason" chapter also have the single letters A, B, and C and thus seem to correspond to the single letters A and B of "Consciousness" and "Self-Consciousness" respectively. This reading renders the following structure:[29]

		[AA. Reason]
in-itself	A. Consciousness	A. Observing Reason
for-itself	B. Self-Consciousness	B. The Actualization of Rational Self-Consciousness Through Its Own Activity in-and-for-itself
		C. Individuality Which Takes Itself to Be Real in and for Itself

The final section of "Reason," which has no previous parallel, would then bring the dialectic to a close by uniting subject and òbject, in-itself and for-itself.

At the end of his account of "Observing Reason," Hegel relates two results of the dialectic examined in that section. His comments there seem to give evidence for this thesis about the structure of "Reason," that is, that the "Reason" chapter is intended in a sense to go back to the beginning of the dialectic and to repeat at a higher level the dialectic of "Consciousness." Hegel says precisely this, explaining that "Reason" "is a completion of the outcome of the preceding movement of self-consciousness. The Unhappy Self-Consciousness renounced its independence, and struggled to make its *being-for-self* into a *Thing*. It thereby reverted from self-consciousness to consciousness, that is, to the consciousness for which the object is something which merely *is*, a Thing; but here, what is a Thing is self-consciousness" (PhS §344; PG 190–91). Here Hegel says expressly that the Unhappy Consciousness at the conclusion of the "Self-Consciousness" chapter reverts "from self-consciousness to consciousness," and it is at this point that the "Reason" chapter begins. Thus, the first section of the "Reason" chapter, "Observing Reason," returns to a treatment of the object sphere and precisely in this respect overlaps with the "Consciousness" chapter.

When seen in this light, the apparently disproportionate length of the "Reason" chapter begins to make sense. This chapter must be longer than the "Consciousness" and the "Self-Consciousness" chapters since it is intended to work through the same material found there, and, in addition, it even adds a third section which is supposed to complete the sequence. When we see that "Consciousness" is supposed to correspond to "Observing Reason" and not to the entire "Reason" chapter, then the disparity in length becomes nominal.

A further parallelism with the preceding chapters can be seen predictably enough with respect to Reason's relation to its object.[30] Here the issue is the *certainty* of Reason, and this is the key to our comparison with "Consciousness" and "Self-Consciousness." In the first section of the "Consciousness" chapter, natural consciousness thought that it had sense-*certainty*, that is, it thought that what was immediately given as a propertyless "This" was true and thus was the object of certainty. In the first section of the "Self-Consciousness" chapter, we saw a new sort of certainty arise: the truth of *self*-certainty. Here natural consciousness, after realizing that it played the crucial role in the account of the determination of the subject-object Notion, deemed itself the true and the certain, whereas whatever was other than the self it considered non-being and something inessential. The analysis thus moves from the objective to the subjective realm between these two chapters. Here in the "Reason" chapter, Hegel explains this relation between "Consciousness" and "Self-Consciousness" as follows:

> There appeared two aspects, one after the other: one in which the essence or the True had for consciousness the determinateness of *being*, the other in which it had the determinateness of being only *for consciousness*. But the two reduced themselves to a single truth, viz. that what *is*, or the in-itself, only *is* insofar as it is *for* consciousness, and what is *for* consciousness is also *in itself* or has *intrinsic* being. (PhS §233; PG 133)

The first aspect mentioned in this passage is, of course, "Consciousness," and the second "Self-Consciousness," which come together in the third, that is, "Reason." Now here at the level of "Reason" we are concerned with the *certainty* of Reason. Reason then constitutes the in-and-for-itself moment which will ultimately bring both subject and object together.

Observing Reason

The general structure that I have sketched so far is made even more precise by Hegel's introductory comments at the beginning of the individual sections of "Reason." In the first of these, he gives us a clear explanation of the way in which the section, "Observing Reason," is intended to fit with what has come before. He writes, "Since Reason is all reality in the sense of the abstract 'mine' and the 'other' is for it something indifferent and extraneous, what is here made explicit is that kind of knowing of an 'other' by Reason, which we met with in the form of 'meaning,' 'perceiving,' and the 'Understanding,' which apprehends what is 'meant' and what is 'perceived'" (PhS §238; PG 136). Here Hegel indicates with his reference to "meaning," "perceiving," and the "Understanding" that the dialectical movements that we have examined from the "Consciousness" chapter, that is, "Sense-Certainty," "Perception," and "Force and the Understanding" will be repeated here at a higher level—at the level of "Reason." Thus, "Observing Reason" will correspond as a whole to the "Consciousness" chapter while its three sections will correspond to the individual sections of the "Consciousness" chapter.[31] Using this as a guide, we end up with the following parallelisms:

A. Consciousness   A. Observing Reason
1. Sense-Certainty   1. Observation of Nature
2. Perception   2. Observation of Self-Consciousness in
                                   Its Purity and in Its Relation to
                                   External Actuality
3. Force and Understanding   3. Observation of Self-Consciousness in
                                   Its Relation to Its Immediate Actuality

However, "Observing Reason" is no mere repetition of the "Consciousness" chapter; despite this important similarity and parallelism, there is also an important difference. Although emphasis is still placed on the object sphere as in "Consciousness," this time the self-conscious subject is not considered atomic. Rather it is the group which is important in the determination of objectivity. Hegel expresses this as follows: "Reason appeals to the *self*-consciousness of each and every consciousness" (PhS §234; PG 134). With respect to natural scientific inquiry, the individual with his own characteristics and idiosyncrasies is not what is important. A scientific experiment must in principle be able to be carried out by a universal subject, and in this sense science is impersonal. Hence, at the level of "Reason," the subject-object Notion is socially determined by a group whose members are parts of a larger social whole, whereas in "Self-Consciousness," for example, it is precisely the isolated individual who determines truth.

The Actualization of Rational Self-Consciousness Through Its Own Activity

Hegel in the introductory paragraphs to this section[32] gives us a fairly thorough discussion of the structure of the "Reason" chapter. Here he summarizes the movement from "Consciousness" to "Self-Consciousness" as well as the movement from "Observing Reason" to the next stage, "The Actualization of Rational Self-Consciousness through Its Own Activity." His comments are instructive in helping us with our reconstruction of the structure of the text:

The *pure* category, which is present for consciousness in the form of *being* or *immediacy*, is the object as still *unmediated*, as merely *given*, and consciousness is equally unmediated in its relation to it. The moment of that infinite judgement is the transition of *immediacy* into mediation, or *negativity*. The given object is consequently determined as a negative object; consciousness, however, is determined as *self*-consciousness over against it; in other words, the category which, in the course of observation, has run through the form of *being* is now posited in the form of being-for-self: consciousness no longer aims to *find* itself *immediately* but to produce itself by its own activity. It is *itself* the end at which its action aims, whereas in its role of observer it was concerned only with things. (PhS §344; PG 191)

In "Consciousness," the category of being was considered in its immediacy as something "merely *given*." Natural consciousness ascribed ontological priority to the object. But then in the course of the dialectic this proved to be inadequate and eventually led us to the dialectic of "Self-Consciousness" where the object was considered to be something negative and inessential over and against the self-conscious subject. In the passage cited above, Hegel then immediately shifts over to a description of the movement of "Reason," indicating that the movement from "Consciousness" to "Self-Consciousness" corresponds to the movement in "Reason" from "Observing Reason" to "The Actualization of Rational Self-Consciousness Through Its Own Activity." As he puts it, "Observing Reason" has just run through the dialectical movement that corresponds to the simple "form of being." Now, however, the moment of negation or otherness is introduced as in "Self-Consciousness." At this point, we will see different forms of the individual self-conscious subject in its attempt to determine itself by distinguishing itself from others. Just as in the "Consciousness" chapter, so too in "Observing Reason" the conscious subject "was concerned only with things." Now we will, as in "Self-Consciousness," be concerned with the sphere of the self-conscious subject.

This supposition is confirmed when we analyze the place and role of this section in the *Phenomenology* as a whole. Since, as we have seen, the individual sections of "Observing Reason" run parallel to the sections in the "Consciousness" chapter, we can infer that the analyses of the present section, following "Observing Reason" as they do, must then correspond to the individual sections of "Self-Consciousness."[33] Hegel confirms this structure rather straightforwardly at the beginning of the present section when he writes, "Just as Reason, in the role of observer, repeated, in the element of the category, the movement of *consciousness*,

The Architectonic of Hegel's Phenomenology of Spirit   459

viz. sense-certainty, perception, and the understanding, so will Reason again run through the double movement of self-consciousness, and pass over from independence into its freedom" (PhS §348; PG 193). Here by "Reason, in the role of observer," it is clear that Hegel means to refer to the section "Observing Reason" as a whole. In this passage he explicitly indicates once again that the three sections of "Observing Reason" correspond to the three sections of the "Consciousness" chapter. Then, referring implicitly to the present section, he says that Reason, just like self-consciousness, will "pass over from independence into its freedom." Here Hegel indicates that the present section, "The Actualization of Rational Self-Consciousness Through Its Own Activity," corresponds to the "Self-Consciousness" chapter, which included first the "Independence and Dependence of Self-Consciousness" (here referred to simply as "independence") and the "Freedom of Self-Consciousness" (here referred to as "its freedom"). Hegel's formulation of the parallel structures here is particularly important. He tells us specifically that the sections run parallel to each other "in the element of the category." By this he seems to mean that although the content of the various dialectical movements changes and gradually becomes richer, nevertheless with respect to the form of the dialectic, certain categorial elements remain the same and in fact are repeated at the various levels. Just as the categories from the various stages of "Consciousness" were repeated in "Observing Reason," so also now we will expect to see the categories and forms of consciousness examined in "Self-Consciousness" turn up once again in the present section. We can briefly sketch the outline of this part of the "Reason" chapter implied by Hegel's remarks here as follows:[34]

B. Self-Consciousness	B. The Actualization of Rational Self-Consciousness Through Its Own Activity
1. The Truth of Self-Certainty	1. Pleasure and Necessity
2. Lordship and Bondage	2. The Law of the Heart and the Frenzy of Self-Conceit
3. Freedom of Self-Consciousness	3. Virtue and the Way of the World

The two units of "Consciousness" and "Self-Consciousness" thus form the basic structures first of the object sphere and then of the subject sphere, units which are repeated here at the level of "Reason." Now the task of the "Reason" chapter is to unify the subject and the object and to overcome the various forms of dualism that have plagued the dialectic up until this point. Thus, the new forms of subject and object which appear here in the first two sections of "Reason" are subsequently unified in the third section.

Individuality Which Takes Itself to Be Real in and for Itself

In this third and final section of the "Reason" chapter, self-consciousness finally comes to realize what we, the philosophical audience, have known all along, namely, the unity of subject and object. What self-consciousness learns from "Virtue and the Way of the World" is that the world is not an evil, external other that stands in contradiction to the individual subject or the moral sphere: self-consciousness, "being now absolutely certain of its reality, no longer seeks only to realize itself as end in an antithesis to the reality which immediately confronts it" (PhS §394; PG 214). On the contrary, the world is in harmony with the individual and allows him to fulfill his needs cooperatively with others.[35] The individual is now able to identify with the external sphere and to see himself in it by means of his work and activity. In this self-recognition in the world of objects, the various dualisms such as universal and particular come together. Here we have "the interfusion of *being-in-itself* and *being-for-itself*, of universal and individuality" (PhS §394; PG 214). Self-consciousness, in viewing the world, implicitly views itself since it sees its own individuality expressed in the external sphere: "it starts afresh from *itself*, and is occupied not with an *other*, but with *itself*"(PhS §396; PG 215).

In making this point about the closure of the dualisms explored heretofore, Hegel indicates the overall structure of the "Reason" chapter and simultaneously locates the present section with a reference to the first two sections that we have just discussed. He writes, "With this Notion of itself, therefore, self-consciousness has returned into itself out of those opposed determinations which the category had for it, and which characterized the relation of self-consciousness to the category in its observational [i.e., 'Observing Reason'] and also active [i.e., 'The Actualization of Rational Self-Consciousness through Its Own Activity'] roles" (PhS §395; PG 215). Both of the two previous forms of consciousness represented "opposed determinations," that is, subject-object Notions which posited an opposition or split. At first, in "Observing Reason" as in "Consciousness," priority was given to the object sphere, and the subject was considered something secondary. Then in "The Actualization of Rational Self-Consciousness Through Its Own Activity" as in "Self-Consciousness," the individual self-conscious agent was given priority, and the world stood opposed to it as something negative. Finally, here this dialectic seems to come to an end since the subject-object split is apparently overcome. It is clear that this final section, "Individuality Which Takes Itself to Be Real in and for Itself," is meant to form a third discrete unit which brings together the two preceding sections. Here in this third section, these two moments of in-itself and for-itself come together as the "real in

The Architectonic of Hegel's Phenomenology of Spirit 461

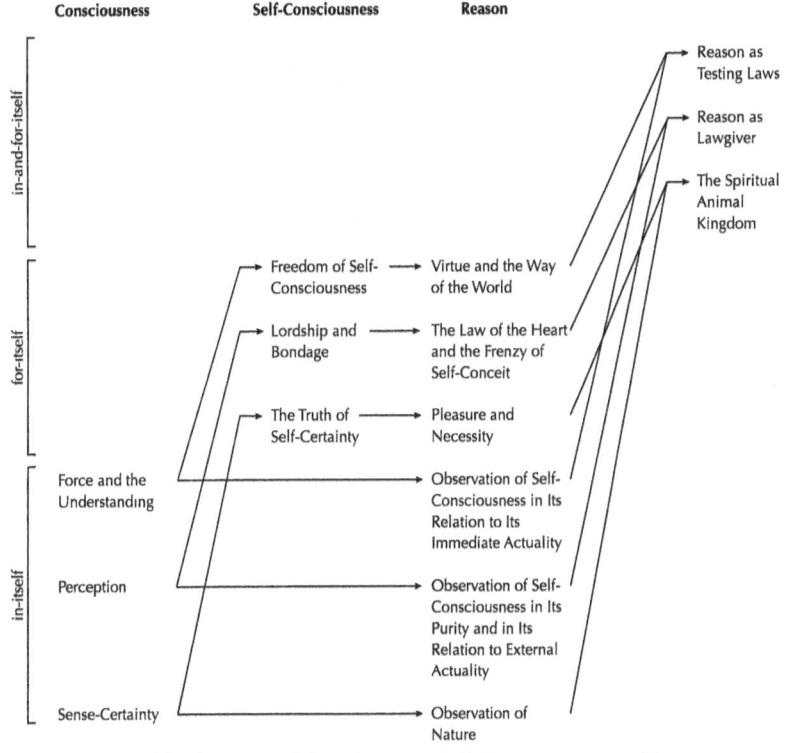

FIGURE 1. The Structure of Consciousness, Self-Consciousness, and Reason

and for itself," where there is no longer any opposition. Thus, this section forms the apex of the pyramid consisting of "Consciousness," "Self-Consciousness," and the sections in "Reason" which run parallel to them. This interpretation can be represented graphically as in figure 1.

The outline in figure 1 should be read starting from the lower left-hand corner where we begin the dialectic at the level of common sense and the dualisms contained therein. The road to Science is an ascending one which I have tried to indicate by vertically representing the sequence of moments of the in-itself, the for-itself, and the in-and-for-itself. Finally, the lines with arrows are intended to represent the parallelisms that we have been following.

Spirit

Let us first turn to the question of what, with respect to content, the "Spirit" chapter adds to the truth problematic. What is the status of the discussions found there *vis-à-vis* "Consciousness," "Self-Consciousness," and "Reason"? After the brief summary of the first three chapters discussed above, Hegel at the beginning of the "spirit" chapter proceeds to answer just this question about the role of "spirit" and to justify the rest of the work. In an important passage, he writes, referring to "Reason as Testing Laws," the third and final section of "Reason,"

> This still *abstract* determination which constitutes the "matter in hand" itself is at first only spiritual essence, and its consciousness [only] a formal knowing of it, which busies itself with all kinds of content of the essence. This consciousness, as a particular individual, is still in fact distinct from substance, and either makes arbitrary laws or fancies that in simply knowing laws it possesses them in their own absolute nature. Or, looked at from the side of substance, this is spiritual essence that is in and for itself, but which is not yet *consciousness* of itself. But essence that is *in* and *for itself*, and which is at the same time actual as consciousness and aware of itself, this is *Spirit*. (PhS §438; PG 238)

Here Hegel makes the distinction between the level of "Reason" and that of "spirit." In "Reason" self-consciousness had only a "formal knowing" of spiritual essence. It was abstracted or alienated from its immediate ethical relations. As he says later, "spirit is thus self-supporting, absolute, real being. All previous shapes of consciousness are abstract forms of it. . . . This isolating of those moments *presupposes* spirit itself and subsists therein" (PhS §440; PG 239). In "Reason" an account of the community and the social whole was given, but this account was always abstract. It was never any particular community. Likewise, the account of self-consciousness was always abstract. For instance, in the final two sections, "Reason as Lawgiver" and "Reason as Testing Laws," we were not concerned with a particular human subject in a particular community, but rather with any rational moral agent at all. These abstracted analyses "presuppose" a concrete social and historical community from which they were originally abstracted. This then forms the next major step in the argument. Now in order to give an account of the Notion, we must include an account of concrete historical communities.

From this analysis we can see that the key point of "spirit" is that it introduces history into the account of the self-development of the subject-object Notion.[36] In the literature on the *Phenomenology*, one of the traditional problems of the continuity of the text has been how to reconcile the epistemological analyses of the first three chapters with the account of history that we find here in "spirit." With the reading I am proposing, we can begin to make sense of this difficult transition by understanding the epistemological import of the historical figures which Hegel analyzes. In order to get beyond the formal account of ethical life examined in "Reason," we need to examine concrete social situations, and this is only possible by an examination of particular historical communities. As Hegel says of spirit in the "Absolute Knowing" chapter, "The movement of carrying forward the form of its [spirit's] self-knowledge is the labor which it accomplishes as actual history" (PhS §803; PG 430).[37] In "spirit" the dialectic departs from the abstract account of the individual and the community found in "Reason" and moves through history, and this movement shapes the truth claims of peoples and historical periods in a way that the "Reason" chapter could not account for. Concerning the content of the "spirit" chapter, Hegel writes, "These shapes, however, are distinguished from the previous ones by the fact that they are real spirits, actualities in the strict meaning of the word, and instead of being shapes merely of consciousness, are shapes of a world" (PhS §441; PG 240). We are now concerned with the actual historical development of communities or as he says "actualities in the strict meaning of the word." In order to give an account of how communities mediate truth claims, we must first give an historical account of how that community developed and how it came to hold certain truths or values. Such an historical account is thus presupposed in any abstract account of the role of the community in the self-determination of truth claims.

The question that this explanation raises for us is how these real or historical forms of "spirit" fit in with our analysis of the architectonic of the work given so far. The most obvious hint is that Hegel divides his abbreviated version of world history here in the "spirit" chapter into three major sections as follows: "A. The True Spirit. The Ethical Order," "B. Self-Alienated Spirit. Culture," and "C. Spirit That Is Certain of Itself. Morality." This would seem to imply a correspondence of "spirit" with the three sections of "Reason" and their respective correspondents in "Consciousness" and "Self-Consciousness." In other words, this would mean that "A. The True Spirit" corresponds to "Consciousness," and "Observing Reason." Similarly, "B. Self-Alienated Spirit" would then correspond to "Self-Consciousness" and "The Actualization of Rational Self-Consciousness Through Its Own Activity." Finally, the third section, "C. Spirit That Is Certain of Itself" would form the apex, corresponding to "Individuality Which Takes Itself to Be Real in and for Itself," the third and final section of the "Reason" chapter. For the sake of simplicity, we can graphically represent the parallelisms that are implied by this reading as in figure 2.

There are a number of important pieces of evidence that support this thesis about the parallel sections. Most obviously, this correspondence is

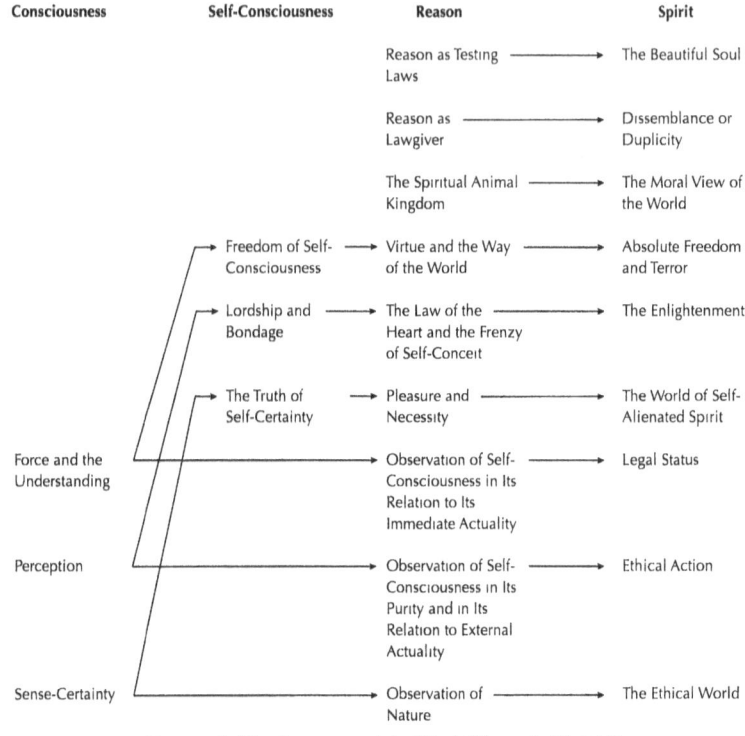

FIGURE 2. The Structure of the Work Through "Spirit"

indicated once again by the double Latin letters "BB" of the "spirit" chapter which are intended to parallel the double letters "AA" of "Reason." In other words, "spirit" will return to the beginning of the dialectic and will then go through all of the same stages as "Reason." These two chapters run parallel to each other as wholes or complete units. This implies that the "spirit" chapter will have *ipso facto* the same parallelisms with "Consciousness" and "Self-Consciousness" as the "Reason" chapter before it. Hegel indicates this parallelism explicitly in a couple of different places. For instance, in the "Religion" chapter he writes, "But the moments are *consciousness, self-consciousness, reason,* and *spirit—* spirit, that is, as immediate spirit, which is not yet consciousness of spirit. Their totality, *taken together*, constitutes spirit in its mundane existence generally; spirit as such contains the previous structured shapes in universal determinations, in the moments just named"(PhS §679; PG 365). Here is it clear that the dialectical movements that we have examined in the first three chapters repeat themselves again in "spirit." Here Hegel says unambiguously, "spirit . . . contains the previous structured shapes." The forms of consciousness in the first three chapters represent what Hegel here calls "universal determinations." In other words, they constitute universal patterns of thought which can assume a number of different forms. These same universal forms are all contained in "spirit" in their historical manifestations as Hegel indicates here. Moreover, these parallelisms are confirmed by the actual contents of the individual sections of the "spirit" chapter.

The first section, "The True spirit," represents the in-itself moment of the dialectic. Here in the discussion of the *Antigone*, for instance, the ethical order is considered to be something objective. The ethical laws and principles are facts about the world that stand over and above all human opinions and authority. Hegel, citing the *Antigone*, writes of these ethical principles, "Thus, Sophocles' *Antigone* acknowledges them as the unwritten and infallible law of the gods. 'They are not of yesterday or today, but everlasting / Though where they come from, none of us can tell'" (PhS §437; PG 236). The moral laws are ontological facts about the world according to this view. This then clearly corresponds to the realms of "Consciousness" and "Observing Reason" where priority is given to the object sphere at the expense of the subject. Hegel writes most explicitly, "spirit, then is consciousness in general which embraces sense-certainty, perception, and the understanding, insofar as in its self-analysis spirit holds fast to the moment of being an objectively existent actuality to itself, and ignores the fact that this actuality is its own being-for-self" (PhS §440; PG 239). From this passage it is, moreover, clear that the individual sections inside of these chapters and subsections also correspond to one another.

The second section of "spirit," "Self-Alienated Spirit," represents the break and the move to the for-itself moment. Hegel indicates this when he writes, "If on the contrary, it [the spirit] holds fast to the other moment of the analysis, viz. that its object is its own *being-for-self*, then it is self-consciousness" (PhS §440; PG 239). Here the historical subject, epitomized for Hegel by Rameau's nephew in his alienation, rejects the accepted traditions and ethical order which were so important in the previous section. He accepts only his own ethical views as valid and negates those of the tradition, which he sees as contradictory or hypocritical. Here we can clearly recognize the for-itself aspect with its rejection of the objective sphere and its insistence on the truth and validity of the individual subject. This then corresponds to "Self-Consciousness" and the second section in "Reason."

Finally, in the third section, "Spirit That Is Certain of Itself," the triad comes to a close with the in-and-for-itself moment. The dualisms of the two previous dialectics are at this point overcome. "Here, then," Hegel writes, "knowledge appears at last to have become completely identical with its truth; for its truth is this very knowledge, and any antithesis between the two sides has vanished" (PhS §596; PG 323). In this third section, the moment of alienation has been overcome and with it the dualism between the inner private law and the external world of nature or culture. In "The Moral View of the World," for instance, nature is not an obstacle to morality; instead, it is thought to be conducive to moral life since obeying moral laws is thought to lead to happiness. Likewise, the beautiful soul's appeal to conscience as the criterion for moral living unites the universally valid moral law with the individual. Thus, the third section represents the reconciliation of the two previous spheres. Hegel explains this as follows: "But as immediate consciousness of the being that is *in and for itself*, as unity of consciousness and self-consciousness, spirit is consciousness that *has reason*" (PhS §440; PG 239). Thus, the historical forms of "spirit" run through the same dialectical movements as the abstract forms of "Reason." It now remains to be seen how the dialectic of "Religion" fits into this picture.

Religion

As we have seen, the movement of the dialectic in the *Phenomenology* tends to be one toward ever greater complexity. In "Consciousness," the role of the self was unrecognized; in "Self-Consciousness" the role of the self as individual was all important; in "Reason" the role of the community was all important; and finally in "Spirit" the role of the historically changing community was essential. "Religion" likewise represents a more complex configuration than what we saw in the "Spirit" chapter. Here in "Religion" spirit becomes aware of itself. This self-awareness is what Hegel calls "universal" or "absolute spirit."[38] "Spirit conceived as object," Hegel writes, "has for itself the significance of being the universal spirit that contains within itself all essence and all actuality" (PhS §677; PG 364). This self-consciousness is implicitly implied in spirit's awareness of its object sphere but must be made explicit in the course of the dialectic. Thus, "Religion" represents a further unpacking of the presuppositions implied in the subject-object Notion. In order to give an account of the Notion we must not just give an account of the development of the historical community. Necessarily implied in this development is the self-awareness of spirit, which, for Hegel, comes about for the first time

The Architectonic of Hegel's Phenomenology of Spirit   467

in "Religion," and specifically in "Revealed Religion." Spirit becomes self-aware in the revelation of God on earth in the Christian religion. Specifically, in Christ, spirit becomes aware of itself. It sees that God and the absolute are not something otherworldly or different from man, but rather God is man or spirit in the world.

Hegel indicates at the beginning of "Religion" that the parallelisms that we have been following up until now will continue in this chapter. He indicates that the forms of religion will correspond to the forms of the chapters we have examined so far: "If, therefore, religion is the perfection of spirit into which its individual moments—consciousness, self-consciousness, reason, and spirit—return and have returned as into their ground, they together constitute the *existent* actuality of the totality of spirit, which *is* only as the differentiating and self-returning movement of these aspects. The genesis of religion *in general* is contained in the movement of the universal moments" (PhS §680; PG 366). In this extremely important passage, Hegel lays out for us in some measure the architectonic of the second half of the *Phenomenology*. He first repeats what we have already learned, namely that spirit encompasses the previous forms and runs through them once again. Hegel then goes on to explain the role of the "Religion" chapter. He tells us that in contrast to the "spirit" chapter, which ran through the various figures of consciousness in their historical or temporal forms, "Religion" will do the same atemporally:

> The course traversed by these moments is, moreover, in relation to religion, not to be represented as occurring in time. Only the totality of spirit, is in time, and the "shapes," which are "shapes" of the totality of *spirit*, display themselves in a temporal succession; for only the whole has true actuality and therefore the form of pure freedom in face of an "other," a form which expresses itself as time. But the *moments* of the whole, consciousness, self-consciousness, reason, and spirit, just because they are moments, have no existence in separation from one another. (PhS §679; PG 365)

All of the previous forms are implicitly contained here in religion, and they all form a unitary whole which is represented by religion. This is what Hegel means when he says that they are moments which "have no existence in separation from one another." The various forms of consciousness are thus organically related and have their meaning only in their relation to the other moments. The conceptual movement of "Religion" thus corresponds to the fundamental structure constituted by the moments of "Consciousness," "Self-Consciousness," and "Reason" which we have already seen. This information now helps us to complete our diagram as in figure 3.

Throughout the "Religion" chapter itself, Hegel is quite forthcoming about the structure of the chapter, and we can thus find evidence in many places for the parallelisms indicated here.

That "Natural Religion" corresponds to "Consciousness" can be seen from the emphasis on the object sphere and above all from a number of explicit references. Here the divine is thought to dwell in the realm of objects. "The first reality of spirit," Hegel says, "is the Notion of religion itself, or religion as *immediate*, and therefore Natural Religion. In this, spirit knows itself as its object in a natural or immediate shape" (PhS §683; PG 368). Hegel confirms this parallelism when he declares that "God as Light," the first section of "Natural Religion," corresponds to the first section of the "Consciousness" chapter: "In the immediate, first diremption of self-knowing absolute spirit its 'shape' has the determina-

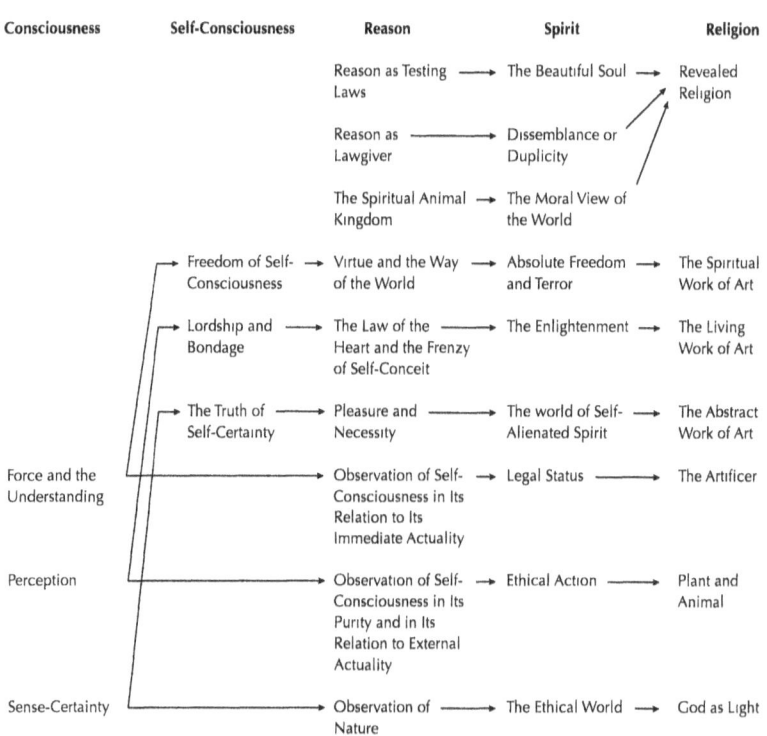

FIGURE 3. The Structure of the *Phenomenology of Spirit*

tion which belongs to *immediate consciousness* or to *sense*-certainty" (PhS §686; PG 371). Likewise, Hegel tells us that the second section, "Plant and Animal" corresponds to the second section of the "Consciousness" chapter, that is, "Perception": "Self-conscious spirit that has withdrawn into itself from the shapeless essence, or has raised its immediacy to self in general, determines its unitary nature as a manifoldness of being-for-self, and is the religion of spiritual *perception*" (PhS §689; PG 372). Finally the third form of natural religion, "The Artificer," corresponds in turn to the third section of the "Consciousness" chapter, namely "Force and Understanding." Hegel tells us this explicitly when writes, "The first form, because it is immediate, is the abstract form of the understanding, and the work is not yet in its own self filled with spirit" (PhS §692; PG 373).

The shift to the for-itself moment and to "Self-Consciousness" comes with "Religion in the Form of Art." Here the divine is thought to be in the self-conscious subject as artist. Hegel introduces this section as follows: "The second reality, however, is necessarily that in which spirit knows itself in the shape of a *superseded* natural existence, or of the self. This, therefore, is the Religion of Art; for the shape raises itself to the form of the self through the creative activity of consciousness whereby this beholds in its object its act or the self" (PhS §683; PG 368). Here the emphasis is no longer on the natural entity as something given, but rather on self-consciousness' reshaping and reworking of it. In the artistic production, self-consciousness becomes aware of itself. Thus, the dialectic is thrown back to the subject sphere. Hegel confirms that this section corresponds to the transition to "Self-Consciousness" that we saw earlier in the dialectic: "The first work of art, as immediate, is abstract and individual. As for itself, it has to move away from this immediate and objective mode towards self-consciousness" (PhS §705; PG 378).

The final section, "Revealed Religion," forms the apex of the triad and represents the in-and-for-itself moment. It thus corresponds to the final third of the "Reason" and "spirit" chapters respectively in which the dualisms and oppositions are overcome. Hegel tells us,

> Finally, the third reality overcomes the one-sidedness of the first two; the self is just as much an immediacy, as the immediacy is the self. If, in the first reality, spirit in general is in the form of consciousness, and in the second, in that of self-consciousness, in the third it is in the form of the unity of both. It has the shape of being-in-and-for-itself; and when it is thus conceived as it is in and for itself, this is the Revealed Religion. (PhS §683; PG 368)

Here in "Revealed Religion" the subject-object split is overcome in the concept of revelation. In revelation man recognizes himself in God and through this recognition becomes reconciled with the world. This reconciliation comes about in the revealed religion, that is, in Christianity, where God is revealed on earth as man. Here God is no longer something transcendent and otherworldly but, instead, is a particular man living in this world. This account contains, on Hegel's view, a deep metaphysical truth expressed in terms of a story. The truth of subject-object unity and the individual self-awareness is expressed by the Christian account of God as revealed. Philosophical or scientific thinking in its turn understands this same truth in a different way.

ABSOLUTE KNOWING

Hegel claims that "Religion" has the same content as philosophical knowing, that is, absolute knowing, but that it understands it in a different way, namely, metaphorically.[39] He says that at the moment of "Religion," "spirit itself as a whole, and the self-differentiated moments within it, fall within the sphere of picture-thinking and in the form of objectivity. The content of this picture-thinking is absolute spirit" (PhS §788; PG 422). Hegel expresses this more straightforwardly in the *Encyclopaedia Logic*: "The objects of philosophy, it is true, are upon the whole the same as those of religion" (EL §1; Enz. 27).[40] What these passages tell us is that, for Hegel, the content that the dialectic has reached in "Religion" is the same as in "Absolute Knowing."[41] Thus, by the time we reach "Religion" the content of our account of the self-determination of truth is complete and exhaustive. This would mean that in a sense our story of the determination of subject and object ends with the "Religion" chapter[42] since at that point a complete account has been given. The upshot of this account was to show the ultimate unity of all the various factors, at first thought to be unrelated, in the overall truth process. We thus see the great unity and interconnectedness of the subject with the object, of the subject with the community, of the community with other historically related communities, in short of everything with everything else in the broadest sense. Hegel explains this as follows:

> Thus the object is in part *immediate* being or, in general a thing—corresponding to immediate consciousness; in part, an othering of itself, its relationship or *being-for-an-other*, and *being-for-itself*, i.e. determinateness—corresponding to perception; and in part *essence*, or in the form of a universal—corresponding to the understanding.... [I]t is from one

side a shape of consciousness as such, and from the other side a number of such shapes which *we* bring together, in which the totality of the moments of the object and of the relation of consciousness to it can be indicated only as resolved into its moments. (PhS §789; PG 422–23)

The dialectic has shown us the totality of the interconnectedness of all forms of subject and object in the attempt to give a complete account of the subject-object Notion. The dialectic has thus demonstrated the truth of a certain sort of epistemic monism in which everything is necessarily related to the whole, and the whole thus corresponds to the ultimate account of the Notion. This is therefore the actual content that the dialectic has produced.

The question is now how to interpret this account of the monistic unity of the world. For Hegel, there are two possibilities: the religious interpretation and the philosophical interpretation. The religious interpretation understands this monistic truth with stories, symbols, and metaphors or what has been translated as "picture thinking." In the figure of God, the religious interpretation personifies the great monistic unity of the universe. For the religious consciousness, these most abstract truths must thus be seen through the veil of simplified concrete examples drawn from normal human experience. The philosophical consciousness, on the other hand, sees these truths for what they are and is able to extricate them from their metaphorical form. Thus, although the monistic content of both interpretations is the same, the difference exists in how that content is understood. Hegel tells us in a fairly straightforward fashion in a number of different places that absolute knowing is merely the understanding of all of these previous modes of knowing in their conceptual form. For instance, he writes, "The realm of spirits which is formed in this way in the outer world constitutes a succession in time in which one spirit relieved another of its charge and each took over the empire of the world from its predecessor. Their goal is the revelation of the depth of spirit, and this is *the absolute Notion*" (PhS §808; PG 433). The absolute Notion is thus the Notion which encompasses all other Notions within itself. It is the complete or exhaustive Notion. In other words, absolute knowing is the panoptic overview of all previous Notions.[43] Hegel thus makes clear that absolute knowing is not the knowing of any particular fact or ultimate piece of wisdom but rather it is merely the grasping of the various forms of thought as a whole. Here we find at the end of the *Phenomenology* a powerful statement of Hegel's holism. Every individual truth or value must be understood in a larger context. Only with this overview of the complex network of interrelations of truth claims, individuals, institutions, and historical events are we able to come to understand the true nature of such claims and give a complete account of objectivity.

The Philosophical Import of a Systematic Reading

Is there anything philosophically interesting that this interpretation of the architectonic of the *Phenomenology* as a whole brings with it, or are these parallelisms simply of interest to the despairing Hegel philologist trying to patch together the Hegelian system for its own sake?[44] The philosophically provocative point that these parallelisms implicitly indicate is that the conceptual logic that governs the development of the object-Notion and the subject-Notion is the same logic that governs world-historical forces. In other words, the moments of in-itself, for-itself, and in-and-for-itself and the dialectic of universal and particular are not categories which apply only to a particular and limited subject matter; instead, they are universal categories or "universal determinations" which govern all human thought and which as such can be found in any subject matter. Thus, the logic which governs our understanding of a Notion of a particular, apparently isolated object is the same as that which governs our understanding of the various epochs of world history with their manifold interrelations and complexities. Precisely this point, which is essential for Hegel's idealism and his monism, is overlooked when we analyze individual arguments of his philosophy in abstraction from their systematic context.

This analysis can by no means by seen as the final word on the systematic structure of the *Phenomenology*. Much work still remains to be done above all with respect to establishing the unity of the content of the work which I could only sketch here in the broadest of strokes. It remains to be seen, moreover, with respect to exactly which "categories" the various sections correspond to one another. This analysis, however, does show us that Hegel in fact had a systematic structure in mind when he wrote the book. One can always dispute the question concerning to what degree he adhered to this structure in any given analysis, but it would be absurd at this point to claim that such a structure simply does not exist. Moreover, we need not find Hegel's structure here philosophically compelling in order to use it to understand the individual analyses which he gives. But, on the other hand, the risk that we run by ignoring his systematic pretensions entirely is not understanding him at all.

Notes

1. The question of the possibility of a systematic philosophy today formed the topic of the International Hegel Conference in 1975. Henrich, Dieter (ed.), *Ist systematische Philosophie möglich? Hegel-Studien* Beiheft 17 (Bonn: Bouvier, 1977).

The Architectonic of Hegel's Phenomenology of Spirit   473

2. E.g., André Léonard, "La structure du système hégélian," *Revue philosophique de Louvain* 69 (1971): 495–524; Johann Heinrich Trede, *"Phänomenologie und Logik. Zu den Grundlagen einer Diskussion,"* *Hegel-Studien* 10 (1975): 173–210.

3. Even as great of an admirer of Hegel as John Dewey writes, "The form, the schematism, of his [Hegel's] system now seems to me artificial to the last degree." John Dewey, "From Absolutism to Experimentalism," in *Contemporary American Philosophy*, vol. II, ed. George P. Adams and W. P. Montague (New York: Macmillan, 1930), 21.

4. Theodore Haering, "Entstehungsgeschichte der *Phänomenologie des Geistes*," in *Verhandlungen des III. Internationalen Hegel Kongresses 1933*, ed. B. Wigersma (Haarlem: N/VH.D. Tjeenk Willink & Zn. and Tübingen: J. C. B. Mohr, 1934), 118–36. Also see Theodore Haering, *Hegel sein Wollen und sein Werk II* (Leipzig and Berlin: Teubner, 1929), 479ff; Otto Pöggeler, "Die Komposition der *Phänomenologie des Geistes*," in *Hegel-Tage Royaumont 1964. Beiträge zur Phänomenologie des Geistes*, ed. Hans-Georg Gadamer, *Hegel-Studien*, Beiheft 3 (Bonn: Bouvier, 1966), 27–74, cited from the reprint in *Materialien zu Hegels Phänomenologie des Geistes*, ed. Hans Friedrich Fulda and Dieter Henrich (Frankfurt: Suhrkamp, 1973), 329–90.

5. Walter Kaufmann, *Hegel: A Reinterpretation* (Notre Dame, Ind.: University of Notre Dame Press, 1978), 158. Cf. "The *Phenomenology of Spirit* is a profoundly incongruous book" (ibid., p. 142). "I should prefer to speak of charades: now a tableau, now a skit, now a brief oration" (ibid., p. 127). Elsewhere, Kaufmann writes in a similar vein, "One really has to put on blinkers and immerse oneself in carefully selected microscopic details to avoid the discovery that the *Phenomenology* is in fact an utterly unscientific and unrigorous work." Walter Kaufmann, "Hegel's Conception of Phenomenology," in *Phenomenology and Philosophical Understanding*, ed. Edo Pivcevic (Cambridge: Cambridge University Press, 1975), 229.

6. Otto Pöggeler, "Die Komposition der *Phänomenologie des Geistes*," in *Materialien zu Hegels Phänomenologie des Geistes*, 372. (My translation.)

7. Cf. L. S. Stepelevich, and David Lamb (eds.), *Hegel's Philosophy of Action* (Atlantic Highlands, N.J.: Humanities Press, 1983).

8. Cf. David Lamb, "Hegel and Wittgenstein on Language and Sense-Certainty," *Clio*, 7 (1978): 281–301.

9. Cf. Gilbert Plumer, "Hegel on Singular Demonstrative Reference," *Southern Journal of Philosophy* 11 (1980): 71–94.

10. Kant, for instance, is by no means less energetic in his insistence on systematic philosophy than Hegel: "As a systematic unity is what first raises ordinary knowledge to the rank of science, that is, makes a system out of a mere aggregate of knowledge, architectonic is the doctrine of the scientific in our

knowledge, and therefore necessarily forms part of the doctrine of method." Kant, *Critique of Pure Reason*, trans. N. Kemp Smith (New York: St. Martin's Press, 1929), A832/B860. Cf. "For pure speculative reason has a structure wherein everything is an organ, the whole being for the sake of all others. . . . Any attempt to change even the smallest part at once gives rise to contradictions, not merely in the system, but in human reason in general." Kant, ibid., Bxxxvii–viii. Cf. also Kant, ibid., A840/B869.

11. EL = *Hegel's Logic. Part One of the Encyclopaedia of the Philosophical Sciences*, trans. William Wallace (Oxford: Clarendon Press, 1975); Enz. = *Enzyklopädie der philosophischen Wissenschaften*, vol. 19 of *Gesammelte Werke*, ed. the Rheinisch-Westfälische Akademie der Wissenschaften (Hamburg: Felix Meiner, 1968–).

12. See Otto Pöggeler, *Hegels Idee einer Phänomenologie des Geistes* (Freiburg and Munich: Karl Alber, 1973), 121–22.

13. PhS = *Phenomenology of Spirit*, trans. A.V. Miller (Oxford: Clarendon Press, 1977); PG = *Phänomenologie des Geistes*, vol. 9 of *Gesammelte Werke*, ed. the Rheinisch-Westfälische Akademie der Wissenschaften (Hamburg: Felix Meiner, 1968–). Cf. EL §16; Enz. 41–42.

14. Cf. also the preface of the *Phenomenology*, where Hegel flatly claims, "The true shape in which truth exists can only be the scientific system of such truth" (PhS §5; PG 11). Cf. also a little later in the preface where he says, "knowledge is only actual, and can only be expounded, as Science or as *system*" (PhS §24; PG 21).

15. I would not wish to claim that my emphasis on Hegel's philosophy as a system is entirely unique or novel. Cf. L. Bruno Puntel, *Darstellung, Methode und Struktur. Untersuchung zur Einheit der systematischen Philosophie G. W. F. Hegels* (Bonn: Bouvier, 1973); Frederic Escaraffel, "Des mouvements parallèles dans la *Phénoménologie de l'esprit*," *L'Arc* 38 (1969): 93–105. Gerd Kimmerle, *Sein und Selbst. Untersuchung zur kategorialen Einheit von Vernunft und Geist in Hegels Phänomenologie des Geistes*. (Bonn: Bouvier, 1978); David Lamb, *Hegel: From Foundation to System* (The Hague: Martinus Nijhoff, 1980); Pierre-Jean Labarrière, *Structures et mouvement dialectique dans la Phénoménologie de l'esprit de Hegel* (Paris: Aubier, 1968); Merold Westphal, *History and Truth in Hegel's Phenomenology* (Atlantic Highlands, N.J.: Humanities Press, 1979).

16. Hegel to Schelling [95], Bamberg, May 1, 1807, *Letters*, p. 80; *Briefe* I: 159–62. *Letters* = *Hegel: The Letters*, trans. Clark Butler and Christian Seiler (Bloomington: Indiana University Press, 1984); *Briefe* = *Briefe von und an Hegel*, ed. Johannes Hoffmeister, 4 vols. (Hamburg: Meiner, 1961).

17. Notably, Johannes Heinrichs, *Die Logik der Phänomenologie des Geistes* (Bonn: Bouvier, 1974); André Léonard, "Pour une exégèse renouvelée de la *Phénoménologie de l'esprit* de Hegel," *Revue philosophique de Louvain* 74 (1976): 572–93; André Léonard, "La structure du système hégélian," *Revue*

philosophique de Louvain 69 (1971): 495–524; Edgardo Albizu, "La estructura de la *Fenomenología del espíritu* de Hegel y el problema del tiempo," *Revista Latinoamericana de Filosofía* 7 (1981): 209–22.

18. See the Suhrkamp edition of the *Phenomenology* for a detailed account of these changes. Georg Wilhelm Friedrich Hegel, *Phänomenologie des Geistes*, Werke 3 (Frankfurt: Suhrkamp, 1986), 595ff. See also the "Nachwort" to the Hoffmeister edition (G. W. F. Hegel, *Phänomenologie des Geistes* [Hamburg: Meiner, 1952], "Zur Feststellung des Textes," 575–78. Also see Otto Pöggeler, "Die Komposition der *Phänomenologie des Geistes*"; Klaus Kähler, and Werner Marx, *Die Vernunft in Hegels Phänomenologie des Geistes* (Frankfurt: Klostermann, 1992), 13ff.

19. I see it as misguided that Labarrière takes both of these versions together in his attempt to reconstruct the unitary structure of the text. Pierre-Jean Labarrière, "La *Phénoménologie de l'esprit* comme discours systématique: histoire, religion et science," *Hegel-Studien* 9 (1974): 143ff.

20. This is of course the thesis of Haering and Pöggeler. Cf. also Walter Kaufmann, *Hegel: A Reinterpretation* (Notre Dame, Ind.: University of Notre Dame Press, 1978), 133–36, esp.: "The table of contents bears out that the work was not planned painstakingly before it was written, that Parts V and VI (Reason and spirit) grew far beyond the bounds originally contemplated and that Hegel himself was a little confused about what he had actually got when he was finished" (p. 135).

21. That is, PhS §§166–77; PG 103–9.

22. Cf. Robert C. Solomon, *In the Spirit of Hegel* (New York and Oxford: Oxford University Press, 1983), 401: "It should be seriously questioned whether these first pages are really a distinct form of consciousness at all."

23. This view is also held by, among others, Escaraffel. Cf. Frederic Escaraffel, "Des mouvements parallèles dans la *Phénoménologie de l'esprit*," *L'Arc* 38 (1969): 93–105.

24. In English as *Hegel's Philosophy of Mind*, trans. William Wallace and A. V. Miller (Oxford: Clarendon Press, 1971).

25. Hegel, *The Philosophical Propaedeutic*, trans. A.V. Miller, ed. Michael George and Andrew Vincent (Oxford: Basil Blackwell, 1986), 59–60; *Hegel Werke*, vol. 4, *Nürnberger und Heidelberger Schriften 1808–1817*. Frankfurt: Suhrkamp, 1986), 117.

26. I have argued separately for this last parallelism in the following article: "Die Rolle des unglücklichen Bewußtseins in Hegels *Phänomenologie des Geistes*," *Deutsche Zeitschrift für Philosophie* 39 (1991): 12–21. Although he interprets it somewhat differently than I, Bonsiepen also points out this parallelism between the Unhappy Consciousness and Force and Understanding: "The opposition between the sensible and the supersensible world, between the here and the

beyond in the 'Force and Understanding' chapter corresponds to the relation between the individual and the Unchangeable." Wolfgang Bonsiepen, *Der Begriff der Negativität in den Jenaer Schriften Hegels*. *Hegel-Studien*, Beiheft 16 (Bonn: Bouvier, 1977), 160. This parallelism is, however, overlooked by Burbidge, who would instead see the section entitled "Legal Status" from the "spirit" chapter as reexamining the material from the "Freedom of Self-Consciousness." John Burbidge, "Unhappy Consciousness in Hegel—An Analysis of Medieval Catholicism?," this volume.

27. PhS §208; PG 122. Hegel uses the same language to refer to God in the *Philosophy of Right*. See PR §270 Remark; RP 350: "It is for this reason that in religion there lies the place where man is always assured of finding a consciousness of the unchangeable, of the highest freedom and satisfaction, even within all the mutability of the world and despite the frustrations of his aims and the loss of his interests and possessions." (PR = *Hegel's Philosophy of Right*, trans. T. M. Knox (Oxford: Clarendon Press, 1952); RP = *Grundlinien der Philosophie des Rechts oder Naturrecht und Staatswissenschaft im Grundrisse*, vol. 7 of *Sämtliche Werke*. Jubiläumsausgabe in 20 Bden, ed. Hermann Glockner (Stuttgart: Friedrich Frommann Verlag, 1927–40.)

28. Cf. Johannes Hoffmeister, "Einleiting des Herausgebers," in Georg Wilhelm Friedrich Hegel, *Sämtliche Werke, Kritische Ausgabe*, vol. 11, *Phänomenologie des Geistes* (Leipzig: Felix Meiner, 1937), xxxv. Cf. also Theodore Haering, "Entstehungsgeschichte der *Phänomenologie des Geistes*," in *Verhandlungen des III. Internationalen Hegel Kongresses 1933*, ed. B. Wigersma, 129ff. Cf. also Robert C. Solomon, "The *Phenomenology of Spirit*: Its Structure," in his *In the Spirit of Hegel* (New York and Oxford: Oxford University Press, 1983), esp. 213.

29. Cf. Solomon who has a glimmering of this structure, which he orders according to categories of theory and practice. Robert Solomon, *In the Spirit of Hegel*, 218. Cf. Escaraffel, who seems to follow these parallelisms but who in my view somewhat confuses the in-itself, for-itself, and in-and-for-itself moments. Frederic Escaraffel, "Des mouvements parallèles dans la *Phénoménologie de l'esprit*," *L'Arc* 38 (1969): esp. 98.

30. See Joseph C. Flay, "The History of Philosophy and the *Phenomenology of Spirit*," in *Hegel and the History of Philosophy: Proceedings of the 1972 Hegel Society of America Conference*, ed. Joseph O'Malley, Keith W. Algozin, and Frederic G. Weiss (The Hague: Martinus Nijhoff, 1974), 52ff.

31. Cf. John Findlay, *Hegel: A Re-Examination* (London: George Allen and Unwin, 1958), 102: "In the treatment of Observation which follows Hegel retraces at a higher level some of the ground covered in his previous study of Sense-Certainty, Perception and Scientific Understanding." See also Charles Taylor, *Hegel* (Cambridge: Cambridge University Press, 1975), 162.

32. Esp. PhS §348; PG 193.

33. See Hyppolite: "*Ce que Hegel nomme 'l'actualisation de la conscience de*

soi rationnelle par sa propre activité' n'est pas autre chose que le développement répété de la conscience de soi dans l'élément de la raison." "Structure de la Phénoménologie," in his *Genèse et structure de la Phénoménologie de l'esprit de Hegel* (Paris: Aubier, 1946), 65.

34. Kline also notes these parallelisms with a slightly different role given to the "Unhappy Consciousness." The fundamental terms on which he bases these parallelisms are "action" and "passion." George L. Kline, "The Dialectic of Action and Passion in Hegel's *Phenomenology of Spirit*," *Review of Metaphysics* 23 (1970): 679–89.

35. With this, the section, "Virtue and the Way of the World," contains roughly the same argument that we find in the *Philosophy of Right* under the heading "The System of Needs," PR §§189–208.

36. Cf. Labarrière, *Structures et mouvement,* 221–31.

37. Cf. also: "Only the totality of spirit is in Time, and the 'shapes,' which are 'shapes' of the totality of *Spirit*, display themselves in a temporal succession" (PhS §679; PG 365).

38. PhS §682; PG 368.

39. Cf. Quentin Lauer, S.J., "Hegel on the Identity of Content in Religion and Philosophy," in *Hegel and the Philosophy of Religion*, ed. Darrel E. Christensen (The Hague: Martinus Nijhoff, 1970), 261–78.

40. Cf. "The content of religion is absolute truth, and consequently the religious is the most sublime of all dispositions" (PR §270 Remark; RP 349).

41. Cf. "The content of religion proclaims earlier in time than does Science, what *Spirit is,* but only Science is its true knowledge of itself" (PhS §802; PG 430).

42. This interpretation is confirmed by Hegel's announcement of the publication of the *Phenomenology* in which he clearly separates "Religion" from the other forms of consciousness and associates it with truth and science: "The *Phenomenology* contains within itself the various forms of spirit as stations along the road by which it becomes pure knowing or Absolute spirit.... The ultimate truth is found at first in Religion and then in Science as the result of the whole.*"* Cited from Hoffmeister's introduction in his edition of the *Phänomenologie des Geistes* (Hamburg: Meiner, 1952), xxxviii. (My translation.)

43. Cf. Detlev Pätzold, "Das absolute Wissen als Theorie des Gesamtzusammenhangs," *Annalen der Internationalen Gesellschaft für Dialektische Philosophie* 1 (1983): 33–37; G. W. Cunningham, "The Significance of the Hegelian Conception of Absolute Knowledge," *Philosophical Review* 17 (1908): 619–42.

44. This is the reproach in Wim van Dooren's review of Labarrière's book. "Zwei Methoden, die *Phänomenologie des Geistes* zu interpretieren," *Hegel-Studien* 7 (1972): esp. 299.

BIBLIOGRAPHY
Works on the PHENOMENOLOGY

COMMENTARIES ON THE WHOLE OR PARTS OF THE PHENOMENOLOGY

Beaufort, Jan. *Die drei Schlüsse. Untersuchungen zur Stellung der Phänomenologie in Hegel's System der Wissenschaft.* Würzburg: Königshausen und Neumann, 1983.

Becker, Werner. *Hegels Phänomenologie des Geistes. Eine Interpretation.* Stuttgart: Kohlhammer, 1971.

Boey, Conrad. *L'esprit devenu étranger à soi-même: Une monographie consacrée à la figur du même nom dans 'La Phénoménologie de l'esprit' de G.W. F. Hegel.* Paris and Bruges, Belgium: Desclée de Brower, 1968.

Claesges, Ulrich. *Darstellung des erscheinenden Wissens. Systematische Einleitung in Hegels Phänomenologie des Geistes.* Bonn: Bouvier, 1974.

Dudeck, Caroline U. *Hegel's Phenomenology of Mind: Analysis and Commentary.* Lanham, Md.: University Press of America, 1982.

Findlay, John. "Analysis of the Text." In *Hegel's Phenomenology of Spirit,* trans. A.V. Miller. Oxford: Oxford University Press, 1977, 479–592.

Fink, Eugen. *Hegel. Phänomenologische Interpretationen der Phänomenologie des Geistes.* Frankfurt: Klostermann, 1977.

Flay, Joseph. *Hegel's Quest for Certainty.* Albany: State University of New York Press, 1984.

Graeser, Andreas. *Einleitung zur Phänomenologie des Geistes. Kommentar.* Stuttgart: Reclam, 1988.

Hansen, Frank-Peter. *G. W. F. Hegel: Phänomenologie des Geistes.* Paderborn: Schöningh, 1994.

Harris, H. S. *Hegel's Ladder.* Vol. 1: *The Pilgrimage of Reason.* Vol. II: *The Odyssey of Spirit.* Indianapolis, Ind.: Hackett, 1997.

Heidegger, Martin. *Hegel's Phenomenology of Spirit*, trans. Parvis Emadt and Kenneth May. Bloomington: Indiana University Press, 1988.

Heinrich, Johannes. *Die Logik der Phänomenologie des Geistes*. Bonn: Bouvier, 1974.

Hessing, J. *Das Selbstbewußtwerden des Geistes*. Stuttgart: Fr. Frommann, 1936.

Hyppolite, Jean. *Genesis and Structure of Hegel's Phenomenology of Spirit*, trans. Samuel Cherniak and John Heckman. Evanston, Ill.: Northwestern University Press, 1974. Originally, *Genèse et structure de la Phénoménologie de l'esprit de Hegel*. Paris: Aubier, 1946.

Jamros, Daniel P. *The Human Shape of God: Religion in Hegel's Phenomenology of Spirit*. New York: Paragon House, 1994.

Kähler, Klaus and Werner Marx. *Die Vernunft in Hegels Phänomenologie des Geistes*. Frankfurt: Klostermann, 1992.

Kainz, Howard P. *Hegel's Phenomenology, Part 1: Analysis and Commentary*. Tuscaloosa: University of Alabama Press, 1976; rpt., Athens: Ohio University Press, 1988.

———. *Hegel's Phenomenology, Part 2: The Evolution of Ethical and Religious Consciousness to the Absolute Standpoint*. Athens: Ohio University Press, 1983.

Kamm, Peter. *Hegels Vorrede zur Phänomenologie des Geistes*. Garus: Tschudi, 1939.

Kettner, Matthias. *Hegels Sinnliche Gewißheit*. Frankfurt, New York: Campus, 1990.

Kimmerle, Gerd. *Sein und Selbst. Untersuchung zur kategorialen Einheit von Vernunft und Geist in Hegels Phänomenologie des Geistes*. Bonn: Bouvier, 1978.

Kojève, Alexandre, *Introduction à la lecture de Hegel*. Paris: Gallimard, 1947. Translated as *An Introduction to the Reading of Hegel*, ed. Alan Bloom, trans. J. H. Nichols. Ithaca, N.Y.: Cornell University Press, 1969.

Krahl, Hans-Jürgen, *Erfahrung des Bewußtseins. Kommentare zu Hegels Einleitung der Phänomenologie des Geistes und Exkurse zur materialistischen Erkenntnistheorie*. Frankfurt: Materialis Verlag, 1979.

Labarrière, Pierre-Jean. *Structures et mouvement dialectique dans la Phénoménologie de l'esprit de Hegel*. Paris: Aubier, 1968.

Labarrière, Pierre-Jean and Gwedoline Jarczyk. *Le malheur de la conscience ou l'accès à la raison. Liberté de l'autoconscience: stoïcisme, scepticisme et la conscience malheureuse. Texte et commentaire.* Paris: Aubier, 1989.

———. *Les premiers combats de la reconnaissance, maîtrise et servitude dans la Phénoménologie de Hegel.* Paris: Aubier, 1987.

Lamb, David. *Hegel: From Foundation to System.* The Hague: Martinus Nijhoff, 1980.

Lauer, Quentin. *A Reading of Hegel's Phenomenology of Spirit.* New York: Fordham University Press, 1982.

Liebrucks, Bruno. *Sprache und Bewußtsein,* Band 5: *Die zweite Revolution der Denkungsart. Hegel: Phänomenologie des Geistes.* Frankfurt: Akademische Verlagsgesellschaft, 1970.

Loewenberg, Jacob. *Hegel's Phenomenology: Dialogues on the Life of the Mind.* La Salle, Ill.: Open Court, 1965.

Marx, Werner. *Hegel's Phenomenology of Spirit, Its Point and Purpose: A Commentary on the Preface and Introduction,* trans. Peter Heath. New York: Harper & Row, 1975. Originally, *Hegels Phänomenologie des Geistes. Die Bestimmung ihrer Idee in Vorrede und Einleitung.* Frankfurt: Klostermann, 1981.

———. *Das Selbstbewußtsein in Hegels Phänomenologie des Geistes.* Frankfurt: Klostermann, 1986.

Naeher, Jürgen. *Einführung in die idealistische Dialektik Hegels.* Opladen: Leske Verlag & Budrich, 1981.

Navickas, Joseph L. *Consciousness and Reality: Hegel's Philosophy of Subjectivity.* The Hague: Martinus Nijhoff, 1976.

Negele, Manfred. *Grade der Freiheit. Versuch einer Interpretation von G. W. F. Hegels "Phänomenologie des Geistes."* Würzburg: Königshausen und Neumann, 1991.

Nink, Caspar. *Kommentar zu den grundlegenden Abschnitten von Hegels Phänomenologie des Geistes.* Regensburg: Josef Habbel, 1931.

Norman, Richard. *Hegel's Phenomenology: A Philosophical Introduction.* New York: St. Martin's Press, 1976; Sussex: Harvester Press, 1981.

Parry, David M. *Hegel's Phenomenology of the "We."* New York: Peter Lang, 1988.

Pinkard, Terry. *Hegel's Phenomenology: The Sociality of Reason.* Cambridge: Cambridge University Press, 1994.

Purpus, Wilhelm. *Zur Dialektik des Bewußtseins nach Hegel.* Berlin: Trowitzsch, 1908.

Scheier, Claus-Artur. *Analytischer Kommentar zu Hegels Phänomenologie des Geistes: Die Architektonik des erscheinenden Wissens.* Freiburg and Munich: Verlag Karl Alber, 1980.

Shklar, Judith. *Hegel's Phenomenology.* Cambridge: Cambridge University Press, 1971.

Smith, Henry B. *The Transition from Bewußtsein to Selbstbewußtsein.* Philadephia: University of Pennsylvania Press, 1947.

Solomon, Robert C. *In the Spirit of Hegel.* New York and Oxford: Oxford University Press, 1983.

Verene, Donald P. *Hegel's Recollection: A Study of Images in the Phenomenology of Spirit.* Albany: State University of New York Press, 1985.

Welker, Michael. *Das Verfahren von Hegels Phänomenologie des Geistes und die Funktion des Abschnitts: 'Die offenbare Religion.'* Heidelberg: Ruprecht-Karls-Universität, 1978.

Well, Karlheinz. *Die schöne Seele und ihre sittliche Wirklichkeit.* Frankfurt and Bern: Peter Lang, 1986.

Westphal, Kenneth. *Hegel's Epistemological Realism. A Study of the Aim and Method of Hegel's Phenomenology of Spirit.* Leuven, Dordrecht: Kluwer Academic Publishers, 1989.

Westphal, Merold. *History and Truth in Hegel's Phenomenology.* Atlantic Highlands, N.J.: Humanities Press, 1979.

Books on Special Themes in the *Phenomenology*

Boey, Conrad. *L'aliénation dans la Phénoménologie de l'esprit de G. W. F. Hegel.* Paris, Bruges: Desclée, de Brouwer, 1970.

Busse, Martin. *Hegels Phänomenologie des Geistes und der Staat.* Berlin: Junker & Dünnhaupt, 1931.

Fulda, Hans Friedrich. *Das Problem einer Einleitung in Hegels Wissenschaft der Logik.* Frankfurt: Klostermann, 1965.

Gretic, Goran. *Das Problem des absoluten Wissens in Hegels Phänomenologie des Geistes.* Zagreb, Croatia: Universitäts-Verlag Liber, 1975.

Jung, Erich. *Entzweiung und Versöhnung in Hegels Phänomenologie des Geistes.* Leipzig: Felix Meiner, 1940.

Lim, Sok-Zin. *Der Begriff der Arbeit bei Hegel. Versuch einer Interpretation der Phänomenologie des Geistes.* Bonn: Bouvier, 1966.

Maurer, Reinhard Klemens. *Hegel und das Ende der Geschichte. Interpretationen zur Phänomenologie des Geistes.* Stuttgart, Berlin, and Cologne: Kohlhammer, 1965.

Ottmann, Horst Henning. *Das Scheitern einer Einleitung in Hegels Philosophie. Eine Analyse der Phänomenologie des Geistes.* Munich and Salzburg: Verlag Anton Pustet, 1973.

Pöggeler, Otto. *Hegels Idee einer Phänomenologie des Geistes.* Freiburg and Munich: Verlag Karl Alber, 1973.

Robinson, Johnathan. *Duty and Hypocrisy in Hegel's Phenomenology of Mind: An Essay in the Real and the Ideal.* Toronto and Buffalo: University of Toronto Press, 1977.

Shklar, Judith N. *Freedom and Independence: A Study of the Political Ideas in Hegel's Phenomenology of Mind.* Cambridge: Cambridge University Press, 1976.

Stiehler, Gottfried. *Die Dialektik in Hegels Phänomenologie des Geistes.* Berlin: Akademie-Verlag, 1964.

Wahl, Jean. *Le Malheur de la Conscience dans la philosophie de Hegel.* Paris: Presses Universitaires de France, 1951.

White, Allen. *Absolute Knowledge: Hegel and the Problem of Metaphysics.* Athens: Ohio University Press, 1983.

COLLECTIONS ON THE *PHENOMENOLOGY*

Browning, Gary (ed.). *Hegel's* Phenomenology of Spirit: *A Reappraisal.* Dordrecht: Kluwar, 1997.

Bulletin of the Hegel Society of Great Britain. *Special issue: Hegel's* Phenomenology of Spirit 29 (Spring/Summer): 1994.

Fulda, Hans Friedrich and Dieter Henrich (eds.). *Materialien zu Hegels Phänomenologie des Geistes.* Frankfurt: Suhrkamp, 1973.

Gadamer, Hans-Georg (ed.). *Hegel-Tage Royaumont 1964: Beiträge zur Deutung der Phänomenologie des Geistes. Hegel-Studien*, Beiheft 3. Bonn: Bouvier, 1966.

Westphal, Merold (ed). *Method and Speculation in Hegel's Phenomenology*. Atlantic Highlands, N.J.: Humanities Press, 1982.

GENERAL BIBLIOGRAPHY ON THE *PHENOMENOLOGY*

Adelman, Howard. "Hegel's *Phenomenology*: Facing the Preface." *Idealistic Studies* 14 (1984): 159–70.

Albizu, Edgardo. "La estructura de la *Fenomenología del espíritu* de Hegel y el problema del tiempo." *Revista Latinoamericana de Filosofía* 7 (1981): 209–22.

Allen, Robert van Roden. "Hegelian Beginning and Resolve: A View of the Relationship between the *Phenomenology* and the *Logic*." *Idealistic Studies* 13 (1983): 249–65.

Altizer, J. J. "Comment on Murray Greene: Hegel's 'Unhappy Consciousness' and Nietzsche's 'Slave Morality'." In *Hegel and the Philosophy of Religion*, ed. Darrel E. Christensen. The Hague: Martinus Nijhoff, 1970, 147–52.

Andler, Charles. "Le fondement du savoir dans la *Phénoménologie de l'esprit*." *Revue de Métaphysique et de Morale* 38 (1931): 317–40.

Andolfi, Ferruccio. "Die Gestalten des Individualismus in der *Phänomenologie des Geistes*." *Hegel-Jahrbuch* 1991: 211–25.

Aschenberg, Reinhold. "Der Wahrheitsbegriff in Hegels *Phänomenologie des Geistes*." In *Die ontologische Option*, ed. Klaus Hartmann. New York and Berlin: Walter de Gruyter, 1976, 211–304.

Asmus, V. F. "The Problem of Immediate Knowledge in the Philosophy of Hegel." *Soviet Studies in Philosophy* 1 (1962–63): 44–50.

Badie, M. F. "La doctrine et la vérité de l'Aufklärung dans la *Phénoménologie de l'esprit*." *Tijdschrift voor de Studie van de Verlichting* (Brussels) 3 (1975): 125–39.

Bahti, Timothy. "The Indifferent Reader. The Performance of Hegel's Introduction to the *Phenomenology*." *Diacritics* 11 (1981): 68–82.

Baillie, J. B. *An Outline of the Idealistic Construction of Experience*. New York: Garland, 1984.

Baur, Michael. "Hegel and the Overcoming of the Understanding." *The Owl of Minerva* 22 (1991): 141–58.

Becker, Werner. *Idealistische und materialistische Dialektik. Das Verhältnis von Herrschaft und Knechtschaft bei Hegel und Marx*. Stuttgart: Kohlhammer, 1970.

———. "Hegels Dialektik von Herr und Knecht." In his *Selbstbewußtsein und Spekulation. Zur Kritik der Transzendentalphilosophie.* Freiburg: Rombach, 1972.

Bednár, Jiri. "Die transzendentale Bedeutung des Hegelschen Begriffs 'Das unglückliche Bewußtsein' im Zusammenhang mit Hegels Religionskritik in der *Phänomenologie des Geistes.*" *Filozoficky Casopis* 14 (1966): 464–82.

Behler, Ernst. "Die Geschichte des Bewußtseins zur Vorgeschichte eines Hegelschen Themas." *Hegel-Studien* 7 (1972): 169–216.

Berenson, Frances. "Hegel on Others and the Self." *Philosophy* 57 (1982): 77–90.

Bernstein, J. M. "From Self-Consciousness to Community: Act and Recognition in the Master-Slave Relationship." In *The State and Civil Society: Studies in Hegel's Political Philosophy*, ed. Z. Pelczynski. Cambridge: Cambridge University Press, 1984, 14–39.

Besse, Guy. "L'utilité-concept fondamental des 'Lumières'." *Hegel-Jahrbuch* 1968–69, 355–71.

Bloch, Ernst. "Das Faustmotiv der *Phänomenologie des Geistes.*" *Hegel-Studien* 1 (1961): 155–71.

Boeder, Heribert. "Das natürliche Bewußtsein." *Hegel-Studien* 12 (1977) 157–78.

Boey, Conrad. "L'aliénation hégélienne: Un chaînon de l'experience de la conscience et de la *Phénoménologie de l'esprit.*" *Archives de Philosophie* 35 (1972): 87–110.

Bonsiepen, Wolfgang. "Erste zeitgenössische Rezensionen der *Phänomenologie des Geistes.*" *Hegel-Studien* 14 (1979): 9–38.

———. "Zu Hegels Auseinandersetzung mit Schellings Naturphilosophie in der *Phänomenologie des Geistes.*" In *Schelling. Seine Bedeutung für eine Philosophie der Natur und der Geschichte*, ed. Ludwig Hasler. Stuttgart, Bad Cannstatt: Frommann-Holzboog, 1981, 167–72.

———. "Dialektik und Negativität in der *Phänomenologie des Geistes.*" *Hegel-Jahrbuch* 1974: 263–67.

Bossart, W. H. "Hegel on the Inverted World." *The Philosophical Forum* 13 (1982): 326–41.

Breton, Stanislas. "La dialectique de la conscience dans la *Phénoménologie de l'Esprit* de Hegel." *Euntes docete* 6 (1956): 323–60.

Brinkley, Allan B. "Time in Hegel's *Phenomenology.*" *Tulane Studies in Philosophy* [*Studies in Hegel*] 9 (1960): 3–15.

Bubner, Rüdiger. "Rousseau, Hegel und die Dialektik der Aufklärung." In *Aufklärung und Gegenaufklärung in der europäischen Literatur, Philosophie und Politik von der Antike bis zur Gegenwart*, ed. Jochen Schmidt. Darmstadt: Wissenschaftliche Buchgesellschaft, 1989, 404–20.

———. "Problemgeschichte und systematischer Sinn einer *Phänomenologie*." *Hegel-Studien* 5 (1969): 129–59.

Buchner, Hartmut. "Hegel im Übergang von Religion zu Philosophie." *Philosophisches Jahrbuch* 78 (1971): 82–97.

Bullinger, Anton. *Georg Wilhelm Friedrich Hegels Phänomenologie des Geistes behufs Einführung in die Philosophie und christliche Theologie*. Munich: Ackermann, 1904.

Burbidge, John. "Man, God and Death in Hegel's *Phenomenology*." *Philosophy and Phenomenological Research* 42 (1981–82): 183–96.

Calvez, J. Y. "L'âge d'or: Essai sur le destin de la 'belle âme' chez Novalis et Hegel," *Études germaniques* 9 (1954): 112–27.

Caujolle-Zaslawskly, Françoise. "Le scepticisme selon Hegel." *Revue philosophique de la France* 98 (1973): 461–76.

Cook, Daniel J. "Sprache und Bewußtsein in Hegels *Phänomenologie des Geistes*." *Hegel-Jahrbuch* 1970: 117–24.

Coreth, Emerich. "Zu Hegels Absolutem Wissen." *Aquinas* 24 (1981): 213–44.

———. "Das absolute Wissen bei Hegel." *Zeitschrift für Katholische Theologie* 105 (1983): 389–405.

Cramer, Konrad. "Bemerkungen zu Hegels Begriff vom Bewußtsein in der Einleitung zur Hegels *Phänomenologie des Geistes*." In *Seminar: Dialektik in der Philosophie Hegels*, ed. Rolf-Peter Horstman. Frankfurt: Suhrkamp, 1978, 360–97.

Cunningham, G. W. "The Significance of the Hegelian Conception of Absolute Knowledge." *Philosophical Review* 17 (1908): 619–42.

Dahlstrom, Daniel O. "Die Quelle der Sittlichkeit in Hegels *Phänomenologie des Geistes*." *Hegel-Jahrbuch* 1987: 256–61.

———. "Die schöne Seele bei Schiller und Hegel." *Hegel-Jahrbuch* 1991: 147–56.

De la Iglesia Duarte, José-Ignacio. "Commentario al prólogo de la *Fenomenología de espíritu*." *Crisis* 18 (1971): 194–200.

De Nys, Martin J. "Sense-Certainty and Universality: Hegel's Entrance into the *Phenomenology.*" *International Philosophical Quarterly* 18 (1978): 445–65.

———. "Force and Understanding: The Unity of the Object of Consciousness." In *Method and Speculation in Hegel's Phenomenology*, ed. Merold Westphal. Atlantic Highlands, N.J.: Humanities Press, 1982, 57–70.

———. "The Appearance and Appropriation of Religious Consciousness in Hegel's *Phenomenology.*" *Modern Schoolman* 62 (1985): 165–84.

———. "The Motion of the Universal. Hegel's Phenomenology of Consciousness." *Modern Schoolman* 56 (1978–79): 301–20.

De Vos, Lu de. "Absolute Knowing in the *Phenomenology.*" In *Hegel on Ethical Life, Religion and Philosophy: 1793–1807*, ed. A. Wylleman. Louvain, Belgium, and Dordrecht, Netherlands: Kluwer Academic Publishers, 1989, 231–70.

Devos, Rob. "The Significance of Manifest Religion in the *Phenomenology.*" In *Hegel on Ethical Life, Religion and Philosophy: 1793–1807*, ed. A. Wylleman. Louvain, Belgium, and Dordrecht, Netherlands: Kluwer Academic Publishers, 1989, 195–229.

De Waelhens, Alphonse. "Phénoménologie husserlienne et Phénoménologie hégélienne." *Revue philosophique de Louvain* 52 (1954): 234–49.

Dobbins, John and Peter Fuss. "The Silhouette of Dante in Hegel's *Phenomenology of Spirit.*" *Clio* 11 (1982): 387–413.

Domenico, Nicola de. "Die 'Verkehrte Welt.' Ein erneuter Versuch, eine reflexive Paradoxie der *Phänomenologie des Geistes* Hegels zu interpretieren." In *Philosophie als Verteidigung des Ganzen der Vernunft*, ed. Domenico Losurdo and Hans Jörg Sandkühler. Cologne: Pahl-Rugenstein, 1988.

Donato, Eugenio. "Here, Now/Always, Already." *Diacritics* 6 (1976): 24–29.

Donougho, Martin. "The Woman in White: On the Reception of Hegel's Antigone." *The Owl of Minerva* 21 (1989–90): 65–89.

Dove, Kenley. "Die Epoché der *Phänomenologie des Geistes.*" In *Stuttgarter Hegel-Tage*, ed. Hans-Georg Gadamer. *Hegel-Studien*, Beiheft 11. Bonn: Bouvier, 1983, 605–21.

Dubarle, Dominique. "De la foi au savoir selon la *Phénoménologie de l'espirit.*" *Revue des Sciences Philosophiques et Théologiques* 59 (1975): 3–36, 243–77, 399–425.

Düsing, Klaus. "Die Bedeutung des antiken Skeptizismus für Hegels Kritik der sinnlichen Gewißheit." *Hegel-Studien* 8 (1973): 119–30.

Eley, Lothar. "Sinnliche Gewißheit, Sprache und Gesellschaft." *Sprache im Technischen Zeitalter* 43 (1972): 205–14.

Escaraffel, F. "Des mouvements parallèles dans la *Phénoménologie de l'esprit.*" *L'Arc* 38 (1969): 93–105.

Escohotado, Antonio. *La conciencia infeliz: Ensayo sobre la filosofía de la religión de Hegel.* Madrid: Ed. Revista de Occidente, 1972.

Ferrari, Oward. "Hegel. Rapport entre *Phénoménologie de l'esprit* et *Science de la logique.*" *Philosophie* 1985: 143–53.

Fessard, Gaston. "Deux interprètes de la *Phénoménologie* de Hegel: Jean Hyppolite et Alexandre Kojève." *Études* 255 (1947): 368–73.

Fetscher, Iring. "Randglossen zu 'Herrschaft und Knechtschaft' in Hegels *Phänomenologie des Geistes.*" In *Wirklichkeit und Reflexion.* Walter Schulz zum 60. Geburtstag, ed. Helmut Fahrenbach. Pfullingen: Verlag Günter Neske, 1973, 137–44.

Finacchiaro, Maurice A. "Dialectic and Argument in Philosophy: A Case Study of Hegel's Phenomenological Preface." *Argumentation* 2 (1988): 175–90.

Fink, Eugen. "Hegels Problemformel 'Prüfung der Realität des Erkennens' (in der *Phänomenologie des Geistes*)." *Praxis* 7 (1971): 39–47.

———. "Die verkehrte Welt." In *Weltaspekte der Philosophie.* Rudolph Berlinger zum 26. Oktober 1972, ed. Werner Beierwaltes and Wiebke Schrader. Amsterdam: Editions Rodopi N.V., 1972, 41–52.

Flay, Joseph C. "Comment on Murray Greene: Hegel's 'Unhappy Consciousness' and Nietzsche's 'Slave Morality'." In *Hegel and the Philosophy of Religion,* ed. Darrel E. Christensen. The Hague: Martinus Nijhoff, 1970, 142–46.

———. "Religion and the Absolute Standpoint." *Thought* 56 (1981): 316–27.

———. "The History of Philosophy and the *Phenomenology of Spirit.*" In *Hegel and the History of Philosophy. Proceedings of the 1972 Hegel Society of America Conference,* ed. Joseph O'Malley, Keith W. Algozin, and Frederic G. Weiss. The Hague: Martinus Nijhoff, 1974, 47–61.

Friedman, R. Z. "Hypocrisy and the Highest Good: Hegel on Kant's Transition from Morality to Religion." *Journal of the History of Philosophy* 24 (1986): 503–22.

Fruchon, Pierre. "Sur la conception hégélienne de la 'religion révélée' selon M. Theunissen." *Archives de Philosophie* 48 (1985): 613–41, 49 (1986): 619–42.

Fulda, Hans Friedrich. "Zur Logik der *Phänomenologie* von 1807." In *Materialien zu Hegels Phänomenologie des Geistes*, ed. Hans Friedrich Fulda and Dieter Henrich. Frankfurt: Suhrkamp, 1973, 391–422. Also in *Hegel-Tage Royaumont 1964: Beiträge zur Deutung der Phänomenologie des Geistes*, ed. Hans-Georg Gadamer. *Hegel-Studien*, Beiheft 3. Bonn: Bouvier, 1966, 73–102.

Furth, Peter. "Antigone oder zur tragischen Vorgeschichte der bürgerlichen Gesellschaft." *Hegel-Jahrbuch* 1984–85: 15–30.

Gadamer, Hans-Georg. "Hegel's 'Inverted World'." In his *Hegel's Dialectic: Five Hermeneutical Essays*, trans. P. Christopher Smith. New Haven and London: Yale University Press, 1976, 35–53.

———. "Hegel's Dialectic of Self-Consciousness." In his *Hegel's Dialectic: Five Hermeneutical Essays*, trans. P. Christopher Smith. New Haven and London: Yale University Press, 1976, 54–74.

Gaete, Arturo. "La idea absoluta." *Dialogos* 22 (1987): 49–91.

Garaudy, Roger. *Dieu est mort: Étude sur Hegel*. Paris: Presses Universitaires de France, 1962.

Gauvin, Joseph. "Plaisir et nécessité." *Archives de Philosophie* 28 (1965): 483–509. Also in *Beiträge zur Deutung der Phänomenologie des Geistes*, ed. Hans-Georg Gadamer, *Hegel-Studien*, Beiheft 3. Bonn: Bouvier, 1966, 155–80.

———. "Entfremdung et Entäußerung dans la *Phénoménologie de l'esprit* de Hegel." *Archives de Philosophie* 25 (1962): 555–71.

———. *Wortindex zur Phänomenologie des Geistes*. *Hegel-Studien*, Beiheft 14. Bonn: Bouvier, 1977.

———. "La critique du salut chrétien par l'Aufklärung selon la *Phénoménologie* de Hegel." *Recherches de Science Religieuse* 68 (1980): 391–417.

———. "La langue de la *Phénoménologie*." *Hegel-Jahrbuch* 1970: 112–16.

———. "Für uns dans la *Phénoménologie de l'esprit*." *Archives de Philosophie* 33 (1970): 829–54.

———. "Les dérivés de Res dans la *Phénoménologie de l'esprit*." In *Res. Atti del III. Colloquio internazionale del Lessico intellectuale europeo*, ed. M. Fattori and M. Bianchi. Rome: Edizioni dell'Atenea, 1982, 313–46.

Geraets, Theodore F. "Hegel: L'esprit absolu comme ouverture du système." *Laval Théologique et Philosophique* 42 (1986): 3–13.

——— (ed.). *Hegel: The Absolute Spirit*. Ottawa: University of Ottawa Press, 1984.

Gerald, Thomas J. "Hegels Familienbegriff in der *Phänomenologie des Geistes*." *Hegel-Jahrbuch* 1984–85: 229–34.

Gloy, Karen. "Bemerkungen zum Kapitel 'Herrschaft und Knechtschaft' in Hegels *Phänomenologie des Geistes.*" *Zeitschrift für Philosophische Forschung* 39 (1985): 187–213.

Goldford, Dennis. "Kojève's Reading of Hegel." *International Philosophical Quarterly* 22 (1982): 275–93.

Goldstein, Leon J. "Force and the Inverted World in Dialectical Retrospection." *International Studies in Philosophy* 20 (1988): 13–28.

Gossens, Wilfried. "Ethical Life and Family in the *Phenomenology of Spirit.*" In *Hegel on Ethical Life, Religion and Philosophy: 1793–1807*, ed. A. Wylleman. Louvain, Belgium, and Dordrecht, Netherlands: Kluwer Academic Verlag, 1989, 163–94.

Gouhier, Alain. "Detresse materielle et conscience malheureuse." *Hegel-Jahrbuch* 1986, 211–22.

Graeser, Andreas. "Zu Hegels Portrait der sinnlichen Gewißheit." *Freiburger Zeitschrift für Philosophie und Theologie* 34 (1987): 437–53.

———. "Hegels Kritik der sinnlichen Gewißheit und Platons Kritik der Sinneswahrnehmung im *Theaitet.*" *Revue de Philosophie Ancienne* 3 (1985): 39–57.

Granier, Jean. "Hegel et la Révolution française." *Revue de la Métaphysique et de Morale* 85 (1980): 1–26.

Greene, Murray. "Hegel's 'Unhappy Consciousness' and Nietzsche's 'Slave Morality'." In *Hegel and the Philosophy of Religion*, ed. Darrel E. Christensen. The Hague: Martinus Nijhoff, 1970, 125–41.

———. "Hegel's Notion of Inversion." *International Journal of the Philosophy of Religion* 1 (1970): 161–75.

Grimmlinger, Friederich. "Zum Begriff des absoluten Wissens in Hegels *Phänomenologie.*" In *Geschichte und System*. Festschrift für Erich Heintel zum 60. Geburtstag, ed. Hans-Dieter Klein und Erhard Oeser. Munich and Vienna: Oldenbourg, 1972, 279–300.

Grlic, Danko. "Revolution und Terror. (Zum Kapitel 'Die absolute Freiheit und der Schrecken' aus Hegels *Phänomenologie des Geistes*)." *Praxis* 7 (1971): 49–61.

Gumppenberg, Rudolf. "Bewußtsein und Arbeit. Zu G. W. F. Hegels *Phänomenologie des Geistes.*" *Zeitschrift für Philosophische Forschung* 26 (1972): 372–88.

Haering, Theodore. "Entstehungsgeschichte der *Phänomenologie des Geistes.*" In *Verhandlungen des III. Internationalen Hegel Kongresses 1933*, ed. B.

Wigersma. Haarlem: N/VH.D. Tjeenk Willink & Zn. and Tübingen: J. C. B. Mohr, 1934, 118-36.

Hanzig, Evelyn. "'Hemmung der Begierde'—Zur Dialektik des Selbstbewußtseins. Die Nahtstelle zwischen Hegel und Freud." *Hegel-Jahrbuch* 1984-85: 309-18.

———. "Die Negativität des Sollens. Zur Konzeptualisierung des Selbst-Seins im Übergang von Hegels *Phänomenologie des Geistes* zur *Logik.*" *Hegel-Jahrbuch* 1987: 284-92.

Harris, H. S. "The Cows in the Dark Night." *Dialogue* (Canada) 26 (1987): 627-43.

———. "Hegel's Science of Experience." *Bulletin of the Hegel Society of Great Britain* 15 (1987): 13-37.

———. "Hegel and the French Revolution." *Clio* 7 (1977): 5-18.

———. "The Concept of Recognition in Hegel's Jena Manuscripts." *Hegel-Studien*, Beiheft 20, 1980, *Hegel in Jena*, ed. Dieter Henrich and Klaus Düsing. Bonn: Bouvier, 1980, 229-48.

———. "Les influences platoniciennes sur la théorie de la vie et du désir dans la *Phénoménologie de l'esprit* de Hegel." *Revue de Philosophie Ancienne* 3 (1985): 59-94.

Hasler, Ludwig. "Hegel und die Aufklärung." *Studia Philosophica* 41 (1982): 115-37.

Heidegger, Martin. *Hegel's Concept of Experience*, trans. J. Glenn Gray and Fred D. Wieck. New York: Harper & Row, 1970.

Heintel, Peter. "Die Religion als Gestalt des absoluten Geistes." *Wiener Jahrbuch für Philosophie* 3 (1970): 162-202.

Hinchman, Lewis P. *Hegel's Critique of the Enlightenment.* Gainesville: University of Florida Press, 1984.

Hirsch, Emanuel. "Die Beisetzung der Romantiker in Hegels *Phänomenologie.* Ein Kommentar zu dem Abschnitte über die Moralität," *Deutsche Vierteljahresschrift für Literaturwissenschaft* 2 (1924): 510-32. Also in *Materialien zu Hegels Phänomenologie des Geistes*, ed. Hans Friedrich Fulda and Dieter Henrich. Frankfurt: Suhrkamp, 1973, 245-75.

Hoffmeister, Johannes. "Einleiting des Herausgebers." In *Georg Wilhelm Friedrich Hegel, Sämtliche Werke, Kritische Ausgabe*, Bd. 11, *Phänomenologie des Geistes.* Leipzig: Felix Meiner, 1937, xxviii-xlii.

Holz, Hans Heinz. *Herr und Knecht bei Leibniz und Hegel.* Neuwied, Berlin: Luchterhand, 1968.

Horn, Joachim C. "Hegel's 'Wahrheit des Sinnlichen' oder die 'zweite übersinnliche Welt." *Kant-Studien* 54 (1963): 252–58.

———. "Absolutes Wesen/Absolutes Wissen." *Kant-Studien* 66 (1975): 169–80.

Hossfeld, Paul. "Zur Auslegung der *Phänomenologie des Geistes* von Hegel." *Philosophisches Jahrbuch* 65 (1957): 232–44.

Hoy, David. "Hegel's Critique of Kantian Morality." *History of Philosophy Quarterly* 6 (1989): 207–32.

Hulbert, James. "Diderot in the Text of Hegel: A Question of Intertextuality." *Studies in Romanticism* 22 (1983): 267–91.

Hyppolite, Jean. "Note sur la préface de la *Phénoménologie de l'esprit* et le thème: l'absolu est sujet." *Hegel-Tage Urbino 1965*, ed. Hans-Georg Gadamer, *Hegel-Studien*, Beiheft 4. Bonn: Bouvier, 1969, 75–80.

———. "La *Phénoménologie* de Hegel et la pensée française contemporaine." In his *Figures de la pensée philosophique: Écrits (1931–1968)*, tome I. Paris: Presses Universitaires de France, 1971, 231–41.

———. "Essai d'interprétation de la préface de la *Phénoménologie*." In his *Figures de la pensée philosophique: Écrits (1931–1968)*, tome I. Paris: Presses Universitaires de France, 1971, 275–308.

———. "L'état du droit (La condition juridique): Introduction à un commentaire." In *Hegel-Tage Royaumont 1964*, ed. Hans-Georg Gadamer, *Hegel-Studien*, Beiheft 3. Bonn: Bouvier, 1966, 181–85.

———. "Situation de l'homme dans la phénoménologie hégélienne." In his *Figures de la pensée philosophique: Écrits (1931–1968)*, tome I. Paris: Presses Universitaires de France, 1971, 104–21. Also in *Les Temps Modernes* 2 (1947): 1276–89.

———. "La signification de la Révolution française dans la *Phénoménologie* de Hegel." In his *Études sur Marx et Hegel*. Paris: Librairie Marcel Rivière et Cie, 1955, 45–81.

———. "Dialectique et dialogue dans la *Phénoménologie de l'esprit* de Hegel." In his *Figures de la pensée philosophique: Écrits (1931–1968)*, tome I. Paris: Presses Universitaires de France, 1971, 209–12. Also in *Entretiens Philosophiques* (Athens) 1955: 184–86.

———. "Structure du langage philosophique d'après la Préface de la *Phénoménologie de l'Esprit*." In his *Figures de la pensée philosophique: Écrits (1931–1968)*, tome I. Paris: Presses Universitaires de France, 1971, 340–52.

———. "L'existence dans la *Phénoménologie* de Hegel." In his *Figures de la pen-*

sée philosophique: Écrits (1931–1968), tome I. Paris: Presses Universitaires de France, 1971, 92–103.

Jamme, Christoph. "Platon, Hegel und der Mythos zu den Hintergründen eines Diktums aus der Vorrede zur *Phänomenologie des Geistes.*" *Hegel-Studien* 15 (1980): 151–69.

Janke, Wolfgang. "Herrschaft und der absolute Herr." *Philosophische Perspektiven* 4 (1972): 211–31.

Jauss, Hans Robert. "*Le Neveu de Rameau*: Dialogue et Dialectique." *Revue de Métaphysique et de Morale* 89 (1984): 145–81.

Jurist, Eliot. "Hegel's Concept of Recognition." *The Owl of Minerva* 19 (1987): 5–22.

———. "Recognition and Self-Knowledge." *Hegel-Studien* 21 (1986): 143–50.

Kaan, André. "Le mal et son pardon." In *Hegel-Tage Royaumont 1964: Beiträge zur Deutung der Phänomenologie des Geistes*, ed. Hans-Georg Gadamer, *Hegel-Studien*, Beiheft 3. Bonn: Bouvier, 1966, 187–94.

Kaan, André. "L'honnêteté et l'imposture dans la société civile (à propos du chapitre V.C. de la *Phénoménologie*: Le règne animal de l'esprit." *Hegel-Jahrbuch* 1971, 45–49.

Kainz, Howard. "Hegel's Characterization of Truth in the Preface to His *Phenomenology.*" *Philosophy Today* 13 (1969–70): 206–13.

———. "Hegel's Theory of Aesthetics in the *Phenomenology.*" *Idealistic Studies* 2 (1972): 81–94.

———. "Some Problems with English Translations of Hegel's *Phänomenologie des Geistes.*" *Hegel-Studien* 21 (1986): 175–82.

Kaufmann, Walter. "The Preface to the *Phenomenology.*" In his *Hegel: Texts and Commentary*, vol. 2. Garden City, N.Y.: Anchor, 1966, 6–110.

———. "Hegel's Conception of Phenomenology." In *Phenomenology and Philosophical Understanding*, ed. Edo Pivcevic. Cambridge: Cambridge University Press, 1975, 211–30.

Klein, Ytashaq. "La *Phénoménologie de l'espirit* et le scepticisme." *Revue philosophique de Louvain* 69 (1971): 370–96.

———. "Conscience de soi et reconnaissance." *Revue philosophique de Louvain* 73 (1975: 294–303.

Kline, George L. "The Dialectic of Action and Passion in Hegel's *Phenomenology of Spirit.*" *Review of Metaphysics* 23 (1970): 679–89.

Kortian, Garbis. "Die Auflösung von Hegels *Phänomenologie* in Hermeneutik. Zum Wahrheitsanspruch eines spekulativen Erfahrungsbegriffes." In *Die Krise der Phänomenologie und die Pragmatik des Wissenschaftsfortschritts*, ed. Michael Benedikt and Rudolf Burger. Vienna: Edition S, Verlag der Österreichischen Staatsdruckeri, 1986, 53–64.

Kozo, Kunio. "Zur Chronologie von Hegels Nürnberger Fassungen des Selbstbewußtseinkapitels." *Hegel-Studien* 21 (1986): 27–64.

Krüger, Gerhard. "Die dialektische Erfahrung des natürlichen Bewußtseins bei Hegel." In *Hermeneutik und Dialektik*, ed. Rüdiger Bübner, Conrad Cramer, and Reiner Wiehl. Tübingen: Mohr, 1970.

Kursanov, G. A. "Hegels *Phänomenologie des Geistes*." *Deutsche Zeitschrift für Philosophie* 10 (1962): 1451–60.

Labarrière, Pierre-Jean. "La *Phénoménologie de l'esprit* comme discours systématique: Histoire, religion et science." *Hegel-Studien* 9 (1974): 131–53.

———. "Belle âme, mal et pardon." *Concordia* 1 (1982): 11–15.

———. "Le savior absolu de l'esprit." In *The Meaning of Absolute Spirit*, ed. Theodore Geraets. Ottawa: Éditions de l'Université d'Ottawa, 1982, 499–507.

Lamb, David. "Hegel and Wittgenstein on Language and Sense-Certainty." *Clio* 7 (1978): 285–301.

Lauener, Henri. "Die Sprache der Zerrissenheit als Dasein des sich entfremdeten Geistes bei Hegel." *Studia philosophica* 24 (1964): 162–75.

Lauer, Quentin. "Phenomenology: Hegel and Husserl." In *Beyond Epistemology: New Studies in the Philosophy of Hegel*, ed. Frederick G. Weiss. The Hague: Martinus Nijhoff, 1974, 174–96.

Lawton, Philip. "Existential Themes in Hegel's *Phenomenology*." *Philosophy Research Archives* 8 (1982): 279–313.

Le Dantec, Michel. "La Conscience Malheureuse dans la société civile." In *Hegels Philosophie des Rechts. Die Theorie der Rechtsformen und ihrer Logik*, ed. Dieter Henrich and Rolf-Peter Horstmann. Stuttgart: Ernst Klett, 1982, 139–50.

Lemaigre, Bernard. "Le saviour absolu comme réalisation de soi dans la philosophie de Hegel." *Études freudiennes* 1–2 (1969): 249–83.

Léonard, André. "La structure du système hégélian." *Revue philosophique de Louvain* 69 (1971): 495–524.

———. "Pour une exégèse renouvelée de la *'Phénoménologie de l'esprit'* de Hegel." *Revue philosophique de Louvain* 74 (1976): 572–93.

Leuze, Reinhard. *Die außerchristlichen Religionen bei Hegel.* Göttingen: Vandenhoeck & Rupprecht, 1975.

Levi, Albert William. "Hegel's *Phenomenology* as a Philosophy of Culture." *Journal of the History of Philosophy* 22 (1984): 445-70.

Liebrucks, Bruno. "Reflexionen über den Satz Hegels 'Das Wahre ist das Ganze'." *Zeugnisse* (Frankfurt) 1963: 74-14.

Link, Christian. *Hegels Wort 'Gott selbst ist tot.'* Zurich: Theologischer Verlag, 1974.

Litt, Theodor. "Hegels Begriff des 'Geistes' und das Problem der Tradition." *Studium Generale* 4 (1951): 311-21.

Livet, Pierre. "La dynamique de la *Phénoménologie de l'esprit.*" *Archives de Philosophie* 44 (1981): 611-35.

Loewenberg, Jacob. "The Exoteric Approach to Hegel's *Phenomenology* (I)." *Mind* 43 (1934): 424-45.

———. "The Comedy of Immediacy in Hegel's *Phenomenology* (II)." *Mind* 44 (1935): 21-38.

Löwith, Karl. "Nachwort zu Hegels Einleitung in die *Phänomenologie des Geistes.*" In his *Aufsätze und Vorträge 1930-1980.* Stuttgart: Kohlhammer, 1971, 204-10.

Ludwig, Walter D. "Hegel's Conception of Absolute Knowing." *The Owl of Minerva* 21 (1989): 5-19.

Luft, Eric von der. "An Early Interpretation of Hegel's *Phenomenology of Spirit.*" *Hegel-Studien* 24 (1989): 183-94.

Luther, O. Kem and Jeff L. Hoover. "Hegel's Phenomenology of Religion." *The Journal of Religion* 61 (1981): 229-41.

Mackay, L. A. "Antigone, Coriolanus, and Hegel." *Transactions and Proceedings of the American Philological Association* 93 (1962): 166-74.

Maker, William. "Hegel's *Phenomenology* as Introduction to Science." *Clio* 10 (1981): 381-97.

Marcel, Gabriel. "Le malheur de la conscience dans la philosophie de Hegel." *Europe* 8 (1930): 149-52.

Marcuse, Herbert. "Leben als Seinsbegriff in der *Phänomenologie des Geistes.*" In his *Hegels Ontologie und die Grundlegung einer Theorie der Geschichtlichkeit.* Frankfurt: Klostermann, 1968, 257-62.

Marejew, Sergej N. "Die Phänomenologie der verständigen Form bei Hegel. Schwierigkeit und deren Ursachen." *Hegel-Jahrbuch* 1975: 374–83.

Marsh, James L. "The Play of Difference/Différance in Hegel and Derrida." *The Owl of Minerva* 21 (1990): 145–53.

Marx, Werner. "Aufgabe und Methode der Philosophie in Schellings *System des transzendentalen Idealismus* und in Hegels *Phänomenologie des Geistes.*" In his *Schelling: Geschichte, System, Freiheit*. Freiburg and Munich: Verlag Karl Alber, 1977, 63–99.

Mayer, Hans. "Herrschaft und Knechtschaft. Hegels Deutung, ihre literarischen Ursprünge und Folgen." *Jahrbuch der Deutschen Schillergesellschaft* 15 (1971): 251–79.

——. "Hegel und das Problem des unglücklichen Bewußtseins." In his *Literatur der Übergangszeit*. Berlin: Volk und Welt, 1949, 7–16.

McCumber, John. "A Mind-Body Problem in Hegel's *Phenomenology of Spirit.*" *International Studies in Philosophy* 12 (1980): 41–52.

——. "Scientific Progress and Hegel's *Phenomenology of Spirit.*" *Idealistic Studies* 13 (1983): 1–10.

——. "Communicative Consciousness and Human Destiny in Hegel's *Phenomenology.*" In *Phenomenology and the Understanding of Human Destiny*, ed. Stephen Skousgaard. Washington D.C.: Center for Advanced Research in Phenomenology and University Press of America, 1981, 143–51.

Metzke, Erwin. "Vorrede zur *Phänomenologie des Geistes.*" In his *Hegels Vorreden mit Kommentar zur Einführung in seine Philosophie*. Heidelberg: F. H. Kerle Verlag, 1949, 137–208.

Miklowitz, Paul S. "The Ontological Status of Style in Hegel's *Phenomenology.*" *Idealistic Studies* 13 (1983): 61–73.

Miller, Arnold V. "Absolute Knowing and the Destiny of the Individual." *The Owl of Minerva* 15 (1983): 45–50.

Monserrat, Javier. "Análisis de la discontinuidad lógico-crítica entre la Introducción y la dialéctica de la conciencia en le *Fenomenología.*" *Pensamiento* 29 (1973): 37–72.

Mougin, Henri. "Hegel et Le Neveu de Rameau." *Europe* 24 (1946): 1–11.

Müller, Gustav Emil. "The Interdependence of the *Phenomenology, Logic* and *Encyclopedia.*" In *New Studies in Hegel's Philosophy*, ed. W. E. Steinkraus. New York: Holt, Rinehart and Winston, 1971, 18–33.

Müller, Ulrich. "Die Erfahrung der Negation. Hegels Wirklichkeitsverständnis in der *Phänomenologie des Geistes.*" *Archiv für Geschichte der Philosophie* 70 (1988): 78–102.

Münch, F. "Die Problemstellung von Hegels *Phänomenologie des Geistes.*" *Archiv für die Geschichte der Philosophie* 26 (1912–13): 149–73.

Munson, Thomas. "Phenomenology and History." *Philosophy Today* 13 (1969): 296–301.

Murray, Michael. "Time in Hegel's *Phenomenology of Spirit.*" *Review of Metaphysics* 33 (1981): 682–705.

Narski, Igor S. "Die verkehrte Welt, List des Verstandes und List der Vernunft bei Hegel." *Annalen der Internationalen Gesellschaft für Dialektische Philosophie* 1 (1983): 136–40.

Neuhouser, Frederick. "Deducing Desire and Recognition in the *Phenomenology of Spirit.*" *Journal of the History of Philosophy* 24 (1986): 243–62.

Nicolin, Friedhelm. "Zum Titelproblem der *Phänomenologie des Geistes.*" *Hegel-Studien* 4 (1967): 113–23.

Okrent, Mark B. "Consciousness and Objective Spirit in Hegel's *Phenomenology.*" *Journal of the History of Philosophy* 18 (1980): 39–55.

Onyewoenyi, I. C. "Self-Consciousness in the Philosophy of Hegel." *Thought and Practice* 2 (1975): 125–34.

Ottmann, Henning. "Herr und Knecht bei Hegel: Bemerkungen zu einer misverstandenen Dialektik." *Zeitschrift für Philosophische Forschung* 35 (1981): 365–84.

Paci, Enzo. "La *Phénoménologie* et l'histoire dans la pensée de Hegel." *Praxis* (1971): 93–100.

Pätzold, Detlev. "Das absolute Wissen als Theorie des Gesamtzusammenhangs." *Annalen der Internationalen Gesellschaft für Dialektische Philosophie* 1 (1983): 33–37.

Philonenko, Alexis. *Lecture de la Phénoménologie de Hegel: Préface—Introduction.* Paris: Vrin, 1993.

Piertercil, Raymond. "Antigone and Hegel." *International Philosophical Quarterly* 18 (1978): 289–310.

———. "De la *Phénoménologie de l'esprit* aux Leçons d'esthétique." *Revue philosophique de Louvain* 77 (1979): 5–23.

Pippin, Robert B. "Hegel's Phenomenological Criticism." *Man and World* 8 (1975): 296–314.

Plumer, Gilbert. "Hegel on Singular Demonstrative Reference." *Southwestern Journal of Philosophy* 11 (1980): 71–94.

Pöggeler, Otto. "Hegels Phänomenologie des Selbstbewußtseins." In his *Hegels Idee einer Phänomenologie des Geistes*. Freiburg and Munich: Karl Alber, 1973, 231–98.

———. "Zur Deutung der *Phänomenologie des Geistes*." *Hegel-Studien* 1 (1961): 255–94.

———. "Die Komposition der *Phänomenologie des Geistes*." In *Hegel-Tage Royaumont 1964. Beiträge zur Phänomenologie des Geistes*, ed. Hans-Georg Gadamer. *Hegel-Studien*, Beiheft 3. Bonn: Bouvier, 1966, 27–74. Also in *Materialien zu Hegels Phänomenologie des Geistes*, ed. Hans Friedrich Fulda and Dieter Henrich. Frankfurt: Suhrkamp, 1973, 329–90.

———. "Ansatz und Aufbau der *Phänomenologie des Geistes*." *Journal of the Faculty of Letters. The University of Tokyo. Aesthetics* (Tokyo) 13 (1988): 11–36.

Preuss, Peter. "Selfhood and the Battle: The Second Beginning of the *Phenomenology*." In *Method and Speculation in Hegel's Phenomenology*, ed. Merold Westphal. Atlantic Highlands, N.J.: Humanities Press, 1982, 71–83.

Purpus, Wilhelm. *Die Dialektik der sinnlichen Gewißheit bei Hegel*. Nürnberg: Sebald, 1905.

———. *Die Dialektik der Wahrnehmung bei Hegel. Ein Beitrag zur Würdigung der Phänomenologie des Geistes*, teil 1. Schweinfurt: Fr. J. Reichardt's Buchdruckerei, 1908.

Rauch, Leo. "Desire, An Elemental Passion in Hegel's *Phenomenology*." *Analecta Husserliana* 28 (1990): 193–207.

———. "Hegel's *Phenomenology of Spirit* as a Phenomenological Project." *Thought* 56 (1981): 328–41.

Roeder von Diersburg, Egenolf. "Die Pseudosyllogismen in Hegels *Phänomenologie*." *Archiv für Philosophie* 12 (1963–64): 46–68.

———. "Konstante und variable Hilfsbegriffe in Hegels *Phänomenologie*." *Archiv für Philosophie* 13 (1964): 50–70.

Römpp, Georg. "Ein Selbstbewußtsein für ein Selbstbewußtsein. Bemerkungen zum Kapital 'Die Wahrheit der Gewißheit seiner selbst' in Hegels *Phänomenologie des Geistes*." *Hegel-Studien* 23 (1988): 71–94.

Rosen, Stanley. "Self-Consciousness and Self-Knowledge in Plato and Hegel." *Hegel-Studien* 9 (1974): 109–29.

Rowe, John Carlos. "The Internal Conflict of Romantic Narrative. Hegel's *Phe-

nomenology and Hawthorne's *The Scarlet Letter.*" *Modern Language Notes* 95 (1980): 1203-31.

Russen, John E. "Selfhood, Conscience and Dialectic in Hegel's *Phenomenology of Spirit.*" *Southern Journal of Philosophy* 29 (1991): 533-50.

Sax, Benjamin C. "Active Individuality and the Language of Confession: The Figure of the Beautiful Soul in the *Lehrjahre* and the *Phenomenology.*" *Journal of the History of Philosophy* 21 (1983): 437-66.

Schacht, Richard. "A Commentary on the Preface to Hegel's *Phenomenology of Spirit.*" *Philosophical Studies* 23 (1972): 1-31.

Scheier, Claus-Artur. "Die Sprache und das Wort in Hegels *Phänomenologie des Geistes.*" *Neue Zeitschrift für Systematische Theologie und Religionsphilosophie* 24 (1982): 94-103.

Schmitz, Hermann. "Hegels Lösung der Paradoxien des Selbstbewußtseins." In *System der Philosophy*, vol. 1. Bonn: Bouvier, 1964, 257-59.

―――. "Die Vorbereitung von Hegels *Phänomenologie des Geistes* in seiner Jenenser Logik." *Zeitschrift für philosophische Forschung* 14 (1960): 16-39.

―――. "Der Gestaltsbegriff in Hegels *Phänomenologie des Geistes* und seine geistesgeschichtliche Bedeutung." In *Gestaltsprobleme der Dichtung*, ed. Richard Alewyn, Bonn: Bouvier, 1957.

Schmitz, Kenneth L. "Substance is not Enough: Hegel's Slogan: From Substance to Subject." *Proceeding of the Catholic Philosophers' Association* 61 (1987): 52-68.

Schütte, Hans-Walter. "Tod Gottes und Fülle der Zeit. Hegels Deutung des Christentums." *Zeitschrift für Theologie und Kirche* 66 (1969): 62-76.

Schwarz, Justus. "Die Vorbereitung der *Phänomenologie* in Hegels Jenenser Systementwürfen." *Zeitschrift für Deutsche Kultur* 2 (1935-36): 127-59.

Seba, Jean-Renaud. "Histoire et fin de l'histoire dans la *Phénoménologie de l'esprit* de Hegel." *Revue de Métaphysique et de Morale* 85 (1980): 27-47.

Secrétan, Philibert. "Le thème de la mort dans la *Phénoménologie de l'esprit* de Hegel." *Freiburger Zeitschrift für Philosophie und Theologie* 23 (1976): 269-85.

Sedgwick, Sally S. "Hegel's Critique of the Subjective Idealism of Kant's Ethics." *Journal of the History of Philosophy* 26 (1988): 89-105.

Shapiro, Gary. "An Ancient Quarrel in Hegel's *Phenomenology.*" *The Owl of Minerva* 17 (1985-86): 165-80.

Shklar, Judith. "The *Phenomenology*: Beyond Morality." *The Western Political Quarterly* 27 (1974): 597-623.

———. "Hegel's *Phenomenology*: An Elegy for Hellas." In *Hegel's Political Philosophy: Problems and Perspectives*, ed. Z. A. Pelczynski. Cambridge: Cambridge University Press, 1971, 73-89.

Siep, Ludwig. "Zur Dialektik der Anerkennung bei Hegel." *Hegel-Jahrbuch* 1974: 366-73.

Simeunivic, Vojin. "Die Aktualität von Hegels *Phänomenologie des Geistes.*" *Praxis* 7 (1971): 73-83.

Sobotka, Milan. "Das Kapitel über den sich entfremdeten Geist in der Hegelschen *Phänomenologie des Geistes* und Ludwig Feuerbach." *Wissenschaftliche Zeitschrift der Friedrich-Schiller-Universität Jena* 29 (1980): 387-93.

———. "Die Auffassung des Gegenstandes in Hegels *Phänomenologie des Geistes.*" *Wiener Jahrbuch für Philosophie* 8 (1975): 133-53.

Soll, Ivan. "Das Besondere und das Allgemeine in der sinnlichen Gewißheit bei Hegel." *Hegel-Jahrbuch* 1976: 283-87.

Solomon, Robert C. "Truth and Self-Satisfaction." *Review of Metaphysics* 28 (1975): 698-724.

———. "Approaching Hegel's *Phenomenology.*" *Philosophy Today* 13 (1969): 115-25.

———. "Hegel's Concept of *Geist.*" In *Hegel: A Collection of Critical Essays*, ed. Alasdair MacIntyre. Notre Dame, Ind.: University of Notre Dame Press, 1976, 125-49.

———. "A Small Problem in Hegel's *Phenomenology.*" *Journal of the History of Philosophy* 13 (1975): 399-400.

Sonnemann, Ulrich. "Hegel und Freud. Die Kritik der *Phänomenologie* am Begriff der psychologischen Notwendigkeit und ihre anthropologischen Konsequenzen." *Psyche* 24 (1970): 208-18.

Sonnenschmidt, Reinhard. "Ist Hegels Philosophie eine Philosophie des Todes? Eine kritische Bemerkung zur Dialektik von Herr und Knecht." *Hegel-Jahrbuch* 1991: 199-204.

Souche-Dagues, Denise. "La raison dans la *Phénoménologie de l'esprit.*" In *Phénoménologie et Métaphysique*, ed. Jean-Luc Marion and Guy Planty-Bonjour. Paris: Presses Universitaires de France, 1984.

Stewart, Jon. "Die Rolle des unglücklichen Bewußtseins in Hegels *Phänomenologie des Geistes.*" *Deutsche Zeitschrift für Philosophie* 39 (1991): 12-21.

———. "Die Beziehung zwischen der *Jenaer Metaphysik* von 1804-5 und der

Phänomenologie des Geistes." *Jahrbuch für Hegelforschung,* Bd. 2 (1996): 99–132.

———. "Hegel's Doctrine of Determinate Negation: An Example from 'Sense-Certainty' and 'Perception.'" *Idealistic Studies* 26:1 (1996): 57–78.

Stiehler, Gottfried. "'Rameaus Neffe' und die *Phänomenologie des Geistes* von Hegel." *Wissenschaftliche Zeitschrift der Humboldt-Universität zu Berlin* [Gesellschafts- und sprachwissenschaftliche Reihe] 13 (1964): 163–67.

Taylor, Charles. "The Opening Arguments of the *Phenomenology.*" In *Hegel: A Collection of Critical Essays,* ed. Alasdair MacIntyre. Notre Dame, Ind.: University of Notre Dame Press, 1976, 151–87.

Thulstrup, Niels. "Hegel's Stages of Cognition in the *Phenomenology of Spirit* and Kierkegaard's Stages of Existence in the *Concluding Unscientific Postscript.*" *Liber Akademiae Kierkegaardiensis Annuarius* 2–4 (1979–81): 61–69.

Thyssen, Johannes. "Kritische Hauptpunkte in den ersten Abschnitten von Hegels *Phänomenologie des Geistes.*" In *Festschrift H. J. de Vleeschawer.* Communications of the University of South Africa, Pretoria (1960), 84–95.

Tran-Duc-Thao. "La *Phénoménologie de l'esprit* et son contenu réel." *Les Temps Modernes* 4 (1948): 492–519. In English as "The *Phenomenology of Mind* and Its Real Content." *Telos* 8 (1971): 91–110.

Trede, Johann Heinrich. "*Phänomenologie* und *Logik.* Zu den Grundlagen einer Diskussion." *Hegel-Studien* 10 (1975): 173–210.

Ulrich, Ferdinand. "Begriff und Glaube: Über Hegels Denkweg ins 'absolute Wissen'." *Freiburger Zeitschrift für Philosophie und Theologie* 17 (1970): 344–99.

Van Dooren, Win. "Der Begriff der Materie in Hegels *Phänomenologie des Geistes.*" *Hegel-Jahrbuch* 1976: 84–89.

Van Dooren, Willem. "Die Bedeutung der Religion in der *Phänomenologie des Geistes.*" In *Hegel-Tage Urbino 1965,* ed. Hans-Georg Gadamer. *Hegel-Studien,* Beiheft 4. Bonn: Bouvier, 1969, 93–101.

Van Riet, Georges. "Y-a-t-il un chemin vers la vérité? À propos de l'introduction à la *Phénoménologie de l'esprit* de Hegel." *Revue philosophique de Louvain* 62 (1964): 466–76.

Vaught, Carl G. "Subject, Object and Representation: A Critique of Hegel's Dialectic of Perception." *International Philosophical Quarterly* 26 (1986): 117–29.

Ver Eecke, Wilfred. "Hegel's Dialectic Analysis of the French Revolution." *Hegel-Jahrbuch* 1975: 561–67.

Verneaux, R., "De la dialectique du sensible selon Hegel." *Sapienza* 21 (1968): 421–38.

Verstraeten, Pierre. "L'homme du plaisir chez Hegel et l'homme du désir chez Lacan." *Revue de l'Université de Bruxelles* 3–4 (1976): 351–94.

Vieillard-Baron, Jean-Louis. "L'idée de religion révélée chez Hegel et Schelling." *Cannocchiale* 1 (1989): 45–58.

Wagner, Falk. "Hegels Satz 'Gott ist tot'. Bemerkungen zu Dorthee Sölles Hegelinterpretation." *Zeitwende* 38 (1967): 77–95.

Wahl, Jean. "Commentaire d'un passage de la *Phénoménologie de l'esprit* de Hegel." *Revue de Metaphysique et de Morale* 34 (1927): 441–71.

———. "La place de l'idee du malheur de la conscience dans la formation de théories de Hegel." *Revue Philosophique* 52 (1927): 103–47.

———. "À propos de l'introduction à la *Phénoménologie* de Hegel par A. Kojève." *Deucalion* 5 (1955): 77–99.

Walter, Eric. "Force and Its Other: An Interpretation." *Iyyun* 19 (1968): 260–61.

Warminski, Andrzej. "Reading for Example 'Sense Certainty' in Hegel's *Phenomenology of Spirit.*" *Diacritics* 11 (1981): 83–96.

Well, Karlheinz. *Die schöne Seele und ihre sittliche Wirklichkeit.* Frankfurt and Bern: Peter Lang, 1986.

Werkmeister, William Henry. "Hegel's *Phenomenology of Mind* as a Development of Kant's Basic Ontology." In *Hegel and the Philosophy of Religion: The Wofford Symposium*, ed. Darrel E. Christenson. The Hague: Martinus Nijhoff, 1970, 93–110.

Westphal, Merold. "Hegel's *Phenomenology* as Transcendental Philosophy." *Journal of Philosophy* 82 (1985): 606–7.

Wiehl, Reiner. "Über den Sinn der sinnlichen Gewißheit in Hegels *Phänomenologie des Geistes.*" In *Hegel-Tage Royaumont 1964: Beiträge zur Deutung der Phänomenologie des Geistes*, ed. Hans-Georg Gadamer. *Hegel-Studien*, Beiheft 3. Bonn: Bouvier, 1966, 103–34.

———. "Phänomenologie und Dialektik." *Stuttgarter Hegel-Kongress 1970, Vorträge und Kolloquien*, ed. Hans-Georg Gadamer. Bonn: Bouvier, 1974, 635–42.

Wieland, Wolfgang. "Hegels Dialektik der sinnlichen Gewißheit." In *Orbis Scriptus. Dmitrij Tschizewskij zum 70. Geburtstag*, ed. D. Gerhardt et al. Munich: Wilhelm Fink, 1966, 933–41. Reprinted in *Materialien zu Hegels Phänome-*

nologie des Geistes, ed. Hans Friedrich Fulda and Dieter Henrich. Frankfurt: Suhrkamp, 1973, 67–82.

Wilden, Anthony. "The Belle Âme: Freud, Lacan, and Hegel." In his *The Language of the Self: The Function of Language in Psychoanalysis*. Baltimore: Johns Hopkins Press, 1968, 284–308.

Wildt, Andreas. "Hegels Kritik des Jakobinismus." In *Stuttgarter Hegel-Tage 1970*, ed. Hans-Georg Gadamer. *Hegel-Studien*, Beiheft 11. Bonn: Bouvier, 1974, 417–27.

Willett, Cynthia. "Hegel, Antigone and the Possibility of Ecstatic Dialogue." *Philosophy and Literature* 14 (1990): 268–83.

Yon, Ephrem-Dominique. "Esthétique de la contemplation et esthétique de la transgression: À propos de passage de la Religion au Saviour Absolu dans la *Phénoménologie de l'esprit* de Hegel." *Revue philosophique de Louvain* 74 (1976): 549–71.

Zimmerman, Robert. "Hegel's 'Inverted World' Revisited." *The Philosophical Forum* 13 (1982): 342–70.

Zuna, Miroslav. "Zur Frage der Kunst in Hegels *Phänomenologie*." In *Hegel. L'esprit objectif, l'unité de l'histoire. Actes du IIIème Congrès international de l'Association internationale pour l'étude de la philosophie de Hegel*. Lille: Association des Publications de la Faculté des lettres et sciences humaines, 1970, 339–44.

Zviglyanich, V. A. "The Inverted World in the *Phenomenology of Spirit* and its Significance for the History of Cognition." *Hegel-Jahrbuch* 1991: 205–9.

Index

absolute Idea, 11, 62
absolute knowing, 17, 64, 66, 67, 126, 140, 141, 149, 174, 205, 230, 280, 284, 361, 399, 433, 434ff., 470ff.
absolute notion, 282, 286, 295, 471
absolute spirit, 224, 238, 337, 352, 353, 361, 376, 396ff., 399, 428, 429, 466, 470
absolute, the, 34ff., 39ff., 42ff., 62, 64, 66, 183, 201, 287, 294, 352, 363, 365, 367, 368, 439, 467
Adorno, Theodor, 231, 251, 266
Antigone, 16, 243ff., 273, 277, 304, 465
appearance, 57, 59, 66, 138, 142, 143, 148, 149, 198
Aristotle, 34, 54, 130, 135, 177, 238, 435
Aufhebung, 28, 108, 243, 252, 256

Baillie, J. B., 56, 193, 194, 195, 197, 200, 226, 319
beautiful soul, 16, 280, 315ff., 336ff., 352, 432ff., 466
being, 67, 68, 69, 128, 143, 453
Berkeley, George, 133
Boehme, Jakob, 359f., 363ff.

Catholicism, 192ff., 197ff.
Christianity, 187, 193ff., 200ff., 236, 252, 260, 276, 284, 292, 341f., 356, 365, 375ff., 399, 404ff., 429, 431, 437, 438, 467, 470
conscience, 16, 310ff., 314, 320ff., 334ff., 432, 438
Critical Journal of Philosophy, 25, 311, 313

Descartes, René, 15, 129, 131, 133, 184, 218, 274, 437
desire, 156ff., 176, 185, 199, 203, 245, 256, 260, 264, 453
determinate negation, 14, 57, 93, 110
dialectic, 12, 52ff., 111
Diderot, Denis. *See Rameau's Nephew*
dualism, 7, 55, 85, 141, 218, 365, 366, 459, 460, 461

end (telos), 31ff., 37, 41, 46, 223, 310, 458, 460
Enlightenment, 16, 124, 182, 192, 200, 205, 275ff., 294ff., 354, 356, 431, 437, 438

Fichte, Johann Gottlieb, 4, 11, 29, 30ff., 176, 177, 182f., 287, 311ff., 314, 320f., 323, 335, 336, 339, 355, 356, 360, 438, 439
for us, 61ff., 123, 126, 139, 379
force, 123, 130, 135, 139, 142f., 453
French Revolution, 16, 181, 183, 192, 282ff., 283, 437
für uns. See for us

God, 27, 29, 34, 167ff., 177, 193, 252, 290, 334ff., 337, 338, 340ff., 356, 357 ff., 368f., 375ff., 401ff., 428f., 432f., 437, 440, 453, 467, 470, 471
Goethe, Johann Wolfgang von, 272, 273, 274, 275, 313, 319ff., 338

Habermas, Jürgen, 283f., 300
Hartmann, Nicolai, 63, 65, 69

Hegel, Georg Wilhelm Friedrich
  Difference Between the Fichte's and Schelling's System of Philosophy, 30, 183
  Encyclopedia of the Philosophical Sciences, 2, 8, 173, 177, 180, 185, 195, 196, 452
    Book I, *Logic*, 8, 11, 107, 177
    Book II, *Philosophy of Nature*, 8, 440, 441
    Book III, *Philosophy of Mind*, 8, 177, 180, 195, 440, 441, 452
  Lectures on Aesthetics, 317, 325, 327, 339, 357, 363, 366, 367, 368
  Lectures on the History of Philosophy, 317, 339, 366
  Lectures of the Philosophy of History, 3, 248
  Lectures on the Philosophy of Religion, 191, 196, 342, 353, 356, 361
  Philosophical Propadeutic, 173, 179, 180, 452
  Philosophy of Right, 2, 3, 8, 16, 173, 185f., 237, 243, 259ff., 284, 298, 322f.
  Science of Logic, 2, 6, 7, 8, 12, 128, 134, 139, 298, 337, 361, 363, 365, 366, 368, 369, 440, 441, 447
Heidegger, Martin, 64, 66-70
Herder, Johann Gottfried von, 183, 313, 355, 357
history, 16, 161, 175, 177, 184, 192ff., 223f., 232, 243, 272ff., 287, 436, 441, 463, 465, 472
Hobbes, Thomas, 232, 237
Hölderlin, Johann Christian Friedrich, 327f., 339
Hume, David, 133, 144, 181, 222
Husserl, Edmund, 129
Hyppolite, Jean, 2, 63, 65, 66, 69, 173, 226, 272f., 274, 304, 316

idealism, 150, 472. *See also* transcendental idealism
immediacy, 34, 60, 108ff., 124, 125, 127, 130, 132, 251, 263, 369, 377, 381, 402ff., 407ff., 415f., 456, 458. *See also* mediation

Jacobi, Karl Gustav Jakob, 313, 314, 321, 329

Kant, Immanuel, 10, 11, 15, 53, 83, 123, 129, 131, 133, 135, 144ff., 147ff., 177, 181, 182, 184, 184, 187, 227, 287, 308, 309ff., 329, 335, 338, 367, 437, 438f.
Kaufmann, Walter, 9, 444
Kierkegaard, Søren, 53, 233, 444
knowledge, 54ff., 79, 105, 108ff., 122ff., 141, 143, 466
Kojève, Alexandre, 2, 10, 15, 173f., 175, 185, 187, 226, 231, 232, 298, 338
Kritische Journal der Philosophie. *See Critical Journal of Philosophy*
Kroner, Richard, 63-67, 69, 181, 352

language, 59ff., 106ff., 278f., 292f.
Leibniz, Gottfried Wilhelm, 318, 437, 438
Lessing, Gotthold Ephraim, 183
Locke, John, 53, 132, 283
logic, 66, 68
lordship and bondage, 10, 15, 16, 156ff., 162ff., 173ff., 195, 201, 229f., 238, 285ff., 362, 369, 451, 452, 453
Lukács, György, 16, 62-63, 64, 65, 67, 68, 226, 232, 235

Marcuse, Herbert, 62, 64, 65, 68
Marx, Karl (Marxism), 1, 2, 15, 173, 174, 185, 186, 187, 204, 205, 232, 234f., 238
mediation, 34, 60, 106, 109, 116, 128, 129, 130, 132, 140
Montesquieu, Baron, 181, 297

natural consciousness, 14, 44, 58, 64, 67, 122, 123f., 125, 126, 139f., 430

Index

negative (negation), 53, 57, 112, 128, 129, 132, 140, 158, 161, 166, 167, 169, 222, 244, 364, 366, 378, 379, 391, 392ff., 402ff., 407ff., 411ff.
Nietzsche, Friedrich Wilhelm, 54, 185, 232, 236, 237, 444
Novalis (Friedrich von Hardenberg), 183, 316, 321ff., 329, 339

object. *See* subject/object
ontology, 67–68

particularity (particulars), 14, 105ff., 243, 244ff., 263, 296ff., 299, 300, 308 ff., 336, 460
phenomenology, 1, 2, 52ff., 68, 174, 185, 307f., 329, 363, 402
philosophical knowing. *See* absolute knowing
phrenology, 15, 213ff.
physiognomy, 15, 213ff.
Plato, 15, 53, 54, 120, 122ff., 177, 187, 228, 317

Quine, Willard van Orman, 115, 121

Rameau's Nephew, 16, 233, 272ff., 293, 465
recognition, 15, 163ff., 169, 175ff., 229, 237, 244, 245ff., 261, 361, 389ff., 397ff., 452
reconciliation, 230, 256, 260, 265, 266, 310, 336, 340f., 369, 410ff., 415
revelation, 252, 360, 404ff., 467, 470
Romanticism, 16, 124, 183f., 278, 280, 282, 307ff., 329, 338, 339, 353, 355, 356, 364, 437
Rousseau, Jean-Jacques, 181f., 185, 296, 354, 355, 356
Russell, Bertrand, 118, 220

Sartre, Jean-Paul, 2, 3, 235
Schelling, Friedrich Wilhelm Joseph von, 4, 11, 176, 183, 184, 239, 291, 352, 357, 363f., 366f., 438, 439, 446, 447

Schiller, Friedrich von, 273, 277, 279, 316, 318ff., 327
Schlegel, Friedrich von, 183, 323, 324ff., 339, 356, 357, 366
Schleiermacher, Friedrich Ernst Daniel, 352ff., 437
science, 5, 7, 26, 34ff., 37, 40, 41ff., 52, 54, 123, 131, 139f., 149, 284, 446, 457, 461
Sextus Empricus, 76ff.
skepticism, 26, 56, 61–62, 76ff., 198, 204, 354
Socrates, 70, 122f., 223, 258
Solger, K. W., 325, 356
speculation (speculative philosophy), 7, 11ff., 66, 402, 408, 412ff.
Spinoza, Benedict de, 29, 31, 33, 110, 135, 365, 437, 438
spirit, 37ff., 44, 46ff., 54, 284, 461ff.
subject/object, 28ff., 35, 37, 43, 54ff., 85ff., 106, 111, 113ff., 163, 434, 435, 440, 441, 450, 451, 453, 455, 456, 459, 460, 465, 470ff.
substance, 28ff., 46, 125, 129, 135, 298, 337, 368, 377, 378, 395, 434, 439
system, 4, 5, 6, 8, 9, 10ff., 29, 34ff., 37, 40, 41, 43, 54, 159, 233, 428, 441, 444ff.

Tieck, Ludwig, 320
tragedy, 16, 256, 258. *See also Antigone*
transcendental idealism, 65, 131, 146, 183
truth, 54ff., 114f., 122, 130, 199, 204, 205, 445f., 466, 470

unhappy consciousness, 15, 178, 192ff., 273, 335, 395, 396, 400, 453, 455
universality, 106ff., 125f., 132, 243ff., 256, 260, 291, 297, 299, 300, 308ff., 336, 342, 377, 391, 429

"we." *See* for us
Wissenschaftslehre. *See* Fichte
Wittgenstein, Ludwig Josef Johan, 70

www.ingramcontent.com/pod-product-compliance
Lightning Source LLC
Chambersburg PA
CBHW030102010526
44116CB00005B/68